To Bob,

(SIMON *ᴜʀ⋯* ER)

When the President Calls

When the President Calls

Conversations with Economic Policymakers

Simon W. Bowmaker

Foreword by Dame Minouche Shafik

The MIT Press
Cambridge, Massachusetts
London, England

This book was set in Stone Serif and Stone Sans by Westchester Publishing Services. Printed and bound in the United States of America.

Library of Congress Cataloging-in-Publication Data

Names: Bowmaker, Simon W., 1971- author.
Title: When the President calls : conversations with economic policymakers / Simon W. Bowmaker.
Description: Cambridge, MA : MIT Press, [2019] | Includes bibliographical references and index.
Identifiers: LCCN 2019005603 | ISBN 9780262043113 (hardcover : alk. paper)
Subjects: LCSH: United States--Economic policy. | Economists--United States--Interviews. | United States--Politics and government--1945-
Classification: LCC HC106.84 .B69 2019 | DDC 330.973--dc23
    LC record available at https://lccn.loc.gov/2019005603

10 9 8 7 6 5 4 3 2 1

Contents

Foreword

Economics is at the heart of politics. That is why all politicians have economic advisers as central players in their policymaking teams. In the United States, there has been a long tradition of drawing on excellent economists from academia, the private sector, and the wider public sector to advise presidents on their economic policies. This collection of in-depth interviews by Simon Bowmaker of NYU and LSE provides insight into who these individuals were, what policy challenges they faced, and how they worked across different administrations. What is perhaps most valuable are the perspectives on how they exercised influence and the important role of individual personalities in shaping major policy decisions.

The chapters cover the major challenges facing the United States, and often the world. This includes the breakdown of the Bretton Woods system and the transition to a predominantly floating exchange rate world, the era of rampant inflation, the collapse of the Soviet Union and the transition to market economics, the shock of 9/11, the financial crisis of 2008, and the Great Recession that followed. The economic judgments made on each of those major issues shaped the world economy in fundamental ways. Learning about the internal debates that enabled those judgments is a fascinating piece of economic history.

One of the most difficult lessons is that ultimately what is economically optimal is constrained and often determined by what is politically feasible. In the UK system, the motto is "civil servants advise but Ministers decide"—meaning that experts give their best technical advice but it is the job of politicians to weigh up the political trade-offs. There are many examples of this dilemma in the chapters that follow. In the US system, the central role of Congress in approving any spending decision invariably involves political bargaining. Often, one is operating in not a second-best world but a third- or fourth-best one. For a well-trained economist, that can be very uncomfortable, and it is interesting to see how different individuals grapple with this dilemma.

Another theme is the importance of relationships—with the president but also with other key players in the policymaking process. It is apparent in these pages that different presidents had very different levels of engagement on economic issues. Some had deep knowledge and wanted to engage in lengthy debates about the issues, others were happy to delegate the details to experts and focused on managing the politics. It is not always clear which approaches resulted in the best policies, but the key seems to be that economic advisers to the president found it most rewarding if they got a fair hearing for their ideas, even if the decision ultimately went against their recommendations.

Harry Truman famously said he wanted a one-handed economist because each one he sought advice from said "on the one hand, and on the other…" It is true that there are many debates in economics that remain unresolved, but there are vast parts of the subject where the consensus is very broad. In areas like trade, competition, and regulation the majority of economists agree on the main principles, although there will be debate on specific details of policy or where new challenges have emerged, such as the digital economy or new forms of monopoly power. Those with policy experience know that often there is no "right" answer, just a choice between different options, each with its own costs and benefits.

The US decision-making process is often decentralized, and economic advice comes to the president from many places—the Treasury, the Federal Reserve, the Office of Management and Budget, the Council of Economic Advisers, the National Economic Council, and many others. The economists in the chapters that follow sat in all these perches. What is called the "interagency process" is key for mediating these different perspectives, and many give examples of how it worked and how their colleagues shaped their views. Where it works well, these different economic perspectives improve the quality of policymaking; where it fails, policies flounder.

Perhaps the most compelling aspect of these individual stories is how participating in policymaking is enriching for all those who do it. I had the privilege of observing many of these individuals from my perches at the World Bank, the UK government, the IMF, and the Bank of England. Academic economists are never the same after a stint in the policy world. It changes their research interests and how they think about economic behavior. Those from the private sector understand how difficult it is to get things done when having to manage so many stakeholders and trade-offs. Economics may be the "dismal science" and politics the "art of the possible," but the marriage of the two makes for some of the most rewarding experiences in a professional life.

Dame Minouche Shafik
Director, London School of Economics and Political Science

Acknowledgments

This book would not have been possible if the thirty-five interviewees had not given their time and energy to the project. I express my sincere gratitude to them. It was both a pleasure and a privilege to have had the opportunity to benefit from their wisdom and knowledge.

Many other people also helped me across various dimensions; from suggesting names of potential interviewees to encouraging their friends and colleagues to be interviewed, assisting in the crafting of interview questions, reviewing the transcripts, providing editorial assistance, and discussing the concept of my book as well as wider questions in economic policymaking. Here, I thank the following: Dick Berner, Tiffany Boselli, Dolly Chugh, Gian Luca Clementi, Tom Cooley, David de Meza, Divyansh Devnani, Michael Dickstein, Nick Drinkwater, Kate Eichhorn, Saul Estrin, Jeanne Ferris, Kelly Friendly, Jason Furman, Bill Greene, Peter Henry, Gavin Kilduff, the late Alan Krueger, Arthur Laffer, Arthur Laffer Jr., Tom McCaleb, Melody Negron, Claire Buchan Parker, Foster Provost, Joshua Reed, Jennifer Roche, Jonathan Rosenfeld, Kim Schoenholtz, Rob Seamans, Bill Silber, Shivaditya Sinha, David Skeie, Gene Sperling, Arun Sundararajan, Dick Sylla, John Taylor, Laura Tribuno, and Robert Wright.

At MIT Press, I thank Jane MacDonald for her enthusiasm and encouragement in the early stages of the project. With incredible patience and great understanding, Emily Taber then took on the responsibility of making sure that I completed the book. I am very grateful for her help and dedication.

I acknowledge the support and collegial environment of the Stern School of Business at New York University and the hospitality of the London School of Economics, where I put the finishing touches to the project.

Last, but not least, I send a special note of thanks to four people—Kim Ruhl, Paul Wachtel, Michael Waugh, and Larry White—who spent innumerable hours helping me throughout the seven years that I worked on this book. Larry, in particular, has always been there for me as a colleague, mentor, and friend.

Introduction

This book provides insights into the personal and professional complexities associated with serving the president of the United States as an economic policymaker. Much has been written elsewhere about the evolution of US economic policy during the half-century discussed in the thirty-five interviews that follow. To be sure, this book contains insights into the causes and consequences of some of the most important economic events of our recent past—including the 2008 financial crisis—and highlights the crucial role economics plays in our daily lives. However, few people have had direct access to the policymaking process, and these interviews provide a window into an environment in which the key players must grapple with difficult trade-offs and understand their myriad implications. What is it like to sit in the Oval Office and discuss policy with the president? To know that your input into his decisions will impact hundreds of millions of people? To know that the wrong advice could be calamitous? Only those who have been there can speak to the intense pressure and constant scrutiny that is involved. In short, this is a book about the human side of economic policymaking.

Selecting the Interviewees

It is important to clarify at the onset that while economic policymakers play a wide range of roles in Washington, including at the Federal Reserve, for the purposes of this book I chose to focus on the specific role that they play in the executive branch of government. The Federal Reserve and the executive branch of government are distinct entities in both their mandate and structure, and thus both cannot be easily addressed in a single book. This is why my interviews with Paul Volcker, Alan Greenspan, and Janet Yellen—whom many people know first and foremost for their roles at the Federal Reserve—focus primarily on their experiences in the executive branch of government during the administrations of Richard Nixon, Gerald Ford, and Bill Clinton, respectively.

While I have narrowed my focus to those who have held one or more key roles in the executive branch, my scope is still comparatively broad. Early in the development of this book, I intended to interview only those who had served on the Council of Economic Advisers (CEA), an agency established in 1946 to advise the president on economic policy. As the project unfolded, however, it became clear that focusing on the CEA alone did not give a full account of economic policymaking. By its nature, the CEA—which consists of a chair, two members, and a staff of junior and senior economists—is an advisory body, but other groups in the executive branch are also responsible for helping the president make policy decisions and actually implementing policy, and I wanted to include these perspectives as well.

For this reason, interviewees for the book eventually included officials of the Office of Management and Budget (OMB) (the largest office in the executive branch, which was founded in 1970 to oversee the performance of federal agencies and administer the federal budget) and in the Department of the Treasury (an agency established by an act of Congress in 1789 to manage government revenue). I also interviewed several people who have held key roles on the National Economic Council (NEC), an entity introduced by President Clinton in 1993 to coordinate the economic policymaking process.

In the end, I interviewed thirty-five former and active economic policymakers who over the course of their careers have served in one or more full-time roles in Washington—including, but not limited to, secretary of the treasury, undersecretary of the treasury for monetary affairs, undersecretary of the treasury for international affairs, chair of the CEA, director of the OMB, chief economist at the OMB, and director of the NEC. The formal roles of these presidential economic team members remain mostly the same across administrations. However, these interviews also show that their informal roles tend to depend upon the president, his management style, and the personalities of other people on his team.

Collectively, the people featured in this book span thirteen administrations. Murray Weidenbaum served as an economist during the administration of Harry Truman before being appointed Ronald Reagan's first chairman of the CEA, while Mick Mulvaney and Kevin Hassett have both held roles under Donald Trump. My specific focus, however, is on those who have served Presidents Nixon, Ford, Jimmy Carter, George H. W. Bush,

Clinton, George W. Bush, Barack Obama, and Trump. Note that I have chosen to organize this book chronologically—beginning with the Nixon administration and ending with the Trump administration—and placed interviewees in the administration in which they were appointed to their first major economic policy roles or in the administration in which they were best known for their economic policy work. I acknowledge that this grouping is somewhat imperfect, but after careful consideration it appeared preferable to any other potential option, such as ordering the interviews by political affiliation or simply alphabetically.

Since this collection spans fifty years of policymaking at the White House, not surprisingly there were several key figures who had passed away by the time I initiated work on this book. Moreover, while I was delighted to secure interviews with the majority of the people I contacted, there were several people who were ultimately unwilling to be interviewed despite my unwavering persistence. Overall, however, the response rate was very high. Indeed, one of my pleasant surprises was how many former and current economic policymakers were willing to share their time and openly reflect on their work at the White House—and even on their relationships with past and current presidents.

This brings me to another small but by no means minor observation: The people interviewed for this book have had remarkably diverse career paths. While some arrived at the White House in junior roles shortly after graduation from college, others got the call to come to Washington after working on Wall Street or in private industry, law, or higher education. A few interviewees—including Gene Sperling, Stuart Eizenstat, Stephen Friedman, Jack Lew, and Hank Paulson—were not formally trained in economics but came to the White House with a strong understanding of economics and policy through their work in business or law. In addition, Mulvaney was a member of Congress before accepting the role of director of the OMB under President Trump. These differences are part of what make the reflections on economic policymaking brought together in this book exceptionally insightful.

Conducting the Interviews

In many respects, it was a daunting task to develop questions for the interviewees in this book. The people included have been top leaders in their respective fields. Many have held prominent positions in the nation's top-ranked economics programs. Others have long been power brokers on Wall

Street. Together, they possess a wealth of experience in economics as well as business, law, and politics that spans the period from the mid-twentieth century to the present. With this in mind, I chose to ask a combination of unique questions (those designed to explore the interviewee's specific role and impact at the White House) and generic questions (those designed not only to bring continuity to the interviews but also to underscore what economic policymakers bring to the White House).

It is important to note that these interviews are also the result of numerous factors that were often out of my own control. For example, a few interviewees could offer only forty-five minutes of their time. In contrast, one interviewee invited me to have dinner with his family and stay overnight at his home, and he gave me six hours of his time.

The location of the interviews also varied greatly. While some interviewees invited me to their homes, others invited me to their offices or met me at a hotel or restaurant. These different contexts, which ranged from very private to very public spaces, may have impacted the content of the interviews, though it is impossible to know for certain.

However, the amount of time initially allotted for interviews and the varying locations in which the interviews took place were not the only factors that structured the final transcripts. Nearly all the interviewees read and made edits to their interview transcripts, and while some edited more intensely than others, I am grateful for their willingness to make candid comments on the record, as their sometimes colorful recollections help bring economic policymaking to life. The interviews were also edited for clarity and in some cases shortened to avoid repetition and keep the focus of the book on the human side of policymaking in the White House.

Another factor that shaped some of the interviews was timing. While former policymakers—especially those reminiscing about experiences during the administrations from the 1970s to the 1990s—were often happy to speak at length about their work at the White House, currently serving policymakers were understandably more reluctant to speak at length on certain topics.

A final factor that undoubtedly molded the interviews was personality. Some people were simply more willing and comfortable than others in opening up about their work at the White House. This relates to something else that might have also had an influence: my background and current location. As an economist who was born and educated outside the United

States, I approached this project from a somewhat unique perspective. As neither a Democrat nor a Republican, but rather a British citizen who has lived and taught in the United States for more than a decade, I viewed myself as an educated and deeply interested outsider—someone who is knowledgeable about and immersed in American economic and political history, but not necessarily someone who was raised to have strong feelings about any of the people, policies, and parties in question. Whether my outsider status afforded me a distinct advantage when interviewing the people who appear in this book is not something I can easily assess. It is certainly possible, however, that my being perceived as somewhat politically neutral may have encouraged my participants to open up more fully.

Readership

Over the past decade, public awareness of the link between economics and policymaking has been on the rise. In short, we no longer live in a world where economists alone are concerned with this relationship. As a result, every effort has been made to develop a book for a general audience that includes anyone who wishes to gain a more comprehensive understanding of how economic decisions in the United States are made, by whom, and under what conditions. That said, the interviewees at times discussed material that is somewhat technical. I have tried to include explanatory information for material that may not be familiar to general readers, but I also recognize that readers may wish to skip certain parts of the interviews or read the interviews in a different order than I have presented them here. My ultimate goal is to increase understanding of economic policymaking, and I hope this book will serve that purpose, both for those who read it cover to cover and for those who may dip in and out of the interviews.

In addition, I hope this book will also serve as a useful resource for students of economics and their teachers. Over the past two decades, I have taught thousands of students—many taking introductory-level economics courses—and I have often wished I had a resource like this collection to share. Students of economics are often eager to understand how economic ideas are implemented in practice and to learn about the very direct ways in which economic policymakers can have an impact on their country's well-being. I am confident that this book will at least help fill this gap. Here, it also likely helped that many, albeit not all, of the interviewees are people who have also spent at least some time teaching economics at the undergraduate or graduate level.

A smaller but by no means insignificant group of readers I hope to reach are future White House economic policymakers. Nearly all the interviewees spoke candidly about the research they carried out to discover what their role at the White House might entail. While some of them stepped into their roles with a clear sense of why they were there—and what they would be expected to do—at least a few confessed that they arrived still somewhat uncertain about the scope of their prospective roles. Perhaps these interviews will also offer insight into the wide range of roles and tasks they are expected to assume when the president calls.

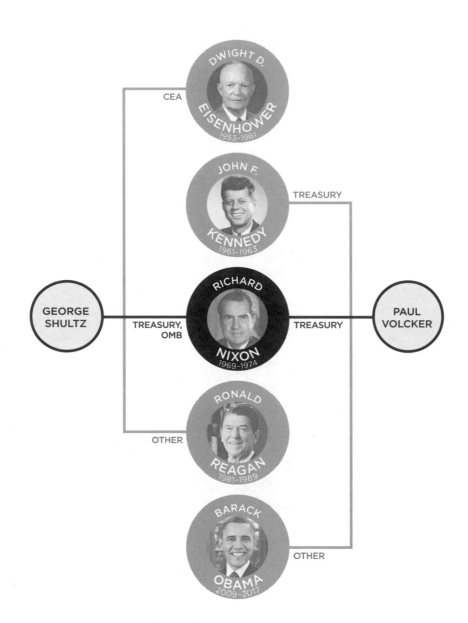

I Richard Nixon Administration

George Shultz (*right*), when secretary of the treasury, meeting with President Richard Nixon in the presidential office of the Executive Office Building on October 19, 1972.

1 George P. Shultz
Born 1920, New York City

George Shultz graduated with a BA in economics from Princeton University in 1942 and obtained a PhD in economics from the Massachusetts Institute of Technology (MIT) in 1949.

From 1948 to 1957 he taught at MIT, taking a leave of absence to serve as a senior staff economist on President Dwight Eisenhower's Council of Economic Advisers (CEA). In 1957, Shultz joined the University of Chicago's Graduate School of Business as a professor of industrial relations, and he was named dean five years later.

From 1968 to 1969, he was a fellow at the Center for Advanced Study in the Behavioral Sciences at Stanford University. He returned to government in 1969 when he was appointed secretary of labor by President Richard Nixon, and in 1970 he became the first director of the newly created Office of Management and Budget (OMB). From 1972 to 1974, he served as secretary of the treasury.

Shultz then left government to become president and director of the Bechtel Group, where he remained until 1982. While at Bechtel, he joined the faculty of Stanford University. Shultz held two positions within the administration of President Ronald Reagan, serving as chairman of the Economic Policy Advisory Board (1981–1982) and secretary of state (1982–1989).

After leaving office, he rejoined the Bechtel Group as director and senior counselor and also rejoined Stanford University, where he is currently the Jack Steele Parker Professor of International Economics, Emeritus, and Thomas W. and Susan B. Ford Distinguished Fellow at the Hoover Institution.

I interviewed George Shultz in his office at the Hoover Institution, in Stanford, California. It was early in the afternoon on Thursday, July 19, 2012.

Background Information

Bowmaker: Why did you become an economist?

Shultz: I grew up in the 1930s, when the country was in a deep depression. Economics was the subject on everybody's minds, including mine. When I went to Princeton as an undergraduate, I took some courses in economics and became even more interested. That's how I got started.

Entering the Policy World

Bowmaker: What does an economist bring to the policy world that others do not?

Shultz: An economist brings a disciplined way of thinking about problems that has been worked out over the years. It helps us understand what kind of data to produce, how it should be organized and then used to guide us to the best policy.

It is also true that economics is a strategic science because it makes us think ahead, take into account indirect consequences, and consider variables that might not be of direct interest.

Furthermore, an economist knows that policies that are enacted today do not have immediate effects: they operate with a lag, which causes a problem in a political context because a politician wants instant results. The economist's lag is a politician's nightmare.

Bowmaker: Your first policy position was senior staff economist at the president's Council of Economic Advisers during the Eisenhower administration. Did you view yourself as having strong policy positions or simply as a hired professional serving CEA Chairman Arthur Burns and, indirectly, the president?

Shultz: I had policy views and I already had a track record of publication in labor economics, which is why I was asked to join the CEA. My predecessor had been another labor economist, Al Rees from the University of Chicago, who I knew very well.

I found it a very exciting year, and I hope that I made a contribution. I certainly benefited so much from the experience. I learned a lot about policy, a little about Washington, and a great deal about federal statistics because Arthur Burns was from the National Bureau of Economic Research [NBER].

He was very interested in those statistics, and I was involved in various committees that tried to improve the time-series data, so that was valuable work.

Bowmaker: How would you describe Arthur Burns's approach to his role as CEA chairman?

Shultz: An early chairman of the CEA was a lawyer named Leon Keyserling, who regarded the council as a place for advocacies of the administration's policies, which led to Congress becoming very disillusioned. But when President Eisenhower was elected, he persuaded Arthur Burns to be chairman of the CEA, and Arthur rebuilt the professional stature of the council. He would not give interviews, make public speeches—and when he testified before the Congress, he would not tell them anything about his views on the economy. His view was that he was not the economic adviser to the American people or to the Congress; he was the president's economic adviser. I would argue that the CEA has drifted somewhat since then, and its members appear to be public figures, but I think that the residue is still fundamentally a very professional organization.

Bowmaker: You returned to academia after leaving the CEA, and in 1962 you were appointed dean of the Graduate School of Business at the University of Chicago. Did this experience prove useful for your high-level government positions that would follow later in your career?

Shultz: Being a dean helps you as a Cabinet member because that role has a great deal of responsibility but practically no authority. You can't order the faculty to do something, you can't order the students to learn, and you can't order the alumni to give money. And so I always felt that I had an advantage over my colleagues who had worked in business or in positions where they told people what they had to do. As a Cabinet officer in Washington, you have responsibility, but the White House is your boss, and you can't spend a dime that the Congress doesn't appropriate. You have to get used to the art of management through persuasion.

As Secretary of Labor

Bowmaker: You were appointed secretary of labor in 1969. How did that position arise?

Shultz: I was out here at the Center for Advanced Study when my year was interrupted by my becoming secretary of labor. I was chairing a task force for candidate Nixon in labor relations. One of the things that he did, which I thought was very intelligent, was to appoint a task force in a variety of these subjects with the understanding that if he was elected, the ideas that were developed during the campaign would be fleshed out in more detail.

Bowmaker: How did your background as a labor economist have an influence on the type of secretary that you wanted to be?

Shultz: I was a labor economist who had written about issues such as emergency disputes, but I had branched out into the real world by becoming involved in mediation and arbitration work, and I also had very vivid experiences in the arena of discrimination on the job. So I definitely brought views to the role of secretary of labor.

Bowmaker: Did you make it clear to President Nixon your intended approach to the role?

Shultz: It was an interesting experience being appointed to the position of secretary of labor. Nixon decided to announce his Cabinet all at once, not one at a time. He told me not to say anything about the appointment until there was an official announcement. I informed him on the telephone that I would like to have a personal meeting with him about the position. He replied, "Well, I'll be in Los Angeles next Monday. Come and meet me at around 10:00 in the morning." I spent the weekend saying to myself, "What kind of secretary am I going to be? I have views about A, B, C, D, and E subjects." When I met him, I said, "I have accepted the job, but I want you to be clear about what you're getting because these are my views, and I'm probably not going to change. If they're not satisfactory, it's best that you announce somebody else for the role." I'm glad I did that because I went through several controversial areas that ended up emerging during my time as secretary of labor, and I was able to do things with Nixon's support that were based in the wake of our conversation.

Bowmaker: Two of those controversial areas included the Longshoremen's Union dispute and the ending of the dual school system in the South. Can you tell us about your work in those areas?

Shultz: Yes, I had to handle the Longshoremen's Union dispute that Lyndon Johnson and the Supreme Court had declared to be a national emergency. I thought it wouldn't be one. I had said to President Nixon in our earlier conversation, "Mr. President, your predecessor and the Supreme Court were both wrong. This dispute will not cause a national emergency, and once people get it into their heads that they're not coming to the White House, I can mediate this dispute and get it settled." And so we then sent a big message to collective bargaining that "you're not going to get bailed out by the White House. You've got to work your problems out for yourself." That succeeded.

The president also decided to end the dual school system in the South, and I was his point man in managing the process. All these years after the Brown decision, schools were still racially segregated in seven southern states. And so we developed a strategy in which we identified people of significance in those states (equal numbers of blacks and whites) and invited them to the Roosevelt Room at the White House to open up the discussion. It was not easy but it worked, and I saw the president do an admirable job up there against a great deal of political advice. That's an example of one of the many terrific things that Nixon accomplished. Unfortunately, Watergate is so dominant in connection with his name that people tend to forget them.

As Director of the OMB

Bowmaker: In 1970, you were appointed director of the newly created OMB. Were you attracted to this role?

Shultz: Yes. There isn't another position in which you get to understand how the federal government works. The budget tells you what the president's priorities are, and of course as an economist it is a big deal to have the opportunity to oversee the expenditure side of fiscal policy.

Bowmaker: What changes did you make at the OMB, which replaced the Bureau of the Budget?

Shultz: We had to develop the M in OMB. One of the things we learned fairly quickly was that the only way to have any managerial impact was through the OMB's budget officers, who had a lot of clout.

Bowmaker: At your first meeting about the job, President Nixon told you that it was his budget, not yours. Your predecessor, Robert Mayo, apparently thought that it was his own budget. Without this conversation in the Oval Office, would you have approached the role differently or not?

Shultz: No, there wouldn't have been any question in my mind that it was the president's budget I was working on, although Nixon didn't like the budget process and tended to be more interested in foreign affairs and so on.

But he also did something interesting in that first meeting. He said, "I'm preparing a new suite in the West Wing. Hold your meetings there. That will give people the geographical notion of where the authority is, and if the meeting is bigger than your office can accommodate, use the Roosevelt Room. But make sure people come to the White House so they know it's my budget." By the way, people kill to get suites in the West Wing. I had two offices and a big reception room.

When I became secretary of the treasury a couple of years later, he told me, "Keep your office and be assistant to the president for economic policy, which means you are responsible for pulling people together who are interested in economic policy. And when you are having your Treasury meetings, have them in the Treasury Room, but when they are intergovernmental meetings, have them in the White House." That worked very well. I wound up having an office in the West Wing for four years, and because of that I got an idea of how the presidency works as well.

As Secretary of the Treasury

Bowmaker: How would you describe the economic environment that you inherited when you were appointed secretary of the treasury in 1972?

Shultz: When I arrived at the Treasury, the exchange rate system was in turmoil after the collapse of Bretton Woods, but I found that there was no alternative plan in place. So I spent the summer with colleagues, such as Paul Volcker, developing one, which was then announced with the president's approval. Although the plan was not adopted as such, you could almost hear the world heave a sigh of relief that the US was in the game with a plan and a proposal.

The second issue was wage and price controls. I had opposed this policy before I became treasury secretary, so I started the process of dismantling them. We were making headway when the president decided to reimpose them. I said to him, "Get yourself a new treasury secretary. I'll stay until you find one, but I'm out of here."

Bowmaker: Why were you so opposed to wage and price controls?

Shultz: When I was director of the OMB, I had given a speech entitled "Steady as You Go." I argued that we have the budget under control, we have a good monetary policy with a lag, inflation will come down, steady as you go. But wage and price controls were imposed, which was a huge intervention in the economy, and so the political process had overwhelmed what I regarded as pretty good advice. The 1970s were a bad decade in economics in this country.

Bowmaker: Do you think economists in government fear having to support political decisions that they do not think are economically justified?

Shultz: Some decisions you win, and some you lose—but as long as you feel that in a broad sense the administration is doing something compatible with your views, that's OK. But economists have to stick to economics and not try to be amateur politicians. They are no good at that. They are better off just saying, "Here are the economic implications," and trying to argue for the right policy on that basis. You can make things more palatable in the way that you phrase things, but stay out of the politics.

As Chairman of President Reagan's Economic Policy Advisory Board

Bowmaker: After almost ten years working in the private sector, you returned to government in 1981 as chairman of President Reagan's Economic Policy Advisory Board. How did that position arise?

Shultz: I had gotten to know Ronald Reagan when I came back from the Treasury. He invited me up to Sacramento for what turned out to be a very long lunch. Reagan grilled me about how the federal government worked, particularly the budget, and then we had a dinner party at my house, where Milton Friedman, Bill Simon, Alan Greenspan, Marty Anderson, and Michael Boskin were present. He argued with all of us and more than held his own when we put him on the spot. I could see how well-grounded he was and how he thought through issues. I was very impressed.

Then he invited me to put together and chair an economic advisory committee during his campaign, which I did, and we produced a report for him, a very big part of which was published in the *Wall Street Journal*. It was very good.

As you said, for the first year and a half of his administration, I then chaired his Economic Policy Advisory Board. It was more or less the same group as the committee, and he paid attention to us because we were his pals from the campaign. We thought the way he did, and in office when there were pressures to compromise, we would come in and say, "No. Stick to your guns." He appreciated that, although his staff didn't.

Bowmaker: You just mentioned that you could see how Ronald Reagan thought through issues. Could you elaborate?

Shultz: Ronald Reagan was not somebody to put his finger in the air to find out which way the wind was blowing. He would dig down and say, "What makes most sense?" And then he would stick with it even if it might be unpopular. He always thought that if it's good for the country, then he could persuade people that it's good for them. An outstanding example was when he took office. At the time, inflation was very high, and in our written recommendation we had said that you couldn't have a decent economy as a result, and that the way to get rid of it was to have a disciplined money supply, which Fed[eral Reserve] Chairman Paul Volcker was in the process of producing. Reagan's political advisers said to him, "Mr. President, there's going to be a recession, and you're going to lose seats in the midterm election." He replied, "Somebody has to do something about inflation." In doing so, he pretty much held a political umbrella over Volcker so that we could do what needed to be done; he knowingly took a short-term hit to achieve a long-term objective. I thought in some ways that was his finest hour in terms of the economy.

As Secretary of State

Bowmaker: Was there anything that you learned in your business career that helped prepare you for your next role as secretary of state?

Shultz: I was in the construction industry, which had a big international component to it. We would go to different countries around the world, hire people, pay them, and occasionally fire them. That allows you to learn so much about how a particular country works, a place that you wouldn't otherwise have had a clue about when you are meeting with government ministers. In that respect, my business background was a very educational experience for me.

Bowmaker: In your Richard T. Ely Lecture in 1995 ["Economics in Action: Ideas, Institutions, Policies"], you said that "I have increasingly realized that my training in economics has had a major influence on the way I think about public policy tasks, even when they have no particular relationship to economics."[1] Can you give some examples of when this was relevant in your role as secretary of state?

Shultz: As I said earlier, economics is a strategy science, which tells you that all kinds of problems are going to come up. When I was secretary of state,

---

1. George P. Shultz, "Economics in Action: Ideas, Institutions, Policies," *American Economic Review* Papers and Proceedings 85, no. 2 (1995): 1.

I had to deal with Americans being taken hostage. The basic strategy, which is almost impossible to follow, is that you lower the value of the hostages and raise the costs of taking them. That's straight out of an economics textbook. If you pay for hostages, you are simply encouraging people to take more of them, and that is bad from a strategic point of view.

I remember when a writer for the *Wall Street Journal*, Gerry Seib, was taken hostage in Iran. The newspaper had been whooping and hollering in their editorials, and they came to see me to ask what we were going to do about it. I said, "I'll tell you, but you won't like it." They replied, "What's that?" I said, "The game here is to minimize the gains they get from what they're doing and maximize the cost. And so the bigger the hullabaloo you make, the bigger the prize for them. You've made your point, so why don't you just shut up? We can work it through the Swiss to their embassy in Tehran or their intersection. We're trying to get the message across to the Iranians that this is going to be very costly for them. If you can keep the benefits that they see down, we have a chance of getting somewhere." They agreed, and after about two or three weeks, we got Gerry Seib out. That was an interesting lesson.

General Thoughts on Economic Policymaking

Bowmaker: Can you give some examples of fallacies, misconceptions, or misinterpretations that affect policy debate in this country?

Shultz: Understanding the effects of taxes is probably the biggest one. Some people think that higher taxes lead to a less vigorous economy, while others believe that you can put a tax on something and it doesn't matter. I remember when they taxed yachts here in California. Somehow, the politicians didn't realize that yachts can move. What a revelation! And so all the yachts went up to Oregon. And the same thing happened with private planes. We collect nothing in revenues because people react to the imposition of the tax. I don't know why it is so hard for politicians to understand that. Or maybe they don't care and instead just pat themselves on their backs and say, "Look what I did—I went after those guys with yachts and private planes."

Bowmaker: Which aspects of the institutional framework for making economic policy in this country work well, and which need to be reformed?

Shultz: I don't think there is an institutional answer to the problems that we have. I do think we would be well off if we had a basic revision of the

GDP [gross domestic product] figures. The categories used to describe the economy were created by some brilliant people at the NBER back in the twenties and thirties, but the economy today bears practically no resemblance to the economy then. When something new is invented, like a cell phone, where are we supposed to put it? When we can't think of a place, we call it a service, which means that today we call ourselves a big service economy. But when your description isn't accurate, you're also not getting the dynamics right. And so I've been recommending to the NBER that we have to start with a clean sheet of paper, redescribe the economy, trace that through, and see whether that changes the way it looks.

Personal Reflections

Bowmaker: What value has your public service had to you, and which aspects of public service do you miss most?

Shultz: I always considered it a great privilege to have had the opportunity to serve my country. When I was secretary of labor, director of the OMB, and treasury secretary, there were things that needed to be done, and it was very rewarding to be part of them. And when I was secretary of state, the tectonic plates of the world changed, and I certainly learned a great deal during those interesting and important times.

I miss working with the president, of course, but also all the wonderful career civil servants. I was told, for example, that a Republican couldn't do anything in the Labor Department because it was a wholly owned subsidiary of the labor movement. But I found that if you give them professional leadership, they'll work their hearts out for you. And it was the same at the OMB, the Treasury, and the State Department. The people there were extraordinarily talented.

Bowmaker: How did your personality affect your style and approach as a policymaker?

Shultz: I had my way of doing things, and it seemed to work pretty well. You need to have a strategy and let people know what it is, and have a structure that emphasizes the importance of what I would call line organization. Too many people hire bright young staff and then try to run things through them. I think that's a bad mistake, and something that the White House is doing more and more. There needs to be a line organization that you can build up and make stronger, which allows you to work effectively. Then, of course, there is the importance of leadership, integrity, and accountability. I'm not trying to be a martinet, but in every job, if you don't do it properly, there have to be consequences.

Bowmaker: As a policymaker, which decisions or outcomes were most gratifying?

Shultz: When I was secretary of state and people asked me about my foreign policy, I would say, "I don't have one. President Reagan has one. My job is to help him formulate it and carry it out. But it's not my policy; it's his policy." I had two private meetings with the president every week in which we talked by ourselves. But I didn't use those meetings to reach decisions. Instead, I used them to share reflections on issues that were coming at us.

Bowmaker: On the other hand, there must be some things, in hindsight, that you'd like the opportunity to do differently. What are they?

Shultz: The worst day of the Reagan administration was when the Marine barracks were blown up in Beirut and 241 servicemen were killed. You look back and think about how that might have been avoided.

Paul Volcker (*center*), when undersecretary of the treasury for monetary affairs, at Heathrow Airport, London, on August 16, 1971. Volcker was in the United Kingdom to discuss President Richard Nixon's action on the floating of the US dollar.

2   Paul A. Volcker
Born 1927, Cape May, New Jersey

Paul Volcker graduated with a BA from Princeton University in 1949 and obtained an MA in political economy and government from Harvard University in 1951. From 1951 to 1952, he attended the London School of Economics as a Rotary Foundation Fellow.

Volcker joined the staff of the Federal Reserve Bank of New York in 1952 as an economist, and he left that role in 1957 to become an economist at Chase Manhattan Bank. In 1962 he joined the Treasury Department during the administration of President John F. Kennedy as director of the Office of Financial Analysis, and in 1963 he was appointed deputy undersecretary for monetary affairs. Volcker returned to Chase Manhattan Bank as vice president and director of forward planning in 1965. From 1969 to 1974, he served as undersecretary for monetary affairs during the administration of President Richard Nixon.

Volcker left the Treasury to become a senior fellow at the Woodrow Wilson School of Public and International Affairs at Princeton for the 1974–75 academic year, and then he became president of the Federal Reserve Bank of New York in 1975. From 1979 to 1987, in the administrations of Presidents Jimmy Carter and Ronald Reagan, he was chairman of the Board of Governors of the Federal Reserve System.

From 2009 to 2011, he served as chair of President Barack Obama's Economic Recovery Advisory Board, which was established by the president to offer independent advice in addressing the US economic crisis.

In 2013, Volcker founded the Volcker Alliance to address the challenge of effective execution of public policies and to rebuild public trust in government.

I interviewed Paul Volcker in his office at Rockefeller Center in New York City on two occasions. The first interview took place during the early afternoon of Friday, January 20, 2012, and the second took place during the early afternoon of Friday, September 23, 2016.

Background Information

Bowmaker: Why did you become an economist?

Volcker: When I went to college at Princeton just after the war, I took economics, and it intrigued me. For some unknown reason, my introduction to the subject was a course on comparative economic systems, which wasn't the kind of Economics 101 version that you see today. Then I jumped into the most advanced economic theory class available, which was about business cycles. It was taught by Oskar von Morgenstern, so I became fully developed in the Austrian school. I also took a money and banking course from Friedrich Lutz, which was attractive because it seemed to have more precision than other economics disciplines in those days—balance sheets had to balance, for example, although I now understand they don't necessarily have to do so.

I didn't know what I wanted to do at graduate school, so I applied to arts and sciences at Harvard as an economist and Harvard and Yale law schools, just in case I wanted to become a lawyer. I was surprised when Harvard asked me why I was applying to so many different places—I didn't think they would realize [*laughs*]. By accident, I also saw an advertisement for Harvard's Graduate School of Public Administration, which gave fellowships. I said, "Aha! Why don't I go there and get my way paid?" I had an interest in public administration, but I mostly took courses in economics at Harvard.

Entering the Policy World

Bowmaker: What does an economist bring to the policy world that others do not?

Volcker: Not as much as economists think [*laughs*]. The contribution of economists to the world at large is their analytical training: identifying cause and effect, primary causes and secondary causes, direct effects and indirect effects, and so forth. Those are benefits of economics education that lawyers don't have, for example. But the discipline is too mixed up with different theories and uncertainties. And so the thought that economists know how to run the economy is a little overreaching.

I had an ideal background as a practicing economist. When I first worked at the Federal Reserve in New York, Bob Roosa, who was its vice president, gave me the chance to work on the trading desk and interact with the market each day. I believe I was the first person with an economics background to do so. It was there that I began to understand the importance of market expectations. That's a big issue. I'm not a believer in the present Federal Reserve theory that you lay everything out so that the market knows precisely not only what you are doing today, but what you expect to do tomorrow, and even two years from now. I think that's a mistake. You want to surprise people occasionally. That also applied when I was at the Treasury. Sometimes when the market was expecting long-term finance, I would say, "Sorry, but we're not going to issue long-term bonds" [laughs]. Internationally, we liked to surprise the market as well, particularly when it was under pressure and we wanted to change expectations. Of course, you don't want to surprise a market every day because they have to trust you, but I don't think it's appropriate to lock yourself in to a long-term policy position in a changing world.

Bowmaker: Your first policy appointment in Washington took place in 1962 when you became director of financial analysis at the Treasury, and shortly after you were appointed deputy undersecretary for monetary affairs at the Treasury. Can you tell us how this came about?

Volcker: In the second year of the Kennedy administration, Bob Roosa, who was by then the undersecretary for monetary affairs, invited me to Washington because of my interest in government and economics. He had established a new group called the Office of Financial Analysis, which intended to bring in some scholars from economics. My job, along with doing the forecasting for the Treasury, was to hire some of those people and put them to work. That was a very exciting opportunity, not least because the Treasury was in a key position at the time, and Roosa was the strong intellectual figure in the department. Then, within a year or two, I became deputy undersecretary for monetary affairs, replacing a guy named Dewey Daane. That exposed me to international negotiations. But I left in 1965 to return to Chase Manhattan Bank, where I had worked for a few years after the Federal Reserve.

As Undersecretary of the Treasury for Monetary Affairs

Bowmaker: How did you come to be appointed undersecretary for monetary affairs at the Treasury in 1969 after the election of President Nixon?

Volcker: I was greatly surprised. I didn't know David Kennedy, the incoming treasury secretary, although I did know Charly Walker, the other undersecretary of the treasury. It must have been Charly who convinced Kennedy to offer me the job, because I don't think Nixon had anything to do with it. It took me about two seconds to say yes, even though I was a Democrat and not a supporter of Nixon.

Bowmaker: Why were you so enthusiastic to take up the position?

Volcker: I had the whole interesting part of the Treasury under me: domestic finance, international finance, debt management, credit programs, and so on. So far as I know, it was the only position (short of the secretary of the treasury) that had clear international *and* domestic responsibilities. And since those things shouldn't be separated—we shouldn't treat, at least organizationally, international monetary policy as distinct from domestic monetary policy—it was great to have the opportunity to see the policy conflicts, as well as the synergies. It's disappointing that the position no longer exists, for extraneous reasons. Charly, meanwhile, dealt with the operational side of the Treasury, and he had the principle burden of managing congressional relations. So it was a very nice division, and the organizational chart was wonderful—there were two lines to the treasury secretary: Charly and me [*laughs*].

When I arrived at the Treasury on my first morning, it was inauguration day. My grand office overlooked Pennsylvania Avenue, and I could see the parade through the window. I hadn't even been confirmed at this point, but I was ready to get to work. It's not like today's crazy vetting process, which means that you end up with a mostly unmanned government for several months. Anyway, the president was sworn in at 12:30, and a memorandum arrived on my desk from the national security adviser, Henry Kissinger, describing arrangements for considering international monetary policy. It said that I was going to be the chairman of a committee [the Volcker Group] that would include Fred Bergsten—one of his staff members—as well as representatives from the Council of Economic Advisers and the State Department. It also said that I should report to Kissinger [*laughs*]. I am sure that Bergsten, who had an interest in international monetary affairs, wrote that memo and got Kissinger to sign it. I ran down and told Mr. Kennedy, "You better do something about this!" I don't think he ever did, but de facto I reported to the secretary of the treasury.

Bowmaker: In June 1969, after five months of work with the Volcker Group, you presented President Nixon with your recommendations for international monetary reform in the Cabinet Room of the White House. Although you still believed in the stability generated from the Bretton Woods arrangement, you recommended a limited increase in exchange rate flexibility and a revaluation of the dollar against several foreign currencies. You also suggested for the first time a contingency plan of suspending the convertibility of the dollar into gold. What was Nixon's response to your recommendations?

Volcker: This wasn't the center of Nixon's focus. He had always said to us, "Go away! I'm not interested in your crises." And when the time came to present the recommendations of the report, which we had worked very hard on, it was obvious that he didn't fully understand them, although de facto he approved of what we were proposing.

Bowmaker: In February 1970, Arthur Burns, chairman of the Federal Reserve, lowered interest rates and the price of gold increased, which meant that you had to revisit your contingency plans from your presentation of a year earlier. What were your feelings at this time?

Volcker: I was annoyed, because I didn't want the system to fall apart. The time is now! In the first year of the plan, Bill Martin was still the chairman of the Federal Reserve, and he was conducting very tight monetary policy, which meant that the dollar improved. But then when Burns became chairman, he didn't pay much attention to what we were trying to do and started conducting pretty easy monetary policy, which wasn't consistent with his views, because he was a big believer in fixed exchange rates [*laughs*].

Bowmaker: In February 1971, John Connally was appointed secretary of the treasury. You have said previously that this made you fear for your job. Why?

Volcker: That's just normal—the undersecretary serves at the pleasure of the secretary. This guy was a politician from Texas who knew nothing about monetary policy, had his own views about international trade, and was a very strong character. I just assumed he would want to bring in his own people, but it turned out I was wrong. He said to us, "I'm not going to fire everybody, but I expect loyalty from you," which was very interesting.

Bowmaker: After a meeting at Camp David in August of 1971, President Nixon announced the new plan suspending gold convertibility and adding a temporary wage-price freeze, both of which were your ideas, as well as an import surcharge, which was Connally's idea. Do you regret ignoring the likely resurgence in inflationary expectations after the temporary wage-price freeze was removed? What did you think of the import surcharge?

Volcker: We had to suspend gold convertibility because there was no other way we were going to get a change in exchange rates, and I favored the three-month wage-price freeze to avoid an immediate inflationary reaction. But like with any devaluation, we had to have a tougher domestic policy, including monetary policy. Unfortunately, that didn't materialize. It's clear that Nixon and Connally had their eyes more on the next election than on stabilizing the system. They thought this was a great opportunity to follow expansionary policies instead of restrictive ones, and that also led to the import surcharge—which, as you say, was Connally's baby. I didn't like it and kept trying to erase it from all the plans [*laughs*]. It was a protectionist measure, which wasn't consistent with multilateral traditions and open markets.

Bowmaker: Arthur Burns was against suspension of gold. Were you concerned that his special relationship with Nixon might have won him over?

Volcker: No [*laughs*]. First of all, Burns's idea that you could have a big exchange rate change and sustain gold at the center of the system didn't make sense—it wouldn't have held together for two minutes. But he kept saying, "I can settle this with my central banking partners." And I presume Connally, who didn't like Burns, was instructed by the president to let Arthur have his chance. I just wanted him shut off.

Bowmaker: Four months of negotiations were needed to produce a new set of exchange rates under a revamped Bretton Woods system. What did you learn about the art of negotiation during this period, and how important was Connally in helping you?

Volcker: I learned not to be too eager to make an agreement just to have one. And you'd better have some levers on your side. Now, Connally was certainly a great negotiator, who could be fairly tough. In fact, he was a bulldozer [*laughs*]. He wanted a three-pronged attack with a change in the exchange rate and concessions with our partners on both trade and defense—which were secondary, but he was serious about them. At some point, the ground was cut out from under him because Nixon became worried about defense, particularly NATO [North Atlantic Treaty Organization], and he told Connally to hurry up with an agreement, and so we got one.

Bowmaker: During the negotiations in the Azores on December 13 and 14, 1971, the import surcharge was removed and the dollar was devalued by raising the price of gold. In the following week in Washington, the Smithsonian Agreement was established. This imposed a new structure of prices and arrangements in international finance, including realignment of exchange rates, where central banks would still intervene to maintain exchange rates—but those rates could vary by 2.25 percent around their central values, compared to the 1 percent leeway allowed under Bretton Woods. You expected the Smithsonian Agreement to collapse sooner rather than later. Why?

Volcker: Yes, yes, yes. I thought the exchange rate did not go far enough to ensure market confidence that it could be sustained. At that point, even I was not interested in restoring any kind of convertibility, because I felt it was unsustainable. But without convertibility, it left us in a very weak position from a psychological point of view, and it is not surprising that the agreement began breaking down within a few months.

Bowmaker: In May 1972 in Montreal, Arthur Burns presented a ten-point program to avert disaster, which included the restoration of some form of dollar convertibility into gold. Less than a week after Burns's statement, John Connally resigned. What did you think about the appointment of George Shultz as secretary of the treasury?

Volcker: To me, George Shultz was a pain in the ass, and vice versa [*laughs*]. I was trying to put the system back together, and he didn't want it put back together because he was a big floater who didn't mind the suspension of gold. Funnily enough, he didn't fire me either [*laughs*]. Shultz was a very interesting guy. He was very ideological in his thinking, but when he was responsible for something, he was all about negotiations and compromise. He turned on a switch! Nixon liked him and gave him a lot of authority, but that only made me impatient because Shultz put together several department heads, including from the Council of Economic Advisers, to periodically discuss international monetary reform and insisted I come up with a plan where everybody was on board.

Bowmaker: The British effectively devalued the pound by refusing excess supply of pounds in the market. Burns was worried about the follow-up speculation against the lira, but President Nixon reportedly said that he didn't "give a shit about the lira."[1] Nixon had hailed previously the Smithsonian Agreement as "the most significant monetary agreement in the history of the world."[2] You must have been surprised at his response to concerns about the lira.

Volcker: I thought it was a perfectly appropriate response [*laughs*]. I don't think the lira was of presidential concern—there was nothing he could do about it. In any case, the lira was getting in trouble every other year [*laughs*]. Now, the devaluation of the pound was important. The British were not under that much pressure, but they had a weak chancellor of the exchequer, Anthony Barber, who took advantage of the situation to sneak in a devaluation. In my view, that created an atmosphere in which commitment to the exchange rate was not very strong.

Bowmaker: In coming up with your plan, can you describe the summer of 1972, mixing fixed and floating exchange rate ingredients to get the right proportions?

Volcker: The Europeans wanted to get rid of the dollar as the reserve currency, which I thought was impractical [*laughs*]. And so in effect, our plan had to have fixed exchange rates at its core, but if countries got into trouble on certain criteria, then they ought to be allowed to float. We also had a system of so-called reserve indicators that would signal when you could give up convertibility or restore it. But George Shultz's heart wasn't really in what we proposed. It was life or death to me, but not to him. When he presented our plan at the IMF [International Monetary Fund] meeting in September of 1972, he was furious that we couldn't say we were just in favor of floating. He wanted to rewrite the speech the night before he gave it. I ended up making the tone a little different, but Shultz still wasn't satisfied [*laughs*].

Bowmaker: In early 1973, you traveled to Japan and Europe for negotiations and engineered a depreciation of the dollar against the deutsche mark and yen. Why did you do this?

Volcker: I was trying to take advantage of the turmoil in exchange markets in Europe. I thought this was our chance to get a big change in the exchange rate. For Shultz, this was the opportunity for him to get rid of all

---

1. William L. Silber, *Volcker: The Triumph of Persistence* (New York: Bloomsbury Press, 2012), 110.
2. Silber, *Volcker*, 110.

the controls, but I told him, "Let's also get agreement on mutually supporting and maintaining the gold price as the vulnerable psychological point."
It turned out that the Europeans were more relaxed about eliminating the
controls than I ever imagined, but they didn't want any responsibility for the
gold price. And so while we got the exchange rate change and the controls
dropped, nobody did anything about the gold price. The market settled
pretty well for two or three days, but then, as I had sensed, the gold speculation began, and that's when we were off to the races.

Bowmaker: The Volcker Agreement, as it was known, lasted less than three
weeks. In the end, a compromise was reached with the Europeans that
involved a joint float. Like Arthur Burns, you believed in fixed exchange
rates, but you realized that time had ran out on the US's options. In March
of 1973, you attended a press conference with George Shultz and Arthur
Burns to answer questions about the European initiative. A reporter asked
Shultz, "Mr. Secretary, what does all this mean for American monetary policy?" The secretary of the treasury gave the microphone to Arthur Burns,
who said, "American monetary policy is not made in Paris; it is made in
Washington."[3] What did you think of his statement?

Volcker: I thought it was stupid. Here's a guy who had conducted weak
monetary policy while the system was falling apart, and then we negotiate a
change, announce it in Paris, and in effect he says, "We're not going to support it by monetary policy." What kind of a signal was that to give [*laughs*]?
He was being deliberately provocative. He wanted to be sure that everybody
knew he was not committed to defending what we had just agreed to.

Bowmaker: You resigned on Monday, April 8, 1974, three weeks after
George Shultz resigned. Is it fair to say you waited for an outside chance of
being appointed secretary of the treasury?

Volcker: Me? No. I knew enough to understand that being secretary of the
treasury is a political position. And so I wasn't looking for the appointment.
I guess I would have taken it if it had been offered to me, but that was never
going to happen with Nixon as president. We had a distant relationship.
I don't think he trusted me, and his political advisers surely thought I was
an outsider because I was a Democrat. And remember I was in the Treasury
at the time of Watergate. It was frustrating being part of an administration

---

3. Silber, *Volcker*, 120.

tarnished by that scandal when I was in the midst of a big effort to revise the international monetary system. There were times when I would think to myself, "What the hell am I doing working for this guy? Maybe I should resign."

Bowmaker: What were the lessons that you learned about policymaking from your time at the Treasury that you were able to take into the rest of your career?

Volcker: I certainly learned the lesson that in those days the United States was clearly the world's leader, and people would have a significant amount of deference to the country. They may not have liked it—even fought with us—but that was the reality. There are big differences, though, in terms of going from the Treasury to being an independent central banker at the Federal Reserve. When you are part of the executive branch of government, you are responsible to the president of the United States. But when you are chairman of the Federal Reserve, you don't have to go to the president and say, "This is what we're planning to do. Do you approve of it?" I never had to write a memorandum at the Federal Reserve—except to my subordinates, perhaps [laughs].

Interactions with Presidents as Chairman of the Federal Reserve

Bowmaker: Did you have the opportunity to interact with President Carter when you were Fed chairman?

Volcker: Occasionally, the quadriad—the secretary of the treasury, the head of the OMB [Office of Management and Budget], the chairman of the Council of Economic Advisers, and the chairman of the Federal Reserve—would meet with the president. And late in his term, when interest rates were very high, and Carter had a budget that was severely criticized, he insisted that I get personally involved. He said he would do the budget again, and so I saw him go over it in some detail—Carter was very detail oriented—but I was just providing moral support; it wasn't my job to help him. Then he imposed credit controls, which I think was a mistake. He had the authority to trigger them, but by law, since the Federal Reserve is an independent agency, we could say we won't implement them [laughs]. We decided that probably wasn't a very wise course of action [laughs]. And so we made a stab at putting the controls in place but tried to deliberately make it as ineffective as possible. We made a huge psychological impact [laughs]. People said, "Oh, my God, we can't borrow any money," and the economy went into recession. But as soon as the controls were taken off, the economy bounced back up. It was not a good episode. I don't know how we could have avoided it. I tried to persuade Carter out of it, but I obviously didn't try hard enough.

Bowmaker: Did you receive any pushback from the White House after the surprise in October 1979, when you announced you would be targeting bank reserves?

Volcker: I had to pull out all the stops. On the way over to an IMF meeting, I told Bill Miller, the secretary of the treasury, and Charlie Schultze, the chairman of the Council of Economic Advisers, what I was intending to do in very general terms. And so, of course, they reported back to Carter. The feedback I got was that the president understood that I had to do something. He preferred that I do it some other way that was more traditional and less striking but made it clear he wasn't going to say anything. I do know there were one or two people in the administration—like Tony Solomon, under-secretary of the treasury—who were supportive of what I was trying to do when they learned about it. But there were others telling Carter that while he should support any discount rate increase that I wanted to do, he shouldn't, on the other hand, be behind any of this unorthodox policy. I didn't want to do the orthodox, though, because it didn't have any credibility [*laughs*].

Bowmaker: You were a Carter appointee as chairman of the Federal Reserve. Did you think President Reagan would make a change when you were up for reappointment?

Volcker: In the first couple of years of the Reagan administration, the sec-retary of the treasury at that time, Don Regan, criticized very publicly the Federal Reserve. And the noises that came out of the White House always seemed to be, "What does that guy Volcker think he's doing?" Blah, blah, blah. I am certain that every time Reagan did a press conference, his people advised him to take the opportunity to criticize the Federal Reserve, but he never did. That doesn't mean he was happy with us all the time, but his instinct was that we were trying our best to deal with inflation. I think it was as simple as that. But when the time came to renew my appointment, there was speculation about what was going to happen. And so I went in to see the president in the upper reaches of the White House. It was the only time I saw him completely alone. I said to him, "Look, my term is up in two months. There's a lot of speculation about it. You're not benefiting from it, and neither is the Federal Reserve. If you don't want to reappoint me, then fine. If you want to reappoint me, that's fine, too. But either way, tell me, and let's get this over with." He didn't say much, and that was the end of the meeting [*laughs*]. After I left, he called in his staff and apparently told them, "Hey, Volcker came over here and said his term is up. He wanted a decision. What should we do?" The next morning I was visited by one of his top advisers, who said impatiently, "What did you tell him? What did he say?" [*Laughs*.] Nothing happened for a couple of weeks until I got a call on a Saturday morning from somebody in the White House to say that my reappointment was going to be announced by Reagan that day on a radio talk show [*laughs*].

Bowmaker: How would you compare and contrast Presidents Carter and Reagan?

Volcker: Carter was a details man, like Obama. I fully warned Carter that I would conduct tighter monetary policy, and so I never actually thought that he would appoint me. But he did, and to some extent I was his child from then on [*laughs*]. Reagan, on the other hand, was a big-picture man. Once in a while, I might be asked why money supply was so high, for example, but there were no briefing papers involved [*laughs*]. I know that he took an economics course in a little college in Illinois—Eureka College— and his professor told him that inflation was a terrible thing. You've got to get rid of it! I think I was the personification of his economics professor, so he wasn't going to criticize me [*laughs*].

As Adviser to President Obama

Bowmaker: I would like to talk briefly about your role as chairman of President Obama's Economic Recovery Advisory Board. How did that position come about, and how would you describe that experience?

Volcker: Initially, I think the president liked to be pictured with me during his campaign to show that he was a solid financial fellow. Then he made me his informal adviser and had the idea of setting up the board with me as chairman. I don't think he understood—and I should have known given my experience—that no informal advisory committee can operate effectively by having public meetings that were announced in advance. It was ridiculous. And while it was a pretty good group of people on the committee, there were certain issues, like Social Security, that we were never going to agree on. We did get some agreement on financial sector reform, so there we did have some influence. But overall it was a frustrating arrangement with limited value.

Bowmaker: How did you come to be identified with the Volcker Rule [which prevented banks from speculating in the markets and from operating and investing in hedge funds and private-equity funds]?

Volcker: I had been head of the Group of 30, and we had our reform plan relating to the financial collapse. It pointed to speculative trading as a problem and included something that came very close to being a full-scale Volcker Rule. I discussed the proposal with the Obama administration, but it wasn't very warmly received by all his economic advisers [*laughs*]. To me, the issue was very simple: When you're dealing with an institution that is government guaranteed, in effect, does it make sense to allow that institution to go out and do speculative trading [*laughs*]? As I say, it was an easy sell from my standpoint, but they weren't interested.

One day, though, out of the blue, I got a call from Vice President [Joe] Biden, who I'm not close to at all. He said, "What about this rule you're proposing? How is it going?" I replied, "It's a good move, but I haven't got any horses." He then told me, "Don't worry, I'm your horse. We'll get it done." And so, clearly, he must have talked subsequently to the president about it, although I had no idea he was going to name it the Volcker Rule [*laughs*].

Bowmaker: You said earlier that you thought President Obama liked to be pictured with you to show that he was a "solid financial fellow." Is there a sense in which he used you?

Volcker: Of course he used me, but I also used him. It was a mutually beneficial transaction [*laughs*].

General Thoughts on Economic Policymaking

Bowmaker: Do you believe that if we were to raise the level of economic literacy in this country, economic policymaking would improve because the people would demand better policy?

Volcker: No. Economists like to believe that's true because they have some broad agreement on issues, but they don't. In any case, you don't need to be an economic genius to understand some of the most important concepts, such as having to worry about deficits and realizing there's no such thing as a free lunch.

Bowmaker: What can be done to improve the mutual benefits between academia and policymaking?

Volcker: All I can say is that economists who have been in government should become better economists. They now have a feel for the real world. I remember when I was a tenured professor at Princeton and the Economics Department was fighting to be number one in the world. Once in a while, I would attend faculty meetings where the feeling was that we couldn't aspire to be the best unless we hired rigorous mathematicians filled with abstract theories.

Bowmaker: I would like to ask a question that relates to one from earlier. When you were president of the Federal Reserve Bank of New York, you had a reputation for paying no attention to the Research Department. Nowadays, the Federal Reserve has hundreds of researchers, and there are many in the Treasury, the Council of Economic Advisers, and elsewhere. Are they of any value?

Volcker: Yes, there are hundreds of economists poring over their computers, but I think they have just demonstrated their inability to be successful forecasters [*laughs*]. There are some horrendous examples, with the recent financial crisis being the most obvious one. And it was the same when I was chairman of the Federal Reserve. I was often told, "We need another $X million to buy computers." I would reply, "More computers? Why?" "Oh, we've got to do more regressions," they would say to me [*laughs*]. I was very cynical. When I arrived in August of 1979, our staff were forecasting in that month that we were on the edge of a recession. Then in September, they were telling us we were in the beginning stage of a recession, and by October, we were apparently in a recession. There was no recession [*laughs*]! But when you receive those forecasts from your staff, what do you do? Are you supposed to not tighten up and just let the inflation go on a little while longer? I resent it. The NBER [National Bureau of Economic Research] actually dated the recession as beginning in February of the following year, when industrial production had turned down. But it was a phony recession, because the credit controls weren't put on until March, and that's when the economy took a nosedive. As I said earlier, though, as soon as the controls were taken off, the economy bounced back up. You rarely see any commentary in textbooks about the artificiality of that recession—it is almost completely lost from economic history.

Bowmaker: Which aspects of the institutional framework for making economic policy in this country work well, and which need to be reformed?

Volcker: Oh, boy! For my money, too much is centralized in the White House now, and in a way that is not very productive. We have had some very weak secretaries of the treasury in recent years. They may not have been weak men as individuals, but they were not treated as principal advisers. I don't think that makes sense if you want to have continuity in policy. A lot has been lost, and not just in economic policy, but in other areas as well. I don't know how it can be restored—I wish I had a magic bullet.

But the policymaking process in Washington has always changed with every administration. For example, when I was at the Treasury, nothing happened organizationally between Treasury Secretaries Kennedy and Connally, but policy influence changed enormously. Connally had a strong personality and was very close to Nixon—in fact, his fair-haired boy—which meant that the Treasury had all sorts of influence that it did not have when Kennedy was there. People from the White House would come over to Connally's office to ask him what to do rather than the other way around [*laughs*].

I am not aware of the relative influence of the economic people in the White House or the Treasury today. But what I do know is that the Council of Economic Advisers always seems to be frustrated that somebody else is making the decisions. That somebody else is very mysterious, it appears—always coming from the political side.

Personal Reflections

Bowmaker: We began our interview with a question about why you became an economist, and you discussed part of your education in economics. When you look back on your career, to what extent has it made you reconsider what you learned as a student?

Volcker: When I went to graduate school at Harvard, I took a course by a strict Keynesian named Alvin Hansen, who lectured continuously about secular stagnation. Even then, I thought to myself, "You are telling me we are incapable of generating enough investment, which means we've got to rely on government securities for all eternity?" That's the same conversation that Larry Summers has now, but he didn't have to listen to Hansen all the time. And then I remember Larry Klein did an econometric analysis of Keynesian economics in a little book called *The Keynesian Revolution*. When

I read it, everything seemed very logical, but I couldn't believe those equations could be a reliable description of reality. There are too many uncertainties [*laughs*]. And so I had skepticism going way back. Now, I was the last Harvard economics graduate student that didn't have to take econometrics, so that may have something to do with my current attitude [*laughs*]. But in the end, I am a believer in Hyman Minsky. He argues that financial cycles are repetitive because there is a certain point when psychology turns from buoyant to depressive. You have a period of good economic activity when people take on more and more risk, but it's inevitable that you'll eventually have a bust. Once that happens, people will become conservative again, and a steady period will then follow until you have your next bust.

Bowmaker: What value has your public service had to economics as a discipline?

Volcker: I prefer the question, "What influence does economics as a discipline have on public service?" During my lifetime, the subject has become much more mathematical, much more abstract, and much more useless in terms of contributing to effective public policy. For example, on some relatively simple problems, regression analysis makes sense, but it has been overdone in many cases.

When I first went into government in the sixties, economists thought they knew the answer. Things went pretty well in that decade and confirmed in their minds that they knew all about the business cycle and how to manage it. When that self-indulgence became improper, there were strong competing theories of approaches toward economic policy. Economists could no longer reasonably claim that they knew the answer [*laughs*]. Demonstrably, things went bad for a while and economists retreated into their shells, becoming junior mathematicians in the process. But as you well know, the profession has been recently shook up through experience, and hopefully we are moving away from being so insular.

Bowmaker: How does your personality affect your style and approach as a policymaker?

Volcker: Personality can destroy everything. I would say that I'm not as good as others at maintaining relationships with people so that they feel warm and fuzzy. I don't bubble with bonhomie.

Bowmaker: What are your strengths and weaknesses as a policymaker?

Volcker: A big problem in government is that there are too many revolving doors. There are people in the private sector who move in and out of

Congress or the administration, which creates conflicts of interest. I avoided that, and I would pick that as a strength.

Weaknesses? I blew too much cigar smoke in people's faces [*laughs*]. And maybe I wasn't as trusting as I should have been.

Bowmaker: As a policymaker, which decisions or outcomes were most gratifying?

Volcker: Getting inflation under control when I was chairman of the Federal Reserve has to be the biggest one.

Bowmaker: On the other hand, there must be some things, in hindsight, that you'd like the opportunity to do differently. What are they?

Volcker: I never succeeded in reforming the international monetary system to the degree that I'd hoped, but I'm not sure there was anything that I could have done differently.

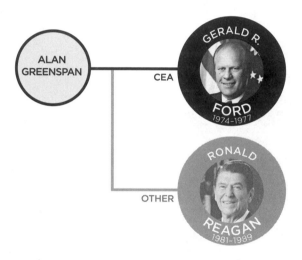

II Gerald Ford Administration

Alan Greenspan (*left*), when chairman of the Council of Economic Advisers, meeting with President Gerald Ford in the Cabinet Room on September 10, 1974.

3   Alan Greenspan
Born 1926, New York City

Alan Greenspan graduated with a BA
in economics from New York University in 1948 and then obtained an MA
and a PhD, both in economics, from
New York University in 1950 and
1977, respectively. He also undertook
advanced graduate studies at Columbia University.

In government, Greenspan served
as the chairman of the Council of
Economic Advisers (CEA) from 1974
to 1977 under President Gerald Ford,
and from 1981 to 1989, during the
administration of President Ronald
Reagan, he was a member of the
president's Economic Policy Advisory
Board, the president's Foreign Intelli-
gence Advisory Board, the Commission on Financial Structure and Regulation, the Commission on an All-Volunteer Armed Force, the Task Force on
Economic Growth, and chairman of the National Commission on Social
Security Reform.

On August 11, 1987, Greenspan took office as chairman of the Board of
Governors of the Federal Reserve System. He was reappointed to the board
to a full fourteen-year term that began on February 1, 1992, and he retired
on January 31, 2006.

In the private sector, from 1954 to 1974 and from 1977 to 1987, Greenspan
was chairman and president of Townsend-Greenspan and Company, an economic consulting firm based in New York City. He currently heads Greenspan
Associates, an economic consulting firm based in Washington, D.C.

I interviewed Alan Greenspan in his office at Greenspan Associates,
Washington, D.C. It was the middle of the afternoon on Friday, September
16, 2016.

Background Information

Bowmaker: Why did you become an economist?

Greenspan: It's very difficult to say, but I can tell you what the sequence is. I was a professional musician at one point and found myself unfulfilled by just being a musician, and so I used to go to the public library and take out books. In a dance band back in 1945, you would get forty minutes on the stand and twenty minutes off. During those twenty minutes, I decided to start reading. As a matter of fact, the first thing I got to read was J. P. Morgan's biography, which I find quite ironic because I was on the board of J. P. Morgan before I went to the Federal Reserve. I had a certain awed nostalgia when they would sit me down in the board room under a painting of J. P. Morgan. I get the notion that they put me there so that they could control me—I would have to vote with the board because I couldn't let those eyes stare at me without consequences [*laughs*]. But I read various books, especially on the stock market and the like, largely because my father was a broker. He tried to get me involved early on, but I was never interested. One thing led to the next, though, and before I realized it, I loved what I was reading, and here I am.

Entering the Policy World

Bowmaker: What does an economist bring to the policy world that others do not?

Greenspan: An economist brings a structured understanding of how the economy is evolving. You begin with a conceptual framework of cause and effect, and then you observe reality and try to anticipate what is going to happen in the future—even though you can never see beyond a certain horizon, and you have to deal with probabilistic events which relate to history. That's how I've always done it, and the way all economists do it, whether they're conscious of it or not.

As Chairman of the Council of Economic Advisers

Bowmaker: You were reluctant on take on the role of the chairman of the Council of Economic Advisers, since you were potentially working for President [Richard] Nixon—whose policies you mostly didn't agree with—and also because you didn't want to interrupt your successful career in the private sector. Which of those two factors weighed most heavily on your mind when you were making your decision?

Greenspan: Back then, Nixon didn't have the reputation that he obtained two years after becoming president. I had no particular objection to him. When I first met him, he seemed staid, almost dull, yet also sophisticated. The problem was that I had my little firm, which was growing very rapidly. And so, when Bill Simon, then secretary of the treasury, called to ask if I would replace Herb Stein as chairman of the Council of Economic Advisers, I told him, "I appreciate it, but let me give you a few other names who will do it." He came back to me a couple of weeks later and said that I had to go to Washington, but again I said that I didn't want to go down there—I was doing fine in New York City. He asked if I would at least go meet with Al Haig, Nixon's chief of staff, at Key Biscayne, Florida, which I agreed to. I told Haig that if the president began implementing policies I wasn't happy with, then I would have to resign as chairman. I mentioned the wage and price controls that Nixon had imposed in August of 1971 as an example—that they were part of the Soviet Union's idea of how the economy functions. I couldn't deal with that kind of thinking. By the time I left Florida, I still wasn't convinced about the job offer, but almost as soon as I got back to New York City, Arthur Burns, my former mentor at Columbia University, called me. "Things are in terrible shape down here," he said, "Someone's got to run the country. You must help." Because of our relationship, when Arthur spoke, I would always say, "Yes, sir; yes, sir," and so he was able to persuade me. I agreed to come down for a month as an interim, and that I would be figuratively, but almost literally, taking on a one-month lease with my bags packed at the door, ready to quit any day. Of course, what eventually happened is that by the time I got down there, Nixon had resigned, and Jerry Ford was about to be sworn in as the president of the United States.

Bowmaker: Prior to accepting the position of chairman of the Council of Economic Advisers, you met Gerald Ford for the first time when you had an hour-long conversation with him about the economy a few weeks before the resignation of President Nixon. What were your first impressions of him, and how would you describe his feel for how an economy worked?

Greenspan: Yes, I had gotten to know him while he was still vice president. We set up an ability to talk to each other in a manner in which I understood what he was doing and could communicate what it is that I thought a CEA chairman ought to do. He had been on the Appropriations Committee of the Senate and for a while had been in the House of Representatives, where he had dealt with the economy—not in a theoretical sense, but in day-by-day practical terms. And so his knowledge of the politics of the way the world works was quite sophisticated. And empirically, because he was involved with the budget and appropriations, he got to learn a good deal about economics. It was easy, then, to work with him in the sense that I could understand his language, and I would try to make what I was communicating with him coherent in his context. We seemed to hit it off remarkably well right from the beginning.

Bowmaker: By your own admission, you were a relatively unusual choice for the CEA role since you didn't have a PhD at the time and viewed the economy differently from most academics. To what extent was this an advantage or disadvantage coming into the role?

Greenspan: I don't think it was either. My reputation was as an economic forecaster of the United States. Through my company, I became an expert in about fifteen different industries. At a very early age, I started off by calculating a fairly accurate series on inventories of steel by product held by customers of the steel industry, and those data had not been available previously. Twelve steel companies, including US Steel, took to that service, and from there I moved on to oil, machinery, aluminum, and other industries. And so I soon became an expert in forecasting a very significant number of parts of the economy and was close to having an aggregated view of the economy as well. I brought to the table, then, types of analysis which no one else had and had developed skills which were very different from those who had come out of university having taken Keynes 101 courses.

Bowmaker: As incoming chairman of the CEA, were you told that you would also be acting as the administration's chief economic spokesperson?

Greenspan: Herb Stein [the former CEA chair] was the chief economic spokesperson for the Nixon administration. But when I went in, I said, "I don't want to be chief economic spokesperson. If I don't agree with what the policy is, I can't effectively communicate it. Let the secretary of the treasury act in the job, since he is a political employee and not apologetic for everybody." And so that's how it worked in the Ford administration.

Bowmaker: Did Herb Stein give you any advice about the role of chairman of the CEA?

Greenspan: Herb was a very special person with a very dry sense of humor. When I sat down at his desk and opened up the drawer, I found a list of instructions that he had left for me, but they were jokes more than anything. He was so funny. One time, he was blind temporarily in one eye and had to be in the hospital. Richard Nixon came to visit him and said, "We're very sorry that you can't read very well." Herb replied, "Mr. President, it doesn't matter. Half of what you read isn't worth reading anyway" [*laughs*].

Bowmaker: The first issue that you had to deal with as chairman of the CEA was the Ford administration's Whip Inflation Now program. Throughout my interviews with CEA chairs, I have heard about bad ideas that needed to be killed. Was this a good example?

Greenspan: Yes, most of the value that the CEA creates is to ferret out the vast proportion of various types of measures which shouldn't go anywhere. And usually when the CEA says something is a terrible idea, more often than not it stops the thing cold. "Whip Inflation Now" was certainly one of them. Basically, it was a voluntary price controls mechanism, and I had literally walked in after it had been spelled out and WIN buttons sent all over the place. In fact, my very first meeting in an economics group for President Ford was a discussion about the issue. As I say, I was the new guy—I had never been in government before—and so I asked myself, "Now, how do I handle this?" I told Ford, "Mr. President, this is an interesting idea, but let me explain to you what the real problems are going to be. If a cotton textile manufacturer is under price pressures and needs to raise his price, he's not allowed to do so. A problem exists then because the basic raw material is cotton. That is not regulated. Why? Because it is a political issue. And so if agricultural prices are rising, this policy says we're supposed to keep cloth prices unchanged. That's all well and good, but the guy will soon be out of business." I think I made a dent with my argument. But very shortly thereafter—within two or three weeks of my arriving in 1974—the problem dissolved itself. The recession took hold, and instead of inflation being the issue, deflation took its place.

Bowmaker: By the latter part of 1974, the economy was weakening. Relative to Nixon, President Ford wanted to slow the pace of policy action; simmer down the deficit and inflation and unemployment; and eventually achieve a stable, balanced, steadily growing economy. You were in favor of a restrained program because it was in line with your own decision-making philosophy.

You have written that in reviewing a policy, you always asked yourself the question, "What are the costs to the economy if we are wrong?" How would you apply this type of thinking to the time that you were at the CEA?

Greenspan: The major problem is that you know what an individual program will do positively, but whether you move forward with it depends more heavily on the downside. If the downside is minimal, then you're more than willing to take risks. If the downside is significant, you have to be very careful irrespective of how big the change of the plus is. In other words, you have to look at both sides of the forecast, and it is a very tricky trade-off. But remember we cannot look into the future, even though human beings are supposed to be able to do it. The oracle of Delphi was invented because people were always looking for somebody to forecast. And how good your forecasts are doesn't matter—people keep coming back. In my own firm, my forecasting record was not very significantly better from anyone else's, but business continued to grow. Why? Because people want to know what the future is, even if they know it is unlikely to occur. It's the same reason why fortune-tellers are in business.

Anyway, you can apply my decision-making philosophy to the major problem that we had right after the issue of Whip Inflation Now, when the economy went into a dramatic swoon. It was a hugely rapid decline that had all the characteristics of inventory collapse, or a final demand collapse, or a combination of the two. We didn't know at the time what it would be, so we constructed a weekly GDP [gross domestic product] set of accounts that enabled us to make a preliminary judgment that it was a major inventory liquidation—which by its very nature has a downside limit [once inventories are at zero, there is nothing left to liquidate]. When the question came up, then, as to what President Ford should do, my immediate reaction was, "Do nothing—it'll cure itself," which is actually a major action, because the conventional wisdom is that when the economy is falling apart, you need a significant stimulus. For example, George Meaney, who was a major labor leader at the time, was advocating that we needed a $100 billion stimulus because, in his view, this was the worst recession since the Great Depression. I thought this would create inflationary pressures when the economy turned around. And so I told the president, "Look, why don't you just do something small? Do a one-shot tax cut and think of it as like a rebate. At worst, it can't do much harm. But most importantly, it will look as though you had taken the recession seriously." He liked the idea and went ahead and did it. That's an example of where I think I made a difference at the CEA. Otherwise, President Ford may very well have felt the political need to put a huge amount of stimulus into the economy, which would have been very unfortunate.

Bowmaker: You unintentionally supplied the buzzword that was used against President Ford throughout the campaign of 1976. The key debate of the campaign was whether the economic recovery had collapsed. You said that the economy was in a pause period. "Pause" was interpreted by the critics of the president that the economic policy of the Ford administration had failed. Do you regret the wording of your statement? If you had your time again, might you have said things differently?

Greenspan: No. In the first quarter of that year, the economy had grown at an annual rate of more than 9 percent but then dropped sharply to a growth rate of less than 2 percent by the summer. I was not concerned, because you cannot achieve an annual rate of growth of 9 percent indefinitely. And so, at a Cabinet meeting, I said, "The recent slowdown in economic growth is just a pause. It will pick up again." But between that statement and growth picking up again was the 1976 election. As an economist, I had to tell the president that it was a pause, because that's what it was. Now, if you're a politician and the economy is growing at 9 percent a year and it slows down to 2 percent, that's viewed as a bad answer. But I don't think it is, because, as I said, the economy can't keep growing at that rate. Eventually, it will begin to accumulate inventory and create the same problem that we had before. It's perfectly normal. I suppose I could have said it's normal, but then the comment would be, "You mean to say that a two percent growth rate is normal?" It was a no-win situation. And so I can't think of how else I would have said it. For years afterwards, Henry Kissinger would tease me, "Are we in a pause now?" [*Laughs.*]

Bowmaker: During the Ford administration, the Economic Policy Board, of which you were a member, would meet to filter different kinds of recommendations coming from various avenues, including Congress, and present the president with a series of options on economic policies. Can you describe the significance of this arrangement?

Greenspan: It was important and useful but also standard procedure, because as far as I know most presidents have groups of people who specialize in certain areas. For example, Reagan had the Economic Policy Advisory

Board during his administration. And you have to remember that the philosophical basis of all the people who work for individual presidents is constant. Those who work with Barack Obama are essentially liberal economists, Bill Clinton's economists were basically centrist Democrats, while our group with Ford were conservative economists. And almost every economist, whether liberal or conservative or something else, has a fundamental view of how the world works—being in favor of free trade and free prices and against protectionism and price control. This meant there were not many differences among the board's members in terms of fundamental goals, only on the tactical implementation of specific strategies. Ford himself was mainly a free trader who believed in market competition and economic freedom, so the Economic Policy Board largely shared his overall philosophy.

Bowmaker: I would like to ask some more questions about your personal interactions with President Ford. First, how did he like to receive and absorb information from you?

Greenspan: I saw him three or four times a week for one-on-one meetings. I would just do what I did for my clients before I got into the cauldron of politics. And he responded like a regular businessman. We had a very good rapport. I knew what he was doing, although I don't think I knew what was actually going on in his head. What was the case is that he increasingly seemed to have ever more confidence in what I was doing, and he asked me not *why* I believed certain things, but *what it is* I believed. And so he wasn't interested in any of the economic details or statistical techniques—which is true of most politicians, with the exception of Bill Clinton. And I certainly didn't put myself in the role of teacher. That would have made me feel very uncomfortable. It's hard to understand, but having just gotten into government, I can remember looking around and saying, "This is the president of the United States in the Oval Office. What am I doing here?" There is a certain aura about being president that you can't get around. I was never, then, going to be a teacher to whoever was sitting behind the table. That would have been inappropriate. And so while he would ask a lot of questions, I didn't put myself in a position in which I said to him, "Now, let me explain to you how this works, Mr. President."

Bowmaker: How would you describe President Ford's style of authority?

Greenspan: I'll tell you about a particular episode that really turned me on to Jerry Ford. When Nelson Rockefeller, the vice president, came up with a boondoggle energy program called the Energy Independence Authority, Frank Zarb, the administration's energy czar, and I went into the Oval Office and told the president, "This is nonsense. It'll be a disaster." He replied, "OK, I'll tell Nelson that it won't go." A week or two later, I received a call from Ford asking me to come back to the Oval Office. When I got there, he said, "I want to apologize to you. I said I was going to stop Nelson's idea, but I was politically unable to do so." I told him, "Mr. President, you're the president of the United States. I work for you." After I walked out of the office, I thought to myself, 'How many presidents could do what he just did? He's so secure in the sense that he knows what he knows, he knows what he doesn't know, and he's not embarrassed by what he doesn't know." That's so atypical in the Washington political arena. And it meant he always acted as though we were equals, which was quite remarkable. I've never run into anything like it before or since.

Bowmaker: How would you compare President Ford to the other presidents with whom you worked or knew?

Greenspan: The two sharpest were Bill Clinton and Richard Nixon. Both had their faults, although Nixon's were a little more egregious than Clinton's. But they were also very smart. After I left government, I remember going to a meeting at the Economic Club of New York. With no notes, Nixon got up and went around the world for forty minutes explaining all the difficulties that were confronting us. It was a tour de force that I'd never seen in my life. Very few people could do such a thing, but he did it all the time. And Clinton is very similar. I had been told that he read three or four books a week as president of the United States. In fact, I talked to him about it, and sure enough there were books that he had probably read in a day that took me two weeks to read. It is an extraordinary intelligence. How he ended up as a politician I do not know, but he is very impressive.

Bowmaker: You have stated many times that President Ford is your favorite president as a *person* for numerous reasons, but some of them are those reasons that would have meant it would be difficult for him to be elected on his own. Can you elaborate?

Greenspan: Yes, Jerry Ford was an extraordinary man, but he could not have been elected president by himself. For one thing, he didn't have the quirkiness. For example, he wouldn't have understood what Donald Trump is talking about at the moment. And in a presidential campaign, there are certain things that you have to do that can be a little bit unsavory. Ford wouldn't have been able to do it—there was too much integrity in the man, whereas Nixon did it to the extreme. Had he not been vice president when Nixon left office, I don't think he would have made it. In other words, I don't believe he could have gotten through the Republican convention. I can't know that for certain, of course, but that's my overall impression. In any case, it turned out that working for Ford was more interesting than my eighteen and a half years at the Federal Reserve. That says a lot.

General Thoughts on Economic Policymaking

Bowmaker: How has the role of the CEA chair changed over time, and how do you think it will evolve in the future?

Greenspan: By the time I came to Washington in 1974, the Council of Economic Advisers had already evolved because its first chairman in 1946 was Leon Keyserling, who was a lawyer. But it tends to be a fairly consistent advisory process for all administrations: you begin with an analytical and conceptual framework of how the economy works, which you then translate into a form that presidents can understand and defend at a press conference. Of course, some presidents are better than others. For example, Reagan, Nixon, and Clinton were superb in that regard, and I have noticed that Obama handles himself very well in a press conference. I'm not sure how much he really knows because he has no real history, but you can tell how his mind is working. Although he pauses when he speaks, he provides a sentence that is structurally correct and an answer that is credible.

Bowmaker: What is your view on the so-called revolving door between Wall Street and Washington?

Greenspan: It's not Wall Street and Washington—it's Washington and the private sector. Wall Street is just a cliché name and only a very small part of the flow back and forth. I am considered one of the "Wall Streets." When Bernie Sanders was in Congress, he was always saying, "You and your Wall Street friends," which seems to have stuck. If anything, though, Wall Street experience is a major plus for monetary policy. Why? Because that's the real world. For example, trying to judge what the Dow or 30-year Treasury yields are going to do is a very valuable idea to have in your toolbox when you do go into government.

Personal Reflections

Bowmaker: How did your personality affect your style and approach as a policymaker?

Greenspan: You're asking me to be introspective [*laughs*]. I'm know I'm a huge public figure but also someone who is very introverted, so that's a contradiction in terms. I think that made me more cautious about going out front and doing things, until it got to the point where everybody was looking at me as the person who is supposed to make the final decision as the chairman of the Federal Reserve. I was acutely aware of what I was doing, but I felt very uncomfortable.

Bowmaker: What were your strengths and weaknesses as a policymaker?

Greenspan: My weakness was that I wasn't omniscient. That would have solved a lot of problems [*laughs*]. I was a sideman. As a musician, I never graduated to being a good soloist, where you have the opportunity to express yourself. I played clarinet, tenor saxophone, or bass clarinet in a band where I sat in the middle reading scores written by other people. Psychologically, I remained a sideman. As a consequence, I did what I had to do, and I made decisions when I had to make them. I could argue with senators when I had to go up to Capitol Hill, and I held my own very well because I knew a lot more than anybody up there. But it wasn't an enjoyable function since none of the people were analytical or conceptual—they had opinions without any reasoning. One of my favorites was Bernie Sanders, when he was a congressman. We had the same routine twice a year, which was hilarious because it never changed. His opening remarks were literally the same one period to the next, so it wasn't very informative. What I didn't do is try to say to someone like him, "Congressman, you're wrong." The one time I decided to say to Barbara Lee, "Congresswoman, let me ask you a question," she stopped me immediately and said, "You're here to answer the questions; I'm here to ask them." I replied that she was absolutely right, and I never did it again [*laughs*].

In terms of strengths, I'll answer that question in a slightly different way. As you know, I was at the Fed for eighteen and a half years. During that time, Paul Volcker never once commented on monetary policy, which I always thought was very thoughtful—because I will tell you to have your predecessor at any job commenting after the fact on what you did is not very edifying. And so I tried to do the same thing. I do talk about what the financial markets are doing, but I never speak about the correctness or failures involved in policy initiatives since I left office. If somebody asks me, "What do you think about the Fed's move the other day?" I stay away from it, but it is a very tough game to play.

Bowmaker: You have stated previously that the three best jobs for an economist in Washington are chairman of the Federal Reserve, chairman of the Council of Economic Advisers, and secretary of the treasury. You have done two of those jobs and have also suggested that you would have loved the opportunity to serve as secretary of the treasury. Why?

Greenspan: Oh, I must have first made that statement when I left the Ford administration, having just been fired by thirty million people. And I probably would've had a reasonable shot at being appointed secretary of the treasury if Ford had gotten elected. At the time, I thought doing that job would've been a very good idea because, technically speaking, you are the senior financial officer in the government, and I liked the notion of having such a broad scope to deal with. But I got all that satisfaction from being at the Fed.

Bowmaker: I have spoken to many economists throughout my interviews who have emphasized your commitment to and fascination with data. For example, Janet Yellen referred to you as a "data hound." Can you elaborate?

Greenspan: I guess that's a compliment [*laughs*]. Data are a measure of what is going on in reality. If you want to endeavor to try to lower the probabilities of forecasting mistakes in the future, the more information you have about the structure of the system, the better off you will be. A conceptual framework without ties to the real world is a very interesting academic exercise, but it ferries you nowhere—which gets us right back to the beginning of this conversation about how I got started as an economist.

By the way, see that gray book right there [*points to a book behind our table*]? That's *Measuring Business Cycles* by Arthur Burns and Wesley Clair Mitchell, which was published by the National Bureau of Economic Research in 1946. I bought it new. Mitchell was the founder—not conceptually, but statistically—of business cycle research, which was data oriented, and I was always attracted to it. I have found that I absorb an awful lot from just looking at data for Lord knows how long. And so Janet is certainly right on this one: I'm a crazy analyst [*laughs*].

Bowmaker: When you look back on your career, can you give an example of an event that made you reconsider how you viewed the economy?

Greenspan: That happens all the time. For example, before the 2008 crisis occurred, I was acutely aware that there was a bubble emerging, but it wasn't until after the crisis that I had enough information to allow me to conclude that while all bubbles burst, not all of them are toxic. On October 19, 1987, the Dow Jones Industrial Average dropped almost 23 percent—an all-time record before or since for one day. I had assumed that was going to have a significant impact on the economy, but in fact it confounded the GDP figures from that day forward. Similarly, when the market collapsed because of the dot-com boom in 2000, we experienced the shallowest recession since before the World War II period. In other words, those two episodes had de minimis consequences. Before we got into 2008, I knew that bubble was also going to blow because, as I say, they all do, but I thought it could well turn out to be de minimis, too. What I didn't realize is that when assets—here, subprime mortgages—crack in a highly leveraged environment, it causes sequential contagious defaults, which blow apart the financial sector as well as the nonfinancial sector because of the breakdown in finance. The same thing happened in 1929, when the asset was highly leveraged broker loans. And so what you can do to avoid any crisis is to have sufficiently high equity in the financial intermediary. Now, the argument against that is that the banks will make fewer loans and generate less profit, but we have data going all the way back to 1869 showing that they have been earning between a 5 and 10 percent rate of return on their equity. This means that, regardless of the level of equity as a ratio to assets, you earned the same rate of return. When you increase the capital requirements, the markets always adjust, so profits stay up even though the capital requirements have risen significantly. My conclusion, then, is that if we had been able to have higher equity to assets, say 30 percent, 2008 would not have been so catastrophic.

Bowmaker: As a policymaker, which decisions or outcomes were most gratifying?

Greenspan: Leading up to the 2000 bubble, there was a big dispute within the Federal Reserve on the issue about whether productivity was rising or falling. I was looking at the data—which I knew very well, obviously—and the published numbers made no sense. I was seeing a very stable general price level and a very rapid increase in profitability, and the algebra of it is that you can only have that if productivity is rising. I said to the Federal Reserve Board staff, "The data have to be wrong," because prices are reasonably accurate to forecast, and wages are similarly forecastable, so it was just not possible for that sequence to be going on without productivity moving very rapidly. The staff argued that the numbers had to be right, but I told them to disaggregate the whole structure of the data. I knew how it would come out because I had done it myself, industry by industry. And so when the staff looked at the numbers in some detail, it turned out noncorporate business productivity in the high-tech area was going down, not up. "Explain to me how that's possible," I asked them. "It's not possible," they replied. And so I finally prevailed. That was important because it affected monetary policy in the sense that if the economy was moving forward, it would have been appropriate to raise the federal funds rate. But it was moving forward in a way in which productivity was accounting for it all, and there were no inflationary pressures. I assume you know what the Phillips curve is?

Bowmaker: Yes, it shows the inverse relationship between the rate of inflation and the unemployment rate.

Greenspan: That works wonderfully well in the classroom, but not necessarily in the real world. Anyway, as the unemployment rate started to go down, everyone was saying, "We've got to tighten up." I said, "Why?" And they told me, "Because of the Phillips curve." I said, "That's never been accurate—it's always after the fact." And so we got down to 4 percent unemployment and no inflationary pressures...we got down to 3.8 percent unemployment and no inflationary pressures. And then finally everybody said I was right [*laughs*]. That was my most enjoyable few months of work with the staff at the Fed.

Bowmaker: On the other hand, there must be some things that, in hindsight, you'd like the opportunity to do differently. What are they?

Greenspan: How long have you got for me to tell you [*laughs*]? First of all, every policy move you make is partially wrong because our understanding of exactly the way the monetary system works is always changing. It's very disturbing when people are coming up with new channels by which monetary policy functions. I say, "How many new channels are there? What about the channels we haven't seen yet?" Economics is a primitive science, if I could put it that way, but we can't do without it because people have to know what the future is, even though we can only know it in probabilistic terms. The only thing you can do is make judgments approximately about how things are likely to arise under conditions which are occurring. Each of us has a model in our heads; some of them work, and some of them don't. For example, the nonfinancial business models all seem to work rather well, but those modeling the financial system are a disaster. Take the so-called liquidity preference function found in the original Keynesian model in the *General Theory* of 1936. When I first read it, I thought, "Oh, this is magnificent." The trouble is it doesn't work, because what you need to measure is continuously evolving. I know that because the Federal Reserve had an extraordinary good and very sophisticated model that was essentially neo-Keynesian, but it did not capture what was wrong that led to the crisis in 2008. I guess we do progress all the time, yet we're always looking back and saying, "We should have done it another way." That's never going to change as far as I can judge.

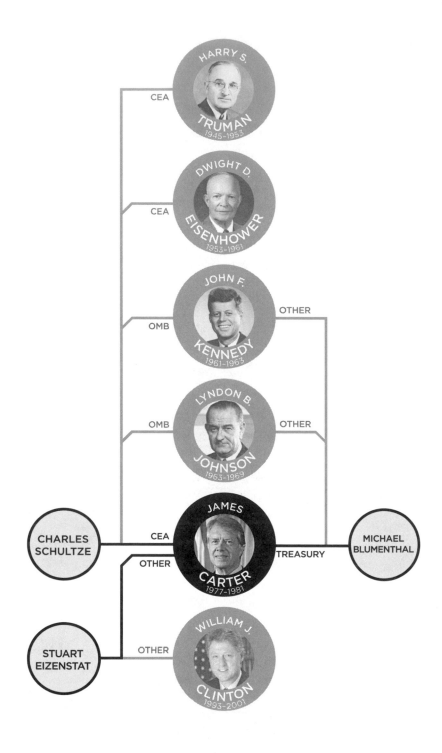

III Jimmy Carter Administration

Charles Schultze, when President Jimmy Carter's designee for chairman of the Council of Economic Advisers, arriving at the Carter family's retreat, Pond House, just outside the small south Georgia town of Plains, on January 2, 1977.

4 Charles L. Schultze
Born 1924, Alexandria, Virginia
Died 2016, Washington, D.C.

Charles Schultze graduated with a BA in economics from Georgetown University in 1948 and then obtained an MA and a PhD in economics from Georgetown in 1950 and 1960, respectively.

He was appointed assistant director of the Bureau of the Budget by President John F. Kennedy in 1962 and was its director from 1965 to 1967, during the administration of President Lyndon B. Johnson. Schultze served as chairman of President Jimmy Carter's Council of Economic Advisers (CEA) between 1977 and 1981.

Schultze also worked as an economist in academia. He taught at Indiana University between 1959 and 1961 and at the University of Maryland between 1961 and 1987. He was a senior fellow at the Brookings Institution in 1968–1976 and 1981–1997 and a senior fellow emeritus in the Economic Studies Program at Brookings.

I interviewed Charles Schultze in his office at the Brookings Institution in Washington, D.C. It was early in the afternoon on Friday, September 7, 2012.

Background Information

Bowmaker: Why did you become an economist?

Schultze: As an undergraduate, I took a course in economics by a professor who was a refugee from Austria. He had an unusual teaching technique. If an argument went from A to B to C to D and the conclusion was F, he would explain the heck out of A and then give you F. And so between classes you would have to figure out B, C, and D. That was a really good intellectual exercise, and I was inspired to go on to take a master's degree in economics. But becoming an economist wasn't something that I had planned. In fact, at one point, I wanted to be a journalist, but that didn't happen ... thank God [*laughs*].

Entering the Policy World

Bowmaker: What does an economist bring to the policy world that others do not?

Schultze: Economics is a structured discipline. That is the key point. While recent research on behavioral economics has demonstrated how people in some circumstances behave differently than traditional economic theory postulated, economists' training nevertheless gives us a solid framework with which to help policymakers deal with economic issues. And economists are incorporating behavioral economic research into their kit of tools.

Bowmaker: Before you began your first major position as assistant director of the Bureau of the Budget in 1962, you served as a staff member at the Council of Economic Advisers. How did you come to be appointed?

Schultze: In 1951, I was teaching at a small college in Minnesota. During Christmas of that year, I came back to the D.C. area, where I grew up, and wandered over to the outfit that ran the Korean War wage and price controls. I was offered a job there and got to know someone who had been closely associated with the CEA and was keeping close tabs on the wage and price controls operation. He recommended me for a position at the CEA. And so I served on the staff during the last year of [President Harry] Truman's term before Arthur Burns came in as CEA chairman and got rid of a lot of us. I worked for a trade association for one year and then came back to the CEA. Initially, Burns wouldn't let me into staff meetings because I was too junior, but eventually I broke that barrier and took on more responsibilities, including economic forecasting.

Bowmaker: How much interaction did you have with Arthur Burns?

Schultze: Plenty. I remember when I received an offer from the trade association to go back and work for them. It was a big jump in salary. I went to Arthur Burns and said, "I've got a wife, one kid, and another on the way. My salary here isn't great. Could I have a raise?" Puffing on his pipe, he replied, "Well, you don't have a PhD, do you?" At the time, I didn't. And then he said, "How many years have you been working in economics?" When I told him for only two years, he replied, "With those credentials, I don't think you deserve a bigger salary." In a smart ass way, I said, "Dr. Burns, there are two ways to think about the determination of a wage. There is the Marxist way, which is how much resources had been put into the worker's background, or there is the modern economic way, which is what you are being offered elsewhere, the so-called market price." He shouted back at me, "Don't you call me a communist!" But I got the raise about three months later [laughs].

Bowmaker: How would you describe his approach as chairman of the CEA?

Schultze: In all fairness, Walter Heller [President Kennedy's chairman of the CEA] and Arthur Burns turned the CEA into an organization of some stature. The person who preceded Burns was a lawyer named Leon Keyserling. He had an idiosyncratic view of how the economy operated. And Truman, the president he served under, didn't give a damn about the CEA. But when Burns arrived, he had a much better idea of how the CEA should work. He hired some good economists and proved to be relatively influential with President [Dwight] Eisenhower. He also raised the status of the CEA substantially.

At the Bureau of the Budget

Bowmaker: How did you come to be appointed assistant director of the Bureau of the Budget?

Schultze: When I was on the staff at the CEA, I had gotten to know Bob Turner, who was a member of the Council. We reached an understanding that he would first take the position of assistant director, and when he left, that I would get it. He only lasted a year and a half in the role before he recommended me to the director.

Bowmaker: When you began your position, was there anything that surprised or frustrated you?

Schultze: Over time, I learned that a large fraction of senators and representatives understand very little economics. For example, they believe that the world is full of corner solutions—the concept of continuous cost and demand curves with nonzero elasticities is alien to their way of thinking. And I would defy anybody to explain the theory of comparative advantage to them.

Bowmaker: How much interaction did you have with President [John F.] Kennedy?

Schultze: I went to around three or four meetings with him before he was assassinated. Academics would have loved him because of his approach to discussing policy. If it was a half-hour long meeting, the first fifteen minutes would be spent on the issue's substance and then we would switch to the politics. You could see his mind working in a very orderly manner.

I remember an issue relating to agriculture when he came down on the political side of the answer. I told him, "Mr. President, this is going to cost you half a billion dollars a year," which was big money at the time. He replied, "You just wait until my next term. I will shake this place up like never before." A few months later, he was dead.

Bowmaker: How would you compare Kennedy to Lyndon Johnson, for whom you worked as director of the Bureau of the Budget?

Schultze: Lyndon Johnson would surround a problem. You didn't know where the hell he was coming from [*laughs*]. It wasn't a linear, logical process at all. If you gave him an economic answer, he would pose a political problem with it or vice versa. But there was nothing more important to him than getting a piece of legislation through Congress. For example, there was a time when the head of the Atomic Energy Commission [AEC] wanted to develop a nuclear rocket, which my staff and I thought was a low payoff venture. LBJ overruled me. But he set up a meeting with four senators who came from areas where the rocket would be built. He staged a debate between me and the head of the AEC. All through the meeting, I would make a point and he would say, "That's a good point, Charlie." But at the end, he said to the senators, "This is a tough decision. You heard Charlie's views. On the other hand, I know that this is important to you, so I am going to go your way." He did so because he wanted them to support his tax bill. And he did the same thing in relation to a proposed change in the cotton price support program. It should have been an open-and-shut case, but he overruled me. The next day I was told by the guy who sits outside his door, "The president asked me to pass on this message to you: when you attend meetings like that again, don't make your arguments so damn convincing" [*laughs*].

Bowmaker: How would you describe President Johnson's style of authority?

Schultze: Johnson's secretary of labor, Willard Wirtz, had a really high opinion of his status. One night, Johnson, Joe Califano [a policy adviser], and a young staff member were discussing a labor problem and came up with a solution. Johnson told the young staff member, "Go out and call the secretary and tell him this is what I want." The next day, the secretary called up the person who sits outside the president's office and complained that a young whippersnapper whom he'd never heard of had told him what to do. Johnson overheard the call on his speakerphone and leaned over and said, "This is the president. From now on, if a charwoman from the White House calls and tells you what to do, you do it!" [*Laughs.*]

Johnson always wanted to show people around his ranch. I was once there with a number of congressmen. Somewhere nearby there was a batch of wet cement in frames. He picked up a stick and said to the congressmen, "I want you to write your names in the cement." And then he looked at me and said, "Do the same, Charlie." As you know, my name has an *e* at the end. I didn't have enough space to put it in the cement. I thought that nobody would notice, but about ten seconds later I heard a voice behind me: "Hey, come over here, guys. You wonder why we have budget problems. The dumb son of a bitch I hired to be budget director can't even spell his own name!" Johnson was a character [*laughs*].

Bowmaker: What were his views on the budget during the Vietnam War?

Schultze: In his early days of the Vietnam War, he was a dove and spent a great deal of time worrying about the right-wing gung-ho guys, including those within his own party, who wanted him to bomb Hanoi. I remember telling his wife that one of the hardest things for a democracy is to run a limited war, and that was certainly true of his treatment of the budget during that period. Johnson went out of his way in the early stages of the war not to give out inside information about how much it might cost. As a consequence, even though we knew that the cost was accelerating, it wasn't until nine months or so after the first major war budget was sent to the Congress in early 1966 that he requested a tax increase to finance it. That was too late and set off a rise in inflation. Everybody says that the reason for the delay in proposing a tax increase was that he didn't want to sacrifice his Great Society programs, which he knew that Congress would make a trade for. But I think a good chunk of it was because he well understood the fact that it is hard to run a limited war in a democracy. To get the tax increase, he would have had to pound the table, whip people up, and go at it like it was an all-out war. He never said that to me, but I think deep down he was scared to death that he would unleash forces that he couldn't control in order to get that war tax.

Bowmaker: What were the main lessons from your time at the Bureau of the Budget that you were able to take into the remainder of your public service career?

Schultze: One of the things that I had learned from my time at the Bureau of the Budget was how to write a memo to the president. I remember one time when Johnson received a long memo from the Treasury, and he sent a note to me that said, in effect, "Would you please explain to me what they're trying to tell me?" To any busy president you need to keep memos brief and in a logical outline form so that he can absorb and evaluate its contents.

As Chairman of the Council of Economic Advisers

Bowmaker: Why do you think Jimmy Carter chose you to be chairman of his Council of Economic Advisers?

Schultze: Before his inauguration, one of his chief staff guys, Ham Jordan, was quoted as saying: "We want to get some new blood in here. The last thing we need is more Charlie Schultzes or Cy Vances [former secretary of the army and deputy secretary of defense]." He had to swallow that comment when Carter called me in to talk about joining his administration. Carter opened up the conversation by asking me, "What would you like to do?" I replied, "To tell you the truth, I would like to run the Bureau of the Budget again." He said, "I'm sorry, but I have a wonderful guy lined up from Georgia, Bert Lance, who is currently director of the Transportation Department." I then asked for the CEA job.

One of the reasons they wanted me in the CEA role was because Carter's number one policy adviser, Stu Eizenstat, thought that without being a politician, I was highly familiar about how the federal government worked. In fact, for the first two or three months in office, one of the advantages I had over anybody else was that I knew how the government worked because of my time at the Bureau of the Budget and could work up rough numbers. And so I had a large role in developing Carter's initial stimulus package. That's an example of a CEA chairman having a bigger hand than would normally be the case. But after the bill got to the Congress the major element I promoted—a refundable tax cut—was dropped.

Bowmaker: Did President Carter make it clear what he expected you to do for him?

Schultze: He told me, "I want you to be my chief economic spokesman." That created a big problem because he brought in Mike Blumenthal as secretary of the treasury who said, "This is going to be awful for me. The secretary of the treasury cannot go around the world dealing with all these other countries and not be the president's economic spokesman." And so we came to an agreement that we would be cochairmen of a committee responsible for economics. That didn't work, and I resigned as cochairman. I thought my role was to bring to the president the views of what I'd call the mainstream of economics—unvarnished advice subject to the realities of the world, if you like. I wanted to minimize as far as possible being put in a position where I had to start off with a compromise between the economics and politics.

Bowmaker: Coming into the role, was your economic philosophy in alignment with that of President Carter?

Schultze: He was inherently somewhat more conservative on fiscal matters than I was. But during his campaign, he had promised a stimulus program to try to speed up the economic recovery from the prior recession. He pushed that hard, but clearly he wanted to keep the budget deficit small. Conversely, he was a good bit more friendly towards environmental regulations than I was. The CEA was particularly worried about how those regulations could raise prices. But there were no major showdowns, and I didn't have any trouble communicating with him. He didn't know a lot about economics as such, but he was very bright and perceptive. He was also the only major politician I knew who would write deltas on memos to denote changes [*laughs*].

Bowmaker: How would you describe the kind of economics that you used in advising President Carter relative to that found in your academic work and teaching?

Schultze: You had to translate basic economics into language that could be understood by the president rather than spell out the latest refinements of theory and econometrics. Richard Schmalensee, a member of the CEA from 1989 to 1991, wrote the following in a letter to Herbert Stein, chairman of the CEA from 1972 to 1974, who was requesting "reminiscences" from CEA members: "The core of my job was not offering opinions honed to perfection in years of academic work. Rather, it was learning about an issue quickly, finding and inhaling some relevant literature (often by calling a real expert outside the Beltway...), applying some basic price theory and common sense (often indistinguishable) and thinking about how to express the core ideas involved orally in a few sentences to a lay audience."[1] That sums up my point nicely.

---

1. Letter to Herbert Stein, May 23, 1995.

I later wrote a book called *Memos to the President* in which I imagined that I was once again chairman of the CEA and the president tells me, "I'm going to give you one hour every week to teach me something about economics." And so I came up with a series of memos that I would send him on a range of issues. It was all about explaining good, solid economics in a way that didn't oversimplify but nevertheless was relatively easy to understand. One reviewer said that it reminded him of Columbus's trip to the new world: "He didn't accomplish what he was hoping for, but it was a worthwhile trip."

Bowmaker: When you were in disagreement with President Carter, did you try to change his mind by presenting new evidence, or did you employ a different strategy?

Schultze: What you don't want to do is reopen old decisions. Part of the game is that sometimes you lose. I remember one case in particular. A new welfare bill was proposed that resulted in a big fight between the Department of Labor and HEW [Department of Health, Education, and Welfare]. The Department of Labor wanted public employment for those who were unemployed. The HEW approach was to expand and improve the current systems of cash payments to the poor. The president asked me to moderate between the two sides. I had two problems with the idea of public employment. First, I was afraid that the unions would push for very high wages in the public employment program. And second, there was the question of whether these jobs would be productive or merely ones that would gain a bad reputation. I thought that I had almost convinced the president of these considerations. But all of a sudden in a discussion about how large the public employment program would be, I could see the president's mind working on something. He was dividing the population of his hometown— Plains, Georgia—by the population of the USA to get how many people in Plains would need a job. And he discovered it was only one! [Vice President] Walter Mondale then chipped in, "Yeah, that's right. I don't know what you're all talking about. It's not a big problem." So I lost that fight [*laughs*].

Bowmaker: Were you satisfied with the formal process by which President Carter received your advice?

Schultze: The only problem with Carter was that he never gave Stu Eizenstat the authority to tell Cabinet officers, "No, you cannot include that as an option." And so instead of being given two policy choices, Carter would receive three or four, many of which had subchoices within them. It got to the point where it was a lousy way to make a decision. And the same thing happened when we initially set up an economic policy committee. We were planning to have the Treasury, the OMB [Office of Management and Budget], the CEA and, when relevant, the State Department on it. But as Carter went down the list of new Cabinet officers to appoint, he promised a number of them, "Oh, yes, you can be on the economic policy committee." I remember the second meeting of the committee in the Roosevelt Room. With principals and staff, there must have been around thirty people there. The president walked in and was absolutely flabbergasted at the size. We told him that he had to do something about it, so we established an executive committee. Unfortunately, that became too big as well! Finally, three or four of us decided to set up a secret committee, called the X Committee, which did the work on economic policy. The decision-making process about major items within government is not efficient when there are too many people stirring the porridge.

Bowmaker: I would like to turn to two specific economic policy issues that you had to confront while you were CEA chairman: first, the problem of high inflation, and second, the run on the dollar that took place in 1978. What was your own view on how to deal with the high inflation?

Schultze: The difficult part of my job was the economic situation at the time. We'd had the two big oil price shocks that led to wage increases and then into prices, which started a spiral and an acceleration of inflation. Simultaneously, the higher oil prices sucked out purchasing power and generated a recessionary threat. It was a terrible dilemma. I used to say to people, "If you want me to get rid of inflation, I can do it. Just let me raise interest rates high enough and make the budget tough enough. But it will give you a huge amount of unemployment." And no administration is ever going to ask the Congress or the Fed[eral Reserve], "Would you help us generate a lot higher unemployment?" And so we tried voluntary jawboning and then something fancy, which was a scheme that involved business firms agreeing to hold wage increases for their employees down to a certain level. If prices rose above that level, then the government would guarantee the workers a tax rebate to make up for it. The Treasury and other members of the economic policy group initially thought that was a great new idea. But as soon as it got up to the Hill, we received a lot of flak and it never went through. What could we do? As I say, I told people that we could solve the inflation problem, but we wouldn't at all like the results for unemployment. This meant that the last two years of the Carter administration were very discomforting for me. I do regret not pushing for more dramatic action to break the back of inflation, but history will say that Fed Chairman Paul Volcker did essentially the right thing in the end.

Bowmaker: How closely was the CEA involved in dealing with the run on the dollar in 1978?

Schultze: On international financial matters, the Treasury, together with the Federal Reserve, were the players. But in this case, the CEA was involved with the Fed and the Treasury. Bill Nordhaus, one of the members of the CEA, managed to convince everybody that if we were to intervene in the foreign exchange market, it should involve big money. The figure that we suggested was $40 billion. The question was whether the Treasury or the Federal Reserve should put up the money. The Treasury had a fund that was a hangover from when gold was devalued in the 1930s. But they said, "We don't have much money left in the fund, so we can't do it." And our contact from the Federal Reserve said, "I can't go back to my board and say that we are going to take this on. We could show a loss." But it was all the government's money! And so it seemed to take us longer to get over the quibbling than to settle the major substantive issue [*laughs*].

Bowmaker: Bill Nordhaus has gone on to become a very prominent economist. Can you tell us a little more about his influence while he was at the CEA?

Schultze: Looking back, I might have brought Nordhaus to more meetings with the president. He had an ability to do great work in a hurry. I remember when we were trying to do jawboning on wages and prices, and there was a threat of a big coal strike. The last thing we wanted was a big settlement in the coal industry. At a weekly Cabinet meeting, the secretary of energy popped up and said, "Mr. President, if this strike doesn't get settled, there are soon going to be two million people unemployed." That number sounded outrageous. And so I asked Nordhaus if he could give me a ballpark number that might be reasonable. Based on some experience of the effect of a big coal strike in the UK, he came back and said to me, "Well, it depends on how long it goes on, obviously, but I would estimate unemployment of around 35,000." I tried to use that number to stop anybody from doing what someone actually did—which was to call the coal mining firms and say, "Settle the strike," which they did with a large compensation increase. It turned out that the Department of Labor set up a way to track the impact of the coal strike, which took place between late '77 and early '78, and the number they came up with was very close to Nordhaus's estimate. I was impressed.

Bowmaker: I would now like to turn in more detail to your interactions with the rest of the economics team. First, how would you describe your relationship with the Treasury?

Schultze: It was good, although there were some moderate disagreements. In 1978, we proposed a tax reform/reduction that was worked on by the Congress in the following year. The reduction component was both for political reasons and because we thought the economy might be soft in the coming year. The Treasury wanted to lower the corporate tax rate, while the CEA was in favor of an investment tax credit on the grounds that it was better targeted. The debate went on for some time. But Carter didn't have any strong opinions about which side it came out on. He just knew it was going to be a business tax cut. And so when he had meetings with business people he would question them on the issue: what did they think? In the end, we didn't get the investment tax credit in the proposal. But in any case the Congress turned it into a capital gains tax cut.

Bowmaker: In the early days of the Carter administration, Arthur Burns was chairman of the Federal Reserve. Why did you recommend to the president that his position should not be renewed?

Schultze: Burns was often hard to deal with. The CEA wanted to set up meetings with the Fed's Board of Governors. Arthur agreed, but then he came up to me privately and said, "Now, the one thing we can't talk about is monetary policy." I understand that is a delicate matter, but what the hell were we supposed to talk about? It was difficult. We also had so-called quadriad meetings every three or four months that involved the president, Burns, Treasury Secretary Blumenthal, and me. They weren't very useful either. I always felt it was like a bunch of dogs sniffing around each other. And it certainly wasn't a place for a real policy discussion.

Blumenthal and I agreed that we'd recommend to the president not to renew Burns's position. But we then made a mistake. Because the Fed job had always gone to someone with a financial background, we felt that we should look instead for a businessman. And so we picked William Miller, who had done quite well in business and was a friend of Blumenthal's. He was bright and a nice guy, but unfortunately he did a poor job at the Fed. He was only there for a year. In late '79, Blumenthal and I both agreed that he was being too loose with monetary policy, even though many people were worried about a potential recession. In any event, Blumenthal kept leaking criticisms of what the Fed was doing, and it was pretty obvious where it was coming from. We both received a note from President Carter: "Keep your hands off Miller." That was all it said [*laughs*]. But Miller became treasury secretary when Blumenthal was fired in 1979, along with four or five other Cabinet members.

Bowmaker: Paul Volcker then became chairman of the Federal Reserve. How would you describe your relationship with him?

Schultze: He was a joy to work with. We disagreed on some important issues, but it was always substantive, never personal—we were good friends. His revolution created a lot of unemployment and pain, but it ultimately worked. I would have preferred a more gradual path, but all in all now I'm glad that he did it. And none of the president's advisers publicly dumped on him—he was pretty much left alone. It's certainty possible that Volcker, who was a very up-front guy, told the president what he was going to do when they first met. And his genius was that he did what he had to do in a way that didn't make it look like every time the interest rate went up it was the Fed that was responsible. Up until that point, the Fed ran monetary policy by agreeing on a target for the federal funds rate and then doing whatever quantitative moving was necessary to get there. But Volcker switched to a monetarist approach that involved setting a "noninflationary growth" in the money supply. And so if interest rates rose sharply, that could be attributed to the market, not the Fed. I have talked to him about this, and he denies that he had a political objective in mind, but I swear I can't imagine he didn't.

Bowmaker: All things considered, can you give an example of where you as an economist, or the CEA as an organization, were able to make a difference?

Schultze: One of the things that a CEA chairman does is to try to quash excessive promises or, conversely, statements of catastrophe. Ultimately, though, you have to accept that you'll never hit any home runs. And you don't even get good singles very often. In most cases, what you're trying to do is take something that is fifth-best policy and make it second best or third best [*laughs*]. You are nudging and pushing towards a solution that is as efficient as possible.

General Thoughts on Economic Policymaking

Bowmaker: Which reforms to the institutional framework for making economic policy in this country have been particularly important?

Schultze: The establishment of the Congressional Budget Office about forty years ago has made a huge difference. My colleague Alice Rivlin deserves a great deal of credit for starting it and keeping it nonpolitical. The idea of a congressional committee that is above politics? Unbelievable. Rivlin also proposed what could be a helpful improvement to the federal budget process—namely, to enact discretionary appropriations only every two years, devoting the alternative years to oversight of federal operations.

Bowmaker: Do you think that the gap between economics research produced in universities and policymaking will increase or decrease over time?

Schultze: While economics has become more and more technical during my professional lifetime, it offers improved tools for public policymakers, albeit with the aid of talented translators. Behavioral economics is a relatively recent field that has already improved economists' policy relevance and will continue to do so in the future. The most urgent research needed at the present time is for further developing the data and the economic analysis to help policymakers understand the intricate and highly interdependent operations of the financial system and its effects on output and employment, both domestically and globally.

Personal Reflections

Bowmaker: What were your strengths and weaknesses as a policy adviser?

Schultze: I was good at framing arguments in a way that wasn't designed to show off my economic knowledge but could be understood by the audience. In terms of weaknesses, I might not have been forceful enough. But one problem facing any economist dealing with policy issues is that in a political environment you don't give your bottom line away immediately. Decision making within government is all about bargaining. This means that you sometimes have to propose 2X rather than your goal X, because compromise will inevitably be involved. But how do you justify 2X when you are pretty damn sure that X is the right thing to do? That goes against your training on how to do and report economic research, and it was an aspect of my CEA role that I found somewhat hard to handle.

Michael Blumenthal (*far right*) when secretary of the treasury, inside 10 Downing Street, London, for a Group of Seven (G7) summit meeting on May 5, 1977. Also pictured are President Jimmy Carter (*second right*) and Secretary of State Cyrus Vance (*third right*).

5 W. Michael Blumenthal
Born 1926, Oranienburg, Germany

Michael Blumenthal spent his childhood years in Germany and China
before moving to the United States in
1947. He earned a BS degree in international economics from the University of California, Berkeley in 1951 and
then attended Princeton University,
where he obtained an MPA in public
affairs and an MA in economics in
1953 and a PhD in economics in 1956.

From 1954 to 1957, he was an assistant professor of economics at Princeton, and from 1957 to 1961 he was vice
president and director of the Crown
Cork International Corporation.

Blumenthal first served in the gov-
ernment from 1961 to 1963 as deputy assistant secretary of state for economic
affairs. During that time, he was chairman of the United States Delegation
that negotiated the Long-Term Cotton Textile Agreement, chairman of the
United States Delegation that negotiated the International Coffee Agreement, and United States Representative to the United Nations Commission
on International Commodity Trade. He then served as the president's deputy
special representative for trade negotiations, with the rank of ambassador,
from 1963 to 1967. In that capacity, he served as chairman of the US Delegation to the Kennedy Round of trade negotiations.

Blumenthal joined Bendix, a worldwide manufacturer serving the auto-
motive, aerospace-electronics, industrial-energy, and shelter markets, in
1967. Within five years, he became chairman, president, and chief executive officer (CEO) of the company. He then served as the sixty-fourth
secretary of the treasury between 1977 and 1979, during Jimmy Carter's
presidency.

I interviewed Michael Blumenthal in his apartment on the Upper East Side of Manhattan, New York City, during the mornings of Wednesday, May 29, 2013, and Tuesday, July 9, 2013.

Background Information

Bowmaker: Why did you become an economist?

Blumenthal: I became an economist because during my early life I witnessed some real economic disasters, which had a personal impact on me. Specifically, in China, I lived through what was at that time the second-worst inflation in world history, and then when I first came to this country after the war [World War II], I was aware of the fear of high-level unemployment with all the returning veterans not being able to get jobs. In fact, the very opposite happened. And that awakened a curiosity in me, and I began to wonder how the economy worked. And when I went to the University of California, Berkeley, that developing interest was heightened by some rather impressive professors.

Entering the Policy World

Bowmaker: What does an economist bring to the policy world that others do not?

Blumenthal: Economics forces you to study the facts and to be rigorous about analyzing them. That is useful because in economic life so much that appears logical is not, and so much that appears illogical is. And so an economist who understands that the subject is frequently counterintuitive has something to contribute.

Bowmaker: You were appointed to your first policy position in 1961 as deputy assistant secretary in the State Department during the [John F.] Kennedy administration. As you began your position, was there anything that surprised or frustrated you?

Blumenthal: I was neither surprised nor frustrated—I was exhilarated. I had spent a few years as a junior faculty member at Princeton and as a junior executive in a company, and this was by far the most exciting, most important, and most fulfilling experience that I ever had. I couldn't have been happier. I had arrived in this country in 1947 as an immigrant, and here

I was fourteen years later as deputy assistant secretary of state. In what other country can you do that? I was so thrilled and proud. And I was the youngest of that rank in the State Department. Everything was wonderful, uncritically wonderful.

Bowmaker: Did you view yourself as having strong policy positions or simply as a hired professional serving the president?

Blumenthal: International economics was one of my fields for my PhD, so I had some relevant economic knowledge, and I had spent four years as a corporate executive in international business, so I also had a little practical experience. But I was put in charge of developing new approaches to commodity policy, which I knew nothing about. I just believed in vibrant, multilateral trade and agreed with President Kennedy that a rising tide lifts all the boats. One of the first things I did was negotiate a world coffee agreement, which the economics profession said was a very foolish and stupid thing to do. But we did it anyway, and it worked—which shows that there is a big gulf between theory and practice.

Bowmaker: Did you have any interaction with President Kennedy?

Blumenthal: The only substantive meeting where I was alone with him was when I was appointed to be the head of the US delegation for the Kennedy Round of trade negotiations. I didn't want to leave Washington because my boss, George Ball, was fond of saying that in politics nothing propinks like propinquity. In other words, you have to be close to the seat of power. I didn't want to go to live in Geneva, and on a couple of previous occasions I had respectfully declined the great honor to run the delegation. Then one day I received a message saying that the president wanted to see me. I knew what was coming, and I rehearsed many reasons for why I didn't want to take the job. I told my wife that I would explain to him that X, Y, and Z are much better suited for the role.

When I went to see the president, he first thanked me for helping him with negotiating other commodity agreements, which had been helpful to him in his Latin American policy. Then he said, "Why do they call this the Kennedy Round?" I told him, "Because you're identified as getting the law passed that enables us to now negotiate on this broad basis." He replied, "You know, I don't think I like that, because if it fails, I've got my name attached to it, and it's going to be a black eye for me." Leaning forward, he fixed me with his nice blue eyes and said, "That's why I want you to go and make sure that it doesn't fail. I have trust in you." And so with all the good intentions of explaining to him why I couldn't, wouldn't, and shouldn't take this job, I heard myself saying, "Yes, sir, I'll do my best"—which was my first lesson in how hard it is to say no to the president in the Oval Office.

I came home and my wife asked, "What happened?" I told her, "Well, we're going to Geneva" [*laughs*]. But I remember Kennedy saying to me, "You get this done in two years, come back, and we'll have a great job waiting for you." Well, first of all, he was dead within a few months after my reaching Geneva, and secondly, it lasted four years, which I thought was very, very long. But in that slow and agonizing process, we achieved a very successful negotiation, which had a lot to do with boosting what is today the European Union.

Bowmaker: Was your training in economics useful in this role?

Blumenthal: Oh, sure. It's always good to remember the theory of comparative advantage [*laughs*]. I got my PhD from Princeton and then taught there from '54 to '57, but I decided that, with all due respect to your great profession, academic life was not for me. But my background in economics did prove to be useful for the trade negotiating role. It trained me to look at things in a certain way, and a Princeton PhD helped in winning a certain amount of prestige. As Dr. Blumenthal, people listened to you and assumed you knew more than you actually did.

Bowmaker: Overall, what were the main lessons from this initial experience in the policy world that you were able to take into the remainder of your career?

Blumenthal: The main lesson was that an individual policymaker who has a good sense of power and an intuitive feeling for how decisions are made, in combination with luck and courage, can sometimes have an outsized impact on the course of events. I came away from the world coffee agreement feeling that without me it never would have happened. And it was the same with the Kennedy Round. But success has many fathers and failure is an orphan, and so in the end, there were many people who claimed they had played a significant role. As I say, though, I felt it might not have otherwise been that much of a success if I hadn't been there. What I learned, then, was that (a) I was good at what I was doing and (b) personalities matter, because I had seen the positive and negative interplays between people and the resulting effect they had on the decision-making process.

As Secretary of the Treasury

Bowmaker: After you left the State Department, you spent ten years in the business sector before being appointed secretary of the treasury during the Carter administration. How were you approached, and why do you think you were considered for the position?

Blumenthal: The Kennedy Round had given me a certain amount of notoriety because it was a very high-profile negotiation. There hasn't been anything like it in your lifetime—it was on the front page of the *New York Times* almost every day. But throughout my career, I have always been appointed to jobs that were more senior than I was entitled to. That was crazy, but just luck. So by the summer of 1976, when Carter had been given the Democratic nomination—I did not support him at the time—I was a somewhat unusual character for two reasons. Firstly, my name had received quite a lot of publicity, and secondly, I was a former stateless refugee and liberal in that bastion of industry, Detroit.

During that summer, Carter assembled a group of Democrats to advise him on economic policy, and I was one of them. I flew down to Plains, Georgia, the little village where he lived, and I spoke a few times during the meeting. But I was one of twenty people, so I had no idea whether Carter even noticed who the hell I was. Then when he was elected in early November, he asked for another meeting of advisers to talk very specifically about the program that he would be launching upon entering the Oval Office. Again, I was asked to come down to consult with him. The newspapers were saying that we were the people he would pick for his economic Cabinet, and all of a sudden there was speculation that I would be appointed to a secretary position. I was a little dubious, but indeed that's what happened. Behind the scenes, my name had obviously risen to the top, and Carter asked me whether I would help him—even though we hardly knew each other.

The only time I was alone with him before my appointment was when I flew down to Atlanta for a twenty-minute meeting. He wanted me to tell him my life story, which is difficult to do in twenty minutes. The one question he threw at me was whether there were any skeletons in my closet he needed to know about. I said, "No. I've always paid my taxes, I've never been in jail, and I've only had one wife." After we were done, he said, "Fine. Fritz [Mondale, his vice president] and Ham [Hamilton Jordan, his principal assistant] will join us. Do you mind?" "No, of course not," I replied. And so they came in, and we ended up having a desultory conversation. The only question that was of any substance was when Fritz asked what I thought about the trade-off between inflation and unemployment. I can't remember what I said exactly, but it was some kind of obvious answer. Carter then excused himself and said, "I'll call you." Fritz went with him, but Ham stayed behind, and we chatted for a few more minutes. "How will you get home?" After I told him I had a company airplane, he said, "Well, goodbye, sir. I hope it works out. I think it will." With that, he left. A few days later, I was in my office at Bendix in Michigan. The phone rang, and it was Carter. "Mike, I've decided to ask you to be my secretary of the treasury," he said. I told him, "Thank you, sir. I'm very honored. I promise I'll do the very best I can for you." That was it.

Bowmaker: What were your first impressions of Carter?

Blumenthal: Very positive, actually. I thought he was an unusually intelligent man. I was impressed that he was very disciplined and that in both the first and second meetings in Plains, he did not act like a politician. He ran them more like a graduate seminar. He asked penetrating questions and was interested in acquiring as much detailed knowledge as possible. He wanted to learn the tax code by heart. Believe me, it isn't easy. He even took seminars from a tax scholar named Joe Pechman from the Brookings Institution. Can you imagine Ronald Reagan doing that?

I also thought he was important for the times. This was in the post-Watergate period, and he had run on the simple notion that "I'll never lie to you." I felt that the country needed that kind of a person. I didn't know many southerners, so it was all very new to me, but I had, on balance, a very favorable impression in those very early meetings. Once we got into the specifics, though, that began to change very quickly.

After he picked the Cabinet, he had a meeting in Sea Island, Georgia, where he got all his people together who would work in the White House. So there were all the Georgians and then the rest of us, like Cy Vance, Charlie Schultze, and myself. That's when I first began to be puzzled by the peculiarly apolitical way in which Carter approached problems, knowing full well what awaited him in Washington was a highly political environment. He would ignore that at his peril, but he didn't seem to understand.

I'll give you one example. He kept describing how he would operate and said, "Send me short memos. I like to read, so I'll read those quickly, and you'll get them back within twenty-four hours, with my notes in the margin." I had been in Washington before, and I knew that the president would be swamped with bits of paper [*laughs*]. He also told us, "I will not have a chief of staff—I will have a hub-and-spokes approach to government. I am the hub, and all my assistants are the spokes, because I don't want to filter anything. You guys will have direct access to me. You can see me anytime." So he had a rather naive impression of how the government works, and it struck some of us who had been in Washington as, "Does this guy know what's it like to be in the White House?" He kept referring to what he had done as a governor of Georgia in Atlanta, which had obviously worked, but it's a big step from being the chief executive of the great state of Georgia to being president of the United States.

During a break in one meeting, I remember saying to him, "Governor, you're going to be up to your eyeballs in paper. Do you think you can manage?" He said, "Oh, don't worry, Mike. I get up at 5:30 every morning. Besides, I like to read." I thought to myself, "Well, maybe he's an unusual guy and can do it." But he had a very, very large agenda of what he wanted to accomplish, and he was determined that all the promises he had made in the campaign would be kept. He had a guy named Stu Eizenstat as his domestic policy adviser, and Stu made a list of all those things. It was called "Stu's List" [*laughs*]. It had about 120 items on it, and he wanted to get all of them done but talked about it without appearing to have a sense that there would be lots of congressional committees involved—that he could propose, but they would dispose. Again, I thought it seemed a bit naive but just said to myself, "Maybe the guy knows something I don't."

And, of course, in the beginning you get carried away by the enthusiasm and don't want to be the skunk at the garden party. Within a few months, though, I realized that he had serious flaws as a leader, and he turned out to be the most difficult man I've ever worked for. I've prided myself on figuring out how to get along with the "not so easy" people in my career, but Carter was something else.

Bowmaker: Did President Carter make it clear what he expected you to do for him?

Blumenthal: No, and that was a big mistake. We never discussed how he saw the job, we never talked about our relationship, and we never talked about how he wanted to organize the making of economic policy. He didn't broach those subjects, and I didn't ask—which I should have done. Maybe I am more to blame than he because I had been to Washington. I should have known this is an important issue and that I better talk to him about it. In his case, he should have known it, also, but perhaps given his lack of understanding of how things worked in Washington, he thought it would be like being the governor of Georgia. I didn't do it because at that point the very idea of being secretary of the treasury was so thrilling. I didn't want to rock the boat.

Bowmaker: Did you have a sense of the type of secretary of the treasury that you wanted to be?

Blumenthal: I knew that it was a very senior job. Within government, the secretary of the treasury has often been the heavyweight when it comes to economic policymaking. On the other hand, I realized the reality is that what happens in Washington has a lot to do with personalities, even though I had a reputation for being a strong guy. What I didn't know is that the president had no sense of what exactly the secretary of the treasury does and would look upon me as just one of his advisers. Getting back to your previous question, I should have asked him, "How do you see my role as secretary of the treasury? How do you want me to relate to the other policymakers? How do you want to be kept informed on the key issues?" But I didn't, unfortunately.

Bowmaker: When I spoke with Charles Schultze, he told me that you were upset that President Carter wanted him to be his chief economic spokesman. Can you shed more light on this matter?

Blumenthal: What do you mean by chief economic spokesman? If you're a sucker for punishment, you can go through my eighty-two boxes of memos at Princeton University and see that in many of them Carter said, "Mike is my chief spokesman on economic issues," and in his mind that was not inconsistent. What he meant was when it came to questions like, "Is the economy going up or down?" then Charlie, as the academic, would be the chief economist. In terms of economic policy, though, he realized that the secretary of the treasury should do it. But he even appointed a guy named Fred Kahn as his inflation spokesman! And when he was still there, he told this strange guy named Bert Lance, who was head of the OMB [Office of Management and Budget], that he was also a spokesman.

So Carter had lots of spokesmen. That's what upset me and explained why the administration developed very quickly an image of utter confusion.

You couldn't get anything done. I kept saying to him, "Somebody has got to be in charge here so that the issues that come to you are ready for a decision." But he was never willing to do that. It's not that I wanted to be the spokesman, it's just there had to be only one. Obviously, the secretary of the treasury was the logical choice, but if he had said, "I'm going to make Fred Kahn my economic coordinator in the White House," I would have understood and told him, "That's fine. At least we now have some order into the process."

Bowmaker: Which policy trade-offs were most challenging coming into the role?

Blumenthal: Carter wanted everything. He had no sense of priority whatsoever. He was constantly torn between wishing to do the right thing for the underdog—he was a born-again Christian—and at the same time being a conservative in that he wanted balanced budgets. Well, we were in the middle of the second-worst energy crisis ever. We had stagflation, high interest rates, and a dollar that was dropping through the floor. He had to make a decision about what to do because you can't have everything. But he wanted to decide for himself, and the result was he always fell between two chairs. His domestic policy advisers would be telling him to do things that are good for the traditional constituency of the Democratic Party, like raising the minimum wage, but I would be telling him not to do it because the dollar would take another beating in world markets. That's the sort of dilemma that Carter was never able to get his mind around.

Bowmaker: Could you describe further President Carter's lack of feel for economics?

Blumenthal: I should tell you that he had probably more knowledge about detailed economic facts and figures than most presidents do. I'll give you a fun example. He wanted to introduce comprehensive—he liked the word "comprehensive"—tax reform by the fall of his election, which he did. As I mentioned earlier, the US tax code is very, very complicated, and there are few people who understand it. So we hired a guy named Larry Woodworth, who was one of its great experts, to be assistant secretary for tax policy. Larry and others worked up a proposal that was to be presented to the president. Tax reform is eternal and involves essentially eliminating loopholes, except each one of them is some particular interest group's lolly [lollipop], and nobody wants to give it up. I had been trained and rehearsed by Larry and his group about what to do when I got up there and spoke. But the president said, "Mike, where is the credit to coal miners afflicted by black lung disease?" Now, there's an obscure provision. Who the hell knows about payments to coal miners who are victims of black lung disease [*laughs*]? That example was very typical of Carter—he prided himself on the detail.

But the president had no real sense of how the economy works, particularly the interrelationships within it, and he had an engineer's faith in statistics. I'll give you another example. Every Thursday, we would have an economic lunch with Carter. It was always the same thing. He would turn to Charlie and say, "Well, what do the latest figures look like?" and he would reply, "We've just run the computers, Mr. President, and unfortunately it looks like there's a slight uptick in wage costs, so we're going to have to revise the rate of inflation." Then, he would turn to me, and I would tell him, "The Treasury has its own computers, and Charlie is right. But you need to be careful, Mr. President. The numbers are based on a model. The problem is that we can't be sure that the underlying circumstances out there are such that the future relationships are going to be exactly the same. I have anecdotal evidence, because I'm the guy who talks to Wall Street, and CEOs come to see me all the time. My contacts indicate that it may well be that things are different. Take what Charlie tells you with a grain of salt. My intuition is that we may be looking at an inflationary rate of increase substantially greater than what the computers indicate." Carter would say, "Mm-hmm, mm-hmm, mm-hmm. Thank you, Mike." And so I got the impression that the statistics spit out from the computers meant a lot more to him than the warnings and anecdotal evidence from Wall Street.

Bowmaker: How would you describe the president's style of authority?

Blumenthal: Carter at heart was an autocrat. He preferred to tell people what he wanted to do and have people loyally carry it out. He didn't like to argue and challenge. I think the reason he relied upon and clung to the very young and inexperienced people around him was because they were totally devoted and always said, "Yes, Mr. President." He didn't like dealing with strong personalities. For example, he picked Cy Vance as his secretary of state, who was a patrician gentleman and not confrontational. There is some evidence that people who disagreed with him and stood their ground made Carter feel a little uncomfortable. Just look at the people who he ended up firing, like [Secretary of Health, Education, and Welfare] Joe

Califano, [Secretary of Energy] Jim Schlesinger, and Michael Blumenthal, who had a reputation of saying what he thought. The media's famous comment at the time of "They cut down the trees and left the monkeys" does have some substance.

Bowmaker: How would you describe your relationship with the Council of Economic Advisers [CEA] during your time as secretary of the treasury?

Blumenthal: I would say we were in agreement 40–50 percent of the time. The Treasury were less concerned about the traditional constituencies of the Democratic Party. But I respected Charlie Schultze as a professional who knew his business. And I liked him as a person. I felt comfortable with him, and I thought he was an honest, decent man. But he was much more cautious in his personal relationships and less willing to make enemies than me. You might say he was more judicious and I was more rash, or that he felt less secure, whereas I felt I had some independent standing. I'll give you an example. During his campaign, Carter had said he would introduce a far-reaching energy bill within ninety days of his presidency. And so he began working with Jim Schlesinger on it early in his administration, but it was being done in isolation. Charlie came to see me—which rarely happened because we usually met in formal meetings—and said, "This has real macroeconomic implications. If we raise the price of oil, then it will have a tremendous impact on the automobile industry. Does the president understand? You call him." In other words, he wanted me to be out in front, maybe because he felt like the Treasury had more muscle, which is true. So I got on the phone in my office and said, "Mr. President, Charlie and I are sitting here. We have no idea of what is happening with this energy bill. All we hear are rumors." The president was always very, very courteous and friendly towards me, but his first reaction, with a note of irritation, was, "Wow, I thought Charlie and you knew everything." I replied, "Well, we don't Mr. President. You've been doing this alone with Secretary Schlesinger, and you need to understand its implications." He said, "All right, I'll see what I can do." And then Charlie and I sat down and worked out a memorandum, which we sent to him. In the end, the bill was not passed until about a year and a half or two years later, and even then it was a pale reflection of what Carter really wanted.

Bowmaker: How would you describe your relationship with the Federal Reserve and the OMB?

Blumenthal: [Chairman of the Federal Reserve] Arthur Burns was somewhat of a bullshit artist. We had a perfectly friendly relationship, but he treated me like a graduate student and was not sympathetic to the administration. He delighted in being different, and I thought he was sometimes contrary for the sake of being contrary. He didn't like the fact that Carter was in the White House and made things difficult for us. And so when it came to the question of reappointment, I, together with Charlie and others, were of the opinion that we had to make a change. But we made a mistake in recommending Bill Miller. He was known to me personally as a very successful, intelligent CEO who I thought would make a good balance wheel. That didn't turn out to be the case.

My relationship with the OMB under Jim McIntyre was perfectly all right. But it was a very, very different story under Bert Lance, his predecessor. Bert was the president's closest friend and the only person who dealt with him almost as an equal. They had known each other a long time, but Bert was everything that the president was not. Carter was cautious, modest, and introverted. Bert was expansive, always good with a southern aphorism, and rode around town with a special vanity license plate that said BERT on the back. Whereas the president prided himself on detailed knowledge, Bert would say to us, almost exuberantly, "I don't know anything about any of these problems. I'm going to rely on you, Mr. Schultze and Mr. Blumenthal, to tell me what to do." He was a small-town banker who cut corners and was just totally mismatched to be director of the OMB. Within a few months of his appointment, he had gotten into serious trouble due to his prior business dealings, and it created a huge scandal. The president made it worse by making the scandal his own rather than distancing himself at the right moment. By September, Bert had to resign, but the problem is that the investigation was done by the comptroller of the currency, which is part of the Treasury. I told John Heimann, who was head of the comptroller's office, "Don't whitewash and don't do a witch hunt." And I said to the president, "This is your friend, and it would be terrible if we tried to sweep this under the rug. I've told the comptroller to go straight down the middle." The president said that that's what he wanted me to do, but his staff in the White House, like Ham Jordan and Jody Powell, never forgave me because they assumed I had tried to shaft the guy. It was just a classic case of shooting the messenger. That created difficulties for me later, because the staff continued to resent my presence and started to leak certain things to the press.

Bowmaker: Can you describe the events that led up to your leaving as secretary of the treasury in 1979?

Blumenthal: When the downward-sloping curve depicting the president's popularity intersects with the upward-sloping curve of the rate of unemployment, it is time for the secretary of the treasury to go [*laughs*]. In the summer of '79, the economy was in very bad shape. The big issue was fear of the dollar declining further, because we were importing enormous quantities of oil due to the second energy crisis. We were under great pressure from our partners abroad in Europe, Japan, and elsewhere to curb energy imports. I was bombarding Carter with memos telling him he had to do something. He had already given various speeches on energy, but when you looked at them, they didn't amount to much. And so he said he would give a stronger one and left his advisers to work out its themes, while he and I went to a summit in Tokyo, where he was under considerable attack.

The message I was getting from Washington was that the boys—the Energy Department, his domestic policy advisers, the Treasury, and the CEA—were not making a whole lot of progress getting the policy together, which was going to be reflected in Carter's great speech. One group was saying one thing, while another was saying the opposite, which is where the problem of not having an economic coordinator comes in. I was desperate. So I thought I would take one more crack at him. On the airplane before we landed, I said, "Mr. President, it's not too late, but to turn this around, you've got to do something dramatic. People have to sit up and say, 'This time, he really means it.' You've got to be seen as a decisive leader, and so here's what you have to do." I gave him a list of seven or eight things. He said, "I like it. Write that up for me." We got back, and the next day we went into a meeting in the White House where all this dissension was apparent. The president said he would go up to Camp David for the weekend and gave instructions to continue to put together the speech. A couple of days later, a draft was sent to him which contained a couple of the things I had given to him, so I was mildly encouraged. We waited for a response, but all of a sudden we heard that the president had called off the speech. He'd gone fishing. That was a thunderbolt in the United States. When the markets next opened, the dollar declined further because people didn't know what the hell was going on. The spokesman of the White House was asked, "What's the president's plan?" He replied, "I don't know"—which wasn't good. I had to draft a statement saying that there would be strong action on energy, and that I would be announcing it in a few days.

I blew my top on the phone to Carter's assistant. I said, "As secretary of the treasury, I want to speak to the president now." I was told, "The president is taking a walk and can't be disturbed." I replied, "I don't care. I need to talk to him." About half an hour later, I finally got him on the phone. I told him, "Mr. President, the markets are plunging. I had to do something, so here is my statement." He proofed it, I put it out, and it stabilized the markets. But what then followed was a week of rumors floating around that the president was dissatisfied with the way things were going and that he was reviewing his whole administration. With the benefit of hindsight, it became clear that people like Fritz Mondale and others were strongly urging him not to do this and that he had to go ahead with his speech, but he just ignored everybody.

I had been wanting to get out for some time. But I had hesitated to do so because I believed it was somewhat disloyal. I had said I would sign on for four years. The president was in deep shit, and I thought that to abandon ship under those circumstances would have been a further black eye for him, so I felt duty bound to carry on. But now I thought, "Ah, this is my chance to get out." I knew that he had asked Cy Vance and Stu Eizenstat to see him about something, and since I'd had trouble getting him on the phone even for an emergency call, I called both of them and said, "Would you please tell the president that I have told you that I'm planning to tell him that I will resign?" I know that Stu definitely told him that and also said, "Don't let him resign. That would be terrible. You ought to keep him."

Then a week later Carter held a Cabinet meeting with principals only, which is very unusual. Normally, the staff sits around the outer edges. It was a very solemn atmosphere. The only non-Cabinet person there was Ham Jordan, who was suddenly wearing a suit and tie, which hadn't happened in a long time. I knew something was up [*laughs*]. He sat next to the president, who then gave a forty-minute speech in which he basically said the country had lost its way and that there had been disloyalty on his staff and in the Cabinet. I remember he really attacked Andy Young, who was the representative to the UN [United Nations] and subsequent mayor of Atlanta, accusing him of doing something that wasn't authorized. It was very unlike the president, and they had a brief exchange before Carter pulled back and said, "Oh, never mind." This business of disloyalty hung in the air, though, because no one knew what he was talking about. Anyway, Carter told us he was going to make some changes. A chief of staff would be appointed, which he had resisted for two and a half years, and he picked

Ham. Most of us were glad he was appointing a chief of staff, but we were a little mystified as to why he chose Ham, whose lack of orderliness and organization was legend. But again, Carter trusted him. Then he dropped a bombshell by saying, "I'm going to replace some of the people in the Cabinet. I want each of you to turn in your resignation, and I will let you know which ones I accept." There was stunned silence. That's never happened before in American history. I was thinking, "Doesn't he know that he doesn't have to do that? We all serve in his pleasure. All he needs to do is say, 'I want you to go,' and then you're out."

The first person to speak after Carter had finished was Cy Vance. He said, "Mr. President, I assure you we're all behind you. We're all loyal, and nobody wants to undercut you. I speak for the Cabinet." Then he said, "As to your request that we all turn in our resignation, I strongly urge that we do not do that. That would be a mistake. It would be misunderstood abroad. In other countries, it would mean the government has fallen." But Carter insisted and then said, "Ham is going to pass out forms that I want you to fill out by evaluating each one of your staffs." These were staffs that he had allowed us to appoint independently, and now all of a sudden he wanted us to evaluate them so that he could see which ones he was going to fire. On that happy note, we left.

Two days later, I was asked to come over to see Carter. I walked in, he greeted me with a big smile, and we went into his little inner sanctum next to the Oval Office. I had hardly sat down when he said, "Mike, I've decided to accept your resignation." I told him, "I understand, Mr. President. That's the right thing to do. You probably heard from Cy and Stu as well. I tried to let you know that I had decided it was time for me to go." You could see he was very uncomfortable with the situation, so he was obviously relieved to hear this. Then we had a pleasant twenty-minute conversation, which—with the benefit of hindsight—was devoid of substance and very akin to the chat I had with him when I was hired. But he did say one or two things that I thought were amazing. He said, "Mike, you did a great job. I admire you for your integrity and for talking straight to me. You've been a lot more right than wrong." He was so full of compliments. It was as if he was going to promote me to vice president. And then he told me, "If I hadn't been able to talk Bill Miller into accepting the position, I would have asked you to stay." Incredible [*laughs*]. He continued by saying, "I had strong advice not to let you go, particularly from the economic team, but some of my staff felt that they didn't get along well with you." That was a peculiar state-ment. While I was listening, I was thinking that he was excusing himself for why he had to fire me. He was hesitating for a long time. When I finally said, "You're busy, I ought to go," he asked, "Will you keep in touch and come and see me?" I said, "Of course, Mr. President. You call me and I'll be right there." Even though that was just a platitude, I could see it made him feel better. So that's how it ended with Carter.

General Thoughts on Economic Policymaking

Bowmaker: Which fallacies, misconceptions, or misinterpretations affect policy debate in this country?

Blumenthal: The basic fallacy is that each person sees the direction of the economy primarily in terms of its impact on himself or herself, rather than understanding the much more complex interconnections—not just within the country, but internationally as well. When the banking crisis ended, I had lunch with the German minister for finance, Wolfgang Schäuble, who is a good friend of mine. We talked about what should be done in Greece, and he said, "This is all very complicated. There are so many interconnections, and I have to deal with so many countries. Some of the other finance min-isters I have to work with have been in this business all their lives. I'm new to this, and I don't understand it too well. What do I do?" I told him, "Rely on your people and study. But don't worry. The other finance ministers may have more experience than you do, but fundamentally, they're in the semi-darkness, too. The world that they're confronting is of very recent origin." You've got to know where everybody is coming from and why, because behind every pursuit of principle there resides a particular selfish interest.

Bowmaker: Which aspects of the institutional framework for making eco-nomic policy in this country work well, and which need to be reformed?

Blumenthal: I think the greatest strength of the institutional framework that we have is the Federal Reserve. Among national central banks, the Fed is the most independent and most insulated from momentary political passions. With the right leadership—and we've been very lucky to have had [Federal Reserve Chairman Ben] Bernanke this time around—it is an institution that has the capacity to lean into the wind. That's very valuable.

The worst part of our institutional framework is the tax system. It's unintel-ligible and highly counterproductive, generating the wrong kind of revenue from the wrong kind of people. It is not accidental that each presidential candidate who runs for office, or each presidential candidate who becomes president, promises fundamental tax reform. We know it is a broken system. Our reliance on income taxation is overdone, and I think the European system of value-added tax is clearly something that needs to be considered here. We tax the wrong things. I think we should be taxing energy a lot more. I remember when Joschka Fischer, the former foreign minister in Germany, came over here and spent a year at Princeton. He said to me, "Your houses are very energy-inefficient. Compared to Germany and elsewhere in Europe, where energy is so much more expensive, you couldn't afford all this heat to escape. And the other thing I still can't get over is the price of gasoline. It's too damn cheap." He was right. And now that we're going to get on to natural gas, it will probably make it even worse in the sense that we don't know what the environmental effects of fracking will be. On the other hand, we'll be importing less, which should be good for any politician running for office. When [President Barack] Obama started his campaign for reelection, I met with him at some point, and he said to me, "The price of gas is killing me" [*laughs*].

Bowmaker: What is your opinion on the so-called revolving door between Wall Street and Washington?

Blumenthal: I think it's unavoidable, because modern life is complex, and not necessarily bad, because it brings in a fresh perspective instead of an encrusted bureaucracy. Thinking outside the box is a good thing. But the only people who are able to ask the right questions and create new initiatives are those with experience in their respective fields. You don't want a secretary of the treasury who has been a medical doctor—it needs to be someone who understands economics and finance. Similarly, you don't want a secretary of transportation who comes out of the agricultural sector—it has to be somebody who knows about transportation network needs in this country. The other side of the coin is that you have to build in walls to insulate the system from the risk of self-dealing and corruption. As long as those safeguards are in place, the revolving door doesn't bother me.

Personal Reflections

Bowmaker: What were your strengths and weaknesses as a policymaker?

Blumenthal: One weakness was that sometimes I wasn't political enough. Having been around government for some years, I thought I understood that politics is the art of the possible. Compared to my former colleagues in the academic world, I was very realistic and cynical. These academics were only concerned with the theory, but I was a policymaker who always prided himself on being practical. But maybe, in the end, I wasn't practical enough in the Treasury.

A big mistake I made when I was there was that I didn't realize the importance of maintaining intimate personal contact with the president's assistants. I didn't have lunch with them. I thought, "I'm the secretary of the treasury. Why do I have to deal with the president's public affairs officer or with his political guru? They've got nothing to do with me." And I probably made mistakes even in my PR [public relations]. I remember how shocked I was when I made some seemingly innocuous remark to the press just before I was being sworn in, and the stock market dropped thirty points that day. I thought to myself, "Wow, you've got to watch what you're saying." As a second example, early in my tenure, I was asked, "What is the ideal level of inflation?" I replied, "What do you mean by the ideal level? I suppose zero is the answer, but it's not achievable." I got blasted in the press who said, "What a stupid thing to say. He knows very well that it wouldn't be good if it were zero." Of course, I didn't really mean zero [*laughs*]. So I wasn't as sophisticated as I might have been in the beginning and had to learn that the job of secretary of the treasury is very different from being an ambassador in charge of trade negotiations or deputy assistant secretary of economic problems in the State Department. You're really out in front.

A good policymaker is also someone who is very good at the black art of bureaucratic maneuvering. I probably wasn't the best in that area. I stood my ground for what I thought was right, but I didn't spend a lot of time romancing the secretary of labor or the head of the OMB, trying to understand their problems and building alliances. After all, policy is the synthesis of compromises between these various positions. In other words, I didn't do enough politicking. But I'm not good at thinking about who I have to buy off to get close to my goal. Who is [*laughs*]? To some extent, it all lies in the eyes of the beholder.

I ask myself often, "Had I behaved differently, would I have been able to be a more successful secretary of the treasury?" History has judged me to have been reasonably effective, but did I fall down in terms of influencing the president to do what he should have done? In the end, I didn't make policy—I suggested it and tried to get the boss to accept it. Clearly, I failed miserably in that regard. Would anyone else have done better? Certainly, Bill Miller didn't, but maybe it's something to do with who the boss is. I remember the first time I met [President Obama's first secretary of the treasury] Tim Geithner. I said to him, "I envy you. You're working with a guy in that Oval Office who is smart and who listens. He may not agree with you, but you can engage with him. That ought to be a pleasure. My problem was that I was secretary of the treasury for someone who listened, but I don't think he heard. He had strong views and he stayed with them." But I've consoled myself over the years by saying, "Don't beat yourself up. It was a hopeless task—Jimmy Carter was hard to move."

My strengths? That's harder. There's a wonderful two-word adage in German which means, "Self-praise stinks" [*laughs*]. I am reluctant to beep my own horn because I prefer to let events speak for themselves. But if you have to ask me, I would say that at the Treasury I was a good leader, which unfortunately is only a necessary but not a sufficient condition of success in that department. Emotional intelligence is one quality of leadership, and I think I stack up pretty well in that respect. I have a sense of what makes other people tick, and I think I hired the right people in the Treasury, like Bob Carswell, Tony Solomon, Fred Bergsten, and Roger Altman. I knew I couldn't hold them on a short leash. I had to trust them and give them the sense that I would rely on their advice. To this day, they all remain my friends.

I also had courage, which is in very short supply in every field. Politicians are cowards. They are followers, not leaders, in most instances. That is true in business as well. Big corporations take risk with other people's money. But I stood up and stuck out my neck for what I believed in, instead of saying, "Oh, I don't want to be associated with failure. I better pull back." For example, under very, very difficult circumstances, we rescued the dollar when I was secretary of the treasury. I was the hero, but I took the risk of being the goat. There was a point when I went to Carter and said, "Mr. President, there's no more time to do this. We have to do the things you've told me you don't want to do. If you don't do them this weekend, I cannot guarantee what will happen, and it's inevitable you will need a new secretary of the treasury." It worked. But, of course, that courage always has to be mixed with a sense of realism and caution as well.

Bowmaker: Which aspects of public service do you miss most?

Blumenthal: It would be nice if I had a relationship with the president. I was in Germany a couple of weeks ago for a dinner hosted by the chancellor.

Obama was present. There was a receiving line, and as we went through I said hi to him. He replied, "Mike, what are you doing here?" Jokingly, I told him, "Well, I had to come all the way to Berlin to see you, Mr. President." He said, "Why did you do that? Why don't you come and see me in Washington?" But if I had tried to see him in Washington, a second assistant down the line would say, "Can I help you? What do you want?" [*Laughs.*]

So what I miss most is having access to the top to understand what's going on behind the scenes. I miss that inside knowledge, plus the capacity to put in my five cents worth and have "eyes only" clearance. It would be great to have a chance to sit down with Obama and say, "Mr. President, why don't we try this instead?" Thinking about it, though, would I really want to be back on the inside? No. It would have to be on my terms, in which the president calls me and says, "Mike, won't you come down and have dinner with me?" If he said instead, "I would like you to be my special assistant in the White House," I would tell him, "Mr. President, you want somebody younger. I've been there and done that."

Stuart Eizenstat (*left*) sitting with President Jimmy Carter on Air Force One during the latter's presidency.

6 Stuart E. Eizenstat
Born 1943, Chicago, Illinois

Stuart E. Eizenstat graduated cum laude with an AB from the University of North Carolina at Chapel Hill in 1964 and obtained a JD from Harvard Law School in 1967.

Eizenstat has held a number of key senior positions in government, including chief White House domestic policy adviser to President Jimmy Carter (1977–1981) and, in the administration of President Bill Clinton, US ambassador to the European Union (1993–1996); undersecretary of commerce for international trade (1996–1997); undersecretary of state for economic, business, and agricultural affairs (1997–1999); and deputy secretary of the treasury (1999–2001). Currently, he heads the international practice of the law firm Covington and Burling, LLP.

I interviewed Stuart Eizenstat at the offices of Covington and Burling in Washington, D.C. It was late in the morning on Tuesday, August 30, 2016.

Background Information

Bowmaker: When did you first become interested in the world of policy?

Eizenstat: I'm sure that in my high school in Atlanta I would have been voted the least likely to become involved in politics. I was very shy. But I went to college at the University of North Carolina [UNC], which had a very well-developed student government, and I became a member of what was called the attorney general's staff that investigated honor code violations. I also wrote regularly for the *Daily Tar Heel*, which is one of the better student newspapers. And in addition, I was particularly inspired by a speech that President [John F.] Kennedy gave at UNC's football stadium in which, among other things, he challenged young people to get involved in the world of policy and politics. When he was assassinated in 1963, I can still remember exactly where I was on campus, and I drove all night from Chapel Hill to Washington with two friends so that we could get prime standing position outside the US Capitol to see the body being taken from the White House to lie in state, and I went up and paid my respects.

Entering the Policy World

Bowmaker: Your first major policy position was as Hubert Humphrey's research director during his 1968 presidential campaign. How did that role come about?

Eizenstat: In the Johnson White House, I worked for Bob Hardesty in a unit that did everything from speeches for members of Congress to support legislation that LBJ [Lyndon B. Johnson] had set up to domestic messages. My office was directly in the executive office building next to the vice president's office, and so I already knew a lot of the staff when Johnson decided not to run for reelection, and they asked if I would join the Humphrey campaign as his research director. I started the first day Humphrey announced his presidential bid at the Mayflower Hotel in D.C. in May of 1968 and worked all the way until the November returns on election night in the Leamington Hotel in Minneapolis. My role was to research all of [Richard] Nixon's positions and to compare them with ours.

Bowmaker: You were then appointed policy director of Jimmy Carter's 1976 presidential campaign. How did that position come about?

Eizenstat: After the election, I went back to Atlanta and worked as a law clerk for a federal judge. I soon met Jimmy Carter, who was a former state senator running a second time for governor against the former governor, Carl Sanders, who was the establishment candidate. I became Carter's policy director in the 1970 gubernatorial campaign, and then in 1974—when Carter was appointed by Bob Strauss, the head of the Democratic National Committee (DNC), to be chairman of the DNC's congressional campaign committee, a position that no one else wanted—he asked me if I would put together a series of papers critiquing the Nixon policy and giving options the Democratic congressional candidates might use for the 1974 election. We put together about a dozen positions with Carter's and the DNC's name on them, and at the end of that process, I called him up and said, "I would like to have lunch with you to celebrate getting this done." And so we met at a restaurant in Underground Atlanta, and I told him, "Look, you should run for president because there will probably be a need for a southerner on the ticket. This is going to be a landslide election because of Watergate. You'll get some credit for it because of your work with the DNC, and if you won a couple of southern primaries, you have a good chance to be the vice president." With a toothy grin, he said, "I'll run, but I'm going to be elected president because I don't want to be vice president. And I would like you to join our staff." And so from that time on, until the very beginning of 1976, I worked part-time with a fellow named Steve Stark, who was a college kid, on actively organizing his [Carter's] issues. I would meet with Carter at the governor's mansion to literally go through everything from abortion to Zaire and flesh out his positions. I came on full-time after Iowa, and we formed an economic task force full of luminaries that was headed by Professor Larry Klein, who we later hoped would come into the administration. But he didn't do so because he wanted to continue to work toward the Nobel Prize in Economics, which he later got. His task force came up with a report, which I helped coordinate, that was the nub of the economic campaign. We focused on the misery index, which Art Okun created by adding inflation and unemployment. But the principal goal was to lower the unemployment rate, rather than the inflation rate, which was Democratic Party orthodoxy.

Bowmaker: What does an economist bring to the policy world that others do not?

Eizenstat: Economists are absolutely critical to any campaign and to any administration. As Jim Baker once said, "There are three issues in a presidential election: the economy, the economy, and the economy." And so you need economists to help develop policies to deal with the major bread-and-butter issues that people are concerned about. The economists that we relied on during our term in office, both those in the administration and outside advisers like Joe Pechman, Art Okun, George Perry, Ed Fried, Henry Owen, Walter Heller, and Charlie Schultze, were Keynesians to the core, and they had all worked in previous administrations, which meant they were not just sitting in an ivory tower being naive to the policy world. But it was not their job to make political judgments. Rather, they had to provide policy advice, and it was my role to then shape it into a politically utilitarian program. However, it is very important to understand that the Democratic Party was, and to some extent still is, a heavily interest group–based party in which big-city mayors, liberal think tankers, minority group leaders, urban leaders, and labor all saw economic policy through the prism of lowering unemployment. For example, until we insisted on it as a condition, the Humphrey-Hawkins bill [known more formally as the Full Employment and Balanced Growth Act of 1978] had no inflation target. It was all about reducing unemployment to 4 per cent—inflation was thought to be a secondary issue.

As Chief Domestic Policy Adviser to President Carter

Bowmaker: Did President Carter make it clear what he wanted you to do for him as chief domestic policy adviser?

Eizenstat: Yes, it was to coordinate all domestic issues. But one of the fault lines was that we created the so-called Economic Policy Group. This was initially cochaired by Mike Blumenthal and Charlie Schultze, an arrangement that didn't work, and so Charlie—being the good guy—let Mike head the group on the condition that he would get an hour every week to talk with the president one-on-one about economics. But the difficulty with the Economic Policy Group was twofold. Problem number one was what its composition would be, because all the domestic agencies wanted to be part of it, and it became very unwieldy. Problem number two was how you would coordinate it, because I have found in both domestic and economic policy, an agency cannot coordinate sister agencies. That's what the White House has to do—to make the trade-offs and present the president with all the agency views. I saw this problem very clearly right up front. And so I went to Charlie Schultze and said, "Charlie, in addition to being chairman of the Council of Economic Advisers, you should be the in-house White House coordinator, like I'm doing on domestic issues." He replied, "No, I'll lose my objectivity"—which gets to your question about the role of economists. In the end, I became the coordinator by default because someone had to pull everything together.

Bowmaker: When I spoke with Michael Blumenthal, he told me that "Stu's List" contained all the things that President Carter wanted to get done coming into the administration. Do you agree that the president had no sense of priority in relation to the issues on the list?

Eizenstat: In terms of economics, the interesting thing is that the president, before almost anybody else, recognized that inflation was a coequal problem to unemployment, and as time went by, a predominant problem. But yes, and this is self-admitted, his biggest problem at the beginning of the administration was that he wanted to do everything, without prioritizing and without having a chief of staff. And so in the first year, we had all of the economic stimulus program, the massive energy bill, tax reform, welfare reform, and hospital cost containment. That was just on the domestic side, let alone dealing with the Panama Canal, SALT [Strategic Arms Limitation Treaty], and the Middle East! The absence of priorities was so striking that by the early fall of 1977, the president got [Vice President] Walter Mondale—very effectively, by the way—to work with me and [National Security Adviser] Zbigniew Brzezinski and his own staff to develop a set of priorities. Priority number one would be those few things that would require serious presidential time. Priority number two would be those things that did not require that much of his time but did require White House involvement. Priority number three would be those things that the agencies could do themselves. But the original sin, so to speak, was that we had a collision of priorities at the beginning of the administration. We got a lot done in the end, but because so much had been thrown up, it looked as if we hadn't accomplished as much as we actually did.

Bowmaker: To what extent could you give personal advice to the president, while at the same time serve as an honest broker and a neutral party from an agency's point of view?

Eizenstat: I remember very early on when I sent in one of my first decision memos that summarized where the agencies stood, but didn't contain my recommendation. The president called me on the red phone and said, "I want you to give me your recommendation." I think that was the right thing to do. I felt I could be the honest broker and still give my advice as long as I told the agencies what that was going to be. In other words, it was important that I didn't use my access to the president to come in at 9:00 at night and tell him, "Forget all the other stuff. Do what I'm saying." And I never abused my privilege—my recommendation was on the decision memo for all the agencies to see.

Bowmaker: How would you describe President Carter's method of making decisions?

Eizenstat: It was too much by paper and too little by interaction with the principals who had written it, so oftentimes he didn't get the feel and the intensity of the arguments. And he didn't just want a summary. In his very clear handwriting, he would check an option and say, "I want more information on this" and then would read the background materials as well—which he should not have had to do.

Bowmaker: How easy was it to predict where he would come down on issues?

Eizenstat: I had worked for him for two years on the campaign, and so I had a pretty good instinct of where he was going to come down. Ham Jordan, who later became his chief of staff, used to joke that the worst way to make sure the president follows your advice, as opposed to someone else's, is to tell him it would be politically beneficial. Carter felt that if he made what he thought was the right decision, ultimately the voters would reward him, and Congress would follow. Unfortunately, the system doesn't work that way.

Bowmaker: To what extent do you think President Carter's training as an engineer shaped his approach to formulating economic policy?

Eizenstat: First of all, President Carter was exceedingly smart. I would say that on an IQ level, there are very few people—maybe only Bill Clinton—who could match him. But he ended up having a group of economists who differed on some very important issues, like whether we should emphasize unemployment versus inflation, and this presented a problem for him because he wasn't an economist. He had to rely on the judgment of those who were advising him. And then when you come to the question of his training as an engineer, you have to remember that he was used to quantifying things. For example, during the preparation of our energy program, as a demonstration of how dependent we were becoming on OPEC [Organization of Petroleum Exporting Countries], he wanted us to convert barrels of oil to square miles, which was an almost impossible task. But he was very fast on the intake with economic data—that didn't overwhelm him at all.

The second point with engineers is that they tend to look at things in a holistic fashion. You can't build half a bridge or half a ship, for example. And so the dreaded word for me at the beginning of the administration was "comprehensive." The president wanted a comprehensive tax reform program, a comprehensive energy program, and a comprehensive welfare reform program, which meant biting off more than the system, particularly Congress, could chew on.

Bowmaker: Do you agree that inflation was the greatest domestic problem that President Carter had to face?

Eizenstat: Yes, it was the greatest domestic problem. In 1977, we proposed a fairly modest $30 billion stimulus program, but we pulled some of it out at the president's demand because he was already beginning to hear from Blumenthal that inflation was a problem, and he felt that himself, too. And so it ended up being a $20–$21 billion stimulus program, which probably didn't do much to kick inflation up.

The president was very tight on budget policy. There was pent-up demand by the interest groups after eight years of Republicans for a new burst of social spending, but that was not Carter. He was fiscally conservative, someone who realized that the country had changed—but the trouble was that the Democratic Party had not. And so despite being constantly pressed by the left to do more on spending, his great goal was to have a balanced budget, and he fought hard for it. He would ask always, even on the stimulus packages, "Is this contrary to a balanced budget?" Charlie would say, "Well, we have to grow to get the revenues for a balanced budget as well." I think the seminal decision was the second stimulus package of 1978, which was done in conjunction with tax reform. The notion was that you cannot reform taxes unless you sweeten it with tax cuts. When the bill came back in October of 1978, it had almost none of our tax reform, and it had almost all of the tax cuts, including a capital gains cut, which was totally contrary to what we had sought in tax reform. The president was the only one who wanted to veto that bill. Blumenthal didn't want it [a veto], Schultze didn't want it, and the political people didn't want it. I mistakenly felt, just coming before the midterm elections, to veto a Democratic tax cut bill was not going to be beneficial, but he held out, and he held out, and he held out, because he instinctively believed inflation was getting out of control.

Bowmaker: In hindsight, should you have urged him to declare inflation as public enemy number one earlier in his administration?

Eizenstat: I think if he had done so he would have run into such a buzz saw with the Democratic Party constituency. As it was, we were on very shaky ground because our budgets were really quite small. Carter did declare that inflation was the number one problem after he signed the second tax cut bill, and up until that point, he did give it equal treatment—which, for a Democratic president, was a hell of a thing to do.

Bowmaker: To what extent was your lack of training in economics a disadvantage when considering issues such as inflation?

Eizenstat: If I had been an economist, I suppose it would have been beneficial, but I had worked around economics and economists for years, so I certainly wasn't ignorant. But I think what happened in this era was a transformational change in the economy. We didn't appreciate until it was too late how inflationary psychology had embedded itself since the oil shock of 1973 and created a wage-price spiral that was unreceptive to traditional fiscal tightening. What you needed was a blunt instrument of interest rates, but no one until, I would say, Blumenthal in 1979 wanted to raise them. Now, Bill Miller turned out to be a decent secretary of the treasury, but not a good Fed[eral Reserve] chairman. He was outvoted on interest rate hikes—he wanted a much more accommodative interest rate policy—and had we acted early on interest rates, even in Arthur Burns's era, we might have squeezed some of the inflation out of the system. But that was so contrary to the whole notion of fighting the Ford recession, and so contrary to the Democratic Party ethos (which was low interest rates), that it was exceedingly difficult to do. And even Carter didn't want it. The president wanted to do more on the fiscal side but not until much later, when [Paul] Volcker was appointed, on the interest rate side. And that's again an example of how economic policy had changed. We didn't fully appreciate the role of the Fed in combating this embedded inflation.

Bowmaker: Was there any tension between the Treasury and the Council of Economic Advisers [CEA] on how to deal with inflation?

Eizenstat: Yes, there was certainly tension between the Treasury and the CEA, because Blumenthal fairly early on saw inflation as a big problem and wanted tighter policies and, ultimately, more interest rate hikes than Charlie Schultze and the other traditional Keynesian economists did. Mike was quite diffident about Keynesian economics. You have to remember he was a German refugee who had inflation from the Weimar Republic stuck in his head, and so he was the principal one in the administration pushing harder on the anti-inflation side. Mind you, we started with our first anti-inflation program in April 1977, which was only three months after we came into office. It's just that the tools we had were not sufficient to deal with the embedded inflation. We had jawboning, voluntary wage and price controls, and tight budgets, but labor was passionately against most of those, and Schultze was opposed to wage and price controls. I wanted the president to have standby wage and price controls starting in the transition; the threat of using them might have been useful. But the experience of them under Nixon was so ghastly and distortive that Schultze and Blumenthal and others didn't want them. And so other than the remedy that Volcker ended up using, there wasn't much else we could do. Carter had to use the tools he was given.

Bowmaker: What was your response to President Carter's energy speech of July 1979 being canceled, which led to the debate at Camp David about the state of his administration?

Eizenstat: Shock and horror. As the Iranian revolution occurred, inflation was rising because of the oil shock, and so we worked on the speech for months. But when he landed after attending the Tokyo Summit, he decided to cancel it, which meant the question then became, "Now what?" Pat Caddell [political pollster], who was the genius behind all of this, said that the public had tuned Carter out on energy—he had given too many energy speeches—and that the real problem was a crisis in public confidence as a result of the assassinations in the sixties, Vietnam, and Watergate, and that Carter not only needed to speak to that kind of issue but also go back to being the sort of populist campaigner he had been in 1976. In fact, it was Caddell's memo that led Carter to cancel the energy speech. And so Carter then decided to have experts come up and talk to him about how to get his administration back on an even keel. I sat in on almost all of those meetings at Camp David and helped develop who should participate in them.

Bowmaker: President Carter had a meeting at Camp David with the economists, including Art Okun, Larry Klein, Walter Heller, and John Kenneth Galbraith. The president said the following: "The session with the economists was a waste of time; they all expounded their own conflicting themes and seemed to be unwilling or unable to consider the views of others or to deal in a practical way with the economic problems I was having to face every day." Were you present at this meeting?

Eizenstat: Yes, I was present, and I think it was just more of the same. No one had any silver bullet of how to deal with what was then stagflation. The most creative proposal was Art Okun's real wage insurance, which we had already heard, and which we proposed to Congress and they rejected. Other than that, as I say, it was more of the same of what we had already been trying to do during the administration. I remember Galbraith talked about tougher wage and price guidelines, which we did. Our first wage and price guidelines were very voluntary, and then we added real sanctions with procurement in late 1978 and early 1979. Companies had to sign up and pledge that they would stay within the guidelines. But I think that Galbraith, along with Heller, were traditional, liberal Keynesian economists who didn't have very many good ideas for inflation. For example, one of the things we talked about—this was the time of gasoline lines—was gasoline deregulation. It would have cured that problem overnight, but at the expense of a price hike, which I believe in the end would have leveled off. The economists, however, were totally against the idea and instead favored import quotas. But it was not a surprise. Carter had reached out several times to Larry Klein and his group earlier in his administration. He was not, nor were we, isolated from the best thinking of economists, at least the best Democratic-oriented economists, but their approach wasn't up to the task of dealing with stagflation. That's why Carter made that comment. He was right.

Bowmaker: What was your view on President Carter's so-called malaise speech of 1979, both at the time and in hindsight?

Eizenstat: At the time, I thought it was a catastrophic mistake, and I was able to get him to agree that he would add the energy piece that we had already prepared onto the "crisis of confidence" speech. By the way, he never used the term "malaise"; Pat Caddell had mentioned it in some memos. I fought like a tiger against Caddell and the political people because they only wanted it to be about the crisis of confidence. I didn't think it was a pseudopsychology problem with the American people, and neither did Mondale. To us, the issue was basic economics: inflation and unemployment were both high, and people were having a hard time making ends meet. And so the compromise I was able to get them to reach was to deal with the crisis of confidence, if it existed, through a solution to a concrete problem: how to make ourselves less dependent on OPEC. The fact was that OPEC was the enemy—it was causing a double whammy of high inflation and lower growth, and therefore we had to unite to get an energy program and the windfall profits tax passed. It worked. Now, to my surprise, and I'm the first to admit, I was wrong about the speech. It was Carter's best. His polls went up dramatically. He touched a thread of what people were thinking, in part because he was very honest at the beginning by saying, "I've had all these experts come up, and here is what they told me I was doing wrong. I've spent too much time on foreign policy and not enough time on you, the American people." It was remarkable, and people gravitated to it. The speech was on the fifteenth of July, and I went out with him the day after to two conventions in Kansas City and Detroit. The reception was wildly enthusiastic. They liked him, and they believed in him. But then the Cabinet firings just threw a wet blanket over the whole thing.

Bowmaker: What did you say to President Carter to try to convince him to retain Treasury Secretary Blumenthal?

Eizenstat: He asked everybody for their resignation, which was a terrible mistake, but he hadn't decided on whose resignations he would accept and whose he wouldn't. It was pretty clear, though, that they had the guns trained on [Secretary of Health, Education, and Welfare] Joe Califano and Mike Blumenthal. [Secretary of Energy] James Schlesinger was going to go anyway because he had bloodied himself on too many energy fronts, but on Blumenthal, I really poured my heart out. Ham Jordan and [White House Press Secretary] Jody Powell both said that he wasn't a team player, but I told them, "Look, Mike has a prickly personality for sure, but he is loyal. I'm the one who works with him every day, not you guys, and I've never had a bad day. We've disagreed on policy, but we have a great mutual respect, and most important—forget me—we have a major inflation problem right now. If you're going to dismiss the person who the financial markets see as the repository of anti-inflation rectitude in the administration, it's going to cause financial markets to go berserk. They'll say, 'You're getting rid of the wrong guy. He's the one who has really beaten the drum on inflation.'" That was my argument, but obviously it was not successful.

Bowmaker: What was your view on the credit controls that were imposed by President Carter?

Eizenstat: We made a horrible mistake. I wasn't the initiator—it was really Fred Kahn's [Carter's inflation czar] idea—but I went along with it. It led, in the election year of 1980, to a deep, one-quarter recession. People thought that the president was asking them to not use their credit cards. Volcker was opposed to the policy, but he said, "Look, Carter has helped us. He's stuck with me on my tough policy. I'm going to do it for him." He hated it, however.

Bowmaker: All things considered, what would you say were the major economic accomplishments of President Carter, and to what extent did they only come after he left office?

Eizenstat: Many economic accomplishments came during office, but the positive impacts were only felt afterwards. First, we deregulated both crude oil, which had been under wage and price controls, and combined it with the windfall profits tax. That was brilliant, because it was a way of saying, "We know there's going to be a big windfall to the energy companies when these artificial controls come off. And so we're going to use the revenues

from the windfall profits tax for alternative energy, like solar, and so forth."
It passed, and Carter did that himself.

Second, as part of the 1977 energy package signed in October 1978, we
deregulated natural gas, which no president had ever tried to do. We inherited
a situation of a dual market in which you had the intrastate market that was
decontrolled—like in Texas and Oklahoma, where gas was plentiful because
it was at market rates—and the interstate market that was controlled. And so
you are talking about the difference between natural gas at 50 cents per Mcf
[thousand cubic feet] to $2.00, which meant it was obvious producers were
not interested in shipping their gas out of state. That was a huge thing that
we got done. The implications for both production and conservation were
mammoth down the road. President Carter championed and signed into law
the first incentives for solar, wind, and biomass production; for conservation;
and for synthetic fuels. He also created with Congress a bill which dramatically reformed the way in which public utilities delivered electricity, making
it more competitive for consumers by permitting small producers of electricity for clean energy sources to have access to the power grid.

Third, we deregulated almost all transportation: airline, trucking, rail—and
bus we came close to. This was transformational for bringing airline travel to
the middle class, to making it possible to have a FedEx and UPS [United Parcel
Service], and to reducing the costs of inputs on rail. Again, that had an enormous impact, and frankly, it was part of our anti-inflation program.

Fourth, we created more jobs—over ten million—in a four-year period than
any previous president and any subsequent president with the exception of
Bill Clinton, while achieving economic growth that averaged about 3 percent.

Fifth, fighting inflation was, ironically, an accomplishment. Why? Because
Charlie Schultze had told him [Carter], "If you appoint Volcker, you're going
to lose the election, because he's going to induce a recession." But Carter
replied, "I've tried everything else—tight budgets, voluntary wage-price guidelines, wage and price guidelines with sanctions, and jawboning. Nothing has
worked. I don't want my legacy to be that I left this kind of inflation." Volcker,
of course, squeezed it out painfully, leaving Reagan to be the beneficiary.

Sixth, Humphrey Hawkins, interestingly, is a positive accomplishment.
Why? Because, unlike the European Central Bank, it created a dual mandate for the Fed, which [Federal Reserve Chairman] Ben Bernanke used
during the financial crisis. The original Humphrey-Hawkins bill had nothing on inflation, but we insisted that it should have a coequal focus with
unemployment. And so, in an ironic way, Humphrey-Hawkins—which is

wrongly viewed as, "Oh, it's that full employment thing"—has actually had an impact on guiding Fed policy.

General Thoughts on Economic Policymaking

Bowmaker: Which fallacies, misconceptions, or misinterpretations affect policy debate in this country?

Eizenstat: People talk about Carter's problems with Congress, but if you look at *Congressional Quarterly* and the *National Journal*, you'll see that they rank him as one of the top presidents, just below LBJ, in terms of legislative accomplishments. We met very regularly with the Republicans, but they were very different to the Republicans of today. We did not have the polarization. What has happened to American politics is that the center has collapsed: all you have are the Tea Party on the right and the liberals on the left. This has created the great difficulty of making economic policy. It is very tough to form a consensus on budget policy, for example. But the point is that there was a middle during the Carter period, and indeed I would say even with Reagan— because some of his most important economic accomplishments, like the 1986 Tax Act, were done with very strong Democratic support.

Bowmaker: Which aspects of the institutional framework for making economic policy in this country work well, and which need to be reformed?

Eizenstat: I think the institutional framework for making economic policy in this country has improved for two reasons. First, we have a greater appreciation of the importance of the Fed, and the Fed itself has a greater recognition that when they see inflation coming, it's whack a mole—they're not going to allow it. Second, structurally, we have a National Economic Council that can coordinate economic policy in the White House to a much greater extent than we were able to do. The creation of such an agency was one of the recommendations that I made to Bill Clinton's campaign staff during his presidential campaign.

Bowmaker: What is your view about the so-called revolving door between Wall Street and Washington?

Eizenstat: Carter had higher disclosure requirements going into office and imposed strict rules through the Ethics Act of 1977 for anybody doing anything wrong during the administration—which, unfortunately, caught Ham Jordan, who had done nothing wrong but ended up with $1 million in legal fees. The Ethics Act also placed much stronger revolving-door requirements in terms of being able to lobby your agencies after you left Washington. And so that is something we certainly thought about even back then. But ultimately when you go to the Treasury and want qualified people, where do you look? Wall Street is the answer. Yes, you can consider the think tanks to some degree, but you need those who understand finance.

Personal Reflections

Bowmaker: How did your personality affect your style and approach as a policymaker?

Eizenstat: I think it affected it positively because I have a low-key personality. I'm not out for self-aggrandizement. My job was to help the president, and that meant being transparent and honest with the agencies. Again, it was important that I didn't abuse my position by being bombastic, someone who circumvented the interagency process. People may have disagreed with where I came out on certain issues, but I think they would say I was always fair to them.

Bowmaker: What were your strengths and weaknesses as a policymaker?

Eizenstat: One strength was that I had considerable knowledge of policy. I'd grown up with it and made it a matter of study. Whether it be housing, agricultural price supports, or energy, I knew a lot about many things. Second, as I've just said, I had a determination to be fair, to not be such an advocate that it overwhelmed the recommendations of others. I was also direct with the president. I was not a shrinking violet. If I felt he was wrong, I said so, like on the malaise speech. In terms of weaknesses—and this is something that isn't related to my personality or intellect—I did not appreciate the inflation problem early enough.

Bowmaker: Would you agree that economic policy is the hardest of all to make?

Eizenstat: Yes, in my opinion, it is the single most difficult policy to make, and I have helped make every kind of policy. There are so many moving parts, and you are always looking at the last quarter of data, which is adjusted. You thought growth was 3 percent, for example, but it turned out to be 2 percent. Similarly, with the employment figures, the Bureau of Labor Statistics might have said we had created 150,000 jobs, but two months later that number is revised down to 100,000. And then you have to consider the psychology of it all. What are 300 million people thinking? Business? Labor? Wall Street? That's something that Mike Blumenthal really stressed. He said the problem with Charlie, the CEA, and the Keynesians was that they didn't factor in psychology into their models. Economics is not just a dark science where you put a lot of data into a computer, and it comes out with the right policy. So much depends on how people perceive their situation and how they react to circumstances. That's really important, and we didn't pay enough attention to it—although Blumenthal, to his credit, did so early on in the administration.

Bowmaker: There must be some things that, in hindsight, you'd like the opportunity to do differently. What are they?

Eizenstat: Look, in defense of all of us in the Carter administration, you cannot have a 100 percent increase in energy prices—they went from $16 to $32 a barrel from February 1979 to February 1980—without paying a price. As I mentioned earlier, it was a double body blow to both growth and inflation and led to stagflation, which is something that had never happened before or, thankfully, since. When you pulled on the inflation end, it hurt unemployment, and when you pulled on the unemployment end, it hurt inflation. This was heavily due to the 1973 and 1979 oil shocks but also due to low productivity. I'm not blaming Charlie Schultze, because he is a great economist, but he kept saying, "I don't understand. We're not getting any productivity growth." There were some periods when productivity growth was zero, and the point is that better performance on that measure would have offset some of the inflation.

In terms of organizational structure, I wanted the president to have a chief of staff from the very beginning, because that would have helped in setting out our priorities. During the transition, Marty Tolchin from the *New York Times* asked me, "Can you describe your evolving domestic policy?" I told him, "It's going to be modest." Why did I say that? Because I remembered John F. Kennedy's admonition, "Great accomplishments don't come on narrow majorities." We had barely won the election and didn't have a mandate for hardly anything. Carter was upset at me only two times, and this was one of them. He said, "It's not going to be modest. It's going to be aggressive and comprehensive." But that, of course, led to the problems with a lack of priorities. And by the way, the second time he was mad at me was when he said, "I relied on you to tell me to veto the second tax bill." That's something I should have done.

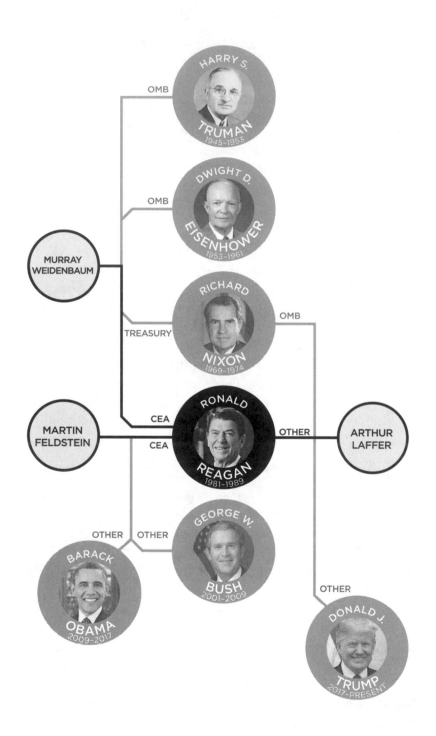

IV Ronald Reagan Administration

Arthur Laffer (*left*), when Charles B. Thornton Professor of Business Economics at the University of Southern California, meeting with Ronald Reagan (then about to become the 1980 Republican presidential nominee) at a business conference in New York City on June 13, 1978.

7 Arthur B. Laffer
Born 1940, Youngstown, Ohio

Arthur Laffer graduated with a BA in economics from Yale University in 1963 and obtained an MBA and a PhD in economics from Stanford University in 1965 and 1972, respectively.

Laffer was a member of the faculty of the University of Chicago from 1967 to 1976, serving as associate professor of business economics between 1970 and 1976. He was the Charles B. Thornton Professor of Business Economics at the University of Southern California between 1976 and 1985 and a Distinguished University Professor at Pepperdine University between 1985 and 1987.

In government, Laffer was the first person to hold the title of chief economist at the Office of Management and Budget (OMB), a position he held between 1970 and 1972, during the administration of President Richard Nixon. He was also a member of President Ronald Reagan's Economic Policy Advisory Board between 1981 and 1989, a member of the Executive Committee of the Reagan/Bush Finance Committee in 1984, and a founding member of the Reagan Executive Advisory Committee for the presidential campaign of 1980. He also advised British Prime Minister Margaret Thatcher on fiscal policy during the 1980s, and most recently he advised President Donald Trump's transition team.

Laffer is best known for the Laffer curve, which illustrates the trade-off between tax rates and actual revenues and is one of the principal theoretical constructs of supply-side economics. A March 29, 1999 *Time* magazine article on "The Century's Greatest Minds" described the Laffer curve as one of "a few advances that powered this extraordinary century."

Laffer is the founder and chairman of Laffer Associates, an economic research and consulting firm.

I interviewed Arthur Laffer at the offices of Laffer Associates in Nashville, Tennessee, in the middle of the afternoon on Tuesday, December 21, 2016, and early in the morning on Wednesday, December 22, 2016.

Background Information

Bowmaker: Why did you become an economist?

Laffer: I did very poorly in my junior year at Yale—I was probably third from bottom in the class—and thought it would be very good for my maturity if I took a year off and went to the University of Munich, in Germany. When I got there, I discovered I'd already taken almost all of their math classes, so instead I took some classes in economics, which was a new subject to me. I liked it. When I came back to Yale more grown-up, I switched my major in my senior year, having fallen into economics out of math.

Entering the Policy World

Bowmaker: What does an economist bring to the policy world that others do not?

Laffer: Hopefully an understanding of incentives, because that's what economics is all about. We tax smokers to get them to stop smoking, we tax speeders on the freeway to get them to stop speeding, and in the same breath, why on earth do we tax people who earn income? Why do we tax people who employ other people? Why do we tax companies that make high-quality products that everyone wants at low cost? We don't tax them to get them to stop earning income or to stop them employing other people or stop them making profits. But don't for a moment think that that isn't the consequence of what happens. It is. It works just like it does with smoking and speeding. And if you tax people who work and you pay people who don't work, do I need to say the next sentence to you? Don't be surprised if a lot of people don't work. And this is the problem with so many of these weirdo economists. Whoever heard of a poor person spending himself into wealth? Whoever heard of taxing an economy into prosperity? It doesn't make sense. It's just amazing the mistakes people make in having a bad model in their brain.

I remember when Marty Feldstein was trying to talk President Reagan into getting rid of the third year of the first tax cut. His logic was if we don't have the third year of the tax cut, there'll be a smaller deficit, and with a smaller deficit, there'll be less borrowing on the part of government from capital markets. With more funds available to the private capital markets, there'll be more investment, more output, more employment, more new houses built, and so on, which will lead to a boom in the economy. The president came to me, presented this exact logic, and said, "Art, what do I say?" I told him, "Well, let me see if I've got that right, Mr. President. If you increase taxes on workers and producers, you're going to get more work and more production." He replied, "Thank you."

Bowmaker: Your first major position within the policy world was as chief economist at the OMB. How did that position arise?

Laffer: George Shultz hired me, like he has done everywhere I've worked. He's just the most wonderful man that has ever walked the face of the earth, and in all honesty, the single most impressive political economic figure in the last century. When you take a core sample of him, it's sterling through and through. He's the only guy, apart from my father, who when he raises his voice at me, I go, "Aah!" I remember one time we were in California with Arnold Schwarzenegger, and it was my sixty-fifth birthday. I said, "Damnit, I'm sixty-five years old." George said, "Arthur, stop right there. I just want you to know I still consider you a promising young man." I said, "Well, I guess, George, that's what Milton Friedman says to you." George replied, "Absolutely not. He's never said the word 'promising'" [*laughs*].

If it hadn't been for George Shultz, I would have gotten nailed in Watergate. All my best friends who I had breakfast with every morning went to prison. I didn't. Why not? Because my boss wouldn't let me do anything that was crooked. He said to me, "Arthur, you can use my name on anything you want, whenever you want to, but if you ever feel that queasy feeling, you can also say, 'I've got to check with George.'" On the couple of occasions when [Special Counsel to the President] Chuck Colson and [Deputy Assistant to the President] Alex Butterfield made me feel that way, I said to George, "Sir, I don't think this is for us," and he told me, "I prohibit you from doing it." Thank you, George!

Bowmaker: At that stage of your career, did you view yourself as having strong policy positions or simply as a hired professional serving the president?

Laffer: I'm a very quantitative economist. I don't see the world in fuzzy grays. And so I came to the OMB with very clear pictures of what is and what is not.

Bowmaker: As you began the position, was there anything that surprised or frustrated you?

Laffer: My first job was to go on a tour of the Far East, on Air Force Two, with George Shultz and [Counsel and Assistant to the President for Domestic Affairs] John Ehrlichman. They saved money by having no windows in the plane, except for a couple in the cockpit [*laughs*]. John Ehrlichman would paint water colors and stick them on the walls [*laughs*]. I got the opium pipe I brought back from that trip right behind the chair you are sitting in. I remember getting it into Andrews Air Force Base, and the guys used pipe cleaners to see if there was any opium in it or not.

I was very shocked on that trip because I fell in love with China. I'm a right-winger from a Midwestern family in Cleveland. My dad headed one of the largest companies in the United States, and so I went into China with my arms crossed, thinking "I'm going to hate these commie bastards." It turned out I just loved them, and I still do. China is one of the most amazing success stories ever, and it's all supply-side economics.

Bowmaker: George Shultz told me he "had to develop the M" in the newly created OMB. How did that affect you?

Laffer: It didn't. They were going to call it the Bureau of the Office of Management and Budget, but they couldn't because that would be BOMB. Then they thought about making it The Office of Management and Budget, but they couldn't do that either, because that would be TOMB. Next, they considered Western Office of Management and Budget, but that was vetoed as well, because that would be WOMB. So it was just OMB. You're bringing back all the humor of the day [*laughs*].

Bowmaker: How much interaction did you have with President Nixon?

Laffer: I met Nixon a couple of times in the White House when I was with George. He was very affable and pleasant. I told my mom once that I wrote a speech for him. "He didn't change a word," I said to her, "Well, not quite. He changed only two words. When I put 'is,' he put 'is not,' and when I put 'is not,' he put 'is.' But other than that, Mom, it's my speech." Everything he did in economics was the opposite of what should be done! He raised taxes, he put on wage and price controls, he put on tariffs, he put on a buy American program, and he went off gold when he should have stayed on it.

After the White House, I got to know him very well. I would go down to Casa Pacifica during the Reagan period, and I'd sit and spend two or three hours with him, just the two of us—with his dog, Timahoe, sleeping in the corner. He'd give me all these things he wanted me to take to Reagan, which I did. He didn't have a good relationship with him, so it was always, "You tell him 'this,' you tell him 'that.'" And so I'd go and tell Reagan, "This is what Nixon said. He wanted to make sure I told you."

I don't remember talking with him on economics specifically at all. We discussed all sorts of topics. He was very smart, very engaging, and fascinating. But also weird and awkward [*laughs*]. He had a hard time hanging up a phone because he had little bitty skinny wrists and shaky hands. Sometimes he would trip over, or when I'd go to leave, he'd stand up and put his hand out, but I'd have to go around the table to say goodbye, by which time he had dropped his hand, so he would then grab mine. Whenever there was a lull in our conversation, he'd open up his drawer where he had some cards, and say, "Give these to your children, Art." I really liked Nixon—it's just that he wasn't good on economics [*laughs*].

Bowmaker: You were part of the Volcker Group that had the responsibility of presenting recommendations for international monetary reform to President Nixon. Can you tell us a little about that experience?

Laffer: Paul Volcker and I were both very strongly enamored with keeping the gold standard. But George Shultz, heavily influenced by Milton Friedman, wanted flexible exchange rates. And he's the boss. My view of a good boss is as long as he listens to you, he is the boss, and if he then votes against you, that's his right. George did just that.

Paul Volcker liked my positions very much—I was almost always the person who supported him—but it was clear I was his subordinate. He considered himself far higher up than me, which was true. But there was one difference: my boss was higher, and my boss liked me [*laughs*]. I don't think he believed I had developed my credentials—I was brought to the White House at a very early age—and he was someone with a big ego who tended to kick down and kiss up. Staffers were treated badly, while superiors were treated beautifully. But he was brilliant. I don't think I've ever agreed with anyone on monetary policy as much as I did with Paul. He understood that you need to have a stable currency—it's not there to stimulate the economy. Period.

Bowmaker: Is it fair to say that when you were at the OMB, George Shultz had the most influence on economic policymaking of anyone working for the president?

Laffer: Yes, he was the single most respected person everywhere I went in the world—far more than Paul McCracken and Herb Stein [chairmen of the Council of Economic Advisers], far more than [Secretary of the Treasury] David Kennedy, and far more than even John Connally when he succeeded Kennedy. Connally was a "if you want it round, I'll make it round, if you want it square, I'll make it square" kind of guy. He was a wonderful person, and I loved him, but if you wanted details and substance, you went to George Shultz. In any professional meeting, he was always the dominant figure, and when something blew, George always had the day because he was so organized. We prepared everything in anticipation of what might happen six months from now. And not only was he prepared, he was also well educated. He asked me to give him a series of lectures on international trade theory when he was the head of the OMB because he understood that you can't have little chitty chatty conversations here, there, and everywhere on the subject. He wanted to learn the material and get it correct, which he did.

Bowmaker: How much interaction did you have with Treasury Secretary Connally?

Laffer: He and I would always swap stories. He was a very funny guy. I remember one time walking with Herb Stein along the little road between the White House and the Treasury on our way to a meeting with Connally. We were talking and giggling when all of a sudden, out of the corner of our eye, we catch this car coming at us like a bat out of hell. Aah! We threw our papers away and ran to the curb because we thought for sure we were going to get hit. The car was a big Mercedes with the license plate JBC1. It was John Connally [*laughs*]! "Scared you, didn't I?!" he yelled. What a character. Now, my boss wasn't like that—George Shultz was wonderful, but he wasn't a laugh a minute.

Bowmaker: How would you describe George Shultz's relationship with President Nixon?

Laffer: George was a loyal trooper to Nixon, although you knew in his heart he disagreed with 90 percent of the president's economics. He didn't like Camp David, he didn't like wage and price controls, he didn't like taxes on imports, and he didn't like job development credits being segregated by whether it's American capital or foreign capital.

A long time ago, I went to his office in San Francisco, and I looked all around. I said, "George, you don't have anything here from Nixon." It was as though that period didn't exist—no pictures, no nothing. "What do you mean there's nothing here?" he replied, "I got that ashtray from Nixon" [*laughs*].

Bowmaker: In 1971, when chief economist, you said GNP [gross national product] would come in at $1.065 trillion, about $20 billion higher than the consensus forecast. In the economics profession, people started mentioning that number "1065," usually to ridicule it. In 1976, however, the revised GNP numbers showed that your forecast was perfect. Can you tell us the story about that forecast?

Laffer: It was the job of the Council of Economic Advisers to do the forecast, which was a very important input to the OMB for budget purposes, and Herb Stein came up with 1065. George Shultz asked me to evaluate the 1065 forecast carefully so that he could have a good grasp of it, and I corroborated the council's number. George and I then had to testify before [Senator] Bill Proxmire of Wisconsin from the Joint Economic Committee. Proxmire began by grilling George on 1065. George kept on saying that we have a "different way" before finally Proxmire said, "What in the hell do you mean you have a different way?" And then George turned to me. From that moment on, I had done the forecast of 1065! No one could correct the records ever again. Herb Stein was superbly pissed [*laughs*]. And of course the damn thing turned out to be right.

Bowmaker: Later in 1971, Paul Samuelson, Nobel laureate, gave a talk called "Why Are They Laughing at Laffer?," in reference to the model used to make your forecast. What do you recall about Samuelson's reported intellectual bullying at his talk at your own University of Chicago? Specifically, as a young scholar, were you hurt by this experience?

Laffer: It was an awful period for me. To be attacked by the top economist in the world as a young staffer was devastating at the time. It was like kicking a crippled kid. As it turned out, though, I wasn't as defenseless as he thought, because I got a lot of surprising support. All the econometricians said the model was professionally done. But Samuelson criticized it for not using seasonally adjusted data. Anyone who knows any econometrics will tell you that you have to use seasonally unadjusted data and co-adjust for seasonality! It's too bad that such brilliant pieces of work like the Stolper-Samuelson theorem, the factor price equalization theorem, and the Samuelson-Rybczynski theorem have to be tied to such a personally flawed human. Samuelson was as mean as the snakiest snake that ever went.

Bowmaker: Can you recount the story of how the Laffer curve got its name?

Laffer: According to Jude Wanniski from the *Wall Street Journal*, he had dinner with me, Don Rumsfeld (chief of staff to President [Gerald] Ford) and Dick Cheney (Don's deputy and my former classmate at Yale) at the Two Continents Restaurant at the Hotel Washington in Washington, D.C., in December 1974. We were discussing Ford's Whip Inflation Now proposal for tax increases when I apparently sketched a curve on my napkin illustrating the trade-off between tax rates and tax revenues. Jude later named the trade-off "the Laffer curve" in an article he wrote for the *Public Interest*. As the years have gone by, my memory of that evening has all of a sudden sprung back to life, but the napkin that's in the Smithsonian Museum is maybe a little too professionally done for my liking. Look at it carefully, and see if you think that's a casual doodle on a napkin, or whether you think it was re-created. When you're sitting with someone and doodling on a napkin, do you then write, "To Don Rumsfeld from Arthur Laffer" because you thought it was some sort of eureka moment? I don't think so. The Laffer curve has been around forever. A fourteenth-century philosopher called Ibn Khaldun wrote about it, and John Maynard Keynes did so as well in the 1930s. But it died in the post–World War II period. I guess I brought it back, and I'm glad I did.

On President Reagan's Economic Policy Advisory Board

Bowmaker: Between 1976 and 1980, you met regularly with Ronald Reagan for lunch. What was he interested in learning from you? What did you learn about him during those meetings?

Laffer: Reagan was in my social circle. We'd have lunch at the Beverly Wilshire and then spend two to three hours in a private room discussing public policy and economics. Reagan was an avid reader and writer—he wrote thousands of words every day—and he always came in prepared with a stack of underlined editorials from newspapers and magazines with paper clips attached. He would flip them over and ask a ton of questions like, "What's the logic underlying the minimum wage? I don't get it." We'd have fun—I guess he found me comfortable to talk to—but I didn't think anything of it at the time, to be honest with you. He was an older ex-actor who'd been governor of California, had run for president, but lost. That was it. Then all of a sudden he was going to run again. I said to myself, "Oh, my God, what have

I told him? I hope I'm right." As an economist, you know there's a great deal of sophistication in a true tax model. But in a conversation with a former actor and politician, you caricature things the way you would in a conversation with someone at a cocktail party, rather than as you would talking to a group of economists. That worried me. And I hadn't done at the time the work I've done now, so I was far less sure that I was right.

It all worked out perfectly in the end, but the worst year of my life was 1980 up until the election. When you're involved in a campaign, it's every minute of every day. Your pituitary gland is squeezing out cholesterol [*sic*] into your bloodstream nonstop. It's very stressful and very unpleasant. And people treated Reagan in that time period like they treated Trump—he was an empty suit who spoke lines other people wrote. Clark Clifford [secretary of defense under President Johnson] referred to Reagan as an amiable dunce. Others talked about him as a California cowboy, a warmonger, and a racist. The bile and derision that they held for Reagan was just amazing. George Herbert Walker Bush accused him of practicing voodoo economics. Everyone trashed him. But then we won [*laughs*]. In fact, we didn't just win, we kicked ass. I was absolutely euphoric.

Bowmaker: Did you have the opportunity to take a formal position within the Reagan administration?

Laffer: There was talk of me being appointed secretary of the treasury, but my first wife left me and our children in late 1979, and I had to raise four kids aged six, nine, twelve, and fifteen alone. There was no way I could go to any job. Period. And I wouldn't have moved to Washington anyway. I hated Washington. When I was with George, I took the work seriously, but it was not fun. I much preferred being on a university campus or working in my home. George Shultz loved Washington. And he was very good at it. Other guys do, too. They love, love, love it. Now, I loved the politics and the economics, but from my own desk, not from one of their desks.

Bowmaker: You did serve on the President's Economic Policy Advisory Board [PEPAB] between 1981 and 1989. In his book *Revolution: The Reagan Legacy*, Martin Anderson described PEPAB, which consisted of twelve members, as a "secret intellectual weapon, one that could be called upon if Reagan's economic program started to veer off track"[1] and an effective

---

1. Martin Anderson, *Revolution: The Reagan Legacy* (San Diego: Harcourt Brace Jovanovich, 1988), 264.

"policy choke point,"[2] which ensured that President Reagan heard "directly from private economists who were independently analyzing and judging his policies"[3] but who were "inside the Reagan tent."[4] Is this an accurate description of the role of PEPAB when it was established in 1981?

Laffer: Yes! PEPAB had two purposes. The first was to reign in potentially renegade people. All of a sudden they had a stake in being with the president, and they were much less likely to go out and bad-mouth him. Bringing all of these people in under the tent to make sure they were on our team was very important. And remember when we came in, while we had won, the Republicans didn't like us very much, just like Trump.

The second thing to note is that the president really loved our sessions. He spent huge amounts of time with us and was very active. I remember when Arthur Burns wanted to get rid of the third year of the tax cuts and said, "Mr. President, if you agree to a small tax increase, you can get very large cuts in government spending." Of course, I had been with the president forever, and I said to Reagan, "Remember that in California, sir. The tax increases are always enacted and the spending cuts are always bypassed." He said to Burns, "Listen, Arthur. These meetings with all of you are just a delight for me. They are so collegial and fun. I think about them, I imagine them, and I look forward to them. They're my one break from being here in Washington. But for some reason, I made a promise that I was never going to raise taxes. And you know, Arthur, I intend on keeping that promise. So never ever mention a tax increase in my presence again. Do you understand?" Boom. That was cold Ronald Reagan to Arthur Burns.

Bowmaker: Were you aware of any resentment from some of President Reagan's senior economic advisers—such as [Chairman of the CEA] Murray Weidenbaum, Don Regan [secretary of the treasury and later chief of staff], and [Director of the OMB] David Stockman—who were concerned about encroachment of policy turf?

Laffer: There was a great deal of personal animosity towards me. They never resented Milton Friedman, for example, even though I was the economist he most agreed with. Why? Because he didn't get into the weeds on policy

---

2. Anderson, *Revolution*, 261.
3. Anderson, *Revolution*, 262.
4. Anderson, *Revolution*, 262.

like I did. Milton was the Yoda of economics. He'd always talk about principles, but he didn't write bills and work on the floor.

Murray Weidenbaum was a nice guy. I liked him. But he didn't like me at all and was at times uncivil. He was very offended by the role that I had with the president—coming in from California once a month to spend two or three hours with Reagan, which might have meant people like Murray had to change their agenda.

I always thought Don Regan was wonderful. I think he was on the right side of the issues, and was the right man for the right job of treasury secretary…but not as chief of staff [*laughs*]. Mrs. Reagan, who was scarier than hell, was a very important part of her husband's life, and you had to kiss her tush. You just had to. Now, Jim Baker was handsome, dapper, and well dressed all the time and would say, "Oh, Mrs. Reagan, you look beautiful today.…" He had all the Texas charm and schmooze. She loved him, but she didn't like Don Regan. He shouldn't have switched jobs.

I knew David Stockman very, very well before the election. He really disliked me, and I really disliked him. He turned traitorous right away with the interviews he did with [William] Greider for that piece in the *Atlantic Monthly* in 1981.[5] I was caught flat-footed by his disloyalty, but I should have known better because [Senator] Pat Moynihan said he was an ass. Here was a guy who worked for John Anderson as his chief of staff, and then when Anderson ran for president, Stockman worked for the opposition against him. That's not what you do—or at least it's not what I do. He liked to get on the inside of something so that he could sabotage it, and he tried to do that with us as well.

I remember when he rolled a scroll in front of the president that had about two thousand categories of tax revenues, and Stockman turned to me and said, "OK, Laffer, show me where your goddamn revenues are coming from. Come on. Here's a pen. Go ahead." I told him, "David, honestly, I'd rather be approximately correct than precisely wrong as you are every day of the week." The president started laughing, and I'd won.

---

5. William Greider, "The Education of David Stockman," *Atlantic*, December 1981, accessed March 5, 2019, https://www.theatlantic.com/magazine/archive/1981/12/the-education-of-david-stockman/305760/. In the article, which was based on eighteen interviews, Stockman was quoted as expressing a lack of confidence in the Reagan administration's economic theories and projections.

But I do thank him for one thing. In those interviews with Greider, he said [paraphrasing], "We all knew what we were doing. We were trying to help our rich friends. There are only two people who believed the supply-side crap: Ronald Reagan and Arthur Laffer. Everyone else understood what it really was." Thank you. I'm very grateful that he did exclude us. At least we were believers. By the way, I was with George Shultz when he said to the president, "Ron, what happened is a terrible thing. What you have to do right away is fire David Stockman." Do you know what Reagan's comment was? He said, "Where will he get a job?" His whole concern was about what would happen to Stockman. Is that not the finest man you've ever heard about in your life? Here's a guy who's just tried to sabotage your entire administration, and you're worried about him losing his income? I find that level of personal involvement to be a wonderful characteristic.

Bowmaker: Herbert Stein was the only member of PEPAB who had not advised Reagan throughout his first presidential campaign, and he also had a reputation as an economist who always favored raising taxes. Do you think a case could be made that the president ought to have been exposed to more debates from economists such as Stein, who had different viewpoints?

Laffer: PEPAB was a case of Milton Friedman, George Shultz, and I sitting together in the corner and conspiring against the other yahoos. Friedman, Shultz, and I never disagreed. Ever. We made that a pact. In that room, they would love nothing more than to separate us, because if we stayed together, there was no way anyone else was going to push anything through.

Herb Stein, who coined the term "supply-side economics," was a lovely man and one of the funniest human beings I've met in my life. At a press conference, he once said, "If you take out all the products that rose in price this month, the price level actually fell" [*laughs*]. Another time, someone said, "It's like a prostitute in a nunnery." Herb replied, "No, no, no, it's like a nun in a whorehouse" [*laughs*]. His greatest line ever was, "The gas lines can never exceed the length it takes to drive through them with one full tank of gas" [*laughs*].

But he wasn't a very quantitative economist—he was one of those chitty chatty Wall Street commentators who would have been great on TV. He'd never presented at a seminar at Chicago, believe me. He was against tax cuts—although Milton only favored them to deprive the government of revenue—and thought we should have more defense spending for Israel and more spending on infrastructure. Herb Stein would've been a Rockefeller Republican back then. We don't have any Republicans like Herb Stein anymore. They're all supply-siders now, every single one of them.

Bowmaker: How would you evaluate the role played by Alan Greenspan on PEPAB?

Laffer: Well, every time I went to the White House—and I went there a lot—I had to sign in. Alan Greenspan had signed in two hours before me. And when I signed out—and I stayed there a long time—Alan Greenspan had not yet signed out. He was going around all the offices, seeing everyone, and lobbying [for the position of Federal Reserve chairman]. Although I had always liked Greenspan, I was a little peeved at him. Yes, he did a great job as Fed chairman, but I thought Volcker was unimaginably good in that role. And who gets to beat the other one out of a position should be based on policy, not personality. However, that's not the way it worked, I believe, and I think you'll find many other people would agree with me.

Bowmaker: How would you assess the relative influence of the three CEA [Council of Economic Advisers] chairmen—Murray Weidenbaum, Martin Feldstein, and Beryl Sprinkel—whom you interacted with when you were on PEPAB? For example, when I spoke with Joseph Stiglitz, he told me that he had the impression that Sprinkel was "not someone who Reagan necessarily turned to for advice." Do you agree with him?

Laffer: In the first term of the administration, Feldstein was far more influential than Weidenbaum. Murray was a good regulatory economist from Washington University in St. Louis, but I don't think he made much of an impression. He wasn't thought of as an expert in all the areas that we were going into, and he was quickly marginalized.

I feel that Reagan thought highly of Marty as an economist. He's a pretty good one, but he's much more cautious and much more of a Keynesian than I am. He believes in the multiplier, for example, and he loves savings. He's also someone who didn't like me. He said many times that I was always arguing that tax cuts raised revenues, which is not true, and he could never document it. Ever.

Beryl Sprinkel was a great, great guy. I knew him forever—he used to come over to my house for dinner when I was at the University of Chicago. I think Beryl was supportive of everything we did, and he was very well liked by all of us. But as Stiglitz said, he was not someone who Reagan would listen to.

You have to remember that by that stage the stone had been set, and the president liked to hang with the old team. If you look at those of us who stayed throughout the administration, we went back a thousand years with the president. It was very hard to be a new person in the Reagan White House.

Bowmaker: In 1982, Murray Weidenbaum left his office as chairman of the CEA and was replaced by Martin Feldstein. The main issue that caused Weidenbaum to leave and to bring in Feldstein, who did not have a prior relationship with Reagan, was the so-called rosy scenarios—macro forecasts that were consistently higher than actual, which became a major PR [public relations] problem. What do you recall of this time?

Laffer: John Rutledge and Larry Kudlow did the forecast, which turned out to be embarrassing in 1981 and 1982. They didn't see the problem of the deferral of the first tax cuts, which I kept trying to explain to everyone. After the tax bill was passed in 1981, the president called me. He was very enthusiastic and very excited, but he could tell I wasn't as enthusiastic or as excited as he thought I should be. So he said, "Art, what's the matter? You sound disappointed. You're not going to pour cold water on this, are you?" I replied, "No, no, sir, I'm not. I'm really delighted you passed the bill." He said, "Well, what's the matter, then? Are you upset that it was only 25 percent and not 30 percent?" I told him, "No, no, I'm amazed you got 25 percent, sir." He said, "What bothers you, then?" I said, "Sir, you've phased in the tax cuts." "Ah, you economists," he replied. "You can't get something passed with Congress by having a massive deficit in the first year. So we phased it in over three years." I said, "Well, can I ask you a simple question?" "Fire away," he replied. I said, "Sir, how much would you shop at a store a week before it had a big discount sale?" His comment was, "Oh, my God. How bad is it going to be?" "It's going to be a barn burner," I told him. Again, economics is all about incentives. If I know there will be a big tax cut next year, why would I earn income this year if I can defer it in the next year? I get to keep so much more of it next year. But everyone was thinking that the boom would occur immediately when the tax cut was passed, not when the tax cuts took effect, and then they really work [*laughs*].

I remember having a debate in Hartford with a professor from MIT [the Massachusetts Institute of Technology] called Les Thurow—Less Thorough, I used to call him. He had a doom and gloom view of everything. I told him, "You better fasten your seatbelt, because this thing is going to take off on January 1, 1983. It'll be like a jet launch from an aircraft carrier." Sure as hell, that's what happened, and it was beautiful. From January 1, 1983, through June 30, 1984, US real GDP [gross domestic product] growth was 12 percent, or a little less than 8 percent on an annual basis. It is amazing what an economy can do with a 12 percent increase in output over a very short period of time. And once that happened, the world was ours.

Bowmaker: What was your view of the Tax Reform Act of 1986, commonly known as the second of the Reagan tax cuts?

Laffer: That was my baby, and I just loved it. It was the best tax bill in US history. We lowered the top tax rate from 50 percent to 28 percent and increased the bottom rate from 12.5 percent to 15 percent—the first time ever that the top tax rate was cut and the bottom rate was raised at the same time. The corporate tax rate was lowered from 46 percent to 34 percent, and the bill also mandated that capital gains taxes would be taxed at the same rate as ordinary income. It was the cat's meow, and it passed [the Senate] ninety-seven to three. [Senator] Al Gore said it was the best bill he had ever voted for in economics. Everyone understood the economics of it, which was about the marginal rate of substitution between labor and leisure. If you have a tax rate of 50 percent, you will spend 50 percent of your time trying to reduce your taxes. But if you can lower that rate, then you will spend most of your time trying to earn income and employ people.

Bowmaker: Related to the previous question, what is your response to economists who have rejected the validity of the Laffer curve? For example, Greg Mankiw has argued that "subsequent history failed to confirm Laffer's conjecture that lower tax rates would raise tax revenue. When Reagan cut taxes after he was elected, the result was less tax revenue, not more."[6]

Laffer: Mankiw has clearly stated time and time again that the Reagan tax cuts on the rich raised more taxes, and yet when I say it, he says I'm wrong on everything. Let me take you through in more detail the economics of why you should cut taxes on the rich and raise them on the poor.

Number one, when you cut taxes on the rich, you're 100 percent marginal, which means that everyone in the highest tax bracket has that tax rate as their marginal tax rate [marginal tax rate is the tax you would pay on your next dollar earned]. But very few people in the lowest tax bracket

---

6. N. Gregory Mankiw, *Principles of Economics* (Fort Worth, TX: Dryden Press, 1998), 166.

have that tax rate as their marginal tax rate: it is inframarginal [not at the margin]. So when you cut taxes on the poor, you're close to zero percent marginal, which means you reduce output and production because it has a positive income effect and no substitution effect.

Number two, the higher tax rates are, the greater the incentive effect is per dollar of static revenue. I will use the [President John F.] Kennedy tax cuts of the mid-1960s as an example. When Kennedy came in, the highest marginal tax rate was 91 percent and the lowest was 20 percent. What the president did was to cut the highest rate to 70 percent (a drop of 23 percent) and the lowest rate to 14 (a drop of 30 percent). Assuming no supply-side responses, the static revenue losses would therefore be 23 percent in the highest bracket and 30 percent in the lowest bracket. Now, let's look at the incentive effects on the highest bracket before the Kennedy tax cut. A person who earns a buck gross pays ninety-one cents in taxes: he is allowed to keep nine cents. After the tax cut from 91 percent to 70 percent, he now pays seventy cents in taxes: he is allowed to keep thirty cents. So his incentive went from nine cents on the dollar to thirty cents on the dollar, which is a 233 percent increase in incentives for a 23 percent static revenue loss, or a ten-to-one benefit-cost ratio. Go to the bottom bracket. A person who earns a buck gross pays twenty cents in taxes: he is allowed to keep eighty cents. After the tax cut from 20 percent to 14 percent, he now pays fourteen cents in taxes: he is allowed to keep eighty-six cents. So his incentive went from eighty cents on the dollar to eighty-six cents on the dollar, which is a 7.5 percent increase in incentives for a 30 percent static revenue loss, or a one-to-four benefit-cost ratio. That is a huge difference in incentives, assuming everyone is on the margin—which, as I just explained, is not true.

Number three, you want to cut taxes on the rich because they are different than the poor. How? They can change the timing of their income (think 401ks and IRAs [individual retirement accounts]), they can change the volume of their income (think about them taking a year off), they can change the composition of their income (think about why Warren Buffet paid a lower tax rate than his staff in 2010), and they can change the location of their income (think about me moving here to Nashville, Tennessee, from Rancho Santa Fe, California, purely and simply because of taxes and buying my house with my first year's tax savings). Woohoo! In other words, the elasticity of taxable income is astoundingly high in the highest tax bracket and low everywhere else.

So that's why you cut taxes on the rich and raise them on the poor. And when you look at the evidence, you will find that every time we have lowered taxes on the rich by a substantial amount, their tax revenues as a share of GDP have gone up. And that's not even counting the secondary, tertiary, and quaternary effects, which are all dramatically powerful. Come on, Mankiw knows it. Everyone knows it, but they all go against it because it's not politically correct. They're such dissembling, disingenuous bastards.

Bowmaker: Was your biggest impact on President Reagan through your personal interactions with him or via your PEPAB meetings with him?

Laffer: PEPAB was as close to a personal conversation as you can get in a meeting, but George Shultz ran it like the chairman of a meeting, and that took away the spontaneity and ambience. But I still met with the president individually or with other groups. He would come out to California four times a year and have a couple of us "kids" over for drinks for an hour or two. It was always an open discussion like PEPAB, only better because it was a social setting. He would have a screwdriver, and we would talk. And I would meet with him on other occasions, too. If he and I were present at an event, for example, he would often pull me over a few minutes and ask me whether I was OK with something that he was doing. Again, you have to remember that I was young at the time and very different from the person whom you're seeing today. It was a cool experience, and I was treated beautifully.

Bowmaker: By the end of the Reagan administration, you had known the president for almost fifteen years. How would you describe how he had changed over that time?

Laffer: I always loved him personally, in much the same way as I loved Nixon. But as governor of California, he was the biggest tax increaser ever [*laughs*]. He raised the personal income tax rate from 7 percent to 11 percent, he raised the capital gains tax rate by the same amount, and he raised the corporate tax rate from 5.5 percent to 9 percent. He was also the biggest social spender at the time. He supported the equal rights amendment. He eliminated, through his own legislation, all the anti-abortion statutes in the state of California. And prior to entering politics, as president of the Screen Actors Guild, he called the first industry-wide strike. This was a tax-increasing, social liberal, former union boss who evolved to be the greatest president of the United States we ever had.

And the thing I loved about Reagan in particular was that he was human, and he learned. I used to tease him by saying, "Sir, when you were

governor…" "I know, Arthur," he would stop me. "I wasn't a very good governor." "Those are your words, sir," I would say. "No, no, I know I wasn't,"
he would admit. "But I'm better than those other damn governors. At least I
learned from my mistakes. They kept making 'em over and over." And that
was the truth about Reagan. I watched him evolve from being governor of
California all the way through to the '86 Tax Act—which, as I said earlier,
was spectacular.

There was just one period when I was really, really worried about him. It
was after he got shot by [John] Hinckley [Jr.]. His personality changed totally.
Reagan was someone who always saw the shining city on the hill, a thousand years from now. He never focused on his mortality, his own little petty
pains…until he was shot. He came back very much worried about himself
and his health. And I at that time thought that there was a very good chance
(maybe 60–70 percent) he would eliminate the third year—the winner—of
the first tax cut. The four anti-Reagans—[James] Baker, [George H. W.] Bush,
[Richard] Darman, and [Bob] Dole—certainly wanted him to do so, but I
thought Shultz, Friedman, and I, in particular, made a difference in telling
him not to backtrack on it. And damned if he didn't just stick with us.

I remember being in the Roosevelt Room when [Congressman] Jack
Kemp came to me and said, "Art, I gotta tell you, Reagan's back." I said,
"What do you mean, Jack?" "I was walking in front of the Oval Office,"
he told me, "and the president called me in and said, 'Go ahead. Put your
finger right here'" (on his chest). [He continued,] "'It's like steel, isn't it?
I've been using the rowing machine, and I've got two inches already back
on my chest.'" No longer was this the mortal man I was worried about—the
guy I thought was going to back off on the tax cuts. He was back to being
the old Reagan. It was just so cool seeing that happen. It was in his eyes and
in his behavior when you were with him.

As I just said, after Hinckley had shot him, it was a devastating hit to his
health. And it was not only life threatening, but the recuperation lasted a
long time and seemed to end only when Jack told me his story. He [Reagan]
was back to being the person who saw the thousand-year kingdom of the
United States—nothing about his own mortality. I just loved that aspect of
the president, and that was the Reagan I knew.

Towards the end of his presidency, he didn't have dementia as many
people have said, but during meetings it was clear he was becoming an
older man. When the environment required it, he could bring himself back

to form and be very alert and very coherent. But those moments didn't last for long. He was tired.

Advising the Trump Transition Team

Bowmaker: You have been advising the Trump transition team. Can you tell us about your interactions with President-Elect Trump, and how you think he compares to other politicians with whom you have worked?

Laffer: I was put in touch with Trump early in the primaries. In all honesty, he didn't know who I was when they first introduced me to him. But I did go on to spend some time with him at the Trump Tower in New York, and by then he had done some research on me. We got along well, but I'm not personally close with him. I was very lucky with Reagan in that our relationship went so, so deep, and so, so far back. I don't have anything like that with Trump—I never will. But what I can say is that, in many ways, he's like Reagan: he's a promoter, he's a circus barker, he's a front man. This is not the guy who you want to head your IT [information technology] department, or to be your CFO [chief financial officer], or to do your cost accounting or file your tax returns. On the other hand, Reagan happened to be a very intellectual person. I beg you to read his book, *Reagan in His Own Hand*. That will provide a good flavor of how amazingly competent the man was on substantive issues and debates.

Bowmaker: Trump's (at least public) stance is very antitrade. You are protrade. How do you change Trump's mind?

Laffer: I had a talk with Jeff Sessions [later appointed attorney general under President Trump] about trade over two and a half hours. Jeff is a good friend, and we have a collegial, friendly, and personal relationship. In fact, Jeff told Bill Hagerty [director of appointments for Trump's presidential transition team] that there will be no economic appointments without Art Laffer's approval. I don't know what approval means, but at least they'll pass them by me, and that's nice. Anyway, Jeff knows I think the world of him. But he's very protectionist, so I went through trade with him very, very carefully and in an intuitive manner.

This is the way that I presented it to him. On countervailing duties, let's imagine we discovered a cure for colon cancer, and let's imagine Japan has discovered a cure for Alzheimer's. Now, let's imagine that Japan, true to form—they're the most protectionist nation around—refuses to let us sell our cure for colon cancer in Japan. Should we retaliate and get even with them and not allow Japan to sell their cure for Alzheimer's in the US? Obviously not. I told Jeff that retaliation for protectionism is not smart because it hurts yourself.

I also went through the following example, where you have someone in Ohio who grows only apples, someone in Costa Rica who grows only coffee, someone in Africa who grows only bananas, someone in New Zealand who grows only kiwis, and someone in China who grows only silk. Each person is fully employed, but no trade takes place. Consumption becomes tedious because in, say, Ohio, it is apples all day long. But what happens when you open up trade amongst them? Then you would see how every person is made better off and how any reduction in trade through barriers hurts everyone. And it's not a case of "I win, you lose"—it's a case of "we both lose."

Then I explained some important points about exports and imports. If you're looking at jobs, you love exports because that's what they're all about. If you're looking at imports, they seem really awful because they substitute for domestic jobs. But when you think about it, exports *are* imports. They are the means by which we get the resources to be able to buy imports. It's like separating work and supply and demand. People work in order to get the income to buy goods and services. Say's Law is correct: supply does create its own demand. And so what I was trying to tell Jeff is that any tax on imports is an exact equivalent tax on exports. This is Lerner's symmetry theorem.

General Thoughts on Economic Policymaking

Bowmaker: As someone who has spent much of his career advising on fiscal policy, what is your view on whether or not the Federal Reserve should be independent?

Laffer: I don't think the Fed should be independent and surely not run by a professor. [Chair of the Federal Reserve] Janet Yellen has never held a job in her life, and she's never had to bear the consequences of her own actions. Ever. The same goes for Ben Bernanke. These are my people; I know them well. You should not allow anything of substance to be in their hands—you really shouldn't. Now, that doesn't mean that you shouldn't listen to them, but you must have accountability for anything as powerful as the Fed.

And while I'm on the subject, who are these yahoos to think they know better than God about how to control our massive, wonderful economy? Think about Charles Darwin and Isaac Newton. They went out to find out about nature, to understand nature, and to love nature...not to override it and boss it. And yet people like Yellen and Bernanke have the hubris to think they can run the economy. To paraphrase Charlton Heston's character in *Planet of the Apes*, I would say, "Get your stinking monkey paws off my economy, you dirty ape." I'm not against doing anything ever, but we need free markets most of all in crises. Policymakers and regulators should put their hands over their ears, shut their eyes, and shout, "I'm not listening, I'm not listening, it'll be over quickly!" But whenever we stick our fingers in, we make it last longer than is necessary. The stimulus package, the regulatory measures, and quantitative easing have all caused the Great Recession to do permanent damage to the world.

Personal Reflections

Bowmaker: How does your personality affect your style and approach as a policymaker?

Laffer: It doesn't have any impact whatsoever. Of course, it matters a lot [*laughs*]. We're humans, and humans like relating to humans, and personalities are very important. Being nice to humans makes a big difference—being respectful of them and treating them with dignity, even when they're wrong. I think everything Jeff Sessions says about trade is wrong, but I like him very much. And he likes me and is willing to listen because we have developed a personal relationship.

Bowmaker: What are your strengths and weaknesses as a policymaker?

Laffer: You're asking the wrong person about my weaknesses. My detractors will tell you what they are. It's surely not a lack of enthusiasm for the topic, and if I thought I had some serious weaknesses, I'd probably try to change them.

What are my strengths? I love being the fly on the wall. I loved having the tête-à-têtes and the dinners and the lunches with Lady Thatcher, rather than being Lady Thatcher. I didn't find her life attractive to live. I found her attractive to be with and to talk to, but then I went home. She had to be Lady Thatcher all the time. It was the same with Reagan. I loved the dinner we had last night. To me, that's really fun, rather than being in Washington every night at a special dinner with other famous people. I think I get much more done being the way I am rather than actually there. And I believe I've had much more influence as a result. The story of the Laffer curve on the napkin at the Hotel Washington took place when I was an adviser. I couldn't have done it as a government official.

Bowmaker: There must be some things that, in hindsight, you'd like the opportunity to do differently. What are they?

Laffer: I should've gone to the bathroom earlier, rather than wetting my pants [*laughs*]. No, I've been very blessed. The worst episodes I've experienced in my life were very formative. When I was close to flunking out at Yale, and I took a year off to see if I could grow up, I came back engines ready to succeed. I'd gotten away from Mom and Dad, not because I wanted to be away from them, but there was a huge protective blanket over me. I was in Berlin on August 13, 1961, the day they built the wall. I'd traveled by bus from Helmstedt, which is a tiny town near Wolfsburg, and they hauled me into the East German Police office there. My Mom and Dad couldn't help me. If I was in trouble in East Germany, I was in trouble [*laughs*]. It scared me. All of a sudden, life became very real, but I think it turned out to be very instructive. And it was the same with that unpleasant moment with Paul Samuelson. If it were the Art Laffer of today, I would have said, "Go for it, dude. I'll shoot you back." But I was a kid.

Murray Weidenbaum (*standing*), when chairman of the Council of Economic Advisers, at a Cabinet Room meeting on December 4, 1981, to discuss the 1983 budget. Also pictured are President Ronald Reagan (*right*); Ed Meese (*center*), counselor to the president; and Martin Anderson (*left*), chief domestic policy adviser.

8   Murray L. Weidenbaum
Born 1927, New York City
Died 2014, St. Louis, Missouri

Murray Weidenbaum received his BBA from City College of New York, his MA from Columbia University, and his PhD from Princeton University in 1948, 1949, and 1958, respectively.

Weidenbaum worked as an economist in government, business, and academia. He was an economist at the Bureau of the Budget in 1949–1957, during the administrations of Presidents Harry Truman and Dwight Eisenhower; assistant secretary of the treasury for economic policy in 1969–1971, in the administration of President Richard Nixon; and President Ronald Reagan's first chairman of the Council of Economic Advisers, in 1981–1982.

Weidenbaum was corporate economist at the Boeing Company in 1958–1963 and was on the faculty of the Department of Economics at Washington University in St. Louis from 1964 to 2014. He was named Edward Mallinckrodt Distinguished University Professor upon his return, after his stint as chairman of Reagan's Council of Economic Advisers (CEA).

I interviewed Murray Weidenbaum at his home in Clayton, Missouri. It was the middle of the afternoon on Friday, June 2, 2012.

Background Information

Bowmaker: Why did you become an economist?

Weidenbaum: I can pinpoint the moment. Professor Herbert Spero was an undergraduate teacher of mine at City College. He was a very inspiring fellow on a very uneven faculty. One day, he was getting into the topic of who are the key players in the development of public policy and pointing out that lawyers were dominant because they were writing the laws and regulations. But he thought that in the future economists would play a much larger role, and that triggered the notion that if I majored in economics I might have the opportunity to improve public policy.

Entering the Policy World

Bowmaker: What does an economist bring to the policy world that others do not?

Weidenbaum: The ability to present details of different government programs within a broader context and using an analytical framework. My field is public finance, where one of the standard tools on the expenditure side is benefit-cost analysis. When I started examining the impact of government regulation, it struck me how useful that tool is. In fact, I believe I'm the first person to introduce and popularize the concept within that area.

Bowmaker: In 1969 you were the first person to be appointed as assistant secretary of the treasury for economic policy. How did you come to be appointed?

Weidenbaum: First of all, let me emphasize that I was not the first person with a strong economics background to be in the Treasury. But it had become apparent in a variety of federal agencies that economic analysis, as personified by a chief economist, was a full-time job. And so I was the first to be tagged by the Treasury to hold that position. I represented the Treasury in subcabinet-level meetings on economic policy. And because of the academic work I had done in the area, Arthur Burns, who was counselor to the president, asked me to be responsible for developing a new program for sharing federal revenues with state and local governments. My work on revenue sharing led to frequent interactions with President Nixon, Vice President Spiro Agnew, and senior members of the White House staff—which, for a young assistant secretary, was a unique opportunity.

Bowmaker: Did you view yourself as having strong policy positions or simply as a hired professional serving the president?

Weidenbaum: By conviction I was just a mainstream conservative economist, so it was a comfortable fit. But I never viewed myself—nor was I viewed—as a narrow technician. As I used to say at Boeing, "I can go a whole day without mentioning GDP [gross domestic product] once" [*laughs*].

Bowmaker: As you began your position, what surprised or frustrated you?

Weidenbaum: You need to appreciate that I started off my career as a peon in Harry Truman's Bureau of the Budget, where I was a member of the team that drafted his annual budget message, and I continued into the Eisenhower administration. I interacted with a very bright staff member of the Council of Economic Advisers, George Shultz, who had an office down the hall. And so I had a feel for what was going on in government and was thrilled to be part of the institution of the presidency.

Bowmaker: How much interaction did you have with Paul Volcker when you were in the Treasury?

Weidenbaum: Paul Volcker was the person with whom I worked most closely, and formally he was my supervisor. I can't say enough good things about Paul. Not only did I learn a great deal from him on the technical side—he is an outstanding economist—but he also taught me the importance of trust and integrity. As you know, he was undersecretary of the treasury for monetary affairs for several years and it was he, not Treasury Secretary [David] Kennedy, who represented the US at major international financial meetings. At one of those meetings, an official from another country was unsure why Paul was in the presence of more senior representatives. The French finance minister, Valéry Giscard d'Estaing, informed him, "He is a minister." Paul was accepted as a peer.

Bowmaker: When I spoke to Paul Volcker, he told me that President Nixon wasn't terribly interested in all things related to economics. Did you get that impression as well?

Weidenbaum: Yes, that's right. But he was extremely interested in revenue sharing, which is why we hit it off, and he kept writing to me after I left the Treasury, which was nice. Early on, Nixon met with the Republican governors near the Louisville, Kentucky, airport, and he brought three people with him to make presentations: myself, [Secretary of Labor] George Shultz, and [White House Urban Affairs adviser and later counselor to the president] Pat Moynihan. George talked about some technical aspect of the Department of Labor's programs, Pat discussed some rudimentary aspect of welfare reform, and I made a presentation on sharing revenues with state and local governments.

I had a series of flip charts—the only ones used at the meeting—and this captured everyone's attention, including the president's. The revenue-sharing program proved to be one of Nixon's successful domestic initiatives.

Bowmaker: What were the main lessons from your time at the Treasury that you were able to take into the remainder of your career?

Weidenbaum: One key skill needed was dealing with other members of the administration who had quite strong views on policy. And I also learned the importance of making a good presentation. You have to know the subject matter and be convincing about it. The people who fall by the wayside are those who can't answer the serious questions. And I'm enough of a ham to enjoy presentations, which ultimately led to my becoming a teacher.

As Chairman of the Council of Economic Advisers

Bowmaker: How were you approached to become President Reagan's first chairman of the Council of Economic Advisers?

Weidenbaum: Not long after the 1980 election, I was part of a group called the Coordinating Committee on Economic Policy, which was chaired by George Shultz. We met in Los Angeles for three days and put together two big loose-leaf briefing books for consideration by the president-elect. The book contained a comprehensive economic strategy, covering budget, tax, regulatory, monetary, and energy policies. It was very much a joint effort by the group—which, along with Shultz, included senior economic statesmen such as Milton Friedman, Arthur Burns, and Paul McCracken. On the third day, Reagan showed up first thing in the morning, walked around the table, and thanked each of us. His staff had told him that we had done good, hard work. If this was Nixon, he would have thanked us, handed the two books to an assistant, and then walked out [*laughs*]. But Reagan sat down and spent the whole damn third day with us, going through our recommendations page by page. This became the guts of the Reagan economic program, and he strongly endorsed it.

During a break in the meeting, one of the senior members of the transition team told me they were keen on my becoming part of the new administration. I told him that I was obviously delighted that Governor Reagan had won the election, but that my public service was behind me. He said, "Oh no, we have lots of important positions, such as deputy secretary of several key departments." When I replied that I still wasn't interested, he asked me what I would like. I told him, "I'm an economist and it's important that I run my own show. I want to be chairman of the Council of Economic Advisers." He said, "Oh, that's all you want ..." A few days later, I was called to Blair House, where the president-elect was living, and he formally offered me the job [*laughs*].

Bowmaker: Why do you think you were approached?

Weidenbaum: When I took a sabbatical from Washington University at the American Enterprise Institute, I started doing work on the many costs of government regulation. At the time, this was something that you mainly read about in law and economics journals, but the institute published my work in a little paperback called *Government-Mandated Price Increases: A Neglected Aspect of Inflation*. It was an instant success and generated significant coverage in the media, including news stories, editorials, guest columns, cartoons, and even comic strips. And that's how I became chairman of the Council of Economic Advisers—because when President Reagan introduced me to the press, he said, "He has advised me economically for over five years. Now, a good share of that time he didn't know he was advising me, but I was following his writings and his utterances and many times referred to them in my own weekly radio broadcasts."

Bowmaker: At your first official meeting, did he make it clear what he expected you to do for him?

Weidenbaum: No. He assumed I knew more about the job than he did—otherwise, I was the wrong guy.

Bowmaker: How did you go about establishing a comfortable working relationship with the president?

Weidenbaum: By listening. The ear is the most underutilized part of the body for many people. I needed to get a feel for how the man operated, and I learned quickly that he welcomed ideas.

Bowmaker: In your initial interactions with the president, what was your perception of his formal knowledge and understanding of economics? Did you get the impression that he was interested in economics in depth or not?

Weidenbaum: He made it clear that he had been an economics major at Eureka College, so he wasn't a total layman in the subject. Let me give you an example. When the White House put together a meeting with the editors of regional newspapers, one of them asked the president about the difference between real and nominal interest rates. He said, "Well, before I turn this over to Murray for a full explanation, here's my take…" When he was finished, there was nothing to add. It was lucid, accurate, and complete. In fact, I made a comment to a press friend of mine about his communication skills, and the lead editorial of the *Washington Star* began by quoting me as describing the president as "the nation's number one economic communicator." He was! But was he interested in economics in depth? No. He was very clever in the sense that he knew how much he needed to know and had a lot of confidence in his own judgment. He used to tease me frequently about Thomas Carlyle's phrase that economics is a "dismal science."

Bowmaker: How did President Reagan like to receive and absorb information?

Weidenbaum: Ronald Reagan was a reader, which was something that the press didn't understand. After I left the administration, I remember how they reported him putting aside two big briefing books—preparing him for an economic summit—to watch some old movies. When I was chairman of the CEA, I recall that he invariably took off from the Oval Office at 5:00 p.m. and went upstairs to his private residence. He loved to say that he lived above the store [*laughs*]. But 6:00 p.m. was the deadline for getting memos to him. Sometimes he would call you later that night about the memo, or more likely as you were walking into the Cabinet meeting the next morning he would comment about the memos you had sent him. So he was obviously a reader and someone who took the job very seriously.

Bowmaker: Did the president reach his decisions slowly or quickly?

Weidenbaum: At first on domestic economic and financial issues, he would often listen to everyone in the room and make his decisions on the spot. But after a while he started getting more than annoyed by the leaking to the press by some member of the team. So he increasingly began to say, "OK, I've got all your views. I'll let you know my decision later." He didn't want the damn thing leaked.

Bowmaker: How much of an impact could you have with the president during your meetings with him?

Weidenbaum: The top staff of the White House, especially Chief of Staff Jim Baker, had a clear view that end runs should be minimized. And so they didn't encourage the treasury secretary, the commerce secretary, or me to make unilateral presentations to the president. This meant that you weren't the only person in the room with him and led Treasury Secretary [Donald]

Regan to complain in his book [*For the Record*] that "to this day I never had so much as one minute alone with Ronald Reagan."[1] But I felt very comfortable with the arrangement. Reagan was presented with a variety of views and never blindsided.

After I told the president in 1982 that I was returning to Washington University, he focused on Marty Feldstein to be my replacement. When Marty came to the White House, we walked into the Oval Office with Ed Meese, then the counselor to the president. Marty asked the president, "Will I have the opportunity to present my views to you?" The president turned to me and said, "Murray, you answer that." And I replied, "I can honestly say, without exception, that on every important issue of economic policy, you will have ample opportunity to give your views to the president, and on a host of lesser policy questions as well. It's up to you to convince the president to agree with you." Reagan inspired loyalty because he gave you a wide berth.

Bowmaker: If you were in disagreement with the president, were you able to change his mind by presenting new evidence, or did you employ a different strategy?

Weidenbaum: My response varied with the circumstances. The president took his campaign commitments seriously—one of which was a strong interest in returning to the gold standard. I was a member of the Gold Commission, which was established under a 1980 law, and when I told him that I would consider this possibility with an open mind, President Reagan said, "Murray, vote your own view." When I reported to him that the majority of the commission was against the restoration of the gold standard, he made no attempt to overrule our decision. (Ron Paul was a member of the minority).

I distinctly recall an occasion when the president and I had a difference of views in relation to seasonally adjusted versus unseasonally adjusted reports on employment and unemployment. As you know, the government releases important economic data on GDP, prices, unemployment, and so on early in the morning. To this day, the head of the relevant agency calls the CEA chair the night before to let him know what's going to be released. And so I would write a one- to two-page memo to the president and call the chairman of the Fed[eral Reserve], the treasury secretary, and the director of

---

1. Donald T. Regan, *For the Record* (New York: Harcourt Brace Jovanovich, 1988), 142.

the OMB [Office of Management and Budget] to brief them. Sometimes the president would call me that night. On this occasion, he said to me, "I feel uncomfortable with these seasonally adjusted data. Why can't I just use the raw data?" He listened to my explanation but decided that he would use the unadjusted data in his speech. I then suggested a sentence to explain his position, "We don't live in a seasonally adjusted world." He liked that phrase and immediately put it into his speech!

Tip O'Neill, Speaker of the House, once said to me, "Damn it, your boss is such a nice man, it's so hard to disagree with him." Deep down, I think Reagan knew that, and maybe he took advantage of it. But I never heard him say anything nasty, even when he was provoked. He was just a good man. You would have liked him [*laughs*].

Bowmaker: If you gave advice that was in conflict with politics, would he point that out to you?

Weidenbaum: Oh, he never put you in a position of weighing political factors against your own professional judgment. I had a designated seat behind him in the Cabinet room and, early on, he told us, "Fellas, I'm the elected politician here. You are my technical advisers. Just play it straight and let me worry about the politics." Reagan was very proud of the fact that he was the only union president [of the Screen Actors Guild] to be elected president of the United States. And so he was used to negotiation.

Bowmaker: How would you describe the kind of economics that you used in advising the president relative to that found in your academic work and teaching?

Weidenbaum: When Robert McNamara was secretary of defense, there was pioneering work done in applying economic analysis to defense decisions. Alain Enthoven, who was deputy assistant secretary of defense, gave a talk called "Economic Analysis in the Department of Defense" at one of the AEA [American Economic Association] meetings that was published in the *American Economic Review*'s Papers and Proceedings in 1963. His main point was that most of the economics was found in a principles class—it wasn't complicated or esoteric. I kept that in mind when I got heavily involved in issues of international trade policy. Even though I carried the banner for free trade, I didn't talk about the theory of comparative advantage to the president, or to the vice president, or to the Cabinet members and senior staff of the White House for that matter. They just wanted my key arguments and a firm conclusion. I think it would have been counterproductive to give them a detailed lesson in economics.

I should mention that I never had to lecture the president on the negative effects of high-bracket income taxation. When that subject arose, he would always recall his days as a Hollywood star. During the fall of each year, his accountant would tell him that he was hitting the top bracket (then over 90 percent), which was the signal to stop working for the rest of the year. And so the president had a very personal understanding of the disincentive effects of higher tax rates [*laughs*].

Bowmaker: Did you work with the president's speechwriters and help vet his speeches?

Weidenbaum: Yes. Let me describe the process of preparing a key speech that the president gave in February 1981, explaining the four pillars of Reaganomics: spending cuts, tax cuts, regulatory reform, and monetary restraint. By the way, that order offended the supply-siders because they thought it showed a lack of faith in the instantaneous nature of the economy's response to tax cuts! Anyway, the first step of the process involved a gathering of his speechwriters, top White House assistants, and key policy advisers. We tossed back and forth the important themes that he would cover, and when he was happy with the basic points that had been developed, the speechwriters came up with a rough draft. Then it was handed to the other members of the group, except for the president. We incorporated our comments into a revised draft, which was sent to the president on the understanding that if he was not satisfied, we would reconvene and start over. What came back was a positive response in the form of a rewrite in the president's own handwriting on a lined, yellow, legal-sized pad! One of the reasons why his speeches were so effective was because he would write them in his own language. When his version was typed up, we went over it paragraph by paragraph at his private residence, with the president holding the master copy. On quite a few occasions, I questioned the accuracy of a statement, but he never pulled rank. Instead, he would invariably say, "OK, how should I make my point accurately?" That hit such a responsive chord with me and is another example of how he inspired loyalty.

Bowmaker: How would you describe your relationship with the upper echelon of the White House staff during your time as chairman of the CEA?

Weidenbaum: My relationship with the White House staff was very good, and I received a host of special assignments. Let me give you an example. In 1981, the military were struggling to meet their manpower requirements, and there was talk of a return of the draft. And so the president established a special Task Force on Military Manpower that was chaired by the secretary of defense, Caspar Weinberger. I wound up on the committee, and we put forward a report proposing that we should improve the compensation and living conditions of the armed forces. The president approved our recommendations; Congress quickly enacted them; and, helped by an upturn in the economy in late 1982, the problem soon evaporated. That was a big accomplishment and, again, very much a group effort.

Bowmaker: How about your relationship with the Treasury and the Federal Reserve?

Weidenbaum: At first, I think Treasury Secretary Regan resented me being up there with him. He was following in the footsteps of Alexander Hamilton [*laughs*]. But there was a press conference at the White House that helped break the ice. We were talking about budget cutting when one of the reporters asked, "Gentlemen, what do you think about all the money that is spent providing limousine service to government officials?" Regan went red in the face. I said to him, "Don, let me handle this one," and told the reporter, "Actually, I gave that subject a lot of thought this morning as I took the bus to work" [*laughs*]. Over time, we learned that we could trust each other. At the Troika meetings, for example, it became quite clear if only Don and I were present, there would be no leaking, but if [Director of the OMB] David Stockman was present, there would be.[2] So it wasn't a matter of high policy that brought Don and me together—it was a personal relationship based on trust.

I continued the tradition of the chairman of the CEA meeting regularly for breakfast with the chairman of the Fed, who at that time was Paul Volcker. At the beginning of the Reagan administration, Paul and I worked on the key monetary policy language for the white paper issued by the White House, laying out the Reagan economic program. We both agreed that in order to fight inflation, we needed to restrain excessive money supply

2. During President Reagan's first administration, Chief of Staff James Baker was part of a senior staff triumvirate with Deputy Chief of Staff Michael Deaver and Counselor to the President Edwin Meese. This group came to be known as "the Troika."

growth. That was important because it maintained the independence of the Fed but at the same time accomplished a crucial part of the administration's economic policy.

In the meetings that followed, the close relationship between monetary policy and fiscal policy became apparent, with Paul often beginning the session by asking about the progress in cutting government spending. Sometimes he would also be interested in the issue of reforming burdensome government regulation. We would almost always discuss current monetary policy, with the implicit understanding that I would use my judgment in briefing the White House. The details of those meetings with Paul were never leaked.

Bowmaker: Did you have much interaction with interest groups as chairman of the CEA?

Weidenbaum: I made presentations to an endless array of interest groups that would come into the White House. It was always predictable [*laughs*]. They would ask me tough, sometimes nasty, questions, but when the president walked in, the tone of the meeting would quickly change. He would shake everyone's hand, thank them for coming, and then say, "Do you have any questions that Murray hasn't answered?" They would toss him a real softball! Once he left the room, of course, they would resume their hostile questioning. But I understood that part of my job was to deflect criticism from the president.

Bowmaker: Can you describe any involvement that you had in international economic policymaking?

Weidenbaum: I was chairman of the OECD's [Organisation for Economic Co-operation and Development's] Economic Policy Committee, which involved working with counterparts in other countries to help draft statements for the annual economic summits. That was an exercise in economic diplomacy! And I also had the opportunity at the OECD meetings to have one-on-ones with my counterparts on serious issues. For example, a senior member of the US Commerce Department had gotten into a shouting match in Washington with his Japanese counterpart on the subject of Japanese trading restrictions on aluminum baseball bats made in the US. I was asked if I could intervene. And so during a recess at the next OECD meeting, I approached the Japanese economics minister to discuss the matter. He told me through his translator that his baseball association adopts rules that the country has to go along with. I said to him, "I'm sure you didn't mean it, but we Americans think that baseball was invented by us, and saying that our bats are inferior is an insult." The translator repeated one word, and I assume it was Japanese for "insult." That short meeting changed the tone of our relationship, and within a few weeks they quietly abandoned their policy.

I remember my first OECD meeting very well. I had a preliminary meeting with Jacques Delors, the economics and finance minister of the new [President François] Mitterrand administration in France. An earlier meeting between Delors and a senior US government official had not gone well, with the American relying heavily on a translator. Since I had a reputation for unruffling feathers, our embassy asked if I would meet him [Delors] in Paris. My French is strictly high-school standard, but I decided to present something in the language. We convened in his office at the Louvre, and I began by saying in fractured French, "What a pleasure it is to meet the new socialist minister in this former grand palace of royalty." I knew I was pushing my luck, but Delors broke up with laughter! And from then on, he referred to me as *"mon ami."* Another example of the importance of personal relationships in the policy world!

Bowmaker: All things considered, can you point to a specific example of where you, as an economist, or the CEA, as an organization, were able to make a difference?

Weidenbaum: As part of a three-man group along with Martin Anderson [domestic policy adviser] and David Stockman, I was heavily involved in putting together the so-called Reagan budget cuts. That was an important part of the Reagan administration's early activity, and as an old budget hand, it was a labor of love. I constantly quoted to the group Harry Truman, who used to remind us during his administration that "I never saw a budget that couldn't be cut." In my public statements about our efforts, I would often cite a former budget director: "Good budgeting is the uniform distribution of dissatisfaction."

The effectiveness of the CEA itself on certain issues partly depended on political economy. For example, we were successful in removing import restrictions on shoes but failed to win the battle on eliminating restrictions on textiles. To be honest, I was guilty of doing a bit of politicking on those issues. When [Secretary of Commerce] Mac Baldridge was trying to get his assistant secretary for economic policy promoted to undersecretary, I was able to help break the logjam, and the House approved of the change. Mac thanked me and said, "I owe you one"—which led to his vital support on the shoe issue.

But it wasn't a coincidence that the congressional delegation to the White House successfully pushing for textile quotas was led by Strom Thurmond, chairman of the Judiciary Committee, who was shepherding through the Senate President Reagan's nominations to the Supreme Court (the unsuccessful shoe delegation was chaired by Northeastern liberal Democrat Edward Kennedy). As I say, the ancient term "political economy" played a role.

Bowmaker: Why did you leave your role as chairman of the CEA?

Weidenbaum: When Reagan overruled our recommendations for budget cuts, I quietly folded my tent and left. Given my role and personality, I knew that if I had stayed, I would be expected to defend the historically high budget deficits—which I couldn't stand to do. The president must have appreciated that, because I'm the only guy who left the CEA during his eight years in office who he brought back as a member of his outside advisory board. As he said when I first left the White House, "We part as friends."

General Thoughts on Economic Policymaking

Bowmaker: Do you believe that if we were to raise the level of economic literacy in this country, economic policymaking would improve because the people would demand better policy?

Weidenbaum: Yes, I would like people to have a better understanding of economics. But policymaking is also subjective, involving difficult choices among important alternatives. For example, take the trade-off between economic efficiency and income inequality. In his book [*Equality and Efficiency:*] *The Big Tradeoff,* my late friend Art Okun argued that transferring money from the rich to the poor was like trying to carry water in a leaky bucket. The poor will not receive all the money that is taken from the rich, and so how much leakage you are willing to tolerate is a measure of your terms of trading off efficiency and equality. Of course, a trade-off in political terms means compromise, which is a dirty word now.

Bowmaker: Do you think that the gap between economics research produced in universities and policymaking will increase or decrease over time?

Weidenbaum: I'm not sure. My younger colleagues, who are very bright, have developed some very high-powered forms of analysis that makes it harder to explain the basic results to a layman and widens the gap between the economics profession and the rest of society. Their work is important in developing the corpus of economics, and I support the effort. But I think we have to be aware that getting it into the decision-making process requires a different combination of breadth of understanding and subtlety of approach.

Bowmaker: Which aspects of the institutional framework for making economic policy in this country work well, and which need to be reformed?

Weidenbaum: The role of economists in government is so fascinating because there are very few issues that are devoid of economic content, and this means that we are heavily involved in the formulation of policy. Specifically, the formulation of policy in the executive branch is far more advanced than the institutional structure of Congress in dealing with issues of public policy. When those issues move to Congress, it is a mess from a variety of viewpoints. First of all, its traditional structure, archaic as it may be, is being abandoned. For example, take the budget process, which is the main way of allocating government resources. Traditionally, the Appropriations Committee in the House plays a central role in that process and relies on its subcommittees to not only hold hearings but also to pass judgment. The full committee rarely if ever sets up priorities; it usually combines the recommendations of the individual subcommittees. Even that primitive system is no longer working. It's been several years since an annual budget has been approved. Instead, stopgap bills are passed to continue the status quo with a few changes. I despair of fundamental change occurring before a crisis forces the country to take effective action.

Personal Reflections

Bowmaker: Which aspects of public service do you miss most?

Weidenbaum: The White House limousine service and telephone service, which can quickly get you in touch with someone anywhere on the globe [*laughs*]. Joking aside, it would be the rare opportunity to help improve public policy of the United States.

Bowmaker: What value has your public service had to you and to your university?

Weidenbaum: Serving Ronald Reagan was the highlight of my professional career. I was involved in a great variety of public policy issues, and I worked with and met a tremendous array of fascinating people. To this day—thirty years later—when I walk down the street here in Clayton or in downtown

St. Louis, someone will stop to thank me for my public service. That's a nice feeling.

It certainly raised the visibility of Washington University—the chancellor even told me so—and I think it made me a better teacher with high enrollments, even though I am a notoriously low grader [*laughs*].

Bowmaker: Do you think academics fear losing intellectual capital during public service?

Weidenbaum: Good point. When I came back to Washington University from the Treasury, I couldn't teach a graduate course in public finance because I had been unable to keep up with the literature. However, I drew on my public service for developing new courses in both the Economics Department and the Business School.

Bowmaker: How did your personality affect your style and approach as a policymaker?

Weidenbaum: When I occasionally went back to the White House, I was told that they missed my sense of humor. Even in the depths of the recession, I would find something to laugh about. For example, I coined the term "rosy scenario," which was first used in 1981—but not originally in relation to the administration's optimistic economic forecast. At a breakfast meeting, a couple of reporters from the *Wall Street Journal* had asked me about the progress in recruiting the other members of the CEA. I told them, "Contrary to rumor, the next CEA member won't be an affirmative action hire known as Rosy Scenario" [*laughs*].

Bowmaker: What were your strengths and weaknesses as a policymaker?

Weidenbaum: I'm not a know-it-all, and I realize that I'm not the smartest economist in the profession. And so I do listen, and on occasion, I will change my mind. The price that I pay for having a very wide range of interests is that other people's knowledge of a given subject area can be far deeper than mine. But it helped that I was an economic adviser to a CEO [chief executive officer] in the private sector because I developed an ability to communicate effectively that I took into the White House. I had learned that a busy CEO appreciates the essence of a story, and so I rarely wrote a memo to the president that was more than two full pages. And I also brought with me the set of voluntary rules that I had adopted at Boeing: number one, don't say anything you don't believe in, either in private or in public; and number two, try to avoid embarrassing the management in public.

Bowmaker: As a policymaker, which decisions or outcomes were most gratifying?

Weidenbaum: Given my hectic and exhilarating schedule at the time, I didn't realize how profoundly we altered the trend of public policy in the United States. The people who thank me in the street understand that those of us who helped Ronald Reagan effectuate those changes made important contributions, which brings a lot of satisfaction. It's a form of psychic income.

Bowmaker: On the other hand, there must be some things, in hindsight, that you'd like the opportunity to do differently. What are they?

Weidenbaum: I waged a two-front war on the issue of defense spending. Externally, I explained why—unlike the Vietnam [War] military buildup—the Reagan expansion on defense spending was not inflationary. Within the administration, I was always on the side in favor of staying within the 5 percent annual real increases proposed by Governor Reagan in his 1980 campaign. But when the Department of Defense put forward higher numbers, the president made it clear that he would never sacrifice national security for economic considerations. "Murray, we don't want to send the wrong signal to the Russians," he would say. In retrospect, we won the Cold War without firing a shot, but maybe we could have succeeded at a much lower cost. Yet Reagan was fundamentally right—he saw the big picture.

Martin Feldstein (*left*), when chairman of the Council of Economic Advisers, sitting next to President Ronald Reagan in the Cabinet Room for a Cabinet Council on Commerce and Trade meeting on October 4, 1983.

9 Martin S. Feldstein
Born 1939, New York City
Died 2019, Belmont, Massachusetts

Martin Feldstein graduated with an AB in economics from Harvard College in 1961 and then obtained a BLitt, MA, and DPhil, all in economics, from the University of Oxford in 1963, 1964, and 1967, respectively.

Feldstein was a lecturer in public finance at Oxford between 1965 and 1967, before spending the remainder of his academic career at Harvard University, where at the time of his passing on June 11, 2019, he was the George F. Baker Professor of Economics. He was twice president and CEO (chief executive officer) of the National Bureau of Economic Research (NBER), in 1977–1982 and 1984–2008.

Feldstein's academic awards include the John Bates Clark Medal (1977), a prize awarded to an economist in the United States under the age of forty who is judged to have made the greatest contribution to economic science.

In government, Feldstein served as chairman of President Ronald Reagan's Council of Economic Advisers (CEA) in 1982–1984, a member of President George W. Bush's Foreign Intelligence Advisory Board in 2006–2009, and a member of President Barack Obama's Economic Recovery Advisory Board in 2009–2011.

I interviewed Martin Feldstein at the Royal Sonesta hotel in Cambridge, Massachusetts, where he was attending the National Bureau of Economic Research Summer Institute. It was the middle of the morning on Tuesday, July 24, 2012.

Background Information

Bowmaker: Why did you become an economist?

Feldstein: I came to Harvard College thinking that I would eventually go off into the world as a lawyer. But I took economics in my first year and liked it because it gave concrete answers and was a useful framework for thinking about both history and current policy issues. Then I went to Oxford as a Fulbright Fellow, discovered the technical side of economics, and became very much interested in the idea of applying economics to real issues.

Entering the Policy World

Bowmaker: What does an economist bring to the policy world that others do not?

Feldstein: Perhaps one should distinguish between different kinds of questions. In macroeconomics, an economist brings a technical understanding of the issues, whereas in microeconomics, it is the ability to think at the margin, for example, and consider opportunity costs—both of which are principles that come naturally to anybody who has studied economics.

Bowmaker: Were you ever interested in working in government prior to your role as chairman of President Reagan's Council of Economic Advisers?

Feldstein: I had certainly expressed my opinions about economic policy issues, but I had no particular desire to go to Washington. In fact, when Gerald Ford was president, Alan Greenspan was chairman of the CEA, and I was invited to become a member of the council. However, I said to the White House, "Gee, I'm just doing too much academic work right now, so I think I'll pass." Of course, there was a big difference between Greenspan's position as chairman and what would be my position as a member. And I was also a little nervous about the prospect of testifying in Congress. What if a senator asked, "The president says the earth is flat. Do you agree?" If I agreed, I was worried that my colleagues would say, "Oh, Marty has sold himself out." But it was never an issue. I quickly learned that you can reply, "Well, it depends on your point of view. If you look at it closely, over a narrow range, the earth is very flat…" The senator would move on to the next question on his list [*laughs*].

As Chairman of the Council of Economic Advisers

Bowmaker: How were you approached to become chairman of President Reagan's Council of Economic Advisers?

Feldstein: Somebody from the White House called me and said, "Come down and meet the president." I knew what it was about because a reporter from the *Wall Street Journal* had already told me that I was on the short list for the job of chairman of the CEA.

Bowmaker: Why do you think you were approached?

Feldstein: I did not know Ronald Reagan before I met him and he offered me the job. But I could well imagine that a variety of my friends played a role: George Shultz, David Stockman, and George Bush Sr., in particular. And of course I wasn't an unknown economist hiding up in Cambridge doing his academic work. By that stage, I had written fairly extensively, had testified in Congress, and had developed policy ideas.

Bowmaker: How much did you know about the history of the CEA before you began your role?

Feldstein: Nothing in great detail. I knew that it existed, that it was created at a time when there was a Keynesian view of the world, and that its role was to advise the president on fiscal policy in order to achieve and maintain full employment. But as professional thinking changed, there was a shift in emphasis from fiscal policy to monetary policy and from the maintenance of full employment to the objective of price stability. That led to a change in the role of the CEA. By the time I arrived in the early eighties, it had taken on a much more important role in advising about the economic effects of government spending, taxation, and regulation. For example, we were involved in a fundamental review of Social Security policy and oversaw a major change in the way that the government paid for health care of the elderly. Macroeconomic issues were still important, but the focus shifted from stabilization to growth, including the role of budget deficits and private saving incentives.

Bowmaker: Did you know what to expect in your role?

Feldstein: Not really. In many ways, the experience turned out to be better than I expected. Since then, whenever young colleagues have had the potential opportunity to serve as CEA chair, I have enthusiastically advised them to do it. There were times during my tenure at the White House when

I would think to myself, "I would give up a day of this week as CEA chair just to see what it would be like in another administration—say, advising [Richard] Nixon or Ford." I was curious.

Bowmaker: Did your predecessor, Murray Weidenbaum, gave you any advice before you began your role?

Feldstein: No, but Murray left on the table a note and two things. The note said, "Good luck," and the two things were a small string of worry beads— the ones that people use in Greece and the Middle East—and a bottle of aspirin [*laughs*].

I'd also had some interaction with two previous chairs, Alan Greenspan and Arthur Burns. I was already president of the NBER, which is a position that Burns had held, and so we had gotten to know each other. He had talked to me about his advising of President [Dwight] Eisenhower. Arthur said that he would go to Eisenhower and talk about different aspects of the economy, so it was kind of a tutorial. I thought that was interesting. But I don't think President Reagan was keen on getting a general education from me. He was more interested in advice about the specific issues and the questions that he faced.

Bowmaker: At your first official meeting, did President Reagan make it clear what he expected you to do for him?

Feldstein: Yes. Reagan was a great delegator, and so he assumed that as part of the larger economics team, I would provide him with understanding and advice about the economy and help him shape economic policy.

Bowmaker: How did you go about establishing a comfortable working relationship with the president?

Feldstein: He was very easy to have a comfortable relationship with. That was just the nature of his personality. When I arrived at the White House, the Mexican debt crisis had just begun, and I had my first session with the president to talk about policy. But he didn't ask questions or take notes! I thought, "Hmm, this is very strange. Maybe it's just a pro forma position. He has to have a CEA chair, and it happens to be my turn." A few days later, however, there was a Cabinet meeting and a subject came up that I had commented on at our first meeting. He said to the group, "No, no, Marty told me the other day that…" So what I learned was that, one, he had a remarkable memory, and two, I came to realize that during our hour-long sessions, it was my job to figure out what I wanted to communicate to him, and if I were clear, he didn't have to do a lot of interrogation.

Bowmaker: When I spoke with your predecessor at the CEA, Murray Weidenbaum, he told me you asked the president whether you would have the opportunity to present your views to him. Did you feel that you were given the fullest opportunity to give your views to the president? When you were in disagreement with the president, were you able to change his mind by presenting new evidence, or did you employ a different strategy?

Feldstein: Yes, I did feel that I had the fullest opportunity to give my views to the president. At the time, there was a lot of debate about the budget deficit, which had exploded partly because we were in a serious recession. His political advisers were telling him not to talk about it because it was bad news, but I wanted him to emphasize his commitment to lowering the deficit, a position that he had held for years. So I would go in to see him and say, "Here are the new numbers. This part of the deficit is cyclical, which will go away, but here is the core that won't unless we make some tax or spending adjustments." I am an evidence-driven economist—I don't have a different way of persuading somebody about an issue.

Bowmaker: As you mentioned earlier, a review of Social Security policy took place when you were in the White House. Given your expertise in Social Security, you might have been expected to be the main leader of the administration's efforts to rewrite the Social Security law to save the system from bankruptcy. Instead, President Reagan turned to Alan Greenspan. Why do you think you were essentially shut out of Social Security reform efforts? Is it reasonable to suggest that was a real snub, since that was one of the main reasons you took the job?

Feldstein: I never felt at the time that I was being kept out of it. A decision was made to do something about Social Security. They wanted to keep the administration's fingerprints off bad news, so they needed a commission— one that was headed by a wise person with a good reputation, and capable of delivering what you wanted. Alan Greenspan ticked those boxes. But it's not as if the Greenspan Commission came up with a plan and the administration said, "Oh, well, I guess that's a good idea. We'll take it." There was interaction between the commission and the folks in the White House; we met with the president, and with [Chief of Staff] Jim Baker and [Director of the Office of Management and Budget] David Stockman, to try to come up with a good package. And so I never felt in any sense that I was left out of it. In any case, I don't think I went to Washington with a specific agenda.

Bowmaker: How would you evaluate the contribution of the President's Economic Policy Advisory Board (PEPAB)? What were your views on the work of Arthur Laffer, who was a member of PEPAB?

Feldstein: PEPAB was a way of rewarding, and keeping in touch with, a number of important people who had been supporters of President Reagan. It was a distinguished group, but I wouldn't say that it had any direct impact on policy. Art Laffer was one of the true-blue supply-siders in the administration who talked about being able to raise revenue if you cut tax rates. I thought that was exaggerated, because even though I was a supply-sider, I wasn't an *extreme* supply-sider. But by exaggeration, I think Art received attention, and he got people to think about the fact that there is a behavioral response. And he would typically do it in terms of examples of people facing, say, 70 percent marginal tax rates. Who were they? They were people on relatively low incomes, and so because of phase-out rules on welfare and food stamps, they could literally be facing such extremely high marginal tax rates. But I do think Art did contribute to an atmosphere that supported bringing down tax rates on the grounds that there would be a behavioral response. To be fair, then, even if it wasn't as extreme a response as he claimed, it was helpful.

Bowmaker: Who do you think represented your greatest competition for the president's ear during the time when you were CEA chairman: his political advisers, the Treasury, or George Shultz?

Feldstein: It was his political advisers, and that was a frustration. In the first budget that I worked on, which was in the early part of 1983, the president accepted a combination of spending cuts and tax increases that would reduce the deficit gradually over a several-year period. The Treasury claimed that the tax increases would be economically counterproductive, while the White House staff argued that they would be politically unpopular and would weaken the identification of tax reduction with the Republicans. This meant that we did not make any progress in negotiations with Congress. I maintained that we should reduce the deficit and argued that the president's budget plan was the way to do it, but I was criticized by the White House staff for my support of his budget.

[Secretary of the Treasury] Don Regan and I had a cordial relationship, but he was very much attuned to what the politicians in the White House wanted. He had no real background in economics and was too persuaded by his staff, particularly the undersecretary for monetary affairs, Beryl Sprinkel, to be critical of the Federal Reserve. For example, during my two years at the CEA, the US trade deficit ballooned because of the overstrong dollar. The Treasury took the view that the strong dollar did not reflect the budget situation but was due to monetary policy being too tight. In any case, it was always hard to know whether you were on the same side as Don Regan on certain issues, because I never felt that his public pronouncements were necessarily what he truly believed.

Regan wanted to be influential—he wanted to be in on things. The best evidence of that was his remarkable decision to give up being secretary of the treasury in order to become chief of staff in the White House. That stunned me. When I was there, he was always nervous about whether there were conversations going on that he wasn't a party to, that he didn't know about, and so on. And it pained him that, unlike some finance ministers in Europe who sit on their central bank's board, he wasn't on the Fed's board. And so Paul Volcker did what Paul Volcker wanted and didn't have to consult with Regan.

George Shultz had a direct relationship with President Reagan and chaired PEPAB for some time. Obviously, I have the highest regard for him. He's an economist, and unlike a lot of very successful people, he's not embarrassed about it. Many would suppress that aspect of their background, but not him. George reminds you that he was a Marine and a PhD economist. In terms of his influence, at any meeting with the president where George was present, George's voice was very clearly heard. He's a very persuasive speaker, and so I thought of him as a very wise man.

Bowmaker: Don Regan did not believe that high deficits caused high interest rates. As you just mentioned, he had no formal training in economics, so how did you try to convince him otherwise?

Feldstein: I never convinced him, and he was really repeating what he heard from Beryl Sprinkel. High deficits do cause high interest rates, and the logic of it seems very clear to me. If the government is borrowing substantial amounts and is expected to continue to go on borrowing substantial amounts, then it's going to take money away that would otherwise go into private investment. And the mechanism that causes that to happen is higher interest rates. That was my argument. I think most people accepted it at the time, and I believe it is still true to this day. Of course, there was no attempt to present statistical evidence, because I don't think Don Regan would have been persuaded by a regression study [*laughs*].

Bowmaker: How would you describe your relationship with the OMB?

Feldstein: David Stockman and I were on the same side in our views about the budget situation. We were trying to persuade the president to make it a higher priority. We worked together to provide him with a forecast of the likely budget deficit in future years under existing tax and spending policies: the CEA did the multiyear economic forecast, while the OMB calculated the revenue implications and resulting budget deficit.

Bowmaker: How would you describe your relationship with the Federal Reserve?

Feldstein: I had a very good relationship with [Chairman of the Federal Reserve] Paul Volcker. There were very few people in Washington whom he could talk to on a confidential basis and who understood what he was doing. It was the kind of conversation that you can only have as an insider. He could trust that what he said to me was just between the two of us.

The lesson I took from Paul is that he conquered inflation in a way that was intentionally unclear. He was very careful not to put the blame on the Fed, or even credit the Fed, for changing policies. It's better to have it all seem as if it's happening because of market forces. That's very different from today's Fed, which debates about whether it's going to raise interest rates by, say, twenty-five basis points. That was not the Volcker way of doing business.

Bowmaker: Looking back, do you regret going public with your philosophical differences with the White House?

Feldstein: I don't know that they were philosophical differences—that seems much too strong. It's hard for an outsider to get a sense of the nature of the debate, but as you know I was in favor of raising taxes as well as cutting spending. The political people did not like the words "raising taxes." And so the president would give a speech in which he would say, "I will never raise taxes on hardworking Americans struggling to make ends meet." And by the way, those qualifying phrases when describing his policy meant that he could go after other things, like business tax increases. Reagan was very clever. I would say, "We need to have more tax revenue if we're going to bring down this deficit." The press would take a clip of the president making his statement and a clip of me speaking someplace about the need to have taxes as part of the package, and they'd say, "Conflict! Conflict!" [*Laughs.*]

In general, I made speeches without a formal written version—I just spoke from notes. But I eventually decided that with all these problems, I better write down my standard talk, give it to the president, and say, "Do you have any reactions to this?" At one point in a draft speech, I said, "And we need to raise taxes and cut spending in order to reduce the deficit." His only comment was, "You should say it in the opposite order" [*laughs*].

But there are two levels of issue here. One, as I just said, was the fact that the political people just didn't like the idea of talking about raising taxes and said to me, "Don't talk about the deficit. Talk about all the good news." But then there is a second thing, which is strictly personal. There were people in the White House who said: "I don't like Marty. Let's discredit him and get him the hell out of here." That obviously didn't work. Yes, it didn't stop leaks coming out of the White House saying how Marty was in big trouble, but certainly if the president didn't like what I was saying, we saw each other frequently enough that he could've said, "Marty, cool it. Stop talking about taxes." He didn't.

Bowmaker: How would President Reagan's policies have been different if the Republicans had controlled both houses of Congress?

Feldstein: Unfortunately, there was a great deal of game playing. Even if we came up with policies that the Democrats would support in principle, they would use them to put the president in a bad light by upping the ante. I'll give you an example. Let's say we wanted to help the disabled and put a price tag on it of X. It would then go to Congress, and they would say, "Oh, you're in favor of helping that group? You ought to do 3X." But the president would respond by telling them that he didn't want to do that. So there you have a situation of instead of looking like a good guy willing to do X, he looks like a bad guy unwilling to do 3X. And that affected the kind of policies that you could even propose in the first place.

Bowmaker: All things considered, can you point to a specific example of where you, as an economist, or the CEA, as an organization, were able to make a difference?

Feldstein: I often felt there was no way to know whether you made a difference. As an outsider writing an op-ed, giving a talk, or going to Washington to testify, you think to yourself, "Did it matter?" As chairman of the CEA, I was an insider, but I still didn't know. Partly that was because of the president's style. For example, when a policy idea was invented at the HEW [Department of Health, Education, and Welfare] level, it would come up to the staff level and I would talk to my colleagues and staff at the CEA about it. But as you know, the power lies with the chair, so it was Marty's view on the advice that we should give at the meeting where a decision had to be made. If it wasn't resolved, the issue would then be bounced up to the Cabinet level, and if we still couldn't reach an agreement, a larger meeting would take place with the president. Very often he listened, he asked questions, but he didn't render an answer. He would say, "OK, I understand the issues, and I'll decide." But when he did decide, you never knew on the basis of which argument because he would not tell us.

Bowmaker: What did you learn from President Reagan?

Feldstein: One of the advantages of being CEA chair is that I would get to meet finance ministers and others around the world. I would go to Paris for the OECD [Organisation for Economic Co-operation and Development] meetings and meet them privately. They were very articulate—people who'd been in parliaments for a very long time. When they were on a trip to Washington, sometimes they'd come to the office and we'd talk. As I say, they were very articulate, and they also seemed very expert. But in the end, I think many of them got the wrong answer in terms of the policies that they were advocating—high taxes and high government spending—despite their ability to talk through them. Reagan was the opposite. He couldn't give a twenty-minute extemporaneous lecture on macroeconomics, but he got the right answer on what the goal should be, and he communicated it very well to the people who worked for him. He wanted low inflation, a smaller-sized domestic government, and lower deficits. His attitude was, "You guys go work with Congress and figure out how to make it happen." So it was a kind of leadership that didn't try to get involved with the details and yet emphasized his ability to sell the program to the American public and to the Congress.

I remember during the '83 budget, Tip O'Neill, Speaker of the House, and a few other members of the Democratic leadership met with us in the White House. O'Neill, good Boston politician, just lit into Reagan. "How could you, Mr. President, put forward a budget to do these things?" he said. I thought, "Oh, my gosh, we're not going to get anywhere with this." After our visitors left, Jim Baker said, "It's clear they're ready to negotiate" [*laughs*]. So Reagan was a great negotiator. And the fact that we got the '86 tax reform, which came as a total surprise to the markets and to the public since we had a Democratic majority in the House, just showed that he was able to take work that had been done by the staff—it was the same with the

'83 Social Security reforms—and move it politically. That's the lesson that one learned from Reagan.

General Thoughts on Economic Policymaking

Bowmaker: Do you believe that if we were to raise the level of economic literacy in this country, economic policymaking would improve because the people would demand better policy?

Feldstein: Yes, and I think economic literacy in this country is greater than it was in the past. The press is doing much more to educate people, and that is partly due to the contributions by good economists. I've been writing for the *Wall Street Journal* since the early seventies, and I think of that as teaching. There are a million-plus readers out there, and I am influencing them.

When I came back from Washington, I taught the introductory economics course at Harvard for more than twenty years, and I would make comments like, "This country needs people like you to understand economics because you are our future thought leaders." And I really believe that.

Bowmaker: Can you give some examples of fallacies, misconceptions, or misinterpretations that affect policy debate in this country?

Feldstein: I'll pick a technical one: trade deficits. Economists know that a country's current account trade balance is the difference between domestic saving and investment, and so a deficit means that your savings are low relative to your investment. You need to explain that to policymakers, because they often believe that it is the result of other countries raising trade barriers or manipulating the exchange rate. A great deal of mischief would be avoided if they could understand that concept.

Another example is the impact of taxes. Economists are pretty good at thinking of them in terms of incentive effects, but policymakers tend to only consider the redistributive effects. Indeed, the way that the Congress scores proposed tax changes gives very little scope for behavioral responses. For example, raising taxes by 10 percent across the board is assumed to raise revenue by about 10 percent. But all the statistical evidence tells us that the response is about two-thirds of the initial change. And so you're not going to get nearly as much revenue as you expected, and you'll create what economists call a deadweight loss, which is a concept that is hopelessly difficult to explain to policymakers. You can teach it to freshmen in college, but policymakers don't have the patience to hear the analytics.

Personal Reflections

Bowmaker: What value has your public service had to you and to your university?

Feldstein: My time at the CEA was a two-year crash course in economics. For example, when I first arrived, we were in the midst of the Latin American debt crisis, so I learned about international finance. And we also had a strong dollar, which meant that I had to be able to contribute to the debate about whether something should be done to bring down its value. At the time, business people wanted government intervention in the foreign exchange market, but we argued that such action combined with looser monetary policy would lead to higher inflation without having any long-run effect on the real value of the dollar. So it was not only an interesting experience to observe the politics of economic policymaking, but also an opportunity to think about a whole range of economic issues that I didn't know much about before the role.

Since returning to Harvard from the CEA, I hope that my students have benefited from the wisdom that I picked up in Washington. And I certainly came back with plenty of problems to work on in my research.

Bowmaker: How did your personality affect your style and approach as a policymaker?

Feldstein: I am an academic kind of guy. I understand that you spoke to Eddie Lazear, who probably told you that he used to go mountain biking with George Bush. I can't imagine having a biking relationship with a president. And that's not because of my current age—it would have been true when I was forty.

Bowmaker: What were your strengths and weaknesses as a policymaker?

Feldstein: I thought I understood most of the issues well because I had been thinking about them for a long time. That's a strength. I also knew a number of the key people in the Congress because I had previously testified there and had talked with them. That meant that I could get along with some of the senior Democrats on the relevant committees, like Pat Moynihan, chairman of the Senate Finance Committee; Al Ullman, chairman of the House Committee on Ways and Means; and Jim Jones, chairman of the House Budget Committee. Overall, I was treated pretty well by both sides of the Congress. Because of my academic work and writing for nontechnical audiences, I think I had their respect. But I do remember testifying at my confirmation hearing as CEA chairman. Senator [William] Proxmire, a senior Democrat, said to me, "You're a very bright man, and I generally vote for very bright people in the other party. But I'm not going to vote for you because I'm afraid that the president will listen to you, and I don't like your views." And he didn't vote for me [*laughs*]!

Bowmaker: There must be some things, in hindsight, that you'd like the opportunity to do differently. What are they?

Feldstein: When I arrived at the CEA, the economy was still very much in a deep recession. But my predecessor, Murray Weidenbaum, had made some very optimistic growth forecasts, which had caused some joking about seeing the world through rose-colored glasses. So I avoided trying to provide an explicit forecast that would make the CEA look overoptimistic by assuming a constant 4 percent a year rate of growth throughout the five-year forecast period. It turned out that the recovery did begin in the first quarter of 1983, but the first year of the recovery posted a 6.1 percent rate of growth—a big bounce back that was partly due to the Fed sharply cutting interest rates. This meant that my first venture into forecasting at the CEA was not well received. It led to criticism that I was overpessimistic and gave fuel to those within the administration who argued that no action was needed to reduce the budget deficit.

Bowmaker: Which aspects of public service do you miss most?

Feldstein: Even though I am a lifelong researcher and writer, being part of the policy decision-making progress is important to me. And so I continue to talk with people at the Fed, the White House, and the Treasury. Unlike, say, the area of national security, in economics there is not a great deal of information that insiders have that outsiders don't. All you know as an insider that outsiders don't know are the policies that are being developed within the administration. Other than that, I am probably as informed and involved as an outsider as I was as an insider. The only difference is that I am not in Washington twenty-four hours a day, seven days a week. In that sense, I have the best of both worlds.

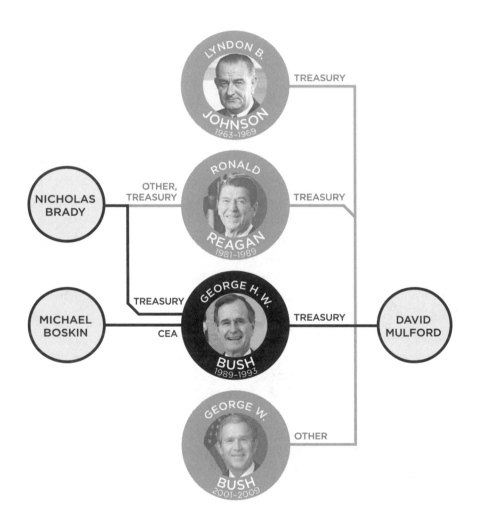

V   George H. W. Bush Administration

Nicholas Brady (*right*), when secretary of the treasury, walking with President George
H. W. Bush on the South Lawn driveway of the White House on May 15, 1991.

10 Nicholas F. Brady
Born 1930, New York City

Nicholas Brady graduated with a BA from Yale University in 1952 and then obtained an MBA from Harvard University in 1954. He joined the investment bank Dillon, Read and Co. in 1954, becoming its president and chief operating officer in 1971 and the chairman of its board in 1974.

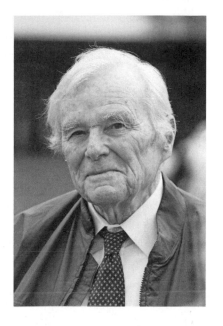

Brady represented New Jersey in the US Senate in 1982 and served on five presidential commissions, including chairing the Presidential Task Force on Market Mechanisms, known as the Brady Commission.

In 1988, he was appointed the sixty-eighth secretary of the treasury, and he served in that role during the administrations of both Presidents Ronald Reagan and George H. W. Bush. During his time in that office, Brady designed and implemented a successful strategy, known as the Brady Plan, to resolve the $1.3 trillion less-developed country debt crisis. The plan offered debt relief to those nations that had defaulted on their international debt by helping them sell dollar-denominated bonds, which came to be known as Brady bonds. Brady is also credited with containing and resolving the US savings and loan crisis through the creation of the Resolution Trust Corporation, and he served as the chairman of its Oversight Board.

Brady is currently chairman emeritus of Darby Overseas Investments, which he founded in 1994.

I interviewed Nicholas Brady at his office in Bernandsville, New Jersey. It was the middle of the afternoon on Tuesday, August 14, 2012.

Background Information

Bowmaker: Before you entered the policy world, what shaped your thinking towards economic policy?

Brady: I am a middle-of-the-road Republican from New Jersey. It is a very populous state, and for most of my life, it has had a large economic base. And so it has all the elements that one has to think about in terms of economic policy—not only to provide the impetus to drive the area, but also to do the right thing for the people involved. Somerset County, where I grew up, has produced a very large number of people who were interested in government service, including Millicent Fenwick, Charles Engelhard, and Douglas Dillon.

Entering the Policy World

Bowmaker: Your first significant economic policymaking position was being chairman of President Reagan's Task Force on Market Mechanisms that was set up to investigate the stock market collapse of October 1987. How did you come to be appointed?

Brady: On Monday, October 19, 1987, the US stock market declined by almost 23 percent, the largest one-day crash in history. Everybody panicked because nobody knew why it had happened. I was walking on the Great Wall of China when I heard about it. I carried on with my trip and then did some business in Paris, where I ran into Jim Baker, who was secretary of the treasury at the time, and we took the same flight back together. A few days later, I was having lunch with a client in the dining room at Dillon Read in Manhattan when Howard Baker, Reagan's chief of staff, called and told me that the president wanted me to look into the collapse. I was given sixty days to complete the report, which didn't seem to be much time to take on something so momentous.

Bowmaker: How did you approach the task?

Brady: It was an unbelievable operation. The New York Federal Reserve gave me an office on the tenth floor of its building. When we went in it only had one desk, but within a few days there were twenty, with computers bummed from everywhere. I convinced business leaders to be members of the task force and picked them from different parts of the markets so that I wouldn't get blindsided. And with so much work to do quickly, I obviously needed a group of people to do the necessary analysis as well. So I appointed Bob Glauber, a professor from the Harvard Business School, to be director of around a hundred staff, who were all volunteers—either taking leaves of absence from their firms or freelancing one way or the other. They were divided into working groups with their own responsibilities, for example looking at the "plumbing" of the markets, describing the bull market that preceded the collapse, and conducting a survey of big traders like Paul Tudor Jones, who was very helpful.

We worked through December, with people yelling and screaming that they had to get home for Christmas. I remember some didn't make it because we had to have the report completed by January 8, and wives were calling on the phone asking where they were [*laughs*]. But we got it done on time and presented it to the president, with 10,000 copies being distributed. Warren Buffett said it was the best report on a financial event that he'd ever read. I certainly don't think there was ever such an important piece of work written in such a short period of time. Half the battle was making sure that the cause and effect was something that could be explained to the public, because once you can do that, then you can do something intelligent about it.

One of the things that we discovered was that there was an arbitrage process taking place between the Chicago and New York stock markets. In other words, everybody thought of them as two separate markets that were a thousand miles apart. But we established that, in fact, they were one market because of the advances that had been made in communications that allowed information to be passed back and forth. At the time, you could engage in arbitrage by buying a futures contract in Chicago and then selling it in the New York cash market. But the New York market wasn't ready for the deluge that came in.

I like to think in visual terms, and so here we were dealing with a water pipe that connected these two huge pools of money. The pipe was far too small, and eventually the pressure inside became so great that it exploded. One of our recommendations was to use circuit breakers to allow the exchange to shut down the market when certain amounts of volume came through. My thinking here was that this thing needed to be slowed down for the future, so that the human mind was capable of operating in such a fast-moving system.

Bowmaker: What did you take professionally from the experience?

Brady: You learn something every time you take a job like that. It expands your vocabulary. It reminds me of going to business school at Harvard. I didn't have extensive business experience at that point, and so my vocabulary was deficient. But the most important thing that I took away from the commission, and something that I'd always had to figure out as an investment banker, is how to get to the bottom of a problem. If someone asks, "Tell me what the problem is," I will identify the essential elements, whittle them down to a few that are more important than others, and concentrate on those. Then you need the discipline to keep everybody on course towards your solution.

As Secretary of the Treasury

Bowmaker: When you were appointed secretary of the treasury in 1988, you hadn't previously served in government. Did you speak with former secretaries about the role?

Brady: No. I must say that Jim Baker is a very close friend of mine, and I also knew Don Regan, George Shultz, and Douglas Dillon, but I didn't speak to them about the role. I had served in the Senate for one year, in 1982, because the governor of New Jersey—a great public servant, Tom Kean—asked me to do so [Brady was filling a vacancy caused by the resignation of Harrison A. Williams Jr.]. I had a very limited idea of the intricacies that were involved, so that was a learning experience and an eye-opener. I had also served on the commission that we've just talked about, so I had a fairly good grasp of how government functioned, and I was confident that I could make a contribution because I knew how to make things work operationally through my investment banking experience. In fact, I didn't think that the role of treasury secretary would be that much different to the job of running Dillon Read, at least in terms of the number of hours per day that you have to devote to it.

Bowmaker: Coming into the role, the country faced many economic problems. How did you begin to prioritize them?

Brady: When President Reagan, through Jim Baker, asked me to take the job, I began to think about the things that could turn the United States economy on its head. And I made up my mind that we needed to address three issues. Number one was Latin American debt, because of its potential effect on our banking system; number two was the savings and loan industry, because it was absolutely broke; and number three was the US budget, because it was well on its way to not being balanced. I viewed them as operational problems, which goes back to my training as an investment banker.

Bowmaker: After serving President Reagan for several months, you then worked for President George H. W. Bush as secretary of the treasury throughout his presidency. Can you tell us how you came up with the Brady Plan to solve the Latin American debt crisis?

Brady: Necessity is the mother of invention. What happened was the finance minister of Mexico showed up at a Treasury board meeting, sat across from me, and announced that his country might not be able to pay the interest on its debt. I knew that all of Latin America was under duress at that time, but I hadn't suspected that Mexico might actually default—which would obviously mean that there would be others behind it, and two or three of our major banks with exposure to the area would have their equity wiped out. In fact, I think our banking system had a very good chance of blowing up in 1989. Not only would that have been a bad thing in terms of its effect on economic activity within the United States, but it would have also had a very large effect all over the world.

So it was a complex problem that needed to be fixed, and people say that a complex problem is hard to solve, but sometimes a simple statement will make a big difference. I took the position that the solution to too much debt was not more debt—what we needed was debt reduction for those who agreed to implement significant economic reform programs. And so I turned the problem over to two incredibly competent professionals from the Treasury, David Mulford and Charles Dallara, who knew very well the highways and byways of Latin America and the world's financial paths. Between us, we developed the Brady Plan, which was a long and complicated process, but essentially it offered banks credit enhancements in exchange for their agreement to reduce claims.

Along the way we devised something called the truth serum, which is an interesting concept. It set out the boundaries of our discussion—you couldn't come in and take up our time with a solution that, while thought to be helpful, involved more debt. In other words, you had to work through the problem as how we defined it.

Bowmaker: Were there any disagreements within the administration about the Brady Plan?

Brady: There weren't too many disagreements because we knew the most about it. And when I took the job as treasury secretary, everybody told me that the best professional staff in Washington are found in the Treasury.

That proved to be exactly correct. Partly that's because they are protected against political change, but in any case, they were enormously helpful in formulating the Brady Plan, which provided a strong path going forward. That's certainly true of Latin America, which is currently one of the main stems of economic activity in the world economy.

Bowmaker: Can you talk us through the cleanup of the savings and loan industry?

Brady: The savings and loan industry was headed on its way to disaster, filled with political influence of one kind or another—it was basically a scam. And so that was an additional piece of the financial structure that needed to be fixed, and I think the last financial crisis would have occurred a lot faster if we hadn't done so. Eighteen days after his inauguration, George Bush 41 presented a legislative proposal to Congress that was governed by four principles: Number one was making sure that people who put their money into insured thrifts got their money back. Number two was restoring safety and soundness to the thrift industry through tougher regulations. Number three was closing down and selling off the insolvent thrifts—around three hundred of them—as quickly and as efficiently as possible. Number four was prosecuting the criminals and fraudulent operators who stole taxpayer money. Those principles were established as a result of a study undertaken in late 1988. It took several months to understand how the industry had incurred such massive losses.

Bowmaker: Who did you hire to help you with the savings and loan cleanup process?

Brady: That's an important question. In my mind, an essential part of getting things done is to hire good people, and then when they made a contribution, you give them credit for it. The political process is filled with people who like to tell you what they have achieved and are always trying to stand in the center of the picture. That doesn't appeal to me at all and makes me feel very uncomfortable. I like the idea of teamwork. For the S&L (savings and loan) cleanup, I relied upon three people: Tim Ryan, the point man; and Bob Glauber and David Mullins, who set out the broad outlines of the process. Again, I viewed it as an operational problem, but since I did not have experience of the political world and all its pieces, I certainly needed them on board.

Bowmaker: What were the main challenges associated with the cleanup process?

Brady: It was highly political because of the cost involved. We had to raise $150 billion from the public under severe criticism from two opposing houses of Congress. Believe me, it was a challenge, because the other side of the aisle wanted many other things to be done. And once we put the thrifts' assets into the Resolution Trust Company, the discussion then centered on what we should do with them. Congress wanted us to keep them there on the grounds that they would get better over time, but we took the decision to auction them to the public. I realized that people would make money, but I also wanted the problem to be over and done with, and by the time I left government, it was. It's true that I've had people come up to me and say jocularly, "We certainly made a lot of money because of the way you did it," and I've replied, "Well, that wasn't my intention, but the country was better off on account of it." I'm very sad that, for reasons that are now becoming clear, the financial system is in disrepair again.

Bowmaker: How would you evaluate the importance of the Budget Act of 1990?

Brady: There is no question in my mind that had George Bush 41 not been willing to allow the Budget Act of 1990 to become law, we would have had a crisis long before the one of 2008. Even though in 1993, President Clinton came in with a strategy to balance the budget, the impetus and origination of the plan all came out of the Bush administration, when the president allowed the issue of revenue enhancement to be put on the table. Of course, he didn't solve the problem to such an extent that he didn't lose the 1992 election. I'm very sorry about that, but he made it clear that when he allowed the Budget Act of 1990 to become law, he was taking a big chance with his reelection prospects.

I must say that it is a real failure of President [Barack] Obama to get the Republicans and Democrats to come forward with a plan that will provide a reduction in the budget. Where is the United States going to get the money to pay off its debts? I believe the answer is abundantly clear: We must harness the energy of the private sector.

Bowmaker: How would you describe your relationship with the Federal Reserve during your time as secretary of the treasury?

Brady: The Federal Reserve was very helpful with respect to the Brady Plan and the savings and loan crisis. But that wasn't entirely the case when I think back to the Budget Act of 1990. If spending out of Congress was going to be stopped, we needed a Federal Reserve that understood the implications and politics of it. Unfortunately, however, our relationship with the Federal Reserve fell apart somewhat on that issue.

I feel strongly that the Treasury Department and the Federal Reserve can operate together for the benefit of the public. I'm all for the independence of our central bank, but it isn't an island off the coast of Virginia—it happens to be part of the United States.

Bowmaker: How would you describe your relationship with the Council of Economic Advisers [CEA]?

Brady: Mike Boskin, the CEA chair for George Bush 41, was very much a team player and did a very good job in my opinion—you could only say he was helpful. The best economists in Washington are those who understand that policy has its own way of working through the system and they're mindful of what those ways are. And it is easy for micro policy issues to unhinge you if you don't have a plan, as my pal George Shultz would say.

Bowmaker: Was there any frustration involved in working with White House staff who only wanted policies that would get the president reelected?

Brady: Everybody who worked with George Bush 41 was absolutely committed to his reelection. They believed in his operating style, his civility, and his world leadership. But nobody from the White House ever approached me to say that if I followed a certain policy, it might affect his reelection prospects. With a man like George Bush 41, there was enough commonality of discourse to ensure that never happened.

Bowmaker: How would you describe your relationship with the media when you were secretary of the treasury?

Brady: People felt that I was inexperienced politically in terms of how I expressed my views. I had a way of looking at things that perhaps short hopped the political policy part of them, if you like, and I'd try not to do that again. Maybe that wasn't very smart, but it was right. For example, I gave an interview on television about the value of the dollar and said, "Markets go up and down." The media made a big joke out of my statement, but markets do go up and down. If the Dow Jones loses 150 points ten days in a row, is that going to change the world? Not really. Pretty soon, you'll find that there's an up kick ten days in a row. In other words, don't worry about it, things will work out in the long run. My philosophy came from the fact that I had lived with the natives for thirty years on Wall Street. I hadn't spent much time translating my views into the arcane language of political rhetoric in Washington.

Bowmaker: You enjoyed a close personal relationship with President Bush. Overall, how did this affect how you went about your role as treasury secretary?

Brady: I want to make it clear that everything that I did as treasury secretary was not only done to further the interests of George Bush 41 but also explained to him. He might have left the details of a given policy to us, but he always knew where we were going and how we were going to get there. If I suggested something, he would often say, "Are you sure you've got this right?" When I told him, "Yes, I have," he would then give me his backing. In other words, once I knew he wanted a problem solved, I would go ahead and do it. But I don't think I led him into anything that he didn't basically understand. It's true that his principal interest was foreign policy, but he'd had plenty of experience in an economic role, having run his own private-sector company successfully. He knew the elements involved, and that was a big help to me as treasury secretary. Of course, though, the close personal relationship that I had formed with him over the years was of enormous assistance.

Bowmaker: How would you describe George Bush 41's legacy as president of the United States?

Brady: I remember having lunch with him about a year after we'd left office, and he said to me, "The things that we did are going to be an asterisk to history." I didn't agree. Look at what we did on the economic side of life: we fixed the Latin American debt crisis; we fixed the savings and loan crisis; and we fixed the problem with Congress and the executive branch spending more money than they were taking in, which is the Budget Act of 1990. And on the political side of life, he oversaw the unification of Germany, the Gulf War, and the collapse of communism in the Soviet Union. So I told him, "Just hang on, my friend, you will be regarded as a very accomplished president." That's proved to be 100 percent correct. Almost every year he goes up in the ratings of former presidents of the United States. He is going to catch Lincoln if he doesn't watch it [*laughs*]. It wasn't just the problems that he faced—it was the exemplary manner in which he faced them.

Bowmaker: Given that you worked for both Presidents Reagan and Bush as treasury secretary, how would you compare and contrast their approaches?

Brady: Ronald Reagan and George Bush were different in style somewhat, but definitely closer in principle than most people might think. Both had a fantastic sense of humor and wide experience. I would say that Bush was perhaps more precise in terms of his language, but not in terms of his view of the world. President Reagan had a mind that had word pictures as the framework for his ideas. They were wonderful and connected with the public, but not necessarily with precision. When he said things like "Make my day" or "Trust but verify," they were expressions of his beliefs rather than a technical treatise. George Bush didn't have that kind of style.

I learned a lot from the six months that I was Reagan's treasury secretary. I think Bush 41 would tell you the same thing. In fact, I heard him say it many times. Getting back to his sense of humor, I remember President Reagan telling me, and this came from his acting background, that when I was having my photograph taken with someone, I should move just before the flash…it makes you look energetic and the other person a dummy [*laughs*].

General Thoughts on Economic Policymaking

Bowmaker: Do you think that if we were to raise the level of economic literacy in this country, economic policymaking would improve because the people would demand better policy?

Brady: My experience at the Treasury taught me two things about government in this country: Number one, those who work in government are better than people are led to believe; they are there for the good of the country. Number two, they are not better in succumbing to the election process—that is, wanting to get reelected, and therefore cloaking things that come out of Washington in terms that the public can't understand. Politicians have a bad habit—and this is increasingly the case—of not being straight about what the issues are, which encumbers democracy. In this respect, I am reminded of the quote by Alexis de Tocqueville: "The American Republic will endure until the day Congress discovers that it can bribe the public with the public's money." However, I do think that the human race and the level of technology has reached a place that gives us an incredible ability to not be confused by what we hear coming out of the political process. Information is so accessible these days, it's literally at the tip of your finger with an iPhone [*laughs*].

Bowmaker: Which aspects of the institutional framework for making economic policy in this country work well, and which need to be reformed?

Brady: It is a tremendous hindrance to the ability of the United States to solve our problems that the FDIC [Federal Deposit Insurance Corporation], the Federal Reserve, the comptroller of the currency, and the SEC [Securities and Exchange Commission] have separate duties over the economy. It is quite clear in my mind that you want to put them all in one place or get rid of some of them. But at least we have the financial authority to provide revenues when needed and the ability to pass laws that make it happen. It took us many years to bring the country into a homogeneous position, which is the difficulty that the European Union has now. It is never going to be successful until it has a fiscal authority to raise revenues and a central bank that is not only independent, but also includes all members of the European Union.

Personal Reflections

Bowmaker: What value has your public service had to you?

Brady: When you shift your parochial concerns in the corporate world to ones where you have a wider obligation to the American people and the rest of the world, it is an experience that you do not forget. I remember George Bush 41 telling me that when his father left the Senate and went back to his role as a partner at Brown Brothers, he realized that once you've been in government it transcends anything you do in business. At the time I thought, "Well, I'm not sure about that," but the truth of the matter is he was right.

Bowmaker: In hindsight, there must be some things that you'd like the opportunity to do differently. What are they?

Brady: I think we solved the problems in the Treasury realm pretty well. But maybe we could have left a stronger legacy for solving international problems, such as trying to make organizations such as the World Bank and the IMF [International Monetary Fund] more responsible going forward. The whole international apparatus that is supposed to aid in rough water is currently flat on its back. But as we faced the '92 election, we didn't spend a lot of time figuring out what would happen if we lost. Certainly I didn't think that way, and neither did George Bush 41.

David Mulford (*left*), when undersecretary of the treasury for international affairs, meeting with President George H. W. Bush (*right*) and Nicholas Brady (*center*), secretary of the treasury, in the Oval Office on August 11, 1989.

11 David C. Mulford
Born 1937, Rockford, Illinois

David Mulford graduated with a BA in economics from Lawrence University in 1959 and then obtained an MA in political science from Boston University in 1962 and a DPhil from the University of Oxford in 1966.

Between 1965 and 1966, Mulford served as special assistant to the secretary and deputy secretary of the treasury as a White House Fellow during the first year of the White House Fellowship Program, in the administration of President Lyndon B. Johnson. Mulford then served as managing director and head of international finance at White, Weld and Co., Inc., from 1966 to 1974, and was seconded to the Saudi Arabian Monetary Agency (SAMA) as a senior investment adviser from 1974 to 1983.

Mulford returned to government service in 1984 when he was appointed assistant secretary of the treasury for international affairs during the administration of President Ronald Reagan. He served in this position until the election of President George H. W. Bush in 1989, when he was promoted to undersecretary of the treasury for international affairs. Mulford served in this role until 1992.

Mulford then joined the London-based banking firm Credit Suisse as chairman international, where he stayed until President George W. Bush nominated him for the role of ambassador to India. Mulford was sworn into office in January 2004 and served in this position for five years. In 2009, Mulford rejoined Credit Suisse to become vice chairman international, a post that he held until leaving the firm in December 2016 to take up his current appointment as distinguished visiting fellow at the Hoover Institution, Stanford University.

I interviewed David Mulford in his apartment in midtown Manhattan, New York City, during the afternoons of Tuesday, September 6, 2016, and Thursday, September 15, 2016.

Background Information

Bowmaker: As an undergraduate, you majored in economics but wanted to drop the subject in favor of a double major in history and anthropology. Why didn't you like economics?

Mulford: In the university teaching format, economics seemed to be a very dry subject compared to the active nature of history and anthropology. In my last year as an undergraduate, I asked the university if I could change my major, but they refused and said I needed to complete it. However, because I had won a Rotary International Scholarship to go over to Oxford, they agreed to arrange weekly private seminars with a Lawrence professor of history, William Cheney, who was English, an Oxford graduate, and an inspiring teacher. These one-on-one tutorials prepared me for the Oxford system and provided a valuable understanding of Western intellectual history that has stayed with me throughout my working life. Later, when I got to Africa [Mulford attended graduate school in Africa and later wrote two books on Zambia], I soon recognized the critical importance of economics and how wrong I had been to see it as a dry subject—it was at the center of understanding countries.

And so when I was invited to Washington as a White House Fellow after seven years away from the United States, I opted for the Treasury assignment. The Treasury was seen by my colleagues as a bit of a backwater in those days—nobody else seemed to want the assignment. My experience at Treasury was outstanding, a really formative year, because President Lyndon Johnson made sure personally that the program worked. I was assigned to the secretary of the treasury's office, stayed at that level throughout the year, and didn't sink into the bureaucracy of the specialized areas. Secretary Joe Fowler took me to congressional meetings and allowed me to sit in on meetings of the Dillon Committee for International Monetary Reform, where I was the only outside observer. About halfway through the year I understood that the life I wanted was in international finance.

Bowmaker: Did you have the opportunity to interact with President Johnson when you were a White House Fellow?

Mulford: Yes, we had four dinners in the White House mess with just President Johnson and occasionally his chief of staff, Jack Valenti. The most remarkable thing was the president's voluntary unloading of his concerns on us. It was moving. Without oversimplifying, he wanted to be loved, and because he was not, it was eating into him. I thought he was a very impressive man when it came to his intellectual commitment to education, civil liberties, and the like, but his Great Society program was being disrupted and diluted by the frightful Vietnam War. You could see the man was torn and in pain. I would say that he let his hair down with us, which was incredible. I've never forgotten it.

I was also amazed by his method of cajoling and convincing people. For example, I recall being present at a large meeting in the East Wing when he met with members of Congress. He was pacing back and forth when he was talking and clapping his hands together. "Gentlemen, you all know what's at stake here…," he was telling them. He had enormous selling capacity because he was such a passionate person, and that was something very appealing to me.

Entering the Policy World

Bowmaker: After a long and distinguished career working in investment banking, you returned to the Treasury in 1984 as assistant secretary for international affairs. How did that appointment come about?

Mulford: I was a seconded advisor to SAMA [Saudi Arabian Monetary Authority] from 1974 until the end of 1983 and headed up our team of advisers, which was hired to create a modern investment program at SAMA and to act as advisers to the Saudis on their large dollar recycling program with major countries and corporations. During that period, I built up a relationship with Don Regan, the chairman and CEO [chief executive officer] of Merrill Lynch. Later, when he was secretary of the treasury and heard I was leaving SAMA, he asked if I would do the international job at the Treasury. He complimented me by saying that I knew more about global capital flows than anybody in the world at that time but also suggested I should feel obligated to help clean up the debt crisis in Latin America, which to some extent was the result of the OPEC [Organization of Petroleum Exporting Countries] countries placing vast funds with Western banks, who became so flush that they overlent to Latin America at unreasonably low rates. This was a high-risk decision for me, because I would be returning to the United States after nine years of total isolation in Saudi Arabia to work for the Reagan administration at the beginning of his last year in office before the election of 1984. But I was very interested in doing the job because I thought I had a unique knowledge of what had gone on in global markets over those nine years. In addition, I felt that as a White House Fellow alumnus, I was part of a program that implied a duty to serve in government in the future, despite the loss of privacy and income opportunities. Looking back, I'm very glad that I did.

Bowmaker: Coming into the role, was your economic philosophy in alignment with the Reagan administration's?

Mulford: Secretary Regan was a strong, opinionated person who was committed to the realities of the global financial world. I was in agreement with the administration's general philosophy and policy format. The only area where I had reservations related to their attitude—and that included Regan's—towards the rest of the major countries. I thought their attitude was arrogant, demanding, and too US-focused. It was almost as if we were saying, "Look at us. We're growing at X percent and creating jobs at Y millions. When you can do things like the United States, we'll sit down and talk to you." My view was different. I believed that if you were going to create a cooperative arrangement with other governments, you had to have a measure of respect, which meant recognizing their own skills and powers and being able to reach some accommodation with them, knowing that their social and political systems were different from ours.

Bowmaker: You worked for Treasury Secretary Regan for one year. Can you tell us a little more about what he expected you to do for him and his approach towards the role?

Mulford: He was a very collegial leader. Every morning at 9:00 a.m., he held action-packed, no-holds-barred staff meetings, in which we spoke out and said what we thought. That was very important for the morale of the Treasury, so I admired his approach. In terms of what he expected me to do for him, as I said earlier he was very focused on the dangers of the Latin American debt crisis and the whole question of world financial stability. He was also alive to the power of capital flows—in that sense, he was a very visionary person. I remember going to Argentina during that year when we put together a bridge loan package for the country to make sure it stayed current with its banks. The money was provided by four major Latin countries but guaranteed by the Treasury, and the package avoided a default in March 1984. There were concerns that a default by Argentina would turn into a major banking crisis, which is why the US approach was to manage the Latin American debt problem for a period of time as opposed to trying to solve it prematurely.

Bowmaker: In March 1985, Jim Baker replaced Don Regan as secretary of the treasury. What was the first thing that you had to do for him?

Mulford: I was asked to go to the White House to meet him and draw up a bunch of hard questions that he would face for his confirmation hearing. My first question was, "Mr. Baker, what in your background qualifies you to deal with all the major global financial issues that are at the heart and soul of the Treasury?" He replied, "Well, the answer to that question is representing the president of the United States at seven economic summits and four years in the Marine Corps." I thought it was a brilliant answer, and it certainly subdued me a little, too [*laughs*].

Secretary James Baker was an utterly different personality to Secretary Regan. He is a meticulous lawyer who was always deeply prepared for meetings, and so when you did a briefing paper for him, you could be pretty sure he would want to talk to you about it. He was hands-on intellectually on policy issues and came over to the Treasury at the exact time when the dollar was peaking against both the deutsche mark and the yen at record levels, which focused even greater attention on the global imbalance problems. Because Secretary Baker was a congressionally oriented person, he understood from day one that the strong dollar was hurting our competitiveness around the world. The growing political response in Congress was a buildup of sympathy for a big omnibus trade bill that would be very disruptive and punitive. Secretary Baker was alarmed about this possible reaction, and so he spent a lot of time thinking about how to get the problem under control—he had a really good grasp of the political economy of issues. We didn't believe that we could manipulate the currency markets, but Secretary Baker was more open to the idea that you could message the markets. That is, you could draw its attention to an unfolding new situation, which is why the Treasury set up a foreign exchange trading desk as a listening post. And Secretary Baker's approach was also to be much more collegial with his peers overseas, the high point in policy cooperation being the signing of the Plaza Accord in September 1985, which established our cooperative effort with full G7 [Group of Seven] participation to depreciate the dollar by 40 percent over the next eighteen months. This remarkable effort, including the macro policy commitments of the countries, effectively derailed the potential destruction that was taking shape because of the strong dollar and protectionist forces in the Congress.

Bowmaker: Can you describe how the Baker Plan emerged to manage the Latin American debt crisis, and your role in its formulation? Why did it essentially fail in the end, and how did it lead to the Brady Plan?

Mulford: Along with one of my colleagues, I wrote the speech that Secretary Baker gave in Seoul, Korea, in October 1985 that announced the Baker Plan. The plan was motivated by the idea behind the Argentina experience of 1984 of keeping the debtor countries current to avoid a catastrophic default crisis. And so it was designed with two objectives in mind: first, to ensure a continued flow of new money to debtor countries in crisis from the large, multinational syndicates of banks to support those countries and their existing IMF [International Monetary Fund] and World Bank adjustment programs; second, to encourage all countries which had lending banks in the syndicates not to take national regulatory or tax actions that would result in banks' recognizing book losses and starting a wave of tax write-offs that would close off potential new money flows. It worked well for two years, but by the end of 1987 it was obvious that it was breaking down. New money flows slowed dramatically, the various countries began to have different ideas about setting up reserves and recognizing losses and taking tax write-offs. Yet in general, banks maintained that the debt of troubled debtor countries was worth one hundred cents on the dollar, even though we saw deep price discounts on small amounts of debt being traded. It was clear that with the sharp rise in arrearages, we were in a desperate situation by the end of that year.

I went up to New York with Deputy Assistant Secretary Charles Dallara to visit investment banking firms like Goldman Sachs and Solomon Brothers and others, who had opened up small boutique windows in Latin American debt. They were purchasing small amounts of bank loan instruments—some at thirty cents on the dollar—from banks who wanted to reduce their exposure to debtor countries. The paper was then resold by the investment banks at significant markups to private investors, who would ultimately insist on being paid one hundred cents on the dollar. This very same paper, of course, represented debt obligations that heavily exposed banks around the world argued was still worth one hundred cents on the dollar, while at the same time they were selling small participations at deep discounts to private holders who would continue to claim that the debt must be paid out at or near par.

Those market realities led me to try out my ideas for resolving the crisis with Secretary Baker in early 1988. They included an element of debt reduction, but the secretary didn't go along with that approach. It was the beginning of the presidential election year, and his view was that it would be unreasonable to get involved in debt reduction/forgiveness at a time when the US had more than $150 billion of official government debt from student loans, small business and farmers' loans. Members of Congress might say, "What's going on? Why are we helping these deadbeat Latin American countries? Why aren't we doing anything similar here?" In other words, it was thought to be an untouchable area during that particular period. Then in August of 1988, Secretary Baker was put in charge of Vice President Bush's election campaign, and the following month, Nick Brady became President Reagan's new secretary of the treasury. As an investment banker, he was very much a realist and market-oriented person who immediately understood what was at stake. That was how my ideas for a resolution to the crisis came back to life.

As Undersecretary of the Treasury for International Affairs

Bowmaker: Nick Brady asked you to stay on as undersecretary of the treasury for international affairs. When I spoke to Mr. Brady, he told me very briefly about the "truth serum," from which the Brady Plan to solve the Latin American debt crisis emerged. Can you describe this in more detail and, in particular, its effectiveness as a problem-solving methodology?

Mulford: You need to remember that I had been managing this seemingly intractable problem for six years. I had experienced a stream of people in my office offering a variety of different solutions for resolving the debt crisis. Most of these were unworkable or ended up with in effect a bailout of debtor countries by governments and taxpayers. When Secretary Brady arrived at the Treasury in August of 1988 and had attended his first meeting of the G7 nations in Berlin, he fully grasped the magnitude of the risk we faced and the lack of understanding among G7 leaders. He decided to bring the economic Cabinet together—secretary of state, the national security adviser, the chairman of the Federal Reserve, and several other Cabinet-level people—to determine how we should proceed.

First, he asked me to write a paper that would set out the reality of the situation we faced. I began to call this paper the "truth serum paper" because it described the unvarnished truth of what we faced. If after discussion we could get the principal participants to accept the paper, then we would radically narrow the range of workable solutions that would comply with the conclusions of the paper. After several meetings, we did accomplish a consensus on the paper's assessment of the debt crisis and how it would play out if radical action was not taken without delay.

Secretary Brady then insisted that in the next phase only proposals or solutions could be tabled that did not violate the conclusions of the "truth serum paper." Secretary Brady was determined that there should be a plan which would solve the crisis without the bailing out of debtor countries by US taxpayers. New money from the bank syndicates had dried up by late 1987. As more countries resorted to allowing arrearages on their debt to build up, it was obvious that the corpus of Latin American debt would grow astronomically, becoming in a relatively short time completely unmanageable and a threat to the world financial system. The banks would have to do their share, and countries would need to make progress on their reform programs. We needed a plan to avoid governments and taxpayers picking up the pieces. This is when and how the Brady Plan emerged as the solution. The concept was clear. Execution in the complex world of global finance, however, was another challenge.

Bowmaker: When you and Mr. Brady met with President-Elect Bush to go through the plan and seek his approval, what was his response, and how difficult was it to explain the various components to him?

Mulford: When we completed the Brady Plan in November of 1988, Nick and I went to see President-Elect George Bush in the White House. After explaining the plan and the need to gain the support of the G7 nations, Secretary Brady told the president-elect that "We'll name the plan after you." The president-elect looked at him and said, "No, we'll name it after you, Nick, and if it is unsuccessful, we'll name it after Mulford" [*laughs*]. But the president-elect clearly understood what we were proposing; he was very knowledgeable and experienced with regard to policy formulation and execution. It was an important meeting, because we needed his authorization to begin conversations with the G7 so that we could work towards a consensus in which all the major national banking systems would play by the same rules.

Bowmaker: In describing the Brady Plan, Mr. Brady told me it was a "long and complicated process." You have suggested in the past that it is difficult to explain but easy to understand. Can you elaborate? How would you best describe the key components of the Brady Plan?

Mulford: I'll explain it to you [*laughs*]. The goal was to find some intermediate amount that the countries could pay, without any bailing out by
the United States. Let's take Mexico as a hypothetical example. Suppose
that Mexico had a nominal debt of $50 billion to the banks that it wasn't
going to be able to pay. The first step would be for Mexico and the banks
to negotiate what the nominal write-down of the debt was going to be. The
United States would not get involved in setting that number. The current
nominal value of the existing debt—at least, as revealed by the back-door
sales by the banks of some of this debt—was around thirty cents on the
dollar. And so a negotiated price that was somewhere between thirty and
a hundred cents on the dollar for the remaining debt would be needed for
an agreement. Let's say that the negotiated write-down was 50 percent, so
that if agreed, there would still be $25 billion of debt that Mexico owed
the banks. Mexico would then issue $25 billion in new 30-year bonds to
offer to the banks. To make these bonds more attractive, Mexico would col-
lateralize these bonds with $25 billion of 30-year zero-coupon US Treasury
bonds issued specifically by the US Treasury to be bought by the Mexican
government on the same terms any other investor would pay. In thirty
years, the Mexican bonds would be paid off with the maturing US Treasury
zero-coupon bonds, although reduced in value from the original Mexican
bonds. Thus, the original outstanding Mexican bonds would be reduced in
value by 50 percent. The newly issued Mexican bonds taken in exchange by
the banks would be a more secure and desirable instrument for the banks
to hold. They also would and turned out to be very much more market-
able for banks which wanted to sell their Mexican bonds. At the relatively
high interest rates that were current for US Treasuries at the time, a 30-year
zero-coupon Treasury could be bought for between 0.07 and 0.09 US cents
on the dollar. This would mean in this example that it would cost Mexico
only $1.75–$2.25 billion to buy the necessary collateral. And it meant that
the principal amount of the original $50 billion in debt, now $25 billion,
would no longer rest on the shoulders of the Mexican people, because its
ultimate payment would be covered by the maturing US Treasury bonds.

Bowmaker: How did you overcome the reaction of the banks to the Brady
Plan?

Mulford: At first, the banks were deeply shocked and unhappy at the idea
of accepting any discount on the debt they had contracted with debtor
countries. The market value of the remaining debt without the Treasury

collateral would have been lower than the $25 billion instrument that they were being asked to accept in the Mexican example above. They were getting a vastly more secure, marketable instrument, which gave them a way to exit the Mexican debt market—which many banks wanted to do. And the fact that the new debt instrument initially went on their books at the nominal value of $25 billion meant that the banks had the timing flexibility as to when they would have to recognize—write down on their books—the remaining amount of their losses by selling the new bonds, if and when they chose to do so. Both the negotiability of the instrument and the timing flexibility had value for the banks, making them more willing to accept the arrangement. And of course, a possible alternative was a total default on the original debt, which would have meant even larger losses for the banks.

To present the plan, Secretary Brady agreed to give a speech at the IMF's annual meeting in Madrid to the chairmen and CEOs of the world's top one hundred banks. I helped write that speech, and my original concept was to say to the banks, "You're on the top floor of a building with one hundred stories. You get into the elevator to descend to a lower floor, but it drops suddenly to the fiftieth floor. When the door opens, you are met by representatives of the US Treasury who offer to provide supports for the elevator—US Treasury zero bonds—to stop it from falling any further. If you reject the offer, the door will close, and the elevator will begin plummeting into the basement. Once you reach there, you'll have to figure it all out for yourselves." In the end, Secretary Brady never spoke so graphically and instead used Charles Dallara's story about Willie the Cook—who, according to the history of the Old West, was part of an early expedition down the Colorado River. The river was hugely turbulent, a frightening experience for all the men. Willie became so frightened that he decided to abandon the group to scale the cliffs and go across country to meet them at their final destination. The expedition went on the next day, and after descending through a couple of big rapids, the group emerged into the solitude and silence of the lower Colorado. They had made it through. Willie's remains were later found in the desert. He had been murdered by Indians. I wasn't present at Nick's speech, but Charles told me that the banks got the message of the story: there was a need for solidarity if they were to reach calm water.

Bowmaker: Can you describe the involvement of institutions such as the IMF and the World Bank in the Brady Plan?

Mulford: The IMF and the World Bank had to be involved in the negotiations, so that the cash amounts the debtor countries needed to buy the 30-year zero-coupon Treasuries for collateral would be made available. The participating countries would need to pay interest on their new bonds, so funds would also need to be budgeted for these interest payments as well. The United States was heavily involved in providing the framework for the negotiations between the countries and the banks but did not get involved in the details of subsequent negotiations. The objective was to avoid the appearance that taxpayers in the United States were involved in bailing out the countries or the banks. To be eligible for the program, countries had to have an IMF reform program in place that was judged to be credible.

Bowmaker: You were awarded the Officer's Cross of the Medal of Merit from the president of Poland in 1995 for your work in leading the negotiations to reduce Poland's official bilateral external debt with the G7 and other countries. Can you tell us about that experience?

Mulford: When the Berlin Wall came down, one of President Bush's greatest strengths was that he immediately sought to bind the Eastern European countries to the West. One important initiative was to reduce Poland's official bilateral external debt. President Lech Wałęsa of Poland asked President Bush for an 85 percent reduction in Poland's external bilateral debt, and eventually we agreed to support a 55 percent debt reduction. I can tell you that it was a brutal and vicious negotiation with the other G7 members, because they didn't want any debt forgiveness for Poland. And to make matters worse, of the $32 billion stock of debt, the United States only had $300 million of exposure, whereas Germany, France, and even Austria had $4–$5 billion each. Their attitude was, "You guys are taking a cheap shot because you don't have skin in this game. You're just leading this negotiation to impoverish the rest of us." And so it didn't make for good relations. Our point was that without acting, Poland couldn't turn around its economy, which would disadvantage them further.

In the end, we achieved a 50 percent reduction and signed the agreement in April of 1991. The result was that by September of that year, Poland announced its first positive quarter of GDP [gross domestic product] growth, and their economy has been very successful ever since. I'm very proud of this deal because it was the way to cure an indebted country that had so much energy and commitment. Mind you, Lech Wałęsa was very tough. When I went to him with the deal, he said, "What's this? It's like a three-wheeled motorcar—it doesn't do me any good at all." I told him, "Mr. President, it's a reduction of 50 percent. That will do you a lot of good. And I just want to say that I lived in London, where there are a lot of three-wheeled vehicles that are very maneuverable and do very well. That's exactly what we're doing for you." And so I went out and later bought him a mini three-wheeled toy car, and when he came over to see President Bush, I rolled it over to him at the end of a meeting: "Mr. President, I want to give you that as a gift." He was hugely amused [*laughs*].

Bowmaker: You left the Treasury in November 1992. During your nine years at the Treasury, you must have had a fair amount of interaction with economists. In your view, what does an economist bring to the policy world that others do not?

Mulford: Economists can be hugely valuable because they are very well trained. But in general I have found that, when giving advice, they have trouble detaching themselves from the philosophical limitations of their ideas. What I like about investment banking is that when you are faced with the brutal reality of a problem, you cannot have a mindless commitment to an idea that does not work. And so you may have to keep an economist adviser at arm's length and develop a relationship with him in which he knows that you're going to have that attitude. You don't go behind his back and say that you took part of his idea, but not the rest of it.

With that said, as a policy practitioner, I used economists every day, and the ones that I found most effective were those who had obtained a broad education in liberal arts with a specialization in economics. I found that economists with a background in liberal arts had a knowledge of history, knew how to write and conceptualize policy issues—which I responded to because that's what I do. I don't want to sound arrogant, but the fact is that if you're in a position of responsibility where important decisions have to be made, you need an understanding of what's going to work, not what you would like to see necessarily because it conflicts with your particular economic theory.

I worked very closely with Beryl Sprinkel when he was undersecretary at the Treasury before becoming President Reagan's chairman of the Council of Economic Advisers. He was an example of an economist committed to a particular type of economic philosophy. He was a die-hard monetarist who believed the very last thing in the entire world that the United States should do is intervene in currency markets. He was a controversial person, but I thought he was such a great guy. I'll tell you a very entertaining story about Beryl. In the autumn of 1983, President Reagan went to Japan, where he agreed to open talks aimed at opening Japan's economy and financial system. The hope was that these changes would promote investment and faster economic growth in Japan and foster its closer integration with global markets.

We met regularly with the Japanese every six months. I chaired the discussions—which were always long and drawn out—for almost nine years. But Beryl led the first of our meetings with the Japanese side, which were headed by Vice Minister [Tomomitsu] Oba. Mr. Oba was explaining for the umpteenth time the importance of his country's gradual step-by-step approach to change when Beryl finally snapped. "Look," he said, "I grew up on a dirt farm in Missouri. Every spring we got new puppies and had to cut their tails off. We didn't cut them off an inch at a time—we just hacked them off once right at the top. That was the end of it!" When the translation came through from the booth in the corner of the room, there was a sharp intake of breath, followed by complete silence from across the table. Mr. Oba looked at everybody for a moment and then broke into laughter. The next day he announced that the Japanese approach would be moving away from "step by step" to "stride by stride." They had understood the "dogs' tails" story! That made a significant difference. Most of our proposed changes were eventually accepted by the Japanese and brought the country into the modern financial world, even if not always in a form that was as effective as we had hoped.

Bowmaker: How would you compare and contrast Presidents Reagan and Bush in terms of their operating styles and modes of economic thinking?

Mulford: President Reagan had a more laid-back personality. He did not take the kind of in-depth policy interest in issues that President Bush did. Instead, he was focused on those broad issues that were priorities for him. He was gregarious and able to deflect in the most remarkable way the inevitable political attacks common in politics, whether from inside his own party, from Democrats, members of Congress, or the media. When criticism became sharp, he would often introduce humor. I was impressed by how he seemed to be protected by that approach. It was not cynical humor, but friendly.

George Bush Sr. was a different personality. He had come up through the policy ranks of government as ambassador to China and head of the CIA [Central Intelligence Agency] and really knew how Washington worked. He was always considerate and respectful of other people, including those who worked for him and those who he dealt with in other countries. He was sensitive to other points of view. As I just said, he also had an appreciation of and working interest in policy, with the Brady Plan being a good example.

I thought they were both effective leaders but with different styles. There was a certain comfort in knowing that Mr. Bush understood the specific details of issues and knew the inner workings of the bureaucracy around the State Department, the Treasury, the National Security Council, and the Defense Department. Mr. Reagan was somewhat more removed.

General Thoughts on Economic Policymaking

Bowmaker: What is your view on the so-called revolving door between Wall Street and Washington?

Mulford: That is an important question. I strongly believe that public service in a democracy and in a complicated system like ours should be influenced by new blood and fresh ideas and by those with hands-on experience. Practical people can make a very significant contribution in Washington by pointing out to the sometimes too confident government officials found in the executive branch that their solutions to a particular problem might not really solve the problem. Of course, I realize that is sometimes a difficult proposition because, as I said earlier, hubris and commitment to certain philosophies or schools of thought run very deep. People don't want to give up their favorite ideas very easily, but I do think that part of the revolving door can be healthy. The part that isn't terribly healthy relates to those who start their careers in Washington at a young age, stay in Washington, only know Washington, and rise in Washington to the point where they believe they can parlay themselves into private-sector jobs as a person of influence and knowledge. But private business doesn't usually view such people as having much value because they have really never run anything, despite having a high opinion of themselves. So one might say there is often an imbalance in the way that door revolves.

Personal Reflections

Bowmaker: How did your personality affect your style and approach as a policymaker?

Mulford: My personality has occasionally been described as abrasive. But some of the complex and substantive issues I had to deal with in Washington could only be done if somebody was willing to stand up for them. It was only natural, then, that I would receive some criticism about being unreasonable or demanding or overbearing—it was part of the job. Looking back, I sometimes wish I hadn't created quite that impression, but I'm always torn. If I hadn't, then the Brady Plan, the Polish debt reduction, and the talks with Japan, for example, would not very likely have succeeded. Why do I say this? Because if you had opened those issues to the full bureaucracy of Washington, there would have been extensive internal debate and dissension; strong and decisive action would not have been forthcoming. On balance, I feel I did the right thing, even though there has been some ongoing cost for me. What you don't want, of course, is to hear that people thought you were totally dictatorial or rude or abusive. I hope that I avoided this impression, but from time to time your patience can be sorely tested. Let me put it that way. In the end, I still believe that those of us who want to accomplish change while in public service cannot just be a comfortable part of the go-along, get-along system of Washington—you may have to step on some toes here and there.

Bowmaker: Relatedly, what were your strengths and weaknesses as a policymaker?

Mulford: I had a keen interest in learning and a very diverse and practical knowledge base of the real world that I could bring to bear on policy issues and judgments. I could quickly grasp the essence of what was at stake in a given situation. Secretary Brady believed in the idea that a good plan this week is better than a perfect plan next week. I was an admirer of that approach. If you can get to the core of what is a good plan as opposed to a perfect plan, then you're probably on your way to solving an issue.

One of my weaknesses was when I didn't know enough about an issue, perhaps I was too anxious to move forward to a solution because of the passage of time. And so there were occasions when I could appear unreasonable to bureaucratic specialists. That's a hard thing to deal with because there is a need to be cooperative. But sometimes, as a hardworking person, you don't allow enough time for something to mature to the point where you could have handled it differently.

Another issue that is hard to describe—and one that I have experienced all my life—is that you have to learn to appreciate that many people around you don't always have the same level of commitment as yourself. That's not easy to accept and understand. I can remember in football being in the huddle during a hard-fought game and realizing looking around at the faces of teammates that they simply weren't believers in the way I was that we could win. It is important to be able to make adjustments in your thinking for the lesser passion. I think having that kind of sensitivity is a very useful trait to possess. For example, President Reagan had clear vision and was deeply committed to certain objectives. He was surrounded by people of diverse views and different levels of commitment. But he found ways to tone them down or brush them off, while at the same time respect them and keep their support. I don't think I developed that art as fully as President Reagan.

Michael Boskin (*left*), when chairman of the Council of Economic Advisers, meeting with President George H. W. Bush in the Oval Office on August 4, 1989.

12   Michael J. Boskin
Born 1945, New York City

Michael Boskin graduated with a
BA with highest honors and the
Chancellor's Award as outstanding
undergraduate in 1967 from the University of California, Berkeley, where
he also received his MA and PhD—in
1968 and 1971, respectively—all in
economics.

Boskin joined Stanford University
as an assistant professor of economics in 1970 and has remained there
ever since, except for brief stints at
Harvard and Yale Universities and four years in the White House. He currently serves as the Tully M. Friedman Professor of Economics and Hoover
Institution Senior Fellow.

In government, Boskin served as chairman of President George H. W. Bush's
Council of Economic Advisers (CEA) between 1989 and 1993. The Independent Council for Excellence in Government rated his CEA as one of the five
most respected agencies (out of one hundred) in the federal government.

I interviewed Michael Boskin in his office at the Hoover Institution at
Stanford University, in Stanford, California. It was the middle of the morning on Tuesday, July 17, 2012.

Background Information

Bowmaker: Why did you become an economist?

Boskin: At the beginning of my sophomore year, contemplating a math
and/or philosophy major, I wandered in to introductory economics 1A. It
was a very boring lecture, but I fell in love with the material. And so I took
1B, became an economics major, and accelerated through the program,
writing an honors thesis that was published and even receiving a nice note

from Milton Friedman about it.[1] But I still wasn't sure whether I wanted to go to graduate school or law school, which I was also considering at the time. And so I went around the country talking to top economics departments about their PhD programs, and I also chatted with some lawyers in Los Angeles, where I was then living. The lawyers weren't very happy with their jobs, which I found compelling, and I realized that economics was more intellectually fascinating to me than law. I liked the combination of bringing mathematical and statistical rigor to problems that were important to the well-being of many people and the fact that there is always something new. We are inventing new ways of thinking about problems or new data sets to study issues empirically, and the economy is constantly changing and generating new information. It is a timely and timeless intellectual pursuit.

Becoming an economist has been a remarkable blessing because there hasn't been a day of my life that I haven't woken up curious about what is going on in the economy.

Entering the Policy World

Bowmaker: What does an economist bring to the policy world that others do not?

Boskin: Economists bring a respect for analytical rigor, data, and information. And the best ones bring a respect for the limitations of what is known, which is a great advantage but one that has to be used wisely in a political context because there, people are prone to make exaggerated claims to bolster their side of the argument.

Bowmaker: Your entry into the policy world took place when you were a member of Ronald Reagan's tax advisory group in his 1980 presidential campaign. How did that position arise?

Boskin: Two of my colleagues here at Hoover, George Shultz and Martin Anderson, were very close advisers to Reagan. They introduced me to him at a dinner at George's house, and we hit it off. On a subsequent visit to San Francisco, I spent an afternoon with him at the Fairmont Hotel talking about taxes, and then in the fall I was asked to help prepare him for the presidential campaign debate. That took place in a barn in Virginia, and I

---

1. Michael J. Boskin, "The Negative Income Tax and the Supply of Work Effort," *National Tax Journal* 20, no. 2 (1967): 353–367.

remember that David Stockman played Jimmy Carter and George Will, Pat Buchanan, and Jeane Kirkpatrick were also there asking questions. I quickly learned how naive I was about the political process, in particular that I had a very inaccurate gauge of what was a successful answer to a question. We had given him [Reagan] three points that he should make in response to a question about the problems in Social Security, and when he answered, he gave them in reverse order of importance. I was crushed! But then I realized that he had thousands of things to contextualize and remember, in foreign affairs, defense, economic policy—down to the difference between Mauritania and Mauritius. And so his answer was actually quite remarkable [*laughs*]—a home run, in fact.

Bowmaker: Did you view yourself as having strong policy positions, or simply as a hired professional serving Reagan?

Boskin: Both. Even by that time, I had written somewhat widely on the harmful effects of high tax rates on incentives, and I was very much in favor of disinflating the economy. During the electoral season, I had a debate with Walter Heller, former chair of the CEA for John F. Kennedy, who thought that we should have an incomes policy and just learn to live with high inflation because the costs of disinflation would be unbearable. I believed those costs would be temporarily high, but that we would reap the benefits in the long run. If you looked at the United States from World War II until 1980, the inflation rate kept ratcheting up in every business cycle, whether comparing troughs, midpoints, or peaks of the cycle, and so we were on our way to inflation rates of countries like Argentina. Many Keynesians at the time thought there was a permanent, stable Phillips curve trade-off between inflation and unemployment, but I felt that was a major misspecification of how the economy worked. Of course, I knew that by raising interest rates substantially, there would be a recession—but, while deep, it was not as bad as some were predicting, and most importantly it was successful in lowering inflation from around 13 percent to 4 percent. Reagan was quite concordant with my views, and I was quite impressed with his command of the big-picture policy priorities. I also thought that we should get spending under control, as did he, and through my teaching and research, I felt that there was a vast opportunity to make spending much more effective and efficient—likewise the tax code, with lower rates, indexing, tax-deferred saving (IRAs [individual retirement accounts]), and so on. I made sure that I explained to him why economists had different views, which is something that presidents need to hear.

Bowmaker: What were the main lessons that you learned from this initial policy experience?

Boskin: Sound economics is an essential input to policy, but the ability to input it depends greatly on the personal relationships between an elected leader and his advisers. That was one lesson. Another was the importance of having backbone. The role of an elected leader is to have some big-picture policies that he or she wants to accomplish and to explain to voters why they are important, even if some pain is necessary. For example, there is no doubt that the only way [Chairman of the Federal Reserve] Paul Volcker was able to succeed in his disinflation policy was because he had the backing of President Reagan. Remember, President Carter went on national TV in the middle of a roaring inflation to say that the Federal Reserve should lower interest rates! And the third lesson was that economics is only a necessary, but not a sufficient, input into the policymaking process.

By the way, I didn't formally go into the Reagan administration because I had just fallen in love with the woman to whom I've now been married for thirty-five years. I didn't think it would be the wisest decision in what might prove to be a lifelong relationship [*laughs*].

Bowmaker: You then served as Vice President George H. W. Bush's chief economic adviser during his 1988 presidential campaign. How did that position arise, and what did you learn about his interest in economics?

Boskin: As with Reagan, we had been first introduced through a couple of people whom I knew, and then he started inviting me to have breakfast with him whenever I was in Washington. Soon I was offered the role of chief economic adviser during his campaign and quickly learned that, even though his first love was foreign policy, he knew a fair amount of economics, having taken classes at Yale, run a business, and been involved in economic policy throughout his career. He was interested in incentives as well as long-term growth and wanted to know how government policy affected both of them. Relatedly, the concepts of innovation and technical change were also something that intrigued him, and I remember having a long discussion about them in relation to antitrust policy because they reminded him of what he called "that Schumpeter stuff" on creative destruction, which he had been taught in college [*laughs*].

Overall, I would say he seemed to like the combination of the analytical with the practical. For example, one time during his campaign, he was asking about which very short-term indicators you would look at to understand what is likely to happen in the next few months. I told him about the importance of business orders for investment goods and capital goods, as well as shipment of goods, but emphasized that since a larger fraction of the economy is now in services, there are fewer things shipped by freight. As the economy is changing, then, this meant that the more volatile indicators, such as those relating to goods, production, and inventories, may not have quite the same validity as they did in the past. He found that quite interesting. The notion, therefore, that he did not pay attention to the economy, or to economics in general, is badly mistaken.

As Chairman of the Council of Economic Advisers

Bowmaker: After George H. W. Bush won the election, he chose you to be the chairman of his Council of Economic Advisers. At your first official meeting, did he make it clear what he expected you to do for him?

Boskin: We had several conversations about the role before I accepted it. He made it clear that he had great confidence in my ability as an economist and communicator and great trust that I would give him honest advice that's best not only for him, but also for his view of what's best for the country. And while he wanted me involved in every decision, he was also adamant that I should leave the politics to him. He told me that a few CEA chairs in the past had played with politicking and, consequently, had been slapped around. And so I always addressed an issue by saying, "Here's what the economics would dictate and why. I know that politics are likely to interfere, but there are things that you could do to still keep it consistent with good economics, if not perfectly congruent. Here are some options." Sometimes you have to develop a less bad option. In fact, reducing or eliminating bad policies is a huge part of good economic policy advising—of advising on any type of policy, for that matter.

Bowmaker: How did you describe the state of the economy to him at that first meeting?

Boskin: I told him that the economy was growing slowly, inflation was still at 4–5 percent, and while the Fed[eral Reserve] wants to get it down to 2 percent, how and when it does it will heavily affect his future. He understood that argument intellectually, but I think he got it on a more political survival level when the economy started having more measurable problems, and of course as vice president he had seen what had happened to Reagan's popularity and the Republican midterm election losses during the '81–'82 recession. And so he knew that when he made some very, very difficult decisions that were in the nation's long-run interests, it would hurt him politically. For example, the decision to go ahead and clean up financial institutions during the savings and loan crisis, as well as enact the Brady Plan to deal with Third World bank debt, would slow credit expansion in the economy at a time when we were dealing with Saddam Hussein's invasion of Kuwait. But I believe that they were major contributors to the long expansion of the 1990s, because those financial headwinds became tailwinds. Of course, we have been going through a larger version of that crisis recently, and you might want to ask where we would be if we had instead seen the kind of decisive action taken by President Bush and by President Reagan before him.

Bowmaker: How did you go about establishing a comfortable working relationship with the president?

Boskin: That came easily, but there was a brief period of three months or so when he was getting hammered on the economy, and I thought he was getting very poor advice from some of his political advisers inside the White House. They held the view that he should be very optimistic about the current state of the economy, which was substantively wrong and politically opened him to the charge of being out of touch. Presidents need to be realistic about the current situation but optimistic and confident about the future if we adopt good—that is, their—policies. But the economy is buffeted from time to time with problems. And during that initial period, we were certainly at a historically unfortunate juxtaposition: we had the savings and loan crisis; the Third World debt issue, making the major banks insolvent marked to market; the stock market collapse that had taken place a year before President Bush was elected; and the oil price shock resulting from Saddam Hussein's invasion of Kuwait—plus an impending defense drawdown following the fall of the Berlin Wall meant that we had a recession on our hands. And so I was at loggerheads with his political advisers because I wanted the president to acknowledge that we faced those problems. Some people would say, "Oh, you're just worried about your own reputation," but I would tell them, "Look, my reputation is fine. It was made a long time ago, and not as an economic forecaster." I had to go to the White House briefing room to explain that the president was deeply concerned about every unemployed person in the country, but that just pissed off some of his advisers, and they tried to squeeze me out. Finally, I went to the president and told him how intolerable the situation was, and thankfully he made sure that was stopped—though of course, I still had some disagreements but could air them more effectively.

Bowmaker: Was your economic philosophy in alignment with the president's?

Boskin: They were close but not identical. I was probably more conservative economically than he was. For example, I was more concerned with keeping tax rates as low as possible. And while we were both in sync about the importance of getting spending under control, as well as controlling the budget deficit late in an economic expansion, he was realistic about the political environment he faced, with the Democrats holding large majorities in both houses of Congress. In the end, he was more willing to strike a compromise, which politically hurt him badly.

There are three conservative positions within the Republican Party on fiscal issues. First, there are low tax rate supply-siders, some of whom don't worry nearly enough about spending. Second, there are the "get spending under control" conservatives who believe that everything else will take care of itself, some of whom don't worry enough about tax rates. And third, there are the budget balancers, some of whom don't care enough about how the budget is balanced—at higher or lower levels of spending and taxes. All three of those points of view are partially valid, more or less so, given circumstances such as the state of the economy. And in the end, we need to do all of them! It's certainly true that if you don't keep tax rates low, the economy will eventually slow. It's certainly true that if you don't get spending under control, you will eventually have to pay higher interest on the debt that you have been borrowing and therefore, eventually, higher taxes. And it's certainly true that you want to keep the deficit and debt under control, otherwise you risk a financial crisis and/or higher taxes. I was always trying to get the three groups to see each other's point of view and to work together, but it certainly wasn't the easiest thing to do.

Bowmaker: You were closer to President Bush than most chairs of the CEA are to the presidents for whom they serve. Can you give a specific example of how this allowed you to push something beyond the bounds of what a CEA chair would normally do?

Boskin: When we wrote the *Economic Report of the President*, we would include content that was consistent with my understanding of the president's philosophy based on many conversations with him. Even though he signs the front part of the report, the view of the White House, however, is that something should be included only if it has been stated explicitly by the president. And so there were a few times when it was questioned that it was the president's policy that we were writing about in the report. But he always backed me up, and then we would push back when other parts of the government were not doing things consistent with his policy. For example, there was a person who was a protégé of a close friend of the president who was siding with something that we thought was antithetical to the president's philosophy. When the time came, then, I took the unusual step of insisting she not be reappointed. I had a lot of incoming mortar lobbed at me as a result, but it sent a message to others that you should take the president's philosophy seriously within the balance of your legal obligations.

Bowmaker: Did you ever seek advice from former chairs of the CEA or other economists during your role?

Boskin: Absolutely. While I have plenty of confidence in my own judgment and analytical abilities, I have never thought that I was a monopolist on wisdom or on knowledge. And so one of the first things I did was to call the former chairs of the CEA to solicit their advice and tell them I had an open phone line any time they thought there was something I ought to know, or when they felt that we were not firing on all cylinders. I made a point of calling not just Republicans but also Democrats like Charlie Schultze, which was very useful. And, of course, I spoke frequently to George Shultz. For example, I was put in charge of our negotiations with the Russians during the move to bail out [President Mikhail] Gorbachev when the Soviet economy was in trouble. President [François] Mitterrand of France, Chancellor [Helmut] Kohl of Germany, and Prime Minister [John] Major of Great Britain kept calling President Bush to tell him we couldn't lose Russia and that we had to lead a huge bailout. There was a big push for the US to put up $100 billion, which was real money even then. And so Gorby, as he was called internally, sent over Yevgeny Primakov [a member of Gorbachev's Presidential Council] along with a couple of others to have this discussion, and I was put in charge of it rather than the State Department. I called Shultz and said, "George, I'm going to be in negotiations with the Russians soon. You have been involved in many high-stakes negotiations over the years. Do you have any advice?" He replied, "You have to press them pretty hard, and if they haven't threatened to walk away twice, they haven't gotten serious." I remember that specifically [*laughs*].

Bowmaker: You talked earlier about President Bush's interest in economics. Did you ever get into theoretical discussions with him about economics?

Boskin: Yes, and sometimes in great detail. For example, during the savings and loan crisis, we discussed the Basel rules on banking regulation in depth, and whether that was one of the reasons why banks had greatly reduced their commercial and industrial lending and were holding a large volume of Treasuries. But of course we also discussed practical realities, like the timeframe involved in cleaning up the banks and the effect on real people.

I'll give you an amusing anecdote about when we made the decision during the Bush administration to shift from using gross national product to gross domestic product. That is a level of detail that even puts economics graduate students to sleep. Commerce Secretary [Robert] Mosbacher had to give a press conference about it, which was just torture for him, so he kept deferring to me. And I also had to explain the difference to President Bush. He said, "OK, I understand, but I just hope that they don't ask me questions on that!" [*Laughs.*]

Bowmaker: Did he ever ask about consensus among economists on certain issues?

Boskin: Yes, and I tried to give him a fair reading of the evidence. For example, I think most economists agree on free trade with clear, enforceable rules and the benefits of markets and, except for those on the extreme left of the profession, that tax rates ought to be as low as possible to fund the necessary functions of government, because the harm from higher tax rates goes up with their square. That's not doctrinal—it's a consequence of the area under demand and supply curves. But of course how those ideas actually map into real-world policymaking is a matter of some dispute.

Bowmaker: Did the president reach his decisions slowly or quickly?

Boskin: I would say he was much more readable than the Supreme Court, but he would often think about something overnight and make a decision the next day or even a few days later. He was also like Reagan in that he liked to receive memos and ponder them in the evening or on weekends. I have been around many other politicians and seen how they like to receive information. For example, Howard Baker was a terrific leader of the Senate, and he would always ask me to walk with him from his office to the Senate floor, because he preferred verbal to written communication.

Bowmaker: How would you describe the kind of economics that you used in advising the president relative to that found in your academic work and teaching?

Boskin: I was just trying to apply good economics based on theory, statistical evidence, and historical experience. [Joseph] Schumpeter once said that history is the most important of those three tools, but I think we need to use all of them.

My microeconomics was always market oriented with limited exceptions, but my macroeconomics was a blend of the schools of thought in that field because I don't think any one of them fully explains how the economy functions or is sufficient to prescribe policy. So I used a combination of new-classical economics, monetarism, new Keynesianism, and supply-side economics. I think the president found my approach very appealing.

Bowmaker: What was the most difficult intellectual economic argument that you had to make as CEA chair?

Boskin: Well, it was to Congress more than to the president: that you cannot treat the budget as just like an arithmetic accounting exercise. Imagine you have a $500 billion deficit. In theory, you could close it with a tax increase and/or a spending cut. However, you ignore the effects of both decisions—especially the tax hike, which has a negative effect on the economy—and so you don't receive all of the expected revenue. If you look at all of the post–World War II fiscal consolidations in the OECD [Organisation for Economic Co-operation and Development], the ones that were successful, in the sense that they consolidated the budget and did not cause a recession—they averaged around $5 to $6 of spending cuts for every dollar of tax increases. More importantly in United States historical experience, however, is the fact that the tax increases occur, but the spending cuts don't wind up fully happening. Either they got changed by a later Congress or the projections were too exaggerated. So we need spending control in reality, not some promise of future changes in exchange for tax hikes now.

Bowmaker: Given that the Republicans did not control either house of Congress, can you give some examples of when politics made it impossible for the president to do something analytically pure or consistent with your economic thinking?

Boskin: On the micro side, the Clean Air Amendment Act of 1990 has been held up as an example of good environmental legislation that respected the economy and dramatically reduced the cost of meeting environmental objectives. But we had to make a variety of compromises for regional voting reasons, because coal from western states such as Montana and Wyoming has a lower percentage of sulfur impurities than coal found in the eastern United States. And the amendment also involved an interagency process that was difficult. I had negotiated directly with the EPA [Environmental Protection Agency] to keep its cost down and make it reasonable, which the president agreed with, but they wound up showing us a draft law that was not what the president had decided. They said that they had decided to make it consistent with the Clean Water Act. When I told them to rewrite it, they replied, "You have no authority to tell us to do that." And so I phoned the president, who was on Air Force One, who said, "I'm going to put [Chief of Staff] John Sununu on the line because he'll be much more colorful in explaining what'll happen if they don't do as I decided." [EPA] Administrator [William] Riley got the message [laughs]. Of course, the president would have preferred not to have had a big argument, but he had made some aggressive environmental statements and viewed himself as a conservationist.

On the macro side, I think President Bush would have been much tougher on spending and might have begun to address the Social Security and Medicare entitlement cost crisis—the massive unfunded liabilities several times the regular national debt—which was always the plan after we had the discretionary part of the budget under control. He would have preferred not to raise taxes at all, not even the small increase he agreed to, but the Democrats demanded that as part of a budget deal that controlled discretionary spending and protected the defense budget. But when he agreed to a small tax hike despite his "no new taxes" pledge in his 1988 convention speech, it became very, very difficult to move further at that stage. It had a small, short-run negative effect on the economy and was clearly a very bad political message for him. A variety of Republican voters (not only the Newt Gingrich conservatives in the House, but also traditional Republicans) were deeply upset. So why did he do it? In part it was to protect the defense budget, which was under tremendous attack by the Democrats at the time. My own view was that virtually everything should have been done on the spending side, and anything related to taxes, had to be as consistent as possible both substantively and politically with his "no new taxes" pledge—for example, some closing of loopholes, tightening of definitions, et cetera. But [Director of the Office of Management and Budget] Dick Darman was always making the case, at least within the administration, for higher taxes. He would often say that government needs more revenue so that it can do "big, bold things." I believe that there are a few, but only a very few, "big, bold things" that make sense for the government to do [*laughs*]. And they could easily be paid for by savings from eliminating failed programs, consolidating overlapping ones, and modernizing technology.

Bowmaker: How would you describe your relationship with the Treasury and the Federal Reserve?

Boskin: I had good relations with both, although I thought the Fed lowered rates a little too slowly. I understood that they were trying to do a second round of disinflation, but the traditional measures were not considering how tight credit conditions were at the time, which were acting as a drag on the economy. And John Taylor [a member of the CEA] and I thought the economy was weaker than the Fed did. The Fed should have taken credit conditions more into account. Unfortunately, we turned out to be correct. It was a mistake, I believe, by Chairman Alan Greenspan—who, however, deserves credit for the second, and more subtle, round of disinflation from 4–5 percent to 2 percent. It was consequential for President Bush in a political sense. I had a straight-up relationship with Alan, who is a personal friend, but I certainly conveyed to him when the president was not thrilled with the actions of the Fed. I had very good relations with the Treasury and worked closely with them—Nick Brady, John Robson, Bob Glauber, David Mulford, and others—on many issues, from the savings and loan cleanup and Brady bonds for the Third World debt of (marked to market) insolvent money center banks to tax policy and our program to help the economy's transition out of socialist central planning. I always tried to be a team player, though there were those who tried to undermine Treasury Secretary Brady in various ways. They would jump on him for certain things he had said, and the Treasury sometimes asked me to provide clarification internally and to the press. But there was bound to be competition for who was going to have Bush's ear, and I think it was difficult for some people to deal with Brady being an old friend of the president's.

Bowmaker: What was your view at the time about the Brady Plan?

Boskin: I thought the notion that we could create a liquid market in zero-coupon bonds that would spread the pain over a longer span of time and allow a form of write-down that Latin governments would agree to was a risk worth taking, and one that had a reasonable chance of being successful. Yes, there were some potential minefields, which I laid out to the team, but on balance it worked out quite well.

Bowmaker: In retrospect, do you have any thoughts on the wisdom of the reduction in government control of Fannie Mae and Freddie Mac that was part of the 1989 savings and loan [S&L] bailout legislation?

Boskin: I pushed for a cleaner resolution of Fannie and Freddie, but at early meetings it was made clear by Lloyd Bentsen, who was chair of the Senate Finance Committee, that we were only doing the S&Ls. And then, right before the end of the administration, the Democrats in Congress tried to push through some expansion of the powers of Fannie and Freddie. I thought they needed to be reined in—having government-sponsored enterprises being so highly leveraged was an accident waiting to happen. As an academic, I had written about how the government had the most inane accounting system for how it dealt with potential contingent exposures to financial institutions involving deposit insurance and implicit guarantees.

Bowmaker: All things considered, can you point to a specific example of where you, as an economist, or the CEA, as an organization, were able to make a difference?

Boskin: We helped a lot on trade—the Uruguay Round, the creation of the World Trade Organization and NAFTA [the North American Free Trade Agreement], which I followed up on through a conversation with Pepe Cordoba, who was Mexican president [Carlos] Salinas's chief of staff, after [Mexico's secretary of commerce and industry] Jaime Serra Puche first proposed it to [US trade representative] Carla Hills. The precise process was as follows. One morning, Nick Brady, Dick Darman, [Secretary of State] Jim Baker, and I were meeting with the president and discussing Brady bonds. The president said he wanted to do something to help the reformers in Mexico, and I suggested we figure out a way to liberalize trade with the country. I remember Baker, in particular, being very supportive, and so there was some thought that we should turn our attention to it after the Brady bonds were launched. Before we had a chance to do anything on a formal basis, though, Jaime Serra Puche and Carla Hills had a meeting in Davos during which Jaime suggested a free-trade agreement with Mexico, since the Reagan administration had already passed one with Canada. Carla brought back the details of that meeting with her, and I spoke with Pepe Cordoba in my office shortly thereafter. I told him I would be in favor of liberalizing trade with Mexico—that it would help them enormously if they opened up their economy—and that President Bush thought it was a great idea.

In terms of our other contributions, John Taylor did a great job in helping to prevent a trade war with Japan. Dick Schmalensee [a member of the CEA] played an important role in applying rigorous cost-benefit analysis and sound microeconomics to environmental policy—for example, the emissions trading in the Clean Air Act Amendments of 1990. We greatly reduced the cost of the Clean Air Act Amendments by instituting a successful emissions-trading scheme.

And I think by recent government standards, we had a pretty accurate view of the economy. I remember telling President Bush at Camp David that we were in a recession before the data even confirmed one negative quarter. I then said so on TV. Other CEA chairmen tell me that it is quite unusual, because they had to wait until the politicos in the White House agreed. But I thought the president would look very foolish if the NBER [National Bureau of Economic Research] dated the recession and people said, "You haven't said anything about this recession that started months ago." And we also predicted that it would be a slow recovery, which it was. John Taylor had great judgment on the macro issues. Of course, I realize that forecasting is a very inexact science, but I think we applied some sound economics.

General Thoughts on Economic Policymaking

Bowmaker: Do you believe that if we were to raise the level of economic literacy in this country, economic policymaking would improve because the people would demand better policy?

Boskin: I think policy would still be primarily determined by people's self-interest. If you have a majority collecting benefits from the government, they will tend to vote not to curtail them. Taxpayers want lower taxes. Of course, people have more complex interests than that simplified description. Some get benefits and pay taxes. Some will pay higher taxes in the future (my students, for example). People care about their parents and grandparents and kids and grandkids, and so on. The place where economic literacy would be most valuable, and where it is currently lacking, is in journalism. Take Obamacare. The notion that you can claim to add medical coverage to tens of millions of people while doing nothing to increase supply (probably decreasing the supply of doctor services) and the cost will fall and quality improve, is patently absurd. You would flunk your midterm if you wrote that in Econ 1A. But how many times have you read that in the newspaper? And how many times do you hear journalists say the government provided something to somebody? But remember, your children will pay for it later with higher taxes to pay the interest on the debt used to fund today's program. That's where economic literacy would help the most—if journalists were honorable and learned economics and utilized it. In 1980, Walter Cronkite asked me to participate in such a program, which I did on several Saturday mornings. This short course for media aired on PBS TV stations across the country by videoconference. We need a lot more of that. Of course, there are some legitimate disagreements among economists, and all journalists should do is inform their readers, hopefully explaining why.

Bowmaker: Do you think that the gap between economics research produced in universities and policymaking will increase or decrease over time?

Boskin: As economics has become more technical and abstract, the gap has definitely become larger, and I think part of the reason is that the rewards for more practical kinds of work have decreased in academia. But a very large fraction of what you need to know to be a good policy adviser in the White House is found in undergraduate economics. In fact, much is in Economics 1, at least as taught at Stanford—especially to knock down so many poorly designed policy options the political process hatches.

Personal Reflections

Bowmaker: What value has your public service had to you and to your university?

Boskin: Playing a character in a historical novel can be interesting and rewarding, despite the fact that you don't get a lot of sleep; you get a lot of grief and harassment; and you sometimes feel that you're wielding a machete until 4:00 in the afternoon, chopping down all the nonsense before you can do anything constructive. Democracy is not a spectator sport, as President Reagan used to say. I learned a great deal about how the government works and, as an economist, about what's important to study in the potential large gap between textbook policymaking and its real-world implementation.

I have also had the opportunity to advise four US presidents, starting with Reagan, both Bush 41 and 43, and I even traveled with Bill Clinton to help on Social Security reform—which was sadly abandoned when he had his personal scandal. And because of my involvement in government, I have been asked to advise in other parts of the world about many issues, from deficits and debt to trade to financial sector reform and cleanup, often with heads of government. And so my intellectual perspective on economic issues has been both broadened and deepened—not just on my traditional public finance and applied macroeconomics areas, but also in concerns about economic measurement, for example, chairing what is now called the Boskin Commission, whose report transformed the way government statistical agencies around the world measure inflation, productivity, and GDP [gross domestic product], and the effects of larger, more intrusive government on economic performance. My role in advising the Russians on economic reform at President Bush's request greatly expanded my interest in comparative economic systems and the economics of transition from communism and central planning to mixed capitalism.

The university gained, too, because I brought back my contacts and experience. I am now able to teach my students classes that are richer in the history of policy debates, which is very useful.

Overall, serving as CEA chair was one of the great highlights of my life. I'm glad that I had the opportunity to do it.

Bowmaker: How did your personality affect your style and approach as a policymaker?

Boskin: I would say that most people found me tough but fair. I always tried to be polite and respectful of others—at least until they proved they didn't deserve it [*laughs*]. Some people told me that I should have been more belligerent because I would have gotten more done, but I don't agree even in hindsight, and that's not my personality. However, there were times when I was very tough.

Bowmaker: What were your strengths and weaknesses as a policymaker?

Boskin: I have a broad interest in a wide range of economics, and I think that was very helpful for the CEA role because I had to advise on almost every issue that you can think of. I recruited two extremely talented economists, John Taylor and Dick Schmalensee, to be the other members of the CEA, and later David Bradford and Paul Wonnacott, which was very important because it is a team effort. And I enjoyed a very good relationship with the president before I went into the White House, which was obviously an advantage. My weakness was that I probably wasn't blustery enough when I first entered the White House. I tried to work with everybody in the administration as a team, and only when it became clear that the president was being given poor advice from some, or his positions were being ignored by others, did I get really tough.

Bowmaker: As a policymaker, which decisions or outcomes were most gratifying?

Boskin: First, warding off the industrial policy of the Atari Democrats, who wanted the government to pick technologies for massive subsidies—which was not based on science and economics but on political payoffs. Second, we put serious market-oriented economics into environmental policy. Third, we made some major moves on trade that were very satisfying, even though they had to be finalized early in the Clinton administration, promoting free trade and limiting protectionism in general. But as a society we need to do a better job of providing transition relief and adjustment assistance to the sectors and citizens negatively affected. Saying no to bailing out Gorbachev and to bailing out Drexel-Burnham. Putting controls on discretionary spending and a marginal balanced budget rule in place. Helping clean up the savings and loans and Third World debt of the money center banks' financial crisis.

I was happy to play a role in a variety of issues that I think were constructive. History can judge whether some of those things were or were not as successful as I think they were, or if they could have been done better by someone else.

Bowmaker: On the other hand, there must be some things, in hindsight, that you'd like the opportunity to do differently. What are they?

Boskin: I gave the best advice I could. There were policy decisions that I would prefer to have been different, but it was always the president's decision, and he was responding to what he thought was right under the circumstances—sometimes reflecting his fairly weak political position in Congress.

It was a frustration that he lost his reelection bid. I think he is a terrific person, and he had a very good batting average as president. In my view, he was dragged down by his agreeing to a tax increase as part of a budget deal and not having a more aggressive growth agenda right after the Gulf War. But at the time, his political advisers were telling him that if he did anything, it would just be stalled by the Democrats who controlled Congress, so he should wait for reelection when there would be more Republicans in the House and Senate. Sadly for him and for the country, he never got the chance.

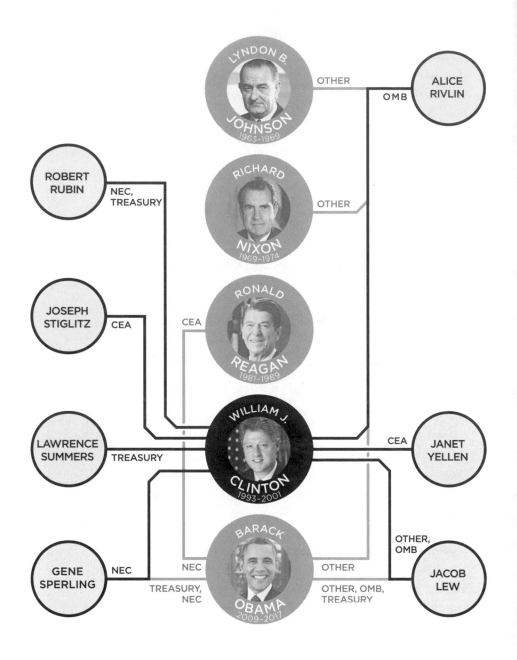

VI Bill Clinton Administration

Gene Sperling (*right*), when director of the National Economic Council, speaking with President Bill Clinton in the Oval Office on February 10, 1997.

13   Gene B. Sperling
Born 1958, Ann Arbor, Michigan

Gene Sperling graduated with a BA in political science from the University of Minnesota in 1982, received a JD from Yale Law School in 1985, and then attended the Wharton School of the University of Pennsylvania.

From 1990 to 1992, Sperling was an economic adviser to Governor Mario Cuomo of New York and served as economic policy director of the campaign of Bill Clinton and Al Gore. Following Clinton's election as president, Sperling served as deputy director and director of the National Economic Council (NEC) in 1993–1996 and 1997–2001, respectively.

In 2002–2008, after leaving the NEC, Sperling served as founder and director of the Center for Universal Education at the Brookings Institution and as a senior fellow at both the Council on Foreign Relations and the Center for American Progress. Sperling was one of Hillary Clinton's top economic advisers during her 2008 presidential campaign.

He then joined the administration of President Barack Obama as counselor to the secretary of the treasury and member of the Presidential Task Force on the Auto Industry (2009–2010). Sperling also served once again as director of the NEC (2011–2014), becoming the first person to fill this role for two presidents. Since leaving government, Sperling has been running Sperling Economic Strategies and has been a contributing editor for the *Atlantic*.

I interviewed Gene Sperling on two occasions. The first interview took place at the Hotel Casa del Mar in Santa Monica, California, from the early morning to the early evening of Friday, January 13, 2017. The second interview took place at his home in Santa Monica, California, from the early afternoon to the early evening of Thursday, March 15, 2018.

Background Information

Bowmaker: When did you first become interested in economic policy, and why?

Sperling: As I entered college, I was already very passionate about policy, but more from the perspective of poverty issues and civil rights. For example, my father, Larry Sperling, had won some important civil rights cases, including the first federal case allowing girls to play on boys' high school sports teams under the Fourteenth Amendment. My mother, Doris, was a major educational leader in Ann Arbor for closing the racial achievement gap. While I was born and raised in Ann Arbor, Michigan, and we are extreme University of Michigan loyalists, I wanted to go away for college. I had gotten into Brown, and then at the very last minute I took a tennis scholarship at the University of Minnesota. It was a very rigorous college life, playing a varsity Big Ten sport, but I had a coach who was very caring, and he allowed me to take a semester off from the tennis team in my senior year to go intern for Senator Carl Levin (a Democrat of Michigan) in Washington, D.C. While I was there, I watched the 1980 presidential elections, and I saw that the Republicans were able to dichotomize the world into people who believed in growth, freedom, and entrepreneurship versus people who cared about poor kids and financial security for families. And I started asking how had we let them be able to control the frame for economic policy? Why does it seem impossible in this frame for a person to believe in the power of entrepreneurship or markets and still believe government should do more in education, in health care, and in fighting poverty? Indeed, I ended up writing my honors thesis on how progressives had to do better in showing how their policies did promote values like freedom and liberty and not allow conservatives to manipulate those terms to be always justifying less government and less aid to the poor.

I continued to go back and forth between civil rights law and economic policy. My time at Yale Law School led me to intern with the NAACP Defense Fund, and I was often mentored by my Ann Arbor friend Paul Dimond, who had litigated many Supreme Court cases. Yet my passion for progressive economic policy led me to work with Bob Reich at the Kennedy School at Harvard. While I was at Wharton Business School, he ended up recommending me to the [Michael] Dukakis presidential campaign to work on economic policy in the winter of 1987. It is amazing how many people I first met there: George Stephanopoulos, Sylvia Burwell, Susan Rice, John Podesta, Larry Summers—I could go on and on.

When I joined the campaign I was actually doing much of the constitutional law portfolio as well as sharing the economic portfolio with my lifelong policy buddy Tom Kalil, who was just starting his rise to being the most influential technology adviser to the Democratic White Houses of his generation. When we got to the general election, Chris Edley, at that time a Harvard Law professor who was head of the policy team and my boss, called me into his office. He told me I needed to give up the legal and constitutional issues and focus 100 percent on economic policy for the general election. When I started to protest, he said, "Gene, this is a compliment. Even if you can convince me that others can only do the constitutional issues 90 percent as well as you, it still doesn't matter. You are the only economic adviser, the chief speechwriter [Bill] Woodward wants to work with. You are the only economic adviser top staffers want to be briefed by. You are the best person I have at getting all the top outside economists on the phone and pounding out a policy we can announce. This is your special value. Embrace it." The funny part is that I reluctantly asked who I should turn over all my legal issues to. He said it was a new staffer that he promised me was good. Her name was Elena Kagan—future Supreme Court Justice Elena Kagan. I can't say Chris Edley was not good in figuring out who showed most promise in which areas.

Entering the Policy World

Bowmaker: What does a good economic thinker bring to the policy world that others do not?

Sperling: Those of us who have been engaged in serious, high-impact economic decision-making bring a very strong appreciation for the rigor that is needed. When you are forced to live with the unintended consequences of your actions, that makes you look down every corner and talk with anybody who might have a different perspective, so that by the time you've given a recommendation to the president, you've done everything humanly possible to ensure that you have not made a mistake. There is a special camaraderie among those of us who have done that, and the interesting thing is that the more you're engaged in it, the more it breeds humility as opposed to arrogance.

Bowmaker: From 1990 to 1992, you were an economic adviser to Governor Mario Cuomo of New York and then were appointed as Bill Clinton's economic policy director during his presidential campaign. How did that position arise?

Sperling: There's no question that as a young progressive policymaker in 1989, getting an offer to report directly to Governor Mario Cuomo was the dream job. First, he was the highest-ranking Democrat in the country at that point, and second, huge amounts of the progressive community were hoping that he would be the Democratic nominee in 1992. When two of his top aides, Ethan Riegelhaupt and Drew Zambelli, told me he was interested in talking to me, I was on a plane to Albany for an interview shortly afterwards. I loved him, and he was enormously good to me. But he was also a tough, strong character. I think working for him really helped prepare me for working for presidents, because you had to be willing to tell him what you thought, stand up to a strong personality, and do so on a one-on-one basis, because Mario Cuomo could call you eight, nine times a day if you were working on something close to his heart at that moment. I was honored that I was one of the handful of people he confided in—usually after playing basketball—on whether he should run for president, and certainly a big part of my job was to advise him on which national economic policies he should support or oppose as governor.

When he didn't run, I was disappointed. To top it off, a month later I see Bill Clinton and George Stephanopoulos [communications director for Clinton's 1992 presidential campaign] walking in a hotel lobby. George came up to me and said, "Ready to come on board?" I said, "It doesn't feel loyal to just leave now." And George patted me on the shoulder and said he understood. I have to admit that as the primary [season] went on, I did have that feeling of life passing you by a bit. But around April, Cuomo graciously called me one night and told me he knew that I should not sit this campaign out, which meant a lot to me. I then let Bob Reich and Mark Gearan know I was interested, but I knew it might now be too late for a big job. So when out of nowhere my assistant said over the intercom in early May, "I have a Mr. George Stephanopoulos on the phone for you," my heart stopped. He said, "Gene, we're going to be putting our policy director, Bruce Reed, on the plane to travel with the president, and we'd like to know whether you would like to become the economic policy director." I had promised myself and my dad I would behave like an adult if they ever called, so I started to ask about details of the job and the pay. There was a long pause, and George said, "Gene, I just offered you the top economic job for the Democratic nominee for president of the United States. Now, you and I both know you would do this job for free." I said, "You know me too well. Whatever you offer is fine." George and I have laughed over my "negotiation" in that conversation for many years.

Bowmaker: You had to write Clinton's economic manifesto, "Putting People First," in two weeks. Can you describe that experience?

Sperling: I had first traveled around in late May meeting existing outside economic advisers, so I actually didn't arrive in Little Rock until about the first day of June '92, and it was definitely trial by fire. The jobs number for May had just been released, and Clinton had the day off. He was exhausted. I came into the office with Stephanopoulos and [James] Carville [lead strategist for the campaign], and said, "This is a really disappointing number. If Governor Clinton speaks out, I think we could be on all three networks"—which back in '92 was the gold standard. Carville, who I barely knew, looked at me and said, "This guy has not had a day off in months. If we're going to go interrupt him on his day off, have him get in a suit and tie and make a statement, you'd better be 100 percent sure." I told them, "I'm pretty sure." Here I am on my first day, driving to the Arkansas governor's mansion, and doing my first campaign briefing with Bill Clinton—by ruining his day off. He was kind and agreed to do it, but I could tell he was exhausted and not thrilled. Thank God, it worked. He made the network news that night saying the economy was not doing well, and I had survived my first trial in virtually my first day.

Almost the next day, Stephanopoulos called me into his office and said, "I don't want you to spend any more time looking for an apartment. We're going to get you a room at the Excelsior Hotel. You should do nothing now but focus on putting together an economic plan." He told me that [presidential candidate Ross] Perot often did big announcements on his birthday [June 27] and that he felt if Perot or [President George H. W.] Bush beat them out with an economic plan it would be a devastating blow.

The biggest challenge was that Bill Clinton had just promised again on *Larry King* that he would balance the budget in five years. I realized that there was no way that he could do the big investments he wanted and balance the budget in five years. What the primary campaign had not really digested was that all of the savings from the so-called peace dividend—the post–Cold War dividend—had already been incorporated in the latest budget projections. Counting them was double counting. So I faced a very big challenge, which is that he had made many major commitments on investments and called for a payroll tax cut and a child tax cut, and he had said he was going to balance the budget in five years. My main realization was that something there had to give, but Carville felt that if he looked like he was breaking a major promise, particularly on a middle-class tax cut, it would be portrayed as a character flaw—which would be very harmful. George soon after told me that they had a serious block of time in D.C. with Clinton that Saturday, and I needed to get on a plane and get here and to work with Bob Boorstin [a deputy communications director] on the wording and the message—in twenty-four hours! I can still remember me writing on scraps of paper and having to send them back to Boorstin as he typed because we couldn't get seats together.

I had basically two major things I was going to tell them that I thought might lead this to be a very bad day for me on the campaign. One, I was going to tell the governor that there was no way he could do his large progressive investments and his middle-class tax cuts and balance the budget, because they had been double counting the defense savings. My recommendation is that he could cut the deficit in half in four years. And secondly, [I was going to tell him] that instead of having to renege on one of the middle-class tax cuts, which Carville did not want me to propose...we could instead offer every American *an option* of a payroll tax cut or a child tax credit. Single people would take the payroll tax credit, and people with children would take the child tax credit. By doing that, we would not be reneging on either promise, but I was bringing the cost of the middle-class tax cut down by nearly half.

I got done with my presentation, and Bill Clinton said, "That is terrific. Politicians always say they're going to balance the budget. If we say we're cutting the deficit in half in four years, it's more realistic and more credible and makes clear how committed we are to our public investment agenda. And solving the tax cuts issue by keeping both and giving people a choice is just smart." He turned to George, who had really pushed for me to be hired, pointed to me, and gave him a thumbs-up. That was I suppose my honeymoon moment you sometimes get as the new guy. George then had me stay in D.C. for a couple of days to meet with the key economic staffers on the Hill, people like Mike Wessel and Joe Minirk, so I understood what options remained from the 1990 budget agreements. Then I flew back to Arkansas, as Bruce Reed worked with me on what policies were most important to Clinton, while people like Paul Begala pulled me back on some cuts that he knew would blow up in our faces as we met Clinton. I remember that our initial title was much longer—more like "Putting American Working Families First" or something like that. But Stan Greenberg, Mandy Grunwald, Carville, Boorstin, and Stephanopoulos decided it should just be "Putting People First." When I raised an eyebrow on that, Stan Greenberg gave me that "you handle the policy, we'll handle the message" pat on the shoulder and said, "Trust me. It will work." Finally, George and I went over to do a final meeting with Governor Clinton and Hillary Clinton. It was really my first substantive meeting with her. She was so sharp and impressive, and I could see how much he wanted to hear her reaction. She asked a lot of tough questions, but we survived. Afterwards she pulled me aside and told me to really make sure that I reached out to senators and other policy types who had previously supported ideas we were announcing. She stressed to me how important it was to listen to them, get their advice, and make sure they get credit and appreciation. "The more mothers and fathers every idea has the better," she wisely advised me.

We put it out that weekend, and it could not have worked more perfectly. Stephanopoulos's worry about Perot ended up being inaccurate, but his instinct on getting a plan out first ended up being a stroke of campaign genius. The week that we put out the plan, Bush and Perot were accusing each other of having put private investigators out—and our message was while they're busy investigating each other, we're investigating how to create jobs for the American people.

A week or so later, Carville told me that according to their internal polls, over 80 percent of Americans were aware that Bill Clinton had put out an economic plan. He later told me that along with picking Gore and the convention, he felt it was one of the three things that moved him—Clinton—from third place into first place in the polls in a single month.

Bowmaker: Can you describe how the origins of the National Economic Council can be traced back to the Clinton '92 campaign?

Sperling: In the years preceding President Clinton's election, there had been some discussion in think tanks that there needed to be an economic counterpart to the National Security Council [NSC]—that there needed to be some kind of coordinating body. Some of the people who pushed that were doing so more out of concern that economics considerations were incorporated into national security, trade, and other issues like that. For Bill Clinton, he had come to much the same conclusion, but based less on any think tank report and more from his own experience as a governor for many years.

I saw this instinct in him from the moment I was hired. The first time he talked to me about how he wanted me to perform the job of economic policy director, he in many ways foreshadowed his thinking for the National Economic Council. He said, "I always want you to give me your advice. I always want you to tell me what you think. But I want all of our top advisers to trust that you have sought out their ideas and that you are presenting them fairly, even if you disagree with them. That has to be your top obligation. I don't want any top advisers feeling like because I have an economic policy director now, their voice is being shut out. I want them to feel they're being empowered and that you are presenting all views fairly to me." He would tell me that he had learned as governor that when trust broke down between different Cabinet members, it could often have a devastating impact on policy. Lack of trust and internal fighting wasn't just a process issue—it affected the actual policy development and actual policy accomplishments. So this was a view he had developed and internalized over many years.

Once when we were on the plane to debate prep[aration] in 1992, Clinton told me how you could see how much trust and good process mattered by looking at the Bush administration. While it was good for our campaign, Clinton found it appalling that President Bush's secretary of treasury [Nicholas Brady] and OMB [Office of Management and Budget] director [Richard Darman] were openly fighting in the newspapers. On the other hand, he told me how even if members of the Bush foreign policy team didn't always love each other or agree, due to Brent Scowcroft they behaved like a coordinated team.

At the NEC during the Clinton Administration

Bowmaker: How were you appointed NEC deputy director by President Clinton?

Sperling: After some of the initial major transition meetings had happened, George Stephanopoulos called me into his office and said, "Listen, you should know that President Clinton plans to make the creation of a National Economic Council his primary innovation for organizing the White House and that he is going for somebody very senior to run that. So while you will be seen as too young for that job, if you are that person's deputy, it could be an amazingly influential job." That seemed right to me. Bob Rubin and I had worked together during both the 1988 and 1992 presidential campaigns. We got along well, and Bob told me he wanted me in the deputy role. He said he knew the president would choose me and that I could be the bridge between the economic team and the strategic team. Bob also thought we should have an international deputy. The person he chose was Bo Cutter, who had been at OMB during the [Jimmy] Carter administration and would therefore bring experience on interagency process. And then Sylvia Mathews—now Sylvia Burwell, and she was amazing even back then—became the de facto chief of staff.

In talking to everyone who had been part of past policy coordination efforts, it was clear that it never worked for someone in a current Cabinet position, like secretary of treasury or OMB director, to try to be that honest broker because they could never shed their agency's prerogatives. And it could also even fail if someone used their proximity to the president to cut others out—as [Henry] Kissinger famously did as NSC director. So when Rubin arranged for a day-long meeting with President-Elect Clinton on the budget, Bob assigned everyone on the core economic team—including myself—a presentation to make to the president-elect. Except himself. That sent the strongest signal that he was going to use this position to create an organized, fair process and not to empower himself at everyone's expense.

Bowmaker: One of your early achievements in your role was to help design and pass the 1993 Deficit Reduction Act. Would it be fair to say that you initially viewed deficit reduction as a political imperative, but once the strategy became successful in promoting growth, you realized the potential it had to help the disadvantaged in society?

Sperling: From the moment we started, we were struggling with this issue of two deficits—an investment deficit and a fiscal deficit—which were by definition in tension with each other. The more he [Clinton] wanted to have significant investments in worker training, Head Start, infrastructure, the Earned Income Tax Credit, the more difficult—or the more pain—it was going to take to lower the deficit. We spent a lot of time in the transition trying to resolve those tensions, but then we learned that the new CBO [Congressional Budget Office] budget numbers were showing the situation was worse than we thought.

As a team, everyone was committed to closing both the budget and investment deficit. That said, there is no question that I was seen as the champion of President Clinton's public investment agenda and was willing to have a somewhat less steep deficit path for that benefit. [Secretary of Labor] Bob Reich was certainly in that camp as well, and so too was George Stephanopoulos. When I presented at an NEC meeting the three options of low, medium, and high success in meeting his investment commitments, President Clinton asked which I recommended. When I told them I supported the high option, somebody said to the president that it "could hurt your ability to get a second term." At that point George said, "Mr. President, I think Gene feels if you accomplished all of your investment commitments at the high level, you wouldn't need a second term." That was a source of laughter.

There is also no question that my most proud battle in that first 1993 budget process was keeping our campaign commitment on pretty much doubling the Earned Income Tax Credit [EITC]. It was hard for me because it meant arguing with our Secretary of Treasury Lloyd Bentsen, who wanted to increase the EITC but just believed the campaign commitment had to be shaved back like everything else. He was not only the most senior member of the economic team, but when I was a young staffer on the Dukakis campaign he was our vice presidential nominee!

I argued that we couldn't cut back on it without backing down on President Clinton's commitment that no parent working full-time would have to raise their child in poverty. Before each meeting, I would spend hours on the phone with Bob Greenstein, the head of the Center for Budget and Policy Priorities, getting all the ammunition I needed to help make my case. After one NEC meeting in the Roosevelt Room where I had argued with Secretary Bentsen quite a bit, I did fear I might have gone too far. But then just before he went back into the Oval Office, President Clinton pulled me aside and said, "You did good. Stay at it!"—hitting me slightly in the chest. Then the lightbulb went off. He preferred that I just win the argument at the table as opposed to him having to overrule his secretary of treasury in his first two weeks. Clinton eventually made the right call. Getting that full EITC increase has probably meant over $250 billion to working poor families since 1993. It might have been my first few weeks, but I will always think it was one of the most important things I was ever involved in.

I will say a few overall things about the 1993 deficit bill. First, while I agree with those who stress that fiscal discipline is often overemphasized and that it always depends on competing priorities and the specific economic context, in the specific case of 1993, it did truly matter. The economists on our team had argued that if Clinton could credibly change the expectation of deficits spiraling up and up, long-term interest rates could drop right away, and that could fuel a lot of additional investment that was at that time being put on hold. Al Gore later said it was the rare case of the "law of intended consequences."

Second, the 1993 budget showed people—and other nations—that deficit reduction did not have to be mindless austerity. Yes, we raised taxes on the top 2 percent and corporations, and yes we did cut back spending where we could, but in that same budget we also increased the EITC, Head Start, WIC [Special Supplemental Nutrition Program for Women, Infants, and Children], training; created the direct student loan program; and expanded countless progressive investments.

Third, the experience in the late 1990s was powerful evidence of the power of tight labor markets and why we should support full employment policies. That amazing several-year stretch of 4 percent growth and 4 percent unemployment truly fueled shared growth. There are few economic things as beautiful as a truly tight labor force that raises wages and that forces employers to really give a chance to workers and communities on the economic fringe. We saw those benefits in the final six years of the Clinton administration, when family income went up significantly across the board—about 20 percent in real terms on average—and even more for African American families. In fact, percentagewise, family income went up even more for the bottom 20 percent than for the top 20 percent and about the same as the top 5 percent.

Bowmaker: Describe what happened from the Democrats' loss in the 1994 midterm elections through to the government shutdown.

Sperling: Election night 1994 was just devastating. Until the election of Donald Trump, it was the single most devastating night of my public service career. We had worked so hard, passed a major budget agreement, and doubled the EITC—and we had big plans to push for things like a well-funded universal training program. Suddenly, you are facing an all-Republican Congress trying to education block grant Medicaid and food stamps; cut and partially privatize Medicare and, no doubt, Social Security—and you are wondering whether you will be sitting in the White House as the Republicans repeal the Great Society. It was a tough time.

When the House Budget Committee under John Kasich put out their budget, it was exactly as we imagined: extremely deep cuts to Medicare, Medicaid, education, and the environment. The strategy that most of us suggested, as well as the Democratic leadership of Dick Gephardt and Tom Daschle, was to spend the entire summer highlighting the harm of their budget before we put forward our own alternative. But President Clinton had a different instinct. It was essentially his version of Tim Geithner's later line, "Plan beats no plan." President Clinton felt that we needed to show that we also had a plan and that our plan was the kinder, gentler plan. While theirs would balance the budget in five years with deep harmful cuts, ours would happen over ten years, but it would preserve education, environment, Medicare, and Medicaid.

And while the economic team was pretty unified, there was serious division amongst his senior political advisers. At one point, Dick Morris pushed Clinton to take a deal where we would win on Medicare, but we would let them deeply cut and block-grant Medicaid. Most of us were horrified by this idea and found the idea of block-granting Medicaid and food stamps the type of thing that would even make some of us ponder resignation. Fortunately, President Clinton completely rejected that idea. He believed deeply in Medicaid. As a son of a nurse in rural Arkansas, it was also personal to him. He strongly believed that once Medicaid was no longer a guarantee, the most low-income people would lose out in every state legislature.

As the drama played out, we started getting closer and closer to a potential budget shutdown. On the day that the CR—the continuing resolution—was going to run out, the Republican leadership was still insisting on sweeping cuts to Medicaid, Medicare, and food stamps—and the president had decided that the negotiations were over and the government was likely to shut down. Hours before that was going to happen, Leon Panetta, our chief of staff, called George Stephanopoulos and me to the office and said we were going to meet with the Republicans at 9:00 o'clock that night. George questioned whether that was going to be jamming President Clinton—putting him in an impossible situation. Leon Panetta said, "Look, my parents came here as immigrants. I think the idea of the government shutting down is terrible, and if anyone's willing to meet at any time to help prevent it, I'm going to take that offer." I remember we felt appropriately chastised and left the office.

That was an historic meeting in many ways. You could see the changing of the guard to a much more conservative Republican party. It started with conciliatory comments from Bob Dole and Leon Panetta. Dole said at one point, "Look, Leon, you and I have had difficult fights. We fight hard. But at the end of the day we put the public first. And this is the time for all of us to put our cards on the table and try to work things out." At that moment, Dick Armey pointed at Bob Dole, the Senate majority leader, and said, "That man does not speak for the House of Representatives." I had never at that point seen a meeting where one congressional leader was so disrespectful to another, and to Bob Dole of all people.

Then Dick Armey started to complain to President Clinton about our advertisements on Medicaid, saying that they were scaring a female relative of his into thinking that her nursing home coverage might be at risk. That led to a fairly powerful exchange back and forth between Armey and Clinton, which ended with Clinton saying, "I'm never going to accept your Medicaid policy. I'm never going to accept your budget. I don't care if it all comes down around me. I don't care if I fall to 5 percent in the polls." And then he points to Dole and says, "You're going to have to put someone else in this chair if you ever want to get your budget passed."

That was Bill Clinton's finest moment. It was the closest thing to a scene out of a movie. He was willing to risk it all and shut down the government to stand up for Medicaid and poor and working people. [Newt] Gingrich was so sure that Clinton would cave that he had no plan B. While we truly did not know if the public would side with us or take a "pox on both your houses" approach, we eventually prevailed policywise and politically. Clinton had gone from the guy schlacked in the midterms to the president who stood up for working families everywhere. Looking back, there is no question the budget shutdown was the pivotal moment in putting him back on path to reelection and a second term.

Bowmaker: How were you appointed director of the National Economic Council?

Sperling: As we were approaching the election, Laura Tyson decided that for family reasons she wanted to go back to California. Ironically, like I am now, she was married to a TV writer and was not helping her spouse's career by being in D.C. It was a new experience, seeing your job prospects debated on the front page of the *New York Times* and even reading anonymous people taking shots at you, especially because I was still only thirty-seven years old at the time. Then I was told by some of my friends in the White House that the transition team was going to recommend that I be promoted to a senior role with an office even closer to the president, but that they go with a senior business CEO [chief executive officer] type for the new NEC director.

Luckily for me, both Clinton and Gore overruled that. Friends told me that Gore said I had gotten up to bat a hundred times and gotten a hundred hits, and that Clinton had agreed. So I was confidentially told that I was now the presumptive choice—but it was a long wait until December 12, 1996, when I was told that I would be announced as NEC director the next day, at the same time as secretary of commerce and United Nations ambassador would be announced. My parents flew in and watched from the first row. And I think my dad was further moved when we walked back to my office and the first call congratulating me was from Senator Ted Kennedy.

I had been made very aware that what makes you a great deputy does not always translate as well to the top job. My reputation was working eighteen hours a day, being very productive—but also looking like I'd never slept and carrying around large notebooks wherever I went. So not being a dummy, I got a good haircut, I got new suits, and for those few weeks I was absolutely trying to be on my best behavior, thinking that nobody really noticed. Well, on the day of my appointment, they were going over Q&A [questions and answers] with President Clinton, and I had the awkward situation of being in the room when he was asked to practice Q&A about me. [White House Press Secretary] Mike McCurry, pretending to be a reporter, said, "Mr. President, you've chosen Gene Sperling as your National Economic Council director. He's only thirty-seven years old. Is he really mature enough for this job?" President Clinton, right in front of me, said, "Since Gene Sperling has been up for this job, his suits have never been better pressed, his hair has never been shorter, his ties have never been nicer, and he's never been more punctual. So I want to pick him for this job so as to continue his personal self-improvement." The place just broke up [*laughs*].

And it was my realization that, yes, all the little things I was doing when I was up for this job had indeed been noticed by the big guy.

Bowmaker: You were one of the negotiators of the 1997 bipartisan Balanced Budget Act. Can you describe the various roadblocks that you encountered and how you overcame them?

Sperling: When we start in '97, President Clinton's got a largely new team. Erskine Bowles is now his chief of staff, Frank Raines is now his budget director, I'm the NEC director, and Rahm Emanuel has replaced George Stephanopoulos as the strategist. President Clinton makes clear to us that he was not content to just have outdueled the Republicans on the budget shutdown. He wanted to actually now get a budget agreement on his terms with the strength and momentum of his reelection. John Hilley—the White House legislative director, who had strong relations on both sides of the aisle—realized that our best shot at starting a serious budget negotiation was with the Republican Budget Committee chairs, John Kasich in the House and Pete Domenici in the Senate.

One thing that confuses people sometimes is there were two rounds of budget negotiations. The first part was negotiating a very detailed agreement, and then the second part was actually turning that detailed agreement into legislation and passing it. I was one of the three lead negotiators for the initial agreement, along with Raines and Hilley. Kasich and Domenici represented the Republicans, and for most of the meetings, Congressman John Spratt and Senator Frank Lautenberg represented congressional Democrats. Two other people who were critical every step of the way were Domenici's top budget guy, Bill Hoagland, and Jack Lew, who was deputy OMB director and would later become OMB director. They were in every meeting.

This was before the age of Twitter and Facebook, and Senator Domenici would almost always host these meetings in his hideaways. Usually, the reporters could not find out where we were. But often at 2:00 or 3:00 in the morning you would leave and see a few reporters waiting for us when the meetings ended.

We had all agreed to two principles. One, we were aiming for a majority of each party. That was really important. In other words, this was not a negotiation where we were trying to get all Democrats and just a few Republicans, or all Republicans and a few Democrats. Our goal was that we were going to try to get a majority of each party. And so both sides had to respect that you were trying to get an agreement that everyone could live with. Second, nothing was agreed to until everything was agreed to. So even if you made a concession on a particular issue, it didn't mean that was agreed to until everything was agreed to. If there was a third principle, it was that everything stayed in the room. When the next day goes by, or the next day goes by, and something still hasn't leaked in the press, then people start to trust each other and believe this is a real negotiation.

For me, one of the most interesting parts was my relationship with John Kasich. In the first term, he was Darth Vader to me. We would debate each other on CNN's *Crossfire*, and I considered him my nemesis. But during the negotiations we developed a personal relationship of trust. There was one day when I brought in an article on a very harsh impact of a restriction on immigrants that Republicans had insisted on being part of the welfare reform package that had passed in 1996 that we wanted to repeal. I was sure Kasich would say, "Who cares about this newspaper article?" Instead, he looked at it and said, "That's horrible. We never intended that. If that's happening, we'll get rid of it." He would then start saying to me, "You have to be honest with me. You have to let me know when you are sure something is important for poor and working people, and when it is just something you have to fight for your Democratic politics."

That was an important experience for me. I would have never believed that with our fundamentally different economic philosophies, we could gain that level of trust or even find areas to agree. Two or three years later, he came to me and said he wanted to help us in our work to pass debt relief for poor countries. This again was shocking from a guy who had just years before asked for a 20 percent cut of the entire foreign assistance budget. Yet the two of us ended up organizing a final White House meeting with President Clinton, Bono, and a combination of very conservative and very liberal members of Congress that helped get the final agreement on debt relief for poor nations through.

Bowmaker: Once the overall agreement was done, what were your biggest personal battles for passing the final legislation?

Sperling: The two issues that were most critical to me in this second stage were ensuring families on the EITC benefited from the new child tax credit and the size of the CHIP—the Children's Health Insurance Program.

Our plan for the $500 child tax credit was to make sure it helped millions of families on the EITC, even if the child tax credit was only refundable for families with three or more children. So how did we do it? Not to be too nerdy, but it involved how you stack tax credits. Let me explain. By applying the child tax credit first, it would lead to far bigger EITC refundable payments for millions of families. Many people do not realize that this was essentially a second major Clinton EITC increase. Unfortunately for us, Gingrich and other Republicans did realize this and started accusing us of just increasing welfare, while a top conservative paper called recipients "lucky duckies." We fought back both publicly and in the budget negotiations, including by showing them all the rookie cops and fire officials who were on the EITC and were not pleased to hear themselves being described as being on welfare.

Sure enough, as we were near completing the legislation, Erskine Bowles brought me into his meeting with Gingrich and Senate Majority Leader Trent Lott to hear what Gingrich was describing as an EITC compromise. When I said it would cut benefits for over eight million families and that we could not accept it, Gingrich got very angry and essentially said he was done. I can still remember driving home with Erskine and John Hilley wondering if I had just blown up six months of work. It was awfully quiet. Erskine said, "You know I am gonna stand by you, but are you sure you are right?" I said, "I am." Erskine to his credit got the negotiations back on track, and we never ended up cutting our EITC proposal a penny.

The second thing that was so important was the creation of the Children's Health Insurance Program, or CHIP. After health care went down, we all worked on a letter that President Clinton sent to Congress saying that he still wanted to make progress on universal health care but would do so in steps as opposed to one swoop—a so-called incremental strategy. As the '97 budget agreement was really the single chance to move the ball forward on health care, we put two ideas into our budget. One was to help millions afford their health care when they lost a job, and the second was CHIP. Our health care guru, Chris Jennings, and I realized that while the two proposals were both important, the two people who wielded the most influence in this space—Hillary Clinton and Ted Kennedy—were far, far more passionate about children's health care. So we wisely consolidated the two proposals in the budget negotiation so our only health initiative in the budget negotiation was CHIP.

While we also got the Hope Scholarship Tax Credit and Lifelong Learning Tax Credit and increased education funding, CHIP was our signature accomplishment. When we finally got bills through both houses, we had gotten $24 billion for CHIP in the Senate and $16 billion in the House. So we all met in the chief of staff's office, and Hilley explained to everyone that the normal course was to split the difference whenever you can.

One thing I have learned: a lot of the most valuable things you ever do involve speaking up and being prepared at a critical budget decision. So when we got to health care, I pressed, "This is our top priority. Why don't we ask for the full $24 billion instead of splitting the difference at $20 billion?" At that point, Erskine Bowles said he thought he could get that done, but looking at me and then around the table, he said that to get it, "I will have to give them a couple of things that would make you puke. So I'll do it, but I don't want anybody to come back and be mad about what I had to give." I said fine with me, and no one objected. We got the full $24 billion, which helped a lot of lives—and the $24 billion was met with such strong approval from Democrats who saw us going the extra mile for this, especially those like Kennedy, [Jay] Rockefeller, and Henry Waxman who had worked so hard on the legislative details.

Bowmaker: What did you learn from your time as NEC director during the Clinton administration that helped you when you subsequently joined the Obama administration?

Sperling: I'd say the basic lesson is that good process is about creating trust. There's a difference between tedious bureaucratic process that can be clunky and hurt productivity and process that is about ensuring that each person believes that their views are being fairly considered and fairly represented. From his experience in the Carter administration, Stu Eizenstat told me that a person could have advocated for an issue for twenty years and seen the president go against them but be loyal if they had felt that they had had a fair chance to represent their views. But he had also seen people who felt they were cut out of a critical meeting on a completely insignificant issue and were still bitter about it twenty years later. I think that's right. How good members of an economic team can feel about accepting and standing behind a decision they might disagree with is directly affected by how much they felt the process was a fair one and not tilted in advance.

At the Treasury and the NEC during the Obama Administration

Bowmaker: From 2009 to 2011, you served as a counselor to Treasury Secretary Timothy Geithner during the Obama administration. How did you come to be appointed to this role?

Sperling: I was a big fan of Barack Obama pretty early on. We met at the convention in 2004, and later two people I knew, Mike Froman and Karen Kornbluh, had both arranged for me to be part of policy brainstorming with him after he was elected senator. I got to know him best when he told me he had read my book and asked if I would read drafts and comment on the economic chapter of his book *The Audacity of Hope*, which I did. Here he was, this first-term senator, and on the nights where he is in D.C. away from his kids, he is writing his own book in his own hand. It was so impressive.

But when he decided to run for president, I had to stay with my first loyalty, which was to Bill and Hillary Clinton. I was pretty much Hillary Clinton's top outside economic adviser in the 2008 campaign and thus was on the other side from Obama during the entire primary campaign. So while I tried to help out candidate Obama's economic team in every way possible during the general election and was in one major financial crisis meeting with him in October, I was not on his original team, like Austan Goolsbee.

Pretty early on, John Podesta, who was head of the transition, asked to meet with me and said, "I've got good news and I've got bad news. The good news is that you are definitely on the short list for both NEC director and OMB director. The bad news is I don't think you're going to get either." He just felt that due to the financial crisis, Obama was likely to need Summers and Geithner for their financial crisis expertise, and with them and Rahm [Emanuel] as chief of staff, that picking another Clinton guy was going to be low priority for Obama. He was very direct. That's what great friends do—they're willing to give you bad news as well as good news.

I then found myself in a bit of the odd situation as being kind of a confidante of both Larry Summers and Tim Geithner, as they were being considered for secretary of treasury. I think Larry first mentioned the idea that while it would be a demotion from my role in the Clinton administration, whoever was secretary of treasury would likely be so focused on the financial crisis that I might play an important role representing Treasury in the NEC process. When Tim got the job, he essentially made that same calculation. He said he wanted me to serve two roles for him. One was to be around the table for major financial crisis decisions, as he would be relying on many people who had little Washington policy experience. Two, that as he had "not spent his life on the domestic economic side" and that he and whoever he chose as deputy secretary of treasury would be absorbed in financial crisis rescue, I could play a lead role representing him on budget, tax, health care, and job issues. And he assured me on those issues, I would be his "plus one"—meaning the person he took with him on those issues for meetings with the president.

Many Washington insider types told me I should not take the job—that it looked weak or even desperate to take a Washington job that is lower ranking than the one you held in a previous administration. My father—who was the wisest man I ever knew—just scoffed at that: "You don't go into public service to be part of a career pecking order. You go in to serve your country. And this is a time of crisis." The fact that it was not as high level or high profile of a job made it all the more a public service. I knew my dad was right in a nanosecond. How could someone like me who cares about economic policy and their country regret being at the secretary of treasury's side and in the room with the president during the worst financial crisis since the Great Depression?

Bowmaker: You served in this role during the peak of the financial crisis. How would you describe that experience—particularly the first few months?

Sperling: I thought it was among the six hardest months of my professional career. One, the stakes were so high. There was nobody at a senior role at Treasury who was not acutely aware that wrong moves could exacerbate the crisis or even lead to a potential depression. And you are moving at the speed of light. In normal policymaking, the timing for between the policy development of an idea, its announcement at the State of the Union [message], its passage, and its being actually implemented is rarely less than twelve to eighteen months.

In the middle of the financial crisis, we were forced to develop high-stakes ideas and implement them in a matter of weeks or a couple of months. And we were doing so at the Department of Treasury with unbelievable demands, and while we were dramatically understaffed. I really believe that during those first six to eight months at Treasury, there was five to ten times more high-stakes demand than a typical presidential year.

I remember one time the president said to me when we were waiting for a meeting to start in the Oval Office late on a weekday night in the middle of the financial crisis, "You did this for eight years before. Is it always like this?" I said, "Well, Mr. President, it's like when people used to ask me whether the TV show *The West Wing* was realistic, and I'd tell them it's pretty realistic—except that they condense what normally happens over ten months into a single hour. That's what your presidency feels like right now." And it did.

One thing that crystallized in my mind during the first six months is that almost any hard issue in life is not that hard to solve if you can relax just one—just one—constraint. So many of the people who weighed in with interesting ideas or criticism from both the left and right would indeed relax or skip over one, two, or three immovable constraints. But we did not have that luxury. When you are in those positions, you are forced like no one else to absorb and digest which constraint cannot be relaxed.

For example, there were many ideas about nationalizing a bank or creating a good bank–bad bank scenario that might have been viable ideas if you had hundreds and hundreds and hundreds of billions of additional dollars to backstop the rest of the system against a dangerous run that could bring us to a depression. But as Rahm Emanuel told the economic team in that well-known seven-hour meeting with the president, the chances of being able to go back to Congress to ask for another $800 billion of TARP [Troubled Asset Relief Program] funding were somewhere between zero and zero. And so we had to play the hand we were dealt.

The other difference when you are actually governing is that you are forced to digest catastrophic risk. An innovative idea during the financial crisis can make a great op-ed if it has a 70 percent chance of being effective. But if that means a 30 percent chance of leading to a global depression or even a systemic event, that's a pretty high risk. If I told somebody I've got an amazing new lighting system for your house, but there's only a 15 percent chance it will burn it down, few people would take that option. Secretary Geithner, President Obama, and the rest of us had to also weigh not only what was the most optimal choice in terms of effectiveness, but also reducing even small risks of economic calamity.

Bowmaker: In the past, you have described the auto bailout decision as both a high point processwise and policywise and a great presidential moment. Can you elaborate?

Sperling: While it was never my primary job or role, I was involved in the auto bailout issue from the very beginning. A close friend, Joshua Steiner, was leading a lot of the transition efforts on the auto crisis, and Brian Deese, who had worked for me for many years and is the example of the protégé who will end up being my boss someday, was chosen to be the all-important third wheel on the auto team leadership under Steve Rattner and Ron Bloom. And finally I was, even at that point, probably the highest-ranking member of the economic team from Michigan, and thus was the source of innumerable calls and pleading from Governor [Jennifer] Granholm and the various senators and congressmen from Michigan on the auto issue. So I feel like I was thrust in the middle of it right from the beginning.

Brian told me after his first several weeks that he thought it was very unlikely that six, seven months from now, there would still be a Big Three. While he thought maybe GM [General Motors] could be saved, Chrysler was unlikely to make it unless we could miraculously find someone to merge with them. When that did happen—when Fiat stepped into the picture—we eventually had to make a decision. Were we going to support taking Chrysler through a bankruptcy with the commitment and support of the federal government to bring them out on the other side?

There emerged a bit of an economic rump group that looked very closely at this issue and was divided. One side, which was largely made up of several of the top economists, felt that if Chrysler went under, it would actually lead to a stronger GM and Ford. Others of us—particularly Ron Bloom, myself, and Brian Deese—argued adamantly that we had miraculously found this partner in Fiat to merge with and that it would be crazy not to make all efforts to save the company. Steve Ratner thought it was virtually a toss-up, and Larry Summers was playing an excellent NEC director role of pressing all sides with the hardest questions and analysis.

One morning, there was what was called the economic daily briefing, and apparently at that meeting the auto issue came up, and some people felt that they shouldn't be having any conversation without having all the players at the table. And so that Friday afternoon we had a meeting in the Roosevelt Room in which all of us who were part of this rump group were seated on the opposite side from President Obama, who had David Axelrod [senior adviser to the president] and Robert Gibbs [White House press secretary] sitting next to him. And he essentially asked for each person's opinion. Ron Bloom, Brian Deese, and I had decided in advance to divide up what each of us were going to say. Bloom made the larger overall case for why he believed a bailout would work and why he believed Chrysler could prevail. I made the argument that whatever the traditional economic analysis of market share going to other companies might be, in this case there was a high risk of a type of manufacturing Lehman Brothers event, where things might spiral down out of control from company to main supplier to small suppliers in ways that could be more devastating than any of us could imagine. After all, there was no precedent for such a decision when you were dealing with unemployment rates that were as high as 25 percent in some of these counties. And Brian presented the argument that when you counted the extra cost in government unemployment and SNAP [Supplemental Nutrition Assistance Program] and other things, it made it even more cost-effective to take the risk on the bailout. Axelrod and Gibbs explained that saving Chrysler was politically unpopular, even though I was sure they were for it. The president listened to everyone and said he wanted to take it under advisement and think about it. Later that evening, we got the word that he wanted to go forward.

That weekend, Rattner, Deese, Summers, and myself huddled with the president in the Oval [Office] as he called each of the governors of the main auto states and the members of Congress from those states to tell them what his decision was. One thing I really admired very much about President Obama was that he did not try to put any easier spin on things than existed. At one point in the call to the Michigan delegation, [Senator] Sandy Levin said, "Mr. President, we're so supportive of what you're doing. Just one thing: you keep saying the word 'bankruptcy,' and I just am worried that if you actually say that word publicly, that you will scare people and cause a panic." You might have expected that a president would say, "Oh, don't worry, I won't use that word." Instead, President Obama said, "You know, Sandy, what I want to do is be honest and direct. I'm going to tell them there are two different types of bankruptcy—one where you're trying to dissolve a company, and there's another where you're trying to strengthen and bring it back, and that this is the latter." And that is exactly what he did and said. I really think the entire episode saved the auto industry, saved a lot of American manufacturing, and was one of the best and bravest economic decisions President Obama made.

Bowmaker: You were the lead person at the Treasury working on the passage of the Affordable Care Act [ACA]. What is your response to those who argue that President Obama should not have pursued the ACA and instead should have focused on rebuilding the economy?

Sperling: I could not disagree more with any assertion that President Obama should not have focused on the Affordable Care Act. First, there are few things so deficient in the economic security framework of our country than the fact that tens of millions went without health care, and over a hundred million went to bed every night knowing that they were one pink slip and one illness away from economic devastation. So I think if you look at the economy as how it affects the lives and economic dignity of real people, there was nothing more important than this effort to provide economic security to all Americans.

Second, it's just not true that it distracted us from more economic stimulus. The Obama economic team was always for creating more economic demand. The problem was that so soon after the Recovery Act [the American Recovery and Reinvestment Act of 2009] and with the huge-sounding amounts of guarantees in the financial rescue plans, there was simply not an appetite in Congress in 2010 for big new stimulus—no matter how hard we pushed. I remember testifying on our small business lending funds and being told by leading Democrats to make clear that they would be paid for, even though the cost was just $1 billion. A new half-trillion dollars for infrastructure or for teacher salaries was just not in the cards in 2010. From a moral, dignity, and economic basis, I will always feel President Obama made the right call on spending in 2010 on the ACA. Its protections for coverage, Medicaid expansion, and protections for preexisting conditions are to me one of the most important domestic economic policy achievements of the last fifty years.

Bowmaker: I know you were very involved in the lame duck budget negotiations after the Republicans won the House in 2010. How important was that, and what was your personal involvement?

Sperling: I think it was a case of making as much lemonade out of lemons as you could. Because they had won the House, they were insistent on not letting the high-income tax cuts be repealed. The issue for us was how much new stimulus and help to struggling workers could we get if we agreed to that. I was quite involved in a few ways.

One was that Vice President [Joe] Biden was put in charge by President Obama of much of the negotiations and selling a potential agreement to Democrats. He decided that he really wanted me and Jack Lew by his side when he was talking to the House Democratic Caucus and Senate

Democratic Caucus because of both of our long-term relationships with so many of the members.

Two, I played a big role in getting the payroll tax in the agreement. In the spirit of getting more stimulus, we had been arguing incessantly that the Republicans might have a hard time saying no to a payroll tax cut, because so many of them had proposed it in the past. When it became clear [Senator Mitch] McConnell would never agree to extend Obama's "Making Work Pay" tax credit, we had a plan B: Biden got him to agree we should at least get some form of payroll tax relief worth $60 billion a year for two years. When Biden, through his Chief of Staff Ron Klain, asked me and Jason Furman to go negotiate it with McConnell's team, I had come up with the idea that perhaps we could—instead of asking for $120 billion spread over two years—ask for the whole $120 billion payroll tax cut in 2011 alone. It was a risk, but my hope was that it would be too hard for them to say no to in 2012, and we would turn it into $240 billion stimulus in 2011–2012. Thank God that gamble paid off.

Finally, Furman, Brian Deese, and I had also worked hard to create the argument that if the well off were going to get their tax cut for two more years, then everybody should—so the Republicans had to agree to extend our improvements to the EITC and Refundable Child Tax Credit. We not only prevailed, we were to make them permanent after I left in 2015—something we are all really proud of.

The other thing I was most proud of then, and later in 2012, was fighting to secure emergency unemployment relief. I really think what we extracted in that negotiation did make a big difference for the stimulus and struggling families, even though it was of course tough to swallow what we had to give up to get it.

Bowmaker: In 2011, President Obama appointed you as director of the National Economic Council, and you took over from Larry Summers. How did that come about?

Sperling: In 2010, just when I was starting to ponder if it was time to leave, President Obama asked me to meet in the Oval Office one-on-one. That always gets your attention. He was so impressive in his candor and transparency. He started by saying he wanted me to first know that he gets it—that he understands that I was playing a bigger role than my title and that he appreciated my contributions in meetings. He told me he planned to make me part of his senior team for the last half of his first term, but that he did not know where yet, and so I should not go anywhere. Around that point, Larry Summers made clear that he was going to leave. And while I would have been honored to have a different type of senior role, for me, there was no job I felt I could contribute more at than returning to NEC director.

The president called me into his office right before the holiday break in December and essentially told me that he was now leaning toward having me replace Larry, who had announced months before that he was leaving as NEC director. He wanted to think about it over the holidays and to keep this to ourselves. It was a hard secret to keep. But about two days after we returned from the winter break, I got the call from him early one evening saying he liked my values, my contributions, and that I was his guy. That was about it. And then I drove home so I could tell my wife in person and then call my dad and mom. Even knowing how difficult it was going to be with such contentious divided government, I felt so blessed to have a chance to do it a second time.

Bowmaker: You ended up being at the table for much of the budget negotiations that surrounded the near default on the debt in the summer of 2011. What was that like?

Sperling: Well, the budget drama in 2011 came in different stages. Initially, we had a strategy for the president to define his terms and push the process early in 2011. But the appropriations process dragged on endlessly into April, which was a great frustration for President Obama as it delayed him speaking out on his larger vision for a budget deal. For me, I was holding NEC meetings to start forging consensus on the parameters for an initial presidential proposal, but it was harder with our OMB Director Jack Lew and our Legislative Director Rob Nabors tied up around the clock on the Hill. After the president finally put out both a serious proposal and a hard-hitting speech at George Washington University, we entered a negotiation stage that Vice President Biden hosted, with myself, Jack, Tim, and Rob also participating and with one of two designees from both the Democratic and Republican leadership in the House and Senate.

When that did not go far enough—that is, when President Obama and Speaker [John] Boehner started dealing with each other directly—we went through two periods where they claimed, incorrectly in my opinion, that we were moving the goalposts, while we felt they were inexplicably walking away from negotiations when progress was still being made.

As to the threat of default, it was both real and scary. We had met with Treasury for a long time on every conceivable option of what would have to be done if the unthinkable came to pass. Still, it seemed sickening and surreal to actually be in the Oval Office while Tim walked through the specific options that he might have to start within thirty-six hours. Fortunately, it never came to that. President Obama told us during this period in one Oval Office pre-brief[ing] before a Congressional negotiation that he wanted us to know that we were never going to do this again: that it was unacceptable that anyone could threaten the default of the nation over a budget issue, and that he felt he would be hurting the office of the presidency if he allowed that to happen again. And he stayed true to that pledge after that.

Almost immediately after the agreement preventing a debt default took place, he called me down to the Oval [Office] and told me he wanted me to drop virtually everything and start putting together a real plan—what we called the American Jobs Act—that would represent his vision. He told me "no self-editing" based on politics, that he wanted a plan that would reflect his values that he would personally sign off on piece by piece. One of the painful things I had to present at our first Roosevelt Room meeting with him and the strategic team was how much the forecast for the economy had weakened—starting with the impact of the Arab Spring, but also due to the default scare. We agreed that the plan we would put forward would have to be able to have independent validation that it would spark growth by an additional 2 percent and two million jobs. We worked tirelessly through August—even with vacations and everyone exhausted—but his speech before Congress announcing it ended up being one of his strongest economic statements. Some key elements of it were passed, but even the ones that failed became part of his stated vision going forward when he ran for reelection.

Bowmaker: Was it frustrating that during those next two or three years when you were NEC director, it was so hard to get as much passed through the Congress?

Sperling: Sure. It made it almost impossible to get the major domestic bills of the scale of the ACA through. But I think one of the things that I had learned my first go-round is that there is enormous capacity for the president to get things done without legislation. To name a few, we used existing funding and competitive applications to create and fund the first several

Manufacturing Innovation Hubs. We held an insourcing round table, helped launch SelectUSA and its big conference, and took on China on illegal auto-part zones. We started a ConnectEd initiative to get billions of more funds for broadband in all areas and created a major College Opportunity Summit that led over a hundred colleges to make new commitments to access. We led a special initiative to fund initiatives for the long-term unemployed and got hundreds of companies to end hiring practices that discriminated against them. We pushed in the right direction fiduciary rule regulations to prevent conflicts of interests, restrictions on predatory for-profits schools, and with my awesome deputy NEC director, Danielle Gray, we helped fight predatory for-profit rip-offs of veterans while moving toward better economic guidance and prep[aration] for those leaving the armed forces. Being from Michigan, one that was personal for me was that President Obama asked me to lead an effort to help Detroit after the bankruptcy. We ended up mobilizing $300 million of existing funds to help them and show Detroit they were not forgotten.

Bowmaker: How would you compare and contrast Presidents Clinton and Obama?

Sperling: Rahm would always say never answer that question: it is like being asked if you love Mom or Dad more. What they shared that I loved the most was their high intellects; that they cared so much about getting it right; and their desire to hear conflicting views, to press everyone to think harder, and to only make big calls when they felt they had done everything they could to make the right call. And while of course the White House is a political place, I saw them both take enormous political risk to make hard calls at tough times. Seriously, if you are a policy wonk like me, it doesn't get much better than working for those two.

Personal Reflections

Bowmaker: As a policymaker, which decisions or outcomes were most gratifying?

Sperling: I guess if I had to single one thing out it has been the efforts I was integrally involved in over two administrations to expand the EITC and other refundable tax credits to working poor families. These are people working so hard to raise their families with dignity. Before President

Clinton's budget in 1993, we devoted about $10 billion to the EITC. Now it is close to $70 billion. That is a half a trillion dollar difference a decade. And overall refundable tax credits are close to $100 billion a year now for hard-pressed families. A single parent with two kids making $17,000 today gets $7,000 more than they did in 1992. That is not good enough, but it is meaningful advancement to economic dignity for tens of millions of workers and their families. The fight in 1993 changed the political landscape on tax credits for working poor families and led to more and more effort by many, and that is very gratifying. So to be part of the fight in 1993 and 1995 and 1997 and then to be able to come back in 2009 and be part of further expanding these tax credits—including refundable portions of the American opportunity tax credit and child tax credit—in President Obama's term is really meaningful. Change does not often come in one blow: it can be working hard, handing off the baton, and then having it handed back to you and then handing it off again. I also think of the pain of losing the health care reform in 1994 but then being part of the budget team that negotiated the Children's Health Insurance Program in 1997 and then being the Treasury lead in working with the Obama team on the Affordable Care Act in 2010 is also gratifying—especially seeing the tremendous impact CHIP had in those years, and now seeing how the ACA that caused President Obama so much political pain and was almost repealed is now both appreciated and safe is something all of us in the Obama administration are really proud of.

But what I said when I left the White House in my final talk is that if you remember—if you visualize—the people you are impacting, you will feel just as motivated to fight when it is 10,000 as opposed to ten or thirty million people's economic lives and opportunities on the line. I always told my team that when I am in the White House, I think back to when I was a ball boy for the University of Michigan's basketball team, and I used to sweep the floors at halftime in Chrysler Arena. I would look up from there and see 14,000 people, which was just an unimaginable number of people from that perspective. So when people felt disappointed and discouraged that an initiative might in the end help only 70,000 children—instead of seven million or some larger number we were hoping for—I would just tell them to imagine all those seats filled with children, five times over, because you fought for them. It was my way of always remembering that while you of course shoot for the seven or seventy million, every life you can help in some way is huge to the person you have provided some security or opportunity to. Indeed, when it would seem like a tough or lonely struggle getting a couple more years of emergency unemployed insurance benefits during the budget fights in the Obama years, sometimes I would just think of even a single home—a single kitchen table—where a parent had to come home to his kitchen table with the fear of hunger or losing a home to motivate me to keep fighting. With all the noise and politics and positioning that goes on, I think you have to force yourself to always keep that focus.

Bowmaker: On the other hand, there must be some things that, in hindsight, you'd like the opportunity to do differently. What are they?

Sperling: Well, the stadium example works both ways. You also agonize about those who did not get the help—or were even hurt—by a missed opportunity or poor political strategy or not seeing a new trend. Sometimes decisions seem right at the time with the knowledge you had, but in hindsight, with new information, you realize it was more complicated or that you didn't see how a future administration might neglect something you fought for or turn it on its head. Going back to the beginning of our interview, that is why when you are in these positions you have to feel the agony of the uncertainty and the human stakes involved: you have to feel that to make sure you are truly driven to look down every corner, check every bias, weigh and test every option, consider every risk so that you can feel that you made the best decision—or presented the best options with the information you had at the time.

The other thing that is always hard is the things you did not do because you and your staff are overwhelmed and overworked and because there are only so many things you can fit on a president's agenda. Sometimes when you pull something out of a hat—like passing the New Markets Tax Credit in 2000 or getting the extra $300 million for Detroit after their bankruptcy in 2013—you look back and feel torn. On the one hand, you look back and worry you pushed your team too hard, and yet on the other hand, you know that without that exceptional effort it likely would have not gotten done. Other times, you look at issues—I have been thinking recently of how little is done for families with children with autism—and wonder, is there anything I could have done if we had tried to focus more on that issue? Back in the late 1990s, when I would run into National Security Adviser Sandy Berger late at night in the West Wing, we would discuss this unsolvable dilemma: the realization of the human limits to what you and your teams can take on, and at the same time the knowledge that for every day you have in a high White House position, you will have so many more days after you leave to ask yourself if there is anything else you could have done to help people while you were there.

Robert Rubin (*standing*), when secretary of the treasury, in a meeting with President Bill Clinton and fast-track advisers in the Oval Office on July 24, 1997.

14 Robert E. Rubin
Born 1938, New York City

Robert Rubin graduated with an AB in economics from Harvard College in 1960 and then studied at the London School of Economics before obtaining a LLB from Yale Law School in 1964.

Rubin practiced law with Cleary, Gottlieb, Steen and Hamilton from 1964 to 1966. He worked as an associate and then a partner with Goldman Sachs and Co. from 1966 to 1992, serving as vice chairman and co-chief operating officer from 1987 to 1990 and as co-senior partner and cochairman from 1990 to 1992.

Rubin was a senior economic adviser to Governor Bill Clinton during his 1992 run for the presidency and played a key role on Clinton's transition team following his election. Rubin was appointed the first director of the National Economic Council (NEC) in 1993 and then served as treasury secretary from January 1995 through July 1999.

After leaving the Clinton administration, Rubin served as senior adviser of Citigroup and then as cochairman of the Council on Foreign Relations.

I interviewed Robert Rubin in his office at Centerview Partners—where he currently serves as a counselor—in New York City. It was the middle of the morning on Thursday, October 11, 2012.

Background Information

Bowmaker: As an undergraduate at Harvard, you majored in economics and found it difficult but engrossing. Could you tell me more about that?

Rubin: When I majored in economics, the subject was much more conceptual than it is today. I found it complex and, as a consequence, intellectually challenging. On the other hand, it was very interesting because it gave you a better sense of how the world worked. I am quite sure that if I had been a student after economics had become swamped with econometrics and heavily based on mathematics, I wouldn't have majored in the subject because you were left with the proposition of learning about models that had little relationship with reality.

Entering the Policy World

Bowmaker: You were appointed to your first major economic policy position in 1993 as director of the National Economic Council. Why were you interested in going to Washington?

Rubin: I had wanted to go to Washington for as long as I could remember, even from my days at Harvard and most certainly in the relatively early stages of my private-sector career, when I became much more conversant with policy. There were certain issues that I cared a great deal about. I felt then, as I do now, that if you are going to have an economy that is successful and a policy regime that works, it has to be grounded on a sound fiscal base. For a variety of reasons, I also got very involved in inner-city issues in a practical way, and I thought it was clearly the case that the most effective way to address those issues was from inside the government.

Bowmaker: As you entered the policy world, was there anything that surprised or frustrated you?

Rubin: Frustrated? No. But that's only because I knew a lot about how government worked. I think if I had come into it from a typical business background, which is what often happens, I would have been enormously frustrated. One reason why so many business people who go into government don't work out is because they are accustomed to systems in which they can make decisions that are implemented in a relatively linear way.

Surprised? Two things. One is that there are extraordinarily good people in government. In fact, it was the most able group of individuals with whom I have ever worked. Two is that while I knew a certain amount about the issues, I didn't realize how much I didn't know. For example, when I first came into the White House, I was astonished about how much there was to know about the federal budget, even in a fairly fundamental way, which does suggest that there is a very real problem in terms of effectively communicating policies in the public domain or, for that matter, in the business community. But I think one of the keys to being effective as you enter the policy world is to know what you don't know. So I had an immensely steep learning curve in all of the six and a half years that I was there, and that was something I liked about being in government.

As Director of the National Economic Council

Bowmaker: Did President Clinton make it clear what he expected you to do for him as director of the NEC?

Rubin: Clinton made it absolutely clear. The reason that the NEC worked is that he expected economic policy to be coordinated through the organization. When he had an issue that he wanted to raise, he wouldn't go to the Cabinet member who was responsible for that area. Instead, he would come to me, the NEC director. And then I would organize a process involving that Cabinet member and whoever else should be at the table, which included an inner core of staff at the NEC. He never actually had to say this, but Clinton expected that I would play the role of neutral broker, which I was.

Bowmaker: How did you balance being the neutral manager of a process and at the same time a substantive participant while at the NEC?

Rubin: I didn't find it very difficult. I had been at an investment banking firm for twenty-six years. In investment banking, you deal constantly with clients, and you don't give them orders. So when I arrived at the NEC, my view was that every Cabinet member and senior staff member at the White House was a client. What I had to do was run the new operation in a way that the clients felt they were better off with it than without it. Once people trusted the process, because it was very neutral, then within that context I felt it was entirely appropriate to express my own views. But very often when I went to the president, I would ask a Cabinet member who had a different view than I did to come along. That's not always the case with an NEC director.

Bowmaker: Did you get the impression that the Council of Economic Advisers [CEA] felt undermined by the creation of the NEC?

Rubin: Initially I think they were troubled by it, which was understandable. But [Chair of the CEA] Laura Tyson and I talked about it. And what actually happened—and I did tell Laura about this very early on—was that the CEA had a more important role because of us. If you look at other administrations, there were quite a few instances where the CEA became rather marginalized. But in our case, they were a core member of the NEC and therefore at the table for every important issue.

Bowmaker: How did you go about establishing a comfortable working relationship with the president?

Rubin: I didn't really know President Clinton very well before the NEC started. I remember somebody telling me at the very beginning that he was very smart, and so you have to be serious and thoughtful when you deal with him. If you are, then your relationship with him can work. If you aren't, there are going to be problems. I don't know whether I was thoughtful, but I was certainly serious. Whatever the reasons, we developed a terrific working relationship.

I would also add that I always told Clinton what I thought. If I disagreed with him, I always made my points clear, which he expected. I would do it diplomatically, of course, because he was the president of the United States.

Bowmaker: Was your economic philosophy in alignment with President Clinton's?

Rubin: Yes. Going back to your previous question, I think this is one of the reasons why our relationship worked so well. Now, there were individual issues on which I had a different opinion. For example, I did not feel that we should have done welfare reform. It's true that I told the president that it was an extremely difficult balance of judgment, but I was just afraid that too many people would fall through the cracks, so we needed a bill to protect against that outcome.

Bowmaker: How much economics do you think Bill Clinton knew before he became president?

Rubin: I think Clinton knew quite a lot of economics before he became president. In the many years before he arrived at the White House, he used to go to the Renaissance Weekend and engage in all sorts of activities that caused him to learn so much.[1] Having said that, I do think that once he became president and had to deal with economic issues of the United States, he greatly enhanced his understanding, but I'm not sure how much I contributed to that.

Bowmaker: Which aspects of the president's economic plan that you worked on reflected your ambitions for the Clinton administration?

---

1. Renaissance Weekend is an exclusive elite retreat for leaders in business and finance, government, the media, religion, medicine, science, technology, and the arts.

Rubin: The three pieces that were most important were those that President Clinton always emphasized. He said that given that he had inherited an unsustainable fiscal trajectory, we needed to reestablish sound fiscal conditions; he also said that we needed a strong program of public investment; and he was very focused on the globalization of the economy, being very supportive of trade, in particular—which is something that business people recognized, although not necessarily those within the political world.

Bowmaker: Which aspects of your knowledge about how Wall Street worked proved to be most useful at the NEC?

Rubin: The single most important value of my time on Wall Street, and something that is missing today among most euro-zone leaders, is the recognition of the psychology of markets, how they work, and an integration of that to framing public policy.

Bowmaker: When you left the NEC in 1995, did you feel that you had accomplished what you wanted in terms of making the organization work?

Rubin: Yes. I believed that we had really done what was needed, and I know that President Clinton thought so, too. But he did say internally that one of the reasons why the '94 election went so badly for us was because he had made a lot of very difficult decisions and the beneficial economic effects, which by that time were well under way, had not been felt yet by the American people. He was right.

As Secretary of the Treasury

Bowmaker: When you were appointed treasury secretary in 1995, did you have a sense of the type of secretary that you wanted to be based on your two years at the NEC and earlier experience on Wall Street?

Rubin: That's a very interesting question. I succeeded Lloyd Bentsen, who had been chairman of the [Senate] Finance Committee and a towering, almost intimidating, figure in Congress with tremendously important relationships in the Senate, in particular. I knew him well before I entered the Clinton administration, but when I thought about how I was going to do the job, I realized that I couldn't be him. I talked to Gene Sperling about the role, and he gave me very good, simple advice: "Look, just be yourself." And that's what I did. Initially people might have said that I wasn't someone with the same presence as Lloyd Bentsen, but you establish your own authority over time.

Bowmaker: When you began your position, how did you prioritize the issues that you faced?

Rubin: I had a tendency then, as I do now to my disadvantage, of not prioritizing very well. I like to do everything. My chief of staff, Sylvia Matthews, came to me one day and said, "What are your five most important issues?" I replied, "My five most important issues are the following twenty-five ..." [*laughs*]. She told me that wasn't a good way to respond, and I said, "No, it isn't, but that's me."

I guess my answer to your question would be that, as it worked out, the most important issues in no particular order were, one, to maintain a sound fiscal policy, which was a struggle throughout our entire administration; two, to continue to support public investment in a broad sense, which was also difficult because we had a Republican Congress that wasn't responsive to our efforts—we even set up a little office in the Treasury for the first time ever to tackle the problems of inner cities; and three, to deal with a hugely important set of issues that none of us ever anticipated having to face, which were financial crises abroad (the Mexican crisis in '95 and the Asian crisis starting in the middle of '97 going into '98 and through '99). But, of course, it was much more than just Asia—it was also Brazil and Russia.

Bowmaker: Which policy trade-offs were most challenging?

Rubin: All decisions are about probabilities and trade-offs. In the whole of the six and a half years that I was in government, the most difficult trade-off was the one between deficit reduction and public investment. All of us would have preferred to have had more public investment, but we inherited a very difficult fiscal situation.

Bowmaker: How did you successfully put policy before politics?

Rubin: President Clinton was often said to be wonkish, which was sometimes meant as a criticism, but I felt it was a great virtue because he cared enormously about policy. It is fair to say that on every important issue, the agenda was driven by the substance, not by the politics. First and foremost, it was a question of figuring out what you wanted to do from a policy perspective and only then recognizing what was politically doable or not. I can think of other presidents where the balance has been different, and Clinton certainly appeared to subscribe to Lloyd Bentsen's view that the best policy is the best politics over time.

Bowmaker: You worked closely with [Chairman of the Federal Reserve] Alan Greenspan and [Deputy Secretary of the Treasury] Larry Summers when you were treasury secretary. How did your approaches to economic policy, and economics more generally, complement each other?

Rubin: We were a terrific combination. For one thing, we trusted other each other. In all of the years that we were in Washington, there was not a single leak from any of our discussions, which was quite extraordinary. But I think our talents complemented each other in the following way: I brought my probabilistic approach to decision making, Larry had a very practical feel for both the economic and political issues, and Alan had a much better sense than Larry or I did of very specific data.

Bowmaker: What did you learn about the role of the media in economic policymaking?

Rubin: The media are critically important—that's how people understand about what the government is doing. That's as true now as it was then. And so as a policymaker, you have to learn how to interact with the media. Mack McLarty [President Clinton's chief of staff] told me, "Never say anything to the media that isn't true." Now, you don't have to say everything that you know, but his comment does mean that, A, anything that you do say must be true; and B, it must not be misleading because of what you don't know. That is a very difficult line to walk.

Bowmaker: When you retired as treasury secretary, [Undersecretary of the Treasury for International Affairs] Tim Geithner, along with two of his colleagues, assembled a list of ten principles that you brought to the Treasury.[2]

---

2. The principles were: "1. The only certainty in life is that nothing is ever certain; 2. Markets are good, but they are not the solution to all problems; 3. The credibility and the quality of a nation's policies matter more for its prospects than anything the United States, the G-7, or the international financial institutions can do; 4. Money is no substitute for strong policy, but there are times when it is more costly to provide too little money than to provide too much; 5. Borrowers must bear the consequences of the debts they incur—and creditors of the lending they provide; 6. The United States must be willing to be defined by what it is against, as well as what it is for; 7. The dollar is too important to be used as an instrument of trade policy; 8. Optionality is good in itself; 9. Never let your rhetoric commit you to something you cannot deliver; 10. Gimmicks are no substitute for serious analysis and care in decision making," Robert E. Rubin and Jacob Weisberg, *In an Uncertain World: Tough Choices from Wall Street to Washington* (New York: Random House, 2003), 251.

Which of the ten principles would you say best characterizes your overall approach to policymaking during your six years in Washington?

Rubin: The first principle: The only certainty in life is that nothing is ever certain. During my career at Goldman Sachs, I first had operational involvement in, and then oversight of, trading operations. The only way you can be successful in that world is to recognize that issues are about probabilities and that there are no certainties. That seems to be true of not only that arena, but also anything related to policy. When Larry and I went to see President Clinton in the Oval Office in January '95 and gave him the reasons for why we should provide support for Mexico during the country's peso crisis, we made it clear that this was the best probabilistically adjusted decision—the expected value, if you like. He understood that it might not work but agreed that we should do it.

Bowmaker: Did Tim Geithner as treasury secretary follow the fifth principle, that borrowers and lenders both must bear the consequences of their deals, in the aftermath of the Panic of 2008?

Rubin: Yes, I think Tim did. But he should have added the caveat that you need to also understand the possible contagion and systemic effects of your actions if you are a policymaker.

General Thoughts on Economic Policymaking

Bowmaker: Do you believe that if we were to raise the level of economic literacy in this country, economic policymaking would improve because the people would demand better policy?

Rubin: I think the level of economic literacy in this country is a terrible problem. I believe economics should be taught in a way that children can relate to in every school, because further down the road poor economic literacy can affect policymaking. For example, when President Clinton said in 1998 that we had a surplus, I told him that we should use it to pay down the debt, not to lower taxes as we were being urged to by the Republicans. And he replied, "It's nice that you have that opinion, but how am I going to do that politically? In a world where people don't know the difference between the debt and the deficit, I am supposed to persuade people to use the surplus for debt reduction instead of tax cuts?" In the end, we had to figure out a way to do that by saying that we would save Social Security first, because it had political traction.

There is also no understanding of trade. I once testified for a Ways and Means Committee hearing and talked about the importance of imports. The leading Republican on the committee said I was the first person who had ever mentioned this during a hearing.

And if we had an adequate level of economic literacy in this country, our political system couldn't have gotten away with the atrocious fiscal policy that we had for the eight years after the Clinton administration—the '01 tax cuts, the Iraq War that wasn't paid for, and Medicare Part D that also wasn't paid for. The idea that most of [President George W.] Bush's policies that affected the budget were deficit financed is not something that the American people seemed to understand, in my view.

Bowmaker: Which fallacies, misconceptions, or misinterpretations affect policy debate in this country?

Rubin: Among mainstream economists, there is almost no support for the propositions of supply-side economics with respect to tax increases. There are some notable exceptions. Marty Feldstein, who is one of the most thoughtful and outstanding economists in the United States, does support the supply-side perspective, but very, very few economists do, and I think it has had an immense effect on public policy.

Bowmaker: When I spoke with Paul Volcker, he expressed concern about the revolving door between Wall Street and Washington. Is there undue influence of industry in the halls of power?

Rubin: I've heard it said that Dick Cheney [George W. Bush's vice president] was very influenced in his thinking by the fact that he had come out of Halliburton in the oil industry, and that there wasn't any counterbalance in the way that the [George W.] Bush administration functioned. I have no idea whether that's true or not, but I certainly can't think of a single instance in the Clinton administration where somebody tried to influence public policy because of the private interest they used to have.

I also believe that for government to be effective, it is critical for people to bring their experiences from other areas. You have to understand the world. Those within the Clinton administration who had worked outside of government were good at recognizing that their views were shaped somewhat by their experiences and acknowledging that there were other perspectives. And so I would say the opposite of what Paul said.

In my view, the problem is when people enter government from businesses with hierarchical structures. Trying to bring that way of doing things to the policy world does not work.

Personal Reflections

Bowmaker: How did your personality affect your style and approach as a policymaker?

Rubin: I do think that in my case I had a recognition that nothing is certain. You may have a strongly held view, but it could be wrong, and so you need to listen to other people. That is very important for a policymaker to be effective.

Bowmaker: What were your strengths and weaknesses as a policymaker?

Rubin: Apart from a recognition of the probabilistic nature of decision making, I also had an awareness that you can have situations where all choices are bad, and so you have to take the least bad choice.

In terms of weaknesses, I will answer the question in a slightly different way. I am not a professional economist. On the other hand, I majored in economics as an undergraduate, and by the time I finished college I had a pretty good understanding of the concepts that framed the underpinning of the subject. And then my whole life at Goldman Sachs involved working with economists because it always interested me.

David Swensen, who is CIO [chief information officer] at Yale and a PhD economist, told me that if you are going to make judgments about economic policy or about economic issues for any reason, what you need to do is understand the concepts in such a way that you can play with them...you don't have to be a PhD economist. On the macro side of policy, there is an econometric business of building models, which sometimes can help inform decisions, but they are almost always far removed from reality. And so given that fact, it was extremely important and tremendously valuable to have professional economists with practical judgment like Larry Summers and David Lipton around when I was in government.

Bowmaker: As a policymaker, which decisions or outcomes were most gratifying?

Rubin: I will give you three answers. One was the restoration of a sound fiscal position for the United States government, for at least what I would call the intermediate term—the ten years in the budget window. None of us ever thought we'd wind up with a surplus, but I think we did feel that if policies worked in the way we hoped they would and contributed to growth, then that in turn would contribute to an improvement in the fiscal position. In other words, our theory was that they would feed each other. Two was the way the US government, which involved many people, responded to the global crises that could have had contagion effects that enveloped all of us. Three related to a small micro area, but it meant a great deal to me—and that was our support, protection, and in some cases expansion of the programs for inner cities. We doubled the earned income tax credit, we created community development banks and empowerment zones, and we protected the CRA [Community Reinvestment Act], which I think is a very good policy and one that the Republican majorities talked about eviscerating.

Bowmaker: On the other hand, there must be some things, in hindsight, that you'd like the opportunity to do differently. What are they?

Rubin: If there is any one thing I would try to do, it is create a rigorous cost-benefit framework for regulation. It is obviously very important to have strong regulation in a whole array of areas where there are externalities that markets don't capture. But you can easily fall short in your regulation or you can overregulate unless you have a cost-benefit framework. Now, a lot of those costs and benefits are hard to measure, but your choice is to do something that is complicated or just to disregard it in your decision making. I do think we could have done much more in that area.

Lawrence Summers (*left*), when secretary of the treasury, speaking with President Bill Clinton in the Oval Office following a small meeting in the Outer Oval Office on May 25, 2000.

15 Lawrence H. Summers
Born 1954, New Haven, Connecticut

Lawrence Summers graduated with a SB in economics from the Massachusetts Institute of Technology (MIT) in 1975. He was appointed assistant professor of economics at MIT in 1979 and was promoted to associate professor with tenure in 1982, the year that he received his PhD in economics from Harvard University. He became a full professor of economics at Harvard in 1983 at the age of twenty-eight, one of the youngest full professors in the university's recent history.

Summers began his forays into public service very early in his career. He worked as a staff economist at the Council of Economic Advisers under President Ronald Reagan between 1982 and 1983, and in 1991 he returned to Washington as vice president of development economics and chief economist of the World Bank.

In 1993, during the administration of President Bill Clinton, Summers was appointed undersecretary of the treasury for international affairs, and in 1995 he became deputy secretary of the treasury, succeeding Robert Rubin as secretary of the treasury in 1999.

On July 1, 2001, Summers took office as the twenty-seventh president of Harvard University and served until June 2006. In 2008, in the administration of President Barack Obama, he was appointed assistant to the president for economic policy and director of the National Economic Council (NEC). In early 2011, he returned to Harvard, where he currently holds the position of Charles W. Eliot University Professor.

I interviewed Lawrence Summers in his office at the John F. Kennedy School of Government at Harvard University, in Cambridge, Massachusetts. It was early in the afternoon on Tuesday, April 18, 2017.

Background Information

Bowmaker: With two parents who were economists and two very famous uncles [Paul Samuelson and Kenneth Arrow], did you ever consider any other field?

Summers: I thought I was going to be a mathematician or a physicist. But then I arrived at MIT and saw what real mathematicians and physicists were like and didn't feel that would be an area in which I would excel. I became very active on the debate team at university and realized that economics was a way of combining my interest in public policy with analytical thinking.

Entering the Policy World

Bowmaker: What does an economist bring to the policy world that others do not?

Summers: Economists bring to the policy world a tendency to be rigorously analytic about dealing with uncertainty, an awareness of trade-offs, an expertise in understanding the effects of incentives on human behavior, and a realization of the way in which the whole system fits together. For example, others tend to assume that if you launch a training program, you can estimate its success by how well the trainees do. But economists would note that perhaps there are only so many jobs available, and so your program may only influence who gets those jobs. That type of general consideration is something that economists are very clear about in their thinking.

Economists tend also to have an understanding of markets. They have contributed ideas ranging from selling spectrum, to charging for carbon emissions, to using market prices to help judge the stability of financial institutions. That orientation to markets is a very useful perspective to bring to the policy world.

Lastly, economists also have a willingness to look at issues in which the causal chain is perhaps less obvious. For instance, most noneconomists view trade principally through the prism of jobs—those created in exports, and those potentially displaced in imports. But economists always put a great amount of emphasis on the fact that real incomes are wages divided by prices, and to the extent that trade is lowering prices by making available cheaper goods through imports, that is a contribution.

Bowmaker: Between 1991 and 1993, you served as chief economist of the World Bank. During the role, you put your signature to a memo that suggested developed countries such as the United States should dump their pollution in poor countries. What did you learn from that experience?

Summers: I learned a few things from my memo. In government, when there is a lot going on, how quickly you review what's being drafted by your office—or whether you review it at all—is a sign of effectiveness. But I learned that speed has a cost, and so you should always read what you sign, because when you're in a position of some prominence, anything you do has the potential to become public. I also learned that ideas have to be framed in such a way that there is a chance for people to hear them. That particular memo was trying to raise the point that there are legitimate issues around not every country being able to afford to set the same standard in every area. As drafted, however, it wasn't written in a form that would allow anybody to think about the relevant issues rather than be shocked by its callousness. But I also learned that there were going to be happier and less happy moments in a public life. And so in the face of an unhappy moment, one had to keep going.

As Undersecretary of the Treasury for International Affairs

Bowmaker: In the fall of 1992, you were offered the position of undersecretary of the treasury for international affairs. How did Treasury Secretary Lloyd Bentsen approach you for the role, and what did he, as a nonacademic, want you to do for him?

Summers: After the election in the fall of 1992, Lloyd Bentsen asked to meet with me, and he and I had several conversations in which he stressed that a huge amount needed to be done in international economic policy. He wanted to be a successful participant in the G7 [Group of Seven] process, there were large issues to deal with around Japan's trade surplus, and there was an awareness that major changes were about to happen with respect to Russia. As someone with knowledge and experience from working at the World Bank, he wanted me to take on that responsibility. I had to think about the offer because it involved significant travel and I had young children, but I decided it was something that I wanted to do.

Bowmaker: During the role, you had to deal with the Mexican peso crisis of 1994 and 1995. What were the main lessons from the Mexican crisis, and would you do the same again?

Summers: I had a pretty substantial role in working with Mexico in 1994, and especially after its currency was devalued and the country went into near financial collapse in late December and January of 1995. I think it's fair to say that I was the leading advocate within the government for a major US support program in conjunction with the IMF [International Monetary Fund] that would provide Mexico with liquidity, coming from an analytic diagnosis that the country had a liquidity program, not a deep solvency crisis. That liquidity problem had been caused by the combination of the fixed exchange rate, the issue of *tesobonos* [short-term obligations of the Mexican government whose peso value was linked to the value of the US dollar], the depletion of reserves, and the mishandled devaluation of the Mexican peso. Battlefield medicine is never perfect, and so one could question whether the mechanism that was ultimately used—the president's exchange stabilization fund—should have been employed earlier or not. But I believe a broad judgment has to be that the program was overwhelmingly successful. American taxpayers reaped a substantial profit, the money that was lent to Mexico came back early, and the process of economic reform in Mexico was greatly supported. Up until that point, the country had had a major crisis at the end of every presidential term for a full generation. But since that time we have had three transitions of power without significant financial dislocation. Mexico is also much more closely allied with the United States in international affairs than it was prior to that time. I think if we had not acted and Mexico had been forced to go into default and moratorium on payments, and impose capital controls, the likely consequence would have been far greater immigration flows into the United States, far more narco failed state risks in a country with whom we share a 2,000-mile border, and far more anti-Americanism in Mexico and in Latin America. Tom Friedman [political commentator] called it the most successful and most important foreign policy act of the Clinton administration to that point, and I think that in many ways it set a template for things that happened subsequently, such as the broad emphasis on the importance of emerging markets, the formation of the G20 [Group of Twenty], the aggregate provision of liquidity to help contain the Asian financial crisis, and the strengthening of the IMF and World Bank. And so I do feel that our intervention was both a substantial event and a substantial success.

As Secretary of the Treasury

Bowmaker: After President Clinton's reelection in 1996, Robert Rubin told the president that he wanted you to replace him when he eventually left the role [of secretary of the treasury]. As part of the plan, you were allowed to attend senior economic meetings at the White House. As the only sub-Cabinet official with access to those meetings, what did you learn from them?

Summers: I think a real strength of the Clinton Treasury was its strong commitment to collegial process that Secretary Rubin had set in place. I learned so much from every meeting I was able to attend, and then from Secretary Rubin generally—who fostered an environment of vigorous interagency discussions on almost every issue and encouraged all participants in those meetings to speak their minds and not be afraid to be contrarian.

Bowmaker: You have said previously that the role of secretary of the treasury turned out to be your favorite position within government. Why was that the case?

Summers: Look, I thoroughly enjoyed my eight years in the Clinton administration and my two years in the Obama administration. I felt privileged to serve two presidents whom I thought were both enormously committed to doing the right thing on the large economic issues, who were extremely curious and extremely smart about grasping economic advice, and who were willing to grapple with analysis and with detail. And so I think it would be fair to say that all my jobs in government were certainly highlights of my career. Once you have studied and mastered a subject, the chance to put your expertise to use on a broad canvas that affects the lives of a very large number of people both in this country and beyond has to be about the most exciting professional opportunity imaginable. But being the president's leading economic adviser and the country's top economic official is something that you dream about as a young economist. When the first dollar bills with my signature came out, I said young actors dream of seeing their name in lights, while young economists dream of seeing their signature on the dollar bill. That's certainly true in my case.

And I'm proud of what we were able to accomplish during my time as secretary of the treasury, such as establishing the index bond program; forming the G20 group, which carries on to this day as the central global convener on economic issues; repurchasing government debt because of the excess of revenue over expenditures; launching the first major program that would scale back international institution debt for the poorest countries; and bringing real information technology expertise into the leadership of the IRS [Internal Revenue Service] for the first time. But while it was enormously personally satisfying to be secretary of the treasury, I really thought of myself as very much continuing on in a stream of policies that I had tried to be a substantial contributor to under the leadership of Secretaries Bentsen and Rubin. In other words, I felt that being there for the whole eight years meant that I had been part of something very, very important.

Bowmaker: In the Clinton years, there was a reluctance to regulate derivatives, and Glass-Steagall [an act passed by the US Congress in 1933 to prohibit commercial banks from participating in the investment banking business] was also repealed. Do you think these were significant contributors to the financial crisis?

Summers: I'm not sure that I quite accept the way your question is phrased. Let me take Glass-Steagall first, and then I'll take derivatives. I don't think it is remotely plausible to argue that the Gramm-Leach-Bliley legislation, which President Clinton signed into law and we worked on, contributed meaningfully to the financial crisis. I'd make the following points. First, Glass-Steagall had effectively been repealed already. J. P. Morgan was involved in almost every investment banking activity before the repeal of Glass-Steagall. Citigroup and Solomon Brothers could combine in a fully legal way under Glass-Steagall as it was understood to be in 1997 and 1998. And so there wasn't the kind of change that many envisaged. Second, there were no transactions that took place between 1999, when Glass-Steagall was repealed, and 2007 that would not have been legal prior to the repeal of Glass-Steagall. Third, if you look at the institutions that were caught up in the crisis, almost none of them would have been affected even by Glass-Steagall in its initial form. Think about Lehman Brothers; think about Bear Stearns; think about Fannie Mae and Freddie Mac, which were government-sponsored enterprises; think about AIG [American International Group], which was an insurance company; think about Wachovia and WaMu [Washington Mutual], which were the major banks that failed. Again, all of those institutions wouldn't have been affected by Glass-Steagall as it existed in the 1930s. Yes, it's true that Citigroup was affected, but Citigroup could already combine with Solomon under the laws that stood. And if you look at the transactions that got Citi in trouble, none of them had to do with the interaction between commercial banking and investment banking. Instead, they had to do with things that would have been entirely legal to do within a commercial bank. Fourth, the solution to the financial crisis was actually in many ways facilitated by the repeal of Glass-Steagall. Think about J. P. Morgan's acquisition of Bear Stearns; think about Bank of America's purchase of Merrill Lynch; think about the extension of the discount window at the crucial moments to Morgan Stanley and to Goldman Sachs; and think about the fact that if you are going to provide insurance to an entity, it's better to provide it to a diversified entity rather than a nondiversified entity. A final consideration is that if you look at the country that had the least financial carnage whilst going through the recession, it's instructive to note that it was Canada—which has a financial system dominated by five large universal banks. They are far more universal and engaged in a far wider range of activities than anything that would have been permitted under even the repeal of Glass-Steagall, but which had the benefit of substantial diversification. And so I don't see how any argument can be made that the repeal of Glass-Steagall contributed to the financial crisis.

We tried very hard on some things that I think were very relevant to the crisis. For example, I'm proud that [Secretary of Housing and Urban Development] Andrew Cuomo and I worked quite hard on the issue of predatory mortgages and identified a major report on the issue that more or less noted everything that happened seven or eight years later in the context of the subprime crisis. But in those days there just wasn't an audience for it, primarily because of opposition from the Republican Congress and concerns from the Federal Reserve. And I'm proud that I was the only treasury secretary to raise major warning flags about Fannie Mae and Freddie Mac prior to their bankruptcy. Again, the politics were too strong, and so we weren't able to legislate in a large way—but I think we were doing everything we could as of that moment.

With the benefit of hindsight, derivatives were obviously substantially underregulated prior to 2008. If we had been able to anticipate all the things that would happen subsequently, we probably would have tried to put in place all the various controls that were put in place in 2008. I ask myself frequently what we could have foreseen that we didn't. But on the other hand, I think the popular narrative on that question does paint with a broad and not entirely accurate brush. At the time that Brooksley Born [chair of the Commodity Futures Trading Commission (CFTC)] expressed her concern, the derivatives that ultimately caused the problem, credit default swaps, had not been invented yet. And even at the height of the financial crisis, the derivatives that Commissioner [Elizabeth] Warren expressed concern about didn't actually pose any serious problems at all. I don't think her warnings did point towards what happened during the crisis, except in a very broad way. What was motivating us—and you can argue whether we were overmotivated by this—was the issue of legal certainty. The actions that the CFTC took created doubt as judged by the civil service general councils of all the major financial regulatory agencies—the SEC [Securities and Exchange Commission], the Federal Reserve, and the Treasury—about whether all the derivatives contracts then in existence would be enforceable. That was obviously a potentially very large source of systemic risk. We felt that it was important to clarify that those contracts were enforceable. That required legislation, and that legislation required dealing with the Republican Congress. The Republican Congress's legislation was not the legislation we would have preferred, but it was the legislation that was necessary to achieve legal certainty. And so on balance, we decided to accept that legislation. It did in some ways limit regulatory power over this issue. But in terms of whether it caused the financial crisis, I find that an almost inconceivable view in light of the fact that the [George W.] Bush administration's regulators stopped far, far short of using all the authorities they had. And so it's hard to believe that if they had had more authorities, they would have used them. And I think one has to understand that the officials in the Bush administration literally allowed themselves to be photographed with rule books holding saws in their hands—the kind of saw that you use to cut wood—with a view to signifying their desire to rip up all that was in those books. Yes, there were various things in our report on LTCM [Long-Term Capital Management] after that episode in 1998 that would have been very good to get into law. But I don't think in that time, with Senator [Phil] Gramm as the chairman of the Banking Committee, there would have been any way of getting them into law. There is no question that if the kind of steps that had been passed in Dodd-Frank had been legislated in the 1990s, it would have been much, much better. Perhaps somebody would have a view as to what we could have done to have made that more likely, but in the political environment at that time, it would have been a different story.

As Director of the National Economic Council

Bowmaker: You returned to Washington in 2008 as director of the National Economic Council during the Obama administration. Can you describe how you were approached for the position?

Summers: President Obama called and asked me serve as director of the NEC. He said he needed someone with my experience and commitment to resolving financial crises to be right by his side. I told him that I thought a lot of the job of director of the NEC was to coordinate the positions of different agencies, and that I was a person with strong views on underlying policy and probably not a specialist in kumbaya. And so I wasn't sure I was right for the position. The president said, "With the crisis we have, kumbaya can be vastly overrated" [*laughs*]. I said that I would be happy do it, because in the end when the president of the United States asks you to do something at a time of substantial national crisis, on my ethics, the answer has to be always yes.

Bowmaker: You had a reputation as being very assertive about your views, sometimes at odds with Cabinet secretaries, the Council of Economic Advisers, and others. Did you see this as your role?

Summers: Were there differences of opinion? Yes. Was I assertive about my views? Yes. I held the strong philosophy, which some people might think was inappropriate, that any Cabinet official, including the chairman of the Council of Economic Advisers, did not have a right to send in a memo to the president with my endorsement if I didn't agree with it. I accept that I had zero standing of any kind to interfere with their sending of a memo, and so I would frequently say that I'm happy to put it through, but if I don't agree, I will note the respect in which I think it's not right. I would also suggest that we could continue to talk about it and see if we can find a formulation that we can all agree on. But I think there were sometimes people who felt they really wanted their memo to go in without there being any view different from theirs in it. That was not my conception of the job. And so there were certainly moments where there were disagreements, but overall I believe the ultimate test is the quality of the policy. If you look at the fact that almost every economic statistic was headed south on January 20, 2009, in a way that looked like 1929 and then see what happened subsequently, it was the sharpest V-shaped recovery in seventy-five years between the second and third quarters. You have to come to the conclusion that whatever it was that President Obama and his team did was very, very important in bringing about an upturn in the economy. That's why I suspect history will give President Obama a very, very high grade for those six months, and I'm happy to have had a chance to help him and the rest of the economic team through that period.

Bowmaker: Given that you have been writing about and pushing the idea of secular stagnation, do you think you should have pushed even harder for stimulus when you were in the Obama inner circle?

Summers: I think I pushed to the limit in emphasizing the importance of fiscal stimulus when I was in the Obama inner circle. There were a couple of times when the president stopped me and said, "Larry, I'm familiar with your views. I think I've heard enough." At the beginning of the administration, the operative statements were that we wanted to get as much fiscal stimulus as we possibly could; there was no danger that we could get too much fiscal stimulus. And the choices about which packages were to be presented were not framed in terms of concern that we could get too much fiscal stimulus, but a concern about what was the maximum opening bid that would be heard. And there was also a need to get fiscal stimulus quickly.

There has been debate about whether the president should have been given a $1.8 trillion option, but I think everybody understood—most certainly the president—that it was all a question of political tactics. We needed to act in whatever ways would get us the most fiscal stimulus, and that was really a matter for the political experts, not for the substantive experts. I was quite focused through the whole time I was there on getting more fiscal stimulus, while others were very focused on the repeal of the Bush tax cuts on long-run deficit grounds—which I felt was a less important issue. There were others still who were focused much more on entitlement curbing, and I thought it might well be the case that showing concern in that direction would be more important in contributing to getting more fiscal stimulus earlier, but that the priority should be fiscal stimulus in the short run, not budget control in the long run. I was as vigorous as I knew how to be on that point.

Bowmaker: How would you compare and contrast Presidents Clinton and Obama in terms of their operating styles and approaches to economic questions?

Summers: Look, there were enormous similarities between Presidents Clinton and Obama. As I said earlier, they were enormously curious, enormously serious about their jobs, very focused on doing the right thing rather than the expedient thing, and very willing to listen to those with expert opinions. I think those were great common strengths. But President Clinton had a less disciplined and more wide-ranging style than President Obama did. His meetings were less likely to begin and end on time; were more likely to range into subjects beyond the immediate agenda; and were more likely to bring in experiences that he had had, or things that he had read or seen outside of the prepared materials for those meetings. President Obama was less wide-ranging and more disciplined about making sure that decisions were reached, and that the decisions that had been reached were effectively implemented. And so they had somewhat rather different personal styles within the broad framework they shared. Many discussions of leadership talk about the right way to be a leader, but what I learned from working with Presidents Clinton and Obama is the reality that to thine own self one should be true. I doubt that President Clinton could have done it President Obama's way, or that President Obama could have done it President Clinton's way. They found approaches of leading that were true to themselves and to their personalities, and I think they were both extremely effective.

General Thoughts on Economic Policymaking

Bowmaker: To what extent can economics research produced in universities help inform policymakers?

Summers: To use a famous phrase about monetary policy, I think economics research produced in universities has great influence on policymaking, albeit with long and variable lags—whether it is Keynesian economics, which shapes the way we think about recessions; whether it is the existence of a poverty line, which shapes the way we think about the question of poverty; whether it is the application of cost-benefit analysis, which we apply as a matter of routine to regulation; whether it is the volunteer army that we now take for granted; whether it is the measurement of correlation and covariance, which is central to the evaluation of the safety and health of financial institutions; whether it is the analysis of and structuring of negotiations, which comes out of the development of game theory; whether it is the thinking about lending of last resort, which was integral to the response to the financial crisis. All of those things have roots in economics research that is done in universities, and so I think it's something that's very, very powerful.

If I had any doubt whether it had relevance, then that was dismissed at the height of the Asian financial crisis when, as deputy secretary of the treasury, I was sent on a trip to Asia to understand what was happening and to provide a certain amount of reassurance on behalf of the United States. I had the chance to meet Zhu Rongji, then the premier of China and the number two person in the country. It was explained to me quite forcefully by the embassy that I was the deputy secretary, not a Cabinet member, and he was the premier of China. And so it would likely be a brief courtesy meeting; meaning that when it was time to go, I had to go. At the meeting, I read my talking points, and he read his talking points, and I felt that after about twenty or twenty-five minutes had gone by, we were done. Then he said, "Are you the same Larry Summers who used to be a professor of economics at Harvard?" He knew the answer, but I said, "Yes" [*laughs*]. He asked me whether I agreed with [economist] Stanley Fischer that in a country experiencing capital outflows, the first priority should be to raise interest rates to stabilize the currency, or whether I agreed with [economist] Joe Stiglitz that the first priority should be to lower interest rates to provide liquidity to the financial system and let the currency take care of itself. We debated those two alternatives for forty-five minutes to an hour, while the people from the embassy sat vaguely slack jawed. The premier of China was spending more time with this American visitor than he had with any other American visitor that year [*laughs*]. I guess what I learned is that it wasn't only in the United States that the kind of academic research that economists do turns out to have a very large influence on economic thinking and on economic policy.

Personal Reflections

Bowmaker: As a policymaker, which decisions or outcomes were most gratifying?

Summers: Ultimately, I suspect the most significant ones will relate to the chance I had to play a role in responding to a variety of crises: the Mexican and Asian crises during the Clinton administration, and of course, the most recent financial crisis during the Obama administration. I was particularly active in supervising Obama's team that presided over the government support program for the automobile industry, and I think if you look at the health of the American automobile industry today, the jobs that were saved, what it has meant for the economy of the north central region, the success we had in replacing management and making other changes in those companies, that stands out as a successful experience in guiding government intervention in the private economy at a time of great crisis.

Bowmaker: On the other hand, there must be some things that, in hindsight, you'd like the opportunity to do differently. What are they?

Summers: It's always hard to know. I don't think anybody can look at where Russia is today and feel satisfied about the way it's all turned out, given the hopes we had for the country back in 1993. Was that a reflection of the economic policies and financial support? Was that a reflection of policies in the security realm? Was that a reflection of forces that were outside our control, because Russia's destiny was always going to be shaped by its own internal forces? Those are questions that historians will debate over time. I'm not sure I know a different course that I can confidently say would have led to a better outcome, but it's an example of where I would like the path to have turned out differently.

And then there would also be regrets over a range of issues during the financial crisis; like the work we did on housing, the work we did after LTCM, and the work we did on fiscal policy in 2009 and 2010—where I look back and like the view that I had but wish I had been more effective in causing it, or something like it, to be implemented.

Joseph Stiglitz (*far left*), when chairman of the Council of Economic Advisers, briefing President Bill Clinton (*far right*) in the Oval Office prior to a meeting on the 1997 budget. Also pictured are Leslie Samuels (*second left*), assistant secretary of the treasury for tax policy, and Lawrence Summers (*second right*), deputy secretary of the treasury.

16 Joseph E. Stiglitz
Born 1943, Gary, Indiana

Joseph Stiglitz graduated with a BA from Amherst College in 1964 before studying for his PhD in economics at the Massachusetts Institute of Technology (MIT) in 1966–1967, during which he also held an MIT assistant professorship. He was a research fellow at the University of Cambridge (1966–1970) and has taught at Yale University (1970–1974), Stanford University (1974–1976 and 1988–2001), Oxford University (1976–1979), Princeton University (1979–1988), and Columbia University, where he currently serves as University Professor.

Stiglitz was awarded the John Bates Clark Medal in 1979 and received the Nobel Prize in Economics, along with Michael Spence and George Akerlof, in 2001 for their analyses of markets with asymmetric information. He was also the lead author of the 1995 report of the Intergovernmental Panel on Climate, an intergovernmental body of the United Nations that shared the 2007 Nobel Peace Prize.

Stiglitz was a member of President Bill Clinton's Council of Economic Advisers (CEA) in 1993–1995 and served as its chairman in 1995–1997. He was chief economist and senior vice president of the World Bank in 1997–2000.

I interviewed Joseph Stiglitz at Henry's restaurant [Boulevard Seafood NYC at the time of writing] on the Upper West Side of Manhattan. It was early in the afternoon on Wednesday, January 30, 2013.

Background Information

Bowmaker: Why did you become an economist?

Stiglitz: I had been a physics major at college, but I was much more interested in social problems like unemployment, poverty, and discrimination and soon discovered that economics provided the analytical skills to understand them. So you might say I began from a social activist perspective, although with a strong theoretical approach having come from physics. In fact, most of my work is much more theoretical compared to others who become involved in policy.

Entering the Policy World

Bowmaker: What does an economist bring to the policy world that others do not?

Stiglitz: Scientists bring something to policy discourse that others do not, which is a clear understanding of theory and evidence and a recognition of the role played by uncertainty, since statements are always tentative. That is the major distinction. When I was in Washington, for example, I interacted a great deal with people from the Office of Science and Technology Policy. I had a natural affinity with them because we were of the same culture, as opposed to the lawyers and politicians.

Well-trained economists, and some scientists, also bring a systemic perspective, seeing things as a solution to a general equilibrium problem—which most others don't have because they are much more partial equilibrium in their framework. Again, that is something I brought from my theoretical background. Many policy economists, on the other hand, tend to be much more mired in partial equilibrium.

The third thing is that economists or social scientists will have thought much more deeply about economic and social problems compared to Washington's lawyers and politicians, whose knowledge is at a level of "journalism plus." When you are doing health care reform, for example, issues of asymmetry of information will arise, but very few people will have read the work by Ken Arrow and me on the subject. That said, there was a large cohort of first-rate academics in the Clinton administration, and so during meetings there was a deeper sense of sharing research findings, which was quite unusual for Washington.

Bowmaker: You began your first major policy position in 1993 as a member of the Council of Economic Advisers. How did you come to be appointed?

Stiglitz: Vice President [Al] Gore played an important role in the appointment of CEA members because of his great interest in the environment, an issue that I had been involved in for quite some time. For example, in the 1980s, I had tried to estimate the cost and, unsuccessfully, to block President Reagan's fire sales of offshore oil tracts to private companies. I must have passed muster with Gore and obviously with President Clinton, whom I also talked to before being appointed.

I think that Larry Summers was also considered for a position at the CEA until it was vetoed on the basis of his absolutely outrageous statement at the World Bank about it being a good idea if we exported our toxic waste to Mexico because the people there die younger, and so the cost is less. Of course, he then went on to the Treasury, where he again demonstrated his apparent lack of sensitivity—but in a different context.

Bowmaker: Did you view yourself as having strong policy positions or simply as a hired professional serving the CEA chair and, indirectly, the president?

Stiglitz: Yes, I had strong policy positions. My views had already been widely articulated because I had written the most popular undergraduate and graduate textbooks in public economics, and in the process of doing those, I had defined what was the appropriate role of the state. I had even written a book called *The Economic Role of the State*, where I weighed in on many issues that came up in Washington like financial policy, cost-benefit analysis, and antitrust laws. But when you take on a job at the CEA, the questions that are posed tend to be more specific or, indeed, very different.

Bowmaker: Did you ask for advice from former members or chairs of the CEA before you began your role?

Stiglitz: Yes. I had known many of the members and chairs of the CEA from preceding years, but their advice was not always relevant because every administration is different. For example, one person from the [Ronald] Reagan administration had emphasized that I should watch out for my back because somebody would always try to stab me [*laughs*]. I can think of only one individual of that kind of character in the Clinton administration— everybody else worked hard to create a cordial environment.

I was also made aware of the fact that the extent to which the CEA was valued within the White House depended on the particular president. For example, my understanding was that Ronald Reagan was so irritated with Marty Feldstein's criticism of his deficit that he wanted to disband the council. After Feldstein left, the vacancy remained open for nine months before he appointed Beryl Sprinkel, who was not a very strong academic and not someone who Reagan necessarily turned to for advice. And my impression is that George W. Bush pushed the council aside, quite literally, by moving it out of the Old Executive Office Building, which is right next door to the White House.

But Bill Clinton did value the views of the council and had a good understanding of the role of the economist: someone who analyzes dispassionately the consequences of policies with a view to the president determining what is feasible given the political climate. In other words, he was smart enough to know that we were the one group in Washington without a special interest.

Bowmaker: You mentioned earlier that scientists bring a clear understanding of theory and evidence to policy discourse. In your American Economic Association annual Distinguished Lecture on Economics in Government, "The Private Uses of Public Interests: Incentives and Institutions," which was published in the *Journal of Economic Perspectives* in 1998, you wrote, "[I had] expected lower standards of evidence for assertions than would be accepted in a professional article, but I had not expected that evidence offered would be, in so many instances, so irrelevant."[1] Can you elaborate and point to a specific example when you were at the CEA?

Stiglitz: Many statements that people would make were based on beliefs about how the economic system worked, perhaps relating to incentives structures—which may or may not have been true. Let me give you an example. In the policy debate, there is a widespread assumption that lowering the tax on corporations will lead to more investment. But most investment is financed by debt at the margin, and debt is tax deductible. And so when you lower the tax rate on corporations, it raises the cost of capital, because when they borrow money, the tax deduction is less. In other words, the marginal return on the investment is lowered, and the marginal cost of the investment is raised, and they net out. Therefore, there is no theory behind the claim that lowering the tax rate is going to lead to more investment.

---

1. Joseph E. Stiglitz, "The Private Uses of Public Interests: Incentives and Institutions," *Journal of Economic Perspectives* 12, no. 2 (1998): 5.

Bowmaker: Was there anything else that surprised or frustrated you as you began your role?

Stiglitz: I was struck by several other things. Firstly, there was a realization that government is very hierarchical relative to academia. In a university setting, it is about the power of ideas, not position. Secondly, I was also a little surprised at how difficult it was to deal with people like lawyers who came from a different cultural background. Thirdly, another thing I found interesting is that although you are an adviser to the president, if you want your ideas to be accepted, they have to go through the Cabinet. You cannot just say that we should do agricultural policy X if the secretary of agriculture wants policy Y. In the end, the president has to pay attention to the people he has appointed to oversee those areas. And so we took our mandate as working with each of the Cabinet departments to formulate policies that were consistent with what we thought was right. We developed strong relationships with most of the departments, although of course some didn't like to take our advice.

I also had to understand that nothing would ever be decided on the basis of voting, which is standard political theory—it was always the consensus of opinion. Lastly, and this is something that I should have known before I went to Washington, winning a battle in the administration would not necessarily win the overall battle, because it had to be approved by Congress. That gave a lot of power to those who claimed they knew how Congress was thinking. Whether they did or not was another question, but it was something that was very important all the time.

As Chairman of the Council of Economic Advisers

Bowmaker: Coming into the role, how did you think your style and approach would be different to Laura Tyson's, your predecessor?

Stiglitz: Laura was a highly effective chair of the CEA. In Washington, you have to constantly fight to be in the room where decisions are being made, and I think she almost always had a seat at the table because she was very strong but nonconfrontational. I wouldn't describe myself as confrontational either, but coming into the role, I felt that I would be more willing to challenge the Treasury, in particular, when necessary.

Laura also had a very nice manner and knew how to speak to the president in a language that he could understand. She was unusually good in that respect. She gave the members of the CEA a lot of discretion and would defer to us on certain technical issues relating to antitrust or financial regulation. Even though she would be well informed about them in general terms, she would not necessarily know all their intricacies. You have to understand that in Washington, there are so many things going on at the same time that it is impossible to be on top of each and every one of them.

Bowmaker: How would you describe the economic environment that you inherited as chairman and the issues that needed to be prioritized?

Stiglitz: By the time I took over as chair, the Federal Reserve had already started to raise interest rates when the recovery from the recession was not on solid foundations. It is important to also mention that the Democrats' loss in the 1994 midterm elections was a disaster. Firstly, if getting good things through a Democratic Congress was difficult, then getting them through a Republican Congress would be impossible. Secondly, there was no coherence, for good reason, about why we had lost. Was it the tax increase for the rich, which was interpreted as a tax increase for everybody? Was it because of health care reform, which was defeated? And since there was no common ground about what we had done wrong, there was disagreement on how we should respond. Should we focus more on investment? Should we address the issue of inequality? Should we adopt the tactic of budget deficit reduction? It was obviously a very challenging time.

Bowmaker: What did you think was the reason for the loss?

Stiglitz: It is hard to believe that those who received a tax cut would be upset because the rich—and remember it was only the very, very rich—got a modest tax increase. And so if I had to pick a reason, it would be the vicious attack against our health care reform from the insurance industry and others. It characterized the administration as being overreaching in the respect that it would take away your right to choose a doctor, and I think that was the issue that probably resonated the most with ordinary Americans. In retrospect, though, the need for health care reform was so apparent, and what we eventually got was not that dissimilar from what we were trying to do with President Clinton.

Bowmaker: What did you believe should have been the appropriate response to the loss?

Stiglitz: While I understood the worry about the deficit, I thought we needed to stimulate the economy. That meant we ought to have pushed ahead with our investment programs. At the CEA, we came up with a number of mechanisms for making low-cost investments—in cities that had been hurt by toxic waste, for example, and even in school buildings. I also believed we should have begun to address the problem of inequality, which was raising its head at that time. On the other hand, I felt that deficit reduction, which is how we did respond, was totally wrong. I didn't think it would by itself lead to a stronger economy and was certainly not the kind of agenda that we, as Democrats, should have been pursuing.

Bowmaker: Was it easy to establish a comfortable working relationship with President Clinton?

Stiglitz: Yes. First of all, Clinton was unusual, certainly from what I can see compared to, say Bush 43, in that he was very bright and always presented himself as having an open mind on almost everything. Whenever I had a meeting with him, he was always listening very carefully, trying to make sure that he understood my argument correctly. Obviously, he brought to bear a lot of knowledge, because as a former state governor he had thought about virtually every problem at a micro level for a very long time. In that respect, it was like a discussion with an informed counterpart rather than somebody who had never dealt with the issues. Of course, he had not read all the relevant empirical and theoretical arguments, but I was particularly struck by his understanding of incentives. I had a meeting with him one day about the design of the unemployment insurance system, and he suggested how we might do it in a certain way so that the incentives were less adverse. I remember saying to myself at the time, "Boy, that was really an interesting approach." Similarly, I was also impressed by the comments that he would make on our weekly economic memo. We used to jokingly call it the periodical that had the smallest but most influential readership in the world [*laughs*].

I should add that, relative to more recent councils, we would consult with economists who had a wide difference of views so that we could present a range of opinion to the president. The fact that he had people in his administration from the left to the right indicated that he wanted to hear a diversity of perspectives, and so we tried to get into the same spirit. Occasionally, this became embedded in the policymaking process. One example was our efforts to reform the legal framework for dealing with toxic waste, which is commonly known as Superfund, where we brought together chemical companies, insurers, environmentalists, and economists in what is referred to today as multistakeholder dialogue.

Bowmaker: During your time at the CEA, you battled hard against the privatization of the United States Enrichment Corporation [USEC]. Why did you feel so strongly about this particular issue?

Stiglitz: What is one of the main things that everybody is worried about today? Nuclear proliferation. Few were concerned about it at the time I was at the CEA, but it seemed obvious to me that nuclear proliferation would be one of the major issues faced by our planet in the future. USEC produced enriched uranium, which is a key ingredient in nuclear bombs. I argued that private incentives to create markets for USEC's product conflicted with national and global interests in nonproliferation. Worse still, they were put in charge of bringing into the United States the enriched uranium from deactivated Russian warheads to then mix it with natural uranium and produce fuel for commercial power reactors. I was worried that as long as the price paid to the Russians was greater than USEC's subsidized—or even unsubsidized—marginal cost of production, then the corporation, as a profit maximizer, would have an incentive to avoid bringing the uranium into the United States. My concerns were fully justified because not only did USEC not take the enriched uranium, but we uncovered through our network that they paid the Russians a bribe to make sure nobody knew about it. That discovery put a temporary halt to the privatization of USEC, but it went ahead in the end because of special interests.

Bowmaker: I would now like to turn to your relationships with the rest of the economic team. First, how would you describe your relationship with the NEC [National Economic Council] when you were chairman of the CEA? Do you think having the NEC is an efficient way of organizing policy? For example, Glenn Hubbard told me that "if a professional economist runs it, it is then very tempting for that person to impose his or her point of view. If a noneconomist runs it, it is then very hard for that person to keep up with all the economic arguments."

Stiglitz: I think Glenn Hubbard's point is correct. But I'd make two further comments. Firstly, the effectiveness of the NEC depends on the personality of who is its head. For example, when Laura Tyson was in charge, she did not very strongly impose her views and did a good job. But I have seen several of the NEC heads not know what they were doing because it was very hard for them to assess the various arguments. On the other hand, I think NEC heads (good ones, at least) are engaged in a coordination role, not a policymaking role. He or she is trying to bring together an organized process for decision making for the president. That means he or she has to synthesize all the arguments—political, economic, and special interest—on a given issue. And so I believe there are big advantages to separating the coordination and policymaking roles and to keeping the NEC position.

Bowmaker: How would you describe your relationship with the Federal Reserve?

Stiglitz: I was concerned that the Fed had an overly restrictive monetary policy because [Chairman of the Federal Reserve] Alan Greenspan thought the economy was recovering faster than I did. That led to the major controversy of whether it was appropriate for the CEA to comment on Fed policy. The Fed obviously made its views known on the administration's policy, but there were those who argued we should not be commenting on an independent central bank. I believed, and still do, that the Fed is a public institution and that there is an interest in promoting open dialogue on what constitutes good policy. But the Treasury felt that would roil financial markets and therefore have an adverse effect on the economy. At the CEA, we handled it by discussing the issues in the *Economic Report of the President* in a sufficiently mild tone. If you weren't a good economist, you wouldn't have recognized that it was a critique of the Fed [*laughs*].

Bowmaker: What did you learn from your one-on-one interactions with Alan Greenspan?

Stiglitz: I thought he was masterful in grasping data from a multitude of sources. He had always a data set that was indicating something that other people hadn't picked up, so it was fascinating to talk to him. It was very much an insight at a microeconomic level, rather like sticking a thermometer in the middle of a turkey to see what was going on. For example, he might use boxcar shipments to try to reconcile what the GDP [gross domestic product] numbers were saying. But he didn't typically think in terms of the standard economic models, which meant it was not easy for somebody like me to go back and think about how each data set fit in with how the macroeconomy works [*laughs*]. And while I thought that something like boxcar shipments were a factoid worth mulling over, I always suspected that if they had proven to be systematically a more reliable predictor of where the economy was going, others would have already used them.

Bowmaker: How would you describe your relationship with the Treasury?

Stiglitz: The Treasury has always been very jealous of its role and less willing to play well with other economic actors. But sometimes it depends on particular personalities and particular people. Take the case when Clinton lowered the capital gains tax rate. As chairman of the CEA, I thought I was reflecting the views of much of the economics profession when I argued that it would contribute to inequality, which is becoming very apparent now, and encourage speculation rather than real investment. But Larry Summers in the Treasury confused the role of economics in politics, which is very destructive, and pushed for it. Even though I would have still disagreed with it, I thought Clinton might have had a targeted capital gains tax reduction for those who engage in innovative activity, but not for speculation.

I'll give you two other examples. During the debate about welfare reform, one issue of natural interest was corporate welfare, such as direct and hidden subsidies for the financial sector—which have terrible distortionary effects on the economy. [Secretary of Labor] Bob Reich and I both agreed that we could not cut back on welfare to the poor without also cutting back on welfare to the rich and to large corporations. We got the president's support to make an inventory of the forms of corporate welfare and to come up with a set of recommendations about what to do about them. But the Treasury and in particular Bob Rubin were very upset both at the idea and even more so at the vocabulary. They felt that corporate welfare sounded antibusiness, rather like the language of class warfare. My own view was that the issue simply reflected the principles of equity and economics. Unfortunately, not much progress has been made in reducing corporate welfare, but at least we were the first ones to raise the issue so vehemently.

Another major point of confrontation with the Treasury was over the repeal of the Glass-Steagall Act. This allowed investment banks and commercial banks to come together. I strongly opposed it on the grounds that banks would become bigger and bigger, to the point where they were too big to fail. Commercial banks would begin to act like investment banks, undertaking risky activities with ordinary people's money, and there would inevitably be conflicts of interest. But when Bob Rubin arrived at the

Treasury in 1995, it was clear those concerns would be ignored, reflecting the interests of Goldman Sachs and Citibank, in particular. The Treasury pushed it by arguing that abolishing Glass-Steagall wouldn't matter because banks had learned how to get around it anyway. I felt that we had articulated our views with sufficient force that the repeal of Glass-Steagall would not prevail, but it got through after I left the CEA. In retrospect, it turns out that my concerns were fully justified.

Bowmaker: A few months before you became chairman of the CEA, the peso crisis occurred. How much interaction did the CEA have with the Treasury in relation to handling the crisis? Where did you stand in terms of the US's decision to intervene? How did the experience of the peso crisis influence your thinking about the subsequent Asian crisis that took place when you were chief economist at the World Bank?

Stiglitz: The peso crisis—as with other international economic policy issues—was handled in a very closed way by the Treasury. They weren't very interested in our views [*laughs*]. I was very suspicious that the US intervention represented a Wall Street bailout rather than a Mexican bailout, and I was not convinced that the crisis would have the traumatic effects that the Treasury claimed. As for how it affected my thinking about the East Asian crisis, we had a number of battles with the Treasury over it wanting to force countries in trade agreements to open up their capital markets. We didn't think it was appropriate use of US capital, you might say, to make countries do so. It wasn't going to be creating jobs in the United States; it wasn't going to be creating global economic stability—probably the reverse; and just because it was going to be creating more profits for Goldman Sachs was not a reason for why it should be a priority element in our international economic policy. So we wrote a paper about the principles of what should govern international economic policy, which things should be given priority, and how should they be prioritized. But the Treasury was very opposed to us even articulating our views, let alone expressing them to the president. And the reason was very clear: we would be giving a higher priority to things other than Goldman Sachs profits. Of course, South Korea was one of the countries over which we had this disagreement with the Treasury about forcing countries to liberalize their capital markets. And so when the East Asian crisis broke out, I thought that was vindication of our position at the CEA.

Bowmaker: All things considered, can you give an example of where you, as an economist, or the CEA, as an organization, were able to make a difference?

Stiglitz: It is not always easy to tell where we made a difference without doing a controlled experiment, but I would point to our creation of inflation-indexed bonds as one of several achievements. Not only did they allow households and the government to reduce their risks, but they also created a market that previously did not exist and gave the government an opportunity to take advantage of this new market in the form of lower interest charges on its debt. Since real risk is reduced, the risk premium should be smaller. This could not have been done without the support of the Treasury, but when we initially proposed the idea to them, they said no, claiming that the English experience of these particular bonds was a failure. People only bought them for their retirement; they did not trade them. And so we did an end run, which got blood boiling, and talked to Vanguard and TIAA-CREF [Teachers Insurance and Annuity Association of America–College Retirement Equities Fund], who expressed great interest in the market. That took away the Treasury's argument, and the bonds were successfully issued in January 1997.

Bowmaker: Can you give an example of when the CEA was able to kill a bad idea?

Stiglitz: I'll give you an example of where we lost the critical vote but in doing so changed the dynamics of the decision-making process. In 1993, the price of aluminum began to plummet for several reasons, including due to the global slowdown, and Paul O'Neill, chairman and CEO [chief executive officer] of Alcoa, wanted to set up a global cartel to help raise prices. I thought that was outrageous. We were supposed to be procompetition! And so we worked hard with the Antitrust Division of Justice to stop it. But the State Department supported the formation of a cartel, and the National Economic Council, led by Bob Rubin at the time, sided with them—even though I had tried to convince them that cartels are bad things. At the end of a heated sub-Cabinet meeting in which the decision to form the cartel was made, Ann Bingaman, the assistant attorney general for antitrust announced, "I may have to indict all of you for conspiracy and restraint of trade!" What a dramatic moment [*laughs*].

General Thoughts on Economic Policymaking

Bowmaker: Can you give some examples of fallacies, misconceptions, or misinterpretations that affect policy debate in this country?

Stiglitz: There are a plethora of fallacies, from the Republican Party's belief that we can somehow ignore the consequences of deficits, to the expansionary fiscal austerity thesis, which argues that cutting government spending in a recession leads to economic growth, and to the policies of the Washington consensus, almost all of which are wrong—including inflation targeting being a necessary and sufficient condition for stability. Many people in Washington also say that free trade creates jobs but don't mention that imports lose jobs. In fact, when I was at the CEA, the administration even had an official figure that was used to translate the value of exports into a number of jobs. But the point is that employment is the responsibility of macroeconomic policy, not trade policy.

Bowmaker: Do you think that the gap between economics research produced in universities and policymaking will increase or decrease over time?

Stiglitz: There will always be a gap. Something that would have helped at the CEA was academic work that was narrowly focused on the specific issues. For instance, there is plenty of research on moral hazard, but at the time there was very little work on the Modigliani-Miller theorem applied to the leverage of banks, or whether Glass-Steagall was a good thing for the financial sector. And so many of the key policy decisions were driven by special interests without the kind of solid academic background that I wanted.

Bowmaker: Which aspects of the institutional framework for making economic policy in this country work well, and which need to be reformed?

Stiglitz: That's a really interesting question. I actually think we have a good overall institutional framework for making policy in this country. My only critique is that we don't have a balanced set of think tanks. The Heritage Foundation and the American Enterprise Institute are on the right and the Brookings Institution is in the center, but there isn't anything that corresponds on the left. This affects policy discourse. In Germany, the government gives support to each of the major political parties to have their own think tank. In other words, it is viewed as a public good to have sound policy research. And so if I had to think of an institutional innovation for this country, that would be the one.

Personal Reflections

Bowmaker: How did your personality affect your style and approach as a policymaker?

Stiglitz: I tried to bring my sense of humor to the role, and I think that was sometimes an effective instrument [*laughs*].

Bowmaker: What were your strengths and weaknesses as a policymaker?

Stiglitz: If you had only looked at my academic work, you might have thought I didn't speak English and just knew how to write mathematics. But I have written textbooks that have been very successful, as I said earlier. I am also a past editor of the *Journal of Economic Perspectives* and was even a debater in high school. So long before I arrived in Washington, I had already spent a lot of time thinking about how to communicate. Yes, there was obviously a learning curve in terms of dealing with strongly opinionated lawyers and politicians, but I think I understood the nature of argumentation and persuasion.

If you were to ask where I might have been more effective, I would probably say I could have been better at managing the staff. Academics don't typically have managerial experience, and I don't think I did. On the other hand, the CEA is a small group, so the management aspect is perhaps not a critical issue and may have in fact turned out for the best because the style was more collegial. In particular, I feel that I got better results from the young people, and I am very pleased that two of my junior staff at the time, Peter Orszag and Jason Furman, later wound up in very senior positions. I made life interesting and vibrant for them when I was there.

Bowmaker: There must be some things, in hindsight, that you'd like the opportunity to do differently. What are they?

Stiglitz: No. The big question you have to ask yourself at the CEA is the following: Am I an inside player or an outside player? In other words, do you work by trying to persuade people in the administration, or do you go out to the press and try to influence public opinion, sometimes in a stealthy way? It is just not consistent with my personality to do both at the same time. In my mind, if you are a public official you work within that sphere, and then when you leave you become a public intellectual and affect policy in another way. But some of my colleagues obviously disagree, because they have gone through the media while working in Washington. I think I made the right decision about how I played that game.

Alice Rivlin (*far right*), then director of the Office of Management and Budget, briefs President Bill Clinton (*seated*) in the Oval Office on May 14, 1996, prior to an interview with the *Washington Post*. Senior staff also pictured in the background include Robert Rubin (*second right*), secretary of the treasury; Alexis Herman (*center, gesticulating*), secretary of labor; and Leon Panetta (*far left*), chief of staff.

17   Alice M. Rivlin
Born 1931, Philadelphia, Pennsylvania
Died 2019, Washington, D.C.

Alice Rivlin graduated with a BA in economics from Bryn Mawr College in 1952 and then obtained both an MA and a PhD in economics from Harvard University in 1955 and 1958, respectively.

During her career, Rivlin held a number of roles in think tanks, government, and academia. Between 1957 and 1966, she worked at the Brookings Institution, and then she became deputy assistant secretary for program coordination at the Department of Health, Education, and Welfare (HEW) from 1966 to 1968. Rivlin then served as assistant secretary for planning and evaluation from 1968 to 1969.

Rivlin returned to the Brookings Institution in 1969 as a senior fellow before becoming the founding director of the Congressional Budget Office (CBO) in 1975, a position she held until 1983. Between 1983 and 1992, she worked again at the Brookings Institution, before being appointed the Hirst Professor of Public Policy at George Mason University in 1992. During the administration of President Bill Clinton, Rivlin served as deputy director of the Office of Management and Budget (OMB) from 1993 to 1994 and then as director of the OMB from 1994 to 1996.

She left the OMB in 1996 and served as vice chair of the Board of Governors of the Federal Reserve System until 1999. Until her passing on May 14, 2019, Rivlin then worked at the Brookings Institution, while also serving as the Henry J. Cohen Professor at the Robert J. Milano Graduate School of Management and Urban Policy at New School University between 2001 and 2003, and as a visiting professor at the McCourt School of Public Policy at Georgetown University from 2003 onward.

I interviewed Alice Rivlin in her office at the Brookings Institution, Washington, D.C. It was the middle of the afternoon on Friday, February 9, 2018.

Background Information

Bowmaker: Why did you become an economist?

Rivlin: As an undergraduate, I started out to major in history, but I took an economics course by a dynamic young professor named Rueben Zubrow, who was then a new PhD at Indiana University. He got me interested in the subject, and it seemed to be more useful than history—particularly because I could see how it might lead to some kind of career.

Entering the Policy World

Bowmaker: You were appointed to your first major policy position in 1968 as assistant secretary for planning and evaluation at the Department of Health, Education, and Welfare during the [Lyndon B.] Johnson administration. How did that position arise?

Rivlin: President Lyndon Johnson observed that the policymaking process in the Pentagon under Robert McNamara, the defense secretary at the time, had gotten very analytical, and decided to move that idea to the civilian agencies. William Gorhan was asked to head the Department of Health, Education and Welfare, but he didn't actually know a lot about health or education or welfare [*laughs*]. So he recruited two deputies, and I was one of them. After a couple of years, Gorhan left to run the Urban Institute, and I became the assistant secretary in 1968.

I was at HEW for three years and stayed over briefly into the [Richard] Nixon administration because what happened between Johnson and Nixon was that Elliot Richardson, who had been secretary of the HEW in an earlier era, had the good idea that they should ask one assistant secretary–level person in each department to facilitate the transition. I was the chosen one in HEW.

Bowmaker: By the time of your appointment, did you view yourself as having strong policy positions or simply as a hired professional serving the president?

Rivlin: I had a strong interest in improving budget decision-making that came from being an applied economist. But we were all very idealistic at the time about how analysis, and particularly economic analysis, if laid before decision makers could improve the process. Since the office was called Planning and Evaluation, we worked on evaluating the slew of new programs introduced by the Johnson administration such as Medicare, Medicaid, the Elementary and Secondary Education Act, and Head Start and used the results in budget decisions. As I say, though, we were enormously overenthusiastic about what could be done at that point. It was much harder than we thought.

Bowmaker: What did you learn about Johnson's approach to the presidency, and how much interaction did you have with him?

Rivlin: President Johnson was very focused on power—that is, getting things done. Having come from the Senate, his measure of success was pushing measures through the Congress. And he knew how to do it. But the only two interactions I had with Johnson actually preceded my HEW job. One of his modes of operation was to appoint a task force on an issue. I worked on one relating to revenue sharing. He didn't adopt the policy—he didn't want to share revenue with states and localities—because he was federal program–oriented, and that gives you some insight into what his criteria were.

My one other interaction with Johnson took place at about the same time. He wanted to demonstrate that women could do things. This was in the early days of feminism—we're talking '64, and even before the Civil Rights Act of '65. He decided that he would make a big announcement that he had fifty highly qualified women in the government. But having announced that he had fifty, he then had to scramble to find the fifty [*laughs*]. At this point I was a rookie Brookings scholar working on an advisory committee to the secretary of the treasury. In scraping the bottom of the barrel to find fifty women, I got on the list and was invited to a big party at the White House as part of the celebration. With hindsight, that story is an illustration of how few women there were at the top of the federal government in those days.

Bowmaker: Did you have the opportunity to meet with President Nixon?

Rivlin: I met Nixon only once, but it turned out in retrospect to be quite significant. Very early on in the administration, he did what presidents often do, which is to go around from one department to another to meet the top brass. When we gathered in the secretary's office and he came in, I was just amazed at how nervous he was. I was standing next to him, and he was quaking. I remember having to restrain myself, because what I wanted to do was put my hand on his shoulder and say, "Relax, Mr. President, we're all your friends here." But, of course, one doesn't do that. Anyway, he got through it somehow. Then we all went downstairs to a room where he addressed a larger audience, and as soon as he was on the platform he was fine. It was in personal interaction that he was so ill at ease. I think that ended up being rather prophetic.

Bowmaker: Overall, what were the main lessons that you learned at HEW?

Rivlin: Something that became most obvious to me at HEW was, believe it or not, the fact that we live in a very big country with very diverse conditions [*laughs*]. We were immersed in trying to make these Johnson-era programs work, especially the education ones, but at that time we had 25,000 school districts—some large, some small, some rural, some urban—and so writing any kind of rules that were applicable in all these different places was really impossible. As a result, I became committed to more autonomy at the state level, and many years later, in '92, I wrote a book called *Reviving the American Dream* which was about devolving some of these programs to the states. I still think that's a plausible idea.

As Director of the Congressional Budget Office

Bowmaker: You were appointed director of the newly created CBO in 1975. Why was there a need for this agency to be established?

Rivlin: The idea came from the Congress, and it was part of the congressional warfare between the legislative branch and the executive branch headed by Nixon. The president and the Congress were at odds about a lot of things, and some of it is familiar in the current context. For example, the Democrats in the Congress wanted more civilian domestic spending than Nixon wanted, and he wanted a bigger military than they wanted. Then Nixon did something which presidents should not do in the view of the Congress—namely, he impounded funds, funds that had been voted on and signed off by him. He just didn't spend them, and that's a no-no under our system.

The Congress reacted very negatively, and that catalyzed something that should have happened sooner. They realized that they didn't really have a way of responding adequately to a presidential budget, and they needed a budget process of their own. And so they then embarked on this very ambitious effort of creating a congressional budget process, and part of it involved establishing the CBO so that they could have analysts on their side who worked for them as the Office of Management and Budget worked for the president. Then they had to figure out who was going to run it. After a long process I was chosen.

Bowmaker: Can you describe that process for us?

Rivlin: Having created this agency, they hadn't worried very much about it. The language and the law about what it should do is fairly short, and they hadn't really created a process for selecting a director except that what the law said was that he or she should be appointed by the Speaker of the House and the president pro tempore of the Senate jointly, on the advice of the budget committees. The two budget committees came up with the dumb idea of having separate search processes, so I was interviewed on both sides. The Senate voted for me, while the House voted for a very qualified guy named Sam Hughes, which meant they had two candidates.

Some months went by during which each side wanted their candidate, but they didn't know what to do about the problem. It was solved by accident because the chairman of the Ways and Means Committee, who was a very well-known congressman from Arkansas named Wilbur Mills, got into trouble. I don't think that many people knew that he was an alcoholic, but he was, and he had a spectacular incident with an exotic dancer named Fanne Foxe, in which Fanne leaped out of his car and into the Tidal Basin. The Tidal Basin is not very deep, so they pulled her out. But that was the end of Wilbur Mills's career because it was a well-publicized event. And that meant that he resigned as chairman of the Ways and Means Committee.

Al Ullman, who was chairman of the House Budget Committee, then stepped up to Ways and Means. He had been a strong proponent of Sam Hughes and very opposed to me. He was said to have said, "Over my dead body is a woman going to run this organization." People said things like that in those days. But with Al Ullman out of the way, the new chairman, Brock Adams, was not committed to the previous candidate. He told Ed Muskie, chairman of the Senate Budget Committee, "If you want a woman, that's OK with me." And so that's how I got the job...I owe it to Fanne Foxe [*laughs*].

Bowmaker: How did you set about creating this entirely new agency?

Rivlin: Starting a new agency with very little guidance was probably the most interesting thing I've ever done in my career. I asked Bob Reischauer from here at Brookings to go with me to the CBO, and I also took a couple of our research assistants and a secretary. Together we drew organizational charts on the blackboard and assembled a small group of consultants to advise us on how to set it up and on what kind of people we needed. In the end, we structured it very much like the Office of Management and Budget and hired very good people who were willing to take a chance on a new organization.

It was also important that the agency was nonpartisan; that's what the law said, and that's what I thought was needed. And so we hired people without regard to political affiliation and stressed the nonpartisanship. But I required the support of the two budget committee chairmen, Ed Muskie and Henry Bellmon [the ranking Republican on the Senate budget committee] to resist any political pressure, particularly on our original appointments. They said to me, "You hire who you think you need, and we'll tell our colleagues that's what we want you to do." That worked, even if it was a little less successful in the House—which is always more partisan than the Senate.

The other important thing was that I decided we should not make recommendations, because if you do, then people are going to jockey to get them. So our rule was that we would always give options and alternatives—we would not make recommendations, except on very technical budget matters.

Bowmaker: Was there anything that surprised or frustrated you in the early stages of establishing the agency?

Rivlin: The press was determined to show that we were partisan and to force me to make recommendations. So I had to learn how to handle questions like, "What do you *really* think?" That wasn't so hard, but there were a few times when a member of the press tried to blindside us in some way. I remember one incident when a reporter that I knew and trusted came in to interview me a couple of days before we were releasing a report. I had agreed to the interview and told him, "But you understand that the report is embargoed for the thirteenth of February." He said, "Oh yes, I understand that." And then the next day he published an article. I was outraged. He argued, "Well, you said the report was embargoed. You didn't say the interview was embargoed." I learned the lesson pretty fast that you can't be too careful [*laughs*].

Bowmaker: Were there any occasions when your bosses were concerned that the CBO was threatening the relationship between Congress and the executive branch?

Rivlin: They didn't want us colluding with the executive branch, and I had one incident in the early [Ronald] Reagan period. We had big differences in the first year of the Reagan administration between the CBO estimates of the deficit and the OMB estimates of the deficit, although as it turned out we were only a little bit more right than they were [*laughs*]. The deficit was much bigger than even we thought it would be as a result of the tax cuts. But in the second year, Dave Stockman, who was Reagan's budget director, called me up on Sunday afternoon at home in January of '82 and said, "We shouldn't go through this again. Can we talk about how you see things and how we see things?" I said, "Sure." And so I took the chief economists of each of the budget committees with me to see Dave at the OMB office. We had a perfectly unexceptional interchange about what we thought and what they thought, and it turned out to be not very different. But the minute I got back to my office my secretary said, "Chairman [Peter] Domenici wants to see you in his office right away." So I went scurrying over to see Pete, and he and Fritz Hollings, who was the ranking Democrat, chewed me out. I was just amazed because I didn't think I'd done anything wrong. But they were furious that I had gone over to see Stockman. I said, "We weren't colluding. We were just exchanging information." They told me, "Well, it looks bad. You shouldn't be meeting with the budget director of the executive branch." So I said, "OK, I won't do it again." I was pretty upset, but that was the separation of powers in action.

Bowmaker: How would you compare and contrast working with the [Gerald] Ford, [Jimmy] Carter, and Reagan administrations as director of the CBO?

Rivlin: We were pretty new in the Ford administration, and they were, too. They only lasted two years, and so each side was feeling their way. But I think we worked quite well with the Carter administration in terms of sharing information. And they liked us. The OMB and other people around Carter thought it was important to have the CBO there as an analytical agency, and that it actually helped to have somebody to communicate with on the Hill that was nonpartisan and reasonably qualified.

The Reagan administration had this kind of explosive beginning where they were suspicious of us because of the supply-side economics obsession. We didn't really care for it. We just thought they were vastly exaggerating the effect of tax cuts and that if you were going to do dynamic scoring of that sort you better do it on the spending side as well, which is actually how it's turned out.

I remember one House hearing where the more extreme supply-siders attacked me specifically as a Keynesian. There was one wonderful moment when Toby Moffett, who was a congressman from Connecticut, stood up on the dais, waved a paper, and said, "Dr. Rivlin, are you now or have you ever been a Keynesian? I have a list…I have a list!" This was a takeoff on the [Joseph] McCarthy era. It just brought down the house. Everybody was roaring with laughter, and it ended the tension [*laughs*].

Bowmaker: How would you describe your professional reputation when you left the CBO in 1983?

Rivlin: I was flying high when I left the CBO, largely because of this confrontation with the Reagan administration. By the end of summer of '83, it was clear that the deficits were going to be huge, and that was not all because we were right about the tax cut—it was much more because of [Federal Reserve Chairman Paul] Volcker raising interest rates and the Fed[eral Reserve] over-doing it and throwing the economy into recession. But it looked like I'd been right, and they'd been wrong [*laughs*]. So that was a high point of my career in many ways. I was on everybody's lists for honorary degrees. And while it was not entirely deserved, it was kind of fun [*laughs*].

At the OMB during the Clinton Administration

Bowmaker: When did you first meet Bill Clinton, and what were your impressions of him?

Rivlin: I first met Bill Clinton in '87 when my friend Peter Edelman called me up and asked if I would be willing to meet with the governor of Arkansas. I said, "Well, I'd like to be helpful, Peter, but who is the governor of Arkansas?" [*Laughs.*] He told me, "Bill Clinton is an up-and-coming young governor. I'm taking him around Washington to meet people that know about federal policy." And so we spent about two hours together, and I thought he was just terrific. He was very enthusiastic, he was very smart, he listened, and he asked wonderful questions. I thought, "Wow, this is a really impressive guy." I didn't see him again until he interviewed me for the OMB job.

Bowmaker: Yes—before taking up the role of deputy director of the OMB in 1993, you were interviewed for the director position. Could you tell us about that experience?

Rivlin: There was a short list of plausible candidates, and I was on it. So I went down to the governor's mansion in Little Rock and met with Bill Clinton. He had read my book *Reviving the American Dream*. I knew that because there'd been a picture in the *Washington Post* of Bill Clinton sitting on a train reading my book. And it was a good enough picture so you could actually see the title of the book, which was very nice publicity [*laughs*]. And not only had he read it, but he'd read it very carefully. Clinton has that kind of mind—he retains detail. So he led with quizzing me about the book, and he loved it because he was still governor of Arkansas, and a governor likes to hear about the idea of devolving power to the states. But I was very nervous during the interview. I wanted to do the job, and he was about to become president of the United States. That's a nervous-making situation [*laughs*]. So I came away with a sense that I hadn't done my best.

I didn't hear anything else for a while, until Vernon Jordan [friend and political adviser to Bill Clinton] called me and said, "The president is choosing Leon Panetta to be OMB director and wants you to be deputy director." I was very disappointed, but I said, "OK." I did consult with my sons and my husband, who told me, "Don't do it. It's a lesser job. You should be OMB director or nothing at all." I said, "Don't be silly. I'd like to be part of this administration, and I want to do it." Then I called Leon, who I'd known quite well on the Hill, and said, "I gather I'm going to be your deputy." They hadn't told him [*laughs*]. He said, "Oh, I haven't heard this. I need to talk to the president." Anyway, it came out in the end, and we all went back to Little Rock, where we had this big announcement of the economic team.

Bowmaker: Can you describe the tension between the economics team and the political team at the beginning of the administration, due to the decision to go for budget reduction when the campaign had been run on the "putting people first" idea? How did the president react to this tension?

Rivlin: There was a lot of tension, and we the economic team, led by Bob Rubin, had our first meeting with the president-elect around the dining room table in the governor's mansion about what was the goal of budget policy. There was some split within the economic team about how strong to be about deficit reduction. Panetta and I were the hawks, and the Council of Economic Advisers were more dovish. We were arguing that we should try to cut the deficit in half in four years, and they were suggesting we cut the deficit in half as a percent of GDP [gross domestic product], which is a lesser goal. It wasn't a big fight or anything, and in the end, we did much better than both.

Then we went through this amazing exercise with the president after the inauguration. We had a series of marathon meetings in the Roosevelt Room—many hours at a time—in which we went through the budget line by line. It was partly a decision process and partly a learning exercise for the president. He knew a lot about the programs that affected Arkansas, and he knew quite a lot about defense, but there were a lot of things he didn't know about. So that was the basis for putting together the first budget proposal. It was kind of isolated in that it was just the economic team and the president talking to each other.

Then the political people began saying, "This is terrible. You can't do this. You're going back on your promises in 'Putting People First.' These budget hawks are going to sink your administration." At one point they focused on me. There was an anonymous quote in *Newsweek*, which was still a serious magazine in those days, under the headline "Dead Man Walking" that said of me specifically, "No one pays any attention to her. She'll be out by the end of the year." The year in question being '93. I had worked at the *Washington Post* and I had friends there, and a couple of times people called me and said, "They're saying these awful things about you." It was kind of childish the way very young people on the political staff who'd been on the campaign thought this was the way to win. It turned out it wasn't, and the president sided with us and went ahead with the program.

Bowmaker: What was the response of NEC [National Economic Council] Deputy Director Gene Sperling, who had written "Putting People First"?

Rivlin: Gene was in an interesting but somewhat awkward position because he was, as you say, the author of "Putting People First." On the other hand, he thinks of himself as an economist—he's very good at economics—and he was working for Rubin. So, he had a foot in both camps. But he was the defender of "Putting People First." He would come not just then but later in the administration to any kind of a budget policy meeting and say, "Remember you said I'm putting people first…" I became really fond of Gene, but he was difficult at first. He was just persistent on the campaign promises, and in some ways he was playing the Steve Bannon role. While that's not fair to Gene, it's true that he was always saying, "This is what you said in the campaign, and this is what you have to do."

Bowmaker: What was your view on the tax increase that was part of the budget deficit reduction package?

Rivlin: In retrospect, the tax raise was quite trivial in many ways. We started out with a very sensible trajectory to mainly do a carbon tax. And that got whittled back to a very small gasoline tax increase—four and a half cents—and then the other piece was raising the top income tax bracket. Both were extremely controversial. After we put the package together, we fanned out in teams of two around the country to sell it. I went with Bob Rubin to New York to a remarkable series of meetings. First, we went to the Stock Exchange, and they assembled all of its members in a big room. That was Bob's territory more than mine, but we both sat at the table with glowering faces looking at us. People were really angry, and Bob made his case. The pushback was extreme. They said it would tank the economy, and that we would have a huge recession—which is of course the opposite of what happened. It was a really grim atmosphere. Then we got in the car and went up to a community center in Harlem. When we walked in, everyone cheered [*laughs*]. But Bob, to whom this was at the time somewhat unfamiliar territory, looked at the sea of black faces and said, "You do it." So I got to do the positive message that everybody wanted to hear in that audience. It was quite an experience [*laughs*].

Bowmaker: How did you feel about the proposed stimulus package that was intended to offset any harm from the aggressive budget reduction?

Rivlin: That was pushed by the people who thought that we were going too far with the deficit reduction. I guess I thought it was OK. It turned out to (a) not be necessary and (b) not to sell well. It got "Christmas treed," as they say—they hung [on it] a lot of small programs that were good things to do, but not essential. That gave the Republicans a chance to make fun of it because we were going to do midnight basketball. Well, midnight basketball was not a bad idea, but it sounds silly [*laughs*]. It was intended to give the young men something to do other than go out and rob people. But in the end, the stimulus package turned out not to matter. The economy strengthened, and it was already stronger at the end of '92 than we realized at the time.

Bowmaker: What was your view on the Clinton health care plan?

Rivlin: At the beginning, the president had said Hillary [Clinton] will be in charge of it. And she pulled together a group of people within the administration like [Secretary of Health and Human Services] Donna Shalala, myself, and a bunch of others to be senior advisers to the health care plan. I thought we'd be heavily involved. As it turned out we weren't, because Hillary and Bill relied on Ira Magaziner, a business consultant that they knew from somewhere, and put him in charge of setting up the process of making a plan. He had very elaborate ideas about the process. He set up all of these task forces of outside people from different parts of the health care industry and academia and came up with a decision plan that had all of these milestones. It was extremely elaborate. I took home a copy of it, and my business school professor husband started laughing. He said, "This is ridiculous" [laughs]. And he was right—it was business consultant over-the-top stuff.

But then there developed within the Magaziner group a great hostility toward the economic team because we were saying, "Wait a minute. (A) this is too complicated. (B) you're being unrealistic about the savings." Magaziner was a real believer in health maintenance organizations and managed care and somehow thought that he could save enough money by introducing managed care to pay for the expansion of coverage. The economic team thought that was pretty fanciful and that you couldn't get savings that quickly. And in any case, these were one-time savings. If you brought down the cost of care, you weren't necessarily bringing down the rate of growth of the cost of care. And so we made all those points and made ourselves very unpopular. We were essentially excluded from the deliberations of the inner circle, except for show-and-tell meetings with the president where I was always invited. The plan got put together and sent up to the Hill, and I did go up and defend it. I testified a couple of times in favor of it giving the best foot forward. But I wasn't terribly surprised when it failed. In retrospect, the [Barack] Obama team actually did a better job.

Bowmaker: Why do you say that?

Rivlin: In part because they co-opted the opponents, especially the insurance companies. The Hillary team brought in a lot of sectors of health care—hospitals, doctors, and so forth—but never got the insurance companies on board. And because the Obama team wanted to use the private sector, and to use competition among private insurance companies rather than this managed competition under a tighter umbrella, they were able to co-opt the insurance companies. And one of the things that ultimately sank the Hillary plan was the series of ads that the insurance companies did with Harry and Louise. That didn't happen with Obama. Now, the

Obama people had other problems, such as the adamant opposition of the Republicans—who by this time had decided to attack anything Obama did. But I think they had a better design.

Bowmaker: What did you learn about Hillary Clinton during the health care plan process?

Rivlin: I think it's a difficult position to put a first lady in. But Hillary was very well informed about the plan and sold it well. I did a couple of listening trips with her. One was to Iowa where we actually sat in farmhouses and listened to farmers talk about their health care problems. She listened— she's very good at that. So I have a generally favorable impression of Hillary, but not of Ira Magaziner. Why they both relied on him so much I never figured out.

Bowmaker: What was your perception of how Bill Clinton interacted with Hillary Clinton?

Rivlin: Oh, they interacted very well. Of course, he would be in the main chair because he was president, but he would call on her. There was never any tension in the room. Back in the early part of the budget process, Hillary was in some of the meetings, and there her role was one of disciplinarian. The president would just let everybody talk and talk and talk. And then she would say, "Now, Bill, we have to make a decision here and move on to the next issue." That was a very useful role sometimes played by her. Hillary is a more disciplined person than Bill is, and I saw that from the very beginning.

Bowmaker: What did you think of welfare reform, and in particular of President Clinton's decision to move health care reform ahead of it?

Rivlin: Some people thought it was a mistake to move health care reform ahead of welfare reform. It may have been. We didn't really get to welfare reform until after the loss to the Republicans in '94. I don't know exactly what I thought at the time, but in hindsight I thought it was fortunate because Democrats would not have supported that kind of welfare reform and Republicans did. In fact, Republicans believed they had thought of it. My colleague Ron Haskins wrote a very good book about the process on the Hill of passing welfare reform.[1] I read the first half of it and said, "Ron, this is very good, but it doesn't mention the Clinton administration. We thought

---

1. Ron Haskins, *Work over Welfare: The Inside Story of the 1996 Welfare Reform Law* (Washington, DC: Brookings Institution Press, 2006).

we were for welfare reform, and we campaigned on it." "Oh, yeah," he said [*laughs*]. He rewrote it so the Clinton involvement was more obvious. But in a sense that was the saving grace of welfare reform—that the Republicans thought they did it, and the Clinton administration thought we did it.

Welfare reform was very controversial within the administration. I think the president vetoed the bill twice, maybe three times, before he got something he felt he could sign. And then a couple of very prominent people at HHS [Health and Human Services], David Elwood [assistant secretary for planning and evaluation] and Mary Jo Bane [assistant secretary for children and families], resigned because they thought it was too tough. I felt it was about right, especially at the time. We had a roaring good economy by then, and unemployment was coming down. It was the correct moment to push people into jobs. And it also turned out that many of the people on welfare were already working—they just weren't reporting it. But then as the economy later turned into recession, it removed a safety net that might have been there. And more important, the obligations that the states took on in return for block-granting the TANF [Temporary Assistance for Needy Families] funds weren't lived up to. So I think that's a negative from my devolution cause.

Bowmaker: How did you end up taking over as director of the OMB?

Rivlin: The president called me one morning. This was June of '94. Leon had been with the president on a trip to Europe to the Normandy beaches, and they'd decided the appointment there. I came in on a Monday morning on a hot summer day in a kind of cotton flowered dress. It wasn't sort of business-like looking as I remember—I didn't have any serious appointments on my calendar that day. The White House called and said, "The president wants to see you right away in the residence." So I went over and he said, "I've decided to make Leon my chief of staff, and I'd like you to be budget director. Will you do it?" I said, "Gulp, yes." I was totally caught unawares. He told me, "I'd like to announce it at 1:00." He did, and then my son called me having watched the proceedings on television, and said, "You didn't know about this, did you, Mom?" I told him, "No." He said, "You wouldn't have worn that dress if you'd known about it" [*laughs*].

I didn't know Leon was leaving. I was aware that there was a problem in the chief of staff area because Mack McLarty, who is the nicest man you've ever met and quite able, had gone to kindergarten with the president in Hope, Arkansas. The last thing you want if you're president is your childhood buddy as chief of staff, especially if he's a very nice man. You don't want a nice man there. You want somebody to say no to you and to other people. And Mack just couldn't do it, and Leon could.

Bowmaker: What was President Clinton's approach to work?

Rivlin: At the beginning of the administration, the president would just run so behind on his schedule that we were wasting enormous amounts of time. If there was a 4:00 meeting in the Oval Office, we'd get there at 4:00, and then we'd stand around chitchatting with each other for an hour. We stopped doing that pretty quickly. You'd have your secretary call over and say, "When is the 4:00 meeting going to start?" And she'd say, "Oh, I would estimate 5:00 or 5:30 or 6:00." And then your secretary would say, "Well, call me when he's about ready." You'd save time that way. That was an example of a lack of discipline again. Because the president likes to talk, and a lot of people wanted to talk to him, he would just get behinder and behinder. That was not the only problem, but it was a symptom of it. And Leon stopped that—meetings would be held on time.

When I went to the Fed, I was really quite surprised. The first day that I was supposed to appear on the Board [of Governors], just as I was about to walk down the hall, I got a phone call that took me about a minute. So I walked into the meeting about one minute late, and boy, I never did that again [*laughs*]. It wasn't that anybody said anything, but they stared. "Who does she think she is?" they were thinking. It was a very much more disciplined situation.

The president had an enormous ability to really focus hard on a policy issue. For example, the amazing thing about his second term was that he was able to appear totally immersed in whatever the issue was—and there were some tough ones—while all this other chaos about impeachment was going on. I realized that he was already doing that when I was working with him because the Monica Lewinsky episode was happening—I just didn't know about it.

Meetings with the president were good policy seminars, and he always wanted to hear different sides. He's a good listener and a good retainer of what people say. When you talk to him one-on-one, you think you're the most important person in his life for five minutes, and then he moves on to the next person. He's just amazing that way, and that makes him very good to work for. Now, he wasn't always decisive. While I thought he was quite decisive in the economic arena, there were other issues like Bosnia which seemed to me to drag on for a long time without a decision.

Bowmaker: Was there ever any concern that the president might be influenced by someone outside the formal decision-making process?

Rivlin: The president had a whole roster of friends. He would call them in the middle of the night and then surprise the staff the next morning by saying, "I was talking to so-and-so last night, and he said..." Of course, there was also this whole Dick Morris episode. He was the consultant that the president turned to outside the regular group. Leon Panetta and the other people right around the president in the White House were quite suspicious of this guy, and it turned out for good reason—he was kind of sleazy. But Bill had worked with him in the past, and after [Newt] Gingrich won in the midterm elections, he [Clinton] began consulting with Dick Morris on the side. I was aware of it because Morris would call me for budget numbers. And he'd call at home on a Sunday afternoon. I don't keep budget numbers in my head very well, and it was always a little unsettling [*laughs*]. I'd give him a ballpark number and then check it.

Dick Morris was the one who had this triangulation idea that after the Gingrich win, Clinton should move back toward more fiscal responsibility. I was basically in favor of that argument, but some of the other people were either against what Morris was saying or just suspicious of him because he wasn't visible. And then he got caught with a prostitute, and it all became very unpleasant.

Bowmaker: Can you tell us the story behind the "Rivlin memo" that took place just before the 1994 midterm elections, and its implications for you?

Rivlin: Bob Rubin had said that in the second term, President Clinton would have to come to grips with the big entitlement programs—Social Security, Medicare, and Medicaid. So I agreed to put together a draft memo to the president that would raise the topic of long-run fiscal responsibility and give him some options, none of which were produced within the administration. We had a series of meetings about it, and in one of them we handed out what we thought was a near-final draft of the memo. We realized that it was sensitive enough that we should collect all of the copies at the end of the meeting. But one wasn't returned. Frank Newman, who was representing the Treasury while Lloyd Bentsen was in Naples, simply folded his copy and put it in his pocket. My special assistant, Matt Miller, saw him do it and started to chase him down the hall. But it was too late, because the next thing we knew it had been leaked.

We found out much later that Newman thought this was a very interesting memo and sent it to Bentsen in Naples on a secure fax. After it got there, on the corner, it was initialed EK—Edward Knight, Bentsen's chief counsel—and it had some handwritten comments by Bentsen, so we knew he had read it. It was then put into a secret pouch to be returned to Washington, and somewhere along the line it got out and into the public domain. The Republicans began saying that Clinton was going to cut Medicare and raise taxes, and that I was this all-powerful person who was pulling the strings. Bill Kristol, the prominent conservative writer, circulated the memo and said it was the Rivlin plan for destroying Social Security. It made me feel like everybody was gunning for me, and I was very uncomfortable.

Bowmaker: In the end, the Democrats lost the midterm elections. Why?

Rivlin: Yes, it was a moment of real depression in the White House, early '95. Some people thought the loss was due to health care. Hillary needless to say thought it was the budget, or at least it was not health care [*laughs*]. But she hadn't been very enthusiastic about the budget trajectory anyway. I don't know that I ever knew what the president thought. But he did not think we were wrong about the budget because we went barreling on with a stronger package that was negotiated with Gingrich. I'm sure he had lots of discussions analyzing the loss, but he wasn't a blamer at all—Trump is, but Clinton isn't.

Bowmaker: Overall, what did you learn from President Clinton?

Rivlin: I learned from what he did well, which was partly the kind of person he was: smart, optimistic, and energetic. And I guess I learned what I already knew: you have to keep things organized and work down a list and get it done. Even if you're president of the United States it's going to be a little more organized than Bill Clinton was. And then his great failure was losing control of his personal life, which was extremely unfortunate. I was very angry with him for that, and so were a lot of other people. We felt he let us down. But I still think he's a great, great guy. I have very positive feelings about him. He could have been a great president—and he almost was—had it not been for his womanizing.

Bowmaker: What did he learn from you?

Rivlin: That's interesting. I would like to know his answer [*laughs*]. I think he liked me and thought I was smart. But I also think he felt I was over-serious and that sometimes I came across as schoolmarmish. He said that to somebody once, who then reported it back to me. I realized that was a product of my nervousness in his presence.

My good friend Donna Shalala got to know him very well and worked with him very closely. She was better able than I was to joke around with him and focus on whatever he was focused on at that particular time. But I remember one wonderful moment. I just happened to be walking down the West Wing corridor, and he was coming toward me looking absolutely as though he was on top of the world. He had just shot a hole in one, and he wanted everybody to know about this incredible thing that he had done. It was just terrific to see how pleased he was [*laughs*].

Bowmaker: I would now like to turn to your experiences with the rest of the economic team. How would you describe your relationship with the National Economic Council?

Rivlin: I never thought that they needed the NEC, which is a symptom of the diffusion of economic decision-making in the US government. Most sensible countries have a finance ministry or a chancellor of the exchequer under whom economic policy gets made. We don't do that. We have the Treasury over "here," the OMB over "there," and the CEA [Council of Economic Advisers] somewhere else. It's all very diffuse, and if you're doing that then you need somebody to coordinate these various centers of power. That was the idea behind the NEC. It sort of worked—Bob Rubin was extremely effective at orchestrating the meetings, including the ones with the president—but the NEC did meddle. One of the problems with welfare reform, for instance, was that there were just too many cooks in the pudding, and it didn't get coordinated very well.

Bowmaker: How would you describe your relationship with the Council of Economic Advisers?

Rivlin: Laura Tyson and Joe Stiglitz were both very good chairs of the CEA. Laura was less exuberant, less maverick than Joe, although Joe for Joe was pretty calm and collected at the CEA [*laughs*]. On the other hand, he was quite shocked that politics played such a role, particularly on issues relating to energy and pollution policy. I remember when we were talking about agricultural runoff waste, and at some point, one of the political people in the White House said, "Stop talking about it. We don't do chickens." Chickens were big in Arkansas, and they cause a lot of pollution. Joe was furious about that kind of thing. He had several causes that he thought were slam dunks from an economic point of view, and he was right.

When I got the job at the Fed, Joe came over to my office at the OMB on a Saturday afternoon, and we sat outside in the sunshine on the veranda. He lectured me on how [Chairman of the Federal Reserve Alan] Greenspan was too hawkish, and that we needed lower interest rates. Actually, he was misreading Greenspan entirely [laughs]. After I had been appointed but not confirmed, during the first conversation I had with Greenspan, he said, "I hope they get your nomination through quickly. I need you to help me with these inflation hawks." So Joe was misreading Greenspan but lecturing me on what I needed to know to go to the Fed. He was often a little professorial in that sense.

Bowmaker: How would you describe your relationship with the Treasury?

Rivlin: I got along extremely well with Bob Rubin and [Deputy Secretary of the Treasury] Roger Altman, but I got along less well with Larry Summers—but that's because Larry is Larry. He lectures people and makes them feel like they're not very bright graduate students who don't quite understand what the great man is saying. That's a universal reaction to Larry, I think [laughs]. I remember one very clear example. The issue was credit scoring of loan forgiveness to low-income countries. What Larry wanted to do was to forgive a bunch of loans to low-income, mostly African countries. That had to appear in the budget. He wanted to use a high discount rate on the grounds that they weren't going to be able to pay anyway, and this wasn't going to cost us very much. But then he wanted to relend to the same countries at low interest rates. My position was, "Larry, you've got to choose. You've got to do one or the other here. We haven't had a regime change or any reason to think these countries are better credit risks than they were. And our job at OMB is to score these loans. If you're going to use a high discount rate on forgiveness, you've got to use the same discount rate when you relend." He was furious [laughs]. We had a big set to and a big meeting with other people in which he just excoriated me—claimed I didn't understand the issue and that I was a captive of my staff. A lot of insulting things were said that were totally uncalled for, especially because I was right [laughs]. I remember this as being a bad moment.

Bowmaker: How would you describe your relationship with the Federal Reserve when you were at the OMB?

Rivlin: The economic team was always trying to restrain the president from attacking the Fed. All presidents want low interest rates. In '94 the Fed was raising interest rates, and the president always wanted to say something negative about it. But the economic team was saying, "No, no, no. They're independent. You don't attack the Fed." One day, Greenspan was due to come over. The president would ask him to the White House every once in a while to chat about the economy. So we were all gathered in the Oval Office—all the economic team and the president—waiting for Greenspan to arrive. Clinton launched into a mimicking of Greenspan, talking about the dangers of high interest rates. And it was so funny. We were all cracking up [*laughs*]. I remember looking at the door to make sure it was closed because I didn't want Greenspan in the other office listening to us. By the time Greenspan was announced and he walked into the room, we were still laughing and couldn't explain what the joke was [*laughs*].

Bowmaker: Why did you leave the OMB for the vice chair position at the Federal Reserve?

Rivlin: I didn't want to leave, but the president wanted me at the Fed. The story that he told me—and I think it was partly right—was that he wanted to reappoint Greenspan and have somebody there who was his person. Alan Blinder was the vice chair at the time, but he wanted to go back to Princeton. So Clinton wanted a package deal, which involved reappointing Greenspan, putting me in, and giving the other open slot to someone else, with Larry Meyer eventually being chosen for it. So it was supposed to be the three of us, and it was, but I initially resisted it. I told the president that I wanted to stay at the OMB because we were in the middle of a budget negotiation. He said that he really needed me at the Fed, and I told him that I would think about it [*laughs*]. And then Laura Tyson, who was by that stage NEC director, gave me the hard sell. She said that I would be good at the job. But I wasn't a monetary policy expert—I cared about the budget. In the end, though, you don't say no to the president [*laughs*]. So I did it, and I loved it. I had a great time at the Fed. It was calmer, more organized, and more collegial—an interesting learning experience. And I got along fine with Greenspan, better than Blinder had. It was a good move as it turned out, but I didn't realize that at the time.

It wasn't until much later that I figured out what they were really doing. Ron Brown [secretary of commerce during Clinton's first term] had been killed in an air accident in Croatia. They were going into the '96 campaign without a major black figure in the Cabinet. Frank Raines, who was an extremely competent person, had been in the OMB in the Carter administration, and I had tried to get him to come back as my deputy at one point, but he was making a lot of money at Fannie Mae, and that was an interesting job and he said no. But they decided it would be a good idea to put Frank somewhere in the Cabinet, and OMB was the natural place. That involved moving me somewhere, and the Fed was a natural place. They had a nice musical chairs arrangement that would get them a black Cabinet member. I didn't figure that out until about two years later [*laughs*].

Bowmaker: In 2010, you were appointed by President Obama to the Simpson-Bowles Commission. Given your experience, how would you compare and contrast Presidents Obama and Clinton?

Rivlin: They're both very smart, but Obama is maybe too disciplined. I was working a lot with Congress in this period and seeing Obama through their eyes, because the Simpson-Bowles Commission had sixteen sitting members of Congress, eight from the House and eight from the Senate. They felt that Obama was distant. Both the Democrats and the Republicans would very often compare him with Clinton, who was not distant. Paul Ryan told me once well into the Obama administration, when he was chairman of the Budget Committee, that he'd never had a one-on-one conversation with the president. That was remarkable. And I was on the Hill at a dinner one night with some senators from both parties. The night before they'd been to dinner at the White House, and they were like kids. They said, "Oh, the president was so nice. The president said 'this,' and the president said 'that'…" It was a demonstration, I thought, of a missed opportunity that Obama had to do this more often and get to know these people well. Clinton had done that, but Obama had not, and neither had Carter. Carter was cerebral and standoffish and didn't get to know the leadership in Congress nearly as well as Clinton did—and Reagan did, for that matter. Reagan understood he needed a relationship with Tip O'Neill, the Speaker of the House, and he had one. I don't think Obama ever quite got it that he needed to really schmooze with these people—he's not a schmoozer.

General Thoughts on Economic Policymaking

Bowmaker: Which fallacies, misconceptions, or misinterpretations affect policy debate in this country?

Rivlin: Europeans don't understand how limited the president's powers are in the economic sphere. I gave a talk at the LSE [London School of Economics] a couple of years ago, and somebody in the question period said to me, "You've talked a lot about the Congress. Do they matter?" That's so European [*laughs*]. It's so not understanding the separation of powers and how important the Congress is. I think the founding fathers got it right. They did want to slow down policymaking and make it deliberate, and they required compromise at every stage between the House and the Senate, and the Congress and the president, and so forth. But that's not the way a parliamentary system works, which means there's the illusion that, "Oh well, the president is the head of the government. He can do anything he wants." That's not true here, and I think that it's something of a misunderstanding in the US as well because there's all this hoopla about the presidential campaign. And then when the president gets into office he realizes, "Wait a minute. I can't do that. I'm going to have to work with the Congress." Trump is finding this very hard to do. Jimmy Carter found it hard to do. I think Clinton didn't, and Obama certainly understood it although he wasn't as good at it as Clinton was. And he had a much harder problem because he had an adamant, angry opposition.

Bowmaker: To what extent can economics research produced in universities help inform policymakers?

Rivlin: When I went to graduate school, which was in the dark ages, we were really focused on what policy should be. And then came a long period in which economics departments were not very concerned with policy—they were concerned with models and working out the implications of these totally unrealistic assumptions about rationality. You got your promotions by being very good at that or very good at econometrics. Economics moved away from sociology, political science, and history and became at its worst an isolated version of applied math, and not terribly useful to policymakers. But what the universities then did was create public policy schools—I teach in one at Georgetown—which has drawn the disciplines back together. And I also think that the emergence of behavioral economics, with all of these outsiders like [Daniel] Kahneman coming into the field, has led to economics being useful again.

Personal Reflections

Bowmaker: How did your personality affect your style and approach as a policymaker?

Rivlin: That's a good question. I think the pluses of my personality are that I work very hard, I'm very persistent, I like to get things right, and I like to write in a way that communicates to noneconomists. All of those skill sets have stood me in good stead.

Like many women, especially women in my age group, I was afraid to lean in, as they say these days, or to assert myself, or to question authority as much as I should have in retrospect. But I think the thing that women suffer from even now is we don't speak up very much in meetings, or we're afraid to say something dumb. Men say dumb things all the time and nobody cares [*laughs*]. But women are afraid to, afraid that the question will sound like they don't really understand it. I think I've only gradually gotten over that.

Bowmaker: As a policymaker, which decisions or outcomes were most gratifying?

Rivlin: I suppose the most satisfying thing was to see that we worked very hard to get the deficit come down, and we ended up with a surplus. But I was happiest in jobs where I was organizing analysis and talking about it to the people who made the decisions rather than actually doing the decision making myself. That's why I loved the CBO.

Bowmaker: Did you enjoy the CBO more than the OMB?

Rivlin: Oh, yes. Partly because I was the boss. I started the organization. It was my baby. I ran it for eight and a half years, and although there were very nervous moments, it was a success. Forty years later, it's still there. The OMB was a much more complicated situation. I enjoyed running it, but the interaction with the White House, while it had its very good moments, was always unsettling partly because there were people gunning for me that would have liked to have seen me embarrassed. I think I overreacted to that in retrospect—I should have just let it go.

But it was also partly because the Clinton White House at the beginning especially was so chaotic. You'd come in to the office as deputy director with a schedule you needed to get done that day. By 8:30 in the morning it had totally exploded because the White House had called and said, "There's a meeting on 'this' and there's a meeting on 'that,' and you have to be 'here' and we want you to go 'there.'" And then you were handing off these other responsibilities to other people and trying to keep your head straight. It was very difficult.

And the OMB is also the crossroads of the government. The number of issues that you have to be an expert on, or at least understand well enough to sign off on, is incredible. It's not just the budget—it's all of the management issues, it's all of the regulatory issues, and it's all of the information control issues. It's just a very big portfolio. It was a relief to get to the Fed where you only had monetary and supervisory policy [*laughs*].

Bowmaker: There must be some things, in hindsight, that you'd like the opportunity to have done differently. What are they?

Rivlin: I've been very lucky in my career. I've been in all of these interesting positions. But I probably would have been a little more aggressive and less afraid of making a mistake—certainly not so nervous about it all the time [*laughs*]. But I think that's true of a lot of people, especially many women.

Janet Yellen (*far right*), when chair of the Council of Economic Advisers, speaking at an economic team senior staff meeting for President Bill Clinton in the Cabinet Room on June 19, 1998. Also pictured are Jacob Lew (*far left*), deputy director of the Office of Management and Budget; Gene Sperling (*second left*), director of the National Economic Council; and Robert Rubin (*second right*), secretary of the treasury.

18   Janet L. Yellen
Born 1946, Brooklyn, New York

Janet Yellen graduated from Brown University with a degree in economics in 1967, and she earned a PhD in economics from Yale University in 1971. She was an assistant professor of economics at Harvard University between 1971 and 1976, served as an economist with the Federal Reserve's Board of Governors in 1977 and 1978, and was on the faculty of the London School of Economics and Political Science between 1978 and 1980. She then joined the University of California, Berkeley, where she became the Eugene E. and Catherine M. Trefethen Professor of Business and Professor of Economics. She is now a professor emerita at the university.

Yellen took leave from Berkeley for five years beginning in August 1994 and served as a member of the Board of Governors of the Federal Reserve System through February 1997. She then left the Federal Reserve to become chair of the Council of Economic Advisers (CEA) under President Bill Clinton through August 1999.

Yellen served as president and chief executive officer of the Federal Reserve Bank of San Francisco between 2004 and 2010. She then became vice chair of the Board of Governors of the Federal Reserve System, and in 2014 she took office as chair of the board. She served in that role until February 2018. Currently, Yellen is a distinguished fellow in residence at the Brookings Institution.

I interviewed Janet Yellen in her office at the Board of Governors of the Federal Reserve System, in Washington, D.C. It was early in the afternoon on Friday, June 21, 2013.

Background Information

Bowmaker: Why did you become an economist?

Yellen: I discovered economics in college, and it combined two things that I like and are important to me. One is thinking very logically and analytically about issues. I was always interested in math, which I contemplated initially as a profession, and found that economics had a similarly rigorous approach. Two relates to the fact that I care about people. I discovered that economics was of enormous relevance to our lives and had the potential to make the world a better place.

Entering the Policy World

Bowmaker: What does an economist bring to the policy world that others do not?

Yellen: A unique way of understanding the consequences of various policies. Thinking through not only their first-round effects, but also what we would normally call their general equilibrium effects, and considering how markets and institutions may respond to the incentives created by systems put in place by policymakers. That is, policies may have unintended consequences that are not immediately obvious, or while it may seem straightforward that they promote a particular goal, they are not always successful in doing so when economists think more deeply about them.

As Chair of the Council of Economic Advisers

Bowmaker: Why do you think President Clinton appointed you to be his chair of the CEA?

Yellen: The Council of Economic Advisers needs someone who understands macroeconomics well. I had been already been appointed a governor at the Federal Reserve, where I had thought carefully about macroeconomic issues and, of course, had developed an understanding of monetary policy. I think that experience was useful and gave me a grounding that most academic economists considered for the role at the council would not have had. But there were many people President Clinton could have chosen, and I was certainly surprised when I got the call.

Bowmaker: Did he make it clear what he expected you to do for him?

Yellen: No, he didn't make it clear what he expected from me. I think he probably took for granted that I understood that I would be involved in anything that pertained to economic policy. In other words, the Council of Economic Advisers would always have a seat at the table when policy was being debated. But we would not have operational responsibilities—unlike, say, the Treasury—and would not take the lead on coordinating policy, because that was the role of the NEC [National Economic Council].

Bowmaker: Did you take any advice from former members or chairs of the CEA before you began your role?

Yellen: Yes, of course. I asked for advice from many people about the workings of the Council of Economic Advisers and its priorities. I knew Joe Stiglitz, my immediate predecessor, very well because he had been on my thesis committee, so I spoke with him. I also talked with Laura Tyson, my colleague from Berkeley; and Alan Blinder, my colleague from the Fed[eral Reserve], both of whom had been on the Council of Economic Advisers. Since I didn't have any previous White House experience, they were able to give me a fair amount of insight into President Clinton. I learned, in particular, that he had a very wide range of interests in economics, as well as a deep understanding of the subject. My predecessors at the Council had also developed a way of interacting with the president that they thought was useful and urged me to continue with it. There has always been a tradition of writing notes to the president about data releases, but what we did was to give him a short publication called the *Weekly Economic Briefing of the President*. This contained very interesting economic research that could help build his knowledge base and influence his views when he had to make policy decisions. It would usually take the form of four or five very succinct discussions of research ideas and findings, often accompanied by graphical illustrations of the main points. It took a great deal of work for our economists to identify things that the president would find interesting and then to write them in a style that was sufficiently concise and clear. And we often did our own research, which ended up in some of his speeches and became an organizing device for conversations that I would lead with the president.

Bowmaker: Did you view yourself as having strong policy positions or simply as a hired professional serving the president?

Yellen: I certainly had strong views about macroeconomics and macro policy. My orientation is more Keynesian, and I had my own perspective, for example, on what drives inflation. What I discovered, though, is that we spent more of our time on micro issues, and I think the disagreement among policy economists on how to think about those is smaller. But as you say, the Council of Economic Advisers is a group of hired professionals whose job is to provide the best possible economic advice to the president. And so I interpreted that as meaning we had to be completely up-to-date with the economics profession's thinking about the policy issues that the president was grappling with, and then based on that understanding, we would provide him with impartial advice.

Bowmaker: How would you describe the economic environment that you inherited as chair of the CEA and the issues that needed to be prioritized?

Yellen: When President Clinton was elected, the economy had relatively high unemployment, but it was beginning to recover. And in 1993, he had put in place a very substantial deficit reduction package, which was pretty controversial because he raised taxes on upper-income earners and undertook significant budget cuts. It passed by only a very narrow majority, and many Democrats who voted for it were defeated in the midterm elections. And so President Clinton was faced with needing to do something about the deficit, but also wanting to see the economy grow. Bob Rubin, who led the NEC, had the idea that it was possible for deficit reduction to also be expansionary. There was a lot of skepticism in markets about whether or not deficit reduction would ever occur, but Rubin's idea was that by phasing the cuts in over time and not all up front, you could regain the confidence of markets and end up with a growth dividend. In other words, in spite of doing fiscal austerity, long-term interest rates would come down. And it really worked like a charm. Before long, the economy was growing quite successfully, and in fact, the Fed had to raise interest rates to stop from overshooting full employment.

So I was lucky in the sense that when I arrived at the White House in 1997, everything from a macro perspective was beginning to turn up roses. But more needed to be done in terms of deficit reduction, which was a major issue on my plate. We had to put together a further deficit reduction package that would complete the job of balancing the budget. Beyond the short term, though, we all well understood that there were very serious long-term issues with the deficit relating to aging populations. Touching those was regarded as the third rail of politics, but President Clinton was very committed to wanting to prepare for the day when deficits would again be rising and they would become unsustainable.

Another huge thing that occurred, of course, was the Asian financial crisis. You could date that from the summer of 1997. We were very worried about how it would hit the United States, as well as the directly affected countries. That was certainly a topic of tremendous importance, but in the end it never had any meaningful impact on our economy. If anything, the spillovers were favorable because the dollar rose in value and oil prices dropped.

But I would say the issue I spent more time on in the White House than any other single thing was climate change. In the run-up to the Kyoto climate negotiations in November 1997, we did a huge amount of analytics trying to figure out what our policy stance should be, and then post-Kyoto, of course, there was huge controversy around climate change. In particular, I had to spend an enormous amount of time trying to devise ways in which we could meet the agreement without it being unduly onerous.

Bowmaker: I would now like to ask you some questions about President Clinton and your interactions with him. First, how did you go about establishing a comfortable working relationship with the president?

Yellen: I think the people who tend to know a president best are those who were with him from the early days of his campaign. I didn't have the opportunity to develop that sort of closeness, and I wasn't even in the White House in his first term, when some of the very important budget decisions were made. So when I came to the Council of Economic Advisers, I never expected to establish a one-on-one relationship with him. And the truth is that a president's time is very jealously guarded in any case, with everybody being very careful about how he has policy issues presented to him. There are many people in the White House who want to be involved in shaping policy. And so, the reason to create something like the NEC is to establish a level playing field. Then everyone can have a seat at the table and put forward their arguments for debate, with the options being narrowed down and presented to the president in a way that is both systematic and fair. What everybody is terrified about is the prospect of the president going off to play golf with one person involved in that process and, while they are buddying around for six hours, being talked into something else. And so much of what goes on in the White House is designed to make sure that doesn't happen, because it really leads to strife. I understood, then, that I was entitled to always have a seat at the table as part of a group to meet with the president, but that it would be a violation of the rules of the game if I was allowed to develop a one-on-one relationship where I would have the opportunity to influence him while playing golf—not that I play golf [*laughs*].

With all that said, I certainly got to know President Clinton well. I was in meetings with him every other day as part of a group of people who were talking to him about one subject or another, and those included my own meetings, which centered on the *Weekly Economic Briefing* that I mentioned earlier.

Bowmaker: Can you give us some insight into President Clinton's specific interests in economics which came out during your meetings with him?

Yellen: There were some topics he found more interesting than others, but he liked in particular anything related to welfare and labor markets. For example, I remember one time when I spoke with him about teen child rearing because we had written about it in a *Weekly Economic Briefing*. We had featured a new paper by Joseph Hotz and coauthors, whose work suggested that among those women who would otherwise carry a pregnancy to term as a teenager, not having a teen birth did not result in improved socioeconomic outcomes in their twenties and early thirties. Instead, teen mothers appeared to pay a penalty immediately following the birth but caught up or even surpassed those who delayed first birth as a result of a miscarriage.[1]

The briefing also mentioned that the results were consistent with earlier work questioning whether teen childbearing had adverse effects. That included other research by Sandy Korenman, one of the council's staff economists, which compared sibling pairs in which one sister had a teenage birth and one delayed childbearing into her twenties. Like the new paper, the findings of sister comparisons showed much attenuated effects of teen childbearing on education, poverty, public assistance use, and so on.[2]

---

1. This working paper was eventually published in 2005 as V. Joseph Hotz, Susan Williams McElroy, and Seth G. Sanders, "Teenage Childbearing and Its Life Cycle Consequences: Exploiting a Natural Experiment," *Journal of Human Resources* 40, no. 3 (2005): 683–715.
2. See, for example, Arline Geronimus and Sanders Korenman, "The Socioeconomic Consequences of Teen Childrearing Reconsidered," *Quarterly Journal of Economics* 107, no. 4 (1992): 1187–1214.

Obviously, these findings were counterintuitive, given the strong presumption that a teenage birth reduces educational and economic prospects for women. President Clinton was totally taken with them. In fact, in the course of talking with him about the research, it was almost like he was becoming a PhD adviser with all of his questions. I had to go to Sandy and tell him, "The president wants to see what similar techniques would show about the consequences of nonmarital, as opposed to teenage, fertility." He said, "Gee, that would be a huge amount of work." But he did it, and I ended up taking him to meet President Clinton, who was genuinely interested in what the evidence would reveal.

During the Asian financial crisis, I also remember him picking up a book by Barry Eichengreen about global financial architecture.[3] He read the entire thing—all 200 pages or so—and then sent it to us with a note saying, "Well, what do you think about the comments I made in the margin?" [*Laughs.*] They were very lively! President Clinton really did have a good instinct for economics.

Bowmaker: How would you describe the president's style of authority?

Yellen: I wouldn't say he was domineering or authoritarian. He listened carefully to the advice he received and was very interactive. Of course, he had his views and sometimes challenged people and pushed them pretty hard on the things they were saying. He might even know more than the experts he was talking to and raise points that they hadn't thought about. In that sense, he could be a little intimidating.

Bowmaker: When you were at the council, how would you describe your relationship with the Treasury?

Yellen: I had a very close relationship with the Treasury. We were the economic agencies that were regarded as being a little more tough-minded than others, and when collaboration was needed or factions formed around policy options, the Treasury and the Council of Economic Advisers were aligned—not always, but commonly.

Bowmaker: How about your relationship with the NEC?

---

3. Barry J. Eichengreen, *Toward a New International Financial Architecture: A Practical Post-Asia Agenda* (Washington, DC: Peterson Institute for International Economics, 1999).

Yellen: I would argue the NEC is more political than the council. It is their job to bring everyone to the table and to forge positions. You don't always win everything. When you are sorting through options, it is sometimes frustrating as an economist to see things dismissed because they are not politically acceptable, and similarly things being done for political reasons that don't embody the absolute best economics.

Bowmaker: Finally, how about your relationship with the Fed?

Yellen: Obviously, I knew the people at the Fed very well from my time there. I stayed in close touch with them and also nabbed staffers to bring over to the council. But monetary policy is an independent Fed task, so it was a very respectful relationship between us. The Rubin Doctrine, I will call it, stated that the White House should always stay out of commentating on Fed policy. This meant that after a monetary policy meeting or when a change had been made, we would issue a statement along the lines of, "We respect the Fed's judgment." In other words, we kept an appropriate distance. But I would often talk with [Chairman of the Federal Reserve] Alan Greenspan about the economic numbers a couple times a week. He was a data hound [*laughs*].

Bowmaker: All things considered, can you point to a specific example of where you, as an economist, or the CEA, as an organization, were able to make a difference?

Yellen: What really makes a difference at the Council of Economic Advisers is shooting down bad ideas. You do that all day long. Now, you may say, "How does that show up? Can you point to that as your accomplishment?" Maybe you want to call that a negative accomplishment [*laughs*], but I feel that it is a very important role of the council. For example, during my time, I remember when there was momentum behind an increase in the minimum wage and thinking it was just a terrible idea because it wasn't going to do anything for the people that you wanted to help.

Similarly, we shot down many potential protectionist measures. During the Asian financial crisis, a number of countries, like South Korea, that had just gotten clobbered were sending lots of steel and other goods into the United States at very low prices, and industry groups were clamoring for trade actions to protect themselves from foreign competition—which was obviously bad on standard economic grounds. At the same time, we were very worried that in response to the crisis, they would also close their own markets. But as a country that had not experienced any discernible effects from the crisis, it would have been extremely stupid for us from a dip-lomatic standpoint to have undertaken protectionist actions while going around the world telling them, "We know you've got all these problems, but don't you dare do anything protectionist as well."

Beyond that, one area where I feel we made a positive difference was climate change. The United States had not been forthcoming on that issue for a long time, and President Clinton and Vice President Gore wanted to change that and play a leadership role on environmental issues. And then it became a question of how it could be done without killing the economy. For example, the president and vice president wanted desperately for the US to sign up for Kyoto, but there were many possible ways of imple-menting it. As I mentioned earlier, we did a ton of work on the issue and developed a set of "must haves" to be included in the agreement. I called it "where, when, and what flexibility." The "where flexibility" referred to the idea that if we were going to agree to targets for emissions reductions, then we had to have flexibility about where the emissions reductions would be done. That meant if it was cheapest to do emissions trading in China, we should be able to meet our obligation by essentially buying emission reductions from the Chinese and getting credit for it. The "what flexibil-ity" referred to the fact that there are different kinds of greenhouse gases, so we should have the flexibility about what types of emissions reductions we were targeting. For example, is it methane, or is it carbon sequestration in forests? And then the "when flexibility" had to do with not having rigid year-by-year targets. We wanted the ability to trade off emissions reductions over time.

We were very insistent about these forms of flexibility, and I think we were successful in building them into basic climate change agreements, and they became tenets of administration policy. But we really had to fight hard to make sure it happened, in part because the economic analysis sug-gested they made an enormous difference to what the costs would be. The administration were motivated to keep the costs down, as they were forced to discuss the issue with Congress and the public and wanted cost validation from a broader community of analysts and economists, including academics. That meant you couldn't say, "Oh, this is going to cost ten cents per house-hold" if the reality was $10,000 per household. There were a bunch of people out there who would tell you, "Here are the following ninety-five studies that say it's going to cost $10,000." And so it was the Council of Economic

Advisers' job to present all of that evidence to the president and vice president. And if they said, "It can't cost $10,000 per household," you told them, "Well, we'll get it down to $500 if we do 'where, what, and what flexibility'" [*laughs*]. So that's an example of bringing economics into the picture in a way that interacts with the politics but in the end makes a difference.

General Thoughts on Economic Policymaking

Bowmaker: Do you believe that if we were to raise the level of economic literacy in this country, economic policymaking would improve because the people would demand better policy?

Yellen: That's a tough question [*laughs*]. Obviously, the level of economic literacy in this country is not very high, with many ideas afoot that don't pass "two plus two equals four" tests. For example, it is always disheartening in terms of budget policy, where people somehow think there is a free lunch. In other words, you can balance the budget without either raising taxes or cutting spending. When I think about how hard we worked on trying to deal with long-term budget issues back in the Clinton administration, it is discouraging to realize how, in all the years since then, we have made no meaningful progress. When you watch every election, it is awfully hard for candidates to discuss the trade-offs that are involved. If the American public was well educated and grown up, it would be able to understand the "no free lunch" principle. You have to make hard choices and be rational in deciding between what is more and less important. Unfortunately, that doesn't seem to happen.

Bowmaker: Do you think that the gap between economics research produced in universities and policymaking will increase or decrease over time?

Yellen: I don't see the gap as being that huge. You have some pretty darn sophisticated economic analysis that underlies policymaking. When you come to things like the budget, it's not that economists aren't at the table. Again, it's that politically, people are not willing to accept either higher taxes or cuts in important programs that they like, or restrictions on their choices that might diminish costs. I feel the problem lies with the electorate and maybe with Congress, as well.

Bowmaker: Which are the most important unsolved economic problems in this country?

Yellen: First, we have a very disturbing, seemingly long-term trend towards rising inequality. But I don't think we thoroughly understand its causes or have a very meaningful approach to dealing with it.

Second, climate change is an enormous problem. I don't think we know how to make adequate progress in dealing with something that is a global externality and one that plays out over hundreds of years. It's like termites eating at the basement. There never seems to be a day when it is urgent to do something, until eventually it is too late. And so how do we get the world to take action on a problem that is tremendously hard to reverse? Frankly, I think it is terrifying.

Third, I am very focused on how we can make the financial system safer, because we don't want another financial crisis like the one we've just had. We are only now beginning to understand the nature of systemic risk and how to address it, and so thinking about the kinds of safeguards and arrangements that will diminish the risk of future financial crises is something we are going to be preoccupied with for a long time. That is challenging from both an intellectual and a policy perspective.

Personal Reflections

Bowmaker: What are your strengths and weaknesses as a policymaker?

Yellen: I'll focus on the strengths if you don't mind [*laughs*]. I think I'm willing to do lots of work to understand an issue and to try to find a way to explain the pros and cons of different alternatives. It helps that I'm a decent teacher and not supertechnical, because I have the capacity to summarize them in understandable and relevant ways to noneconomists.

I also think I'm a reasonably good listener who works reasonably well with other people. I don't feel that I have to be the dominant personality in the room. Making economic policy always involves bringing together people from different backgrounds with different points of view. I'm good at developing strong relations with those people and at looking for options that will satisfy them. That's partly what I do here at the Fed, when I participate in a committee with nineteen strong-minded people. I listen carefully to what is being said and then think about how to forge positions that will command reasonable consensus and be, if not first best, at least fourth best [*laughs*].

Bowmaker: As a policymaker, which decisions or outcomes were most gratifying?

Yellen: I haven't said much so far about my time at the Fed. Obviously, this is a very different organization. Politics doesn't play any role; we have the advantage of a huge professional staff who can do work in a very thorough, analytic, and thoughtful way; and there is time to debate things more carefully than is possible sometimes in a White House setting. We have made a lot of advances in policymaking that I have been part of and feel very good about. For example, our communications to the public have come a long way, to the point where they are now central to policy. That's not to say that we always communicate perfectly, but we have established clear statements of our goals and strategies for achieving them.

Bowmaker: On the other hand, there must be some things, in hindsight, that you'd like the opportunity to do differently. What are they?

Yellen: The Clinton years were great, at least in terms of macroeconomic performance: unemployment and inflation were both low, and we didn't see a huge exacerbation of trends towards rising inequality in a strong economy. But as part of the economics profession more broadly, I feel we should have been more on top of the dangers that were building in the financial system in the run-up to the crisis. Supervision of the banking organizations ought to have been better. As I said earlier, in the aftermath, we are now trying to build the apparatus and knowledge base that is necessary to think about things differently, like monitoring of the financial system appropriately and putting in place safeguards that will make it less likely to collapse if there is an adverse shock. But I think anybody who lived through the financial crisis with any responsibility for any part of it beforehand has to feel sobered by the experience and must ask themselves what they might have done to have made a difference.

Jacob Lew, when director of the Office of Management and Budget, during a hearing on February 2, 1999, before the Senate Budget Committee on President Bill Clinton's fiscal year 2000 budget proposal.

19 Jacob J. Lew
Born 1955, New York City

Jacob "Jack" Lew attended Carleton College for a year and then transferred to Harvard University, graduating with an AB in 1978. He obtained a JD from Georgetown University in 1983.

Lew began his career in Washington in 1973 as a legislative aide to Representative Bella S. Abzug. In the following year he became an aide to Representative Joe Moakley. He served as principal domestic policy adviser to House Speaker Thomas O'Neill from 1979 to 1987. From 1987 to 1991 he worked as a partner at the law firm Van Ness, Feldman and Curtis, and from 1992 to 1993 he was executive director for the Center for Middle East Research.

In 1993, Lew entered the administration of President Bill Clinton. He served as special assistant to the president for one year and then worked as executive associate director and associate director for legislative affairs in the Office of Management and Budget (OMB) from 1994 to 1995. He served as deputy director and director of the OMB from 1995 to 1998 and from 1998 to 2001, respectively.

Lew left public office to serve as the executive vice president for operations at New York University and a clinical professor of public administration at the university's Wagner School of Public Service from 2001 to 2006. He worked as managing director and chief operating officer for two Citigroup business units from 2006 to 2008.

Lew returned to public office to serve as deputy secretary of state for management and resources in the administration of President Barack Obama from 2008 to 2010. In late 2010, he became director of the OMB, and he served as Obama's chief of staff from 2012 to 2013.

Lew was sworn into office as the seventy-sixth secretary of the treasury on February 28, 2013. He served in this role until January 20, 2017.

Lew assumed his current position as partner at Lindsay Goldberg LLC, a private equity firm, in late 2017.

I interviewed Jacob Lew in his office at Columbia University, where he is also a visiting professor of international and public affairs. It was early in the afternoon on Thursday, September 14, 2017.

Background Information

Bowmaker: When did you first become interested in economic policy, and why?

Lew: I took economics both in high school and in college, and I quickly saw that economic policy encompassed most of the major policy areas I cared deeply about. When I started working on Capitol Hill as a legislative aide, I also learned that opportunities for action gravitated around economic policy–driven events, whether it was a tax bill or an appropriations bill. My primary focus became economic policy when I went to work for Speaker O'Neill in 1979. I ended up being his policy adviser on most major economic policy issues, such as those relating to tax, trade, and health.

Entering the Policy World

Bowmaker: Can you tell us about what you learned from your initial experiences working for Speaker O'Neill?

Lew: One of the first projects that I did for the Speaker, and it became a regular one, was to provide a periodic economic overview. He was always concerned with the risk of a recession and with what policies could control inflation and unemployment. On a regular basis, I would call the dozen smartest economists in the country, both Democrats and Republicans, who were all generous with their time, and I got to know them—people like Otto Eckstein, Leon Keyserling, Marty Feldstein, Alan Greenspan, Walter Heller, Arthur Okun, and Joe Pechman. For a twenty-five-year-old like myself, it was an education in macroeconomics from the giants of their generation. They all had a macroeconomic model of the United States and the world in their head; they all had their own view on what economic indicators to watch closely. Experience bore each of them out on some things more than others, like all forecasting endeavors. But what impressed me most was their passion for having academic work make a difference in the policy world. It really mattered to them for the Speaker of the House to know what they thought. And it wasn't out of ego or pride—it was because they wanted to be able to contribute to the policy process. I think that it has become more challenging for economists in this day and age to feel that same passion, both because their careers sometimes are not always enhanced by their involvement in the policy process and because of some disillusionment about the possibility of making a difference.

Bowmaker: Were there any particular skills that you developed in this role that proved useful for later in your career?

Lew: I found early on that I had an ability to go back and forth between academic scholars and policymakers and sometimes act as a translator between them. In scholarship, there's a high premium on technical and sometimes esoteric knowledge—things that are complicated and perhaps not as accessible to the outside world. It is a very important role in public policy to act as a mediator between experts and political decision-makers. I never stopped feeling that this was an important function, even as I rose to leadership positions myself.

Bowmaker: During your role with Speaker O'Neill, you were influential in forging the Social Security deal made between him and President [Ronald] Reagan in 1983. Can you tell us about the issues that were involved, and how they were resolved?

Lew: Richard Schweiker, secretary of HHS [Health and Human Services], put forward a Social Security proposal which involved broad cuts in benefits to deal with the long-term Social Security financing problem. It became the grist for a political campaign to save Social Security. Coming out of the 1982 midterm elections, there was a different political lay of the land: Democrats won enough seats that the White House could no longer press ahead without bipartisan support. And you had a president and a Speaker who maintained a cordial relationship while they did political battle. They had their staffs behind the scenes figure out ways to lay a foundation to work through this problem that became known as the third rail of American politics, because it was so dangerous to touch.

The first step was to reschedule the date of the crisis. The old age fund was running out of money, while the disability fund at that time had a big surplus. By transferring money from one fund to the other, you could pretty much schedule what month the old-age fund would run out of money. We collectively picked a date that was squarely between political cycles to create a moment that might lend itself towards working together. The Greenspan Commission was appointed, with both parties choosing members, and at first it was not clear that it would be more than a technical study. As it got closer and closer to the new deadline, though, there was one member on the commission, Bob Ball, who by dint of his own personal credibility and reputation became a shuttle diplomat. He was the last of the founding generation of Social Security and was close to many Democrats. He had been Social Security commissioner under [Richard] Nixon and was trusted by members of the Reagan team who knew him from that time. He would go back and forth and test ideas with each side. We didn't have to negotiate directly with each other, so with no fingerprints we could explore where there might be a meeting of the minds.

Despite the trust built during the process, there was still a fair amount of fear that if anyone went out in public before the other, the finger-pointing could begin, and instead of it being something that both sides owned together, it would become the source of another political battle. So there was this heavily choreographed set of statements on a Saturday where in different cities, the president and Speaker at the same moment endorsed the plan, which essentially took the electricity out of the third rail of American politics.

When it came to writing legislation, the Ways and Means Committee drafted the commission's recommendations into bill form, and there was a last gap to fill and a disagreement on how to fill it. One view was to raise the retirement age, while another view was to raise payroll taxes, particularly on higher-income people. Rather than resolve this issue in committee, the decision was to let the full House make a choice. Many Democrats, including the Speaker, supported the idea of doing it through taxes, but when the House voted, the decision was to raise the retirement age.

Now, why am I telling that story? Because that was in an era when the Speaker of the House considered it a fundamental principle that a majority should be able to work its will. It wasn't just about winning or losing. And here we are in 2017, pushing fifty years of stability in the trust fund, because we managed to come up with a bipartisan plan and take it to the floor to let a majority decide on the outcome. If leaders today would permit a majority to make decisions, you could solve some hard problems, like immigration reform. But we have seen a change in philosophy where it's hard to imagine in 2017 a Speaker putting a choice like that to the House—even at the risk that the outcome might not be his or her preferred position. I think democracy requires that we get back to the approach that Mr. O'Neill considered sacred.

At the OMB during the Clinton Administration

Bowmaker: You were a member of the Clinton administration team that negotiated the 1997 Balanced Budget Act. Can you describe the various roadblocks that you encountered, and how you overcame them?

Lew: Discussions on what became the Balanced Budget Act of 1997 started in the period between the 1996 election and the opening of the new Congress and the second inaugural in January 1997. President Clinton had a new team taking over at the White House, many of whom had not participated directly in the previous battles. Erskine Bowles, who was taking over from Leon Panetta as chief of staff, and Frank Raines, who was coming in as director of the OMB, quietly started conversations with the members of Congress who would be lead negotiators on the other side—Senator Pete Domenici, who would represent Majority Leader Trent Lott in the Senate, and Congressman John Kasich, who would represent House Speaker Newt Gingrich. It was a complicated process because the shutdown did not lead to a lot of trust. Before you can talk policy, you first have to be able to talk to each other, which meant there was a great deal of time spent developing relationships to convince each other of the seriousness of the endeavor. It helped that another shutdown was no longer an option, because it had failed so recently. The only way to get something done would be through a process of give-and-take where everyone could agree, and a complicated negotiation was set up that involved much of the economic team.

As I think back over the 1997 budget negotiation, it was managed about as well as a White House executive branch engagement with Congress could be managed. It's hard to do a tax bill, but the treasury secretary working with the White House can do that. It's hard to negotiate appropriations, but the OMB director does that job. In other words, every element has a central player. But the balanced budget agreement spread across a great expanse of policy. It involved major tax provisions and new spending limits for appropriations; it involved going into individual entitlement programs and major health changes, including not just savings but also creating the Child[ren's] Health [Insurance] Program. And there were no fewer than four centers of negotiating activity at any given time. It was coordinated out of the chief of staff's office, and we were able to make trade-offs within and between the different areas to reach the best possible outcome because we all came back to home base, and we all went out as one team. It was the days before BlackBerrys and iPhones, but I remember being in the basement of the Capitol—in Pete Domenici's hideaway—and the new phenomenon was that we could share information with negotiators in other rooms using pagers with text capabilities. We were also in touch with what was happening in the world outside the negotiations, what was running in the press, and what members outside the room were saying. And because we always came back to home base, we could make the strategic and tactical trade-offs. It's inherently hard to do that on the Hill because a leader, at least in those days, could not tell all the committee chairmen exactly what to do on every detail in their area jurisdiction.

I'd say the administration worked as a seamless team, and we individually and collectively were able to build relationships of trust on the Hill. We were not all doing each element—Bob Rubin, Frank Raines, Gene Sperling, Larry Summers, and I each had elements that we took the lead on. And periodically we would have meetings to take key issues back to our principals. Lott and Gingrich have very different personalities. Gingrich is a detail guy. He and President Clinton could go for hours on technical issues. Speaker Gingrich was also prepared to spend hours with our economic team. But Lott was much more impatient and started tapping the table when he was ready to finish. So on their side you had this dynamic: both wanted to get it done, but with very different styles.

The balanced budget agreement was reached in two stages. There was an agreement in principle before Memorial Day, and then from Memorial Day until August we worked out all the details in what were often around-the-clock negotiations. It is actually a very short time to craft so much complicated policy, but unlike a government shutdown or a debt limit crisis, it is an energized setting where you are motivated by the idea that you are getting something important accomplished, as opposing to averting a self-inflicted crisis. But this does not mean it is easy—the give-and-take was very hard. We didn't want to reduce the capital gains tax. They were not eager at first to agree to child health coverage. So we traded back and forth across areas. And this is where coordination was so essential. The team in the health room couldn't have possibly known what to give on capital gains.

And the people in the capital gains room didn't have the technical knowledge of what to do on health. And at the back of it all was what to do about funding levels for all domestic and defense spending.

So it was really a very complicated undertaking. As deputy director of OMB, I played a very active role in the policy negotiations, but part of my job was to keep the pieces organized so we all knew where we were at any point. That was quite challenging. Domenici's staff director Bill Hoagland did the same job for the Senate Republicans, and in the end we took the toughest issues upstairs, to the president and the leaders. It was a model for how to directly engage and get things done. People feel pretty good about having been part of it. I don't think anyone looks back and says, "Oh, I was taken to the cleaners." As I say, I did not like the capital gains provisions that we agreed to, but overall the package was really good for the country. And you live to fight another day. Compromise is about winning the things that are most important, and you make concessions on other things to get there. And it's all rooted in trust. You have to be in a room with people who you trust to keep their word and execute on it.

At the OMB during the Obama Administration

Bowmaker: In the summer of 2011, it appeared to some observers that House Republicans were going to force the country to default on its debt. In Bob Woodward's book *The Price of Politics*, you were portrayed as being too tough and stubborn during those negotiations. For example, he notes that, "[Ohio governor John] Kasich called [economic adviser Gene] Sperling at the White House, suggesting that he meet with [House Speaker John] Boehner. Lew, he said, did not know how to get to yes."[1] Ahead of time, did you think about the degree of toughness that you would show in negotiations? Looking back, is there anything you would have done differently?

Lew: My first negotiation with John Boehner came a few months before on a spending bill to keep the government operating until the end of September. We had meetings in the Oval Office with Speaker Boehner, the president, and other leaders where we laid out very clearly what we could and couldn't live with. They were asking for more cuts than we thought

---

1. Bob Woodward, *The Price of Politics* (New York: Simon and Schuster, 2013), 235.

you could responsibly implement on either the defense or the nondefense side. They said, "If we can't do that, we have to do something else to pay for that much spending. In other words, we need offsets to pay for it." When we reached our bottom line, the Speaker said he needed more cuts, that he could not go back to his Freedom Caucus without a bigger number.

I remember making the case to the Speaker that this was the first round of negotiations, and he was already getting bigger cuts than we were comfortable with, so the only alternative was to find other ways to offset spending with policies that would be treated as savings by the scorekeepers. At the time, I said, "I have to warn you, Mr. Speaker, your hard-liners are not going to be happy with these offsets. CBO [the Congressional Budget Office] will score them, but somebody's going to call them gimmicks. I don't want you to be surprised." And he said, "I need the bigger number." Leave aside whether the offsets are gimmicks or not—that's not the real point here, because you could argue that either way. He went back to his caucus, and they looked at the offsets, and they said, "We wanted spending cuts. You got taken to the cleaners." And it was terrible for him. His credibility was hurt, and his ability to reach an agreement with me was damaged. If he was taken to the cleaners, I had to be the one to blame. Even though I had briefed him on what the reaction might be, it didn't change the political effect when he went back to his caucus, and that became the lens through which people saw our relationship for a long time. He and I had a warm personal relationship and in private had many long and confidential conversations. But in public, he had to be very tough on me in his caucus. And I think that the Woodward book reflects that toughness. But my reflection on it is not that I bargained tougher than I did in the past. I was bargaining with someone who was more nervous about his own credibility in his own caucus, and I had to be the bad guy. And that's sometimes the way things work out in politics.

In 2011, the issues were hard. Many Republicans were again saying, "We're going to not just shut down the government, we're going to default if we don't get our way." What became known as "grand bargain" negotiations began very privately, but what John Boehner said in public also shaped the private discussions. He publicly said that he would need one dollar of savings for every dollar that he would raise the debt limit. It was an enormously high bar that made no economic sense, and it was possibly unachievable. Moreover, if that became the rule going forward, it would become a mechanism to grind the government down to a smaller and smaller size just to keep paying old bills.

Over many weeks we worked through the elements of what could have been a grand bargain, including revenues, entitlement reforms, and limits on discretionary spending. On the entitlement side, there are the big entitlements—Social Security, Medicare, and Medicaid—and then there's everything else, often called "other mandatories."

In terms of spending issues, the Speaker was engaged mostly on Medicare and Medicaid, Social Security, and overall discretionary spending limits. Everything else was left for something that became known as the Biden group, chaired by Vice President [Joe] Biden and House Majority Leader Eric Cantor. I briefed the whole group on dozens of options to save money, and we came up with a bit over $200 billion of possible savings that we could in concept agree on. And Eric Cantor was one of the more conservative members of the House. I developed quite a good working rapport with him and his staff. While the overall grand bargain did not come together all at once, if you look at later budget agreements like the [Patty] Murray–[Paul] Ryan agreements, most of the savings provisions had been agreed to in the Biden group.

In the big conversation with the president and Speaker Boehner, the question was how far can you go on taxes, and how far on Social Security, Medicare, and Medicaid? We were willing to make some pretty substantial concessions on entitlements, including technical changes in how cost of living increases would be calculated, knowing that it would mean lower COLAs [cost of living adjustments], and means-testing Medicare premiums so that higher-income retirees pay more of the cost of Medicare. While Speaker Boehner considered this barely scratching the surface, we knew that taking this back to congressional Democrats would be like going into the Colosseum and having the lions come at you. They didn't think of it as technical. But we were prepared to make the case for a balanced package and believed we could bring enough Democrats with us, if there was a significant increase in revenues—particularly by repealing tax cuts for the most wealthy.

We explored other structural changes in Medicare but were not able to find common ground without, in our view, undermining the economic security of vulnerable people. At each stage, Speaker Boehner described how hard it would be to go back to his caucus for new revenue and that he could only do so if there were enough savings from reforms.

There were moments when the president and Boehner seemed very close, but sometimes things happen that you don't control. There was a bipartisan group of senators who came up with their own alternate plan for a grand bargain. That plan, which had several significant Republican cosponsors, included more revenues than the Speaker had been willing to take back to his caucus. The reality was if there were Republicans willing to agree to a higher revenue number than what the president and the Speaker could agree to, it reduced the number of Democrats who would support a lower revenue number. The president told the Speaker he would stick to the deal but that there would be fewer Democratic votes. Since the Speaker was already unsure that he could muster the necessary number of Republican votes, this led to a collapse in the talks. On both sides there were bad feelings, with questions about good faith and the ability to deliver. It wasn't a great outcome.

We did avoid the default through a miserable process called sequestration, which was really just kicking the can down the road on the principle that if the outcome would be bad enough, everyone would later agree to an alternative to avoid it. So far, mostly that's been true. The Murray-Ryan agreement has twice avoided the worst of sequestration. But it's not a great way to run things. In the eighties, when the first sequestration was put together by Phil Gramm, Warren Rudman, and Fritz Hollings, I hated it. And fast-forward to 2011, when we were hours away from default, I remember Gene Sperling and I were the only ones on the White House team who really remembered sequestration. I said, "Gene, I have no other idea for how to get out of this. Do you?" He said, "Nope, I don't either." And the two of us, who hated it, made the case within the administration that we can't default and this was the only way to avoid that catastrophe.

At the end of the day, if you look at what would have been a grand bargain, most of the pieces have been addressed in one way or another. There was a big cut in discretionary spending in 2011. In 2013, there was a tax increase that was on the scale of what we were talking about doing. And the Biden-Cantor group's ideas in other areas were enacted later to avoid sequestration. It was not a process that helped restore confidence in stable policy, and that delayed our economic recovery in my view. And because Republicans insisted that the 2013 tax cut be a Democratic-driven policy, there was no balanced approach between taxes and entitlements, as we saw in many earlier budget agreements.

As Secretary of the Treasury for President Obama

Bowmaker: Why do you think President Obama chose you to be his secretary of the treasury?

Lew: While we did not know each other before, he and I had worked very closely during his first term. I'd been his chief of staff and his OMB director. But you'd have to ask him why he wanted to nominate me to be treasury secretary. After four years of commuting between New York and Washington almost every week, I was prepared to go home.

Bowmaker: How were you approached?

Lew: As chief of staff at the time, I was coming up with other names [*laughs*]. The president knew that my wife and I were ready to return to a more normal life. It was particularly hard to live in two cities as chief of staff. As the president kept ruling out other candidates that I brought him, he said, "What would you say if I asked you?" I said, "Oh, Mr. President, you know that that's an offer that would be hard to refuse, but I still have somebody else I have to talk to." I'd come down to Washington thinking I was going to be in the State Department for a year and a half or two, and I'd already been there for four years in the highest pressure roles you could imagine. And signing up to be treasury secretary meant I'd be there for a good long while. But I am lucky to have a spouse who's also a patriot and a good citizen, who put what was easiest and best for her second.

Bowmaker: Did he make it clear what he wanted you to do for him?

Lew: We knew that there would be a debt limit issue coming up. We hoped that there'd be tax reform and still hoped there might be a budget agreement. Four years after the financial crisis, it was essential to avoid another one and to develop the relationships of trust in government, internationally, and in the business world to manage it effectively if there were another problem.

No treasury secretary comes in with equal experience in all aspects of the job. With a background that was heavy in fiscal policy, I needed to quickly dive into all of the financial regulatory issues and many of the international issues. I probably knew more of the pieces than many of my predecessors but still had a great deal to learn. I invested a great deal of effort in the beginning to making sure that I knew the finance ministers and central bank governors in the G20 [Group of Twenty], and the CEOs [chief executive officers] across the financial and industrial sectors. I called them for advice and invited them in to talk. It turned out that the relationships all worked very well, and we managed to get through some pretty dicey moments. We went through four years without a major financial crisis, and I'm never going to complain that I didn't get to test my ability to deal with a situation like 2008. I hope nobody in my lifetime ever has to do that again.

Bowmaker: Did you speak to former treasury secretaries about the role?

Lew: Yes. I'd also done that as chief of staff and as OMB director. And I made myself available to successors as well. Most of the people who serve in these roles develop an institutional sense of responsibility and want to be available to advise whoever comes next. I actually reached out to Republican predecessors, if anything, more than Democratic predecessors. I'll give you an example. It was natural for me to talk to Bob Rubin, Larry Summers, and Tim Geithner. We were long-time colleagues and friends. But I got to know Hank Paulson and George Shultz very well, too. Hank in particular would call whenever he had something on his mind, and I enjoyed talking to him. I found his observations to be thought provoking and helpful. He often had intelligence from things that he had done or seen. Most of the time he was not advocating a specific policy but helping me to think through hard problems.

George Shultz was always very available. I've worked in three organizations—Treasury, State, and OMB—where when you ask who can help you learn how to do the job the right way, his name always comes up. Hillary Clinton had the same experience when she became secretary of state. I think she found her conversations with George Shultz to be among the most helpful in understanding how you get your hands around that far-flung bureaucracy to manage it effectively and to pursue policy directions while you're nurturing it as an institution. Our political views are not the same, of course, but I deeply respect his wisdom and his judgment. And there was one year while I was treasury secretary when I saw him in three different cities, while he was in his nineties.

Bowmaker: As secretary of the treasury, you continued the trend of using economic sanctions as a major tool of foreign policy. Do you think there is a danger that they can be overused?

Lew: Yes. Sanctions are an enormously powerful tool and should be treated with the care that powerful tools and weapons deserve. We are accustomed to thinking about the cost of warfare in terms of lives put at risk and dollars spent. We also need to think of sanctions as powerful weapons that have costs and collateral consequences.

The purpose of sanctions is to use economic pressure to convince another sovereign to change its policy. Whether it is Iran or the DPRK [Democratic People's Republic of Korea], the goal is to change how they define what is in their sovereign interest. The most effective approach is multilateral in a global economy: a unilateral approach is unlikely to produce sufficient pressure and is very hard to police. Iran sanctions were effective because most of the world joined with us. On the DPRK, last year and again this year, China worked with us to approve multilateral sanctions at the UN [United Nations]. China needs to do more, but in the end we need China as a partner—not an adversary—to be effective in putting pressure on the DPRK.

Because the dollar is the world's reserve currency, and most complex or global transactions at some point involve dollars, the United States has the ability through secondary sanctions to cast a wide net. That is a very powerful weapon and needs to be used with care. Today, there is no real alternative to the dollar, but over time that could change, and we should not encourage that process to accelerate. We should always reserve the right to act unilaterally but make every effort to work through multilateral diplomacy.

I gave a speech at the Carnegie Endowment [for International Peace] towards the end of my tenure to outline our approach on this issue. During the years I was in Treasury, we developed very sophisticated tools to target sanctions effectively, while limiting undesired spillovers, and worked through diplomatic channels to build and sustain broad support from other nations. The sanctions on Russia after the seizure of Crimea were carefully constructed to do a number of things: to put pressure on the Russian regime, to put pressure on the Russian economy, but not to hurt the Russian people any more than we had to. We also took care to avoid spillover effects that might cause an economic shock to our partners in Europe. If you look at the way we put the sanctions in place, they actually accomplished that goal. We maintained broad international support, and while Russia did not withdraw from Crimea, sanctions became a serious factor limiting how far they were prepared to go, and they helped bring the Minsk Accords into being. Although Minsk has not been fully implemented, it remains a diplomatic blueprint to resolve the conflict.

Sanctions are most effective when you have credibility that you will take the steps you say you're going to take, and then if you need to, you'll do more. And you have to keep your word. Sanctions only work if complying with demands leads to promised relief of sanctions. In the case of Iran, it was economic pressure that brought them to the table, because they wanted relief from sanctions. Iran agreed to take a series of steps to end its development of nuclear weapons, and the agreement was verifiable. We only removed sanctions after Iran took the promised steps to unwind their nuclear weapons program. As long as Iran is complying with the agreement, it is important that the US also comply. This is important beyond Iran. If it becomes clear that after complying with demands a country cannot rely on sanctions relief, sanctions would be less effective in the future as a tool to force policy change.

Bowmaker: Returning to an issue that was discussed earlier, the US experienced another debt ceiling crisis during your tenure as secretary of the treasury. Why do they keep happening? Why do you think it necessary to raise the debt ceiling? Should we eliminate the debt ceiling?

Lew: I think the debt ceiling is an anachronistic tool. You go back to the history of the debt limit—it was put in place to make it easier, not harder, to efficiently issue US debt. Before World War I, every time the US government borrowed money, Congress needed to approve each debt issuance. The debt limit was a reform to say, "You can borrow until you hit the debt ceiling, and that could be a very long time." It became a moment for members of Congress to gain leverage many decades ago but was not used as an extortionary tool—it was a "must pass" bill that created both a deadline and a negotiation where other business could be addressed. It wasn't great in the eighties, when Gramm-Rudman, the original sequestration, was done on the back of the debt limit increase. But no congressional leader called for default if demands were not met. It changed materially in the nineties, when Speaker Newt Gingrich raised the threat of default as a real possibility. But even then it was largely treated as an empty threat because the consequences were considered catastrophic. That changed in recent years. In 2011, and then again in 2013, a serious argument was made by those demanding concessions that we should default if they did not get their way. I had long conversations with the president about this. We believed deeply that this could not be allowed to continue, and that even if we could negotiate our way through the current crisis, unless this brinksmanship stopped, at some point there would be a default. Even the risk of accidental default because of miscalculation was a real worry.

In resolving 2011, [Senate Minority Leader] Mitch McConnell quite cleverly created a procedure that permitted almost every Republican to vote against raising the debt limit, so that the president and Democrats in Congress had to take full responsibility. This solved the crisis of the moment but does not address the underlying issue: When the US government makes commitments it needs to keep them, and you cannot decide not to pay your bills after spending was lawfully undertaken. In 2013, we took a different approach. We said, "Congress has to do its job. This is not something that we're going to negotiate over. If you want to attach it to something else that is mutually accepted, that's fine. But there's not going to be a quid pro quo to raise the debt limit. The debt limit is just your job to do, and you have to do it."

A debate ensued about another dangerous idea called prioritization—pay some bills but not others to avoid defaulting on the debt. We made the case that picking and choosing which bills to pay would just be default by another name. Would the federal government stop paying doctors for treating Medicare patients, or electric companies for lights in the federal buildings? What about veterans' disability benefits? Even if technically you could pay the debt and not other bills, we did not have the capacity to pick and choose among normal spending. And it is almost impossible to imagine the level of public outrage if we ever got to the point that we were paying foreign bondholders but not US veterans and health care providers.

When I worked for Speaker O'Neill, we crafted a rule called the Gephardt Rule, where a debt limit increase popped out of the budget resolution when you adopted the budget resolution, so the spending and financing decisions would be linked. There are a lot of ways to defuse this political weapon, and I hope that Congress adopts one of these approaches before we face a crisis that careers out of control.

Bowmaker: As secretary of the treasury, you chaired the FSOC [Financial Stability Oversight Council]. What was the accomplishment of the FSOC that you believe was most important? What FSOC issue was the most difficult? What FSOC issue was the most frustrating?

Lew: By the time I came into the role, we were just coming out of the financial and economic crisis. Dodd-Frank [legislation intended to decrease various risks in the US financial system] and Wall Street reform had been passed. But in a world where you have five independent regulators with different responsibilities, it was not straightforward to get it implemented—keeping them at the table, coordinating and working with each other. It was important to implement the reforms effectively and with consistent approaches to avoid creating a hydra-headed monster, with different approaches to major initiatives like liquidity standards and the Volcker Rule. I did not have the

authority to order any of them how to proceed because they are independent regulatory agencies, so I used my convening authority as FSOC chair
to shepherd them. And I think we did a pretty effective job. I'm not saying
that everything was done exactly the way I would have done it, if it all
came to a head in one place and I was the final decision maker. But when
I talk to financial regulators around the world, I think we get pretty high
marks.

The work on designations is both something I'm proud of but also a
frustration. If you look at the venom that has been generated in terms of
criticism, you would think that hundreds of entities had been designated as
SIFIs [systemically important financial institutions]. In terms of the nonbank
insurance companies, it's four, and one has already been dedesignated with
another pending in litigation. We were very careful about who to designate
and about the analysis that was used to get us there. The anti–Dodd-Frank,
anti–Wall Street reform campaign has distorted what we actually did in a way
that is dangerous. FSOC for the first time brought together in one place all of
the senior financial regulatory authorities, so that as a group they would say,
"What are the risks we face in terms of financial stability?" It didn't used to
exist, and regulators missed the financial crisis. Would we have seen it coming if that group had been charged with asking the hard questions? Going
forward, we need to have a body where you ask questions like we did. Is there
something going on in a nontraditional bank area that we need to worry
about? Are we asking the right questions about asset management? Are we
asking the right questions about hedge funds? We didn't designate any firms
in those areas, but the standard is not how many designations were made.
Rather, the standard should be, "Did we ask the right questions, and today
are we continuing to ask the right questions?" If a problem is developing,
you need to see it early enough to do something about it.

The myth of zealous overreach is dangerous. I don't think the authority
will probably be eliminated, but if it suffers from disuse for long enough,
the difference between repeal and nonrepeal may not be a real one. What
I think FSOC represents is a responsibility to look through the front
windshield at what's coming at you, not in the rearview mirror at what
occurred in the past. Anyone who is ultimately responsible for dealing
with a financial crisis should want to have that. And I think FSOC has
been judicious and careful. Could it do things better? Sure. Any group of
humans can always do things better. But I actually think it's done a pretty
good job.

Bowmaker: How well did the Treasury coordinate with the Federal Reserve on financial regulation issues?

Lew: Very well. The regulatory area tends to be more at the technical level than at the chairman of the Fed and secretary of the Treasury level, but when the teams would start reaching points where they might have different views, whether it was me talking with Ben Bernanke or Janet Yellen, it elevated discussions so our teams could go back and work through issues.

The Fed and the Treasury have a very good, close working relationship. It's one of trust and respect. The Fed never tells the Treasury what to do, and the Treasury never tells the Fed what to do. These are the two places in our government where you have the highest level of knowledge on these issues, and people from the top through the ranks treat each other as peers. It's not a party line issue. Ben Bernanke was a Republican, and I developed a very close relationship with him. And I think Janet Yellen has done the same thing with my successor.

Bowmaker: As you just mentioned, during your time in Washington you had a significant amount of interaction with economists. In your view, what does an economist bring to the policy world that others do not?

Lew: Economists bring to the table knowledge and analysis that help to inform many important decisions. Economic analysis often depends on assumptions, and basing your analysis on what happened in the past can miss an inflection point, so you cannot see perfectly how things are going to be in the future. But good economic analysis can help you construct the best possible approximation of where you stand and where you're going on important issues. It's data based and analytically driven. The standard is not whether economists are always right, but are they using the best information and analysis available to get as close to right as possible. I think good economic analysis helps you do that.

Bowmaker: What did you learn from Presidents Clinton and Obama?

Lew: The president always has to step back and remind everyone to look at the big picture. That is sometimes hard to do when you are working around the clock in the trenches every day. As president, you need to focus on big ideas as well as details—not just what our policy choices may be, but how our country got to the point we are at, and where we need to go. It was a reminder to me to always sweat the details to get it right but not to get overtaken by the details and miss the big point—to make sure that the details are serving the higher purpose.

General Thoughts on Economic Policymaking

Bowmaker: What is your opinion on the so-called revolving door between Wall Street and Washington?

Lew: I think having a high standard of ethics and not having conflicts is very, very important. I also think it's very important to have people who have broad and deep experience in the areas that they're working in, and I don't believe that it's inconsistent to find talented people who do not have conflicts, who have high ethical standards, and who bring broad and deep knowledge into government.

The jobs in many of these areas are very technical. It's not something that you would want your top people to be learning on the job in many cases. And I think that when it is done right, it can enrich the team you have in government.

Now, if you disregard concerns about conflicts, that's a different story. So conflict reviews are very important, but we need to be careful not to make all prior business experience as a disqualification for public service.

Personal Reflections

Bowmaker: How did your personality affect your style and approach as a policymaker?

Lew: I'll leave it to others mostly to evaluate the impact of my own personality and analytic approach. The difference in my career path and many other people's career paths is that I really worked my way up and learned the vast reaches of activities in the federal government. And one of the things that I found quite gratifying is that a lot of people who devoted their own careers to public service have said to me over the years that it means a lot to them that I was able to hold these very senior positions. I am glad that my own career helps to validate the work of career public servants and the many good people in appointed positions that work on the Hill and in the executive branch. I was promoted because of my understanding and experience in the business of government. The knowledge and analytic and political skills to get the job done are important skills for government leaders. But so is the ability to work respectfully with people at all levels. I always say to people, "Just remember who you are going in, because that's the person you want to take out." Transitions are much more painful for people who start to confuse who they are and the office they hold. And I pride myself on coming and leaving as the same person.

Bowmaker: As a policymaker, which decisions or outcomes were most gratifying?

Lew: I've held many of what people would say are the best positions one could have in government: a very senior policy adviser at a young age to the House Speaker, OMB director twice, [president's] chief of staff, and secretary of the treasury. If I had done any one of those jobs and none of the others, I would have had a fulfilling career.

Treasury is a very special place, but then again, so are OMB, the White House, and the Speaker's office. Serving as secretary of the treasury was a particularly unique opportunity and privilege. In addition to your formal responsibilities, you have a bit of a bully pulpit to take on issues and drive action. It might not be a front page of the *New York Times* issue, but IMF [International Monetary Fund] quota reform would not have gotten through Congress if I hadn't just constantly been out there making the case that it was essential to do, and I deeply believe that our leadership in the world was at stake in terms of the outcome of that.

Much closer to home is the financial crisis in Puerto Rico. We knew that four million Americans would go through absolute misery if we could not do something about it. And so I used the combination of raising the issue in negotiations, dealing with it publicly, and going to Puerto Rico and was proud that it came to be seen as legislation that must pass. You don't have the ability to do that in every job.

The work we did on Iran sanctions was incredibly important, and assuming the deal is honored by all sides, it leaves the world a safer place.

Obviously, avoiding a debt limit crisis was a very significant accomplishment. One doesn't take a lot of joy out of it, but you know that the alternative would be a disaster and do take pleasure in avoiding a catastrophe.

Bowmaker: On the other hand, there must be some things that, in hindsight, you'd like the opportunity to do differently. What are they?

Lew: I had the privilege to hold a number of very senior positions. In each, I did my very best to leave the country in better shape than I found it, even when perfect outcomes were impossible. The work is never done, and there are many challenges left.

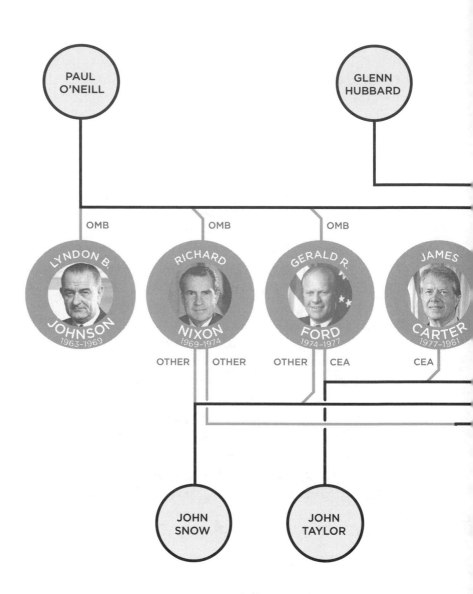

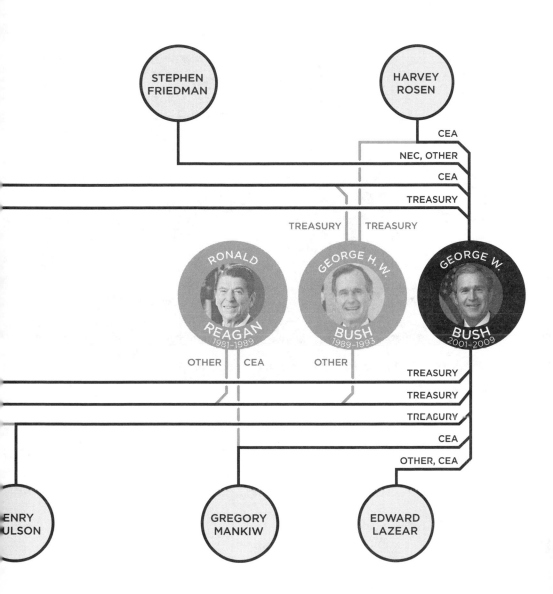

Paul O'Neill, when secretary of the treasury, sitting in his office in Washington, D.C., on September 19, 2001.

20   Paul H. O'Neill
Born 1935, St. Louis, Missouri

Paul O'Neill graduated with a bachelor's degree in economics from
Fresno State College in 1960, studied
economics at Claremont Graduate
University in 1961, and received a
master's degree in public administration from Indiana University in 1966.

O'Neill began his public service
as a computer systems analyst with
the US Veterans Administration from
1961 to 1966 and served on the staff
of the Office of Management and
Budget (OMB) from 1967 to 1977. He
was deputy director of OMB from 1974 to 1977. From 1977 to 1985 he was
vice president of International Paper Company, and from 1985 to 1987 he
was the company's president.

O'Neill served as chairman and chief executive officer of Alcoa, the
world's leading producer of primary aluminum, from 1987 to 1999, retir-
ing as chairman at the end of 2000. From 2001 to 2002, during George W.
Bush's presidency, he served as the seventy-second secretary of the treasury.

O'Neill founded Value Capture LLC, which advises health care executives
and policymakers, in 2005, and currently he is the non-executive chairman
of the firm.

I interviewed Paul O'Neill in the DoubleTree by Hilton Hotel Metropoli-
tan in midtown Manhattan, New York City. It was early in the afternoon on
Wednesday, April 3, 2013.

Background Information

Bowmaker: Why did you study economics as an undergraduate?

O'Neill: Before I studied at Fresno State, I worked for two and a half years as
an engineer in Alaska. And so I went to school with the idea of majoring in

engineering. Along the way, I also had to enroll in some economics courses and soon became fascinated. I ended up taking 80 course hours out of 124 in economics and business and dropped engineering. Then a couple of professors at Fresno State were determined that I should be a professor of economics and arranged a fellowship for me at Claremont Graduate School in Pomona. I was planning to earn a PhD in economics at the school when I accidentally stumbled into the Federal Entrance Examination. At the time, there existed something called the management intern option, in which they hired 300 people out of the 300,000 who took the test for middle management positions in government. That fluke took me away from my graduate work.

Entering the Policy World

Bowmaker: You joined the Bureau of the Budget in 1967 and were appointed its deputy director during the [Gerald] Ford administration. By the time you took up the deputy director role, did you view yourself as having strong policy positions or simply as a hired professional serving the president?

O'Neill: The standard of excellence for people who worked in the Bureau of the Budget in those days was to be able to deal with questions about anything and everything that the president could conceivably need the answer to. There was no ideology. If there was one, it was the pursuit of the truth, driven by facts and analysis. There were no exceptions. Four hundred people practiced that religion.

Bowmaker: Tell us about your interaction and work with two of our interviewees, Charles Schultze and George Shultz, at the bureau, which later became the OMB.

O'Neill: Charlie's approach was to know everything. I remember going to the old Roger Smith Hotel on Pennsylvania Avenue to have a press availability when the president's budget was released in January of 1967. It was full of media. They started heckling Charlie with questions, and he would frequently say to a reporter, "Well, if you look on page nineteen of the federal budget, you will find a full explanation…" He literally knew where everything was in the budget and what it said. He was an amazing standard of excellence for people to aspire to. Quite simply, he thought you should hold yourself accountable to know everything.

I had gotten to know George fairly well when he was secretary of labor because I worked with him on the Family Assistance Program, which was one of the great set of initiatives of the [Richard] Nixon administration. After he had been at the OMB for about six months, he called me and said, "I want you to give up your career service." So I accepted a position of assistant director, and there were many things going on that caused me to have a really close involvement with George. For example, I saw him in action with the assignment that Nixon gave to him of achieving desegregation in schools in the South. I was one of the people that George picked to work with him on trying to figure out that problem. We met with the leaders from the communities—both black and white—and created a small pool of funds so that they could also get together out of public sight. It worked wonderfully well. It was one of the many examples of George using his people selection and convening skills in just the right blend to work on complicated problems to produce a desirable, laudable outcome.

Bowmaker: You worked closely with Alan Greenspan, chairman of the Council of Economic Advisers, when you were at the OMB. How would you describe your relationship and how he thought about economics?

O'Neill: Alan and I have been friends for a very long time. We are both fact-driven people, analytic, and willing to learn from each other. He is also not bombastic. I don't think I have ever heard him raise his voice or try to make a point with something other than facts. That's a quality I admire. But it is not infrequently that we challenge each other's fact base or the way we do analysis. Even after I left government and went to the private sector and he became chairman of the Fed[eral Reserve], I would be invited to talk to him about the real-world economy. I think I made a significant contribution to his awareness of what was going on in the private sector in the nineties because I was part of it.

Bowmaker: I understand that President Ford liked to have you and Greenspan talk about various issues while he listened. What do you think the president was trying to learn from these meetings?

O'Neill: I spent an unbelievable amount of time with President Ford, and Alan was often there, too. The president was also a fact-driven person, and he knew a lot. I don't think that history has captured his depth of understanding of government and society. People forget he was in the House for twenty-five years, and through almost all of that period he was on the Appropriations Committee. He did his homework. And so he would seek out anybody who had a point of view and facts to back it up, like Alan and I.

Many meetings with President Ford were like graduate seminars. It was great. One that sticks in my mind took place shortly after he became president and the economy was in tough shape. He called a meeting in the East Wing of the White House, and every economist of note in the world was sitting around the table—people like Paul Samuelson, Milton Friedman, and Ken Arrow. Unlike others I have attended in other presidencies, none of it was fake. People were told that the president wanted to hear their views about the economy. The thing I found fascinating was the degree to which they had markedly different opinions, and of course they could not all be right. Some were arguing we needed a massive stimulus program, while others were saying the budget had to be balanced immediately. Those were the polar extremes, with the economists selectively pulling out the data that they liked the most to make their case. President Ford spent all the time asking them for the reasons why they advocated what they did. It was a lesson in economic thought and presidential advice from those with the biggest reputations in the world.

In my experience, President Ford constantly operated in such a way. Back in 1918, there was a swine flu epidemic in the world, and about half a million people died in the United States. So when they had an affirmative diagnosis of seven army recruits at Fort Dix, New Jersey, during his administration, there was a huge scramble of the scientific and medical community. Again, the president was getting conflicting advice, with some advocating a "wait and see" approach and others saying that we needed to inoculate the whole population right away. The situation was so fraught with danger that the top epidemiologists and virologists in the world were invited to the White House. They sat around the Cabinet table, and to a person they argued for the immediate creation of a national program to inoculate the whole population. At the end of the meeting, President Ford said to them, "I am going to go through that little door over there and back to my office. If any of you have an even slightly different opinion that you don't want to say in front of your colleagues, speak to me privately." Nobody came. So later on that same afternoon, he went down to the pressroom and announced the national program, which was a long, complicated story. They had to eventually stop it because the inoculation was causing facial paralysis in some people. In any case that was another example of President Ford wanting to hear from everybody before he decided what needed to be done. But he never asked the question, "Could this backfire politically?" With President Ford, it was almost never about politics—it was about doing the right thing for society. By my calculation, he was the most value-based significant person I have known in my life.

Bowmaker: Overall, what were the main lessons that you took away from your time at the OMB that you were able to use in the rest of your public service career?

O'Neill: Each day I spent there reinforced my belief that you should start every issue with a search for the facts. A question that provided great utility throughout my entire work career was the following: If we can imagine the perfect answer, what would it be? Then you work back from your perfect answer to what is possible. You should never start with what is possible or what is politically valuable. Instead, begin with the question, "How do we advance the condition of society?" That has served me well…although it has got me in trouble, too [*laughs*].

Bowmaker: You mentioned earlier that you advised Alan Greenspan in the 1990s. I also understand that during the same decade you advised President [Bill] Clinton. Can you tell us about that experience?

O'Neill: I was invited to go to the Clinton advisory meeting in Little Rock right after the election. One of the things I talked to him about was global climate change and how we needed to fix the growing unfunded liability for Social Security and Medicare. And so when he and Hillary were creating the Clinton health care plan, which was a 1,452-page bill, they called me into a meeting in the Roosevelt Room with about six or seven other people. Hillary was sitting next to me, and as always Bill Clinton came in late [*laughs*]. I said to them, "This thing is not going to fly. It's an overreach in terms of regulation and intervention." In the end, I was right.

I also remember being called to a meeting with about thirty people in a Cabinet room to talk about global climate change. We went around the table and asked everybody what their opinion was. I started my comments by saying to President Clinton, "Be wary of scientists who have 100 percent confidence in their point of view." I told everyone that they should read a book called *The Swine Flu Affair* by Dick Neustadt [and Harvey Fineberg].[1]

---

1. Richard E. Neustadt and Harvey V. Fineberg, *The Swine Flu Affair: Decision-Making on a Slippery Disease* (Washington, DC: US Department of Health, Education, and Welfare, 1978).

One of the points he [they] made was about the scientists being unanimous in their view about swine flu inoculation and their being wrong. And so I told President Clinton that we still needed a better understanding of what is going on in the atmosphere. We had to create a smorgasbord of intervention ideas with the probable consequences of those interventions, and then we needed to seriously decide how to allocate substantial resources to get at those problems. I didn't like where they were going, because this was in the days before Kyoto. If you dug into the details of that policy, you discovered that it was going to cost a bloody fortune and would do practically nothing to slow down the accumulation of greenhouse gases in the atmosphere. The environmentalists declared it a great success, but I thought it was a tragedy because it appeared to do something when, in fact, it didn't do anything.

I will tell you, though, I really enjoyed doing things with President Clinton. That same night when I was with him in the Roosevelt Room, there was a business round table at the Hyatt Hotel on 24th and M Street in the downstairs ballroom. He came to speak to the group, and afterwards he came over and stood by me when pictures were being taken. Out of the corner of his mouth, he said, "I do appreciate that you always tell me what you think." There is no question he is the greatest policy wonk of all time. I don't think any individual has ever known more or thought more deeply about the scope of issues that Bill Clinton commands. It was also interesting to me that when he does the analysis, oftentimes he doesn't care how it comes out [*laughs*].

As Secretary of the Treasury

Bowmaker: After a long and successful career in the private sector, you were appointed secretary of the treasury during the George W. Bush administration. How were you approached for the role?

O'Neill: [Vice President] Dick Cheney called me. He said, "We want to talk to you about coming back into government." When I told him, "I don't think so," he said, "You need to let me tell you what it is: it's for the secretary of the treasury position." I replied, "Well, I need to think about it for a few days and discuss it with my family. I'll get back to you." I was then coming over to New York for something or another, and when I checked into my hotel, I had a call waiting from Alan Greenspan. I called him back, and Alan said, "I know they've offered you the Treasury post, and it's your obligation to take it. And just incidentally, we'll have a good time working together." So I talked to my wife about it, and honestly she was against the idea. She had a much better understanding of how things had changed since I had last been in Washington. I had a somewhat naive view that if you were principled with facts, values, and analysis, you could play an important role. Anyway, as I was finishing my time as chairman and chief executive officer of Alcoa, I finally said to her, "The country needs some help and I'm going to do it." So I did.

Bowmaker: Did you speak to former treasury secretaries or other high-ranking officials about the role before accepting it? If so, which information or advice proved to be most helpful when making the decision?

O'Neill: After I decided to accept the role, Nick Brady called me. He had advice about people he thought would be of high value working with me in the Treasury Department. It was all about people, not about politics. Of course, he and Greenspan had a serious difference of opinion during the Bush 41 administration. Nick thought the Fed should be easing monetary policy in 1992. Alan did not think so, and Nick then felt that the Fed's policy position contributed to Bush 41 not winning reelection.

George Shultz was also good enough to send me a three- or four-page paper of recommendations for me to think about while I was secretary of the treasury. I remember it being very sage advice, but it also reinforced what I already thought. It is interesting that policy issues have not changed much in over fifty or sixty years. Since 1965, we have had three balanced budgets. There are economists like Paul Krugman who don't think that is a problem, but I don't agree with him. I came to the role with the conviction that we should have a policy declaration that said, "Over time, we, the American people, have to pay for the things we want and need." Yes, there are circumstances when it is OK to run a deficit, but it cannot be done habitually. Ideally, we want the economy someplace around full employment, with decent real GDP [gross domestic product] growth and a surplus so that we can afford to run a deficit when we need to.

Bowmaker: Did you make it clear to President Bush at your first official meeting about your intended approach to the role?

O'Neill: I didn't think that was a necessary thing to do. I felt Cheney knew enough about my background that they would not expect me to be something different just because of the title. In fact, before I said yes to the appointment, I had a luncheon meeting with President Bush and Cheney and told them, "One of the downsides for you to appoint me is that I have a strong 'on the record' public position about a lot of issues, including advocating a gasoline tax in 1986 and other points of view about workplace safety and the environment. It's all hanging out there, and there are people in politics who are going to say, 'Oh, my God, what are you doing appointing him?'" But they basically said, "We know about all that stuff. We don't care."

Bowmaker: Why do you think you were appointed to the role?

O'Neill: I had a reputation when I was at the OMB of being able to deliver on the idea of organizing information and analysis so that it is pretty bulletproof. It was my impression that is what they wanted. And over the years I had gotten an awful number of accolades for the fact that when I was at Alcoa, its market value increased 1,000 percent, while at the same time it became one of the safest and most environmentally responsible companies in the world. Some of the strongest supporters of my appointment were the president of the steelworkers' union, leading environmentalists, and business leaders. If you go back and read the newspapers and media commentary from that time, you will see it is positive. I will never forget when a friend of mine read the front-page story from the *New York Times* announcing that I was going to be appointed. He said, "My God, it looks like your mother wrote the piece" [*laughs*].

Bowmaker: What were your first impressions of President Bush when you began your role?

O'Neill: At the beginning of the administration, his staff decided that I should have an hour a week of the president's time and talk about whatever I had on my mind. And so at my first meeting, I spoke with him about education, because one of his strongest policy positions during his campaign was "no child left behind"—which I thought was a good idea. But I did not believe then, and it is still true now, that we are not going to get there until we rethink how we do primary education. There is a long story in the paper today about our failure to reduce the fact that 30 percent of our ten-year-olds cannot read, write, or compute. And since education is a cumulative process, if they don't get it by the time they are ten, it becomes decreasing in likelihood that they are ever going to have the right skills that they need. I believed for a long time that we should assess children when they are four and a half or five and fashion an intervention for them individually to get them there by age ten. But the president didn't understand the distinction that I was making between advocating for "no child left behind" and having a real analytic set of ideas about how to change the process. I don't know why. To me, he had a superficial characteristic. When I say that, though, I am mindful of when there was a big fight over a medical issue. I remember thinking at the time when he talked about that issue how impressed I was at his command of the subject. I would have to go back and look at my notes for the specific details, but as I say, I remember thinking, "Wow, this is different." I just didn't see it in other areas, like in that first meeting.

Bowmaker: It is common knowledge that during those weekly meetings he didn't seem to be very inquisitive or ask many questions. At the time, why did you think that was the case? How would your answer differ with the benefit of hindsight?

O'Neill: I honestly didn't know at the time. But I do have one hindsight. One of the defining things during the time I was in the Nixon and Ford administrations was the preparation of decision memos on anything of consequence. At the top of the paper was the issue to be decided, and underneath that was an identification of all the policy options—whether federal, state, local, or private—and then an analysis of the pros and cons of each alternative with facts. No opinions were allowed. After that was prepared, there was an opportunity to express your opinion. It was a fantastic discipline, because the papers were shared among everyone in the government to add a legitimate reason to be involved. But during the Bush 43 administration, I never saw a policy decision paper about anything. I guess I have fought myself a lot for not creating those kinds of papers for other people to shoot at.

The other thing I found really strange was that when I was at the Bureau of the Budget and the OMB, there was never ever a presidential statement of policy or policy position paper issued that didn't come to me for comments, editorial suggestions, and facts. As secretary of the treasury, however, I never ever saw presidential decision papers for things that the president was going to say before he said them.

Ultimately, I would say President Bush got what he wanted, but I don't think it served the nation well. For example, if there had been a thoroughly vetted paper on the issue of attacking Iraq, it would have become clear that there was no evidence of weapons of mass destruction. There were only allegations and assertions. But the value of a more disciplined decision-making process is that it makes you think more deeply about the difference between facts and suspicion. As another example, I don't think they would have had Medicare Part D if they had had a preclusion memo, because somebody would have had to say, "We don't have any money to pay for this. It's an eight trillion dollar obligation. Anybody here got it?" Do you know we created an eight trillion dollar obligation with Medicare direct coverage? Did you know how much money we raised in line with that new obligation? Not a penny. We would never have done that with a decision memo of the kind that I am suggesting to you because they would have had to decide that this thing is not financed, and there is no way to pay for it.

Bowmaker: Did you ever get an insight into how he thought about economics?

O'Neill: I honestly have no clue how Bush 43 thought about economics. My meetings with him were absolutely unmemorable. I don't recall him ever advocating or articulating a position about economic policy matters—only the tax cut, the tax cut, the tax cut. And then after the tax cut, more tax cuts. He can't be very proud of what he did. We ended up in a dreadful place. I have talked to my friend Alan Greenspan about this. It was clear in the first six months of 2007 that we were headed for the wall, because 30 percent of people who had taken out a mortgage in that period never paid the first payment. People in the administration were sitting there looking at the situation and then were surprised when things started unraveling. How could they be surprised? I was an outsider, and I could tell. It is astounding.

When I was there, I remember a meeting with Glenn Hubbard [chairman of the Council of Economic Advisers], Larry Lindsey [director of the National Economic Council], Karl Rove [senior adviser to the president], the vice president, and the president. I can't recall the subject, but I do remember saying at one point something like, "I don't care about the politics. That's Karl's job." Again, my view is that when you are in those kinds of positions, your job is to figure out as best you can what is the most beneficial thing to do for the future of society. Then politics is about figuring out how to get enough people in the House and the Senate to agree with you. And so I think the disjunction I had with that crowd is they thought politics was the dominant variable. It was about winning votes and winning elections. Doing the right thing was more an afterthought.

Bowmaker: Vice President Cheney had a strong interest in economics. Can you elaborate?

O'Neill: Cheney is an enigma to me because I have known him for a very long time. I first started working with him when he was a staff assistant to Donald Rumsfeld at the Office of Economic Opportunity, and I worked with him closely when he was chief of staff to President Ford. I always thought we were in the same place on economic matters. That turned out not to be right. He is the one who said to me, to my astonishment, that Ronald Reagan proved that deficits didn't matter. I was staggered. I couldn't believe anybody who knows anything about economics would think that was correct.

Bowmaker: I would like to talk about how you interacted with the rest of the economic team. It is well known that you felt that the head of the National Economic Council [NEC], Larry Lindsey, did not act as the honest broker. Can you give some specific examples of when this first came to light?

O'Neill: I thought the principal role of the NEC was to get the views of the secretary of the treasury and the respective heads of the CEA [Council of Economic Advisers] and the Department of Commerce. Departments and agencies have insights that should be included in any kind of analysis. But none of that happened, and I thought the NEC was largely irrelevant. I have to say, though, that Larry and I got off to not a very good start. In the first couple of weeks, I received a letter from him, which was copied to the president, saying that my staff were using static analysis of tax changes instead of dynamic analysis, which went against the administration and its way of doing things. I thought that was a little strange, since I was back and forth between my office at the Treasury and the White House maybe five or six times a day, every day, including Saturdays and Sundays. And so when I got the letter, I took my pen and wrote on the upper right-hand corner, "Larry, this is bureaucratic chicken shit. If you've got something to say to me, call me on the phone." I didn't think that was how a collegial administration ought to work together. If he had a problem with what my people were doing, and he thought it was negative, he should have called me up and said, "Hey, Paul, what is going on? Do you have a point of view about this?" But he didn't do that, and so we didn't get off to the best of starts.

Bowmaker: How would you describe your relationship with the CEA, in particular Glenn Hubbard?

O'Neill: We had a personally cordial relationship. He was analytic and had a strong, ideologically driven point of view about economic policy. I think he and Larry were in partnership with the idea of what they called "starving the beast," which is cutting taxes so much that the ideologists on the other side wouldn't have any money to spend. The president was sympathetic to it. Let somebody else pay the bills! That hasn't turned out too well [*laughs*].

Bowmaker: How would you describe your interactions with the political team in the White House?

O'Neill: I was not really part of their group, but again we got off to a bad start. Just after I was announced as secretary of the treasury, I got a phone call telling me they were going to invite a bunch of business people to meet with the president in Austin so that they could tell him their economic advice. But they set up the meeting and the schedule without talking to me. And so I called Karl Rove and said, "Hey, Karl, I can't make this meeting because I have got other obligations with getting ready to move to Washington." He said that was OK, but I also told him, "I've seen the composition of people you've invited, and I don't think it is right. You ought to include labor leaders and other prominent people in society so that the president can be seen to be soliciting advice from everyone." He said, "You don't understand. This is about political payoff for people who helped us during the campaign." Now, when you go back to what I told you earlier about President Ford having people of every intellectual stripe and political persuasion advising him, you might see how I could find what they were doing to be dreadful.

Bowmaker: How did your close relationship with Alan Greenspan, chairman of the Federal Reserve at the time, affect how you went about your role as secretary of the treasury?

O'Neill: We made it a point to have a breakfast meeting either in his office or mine at least once a week—no interruptions, no phone calls, no nothing. We would talk about the day's economic data, employment in different sectors, inflation rates, and what was happening in Japan, for example. We both learned from the different insights and knowledge that we had. I will tell you, though, that he was not as helpful as I had wished with the first Bush 43 tax cut. I believed the tax cut was warranted, but it might have been desirable to have a trigger so that if economic conditions deteriorated in a major way, we would have an automatic suspension. I think he agreed with me, but not enough to get the members of Congress to put a trigger in place.

Bowmaker: Can you give some examples of when politics made it impossible to do something that was analytically pure or consistent with your economic thinking?

O'Neill: In early 2001, there was a clamor from the members of Congress to impose tariffs on steel imports. So I called up my friends at the Boston Consulting Group and told them I needed a piece of pro bono work in three weeks. I asked for a world supply cost curve for the entire steel industry, done plant by plant, with fixed cost and variable cost, and including their environmental footprints. They produced a fantastic supply cost curve which showed that 75 percent of the capacity that was both high cost, as measured by the variable cost curve, and environmentally damaging was in two countries—the US and Japan. So I said we should not impose tariffs because what we would do is create protection for our 37 percent of the offending high-cost capacity. It would also be done on the backs of unwary consumers who would have to pay more than they ought to, and into the bargain, we would also be protecting capacity that is creating environmental damage. But they imposed them anyway. I believe we should have said that there is some capacity in the US that needs to be shut down, and we, the people, should have a robust program of relocation, retraining assistance, and financial support for people who are displaced by the closure. It will cost us a fraction of what the tariffs are otherwise costing the American population. But it was not a winning argument. It was one of those cases where right did not win.

Bowmaker: What did you learn about the role of the media in economic policymaking during your role?

O'Neill: I was significantly disappointed in the media. I expected them to be more fact-based and interested in analysis. I found them to be repellents for ideological arguments rather than independent referees about what is right or wrong. Early on, I had a dustup. A reporter came in and asked me about the strong dollar policy. Bob Rubin had created a mantra that whenever he was asked about exchange rates, he would reply, "Our policy is a strong dollar." That's all he would say. I always thought that was intellectually vacuous because, if you really mean it, it has the connotation that you are prepared to do whatever is required to have the appearance of a strong dollar. If there is a lot of pressure on the currency because of fundamental economics, then the only way to do anything about it is by massive fundamental intervention, which history tells us does not work. So I said to the reporter, "A strong dollar is a consequence, not an objective. It is a consequence of a highly productive economy, which in turn creates strength in your currency compared to other places where productivity is not good." I couldn't believe the attacks I received. And it roiled the markets. It was amazing to me that people sitting on a trading floor took all that in like it was an abandonment of our economy.

Shortly after the steel tariff issue, I was invited to give a speech to the Council on Foreign Relations here in New York. I was introduced by Les Gelb, Pete Peterson, and Paul Volcker, and as each of them got up, they said to me, "We have a great tradition here which is always honored: whatever you say is off the record." During the Q&A [question-and-answer] period, somebody asked about the steel tariffs, and I explained the thought process to him. The very next day the *New York Times* ran a story about what I had said.[2] I considered that to be unethical.

Bowmaker: In the end, was your wife correct about how Washington had changed since you had last been there?

O'Neill: She was absolutely right [*laughs*]. It was much more ideological and almost thoughtlessly free of facts. If you ever have an opportunity to sit in the galleries of Congress and listen to what is being said, you will be amazed at how detached it is from reality. And of course, Washington-related talk shows are an embarrassment. I will give you an example. Some people say, "The defense budget ought to be 4.5 percent of GDP." When I hear something like that, I want to scream at the TV, "How do you know what percent defense should be? In fact, how do you know what percent anything else ought to be of GDP?" It is a fraudulent way to think about the issue.

Bowmaker: How would you describe your emotions when you lost the position of secretary of the treasury?

O'Neill: I was ready to go. During the time I was there, I kept saying there was no evidence of weapons of mass destruction and that we needed fundamental tax reform instead of another marginal tax rate cut. I was clearly at odds with what the president wanted to do, so I was actually delighted to not be a part of it. But I will tell you that I have had leadership roles for a long time in my life, and I never had a surrogate tell someone they were done. The president didn't tell me. He had Cheney call me on the phone—he didn't even come and see me. When I had to dismiss someone who worked for me in the private sector, I would look them straight in the

2. Joseph Kahn and Richard W. Stevenson, "Treasury's Chief Is Said to Fault Steel Tariff Move," *New York Times*, May 16, 2002.

eye and say, "It's time for you to go, and here are the reasons why..." And so I consider that to be a mark of a nonleader—not having the courage to tell people, when you are in a superior position, "I'm firing you." I think a real leader would have called me in and said, "You're doing and saying things that I don't approve of, and here's why...you need to leave."

Bowmaker: Do you regret taking the secretary of the treasury position?

O'Neill: No, but I have regrets about not influencing policy in the right direction. We are now twelve years down the road, and where we were in the beginning of 2001 represented an enormous opportunity. If we had not had the third tax cut, if we had not gone to Iraq, if we had not done Medicare Part D, and if we had not had a housing debacle, we and the world would be in a remarkably different place.

General Thoughts on Economic Policymaking

Bowmaker: Can you give some examples of fallacies, misconceptions, or misinterpretations that affect policy debate in this country?

O'Neill: That the government somehow has an independent source of means. One of the fundamental principles we need to get everybody in the country to understand is that the federal government doesn't have any money. Yesterday, the president said that the federal government was going to supply $100 million for brain research. But he didn't say, "I am going to take $100 million away from the people so that we can commence this work." I think if you asked people the question of where the federal government gets its money from, most wouldn't know the answer.

Bowmaker: What is your opinion on the so-called revolving door between Wall Street and Washington?

O'Neill: I like the idea of people tracking back and forth between the public and private sector. But before you have decision-making positions in Washington, ideally you should have had contributor positions on the ground. For example, before you are appointed agriculture secretary, I would like you to learn how to plow, grow corn, smell figs, and understand what subsidies mean so that you can be better informed by the time you are making decisions about whether we ought to have more or less of them.

Bowmaker: Which institutional changes would you make to the policy-making process in Washington?

O'Neill: I think it would be enormously beneficial if we had a rigorous decision-making process so that we can create a basis for evaluating ourselves—it wouldn't be mysterious. We would be able to look back and say, "This is what we thought and were wrong. Is there a generic theme we are wrong about that we can set out to improve, so that we don't make the same mistake again?" My friend Roger Porter from Harvard, who was in the Reagan administration, was one of the best decision-paper writers I have ever known who meets all the standards that I mentioned earlier about clarity, facts, analysis, and plumbing everybody's intellect to make sure it is correct. There was a lot of that work done during the Reagan administration, and it meant they were not flying by the seat of their pants.

Personal Reflections

Bowmaker: How did your personality affect your style and approach as a policymaker?

O'Neill: I have a fundamental belief, which has occasionally been dented, that over time the truth will win. I am still driven by trying to find the truth, and making sure people are acquainted with it.

Bowmaker: What were your strengths and weaknesses as a policymaker?

O'Neill: Factual analysis is my strength. Zero tolerance for ideology is my weakness. I think ideology is the enemy. Let us take an extreme example. Fascism was an ideology that galvanized people. And there are other kinds of ideologies that push facts into the background or make them irrelevant. I believe logic, facts, and analysis are the friends of a broader society.

Bowmaker: As a policymaker, which decisions or outcomes were most gratifying?

O'Neill: When I was secretary of the treasury, one was to reduce the injury rate in the workplace by 50 percent. I thought it was shameful that it was forty times higher than Alcoa's. Nobody cared. At the US Mint in Philadelphia, people didn't have the last joint on their little finger because they had it cut off in the stamping machine. I didn't have factories at Alcoa where people lost a finger! Why not? Because we put protective equipment on the people and the machines, and we trained workers how to avoid inherently dangerous situations. And so I said to those in industry leadership positions, "We will work together to do what Alcoa does. If there is an injury, we are going to figure out why within twenty-four hours. And then we will correct whatever it was that created the injury so that we don't have to do it over and over again." Within twenty-three months, we had reduced the injury rate by 50 percent.

When I was at Alcoa, I also had a process by which I got reports every Friday from forty-three different countries about what had happened in terms of real economic activity during the past week. So I set up that same process when I was at the Treasury, which meant I knew better about what was going on in the world economy than anybody else—certainly better than the people at the Commerce Department, with their six-month-old data that was aggregated in indecipherable ways. After 9/11, I knew we were not going to have a negative quarter because I had on-the-ground data for real automobile sales, credit card billings from the close of business each day, and so on. I kept saying that to Glenn Hubbard and everyone else, because they were wringing their hands that we were going to have a negative quarter. I still have someplace a handwritten note from Glenn saying:

> My math on 2001: Q4 is -1.1%.
> Officially eating crow.
> Glenn
> [O'Neill laughs.]

Bowmaker: On the other hand, there must be some things, in hindsight, that you'd like the opportunity to do differently. What are they?

O'Neill: I wouldn't have done anything differently in my earlier time in government. During my Treasury stint, I should have drafted legitimate decision papers, which would have forced discipline in the system, at least in economics. That was a mistake.

Glenn Hubbard (*second left*), when chairman of the Council of Economic Advisers, meeting with President George W. Bush (*left*) in the Oval Office on September 17, 2001. Also pictured are Lewis "Scooter" Libby (*right*), the vice president's chief of staff; and Lawrence Lindsey (*second right*), director of the National Economic Council.

21   R. Glenn Hubbard
Born 1958, Orlando, Florida

Glenn Hubbard graduated with a BA and a BS in economics from the University of Central Florida in 1979 and obtained an AM and a PhD in economics from Harvard University in 1981 and 1983, respectively.

After graduating from Harvard, Hubbard began his academic career at Northwestern University before moving in 1988 to Columbia University, where he has remained ever since. He served as dean of the Columbia Business School between 2004 and 2019. He is currently the Russell L. Carson Professor of Finance and Economics at the Columbia Business School, and he is also a professor of economics in Columbia's Faculty of Arts and Sciences.

In government, Hubbard served as deputy assistant secretary (Office of Tax Analysis) of the Treasury between 1991 and 1993. Between February 2001 and March 2003, he served as chairman of the Council of Economic Advisers (CEA) under President George W. Bush.

I interviewed Glenn Hubbard in his office at the Columbia Business School in New York City. It was the middle of the afternoon on Monday, July 2, 2012.

Background Information

Bowmaker: Why did you become an economist?

Hubbard: Nobody grows up wanting to be an economist [*laughs*]. I started my training in math and engineering at college but realized that I had a major interest in public policy. And so I applied to graduate school in economics because I saw it as having a big potential impact on people's lives.

Entering the Policy World

Bowmaker: What does an economist bring to the policy world that others do not?

Hubbard: I think economists bring a way of thinking that is distinctive and advantageous. If I were sitting around the table with people from the political world, they would often be looking at a series of random things and having one-off discussions. Economists have models that they use to organize the world. That doesn't make us better, because sometimes our models are wrong, but I have found that you can win a lot of arguments simply by having structure.

Bowmaker: You began your first policy position in 1991 as deputy assistant secretary of the Treasury. How did you come to be appointed?

Hubbard: I don't know. I remember that Mr. [Nicholas] Brady, the treasury secretary, asked me if I wanted to do the job. At the time, the Treasury was undertaking a very big study of corporate tax integration, which had been an area of my research. And there aren't many Republican senior economists either, so it may have just been a confluence of those factors that led to my appointment.

Bowmaker: As you began your position, was there anything that surprised or frustrated you?

Hubbard: A lot. Aside from understanding how the Treasury fitted into a big machine, I was pleasantly surprised at the power of my unit. For example, the revenue estimates for a policy proposal came from us. But it was a challenge interacting with my staff, because some of them held the view, "Here's my number, and I'm not going to tell you how I got it." I came from a university environment where you just can't do that—if I say the answer is X, I have to defend it. Several years later, it occurred to me why the staff behaved in this way: smart political officials would come in and decide to cherry-pick assumptions or manipulate their cleverness with them. It was a real learning experience.

Bowmaker: What were the main lessons from your time at the Treasury that you were able to take into the remainder of your career?

Hubbard: There were two main lessons. One was that even though I'd considered myself an applied economist at Northwestern and Columbia, I didn't have a feel for how tax policy was made until I was in Washington. That changed the way that I subsequently studied and conducted research. And there were also several occasions when senior officials would ask questions that the economics profession could not answer well. I thought that was very unfortunate. If a question is important enough that the president or the secretary of the treasury asks it, shouldn't we be able to respond? And so that too changed some of the topics on which I worked in my research.

As Chairman of the Council of Economic Advisers

Bowmaker: You worked for Governor Bush during his presidential campaign. When he became president and asked you to be his first chairman of the Council of Economic Advisers, did he make it clear what he expected you to do for him?

Hubbard: Absolutely. First, he asked me what I thought the job was all about. I said, "Well, sir, I see it as a consulting firm for you. We have three people on the CEA—two members and the chairman—and a small staff that are here to work on problems that you think are important." And so I think he expected good-quality economic analysis, being on an economic team, and most of all, telling him what we actually thought.

Bowmaker: How did you go about establishing a comfortable working relationship with him?

Hubbard: I was lucky because I had worked with him during his campaign, so I started out with some advantages that other CEA chairs maybe didn't have. I had gotten along well with him, and there was mutual respect. And over time it was just a question of trying to engage him and present an economic point of view either during regular briefings or on policy topics that he found interesting.

Bowmaker: What was your perception of his formal knowledge and understanding of economics?

Hubbard: He had a fascinating worldview. When I first talked to him about economics, I asked about how he thought the economy worked. He described what I would call an economy of dynamism, innovation, and entrepreneurship, which was very spot-on with what the American economy at its best can be. Clearly, he had very significant knowledge of how businesses and economic institutions operated, and as a former governor of a state, he had certainly interacted with economic policy. Among politicians with whom I've worked, I would say he's close to the very top in terms of his feel for economics.

Bowmaker: Was he interested in economics in depth?

Hubbard: If it served a policy question. For example, I don't think he would care about whether there are different theories that say different taxes are capitalized in stock prices. But if we were talking about an actual policy reform and it turned out that changing dividend or capital gains taxes move stock prices, and that's something he cared about, then he liked to hear about it. Like many practical people, he was driven more by the question. And if you were answering his question, you could take all the time in the world.

Bowmaker: Did he ever ask about consensus among economists on certain issues?

Hubbard: Yes, and I always told him. That would be on a universally agreed-upon concept such as the disadvantages of imposing steel tariffs, as opposed to something where reasonable people might disagree over the size of a particular elasticity.

Bowmaker: How much of an impact could you have with the president during meetings?

Hubbard: If you have a good relationship with someone in power and you can persuade them with cogent arguments that meet them at their point of need, I think you can have a considerable impact. Most of the people sitting around the president don't have an economic organization to their arguments—they are advising him on politics or strategy—and this is where a good economist can be enormously effective. At the end of the day, though, presidents make decisions that are political, and I don't mean that in a bad sense at all. He has to trade off all kinds of advice, and he may decide on something that's against an economist's argument, but that doesn't make the president antieconomics.

Bowmaker: How would you describe the president's style of authority during those meetings?

Hubbard: The trappings of the Oval Office make it clear who's running the show [*laughs*]. The president had a natural way about him that wasn't commanding or imperious. You just had a view of a leader who was going to make a decision.

Bowmaker: Did he reach those decisions quickly or slowly?

Hubbard: I'm not sure. When a decision took a while, I don't know whether he was simply working on five other things and then finally got to mine, or whether it was quick. What I do know is that he could *react* very quickly. I could always tell in a policy briefing on a subject whether I was going to win or lose. And he hated to relitigate issues. Once a decision was made, unless there was a huge change in the environment, that was the end of the matter. For example, if you forgot one of your arguments yesterday, too bad.

Bowmaker: Could you see how his fundamental values shaped his economic thinking?

Hubbard: Definitely. He was very much a believer in the dynamic, Hayekian economy of business people groping toward a solution. And he would not be very open to big government economic interventions. Again, though, you have to understand that a president thinks about everything from a political perspective. For him, economics is an input. For me, it is an output.

Bowmaker: If you were in disagreement, were you able to change the president's mind by presenting new evidence, or did you employ a different strategy?

Hubbard: When I had an economic argument to make, I made sure that I presented it to everyone around first, because if there was going to be opposition to it, I wanted to know where it was coming from before I sat with the president. Those people included his chief of staff, his political advisers, and Vice President [Dick] Cheney, who had a very strong interest in economics and was always present in the room at briefings.

I'll give you an example of where I failed with my argument and one where I succeeded. I failed on steel tariffs, which in addition to being very bad economic policy were probably also bad politics for him. I came at the economic arguments almost every which way you could imagine, and to try to make a political argument, I then presented him with a map showing job losses by state that the staff had calculated. But his political advisers beat me.

I was more successful in arguing for big tax policy interventions. There the president didn't have a strong prior one way or the other—he was willing to listen to the arguments pro and con. And although there was certainly disagreement within the administration, I was able to persuade him on that issue.

Bowmaker: You just mentioned the tax policy interventions. In hindsight, are there any aspects of the tax cuts design that might have been done differently, and to what extent were they less than ideal from a policy perspective?

Hubbard: Two things. One is that from the very beginning, I felt that doing Social Security reform and funding accounts might have been a better idea. However, President Bush's view, which may well have been right politically, is that was just not going to happen, and so tax changes were easier. Two is that maybe there should have been more focus on business tax reform.

In terms of whether they were less than "ideal" policy, once again you need to remember that politics and economics are just so different. Economic benefits come from cutting marginal tax rates, and distortions rise with the square of the marginal tax rate. That means lowering the highest rates has the biggest economic benefit, but of course that's politically the toughest. Whereas cutting infra-marginal tax rates has a very small bang for the buck but is widely viewed as popular.

Bowmaker: You were chairman of the CEA on the day of 9/11. Which were the key questions and issues that you had to consider in relation to the attack's impact on the US economy?

Hubbard: For me, right away that day was focused on airlines and financial services. The main questions I had to think about related, for example, to what would happen to the risk premium and to what would happen to the stock market when it reopened. I wrote an op-ed the day of the reopening, which was about a week later, and argued that stock prices shouldn't decline by that much, because as terrible as the event is, the actual economic impact of the crash isn't so great. But it turned out that they did drop a lot that day.

Bowmaker: Did the White House have an economic contingency plan in place should the United States ever be subject to a major terrorist attack?

Hubbard: We did. We had looked at both terrorism and bioterrorism, which is something that could have affected public health. Most of our work was on first responders and on some economic responses. With respect to terrorism, for example, we focused on transportation (although not necessarily airlines per se), financial services, and market effects. But we certainly didn't predict 9/11. I'm sure you can always do more scenario planning, but I don't know how anyone could have envisioned that particular act of terrorism.

Bowmaker: One can argue that 9/11 led to the Iraq War. What questions did the president ask you in relation to the economic impact of the Iraq War—for example, in terms of cost, the domestic economy, and economic reconstruction of Iraq? What did you tell him?

Hubbard: I haven't answered those questions for years. Yes, he asked questions, and yes, I answered them, but given the context, I don't think it's responsible or appropriate to talk about them any further.

Bowmaker: Turning to a very different issue, do you think there is anything that the Bush administration could have done to prevent the financial crisis?

Hubbard: I saw three things as being responsible for the crisis: the persistent global imbalances that led to very low levels of the real interest rate, monetary policy being too easy from '03 to '05–'06, and regulatory arbitrage. So if you ask, "What could the administration have done?" I suppose promoting domestic saving would have been a good thing, but I would have said that's a good thing anyway. The Fed is in charge of monetary policy, so I'm not sure the administration could have done anything differently there. And then in terms of regulatory arbitrage, I think there should have been more attention inside the administration, and more generally just better financial surveillance—just sort of asking yourself where risks lie. Currently, there's the FSOC [Financial Stability Oversight Council] structure, which I don't think is a particularly good one. But even in the old days, there was a financial markets working group that could have done a lot more.

Bowmaker: I would like to ask a couple of questions relating to your interactions with the rest of the economic team. First, how would you describe your relationship with the National Economic Council [NEC]?

Hubbard: On a personal level, it worked fine. Larry Lindsey [director of the NEC] and I were friends from school. But the structure of the NEC is complicated. If a professional economist runs it, it is then very tempting for that person to impose his or her point of view. If a noneconomist runs it, it is then very hard for that person to keep up with all the economic arguments. And so I did not see the NEC as being an efficient way of organizing policy, though Larry himself was an excellent colleague.

Bowmaker: How would you describe your relationship with the Treasury and the Federal Reserve during your role?

Hubbard: Very close. I had worked previously at the Treasury, so I knew the staff and all of the key offices. I had a good professional relationship with Treasury Secretaries [Paul] O'Neill and [John] Snow, although we did not always agree. For example, the most complicated issue was the crisis in Argentina, because the CEA and the NEC had a very different point of view than the Treasury. I was not a fan of the bailouts and of the IMF's [International Monetary Fund's] intervention, and I remember cautioning the Treasury and the IMF on the implications of the Modigliani-Miller theorem. Treasury Secretary O'Neill was confident that he could turn small amounts of money into large amounts of money. I told him that theory says that can't happen.

Alan Greenspan [chairman of the Federal Reserve] had a regular lunch with the Federal Reserve Board members and the CEA, which was a good chance to have a frank discussion of policy, including Fed policy—as long as it was private and stayed in that room.

Bowmaker: In your meetings with Alan Greenspan, what did you learn about your similarities and differences in terms of your approaches to understanding the economy?

Hubbard: I am an admirer of Alan's in many respects, and I think what I learned from him was the value of adding more real-time information throughout the '01-era recession. I created both a business economist and a CEO [chief executive officer] working group that I talked to regularly to get high-frequency information. What I think was different about us is Alan viewed everything through the lens of real data, and because I'm an academic, I viewed everything through the lens of my models. Now, sometimes, that can lead me astray, because a model doesn't capture the world necessarily perfectly, as I mentioned at the beginning of our interview. But I would argue that since they tell you the factors to look for, models are better than no models, and I certainly think you need a model-based framework if you're a Fed chairman.

Bowmaker: All things considered, can you point to a specific example of where you, as an economist, or the CEA, as an organization, were able to make a difference?

Hubbard: I always say that the biggest value for an economist in Washington is killing really bad ideas. Thankfully, you will never even know about them. I'll give you an example of one that was proposed when I was there: guaranteeing 401(k) plans when the stock market goes down—a monstrously bad idea [*laughs*].

But affirmatively, I think the CEA, and to some extent myself, played a big role in President Bush's health care and tax agendas. It wasn't just a matter of persuading the president; it was a case of showing that economics can give you the right answer.

General Thoughts on Economic Policymaking

Bowmaker: Do you think that the gap between economics research produced in universities and policymaking will increase or decrease over time?

Hubbard: I worry about two disturbing trends. The first is that the economics profession is moving away from practical policy questions and focusing on problems that are relatively narrow, but more easily solved. The second is that I see too many economists, including very well-known ones, offering political commentary. That's just not appropriate for an economist. If you are providing professional advice, it needs to be on something in which you have expertise.

Bowmaker: Which aspects of the institutional framework for making economic policy in this country work well, and which need to be reformed?

Hubbard: I am writing a book with Tim Kane on this very issue.[1] The thesis is that when great powers stumble, it is most often cases in which political institutions don't keep up with economic reality. If you were to go back to the American Revolution and plot the debt-to-GDP [gross domestic product] ratio over time, you would see that up until around 1970 it looked just like war and peace. And so our budget institutions were built for that era—you borrowed money to fight a war, you paid it off over time, and by and large, you had a stable fiscal situation. However, the growth of the modern welfare state changed the environment dramatically, not only in the United States but in much of the industrial world as well. Beginning in around 1970, the debt-to-GDP ratio started to rise sharply, and that had nothing to do with military spending—our budget institutions were simply designed for a different period. And so if we're going to confront our current fiscal problems, we must change our institutions.

---

1. Glenn Hubbard and Tim Kane, *Balance: Why Do Great Powers Lose It? How Can America Regain It?* (New York: Simon and Schuster, 2014).

Personal Reflections

Bowmaker: What value has your public service had to you and to your university?

Hubbard: It has benefited me enormously. I developed new research interests when I left the Treasury and the CEA. And I think it has also made me a better teacher because I can relate to MBA students on a more applied policy level, which is a big plus for the university, too. Academic economists are making a mistake when they push away the potential benefits of public service.

Bowmaker: It is almost always the case that the chair of the CEA is an academic, and there is a fairly fast turnover. What are the consequences of this arrangement?

Hubbard: I would argue that because the chair of the CEA is typically a college professor, he or she will be the one person in the room who will provide a straight, clinical answer to a question. For example, I may have lost the argument on steel tariffs, but I think it struck the president that I was able to give such an unequivocally and unrelenting negative response.

The quick turnover of chairs means that you're more likely to get academics who want to return to the world of scholarship. That's a good thing. The downside, of course, is that by the time you've learned all of the ropes, it's time to go home.

Bowmaker: Might they also fear having to support political positions that are not economically justified?

Hubbard: When the president made his decision on steel tariffs, I told him that I would not publicly attack him, but I certainly would not defend him either. As an economist, I'm not going to take a position that I don't buy. It might get me fired, but so be it [*laughs*].

Bowmaker: How did your personality affect your style and approach as a policymaker?

Hubbard: I would say it's not so much personality as what you're used to doing for a living. I'll give you an example. Sometimes CEOs come to Washington thinking they will have a very significant impact because they have run big command-and-control business organizations, but the truth is government is a very different animal, and universities are better training for it. I always laugh when, as dean of Columbia Business School, business people say to me, "Oh, you're the boss." A dean is not a boss. The boss are my colleagues, and I'm simply the managing partner. And so I think academics enter public service with a greater sense of the team sport aspect of policymaking, and those who have been outstanding teachers tend to do well, too. After all, part of the art of policy advice is teaching without appearing to be didactic. I am a big believer in the policy process and know that if I can't make the argument in the same way that I would in teaching freshman economics, then I'm probably going to lose. You can present a relatively complicated viewpoint, but you have to do so intuitively and not necessarily with the same formalism found in graduate school. Any argument that can't be easily distilled like that isn't likely to persuade. And that's true if you are talking to not only presidents, but also business people or other practical leaders.

Bowmaker: What were your strengths and weaknesses as a policymaker?

Hubbard: My strength is that I'm pretty good at making arguments and persuading people to go along with them. The flip side is that I don't think we were as good an economic policy team as we should've been. Each of us might have worked harder to develop our team relationships, because I'm not sure the president was well served. He had a group of very intelligent, smart individual advisers from whom he heard, but I could have been more effective if I had been part of a stronger team.

Bowmaker: Which aspects of public service do you miss most?

Hubbard: There are issues that I care passionately about, and I miss not being directly involved in trying to find solutions to them. I had the pleasure of being at the very pinnacle of the economic policymaking process. I sat at the table with the secretary of the treasury, the director of the OMB [Office of Management and Budget], and the president himself. That is a way of taking your ideas right to the top. When I took the position as chairman of the CEA, my old friend Alan Blinder said to me that every day I would be commiserating over a problem in Washington, but once I left, I would think it was one of the best jobs I'd ever had. He was right.

John Taylor (*right*), when undersecretary of the treasury for international affairs, speaking with Paul O'Neill (*left*), secretary of the treasury, and Alan Greenspan (*center*), chairman of the Federal Reserve, on February 9, 2002, prior to the start of the G7 (Group of Seven) finance ministers and central bank governors meeting at Meech Lake, Ontario.

22 John B. Taylor
Born 1946, Yonkers, New York

John Taylor obtained an AB in economics from Princeton University in 1968 and a PhD in economics from Stanford University in 1973. He taught at Columbia University between 1973 and 1979, becoming a professor of economics in 1979. Between 1980 and 1984, he was a professor of economics and public affairs at Princeton. He then moved to Stanford, where he has remained ever since. He currently serves as the Mary and Robert Raymond Professor of Economics and the George P. Shultz Senior Fellow in Economics at the Hoover Institution.

In government, Taylor served as senior staff economist of the Council of Economic Advisers (CEA) in the administrations of Presidents Gerald Ford and Jimmy Carter (1976–1977). In the administration of President George H. W. Bush he served as a member of the CEA (1989–1991). And from 2001 to 2005, he served as undersecretary of the treasury for international affairs during the George W. Bush administration.

I interviewed John Taylor on two occasions. The first interview took place in his office at the Hoover Institution in Stanford, California, in the middle of the morning on Thursday, July 19, 2012. The second interview took place at the Hyatt Regency hotel in Chicago, where he was attending the Allied Social Science Associations meetings, in the middle of the afternoon on Saturday, January 7, 2017.

Background Information

Bowmaker: Why did you become an economist?

Taylor: I majored in economics as an undergraduate and was fascinated by how various quantitative techniques could be applied to economic issues. I was very attracted to the science and elegance of the approach, but I don't think I would have become an economist without the accompanying policy aspects.

Entering the Policy World

Bowmaker: What does an economist bring to the policy world that others do not?

Taylor: Economic science, including theory and history, brings guidance about what good policy should be. It is quite substantive in terms of its ideas about the importance of markets and individual choice and, more generally, in providing a cost-benefit analysis of government.

Bowmaker: Your first policy position was as senior staff economist at the Council of Economic Advisers between 1976 and 1977. Did you view yourself as having strong policy positions or simply as a hired professional serving the CEA chair and, indirectly, the president?

Taylor: At the time, I had been doing academic research on policy issues as a professor at Columbia and was anxious to understand how policy worked in practice. I didn't have tenure yet, but I talked to one of my senior colleagues, Phil Cagan, and he recommended that I take the opportunity because working in the White House gives you a sense of translating economic ideas into action that you can't get elsewhere.

Bowmaker: As you began your position, what surprised or frustrated you?

Taylor: First of all, being part of a very small group of people advising the president of the United States is in itself a surprise. You are very close to the president and very much part of the policymaking apparatus. The second surprise is the very complex way in which economic policy decisions are made, because there are so many influences to consider—including those relating to politics and national security.

Bowmaker: When you were at the CEA for the first time, Alan Greenspan was its chairman. How would you describe his influence with President Ford?

Taylor: He enjoyed a special relationship with President Ford, and therefore he had a great deal of influence—which helped morale among the CEA staff. For example, Alan weighed in on the 1975 tax rebate when it was under consideration. Ford asked for two messages, a veto message and a signing message, to give him time to make a decision. He then requested written opinions about whether or not to sign the bill. Treasury Secretary Bill Simon was against it, but Alan went with it, I believe, in order to achieve other objectives such as discipline of the budget. In the end, President Ford signed the bill, which was bad policy in my view because it represented a compromise: some principles were given up in exchange for others, such as reining in the growth of government spending, as Alan had recommended in his memo. But it is a clear case of Alan having a direct influence on a decision made by President Ford.

Bowmaker: How would you describe Alan Greenspan's general approach as an economist?

Taylor: Alan was a business economist, and while many academics might not have appreciated the way he went about things, I thought he was very careful in his analysis of data. And he even tried to generate new numbers, because he had this sense that that would allow him to go further on an issue than other people. For example, when I returned to Columbia, I worked for his consultancy firm on a model of coffee consumption, which involved estimating short-term movements in inventory. Of course, you can find inventory at the stores, but Alan argued that one of the largest inventories of coffee is what people have on their shelves at home. And so we made a big effort to estimate that particular stock.

Bowmaker: You returned to the CEA in 1989 as a member, where part of your role was to liaise with the Federal Reserve—which by that stage was headed by Alan Greenspan. Can you describe what that entailed exactly?

Taylor: One important aspect was keeping a close association with Greenspan. I had to make sure that the White House knew what was going on with monetary policy. The second thing, which is maybe more important historically, was an attempt to think about the Fed as a more rules-based institution under Greenspan. At the time, many people were viewing it as just being a Greenspan standard in that it was very ad hoc, informal, and discretionary. To me, it didn't operate that way—there was a method in the decisions, even if it wasn't entirely visible. For many years, I had thought about the idea of having monetary policy guided by a rule. This was very interesting to me. And so in the year that I returned to the CEA, the *Economic Report of the President* had a whole section on policy rules at the Fed. It was a case of us putting our toes in the water to not only think about monetary policy this way, but to encourage it as well. In other words, it was one of the first efforts to make technical work on this issue operationally useful. The language in that section was approved by the Fed, and I remember when I left the Treasury as undersecretary many years later, Alan Greenspan made the comment that the Fed deserves an assist in relation to the Taylor Rule that I later developed [a mathematical formula to provide guidance for how central banks, such as the Federal Reserve, should set short-term interest rates based on economic conditions] because of that connection when I was a member at the CEA.

Bowmaker: When I spoke with Michael Boskin, who was chairman of the CEA when you were a member, he told me that you helped prevent a trade war with Japan. Can you tell us a little about your specific role?

Taylor: Yes. I was involved in trade negotiations relating to the Structural Impediments Initiative, which was an effort to reduce the great deal of friction that existed over our bilateral trade deficit with Japan. This was a basic macroeconomic issue because a trade deficit is an imbalance between saving and investment: if you're saving more, then you're running a smaller trade deficit, while if you're investing more, you're running a larger trade deficit. Many people were arguing that we should deal with the situation with protectionist or retaliatory measures, but I thought a better way to come at it would be through structural changes, of which savings and investment were examples. In return for dealing with some of our regulatory issues, then, we asked Japan to deregulate its retail sector to induce more consumption—which would reduce saving, of course, and move the trade deficit in a direction that was more favorable for the US. I remember having a conversation about these talks with Bush 41 in the small dining room just off the Oval Office. He said, "Well, I hope you're not saying we should save less. We should save more!" I told him, "That's exactly right, Mr. President, you've got it. We're trying to get our own savings rate up so that we can reduce the deficit."

Bowmaker: What were the main lessons that you learned from your time at the Council of Economic Advisers?

Taylor: I learned that relative to the shifting political winds, the economist is nearly a fixed point in Washington. My first stint at the CEA began with

President Ford in the White House and ended with President Carter being elected, and you could only see a big change in politics relative to the economics in moving from Republican to Democrat. That's the way it should be. Our job is to give objective economic advice.

As Undersecretary of the Treasury for International Affairs

Bowmaker: In 2001, you were appointed undersecretary of the treasury for international affairs. Were you always attracted to the role?

Taylor: Yes. Historically it has always been a very important position—Paul Volcker had the job in the past—and I think it is also the most interesting economic role in government. It involves operational issues with respect to currency markets, the IMF [International Monetary Fund], the World Bank, and the relationship between the US and the rest of the world. The undersecretary is effectively the top financial diplomat for the US government, and so the role comes with a huge amount of responsibility.

The natural job for me would have been to run the CEA for the incoming Bush administration, and I was offered the role. But that is largely an advisory position without any operational duties—unlike the undersecretary job, which I was thrilled to take. Of course, when 9/11 hit, the role changed completely. We had to develop strategies to deal with terrorist financing, reconstruction in Iraq, and fund-raising for Afghanistan. In each of those cases, new operations had to be established. For example, in our mission to freeze terrorist assets, we created a new office in the Treasury that was responsible for monitoring the cooperation of other countries.

Bowmaker: Can you describe the initial challenges in moving from being an adviser in the three earlier presidential administrations, and a developer of policy ideas in academia, to being responsible for implementing decisions?

Taylor: Yes. There is a very significant difference between economic advice and policy operation. People often forget that fact. During my second stint at the CEA, I had enjoyed quite a bit of interaction with the Treasury, so that was helpful in bridging the gap. But it was really a question of learning as fast as I could, which involved talking to experienced economists, like George Shultz, who had served in similar operational roles and developing an approach to the job that made use of sound economic principles.

Bowmaker: What advice did George Shultz give you?

Taylor: I've known George for a long time, and he was helpful in encouraging me to accept the job in the first place. In some sense, he is a model policymaker as an economist in that he has strong principles that he uses to guide decisions and knows about incentives, which he also takes to the job. One very specific piece of advice that he gave to me was about something he calls "gardening," which means that you have to work on your relationships with other people and countries, even when there is not a crisis at that moment in time. In other words, you have to be ready for when there is one. As it says on a tie that George gifted me when I took the job, "Democracy is not a spectator sport."

Bowmaker: You just mentioned the importance of knowing about incentives as a policymaking economist. Can you describe how this applied to your role?

Taylor: Part of my basic research on monetary policy concerns commitment and expectations, and the need to get incentives right. This can be applied to financial crises, where bailouts create terrible incentives and ultimately make things worse. And so I thought it was very important to convince the IMF to shake off this bailout mentality with respect to the emerging markets. There had already been a Mexican bailout and Russia had been helped for a while, and my research told me that this was a very bad situation. Of course, fixing it is incredibly more difficult than writing a paper, because you have to resist the temptation of a bailout and find a way to make the other countries agree. This policy problem is a fascinating application from economics called time inconsistency, which in this case means that it is hard for governments to commit now because circumstances will change in the future. In other words, we can say that we are committed to not bailing out a country, but when times get tough and the country's leaders and creditors around the world are screaming, we give them a bailout. And so we had to deal with that time-inconsistency problem, and economics tells us that you can find a way of staying more firmly committed to saying no. We had the idea of changing the terms of the debt contracts of the emerging markets when they borrowed from investors so that if a country got into trouble with its creditors, the financial terms of the contract could be adjusted without a default, and therefore without the need for a bailout. That is a very concrete application of ideas found in the economics literature. Of course, it was a very sizable task to get other countries in the emerging markets to issue debt with these new financial terms, which are called collective action clauses. But ultimately they did, and I think it changed the nature of the IMF's relationship with them dramatically and led to major improvements. We didn't have serious financial crises in the emerging markets after 2001–2002, and they went through the recent financial crisis much better than anyone could have expected.

Bowmaker: As you noted earlier, part of your role included setting up a new monetary system and currency in Iraq. Can you describe how you went about that task?

Taylor: That involved a huge amount of delegation and feedback mechanisms to make it work. We had to stick to our principles, particularly the importance of stability, which meant that we first had to ask ourselves, "What is the best way to create that stability?" And that led to the question of whether we should introduce a new currency overnight or hold off until later. Going too fast was probably not a good idea on stability grounds, and in any case we didn't even know who could implement it, because the intelligence at that time was very poor. So we decided on a two-stage plan. First, we would use US dollars to pay people, like civil servants and pensioners, and make sure that we did not cause a hyperinflation. That would create stability and confidence, and I think it worked pretty well. We were able to get the funds to make those first payments from the assets that had been frozen in US banks in the first Gulf War. Once the president issued an executive order, the funds could be used. When the time did come to introduce the new currency—which was the second stage—we wanted the Iraqis to choose its design, because currency is frequently something of nationalistic significance. It took a little longer that way, but again I think it worked quite well.

Bowmaker: You were handed this task having just come from an academic environment. Was this an advantage or a disadvantage?

Taylor: It's hard to believe that my academic experience was a good thing because there were so many moving parts and so much reporting responsibility involved, including dealing with the military and Foreign Service. However, at the same time, I had the advantage of being able to lay out the principles of what needed to be done rather than how it should be done. That is something I learned from my previous experiences and through talking with people. But it also comes out of economics because when you're a leader in an organization, it doesn't make sense to try to lay out all of the details about what everyone should do—it's really not possible. There is evidence from the organization and management literature that microman-aging in such a situation causes problems. And so you have to find a way to hire good people, give them a mission, and let them make on-the-ground decisions. We were fortunate enough to find a good person to head up the currency exchange in Iraq, which had been experiencing some glitches. He was a former brigadier general, Hugh Tant. He did certain things that I couldn't possibly have known about, and I only learned about them later. For example, because of his military background, he was very good friends with General [Ricardo] Sánchez, and when there were security concerns with shipping currency, he was able to call him for help. I certainly couldn't have done that, and so that is definitely a case of where delegation was preferable to micromanagement.

Bowmaker: What did you learn about the intersection of economics and foreign policy when you were at the Treasury?

Taylor: When most people think about foreign policy, diplomacy and the military spring to mind. But when I was at the Treasury, I argued that eco-nomics is the third leg. It's still a concern to me that we don't focus enough on economics in our foreign policy. When discussing with my counterparts about how to set up a good process for creating more freedom in Iraq, I would be the one who piped in, "Don't forget about economic freedom." When we ignore the economics, things don't work quite so well.

Financial crises also interact with other parts of our foreign policy. For example, if you are the United States, you might be tempted to give a bail-out to a country in Latin America, while the Europeans may be more con-cerned with helping a country such as Turkey. And when we were thinking about forgiving the Iraqi debt that had been run up by Saddam Hussein, the internal debate centered on the "odious debt" argument, because Saddam was a bad guy. But my feeling was that you didn't need a special rationale in this case, you could just do it on the basis of the economics—such as whether it made sense for future borrowing, and how it would not be fea-sible for the country to get started again if it had this gigantic overhang of debt. Ultimately, those simple economic arguments carried the day.

To some extent, I think many of the issues relating to economics in the foreign policy examples I just discussed worked well because of the com-fortable personal relationships that I had with Condi Rice, director of the National Security Council, and President Bush. I had worked with the presi-dent during his electoral campaign, and I think that contributed to him emphasizing the important role of the Treasury in foreign policy. In fact, after 9/11, he gave a talk in the Rose Garden in which he said that the first shot in the war against the terrorists was the Treasury freezing their assets.

At that time, the best international network in the area of finance was the G7 [Group of Seven]. A lot of its operations were run by deputy secretaries of the member countries, and I thought it was very important to have a good rapport with them. And so we made a big effort to have summer retreats out here in California, away from the capitals, which is an example of the "gardening" that I mentioned earlier. That was pretty beneficial, because it enabled us to continue to work when things got tough—especially in Iraq, when there was the dissension of the French and the Germans. They were not interested in helping the Iraqis establish a new currency or giving the country a new start by writing down their debt as much as possible.

Bowmaker: Turning to your relationships with your colleagues at the Treasury, how would you describe your experiences with Treasury Secretaries [Paul] O'Neill and [John] Snow?

Taylor: Both of them were hands-off, which I appreciated quite a bit, but Paul was more outspoken, which was something that I had to deal with occasionally. For example, in the previous administration, [Treasury Secretary] Bob Rubin had made a point of saying that the US had a strong dollar policy, but Paul indicated that that was not so important to him. I think, quite rightly, he was thinking, "What are you talking about? We just want a flexible exchange rate." But the problem was that the concept of a strong dollar was a signal that we were going to have a good policy overall. And so appearing to go back on that so-called mantra made people worry, and the exchange markets did react. I was asked by people several times whether we should be intervening in the markets, which we did not do, and eventually Paul made the following statement: "I believe in a strong dollar, and if I decide to shift that stance I will hire out Yankee Stadium and some rousing brass bands and announce that change in policy to the whole world." That was his way of saying that we still had the same old policy. And so we got over it in the end.

Bowmaker: What did you learn about the role of the media in policymaking?

Taylor: That's a big part of the environment. Take the Argentina situation in 2001. In the summer of that year, the country received a bailout one month before I began my role in the Treasury, and its economy had deteriorated even more. Our feeling was that we would grant them one final bailout, which we did in August. But given my statements about bailouts prior to entering government, we were heavily criticized by the media for that decision. It was a case of, "Those guys talked a good game, but when push came to shove, they did the same thing again." And there is no question that can have an influence, from the public's perception of whether you continue with your commitments to perhaps even affecting the thinking of other government agencies who might have read about it in the newspaper. And so you have to be aware of this part of the job and even be prepared for it.

Bowmaker: The previous four undersecretaries lasted an average of two years in the position. You served for four years. What was the secret of your longevity?

Taylor: Oh, I think it was just the circumstances and a sense of making sure that as much of the job was done as possible. Those were exhilarating and grueling times because of all of the things that were happening, but I can't tell you enough about the spirit of the people with whom I worked. There was a great sense of patriotism and friendship for the United States given the attacks of 9/11, and I made many, many trips all over the world because it just seemed so important to get it right.

General Thoughts on Economic Policymaking

Bowmaker: Do you believe that if we were to raise the level of economic literacy in this country, economic policymaking would improve because the people would demand better policy?

Taylor: Yes, to the extent that what people learned was consistent with good economic policy. There are so many commonsense, pocketbook concepts that we teach in Economics 1, such as the advantages of markets and the harm caused by national debt, which are important for voters to learn. The greater people's understanding of them, the better off policy would be. And I would also add the intertemporal issues associated with policymaking. It's very easy for policymakers to do something now and not take into account the future ramifications of their decisions. For example, you see it in local government when the promise of big pensions does not materialize because the decision makers are no longer in office. It would be tremendous if policymakers could be held more accountable on this dimension, and I think this is where the economic literacy of the voting public is a useful input.

Bowmaker: Do you think that the gap between economics research produced in universities and policymaking will increase or decrease over time?

Taylor: Economists inside and outside of academia have to work together on that, because there is a natural tendency for us to drift apart for several reasons. One of them is that policymaking sometimes involves a great deal of nitty-gritty work, including managing people—which is not something that academic economists are typically going to think about during their careers in universities. And there are also complicated issues that are very difficult to get into policy. Again, think about the time-inconsistency problem. That is a beautiful theory, but it is perhaps not as exciting when you face the task of trying to apply it to different countries at difficult times.

Bowmaker: How important is the role of prominent economists who act as independent critics of the policymaking process?

Taylor: They are very important. Part of our democracy is to have people outside government kibitzing through op-eds and articles, and we need to preserve that as much as possible. I think there is a temptation in government to not pay attention because one feels that the writer is just sitting in an ivory tower. A good example of the importance of a civil society comes from my experience in Iraq. In setting up a new financial system for the country, my staff recognized that it was impossible for the small, independent banks to communicate their views to the finance ministry. Freedom of assembly had been forbidden under Saddam Hussein's regime. And so we had to recreate a banking organization for them. I don't think people realize how lucky we are in the US to have the freedom to speak out and criticize government policy when we see it is appropriate.

Bowmaker: Which aspects of the institutional framework for making economic policy in this country work well, and which need to be reformed?

Taylor: One thing that has happened in recent years is that there is a greater tendency for the White House to micromanage the government agencies, such as the Treasury, the State Department, and the Commerce Department. This is happening for a number of reasons, one of which is that it is very difficult to get people confirmed in top jobs in those agencies. It is a very long and painful process. One simple idea would be to go back to the situation where the president appoints these individuals, who are then confirmed by the Senate.

I mentioned earlier that the third leg of foreign policy is economics. I think if there was a way to recognize that fact within the institutional framework, that would be a good thing, too. Some progress was made when Condi Rice was director of the National Security Council [NSC]. She included the Treasury Secretary on the NSC's Principals Committee. But there is more to be done along those lines to help economics have a bigger voice in international policy. I have heard it said that the reason economics is not more front and center is that economists are too narrowly focused in their questions, but I've always thought that the foreign policy people's eyes become glazed over too much with economic issues. Whichever side is at fault, though, more does need to be done.

Personal Reflections

Bowmaker: What value has your public service had to you and to your university?

Taylor: It has made my career as an economist more complete. As I said at the beginning of our interview, I was always attracted to the policy side of economics. Of course, there are many beautiful theories and interesting empirical approaches that are not policy related, but if I had not worked in government, that would have been a major missing component in my work. And having the policy experience has helped in deciding which paths to follow in my research. To the extent that my research is better as a result, that benefits Stanford, too. There is no question that my teaching has been improved, because I am able to better explain the policy process to students.

Bowmaker: How did your personality affect your style and approach as a policymaker?

Taylor: In government, many of the people who are working for you have been there a long time—they are career civil servants. And so you have to think about the incentives they have to do a good job, or the ways in which you can motivate them to do a good job. I think you have to show them great respect and emphasize the importance of their own job. The personality trait that is most crucial is enthusiasm, and for me that often meant putting the stress on the economic importance of issues.

Bowmaker: What were your strengths and weaknesses as a policymaker?

Taylor: I would say the pluses and minuses are related to our system of government, in particular the quite unusual way in which people from academia are put into positions of responsibility. Take the job as under-secretary. All of my counterparts in the G7 had been in government for many years. I didn't have their experience, which was a disadvantage, quite frankly. But I think an advantage is that you aren't captured by the way things are done—you come in with new ideas and try to make them work.

Bowmaker: As a policymaker, which decisions or outcomes were most gratifying?

Taylor: The most satisfying ones are those when you stick to your economic principles even when people are skeptical that they will work, but ulti-mately they turn out to be successful. One example was the major financial crisis of Argentina in 2001. The biggest concern was that this would lead to contagion around the world, just as Russia's default had done a few years earlier. One reason that Russia's crisis had spread was that the international community changed its policies quickly without much warning, so the default was unanticipated until very close to its actual date. Therefore, our strategy to reduce the chances of contagion from Argentina was to change policy gradually, or at least signal our intentions in advance so that mar-kets could anticipate and adjust to the news. In addition, we had to help countries with financial connections to Argentina, such as Uruguay, absorb the shock. Our strategy worked, and we were able to contain any global contagion.

Bowmaker: On the other hand, there must be some things, in hindsight, that you'd like the opportunity to do differently. What are they?

Taylor: I would say locking in some of the changes that were made during the time I was undersecretary. We were moving in the right direction on the bailout mentality, especially for the emerging markets, but with the ampli-fication of the issue of "too big to fail" in large financial institutions and the reemergence of bailouts in Europe, we have gone backwards.

More generally, when I think about being an economist over the last forty years, I feel a sense of disappointment at our fitful progress in eco-nomic policymaking in the United States. The late sixties and entire seven-ties were terrible for the economy, mainly because macroeconomic policy was terrible. Then we made real progress with monetary and fiscal poli-cymaking in the 1980s and 1990s until recently, and things then worked quite well for the next twenty-five years. But we are now back in a very bad situation. I think that is due to a slippage away from good economics, and I am hoping we move back to good economics soon.

John Snow (*left*), when secretary of the treasury, sitting next to President George W. Bush, who was speaking to reporters after a meeting in the Oval Office on December 9, 2004, with the Trustees for Social Security. The president was promising a bipartisan effort to reform the Social Security system.

23 John W. Snow
Born 1939, Toledo, Ohio

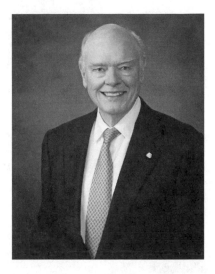

John Snow attended Kenyon College and the University of Toledo, where he earned a BA in economics in 1962. He pursued graduate studies at the University of Virginia, obtaining a PhD in economics in 1965. He was an assistant professor of economics at the University of Maryland from 1965 to 1968. He received a JD from the George Washington University Law School in 1967 and subsequently worked at a Washington, D.C., law firm until he joined the general counsel's office of the US Department of Transportation in 1972. He subsequently served in a number of different roles, culminating in his appointment as deputy undersecretary (1975–1976) and administrator of the National Highway Traffic Safety Administration (1976–1977).

Following the administration of President Gerald Ford, Snow became a visiting professor of economics at the University of Virginia and a visiting scholar at the American Enterprise Institute. From 1978 to 1981, he was a distinguished fellow at the Yale School of Management.

During the presidential campaign of 1980, Snow was a member of Governor Ronald Reagan's four-man advisory group on regulatory policy, and as president-elect, Reagan named Snow vice chairman of his transportation transition team.

During the administration of President George H. W. Bush, Snow was appointed cochairman of the National Commission on Financial Institution Reform, Recovery, and Enforcement on the causes of the savings and loan crisis (1991–1992). He was a member of the national tax commission chaired by Jack Kemp in 1996, and in 2002 he cochaired the Conference

Board's blue-ribbon Commission on Public Trust and Private Enterprise. Snow served as the seventy-third secretary of the treasury from 2003 to 2006 during the George W. Bush administration.

Snow held multiple positions with CSX Corporation (formerly Chessie Systems, Inc.) including president, chief executive officer (CEO), and chairman (1989–2003). He was chairman of the Business Roundtable (1994–1996). Snow assumed his current position as chairman of Cerberus Capital Management in late 2006.

I interviewed John Snow at the offices of Ceberus Capital Management in New York City. It was early in the afternoon on Tuesday, December 20, 2016.

Background Information

Bowmaker: Why did you pursue a PhD in economics?

Snow: I developed an interest in economics early on from my father, who had studied the subject at the LSE [London School of Economics] and Cambridge. He was a lawyer specializing in regulatory and antitrust issues, and we had regular discussions around the dinner table about economics, politics, philosophy, and world affairs. I wanted to be a lawyer, too, but in talking to my father I recognized that the substance he was dealing with underneath the formality of the law was really economics. And so I set out to study both law and economics.

Entering the Policy World

Bowmaker: What does an economist bring to the policy world that others do not?

Snow: Economics provides a unique framework, a set of tools, and a mindset that is useful in addressing public policy questions. The economist thinks in terms of costs and benefits and trade-offs. The core ideas of economics—opportunity costs, optimization, comparative advantage, externalities, public goods, moral hazard, equilibrium, and so on—provide an extremely useful methodology in thinking about public policy issues. Economics is essentially about choice, and the choices we make individually and collectively lie at the heart of public policy. Training in economics also breeds skepticism over easy answers to complex problems and puts great emphasis on quantification. That's valuable in public life, where there is a tendency to go with easy answers and to overlook or downplay quantification.

Bowmaker: You joined the legal department of the US Department of Transportation in 1972 and were appointed deputy undersecretary of the department in 1975 during the Ford administration. What did you learn about the interface between law and economics in policymaking in this role?

Snow: I got a good practical education to supplement what I had learned in grad school at the University of Virginia, studying under a group of brilliant thinkers including Ronald Coase—who pioneered the whole field of law and economics, changing the way we study both law and economics today. His fundamental point was that the law establishes the social arrangements through which economic concepts get expressed. In other words, if you want to know what is happening in a given situation, you need to understand the institutional framework within which the participants are engaging.

At the Department of Transportation, President Ford was facing a weakening economy, and he badly wanted to get at the problem. So he set up a task force to identify ways in which the government was getting in the way of better economic performance through its rules and regulations. I was appointed as the representative for the Department of Transportation. The lead White House participant was a member of the Council of Economic Advisers named Paul MacAvoy, who was on leave from the Yale economics faculty and whose specialty was the economics of regulation. Under Paul's leadership the interagency representatives would meet—sometimes with the president himself, who took a great interest in our undertakings.

As our efforts proceeded, it became clear that the transportation sector offered real opportunities for reforms by eliminating unnecessary regulation. Our studies demonstrated that transportation was a naturally competitive industry, but it had been put into the wrong framework—a regulated public utility framework—rather than in an open marketplace. We advanced the view that society would benefit enormously if the transportation industry were deregulated, so I became an advocate for deregulation, which was met with fierce opposition within the transportation industry. I saw firsthand the natural alliance of market incumbents with politicians and the idea of regulatory capture in practice, and with it the heavy burden of proof required to change the system over the objections of the established players. Before coming to the department, I had been well exposed to the theory of rent seeking and regulatory capture, but now I saw it up close and personal. In one meeting in the Roosevelt Room of the White House, Frank Fitzsimmons—the head of the Teamsters Union—reminded me and Paul MacAvoy that the teamsters had supported [Richard] Nixon and were prepared to support Ford's election effort in 1976, but he couldn't do it if truck deregulation continued to be a priority for the Ford administration. But despite knowing the political risks, Ford remained committed to the policy, so our efforts continued and ultimately bore fruit a few years later, with the deregulation of motor carriers, airlines, and railroads.

Bowmaker: By that stage, did you view yourself as having strong policy positions or simply as a hired professional serving the president?

Snow: Both. I was doing a professional job serving a president who wanted to find out what the obstacles were to higher productivity and greater prosperity. But you couldn't study economics as I had without having a strong predisposition toward markets and a skepticism about economic regulation. And so as we studied closely the effects of regulation—and I saw the evidence mount up—it was easy for me to be an advocate for a more competitively structured transportation system.

Years later, Alan Greenspan told me that he felt that the deregulation movement was an important reason why the performance of the US economy improved so much in subsequent decades, becoming much more resilient and adaptive—a view that as we know greatly influenced monetary policy.

Bowmaker: As congressional liaison for the Department of Transportation in the 1970s, what did you learn about how Washington worked that would prove useful later in your government career?

Snow: Members of Congress respond to their constituents, and they read political tea leaves very well. And so if you want to influence a member of Congress, don't simply tell them you've got a great idea in the abstract—tell them how it's going to help their constituents. And then you need to ask the constituents to tell their member of Congress: "You need to get behind this idea, because it helps us." And of course if you want to influence the course of events in Washington, advocates for a particular position need to amplify their voice through grassroots outreach, coalition building, and finding a powerful champion in the Congress.

People in Congress respond to their colleagues on legislative matters, particularly those who are well informed and well respected. Having people like that in your corner is extremely helpful. In addition a popular, persuasive, and committed president like Reagan really changes the dynamics in Washington.

As Secretary of the Treasury

Bowmaker: Following a career spent mostly in the private sector, you were then appointed secretary of the treasury in 2003 during the George W. Bush Administration. Why do you think you were approached?

Snow: That's probably a question better put to others. But recall the time— the president was on watch for the American economy because it was still struggling in the aftermath of 9/11 and the corporate scandals and was looking to rebuild his economic team, which had been plagued by discord. He wanted a team player at Treasury who could help communicate his economic policies, particularly the big tax bill, to Main Street and Wall Street. I guess the folks who made and influenced such things in the White House felt that I had the necessary qualifications and was suited to the role. In addition, I guess I was pretty well known to them as I had prior connections from the Reagan and Ford years with many of the Bush administration people. And, of course, I had kept my hand in public policy issues over the years through my involvement at AEI [the American Enterprise Institute], chairing the Budget and Tax Committee of the BRT [Business Roundtable], and later becoming chairman of the BRT. In these roles I was active in trade policy—including the passage of NAFTA [North American Free Trade Agreement]—as well as the budget accord achieved during [Bill] Clinton's presidency. My work on things like the S&L [savings and loan] crisis, tax reform with the Kemp tax commission, and corporate governance with the Conference Board were probably noted as well. So I had kept my hand in Washington matters and was reasonably knowledgeable about how the place worked.

Bowmaker: How were you approached?

Snow: I was in London as part of my corporate governance work when I got a call from Chief of Staff Andy Card, who asked me to come in for a visit without specifying the purpose. Of course, there was already a sitting treasury secretary, Paul O'Neill, who also was somebody I'd worked with in the past, and we are good friends. Upon returning to the States a week or so later, I visited the White House in November 2002 and was taken first to the personnel office—which should have made me suspicious—and in the course of things was asked if I would be interested in being chairman of the SEC [Securities and Exchange Commission], a position that was then open. I told them no, leaving no doubt in anybody's mind of my lack of any interest. As I was leaving that meeting, someone suggested, "You shouldn't be so preemptive about not wanting a government position." Next, I met with various members of the White House leadership team, where again I was asked about my interest in the SEC. I told them, "No, absolutely not." At that meeting, we also discussed the economy, the upcoming debate over taxes, and other such things. After an hour or so, I was taken into the Oval Office to meet the president. Having a great sense of humor, the president said to me as I walked in, "Hey, nice to see you. I guess you're not interested in the SEC, are you?" I replied, "Mr. President, news travels fast, doesn't it?" and we both laughed.

In the course of the conversation with him I said, "I see from today's *Washington Post* that you've got a real issue on your hands within your economic team on your tax proposal." The article was about the conflict between his advisers who wanted a total elimination of the tax on dividends, and those who were proposing a 50 percent tax cut on dividends. He asked, "What do you make of that?" I said, "Well, Mr. President, there's a principle in tax policy that you should tax income once, but only once. I've never heard of a principle that said you should tax something one and a half times." "I like to fight from principles," he said. We went on from there to a far-ranging general discussion, where I guess he was taking my pulse. As I was leaving, he remarked, "There may be something here that we'll need to talk about further. Let's just say for now we're sniffing you and you're sniffing us."

Andy Card called me later and asked me what I thought about being secretary of the treasury. I told him I would have to think about that. He said, "Well, you've got three hours to think about it, because the president is calling you then."

Bowmaker: What did you think about during those three hours?

Snow: I thought about my family obligations and perhaps needing to put plans for retirement on hold. I thought about the job itself, what a great honor it would be, and what a great responsibility. In particular, I thought about the state of the US economy and the administration's then forthcoming tax bill, as the president had indicated that would be a priority. As treasury secretary, I knew it would fall to me to lead that effort, which it did. And the more I thought about it, the more comfortable I became with the whole idea of using fiscal policy to strengthen the economic outlook for the country at that time.

Bowmaker: Popular perception is that the Treasury had suffered a loss of prestige before you accepted the role. Do you agree?

Snow: That perception is understandable but incorrect. Treasury had lost many of its roles to the new Department of Homeland Security and DOJ [Department of Justice] after 9/11. But in a sense, that was a clarifying event for the department, allowing it to focus on its primary mission of shaping national economic policy, which is the department's essential role. The Treasury is never going to be very far away from the center of the action on economic policy just by the very nature of policymaking, as the essential expertise lies in the department. Who do you turn to on jobs, the economy, taxes, the financial system, pensions and Social Security, and Medicare and Medicaid? The Treasury. It's the factory of ideas that deals with all of those issues and so many more. So shedding those law enforcement roles in retrospect made a lot of sense, as the Treasury Department became a true ministry of finance.

Bowmaker: It is well known that your predecessor, Paul O'Neill, did not have an enjoyable or successful time during his two-year tenure. How conscious were you of his experience before you accepted the role?

Snow: Paul is a wonderful guy, but he had a different view of things than the president. Paul was much more of a budget hawk than he was a supply-sider. And the president was much more of a supply-sider than a budget hawk. That made for some understandable tension.

Bowmaker: Did you speak to Paul O'Neill before you accepted the role?

Snow: Yes. I called him up and said, "Look, I want you to know I had no part in this." He said, "Oh, I know that, and no hard feelings." And then we talked about the transition. He was helpful and supportive.

Bowmaker: Who else did you speak to?

Snow: A number of people, including economist friends, members of Congress, and some people who knew the Treasury Department well. Perhaps the most useful advice came from George Shultz. He said you will find it very flattering when you get the question, as you will, "Mr. Secretary, what's your policy on X?" He said, "The answer always is, 'Thanks for the question. I'm pleased to be an adviser to the president, but the policies are the president's, not mine.'" His point was that it can only work if you are the voice of the president's policies, that you don't appear to be usurping that chain of command, and that you and the president are on the same wavelength. It's the only way a successful administration can work. You can't have one policy on the dollar or trade or the yuan coming from Treasury and a different one from the White House.

Bowmaker: In your first official meeting with President Bush, did he make it clear what he wanted you to do for him?

Snow: Yes, he did—good, strong, effective leadership and communication on the administration's economic agenda, and in particular getting the tax bill done. He also warned me about freelance off-the-cuff comments by saying, "The staff here tells me you're a good communicator—someone who can speak extemporaneously and without notes. That's a marvelous skill." I said, "Well, it comes from having been a university professor with a class of 500 students at 8:00 in the morning and realizing if I use notes I'd lose them all. That greatly helped my rhetorical skills, because you've got to learn to tell stories and capture the audience." He said, "Yes, that ability to speak without notes is such a wonderful, wonderful thing." And then he looked at me sternly, and told me, "In this job, use notes" [*laughs*]. A treasury secretary who goes off script is someone who is loved by the currency traders, but the consequences for world markets are serious and to be avoided. He was right [*laughs*].

Bowmaker: I would now like to turn to several economic issues that you faced during your time as secretary of the treasury. I have two questions about the tax cuts. First, in light of the growing budget deficit, why were you such a staunch advocate of them?

Snow: I was concerned that we were going into a double-dip recession and we needed to take action, a thought I expressed at an economic forum called by President-Elect Bush in Austin, Texas in December 2000, where he had gathered some economists and business leaders. Governor Bush asked the participants to offer some thoughts on the economic outlook. When it was my turn to speak, I said, "Mr. President, you're not going to want to hear this, but I think you're inheriting a recession." Being in the transportation industry, you can see a downturn earlier than almost anybody else by looking at container loads and global shipping activity. So I saw the tax cuts as a good insurance policy against a possible weakening in economic outlook, and I saw it as good fundamental economic policy as well.

I also saw the tax bill as a way to promote reform of government. Like Milton Friedman, I believe it puts discipline on government when less revenue is available and government is required to live within its means. I also think you get better results when the people can keep more of their own money and decide how best to use it.

I also saw our tax policies as a way to promote productivity, higher growth, and greater efficiency in the economy. Eliminating double taxation of corporate profits was a good fundamental tax reform idea. By raising the cost of equity, which is what double taxation does—versus debt, which is all deductible—you encourage excess reliance on debt. Ideally, you want a tax system that's as neutral as possible between debt and equity. And so the Bush tax cuts not only put oxygen in the economy but also enacted reforms that created better long-term incentives, because it mitigated a bias in the code to use debt rather than equity. That all made good sense to me, but of course we recognized that while well-conceived tax reductions will create some additional government revenue as growth spurts, they don't fully fund themselves, so we needed to deal with the resulting gap.

Bowmaker: How do you respond to the work of some scholars that suggested the tax cuts widened the gap between the after-tax incomes of rich and poor Americans?

Snow: They're just wrong. The tax tables show that the higher-income people paid a larger proportion of total taxes after the tax bill than they did before. And lower-income people found that their taxes were either eliminated or greatly reduced.

Bowmaker: Where did you stand over the issue of prescription drug benefits for Medicare?

Snow: While I had some misgivings at the time, I went along with the president because of his view that unless we had some sort of a prescription drug program, the Democrats would put one in place, and it would be much more costly and much less market-oriented than ours. And he turned out to be right—Medicare Part D has cost a lot less than people forecasted, and it's gotten a lot of popular political support.

Bowmaker: President Bush wanted to privatize Social Security. Did you believe this was always a feasible proposition?

Snow: You are probably referring to the so-called carve-out Social Security reform proposal, which would have created personal accounts by diverting funds from traditional Social Security. This always bothered me, especially as somebody who had to be responsible for trying to make it appealing to Congress. While you could argue that in the long run it would be self-funding, you would have had to borrow an awful lot of money in the interim. For that reason alone, it was a very tough pitch. The Democrats in Congress wouldn't talk to us, and the Republicans didn't like it. So it wasn't exactly well received. For that reason, my view was that we should pivot and focus on changes that would make Social Security self-sustaining, and in effect make the personal accounts optional—the add-on approach. That would have been a more salable position.

Bowmaker: Some economists have argued that the Bush administration should share part of the blame for the financial crisis since it avoided regulation of banks and mortgage brokers, and also its fiscal policy made the economy more dependent on foreign capital, which fueled the bubble in housing prices. What is your response?

Snow: No, that is a misreading of history. Looking back, the Treasury, and with the support of the White House, focused considerable attention on probably the single greatest systemic risk in the system, which was Fannie [Mae] and Freddie [Mac]. I was outspoken with the Congress and in public on the fact that Congress had to deal with Fannie and Freddie. I could not have been any clearer. Fannie and Freddie were right at the center of fueling the housing bubble, which brought the financial system down, because they were systematically reducing the cost of mortgages through buying them up in the secondary market. Then along came the clever folks who created the CDOs [collateralized debt obligations] and all of the slicing and dicing of the derivatives based on housing paper. I was adamant that we had to put a stop to this hedge fund arbitrage game that Fannie and Freddie were playing. So I spoke out about Fannie and Freddie, and I told Congress it was the biggest systemic risk in the system, and that they had to be reined in. I was calling for regulation, not deregulation. If Congress had listened to us and put a strong regulator in place, that whole unfortunate chapter in our financial history may have been much different. But Congress never points back at itself [*laughs*]. And so the criticism is misplaced.

Bowmaker: Might you have pushed harder on banking regulation?

Snow: In early '05 we were hearing about some questionable practices, like the liar loans, that were going on in the lending markets. So I called in all of the financial regulators to the Treasury. A meeting of that kind was unprecedented, because at the time Treasury by law had no operational role over the independent financial regulators. Some resisted, but I persisted because we had to find out what was going on. I asked each of them what they were seeing and what they were doing. What I learned was that they all had a grasp of their narrow area, but they were not looking at matters outside of that. It was like the parable of the blind men touching the elephant: they were all touching different parts of the elephant, but nobody knew it was an elephant. Financial market regulation had been siloed with so many different regulators who didn't talk to each other. So none of them had a complete picture of what was going on. There was a huge blind spot.

Following the meeting, the regulators started to put out guidance to begin to rein in the excessive practices. In addition to goading the regulators on, I also asked the undersecretary for financial markets to craft a plan for reorganizing financial regulation, which resulted in the Treasury Blueprint ["for a Modernized Financial Regulatory Structure"]. But of course the financial regulatory agencies had no interest in being restructured, and later on in Dodd-Frank very little was done in that regard.

The deeper problem of the elephant—the "too big to fail" banks as well as the GSEs [government-sponsored enterprises]—still persists: how to prevent them from bringing the economy down and putting taxpayers on the hook yet again is still at issue. No one has come up with an answer despite the efforts since then, including Dodd-Frank. That seems to me to be a huge failure.

Bowmaker: Some have suggested that since you did not have a background in finance, this made it harder for you to understand what was going on in the markets, and therefore to perceive in advance some of the things that happened. Do you agree with that assessment?

Snow: No. As the CEO of a major global corporation, I had had a lot of experience with financial markets. But the fact is no one can foresee a financial crisis, and of course if they could, steps would be taken to prevent it. But in the nature of things that can't be done.

This idea is well developed in Mervyn King's book, *The End of Alchemy*, which makes the point that financial crises simply can't be foreseen.[1] Yes, you can take steps to be better prepared, like having more capital in the banks. But the whole concept of eliminating systemic risk—and that's behind Dodd-Frank, that you can somehow let the animal spirits in the market go up to a certain point, and then somehow know precisely when to intervene to shut them off so they don't spin out of control—seems to be naive and inconsistent with the history of finance. In fact, such actions could very well bring about the crises that they seek to prevent.

Bowmaker: In the international arena, can you tell us about the challenges that you faced in helping postwar Iraq establish viable financial institutions and how you interacted with John Taylor on this issue?

Snow: The first thing we had to do was assist the Iraqis in replacing their currency and then lead the international effort to reduce the unsustainable level of sovereign debt that would make Iraq's recovery impossible. I will always be indebted to former German finance minister [Hans] Eichel for the critical role he played in making the debt forgiveness agreement possible. We also needed to help build the basic institutions of a modern economy—a system of national accounts, a central bank, a ministry of finance, and so on. My primary role was leading the Iraq debt restructuring effort, interacting closely with Ali Allawi, Iraq's finance minister, and supporting John Taylor and his team in their efforts to rebuild the Iraqi economy. I was told by Ali—and this was credit to John Taylor and his team—that of all the efforts on the part of the US government to support Iraq, none approached the importance of what the Treasury had done. A major accomplishment we spearheaded was the massive reduction in Iraqi debt, which required a great deal of financial diplomacy.

---

1. Mervyn A. King, *The End of Alchemy* (New York: W. W. Norton and Company, 2016).

Bowmaker: I would now like to turn to your interactions with President Bush. Can you give us an insight into how he thought about how an economy worked and how economic policy fitted into that context?

Snow: The president was a traditional conservative on economic policy, favoring low tax rates and limited but effective government. He used to say that people can make better choices of how to spend their own money than the government, so let's give their money back to them. For that reason, I think he fundamentally supported smaller government.

President Bush was also a believer in the American enterprise system. He believed in people taking risks and entrepreneurship. He felt strongly that we needed to help small business burdened by overregulation and high taxes, which led directly to our enhanced expensing provision for small business. He aligned with small business and saw it as the engine of the economy.

He was a very quick study who put things together fast and was impatient with formalities. He decided at some point to end a regular meeting with certain of his advisers because the meetings had become overly choreographed set pieces. He already knew what each of them was going to say, because they always made the same arguments.

I saw the combination of his analytical and political skills at work when we did the 2003 tax bill. When the bill reached an impasse between the House and Senate, the president was pragmatic: when you can't get it all, get as much as you can. Working with [Chairman of the House Ways and Means Committee] Bill Thomas, in fact we ended up with a bigger tax cut than we had initially proposed by making it temporary, which was a major concession. And we got capital gains down to 15 percent, which was a huge win, but the president had to overrule some of the purists in the White House who held out for the original proposal providing the 100 percent exclusion. Like Reagan, Bush was very pragmatic and principled. He had also observed firsthand his father's reelection bid in 1992, where the perception of a slowing economy proved so harmful: "It's the economy, stupid." He was keenly aware of the fact that jobs and growth are the most important political barometer for any administration and focused hard on the tax bill because of the economic implications.

Bowmaker: When I spoke with Paul O'Neill, he said that during the Bush administration, "politics was the dominant variable. It was about winning votes and winning elections. Doing the right thing was more an after-thought." How do you respond to that statement?

Snow: I think the president saw politics as a way to do the right thing: the two were married in his mind. Just think about what he took on with Social Security—that's the third rail of American politics. I asked him once, "Why do you want to do this, Mr. President?" He said, "It's the right thing to do, and I've got some political capital coming out of the election, and what's political capital for but to spend it?"

Bowmaker: What did you learn about the importance of the media in economic policymaking during your time as secretary of the treasury?

Snow: You learn that you need to choose your words carefully because you have a wide audience. You learn that you have to always talk in a way that avoids surprises and continually reassures markets. You come to understand that the media have a job to do, and that working well with the media is a big part of your job as secretary. You appreciate that there is a natural and healthy tension with the media. They are always looking for a story line, and government officials are always open to questions and serve as a fair target. You need to learn to accept that as a fact of life in the public sector.

When I first came in, the media were focused on the issue of slow growth, so I was frequently asked, "Mr. Secretary, aren't you concerned about the low growth rate of the US economy?" I responded that of course I was concerned, but with the tax cuts and natural resiliency of the economy I was confident we would see higher growth. When we got higher growth, the questions shifted, "Mr. Secretary, higher growth isn't doing much to raise employment. Aren't you concerned about high unemployment?" Again I responded "sure," but with higher growth we would expect to see better employment numbers. Then when unemployment fell, the question became, "Well, Mr. Secretary, aren't you concerned about stagnant wages?" And then I would respond "yes," but with higher growth and rising employment we can expect wages to rise as well. And as wages rebounded, it was then, "Mr. Secretary, aren't you now concerned about inflation?" You never win [*laughs*]. I kept waiting for the question, "Mr. Secretary, aren't you pleased…"

Bowmaker: How did you handle the speculation over your position towards the end of your tenure as secretary of the treasury?

Snow: After getting reelected, the president asked me to stay on after my first two years. I told him I'd continue for another year or so, and by then I would be ready to go. I felt that I'd done my time and accomplished what was asked of me.

Bowmaker: You worked closely with four presidents: Gerald Ford, Ronald Reagan, George H. W. Bush, and George W. Bush. How would you compare and contrast their operating styles and approaches to thinking about economics?

Snow: President Ford had conviction: he put doing the right thing first—like pardoning Nixon, which saved the country from a hellish turmoil. He was a godsend for the country, the right man at the right time. Ronald Reagan is, of course, the great president of modern times who changed the course of world history and American politics. He understood the office and sets the standard for all who followed. A true statesman and a great gentleman, Bush 41 was probably our best president on foreign policy since Nixon and, as a result, he will be greatly honored by history. And Bush 43 was principled, pragmatic, and determined, uniting the country as he did after 9/11 and making the hard choices that followed.

General Thoughts on Economic Policymaking

Bowmaker: To what extent can economics research produced in universities help inform policymakers?

Snow: Unfortunately, I think a lot of current economics is going in the wrong direction, with overreliance on complex mathematical models that don't give us a clear understanding of how the world really works, and how and where it is going. Sometimes the conclusions of these models are deeply suspicious and even unscholarly, as with the much-publicized work on rising income inequality—which on closer examination wasn't supported by the evidence.[2] The same was true of the study concluding that countries with debt levels exceeding 90 percent of GDP [gross domestic product] were effectively doomed—another case where the data didn't

---

2. Snow is referring to work by Thomas Piketty on income inequality. See, for example, Piketty's *Capital in the Twenty-First Century* (Cambridge, MA: Harvard University Press, 2014).

support the conclusions.[3] Economists need to be modest in their counsel to the world and make sure it's based on sound theory and research with quantifiable results—and remember to check the coefficients.

Bowmaker: Which aspects of the institutional framework for making economic policy in this country work well, and which need to be reformed?

Snow: I think the Fed[eral Reserve] and the Treasury work together pretty well. And any White House would be well served by more reliance on Cabinet agencies, where so much of the real expertise lies. Of course, we have the age-old problem that people seeking office have powerful incentives to promise the voters benefits while never adding up the underlying costs, which explains the impending implosion of entitlements that are leading to exponentially rising deficits. Maybe this calls for a constitutional balanced budget amendment as championed by many—including former President George H. W. Bush. Somehow we have to confront the issue.

Personal Reflections

Bowmaker: What were your strengths and weaknesses as a policymaker?

Snow: Again, that's a question that's probably better answered by others. My prior government experience was certainly an advantage. The training in economics and law was certainly helpful, as was my long career as a corporate executive—which gave me a pragmatic business approach to things, and of course a good background running large organizations. I also came to the Treasury job with a lot of experience in dealing with Congress and many good relationships developed over the years. So these were all pluses. But as President [John F.] Kennedy once remarked, there is no effective prior training for the Cabinet positions, which means a good deal of on-the-job training goes with it. And of course Washington can also be a rough place, and perhaps some sharper elbows were called for on occasion. But that's just not the way I choose to operate.

Bowmaker: As a policymaker, which decisions or outcomes were most gratifying?

---

3. Snow is referring to Carmen M. Reinhart and Kenneth S. Rogoff, "Growth in a Time of Debt," *American Economic Review* 100, no. 2 (2010): 573–578.

Snow: From my earlier experience, my work on the deregulation of the transportation sector was very gratifying as it has made a big and lasting impact. As treasury secretary, I would point to the tax cuts, which improved the economy and led to jobs; to our focus on the systemic threat the GSEs posed; to our role in getting the Chinese to move to a more flexible currency regime; and to our actions that gave Treasury a greatly enhanced role in the financial war on terrorism and thus made the country safer. That said, the Iraq war drained the energy and political capital from the Bush administration, and important matters were left undone—like Social Security reform and tax reform. But our efforts on both paved the way for future action.

Stephen Friedman (*left*), when director of the National Economic Council, walking on the South Lawn of the White House with President George W. Bush, who was en route from the Oval Office to Marine One on September 30, 2003.

24   Stephen Friedman
Born 1937, New York City

Stephen Friedman graduated with a
BA from Cornell University in 1959
and obtained a law degree from
Columbia University in 1962. He
joined Goldman, Sachs, and Co. in
1966 and became a partner in 1973.
He was the company's vice chairman
and cochief operating officer from
1987 to 1990 and cochairman or
chairman from 1990 to 1994. He was
chairman of the Federal Reserve Bank
of New York from 2008 to 2009, and
since 2005 he has been chairman of
Stone Point Capital LLC, a private equity firm.

In government, during the George W. Bush administration, Friedman was
assistant to the president for economic policy and director of the National
Economic Council (NEC) from 2002 to 2005, and from 2006 to 2008 he was
chairman of the President's Intelligence Advisory Board and Intelligence
Oversight Board.

I interviewed Stephen Friedman in his office at Stone Point Capital in
New York City. It was the middle of the afternoon on Wednesday, February
6, 2013.

Background Information

Bowmaker: When did you first become interested in economic policy?

Friedman: My intellectual interest stirred when I went to law school. I wasn't
a serious student up until that point. Then I entered a career in investment
banking, and as I became more senior, my lens widened. I was traveling the
world and observing the economy in different countries, which led to more
focus on economics—not in an academic sense, but from what you might
call a street-corner perspective.

Entering the Policy World

Bowmaker: How were you approached to become director of the National Economic Council?

Friedman: During the first two years of the Bush 43 administration, when clearly there were some bumps in how the economic area was working, one of my former partners asked if I would have a conversation with someone he was quite friendly with, George H. W. Bush. And so I remember having a long talk with him on the phone. He was an extremely gracious and charming man, and I was very open about certain things that, as a Bush 43 supporter, I found troublesome. I thought that I was just giving friendly advice from the peanut gallery, but I subsequently learned that he passed it on and suggested that if they were thinking of making changes, I should be approached. And that's what they did. The concept was that either John Snow or I would take over as secretary of the treasury, and the other would be director of the National Economic Council. I took the role at the NEC.

Bowmaker: Were you formally interviewed for the NEC position?

Friedman: I don't know how formal it was, but I had breakfast with Josh Bolten [deputy chief of staff for policy] and Karl Rove [senior adviser to the president], and I'm sure that I met Andy Card [chief of staff to the president] at some point. One of the things I think they were trying to assess is whether I had an ego that would fit into the environment—that I didn't suffer from CEO [chief executive officer]-itis, if you will. One can always just look at your background to form an opinion as to whether you are a competent person or not.

By the way, if you come from the private sector, the financial disclosure forms and divestiture requirements are a monstrosity and would discourage many people from taking a job in Washington. It is a very, very difficult process.

Bowmaker: You were cochairman with Robert Rubin at Goldman Sachs. He was director of the NEC during the [Bill] Clinton administration. Did you take any advice from him either before or after you accepted the role?

Friedman: Yes, I spoke at length to him. He did not say anything that was inconsistent with my intuitive approach. I have a mantra that any organizational structure is about three things: the quality of the people, the quality of the culture (the two most important ones), and a little bit about strategy.

The latter was straightforward. In Washington, I knew my job would be to identify the issues that most needed to be on the president's plate and/or that he was most focused on.

The culture is interesting. What would that be like? In the NEC—a small group, to a large extent—it was what I encouraged it to be. That is much easier to say than when you are parachuted into a major corporation that has been around for one hundred years, with decades of people at the watercooler perceiving life should be run a certain way. Woe to the outsider who puts something on the bulletin board that says we are going to change your cherished practices.

How about the quality of the people? I was very pleasantly surprised. I thought that I had absolutely crackerjack staff.

Bowmaker: How did you think your style and approach to the role would be different to Rubin's?

Friedman: Most people would say that our personalities are quite different, but I think our similarities are probably greater. We both tend to be quite analytical and probability-weigh decisions, which means that we don't fall in love with single outcomes as necessarily going to happen. We also spend a lot of time trying to size up people and deciding whom we have confidence in and in whom we don't. In the end, we are comfortable with people who are substantive as opposed to having too much salesy gloss.

Bob and I have worked together very well over a long period of time. In many ways, I think our respective approaches to running the NEC were the same as when we were heading the Goldman Sachs Management Committee.

Bowmaker: Coming into the job, how conscious were you of the way that your predecessor, Lawrence Lindsey, went about it—which ultimately led to his dismissal?[1]

Friedman: Only in the most general way. I didn't spend much time thinking about it, because we are very different people. He is an accomplished economist, whereas I am a generalist who tries to run a process that arrives at good decisions, having heavily harnessed the specialist inputs of others.

---

1. Lindsey left his position in December 2002 after a dispute over the projected cost of the Iraq War. He estimated that the total cost could reach $200 billion, while several of President Bush's other advisers argued that the cost would be much lower. It turned out that given the length of the war, Lindsey's estimate in fact was low.

But I do remember Larry telling me to give his staff a fair chance before making judgment on them. I felt that was good advice, and I am glad that I took it. If I'd had to start recruiting from scratch, it would have used up a hell of a lot of time. But as I just said, the staff were very good people—they really understood Congress and the substance of their areas of expertise. I was proud to have a chance to lead that group.

As Director of the National Economic Council

Bowmaker: Did President Bush make it clear what he expected you to do for him?

Friedman: Yes. However, it was pretty clear what had to be done. Anyone who is functioning as the head of staff, whether in government or in the business world, has to first—as I mentioned earlier—understand his boss's agenda and identify the issues that need to be prioritized. Then you have to come up with the options to deal with each of them, including their pros and cons, and make the necessary recommendation. This particular part of the job seemed self-evident to me. That doesn't mean easy. It is also part of the job to introduce certain policy issues to the president that are worthy of being on his agenda.

Bowmaker: How did you balance being the neutral manager of a process and at the same time a substantive participant while at the NEC?

Friedman: I felt no tension whatsoever. The natural quarterback for the economic policymaking process in the White House is the NEC. I can't think of a major issue that the president has to deal with that doesn't involve a number of different Cabinet departments or agencies, and so the role of the NEC is to coordinate them. I would have had my own opinion, but I made sure that everyone's point of view was fully and accurately reflected. I knew that you can get one hell of a lot of buy-in from people if they felt their ideas were listened to respectfully and taken into account. I used to try to explain to people at Goldman Sachs that if you find a piece of business, close the sale, and collect the fee (you do it all yourself), then you will receive applause. But if you recognize that you have a better chance of being successful if you bring someone else on board (you don't do it all yourself) then you will receive even more applause. Now, how does that relate to policy? If you have people in Washington thinking that the NEC just wants to be the honest broker, you will get much more support from them, even if they are ultimately on the losing side of the debate. The word is "teamwork"—desirable, but not ever present in Washington.

Bowmaker: What was the most difficult aspect of the job?

Friedman: The most difficult aspect of the job was pulling together a recommendation for the president in the knowledge that we had a meeting with him that afternoon or the next morning. You had to articulate and frame participants' various views in such a way that a vote could be taken—that is, turn conversation into a viable proposition. And so we would have a meeting around a big conference table in a big office with the objective not being to hit the lowest common denominator, but rather to get to the ultimate policy points of view. Enabling the group to absorb the facts and different views, hearing everyone out, then framing the relevant points to be decided, all the while looking up at the clock, conscious of the time pressure. I recall early on telling the president that I would be coming to him with an issue on which there was a significant difference of opinion. He just said, "That's what I'm here for," which was a very liberating moment for me. I wasn't interested in a mushy consensus. We gave him the options, the pros and cons of each, and who favored which one.

Bowmaker: Which aspects of your knowledge about how Wall Street worked proved to be most useful at the NEC?

Friedman: The fact that we live in a world of probabilities. And so I constantly pushed my staff and others to put probabilities on things. You need to prepare for tail risk and a range of possible outcomes. Now, I totally understand that is a highly imperfect art, and I would not recognize a Bayesian algorithm if you brought it in here and put it on the blackboard, but I do know that the financial cemeteries are littered with people who were dogmatic in their beliefs that a particular outcome was certain to happen. I don't think that you have intellectual rigor unless you have weighted your confidence in the various outcomes of interest. And it's a very revealing process. Take half a dozen knowledgeable people, have them talk through a certain topic, and then ask them to write down on a piece of paper the odds of a particular outcome taking place. You would be surprised how close the band typically is—it is likely to be something like 20 percent to 30 percent, rather than 20 percent to 90 percent. Of course, I can't guarantee that it always happens, but I have seen it many times during my career.

Bowmaker: Was there anything that surprised you about the way Washington worked relative to Wall Street?

Friedman: I remember one of my staff members saying to me, "You are always asking, 'How is this piece of legislation actually going to work after it is passed by Congress?'" I don't think that question is a very profound one, but it appears that it is not often really probed in Washington. It reminds me of the difference between working in mergers and in private equity on Wall Street. When a deal closes, the agent involved in the merger gets his check and then moves on to the next one. But the person from private equity now has five to seven years of work to see if it was a good deal or not. And so Congress is like the person working on the merger: once we get the legislation through, we put out a press release and have a signing ceremony. But will it be successful down the line? That's an entirely different question. That's after the next election—not often considered a relevant time frame.

Bowmaker: Despite your role being an honest broker, there must have been some policies that you coordinated and implemented that you probably wouldn't necessarily have chosen. Are there any examples that come to mind?

Friedman: Although I did believe in tax reduction, I would have been sharper with the scalpel on costs, particularly in relation to the Medicare drug bill and the highway bill. That was just my personal bias. At the end of the day, you lay out your recommendation to the president and he makes the final decision—which, by the way, is something that you have to get your mind around: you only *recommend*, even if you are a Cabinet member.

Bowmaker: How would you describe the president's style of authority?

Friedman: Contrary to myth that many of his political opponents have spread, George W. Bush is a smart and decisive man. I know this because I sat with him in the Oval Office after he had read our memos, and he asked very good, aggressive questions and expected hard-reasoned answers. He was fond of saying to people in meetings, "Enough of the 'on the one hand ... but on the other hand ...' What's your vote?" After listening to the arguments, he would often make a decision on the spot. The idea that the president was force-fed predigested decisions by other people is purely a canard.

I would also say that he had an extremely keen political sense. For example, I remember talking about something that Congress wanted to do in the area of taxation, and the president said, "I can't really explain this to a guy running a machine shop in Milwaukee." As soon as he said it, the nickel dropped, and I thought, "You're right, that's not going to come across as fair to him." In that respect, he was as good as anyone I saw, including those who had spent their whole lives in Washington.

Bowmaker: You spent a great deal of time interacting with economists. How, in general, did their approach to analyzing a problem differ from yours?

Friedman: First of all, Glenn Hubbard, Greg Mankiw, and Harvey Rosen have a very structured way of thinking, which I found very useful, and I leaned on them very heavily for advice. It's true that there may have been times when I had a sense that the world may not work in such an orderly fashion, but I don't recall ever talking to them and thinking, "You guys are not making a contribution." As I say, they were very helpful. In many ways it might have helped that I wasn't an economist, because there was never a feeling that we were competing with each other.

I should add that I also spent a lot of time with Alan Greenspan. He is a very smart and very wise man who was very highly regarded in the White House. He has been around Washington for a long time and possesses a very astute sense of what Congress is likely to do in certain circumstances, or what Pandora's boxes might be a bad idea to open up. I was astounded by his ability to draw upon an almost encyclopedic knowledge of events from the past and recall things from his career that were extraordinarily granular and cast light on present issues. He was a remarkable resource.

At the end of the day, though, economics tends to get trumped by politics in Washington. Just open your daily newspaper. Do you think that we would see today's fiscal situation if economics prevailed over politics? I think not, sir.

Bowmaker: What did you learn about the role of the media in policymaking when you were in Washington?

Friedman: To be careful. In my first week, I passed an NEC rule that nobody would talk with the media without having it coordinated by the White House Press Office. Not only did I never want my staff or me to be suspected of leaking a story to the media, but I also knew it would be enormously valuable to have the press office prepping us before any interviews, because it is so easy to unwittingly use a poor choice of words that could be taken the wrong way. Now, I might have needled the press office from time to time by saying, "OK, I intend to talk to the media about the tremendous value to the economy of gales of creative destruction …," but they were pleased with the rule. My question was, "Why didn't you make this change two years ago?" It just seemed so obvious to me that it was a perfectly sensible thing to do.

Bowmaker: When you left the NEC, Gene Sperling suggested that while you were serious about policy, it was very difficult for those on the outside to know how you and the NEC functioned within the White House. What is your response?

Friedman: Was it part of my mission to help Gene understand how I functioned within the White House? No. My mission was to be sure the best unfettered, candid advice got to the president, whether he wanted to hear it or not, and whether he chose to take it or not. Sometimes there seems to be an attitude in Washington that if you are not highly visible and getting publicity, what can you be doing? That may be true of certain jobs, but I felt as the quarterback of the policymaking process, it would be much more effective if I stayed out of the limelight. And so while I would make speeches or go out in front of the cameras whenever I was told to, I preferred to minimize it and let the relevant Cabinet secretaries maximize their time doing it instead. I think it worked well. I realize that's a self-serving statement, but I also know that the most important person measuring the performance—the president—was happy.

General Thoughts on Economic Policymaking

Bowmaker: Which fallacies, misconceptions, or misinterpretations affect policy debate in this country?

Friedman: I'm afraid that there is a gross lack of education about very fundamental economics among the overwhelming majority of the public and in large parts of Congress. But, in the words of Upton Sinclair, "it is difficult to get a man to understand something, when his salary depends upon his not understanding it!"[2] So it is hard to get someone to understand that we have to means-test Social Security if he is a beneficiary who would rather not be means-tested. And in Congress, if something is longer than a bumper

---

2. Upton Sinclair, *I, Candidate for Governor: And How I Got Licked* (repr. Berkeley: University of California Press, 1994), 109.

sticker, it is too academic. I can remember going up the Hill to talk to them about the tax bill, and they were asking about the arguments so that they could explain it to their constituents. Finally, one of them shouted, "John, it's all about jobs, jobs, jobs! That's all you have to know or say." That may be the most important part of it, but it's not something that would work well in the faculty lounge at a good university.

Look at our fiscal situation. If you listen to those speaking at town hall meetings, the public seems to think, "Yes, we have a fiscal problem, but the way to deal with it is to cut down on foreign aid." But that's just a tiny sliver of the issue. Yes, we are all entitled to our biases, but it is indisputable that harsh medicine is going to be needed, and reasonable people can debate how much should involve cost cutting versus revenue generation. In Washington itself, though, there is also a propensity to ignore the tremendous unfunded liabilities that we have in the entitlement system: pension plans don't enter into Congress's budget.

I do think that the public gets the government it deserves. As a leading politician once said to me, democracy is the only alternative to violence [*laughs*].

Bowmaker: Which aspects of the institutional framework for making economic policy in this country work well, and which need to be reformed?

Friedman: The fact that we had a debate on whether the United States of America should tactically default on its debt should give you some clue that we don't have an institutional framework for making policy that is working well. President Bush tried to take a reasonable and negotiable approach to dealing with Social Security, but it was demagogued by some as a ploy to fatten Wall Street. Baloney. I don't know anyone in Wall Street who was waiting for any benefits from that policy. It was an attempt to deal with what is, actuarially, an unsustainable situation. I doubt that we will be able to resolve it until it is patently clear that the locomotive is coming through the tunnel at us. There is an old saying in the financial world that you don't get major constructive change until "the fear of the future exceeds the pain of the change." But if you have a political system in which the most radical groups of the right and left are dominant in the primary elections, and politicians feel a need to cater to those extremes, then it is going to be very, very difficult for pragmatists to pull things towards a compromise.

Bowmaker: What is your response to those who express their concerns about the so-called revolving door between Wall Street and Washington?

Friedman: I will accept that if you pick people who are looking to spend a few years in Washington just to polish their résumé, go back to industry, and call in some favors, then you've made a mistake. But take someone like Bob Rubin or Hank Paulson. By the time they went to Washington, they had already had successful careers. They only wanted to do the best job they could in government. I strongly believe that you need people who understand the give-and-take of a competitive economy. To use a baseball analogy, you don't want your team to be run by those with no real-world experience on the field. Also, I like having some people in government who don't need or lust after the job—in fact, who are making a considerable sacrifice to take them and preserve their intellectual independence while in office.

Personal Reflections

Bowmaker: How did your personality affect your style and approach as a policymaker?

Friedman: My respect for bona fide experts was helpful. I think the White House was pleased that I didn't feel obliged to do all the talking for the NEC. I did that for a very basic reason: there were experts who were in a much stronger position than I to discuss certain topics. And so I would sit, watch, listen, and redirect only when it was necessary. Of course, we would very actively prep and interrogate them before those sessions with the president.

Bowmaker: What were your strengths and weaknesses as a policymaker?

Friedman: I don't recall any criticisms that made me think, "Gee, the president wants me to be better in this area…" One important ability that I had was the running of a meeting. It is possible to have long, rambling, and inconclusive discussions in Washington if you don't push for a clear focus and actionable positions. And so before important meetings I would have private sessions with the relevant people from the Cabinet offices to see if we could get ourselves into the same ballpark. We had a weekly lunch in the White House Mess with key economic Cabinet members and advisers, often with the vice president attending. These were very helpful in sharing information and bonding. Something else that we avoided with great success was re-litigation, which I feared when I went there. But that was one of the virtues of having people feel that they were on board.

Bowmaker: As a policymaker, which decisions or outcomes were most gratifying?

Friedman: I thought the whole process of the tax bill, which I heavily inherited from Josh Bolten [in his role as director of the Office of Management and Budget], worked particularly well.

Bowmaker: On the other hand, there must be some things, in hindsight, that you'd like the opportunity to do differently. What are they?

Friedman: I'm a big hindsight person. But I can't say anything major about my two years at the NEC. We worked hard, stayed out of the limelight, and got the job done.

Gregory Mankiw (*second right*), when chairman of the Council of Economic Advisers, meeting with President George W. Bush (*second left*) in the Oval Office. Also pictured are Vice President Dick Cheney (*far left*), and Stephen Friedman (*far right*), director of the National Economic Council.

25 N. Gregory Mankiw

Born 1958, Trenton, New Jersey

Nicholas Gregory Mankiw graduated
with an AB in economics from Princeton University in 1980 and obtained
a PhD in economics from the Massachusetts Institute of Technology (MIT)
in 1984. In 1985 he became an assistant professor of economics at Harvard
University and has remained there ever
since, currently serving as the Robert
M. Beren Professor of Economics. In
government, Mankiw served as staff
economist at the Council of Economic
Advisers between 1982 and 1983 and
as chairman of President George W.
Bush's Council of Economic Advisers
between 2003 and 2005.

I interviewed Gregory Mankiw on two occasions. The first interview took
place in his office in the Department of Economics at Harvard University,
in Cambridge, Massachusetts, on Monday, February 4, 2013. The second
interview took place at the Hyatt Regency hotel in Chicago, where he was
attending the Allied Social Science Associations meetings, in the middle of
the afternoon on Friday, January 6, 2017.

Background Information

Bowmaker: Why did you become an economist?

Mankiw: I had no idea when I went to college that I would become an economist. But during my freshman year, one of my friends told me about what
she was learning in an economics class. I looked through one of her textbooks and thought it was pretty interesting, and so in my second semester
at Princeton I took the introductory courses in microeconomics and macroeconomics. I was off to the races!

The micro professor was Harvey Rosen. He was a great teacher, and it was his ability to clearly exposit simple, but profound, ideas that drew me to the field of economics. I remember that he once assigned a chapter on educational vouchers from Milton Friedman's *Capitalism and Freedom*, and I would say that to a large extent, the beginning of my policy views came from his tutelage.[1]

Entering the Policy World

Bowmaker: What does an economist bring to the policy world that others do not?

Mankiw: I view an economist in Washington as an ambassador for the economics profession—someone in a unique position to translate academic articles for a policymaker who is typically a lawyer and not a regular reader of the *American Economic Review*. It's true that not all of those articles in top journals have policy relevance, but many of them do, and so an economist plays an important role in figuring out the parts of the academic literature that can inform the policy community.

Just as an aside, I think economics is a wonderful major for someone who wants to become a lawyer, because it provides a good foundation for thinking about how society is put together.

Bowmaker: Your first experience of the policy world was as an undergraduate, when you worked at the Congressional Budget Office [CBO] for two summers. Can you tell us a little about that?

Mankiw: That was a great experience. I was hired by the group that is now known as the Macroeconomics Division. It involved working with economists who had spent a large fraction of their careers in the policy world, and it was fascinating to see how they harnessed their economic models to do forecasting and policy analysis. When I took those introductory courses in my freshman year at Princeton, I liked micro better, but working at the CBO for those two summers cemented my interest in macroeconomics.

Bowmaker: After a year as a PhD student at MIT followed by a year at Harvard Law School, you took up a position as staff economist at the Council of Economic Advisers [CEA]. What motivated your decision to join the CEA?

---

1. Milton Friedman, *Capitalism and Freedom* (Chicago: University of Chicago Press, 1962).

Mankiw: When Marty Feldstein was appointed by President [Ronald] Reagan to be his chairman of the CEA in 1982, he hired Larry Summers to be one of his senior staff economists. I had just taken a course from Larry at MIT and, along with Julio Rotemberg, we had written a paper together on intertemporal substitution in macroeconomics. He asked me if I would like to spend a year in Washington on the junior staff at the CEA. I don't think the world had realized it yet, but I could see that Larry was already a fantastic economist, and so the opportunity to work with him was one that I couldn't pass up.

I had great respect for Larry's approach to economics of combining very powerful intuition with a thorough understanding of economic models and a true commitment to data. When I look back at some of my favorite economists, like Milton Friedman and Robert Hall, they all fit into that mold. During that year, Larry also gave me input on how I should revise my paper, "Small Menu Costs and Large Business Cycles," which was eventually accepted by the *Quarterly Journal of Economics*.[2] In addition, I wrote two articles around that time on preliminary economic data, which was motivated by the fact that I was constantly being bombarded with those numbers while at the CEA. I wanted to understand their relationship with final data.

More broadly, it was wonderful to be in an environment that was particularly cognizant of how economic research can be useful in shedding light on policy issues. I think it is a good idea for young academics interested in policy to spend some time in Washington, so that when they go there later in their careers, they are not complete novices.

As Chairman of the Council of Economic Advisers

Bowmaker: You were appointed chairman of the CEA in 2003. I understand that your predecessor, Glenn Hubbard, recommended you for the role. Why do you think he did so?

Mankiw: I don't think it was a personal friendship that generated the recommendation, because we weren't very close at that time. I assumed that he had read my work and felt that I would do reasonably well in the role. He had contacted me back in 2001 about a position at the Treasury that he

---

2. N. Gregory Mankiw, "Small Menu Costs and Large Business Cycles: A Macro-economic Model of Monopoly," *Quarterly Journal of Economics* 100, no. 2 (1985): 529–538.

thought that I should interview for, but I took my name out of the running because my youngest child was then three years old. He was our third, and my wife suggested that it would be a particularly hard time to leave her alone with three children—which is what I ended up doing two years later when our youngest was five [*laughs*]. I thought that would be somewhat easier for my wife, and given that the CEA position was one level up in the hierarchy, I jumped at the chance to replace Glenn.

Bowmaker: Coming into the role, how did you think your approach might be different to Glenn Hubbard's?

Mankiw: He and I came into the administration in very different ways. Glenn knew all of the players, having worked on the Bush campaign, but when I arrived, I was the new kid on the block, and it was a learning curve to get to know the people. I was aware that Glenn had done a fantastic job, and to a large extent, I thought of myself as trying to emulate him because he had worked well with the staff and was quite effective at getting his voice heard by the president. In a sense, making economic policy is like a relay race, where you grab the baton from the person who goes before you.

One of the most important things that Glenn gave me was his chief of staff, Phill Swagel. Phill had been hired for that job about six months before I joined the CEA. I had known Phill a little bit when he was a PhD student here at Harvard, but we became very close friends during my two years at the CEA. He was terrific at helping me navigate many of the personalities and institutions of the White House, because he understood how the council fit into the overall hierarchy. For example, one of the most important relationships that we developed was between the council and the [White House] press office, since I was supposed to be one of the public spokesmen for the president. Phill proved to be very important in acting as a liaison officer between those two parties.

Bowmaker: Did you view yourself as having strong policy positions, or simply as a hired professional serving President Bush?

Mankiw: I don't view myself as dogmatic. Of course, before I arrived at the White House, I had spent a lot of time writing and speaking about certain issues, but I recognized that I was a hired adviser who was there to help the president implement his policies, and to maybe change his mind when I thought that was appropriate. Being pigheaded is a terrible attribute for a policy adviser. I was probably not 100 percent successful in remembering that fact, but at least I tried.

Bowmaker: Did you take any advice from former chairs of the CEA before you began your position?

Mankiw: One of the things that happened shortly after I went there was that they moved the council out of the Old Executive [Office] Building. I was pretty annoyed at the time because I hadn't been warned about it or given any input into the decision. But I talked to Marty Feldstein, and he calmed me down. It turned out that the reason for the move was that after 9/11, major renovations of the Old Executive Building had to be completed, which meant that large parts of the building had to be vacated. And so for the two years that I was in Washington, a good fraction of the staff were off campus, so to speak, or located about a block and a half from the White House. I was worried that was going to reduce the council's access to meetings and, more generally, to the policy process, but my concerns were not realized. It still wasn't ideal, because my life was made even more hectic by having to regularly walk between my two offices—the one in the White House complex and the other where most of the CEA staff were parked. Thankfully, the weather in Washington tended to be relatively good [*laughs*].

Bowmaker: Did President Bush make it clear what he expected you to do for him?

Mankiw: It was made clear that the president wanted the economic team to work more closely together. In the first two years of the Bush administration, that certainly hadn't been the case. Yes, people can disagree with each other, but at the end of the day the president wanted us to reach a consensus on issues and simply get along. And I think we did when I was there. For example, I had never met the NEC's head, Steve Friedman, before taking the job, but after two years of working with him, he is one of my favorite people in the world. He is a really nice guy and both smart and open-minded. Many smart people in academia are excessively taken with their own intelligence, but Steve was always ready to learn and listen to other people's opinions. He was such a great person for that role.

Bowmaker: How did you go about establishing a comfortable working relationship with the president? I understand that early into your position you sent him a copy of Milton Friedman's book *Capitalism and Freedom*.

Mankiw: Yes, I did. President Bush is extremely social, and not long after I arrived in Washington, he invited the economic team to Camp David as a team-building exercise. I sent the book as a thank you, but I also thought that it would be a fun read and one that would help him formulate some of his own ideas. What I learned early on when giving briefings to him was that graph-heavy presentations tended not to resonate. After all, he was a history major, and so words and stories were likely to be more useful. Mind you, one of the most abstract presentations that I gave to him was about the exchange rate and the relationship between capital flows and trade deficits. Treasury Secretary John Snow was shocked that I included an equation! It was a basic accounting identity of savings, investment, and the trade balance. John said, "You don't usually refer to equations when you are briefing the president of the United States..." He was probably right [*laughs*].

Bowmaker: How would you describe the economic environment that you inherited as chairman and the issues that needed to be prioritized?

Mankiw: President Bush inherited an economy that was in a recession. By the time I arrived in Washington, it was over, but the recovery was slow. And so in 2003 he passed a second tax bill that accelerated some of the tax changes found in his 2001 bill and also reduced the taxation of corporate capital income—dividends and capital gains—to 15 percent. Those were probably placed highest on the agenda in my first year at the council.

To this day, I am glad that he reduced the taxation of corporate capital income. Many economists had long thought that it was excessively taxed relative to other forms of capital. Even though the [Barack] Obama administration has subsequently increased it to 20 percent, that is still lower than ordinary income taxation and represents an improvement in policy—which I hope will persist. I've always been a big believer in moving the tax code in a more pro-growth direction.

Bowmaker: How do you respond to those who argue that the administration's tax cuts were costly in light of the growing budget deficit, and that they widened the gap between the after-tax incomes of rich and poor Americans?

Mankiw: The economy was weak, and so it made sense to increase aggregate demand through expansionary fiscal policy. In terms of the second point, there is a classic trade-off between equality and efficiency, and you're balancing those competing objectives when you're designing a packet of tax changes. Those tax cuts were clearly designed to promote faster economic growth, both in the short run through aggregate demand and in the long run by having a more pro-growth tax structure. But parts of the tax code, like the child tax credit, probably did less to promote economic growth than others, such as reducing taxes on dividends.

Bowmaker: Some economists have argued that the Bush administration should share part of the blame for the financial crisis. Was there any discussion in the White House regarding the seeds of the financial crisis to follow—for example, relating to the rise in volumes of lightly regulated over-the-counter derivatives markets and the ballooning balance sheets of Fannie Mae and Freddie Mac?

Mankiw: If you go back and find some of the speeches that I gave at the time, you'll see that I talked about how we needed a better regulator for Fannie Mae and Freddie Mac and suggested they were a source of financial fragility for the economy. In other words, we were aware that there were certain features of the housing finance system that probably weren't robust and needed to be reformed, and I think we were on the right side of the argument. But we faced a lot of congressional resistance. It [Congress] was much more concerned about ensuring that Fannie Mae and Freddie Mac continued to promote home ownership. That said, I don't think those government-sponsored enterprises were the only source of the crisis that subsequently unfolded. For example, I certainly had no idea that banks were as highly leveraged to the housing market as they were. With the benefit of hindsight, that would have been useful to know, so that we could have figured out an appropriate regulatory response. But I don't think anybody fully appreciated the extent of the financial fragility in the economy at that time.

Bowmaker: When you look back at the offshore outsourcing furor that took place in 2004, what are your memories? Do you remain satisfied with the wording that you used in the *Economic Report of the President*?[3]

Mankiw: The reaction was certainly unexpected. The basic idea that outsourcing of services is a form of international trade, and that international trade is positive for the economy in the long run, is something that most economists agree upon. And so I thought what I wrote at the time was not

---

3. The 2004 *Economic Report of the President*'s chapter on international trade included a section on trade in services, containing the following wording on outsourcing: "One facet of increased services trade is the increased use of offshore outsourcing in which a company relocates labor-intensive service industry functions to another country.... When a good or service is produced more cheaply abroad, it makes more sense to import it than to make or provide it domestically." The last sentence was viewed in the press and on Capitol Hill as an insult to American workers (Council of Economic Advisers, *Economic Report of the President (2004)* [Washington, DC: US Government Printing Office, 2004]).

very controversial, and I still believe that is the case today. But whenever you say something that is controversial among the general public, but not among economists, it does suggest that perhaps we haven't explained ourselves fully. If you look at my principles of economics textbook, you'll see that I spend a lot of time discussing trade, and we do it quite early in the book because I think teaching people about the basics of trade—as proposed by Adam Smith and David Ricardo—is very, very important fundamentally for understanding the world. And so with the benefit of now knowing the emotional response to my wording in the *Economic Report of the President*, I probably would try to write it differently. I'm just not sure how.

Bowmaker: How did the White House itself respond to your comments?

Mankiw: The president was extremely nice to me. In fact, during my two years at the CEA, the only time he and I were in the Oval Office by ourselves was over this issue. He told me not to worry about it. He wasn't particularly concerned with anything that I said because he realized it was just a political firestorm that would eventually die down.

Bowmaker: So it's not true that the administration wanted to restrict your public appearances?

Mankiw: That's not true at all. I did the same number of public speeches, for example, and probably received more invitations to do them because of the political firestorm that I created.

Bowmaker: What did the whole experience teach you?

Mankiw: It probably taught me to be a little more careful in expressing myself. As I say, when I wrote that section in the *Economic Report of the President*, I didn't think any of it would turn out to be controversial. And so be ready to be surprised when you are in Washington, because clearly there are many things that are hard to predict—including political firestorms [*laughs*].

By the way, speaking of the *Economic Report of the President*, that's something I left Washington skeptical about, because it takes an enormous amount of work to put together every year. I often wondered whether it was a worthwhile use of our time because it took the attention away from internal issues relating to the White House policy process.

Bowmaker: I would now like to turn to a series of further questions about your interactions with President Bush and with some of the other members of the economic team. First, what did you do when you disagreed with the president, and can you give an example of when you disagreed with his policy position?

Mankiw: In a closed-door meeting, you tell him straight up, "Mr. President, I don't agree with you." But when you're in public and somebody says, "Professor Mankiw, what do you think of X?" and you disagree with the president about X, you reply simply, "The president believes fundamentally about X…" Before I went to Washington, I was actually a little worried that if I ever disagreed with the president, I might end up in an uncomfortable situation with a reporter. But one thing that I learned fundamentally was that the media didn't care what I thought—it was only the president's view that mattered.

There were certain areas where I didn't agree with the decisions he made, but I understood why he made them. Take the big debate over prescription drug benefits for Medicare. Along with most of the economic team, I held the view that we had an entitlement system that was fiscally imbalanced in the long run, and so it didn't make sense to make it more generous. But there were health policy advisers who made the basic argument, not unreasonably, that it didn't make sense to have a health system for the elderly that excluded prescription drug benefits. In the end, the president sided with those in the Department of Health and Human Services rather than the green eyeshade economic team.

The president knew that I disagreed with him on this issue. I only flew on Air Force One once, and I have a picture of me sitting in his office on the plane. I know exactly what the conversation was about … prescription drug coverage for Medicare [*laughs*]. He believed at the time that it was not going to be as costly as the initial estimates indicated, because we had moved to a more rational health care system. In some ways, he turned out to be right. But the fact is that it did cost something, and so it added to the country's long-term fiscal imbalance.

Bowmaker: Overall, what did you learn from President Bush?

Mankiw: The president had extraordinary interpersonal skills—he was very, very good at making people feel important and connected to him. When you go into a meeting with the president, in say the Oval Office or the Roosevelt Room, typically there are twenty to twenty-five people in the room. Everybody has assigned seating, with those higher up the hierarchy being seated at the main table. When the president walks in, everybody stands up and then eventually sits down. The president would often look at somebody at the very back of the room who was probably the most junior person there and say, "Hi, Bob, how's Mary and the kids?" Bob was probably lucky to have been at that meeting at all, but now the president of the United States is calling him out personally because he hadn't seen him in several months. That probably makes Bob's day, month, and year [laughs]. And so the president really went out of his way to make even the junior people who worked for him feel appreciated. As a result, I think that generated a great deal of loyalty to him, even when he made decisions with which you didn't agree. That's not something I would have known how to do had I been in his position.

Bowmaker: You mentioned earlier that Steve Friedman was a great person for the role of director of the NEC. Can you elaborate?

Mankiw: Steve had a great deal of market experience at Goldman Sachs, but he didn't have much academic background in economics. In some sense, then, he was a perfect foil because he would need people to explain economics to him in a way that a broad audience could understand. He was very good at asking questions and trying to get to the nub of the matter. And I certainly learned a lot from him in terms of how to handle other people, because he had great interpersonal skills. In academia, we tend to sit in our offices writing papers and engage in a relatively introverted activity, whereas Steve came from a background in which he had to run a large organization, listen to people with many different points of view, and reach a meeting of those minds. Watching him in action made me not only a better person, but also a more effective chair of the Economics Department at Harvard a few years later. Steve didn't try to assert his own way; he wanted good decisions to come out organically from the policymaking process. It was never a case of, "I'm Steve Friedman, I'm smart, and so I want my own way." Instead, it was always, "I'm Steve Friedman, I want all these smart people around me to interact in a way that's useful, so that we as a group can together reach the right decision." He didn't have strong opinions in the sense of wanting things to go in a particular direction. He was just a big believer in a process, and I think by the end of our meetings most people were on board.

Bowmaker: Next, I would like to discuss the intersection between economics and politics, and your interactions with those outside the economic team. First, can you give an example of when politics made it impossible for the president to do something analytically pure or consistent with your economic thinking?

Mankiw: There was once a tax provision on its way through Congress that would mean manufacturing firms would face a different corporate tax rate than nonmanufacturing firms. We at the council were opposed to it because we didn't want to create a nonlevel playing field for different kinds of firms, and we convinced the president of that argument. At the end of the day, though, we did get a special tax credit to manufacturing firms because Congress attached the tax provision to another piece of legislation that the president wanted. And so he had to either sign the whole bill or veto all of it—he couldn't pick and choose. Given the pros and cons, he quite reasonably decided to sign the whole bill. Something that is frustrating, then, for everyone who works in the White House is that it is much harder for it to work its will than people on the outside think it is. I lost count of the number of times when the economic team would say to the president, "Here are options A, B, and C," only for the person from legislative affairs to tell us, "There is no way that Congress can pass A, I doubt they will pass B, and so we are left with C." However, if you step back and think about it for a moment, you should realize that it is not a bug in the system, but a feature that was put in place by the founding fathers. They wanted it to be difficult for the president to get his legislation through Congress. That is a key part of the system of checks and balances.

Bowmaker: Was there ever any frustration involved in working with White House staff who only wanted policies that would get the president reelected?

Mankiw: Not really. The president always acknowledged the political trade-offs associated with a given policy, and I don't think it was something that he was doing to get a few extra votes. The one time my own personal views in politics went squarely against the president's was when, during his campaign, he ran some ads against gasoline taxes. By that point, I had written several articles in my career advocating high gasoline taxes, which led Karl Rove [senior adviser to the president] to call me and say, "Just to warn you, Greg, we're running some ads criticizing John Kerry for being in favor of high gasoline taxes. You might get some pushback because we know you've taken this stance in the past." But it turned out not to be a very big deal. Very few voters knew who Greg Mankiw was [*laughs*].

Bowmaker: All things considered, can you point to a specific example of where you, as an economist, or the CEA, as an organization, were able to make a difference?

Mankiw: Let me give you an example that probably hasn't been told until now. A question that arose when I was at the CEA was whether corporations should have to expense stock options for the purpose of computing earnings. Many high-tech companies were taking the view that giving out corporate options to executives was not really an expense to the firm, and so they shouldn't be counted. It mattered a lot to them because if you did count options, it had the potential to significantly reduce their earnings. But some regulators were in favor of expensing of stock options on the grounds that it is a form of compensation. In response, the high-tech industry was pushing a bill in Congress to prohibit the regulators from doing that, and the administration was debating whether or not to back that bill. What made it tricky was the fact that several years earlier, during his campaign, the president had expressed the opinion that he didn't think stock options were an expense. In other words, he sided with the high-tech industry and against the regulators. The economic team looked at the issue and decided that the regulators were right and the high-tech industry, along with President Bush, were wrong. But it is always hard to tell the president that he has made a mistake [*laughs*]. I remember vividly the meeting with the president over this very issue. Steve Friedman ran the meeting and tried to convince him that he shouldn't back the bill in Congress. There was a great deal of hemming and hawing, and at one point the president said, "What exactly are you trying to tell me?" I told him, "Mr. President, we are trying to tell you that you were wrong. Options are compensation, and compensation is an expense." After listening to our arguments, he said, "Let me think about it." Ultimately, he remained silent while the bill was going through Congress, where it died.

General Thoughts on Economic Policymaking

Bowmaker: Do you believe that if we were to raise the level of economic literacy in this country, economic policymaking would improve because the people would demand better policy?

Mankiw: Our politicians are as much followers as they are leaders. In other words, they do what the public wants. And so if we wish for the president to worry about the long-term fiscal imbalance, then we have to talk to the general public about the risks of growing government debt. It is obvious that economic literacy is crucial, which is why when I think of all the things that I have done in my career, writing a freshman-level textbook is probably my most important legacy.

You need to remember that the median voter determines political outcomes. How many economics courses has the median voter taken? My guess is zero. I think what we should do therefore is move towards a situation where universal economic education is part of general education. Start by making freshman-level economics a high-school junior or senior course. It is often said that we need a year of American history to be a smart voter. I think the same is true of economics.

Bowmaker: Can you give some examples of fallacies, misconceptions, or misinterpretations that affect policy debate in this country?

Mankiw: When I teach the freshmen here at Harvard, I go through the theory of comparative advantage before supply and demand. The gains from trade are so counterintuitive that it is worth hitting them home as early as possible. You need to get people away from what tends to be a mercantilist view of trade. Thankfully, the Bush administration was very free trade–oriented, and I didn't find it too difficult to explain the arguments in favor of it. But most people believe that trade is good because exports create jobs, and so imports are merely a burden that you have to bear in order to get those exports. As economists, we recognize that imports are one of the things that you gain from trade.

Bowmaker: Which aspects of the institutional framework for making economic policy in this country work well, and which need to be reformed?

Mankiw: I think the Council of Economic Advisers is too small. I remember kidding with my friends at the Federal Reserve that they had two hundred PhD economists doing monetary policy, while we at the council had twenty staff doing everything else [*laughs*]. Joking aside, although I think that the Fed works quite well as an institution, it is very, very large compared to the CEA, and in an ideal world, that balance could be shifted.

More generally, I think the institutional framework in this country is reasonably sound. As I mentioned earlier, I'm a big believer in checks and balances, and in my view the founding fathers were very wise. The fact is that politics will always be ugly, and I don't think it can be made beautiful.

Personal Reflections

Bowmaker: What value has your public service had to you?

Mankiw: It was a great break, because I had been at Harvard ever since finishing my PhD. I enjoyed the opportunity to be in a different environment, and it was one of the most intense two years of learning that I had ever done in my life. When issues came up that I didn't know the answer to, my staff had to do the research and teach me about them, which was tremendous fun. Take the example of nuclear power. Before I went to

Washington, I knew very little about energy economics and certainly nothing about nuclear power. Several questions needed to be addressed: Why were we not building nuclear plants in this country? What could we do to promote nuclear power? Should we do anything to promote nuclear power? At the beginning of the process, the administration held the view that nuclear power is relatively inexpensive and environmentally safe from a carbon standpoint. However, when my staff did some research, it turned out that the real reason we were not building nuclear plants in this country was because that form of energy was relatively expensive compared to the alternatives. We realized that the electric utilities were not going to build nuclear plants just by streamlining the regulatory hurdles; they would want massive subsidies from the government. At the end of the day, the president agreed that we shouldn't give vast sums of money to them. I must admit that I was surprised by the findings of our research. Before I started learning about it, I thought that a better regulatory system could promote nuclear power, but the truth was that nuclear power simply wasn't cost-effective.

Bowmaker: How did your personality affect your style and approach as a policymaker?

Mankiw: I'm someone who gets along with other people pretty well. As a result, I think that contributed to the fact that the economic team was very collegial. But one thing that I would say about personalities is that I view myself as a relative extrovert among academics…grading on a curve [*laughs*]. When I went to Washington, though, I realized how much of an introvert I was. Everyone there was so friendly and gregarious. It was something that really struck me.

Bowmaker: What were your strengths and weaknesses as a policymaker?

Mankiw: I was pretty good at saying what I thought even when I disagreed with people, including the president. I didn't have much trouble being direct partly because I came from an academic setting at Harvard where one needs to have thick skin. In seminars here, nobody hesitates to argue with you, and I think it's better to say what you think than not. That said, early on in Washington, I was probably a little too direct on occasion, but as time went by I think I figured out when it was better to bite my tongue.

Let me give you a story that I don't think has ever been made public. Not long after I arrived at the CEA, the president OK'd a trade restriction that the Department of Commerce had recommended. I thought that was a mistake and it hadn't gone through the right channels. And so I wrote a memo to several people involved in the decision, including the secretary of commerce and the secretary of the treasury, explaining why I felt it was a bad move. As soon as it was circulated, I received a call from Andy Card [chief of staff to the president]. It was the only time that he was ever mad at me. He said, "You could have disagreed with the decision, but why didn't you just call us up and do it verbally? Keep it off paper, because phone conversations can't get leaked as easily." He was right. Thankfully, it didn't get leaked, but the possibility that it could have gone to, say, the *Washington Post* hadn't crossed my mind. My judgment about how to handle situations like that probably got better over time, and I would say that experience has helped somewhat in making me a better chair of the department here at Harvard.

Bowmaker: There must be some things, in hindsight, that you'd like the opportunity to do differently. What are they?

Mankiw: I'm someone who likes to look forward rather than backward. But I might have worked harder to try and convince my wife to move to Washington for two years. I flew back almost every weekend, but leaving my family up here was hard, and I missed my three kids. In that respect, I am grateful that Harvard has a rule that allows you to work in Washington for only two years. From the perspective of policy, however, I think that having people stay longer is probably better. That's because there is such a big learning curve in terms of getting to know the players and the institutions. Another thing is that the same issues always come back in Washington. It's true that it's not as edifying to revisit them, but you're probably better at explaining them after you've done it a few times.

Bowmaker: Which aspects of public service do you miss most?

Mankiw: That's easy. I miss most the camaraderie with the CEA staff. I really loved it. In a sense, the staff was more collegial than one's colleagues in an academic setting. As a professor, you write your own papers, do your own research, and teach your own classes. But at the CEA we worked closely together. One of the things that I tried to do was foster that close-knit feeling by buying a foosball table for the staff. Both Phill Swagel and I were undergraduates at Princeton, and foosball is very popular at the eating clubs. And so I paid for it, Phill arranged the shipment and assembly, and we put it in the lounge area for the staff to play with at break time. I think it worked. It did create a lot of camaraderie. I've heard from more recent members of the CEA staff that it is still there, and some have thanked me for it. I feel proud for having made that small contribution to the CEA as an institution [*laughs*].

Harvey Rosen, as a member of the Council of Economic Advisers, appears before the Joint Economic Committee on Capitol Hill in Washington, D.C., on February 10, 2004.

26 Harvey S. Rosen

Born 1949, Chicago, Illinois

Harvey Rosen graduated with an AB in economics from the University of Michigan in 1970 and obtained an MA and a PhD in economics from Harvard University in 1972 and 1974, respectively. Rosen joined Princeton University as an assistant professor of economics in 1974 and remained there until his retirement in July 2019, by which time he was the John L. Weinberg Professor of Economics and Business Policy.

In government, Rosen served as deputy assistant secretary (Office of Tax Analysis) of the Treasury between 1989 and 1991, as a member of President George W. Bush's Council of Economic Advisers (CEA) between 2003 and 2005, and as the council's chairman for the first six months of 2005.

I interviewed Harvey Rosen in his office in the Department of Economics at Princeton University, in Princeton, New Jersey. It was the middle of the afternoon on Tuesday, January 15, 2013.

Background Information

Bowmaker: Why did you become an economist?

Rosen: When I was an undergraduate, I was casting about for a major. Economics appealed to me because of its focus on social problems, and it allowed me to take advantage of the fact that I was pretty good at math. Once I became a senior in college, I decided that I would go on to graduate school because I had been enjoying economics and thought it would be interesting to continue studying it. As far as career choice, one of the nice things about our discipline is that there is a lot of flexibility with respect to career choice. I wasn't sure about whether I wanted to be an academic or a government economist, but when I went on the job market, I received an attractive offer from Princeton and accepted it.

Entering the Policy World

Bowmaker: What does an economist bring to the policy world that others do not?

Rosen: An economist brings a coherent worldview that allows important questions to be asked about benefits and costs. We are forced to think hard about what our opinions entail. Related is the fact that economics provides a template for thinking about whether government should be involved in a given issue in the first place. Conventional welfare economics tells us that we should let the market work unless there is at least one of a specific set of problems: some unfairness in the income distribution, market power, or the failure of a market to emerge. It's remarkably useful to have that checklist in your head when an issue arises, because not only will it lead you to a sensible answer but, as an economist in Washington, it will allow you to be consistent from meeting to meeting. For example, it will ensure that what you say about the minimum wage today will follow the same underlying principles as your view on airline regulation tomorrow.

Bowmaker: You took your first policy position in 1989 as deputy assistant secretary of the Treasury. How did you come to be appointed?

Rosen: My model of how jobs are allocated in the executive branch of government in this country is that there is a list of people who worked on the campaign, and the Office of Presidential Personnel wants those individuals to be appointed to as many jobs as possible. However, there are some positions that require specific technical skills, and it's not terribly likely that those who worked on the campaign have them—in which case they need to ask the nonpolitical staff if they have any names in mind. My impression is that the Office of Tax Analysis maintains a list of economists whom they would like to see lead their office. And so if your name is on the list, sooner or later someone is going to approach you about filling a vacancy.

Bowmaker: As you began your position, was there anything that surprised or frustrated you?

Rosen: These days, I don't think anyone who is even vaguely aware of what's going on in the world holds a naive *Mr. Smith Goes to Washington* view in which they go to D.C. and say, "Oh, my gosh, people are motivated by things other than the public interest!" That said, I was taken aback at how blatant it was. For example, one Saturday morning, we were working on capital gains legislation, and an important Republican on the Finance Committee sent his staffer to talk to us. She arrived at the meeting and said, "The senator cares about something for timber. That's it!" She then walked out. I found it breathtaking [*laughs*].

Bowmaker: One of the main political selling points of the Tax Reform Act of 1986 was that it would shift $120 billion in taxes from individuals to corporations in the first five years. In the first three full years that the law had been in effect, the increase in corporate tax revenues was $20 billion to $30 billion below expectations. You were asked by the Senate Finance Committee, chaired by Lloyd Bentsen, to explain this shortfall. Can you tell us about that experience?

Rosen: Yes. The Democrats wanted to find some malfeasance on the part of the Republicans when they passed the Tax Reform Act of 1986. They said, "Aha, you promised there would be more tax revenues than really happened." But of course these projections are always guesses, because they depend on what the economy is going to be doing. In general, testifying is a stressful and unpleasant experience. What I learned was that the purpose of a testimony is not to educate or inform—it is to serve as a kind of pincushion for members of the Senate or House who are unhappy about something. So they dump on you. You just have to sit there, take it, and hope to keep your skin on.

Bowmaker: What were the main lessons from your time at the Treasury that you were able to take into the rest of your career?

Rosen: The main lesson that I took away is how helpful economic analysis is when tackling problems. When I came back from the Treasury, I was often asked, "Well, how useful was your academic expertise when you were there?" I think the subtext of that question is, "You were in the real world. I bet airy-fairy academics didn't help in the trenches." But honestly, I left the Treasury more impressed with the power of the economist's way of thinking than beforehand.

As Member and Chairman of the Council of Economic Advisers

Bowmaker: You were appointed a member of the CEA in 2003. Did you take any advice from former members or chairs of the council before you began your role?

Rosen: I sure did. I spoke to both Alan Blinder and Glenn Hubbard before I joined the CEA. However, what I learned is that some of the advice was useful in general, but other advice was situation specific, and therefore not too helpful. I'll give you an example of both kinds. Alan Blinder told me that for most issues, there would be more agreement between CEA members of different administrations than they would have with their respective political masters. That information—I guess it wasn't exactly advice—turned out to be quite correct. On the other hand, Glenn Hubbard gave me advice on how to operate and be effective in Washington. He said that you were not guaranteed that your voice would be heard if you went through official channels, and so you had to find alternative methods of communication. However, it was almost entirely useless advice because the players on the economic policy team had changed so much. When Glenn was at the CEA, I think he was dealing with a group of people who didn't get along very well. But when I was there, John Snow, treasury secretary; Steve Friedman, director of the NEC [National Economic Council]; and Greg Mankiw, chair of the CEA, were great guys. They followed the rules, and everyone got along. It was a big relief to me that I didn't need to worry about what Glenn had said.

Bowmaker: Were the responsibilities of the position made clear to you?

Rosen: Yes. The responsibilities were laid out very clearly by Josh Bolten, who interviewed me for the job. At the time, he was deputy chief of staff for policy. He said, "There are many people around here who know how to spin advice. But the CEA members are viewed as the resident truth tellers." I felt very comfortable with that role. Under the Mankiw regime, therefore, we viewed ourselves as the West Wing's in-house economics consulting firm, although we understood that we were operating in a politically sensitive environment. In other words, we positioned ourselves as the West Wing's nerds who weren't going to talk about politics. Ultimately, the effectiveness of that strategy depends totally on who the political people are in the West Wing. And given the particular cast of characters in our case, it turned out to be an incredibly effective strategy because they respected the fact that we were giving them the straight dope.

Bowmaker: During your two years as a member at the CEA, Greg Mankiw was the council's chairman. He has described you as someone who taught him how to practice economics as a student at Princeton. How did this personal relationship affect how you interacted with him at the CEA? Did you feel that perhaps you were able to have more involvement and influence in policy advising relative to the median CEA member?

Rosen: The CEA was exceedingly collegial under the Mankiw chairmanship. Greg ran it more like an academic institution than a governmental or hierarchical one. It's hard for me to think of a single substantive issue on which we disagreed, which is remarkable over a two-year period. One reason is that Greg is so brilliant at economics, he'd generally be able to convince me that I was wrong. But that rarely happened—we are mainstream economists who tend to come to the same conclusions. To the extent that we ever disagreed, it would be about issues that had nothing to do with economics. I'll give you an example. When you go to a meeting that the president will attend, a name card is always placed in front of you on the table. We had a discussion about whether we should put "Dr." in front of our names. I felt very strongly that it would make us look pompous, but Greg thought it would buy us more credibility. He eventually pulled rank on that one [*laughs*].

Bowmaker: How did you come to be appointed as chairman of the CEA in 2005, and what did the previous two years as a member of the CEA teach you about the role of the CEA in policy advising in Washington?

Rosen: Greg was going to return to Harvard, and they needed someone to do it. When they asked me if I would take over, I agreed but told them I would need to go back to Princeton during the summer. Of course, I was thrilled to receive the offer. Like Greg, I felt it was very important to represent mainstream economics, and it meant much more interaction with the policymakers. By statue or tradition—I'm not sure which—the way the CEA communicates to the president is through the chairman. So I didn't have very much face time with President Bush [as a member]. Often, I was sitting in a room along the wall, while the grown-ups were at the table.

In terms of the role of the CEA in policy advising in Washington, I had seen Greg's model at work, and I loved it. But let me add something that Greg and I have in common: we are both textbook authors and teach introductory economics. This means that we have developed some facility in explaining the subject to noneconomists, which is incredibly important in Washington. Unfortunately, due to their own experiences, policymakers view economists as incomprehensible spewers of jargon—that's what they are expecting when you open your mouth. The fact that Greg expressed himself beautifully, both in writing and orally, was in part due to his experience as a

teacher and textbook author. And I think it made me much more effective
as well. When a problem came to the CEA, the first step would usually be to
designate several staffers to deal with it. They would then write a draft memo
which had to be reviewed by a member of the council before being sent to
the West Wing. The staff were marvelous when I was there, but I would say
that probably three-quarters of the time I spent editing their memos, trying
to improve the exposition. I knew that they would get the economics right,
but I was really fussy about clarity because I had seen Greg in action.

Bowmaker: How would you describe the transition from being a member of
the CEA to being chairman?

Rosen: The most challenging aspect is when an economic issue arose, as
the chairman of the CEA, you would often be the one in the Oval Office
briefing the president. And those briefings were certainly very challenging
events. Let me elaborate. I was talking earlier about how the economics
team in the first two years of the Bush administration didn't get along very
well. From what I've heard, Treasury Secretary Paul O'Neill in particular
didn't seem to get along with anybody. In a book that came out while I was
at the CEA, he said that President Bush was disengaged, especially on tax
issues.[1] And so I thought to myself, "It's going to be a breeze briefing this
guy because he doesn't care." I was totally wrong. I could barely open my
mouth before he was shooting questions at me. They were aggressive, really
great questions, and he was clearly engaged. It was like the most intense
oral exam you can imagine. And so I was mystified because Paul O'Neill had
said one thing, but with my own eyes and ears I had experienced the other.
I brought up this issue with Alan Greenspan during one of our monthly
lunches at the Fed[eral Reserve]. He told me, "Harvey, this is actually very
simple. Fairly early on, President Bush had been a bit turned off by Secretary O'Neill. Well, what do you do when someone like that is in your office?
You say to him, 'Yes, that's fine, I've got to run…'" [laughs].

Bowmaker: Was it an advantage or a disadvantage to enter the role following the reelection of the president?

Rosen: I think it was an advantage because it made it more exciting. But
I will tell you about something that I was not expecting. When I went to

---

1. Ron Suskind, *The Price of Loyalty: The White House, George W. Bush, and the Education
of Paul O'Neill* (New York: Simon and Schuster, 2004).

Washington in 2003, everyone was telling me, "Oh, boy, there's an election coming up. You are going to be pressed to become very political. You better watch yourself." Well, it turned out that the folks in the West Wing were extremely conscious of the Hatch Act, which states that political appointees are not allowed to be part of a campaign. They sent over someone from the White House counsel's office to tell us what we could and couldn't do. It was really confusing. Apparently, the folks in the West Wing were scared of asking about things that might bring us into violation of the law. So the two months before the election turned out to be my quietist time at the CEA. But the day after the election, it was as if a switch went back on. We went straight back to work.

Bowmaker: You served as chairman of the CEA for six months. Was there sufficient time to establish a comfortable working relationship with the president?

Rosen: I certainly think that six months was long enough to get a sense of how he thought about economic problems. The president and I had a cordial, professional relationship. We both liked each other, even though he likes to tease you [laughs]. I'll give you a couple of examples. I remember once there was a meeting when the secretary of health and human services, Michael Leavitt, was talking about what we should be doing to improve health-care technology. I don't have a poker face, so I was just sitting there shaking my head. The president said, "All right, Harvey, what's wrong?" I told him, "Well, I'm a free-market guy, and I don't think the government should be imposing a set of standards on the economy relating to this issue." He replied, "I bet you didn't even like President [Franklin D.] Roosevelt's Social Security Act, do you?" I said, "It's fine, but it could have been designed better" [laughs]. Another time I was speaking about immigration, which is not one of my areas of expertise, so I had written down some notes—I didn't want to screw it up in front of the president. I went through my notes, and he said, "Harvey, you're just reading what your staff told you to say" [laughs]. That sounds mean, but it wasn't meant to be.

However, I don't believe I was ever in a room with the president when there were fewer than fifteen other people present, and so it would be disingenuous to say that we were intimates. As far as my impact on policy, I certainly had no illusions that I would walk into a room and say, "Hey, I'm an official economist. Here's what you should do…" and everyone would reply, "Oh, thank you" [laughs]. I felt that as someone without political experience and no prior relationships with anyone in the government, I was ahead of the game if I received a respectful hearing. I was quite satisfied that I got that most of the time. In that context, I thought that the atmosphere was, to use a slightly old-fashioned term, gentlemanly. For example, if you were having several meetings on a contentious issue, and someone had come up with a new argument that they could use against you, you might be told in advance. I thought that was pretty cool.

Bowmaker: You just mentioned that you were able to get a sense of how President Bush thought about economic problems. Can you elaborate?

Rosen: In broad terms, his instincts for economics were very good. He tended to think that markets worked well, and if they didn't, he would say, "What's the problem here?" Of course, that is the same question that an economist would ask. And he displayed a lot of intellectual curiosity. I'll give you another couple of examples. I remember briefing him on inflation and noting that the Fed's comfort zone is 1–2 percent. It didn't want inflation to go below 1 percent because a negative shock would lead to deflation. He thought about that for a second and said, "Well, if 1–2 percent is better than a lower number, what's wrong with 3–4 percent?" I was actually taken aback and not sure how to answer, because that is a very fundamental and unsettled question in macroeconomics. And the very last briefing I gave him was on the so-called legacy industries, like airlines and automobiles, where there is a big overhang of debt and union and pension obligations. At one point, he said, "Well, are they profit maximizing? Are they competitive?" I began by saying, "Uh..." and he told me, "Harvey, don't waffle" [*laughs*].

I was talking about this with Ed Lazear once, and he thought that the president just loved talking about economics. I found the experiences scary, but he was clearly enjoying himself.

Bowmaker: When you were at the CEA, President Bush was committed to the idea of privatizing Social Security. As a public finance scholar, what was your view?

Rosen: First of all, that's not the fairest way to characterize the plan. What was being proposed was that people could take some of their Social Security taxes and allocate them to mutual funds. In return, there would be an actuarially fair reduction in the benefits that they would receive when they retired. I thought it was a fine idea. A very high proportion of households have no exposure at all to the stock market, and I don't know of any portfolio theory that says that's a wise thing.

But here's what is interesting about the politics of the issue. The Republicans believed that if you gave people some interest in the stock market, they would become good little capitalists. And the Democrats believed the same, which is why both parties fought about it so hard. I never bought into that view. I just thought that any notion that your decision to be a Republican or a Democrat might be dominated by the fact you have a few thousand dollars in a mutual fund seemed implausible to me.

Bowmaker: Where did you stand over the issue of prescription drug benefits for Medicare?

Rosen: I wasn't happy. I thought that what we should be doing in this country is figuring out a way to rationalize entitlements and getting spending under control. And here we were introducing a new entitlement without any thought about financing. Mind you, it makes perfect sense to include drugs. When Medicare was first started, drugs just weren't that important in terms of the finances of the medical system. But in terms of them being an add-on, I didn't like the idea very much at all.

Bowmaker: I would now like to turn to your interactions with the rest of the economic team in Washington when you were at the CEA. First, how would you describe your relationship with the National Economic Council?

Rosen: I loved the NEC. Our slogan when I was in Washington was "There is no 'E' in the NEC." They had no economists on their staff, which I viewed as a big plus because they weren't playing amateur economists. Again, this goes back to personalities. During my time at the CEA, Steve Friedman from Goldman Sachs was the director of the NEC, and then Al Hubbard, an Indianapolis businessman, took over the role. They had very different personalities, but both took their "honest broker" mission with the utmost seriousness and believed that finding out what economists had to say was part of that mission. They wanted to check that box. And so if they wrote a memo to the president and we dissented, it was noted. The NEC were our de facto boss, and we happily accepted that relationship.

Now, if you talk to Glenn Hubbard about his relationship with the NEC, you might get a different story, because Steve Friedman and Al Hubbard are not Larry Lindsey. And it is common knowledge that the economic policy apparatus at the beginning of the [Barack] Obama administration was totally dysfunctional because Larry Summers and Christina Romer [chair of the CEA] did not get along well. He thought he was a better economist and was not particularly interested in hearing what she had to say. And according to what I've heard, Austan Goolsbee had issues with both of them.

Bowmaker: How would you describe your relationship with Treasury Secretary John Snow when you were at the CEA?

Rosen: I thought he was a smart and articulate guy who was also a good listener. I liked him very much. One of the great mysteries to me was that someone was trying to get him. Someone in the White House was planting stories in the *Washington Post* about how ineffective he was, and that they were thinking about firing him. I never understood why that was happening or who was behind it. Perhaps this just shows that I'm naive about politics, but if you want to fire someone, why don't you simply call them into your office and say, "You're fired," instead of torturing them by leaks to the press? I thought John Snow acquitted himself very well.

Bowmaker: Based upon your interactions with Alan Greenspan when you were at the CEA, how would you describe his approach to understanding the economy?

Rosen: In his own way, he was a genius. But he didn't think about things the way I do or the way a conventional academic economist does: What's your model? What are the parameters of your model? If we follow this particular policy, given the parameters of your model, how is the world going to change? Instead, Greenspan was a sponge for data—the entire staff at the Fed were constantly feeding him numbers—and somehow he just had this sense of how they all fit together. I thought it was very impressive. For example, I might think, "What do I care about pig iron shipments?" But he would latch onto them and say, "They are significant. When they go up or down…" But I did come to the conclusion, "Don't try this at home." He could bring it off given his experience and the way his mind worked, but for most people, conventional academic modeling would be a more sensible approach. Why do I say that? Because if you don't have super intuition, then you need some way to ground your ideas—to see whether they're consistent, whether they hang together, and whether they can be tested. That's what formal modeling does for you.

Bowmaker: How would you describe your relationship with the media when you were at the CEA?

Rosen: The media are awful. Firstly, the journalists who are assigned to business probably don't want to be there—they would prefer to be writing the great American novel. And so for the most part, they don't understand economics. Secondly, they think that because you are in the administration, you must be lying to them. And thirdly, if they have a theme for a story, they are going to write it, even if it is not true. I'll give you an example. President Bush formed a commission on tax reform when I was at the CEA. Word got out that I was going to be appointed its executive director. That had to be false, because you couldn't hold those two positions at the same time. In any case, I wouldn't have taken the job even if it had been offered to me. A reporter from the *Washington Post* called up the CEA and talked with my chief of staff, who told the reporter that the rumor wasn't true...but they wrote the story anyway [*laughs*]. And so let's just say that nothing happened during my time in Washington that increased my respect for the press.

Bowmaker: How would you compare the environment at the CEA relative to the Treasury?

Rosen: When I was at the Treasury, there were several dozen professionals with PhDs who were smart and conscientious. They had also been there for a long time and were not going to leave in the near future. At the CEA, practically every professional was an academic like me who planned to stay for only a couple of years. That led to some important differences. Number one is that at the CEA, there is almost no institutional memory, but at the Treasury, it seems like it is infinite. There are both disadvantages and advantages to having a long institutional memory. At the Treasury, there are benefits to knowing that someone had come up with some idea during the [Jimmy] Carter administration and that didn't work then, and so it probably wouldn't work now either. On the other hand, when confronted with exactly the same proposal, people at the CEA might say, "Wow, that's a cool idea. Let's see what happens." In other words, they would bring a freshness to the idea. I loved the excitement at the CEA. It's just not possible to maintain that kind of enthusiasm for a job over decades. But at the CEA, you sometimes felt that you were reinventing the wheel, which would never happen at the Treasury.

Bowmaker: All things considered, can you point to a specific example of where you, as an economist, or the CEA, as an organization, were able to make a difference in your time at the CEA?

Rosen: The one thing that I'm really proud of was the relationship with the government-sponsored enterprises [GSEs], Fannie Mae and Freddie Mac. I knew next to nothing about Fannie and Freddie before I went to

Washington, but I became the point man on the CEA on this issue. It was fascinating because the Republicans had a natural disinclination towards them for two reasons. One is that they are at least vaguely promarket, which Fannie and Freddie were not. And the other is that Fannie and Freddie were in bed with the Democrats. And so the instincts of the West Wing crew were to try and rein them in. But they were spooked by the possible economic consequences of doing so. They had been fed this line that if you did anything to rein them in, all hell would break loose: the housing market would collapse, interest rates would go up, and the economy would be wrecked. That's nonsense. We began an education campaign to convince them that sensible steps could be taken to rein in the GSEs in such a way that the economy would not tank. Over time, I think that the arguments we made—for example, noting that some of the non-GSE part of the mortgage market could pick up the slack—helped the policymakers follow their instincts. In other words, it was one of those rare instances where the politics and good economics were both pointing in the same direction.

Bowmaker: Were there any very poor policy ideas that the CEA were able to kill?

Rosen: I think "kill" is too strong of a word, because bad ideas never go away. But let me talk about an idea that we at least helped put off, and I remember it well because it was one of the first things that happened when I went to Washington. The "no child left behind" policy had already been done for grade school and high school. It was essentially about testing students every year to make sure that they were meeting certain goals. One of the president's advisers, Margaret Spellings, had been very involved, and she said, "Now, let's do college." We thought that was totally misguided. This goes back to my point about economics providing a template to think about issues. When you look at K[indergarten] through 12[th grade], it is a monopoly, which means that there will be problems that the government may be able to solve. But higher education is a vibrant, successful market with a wildly diverse set of institutions. What kind of national exam are you going to set for students at, say, the Philadelphia Bible College and Stanford University? It's absurd if you think about it. You can tell if they are not meeting their respective goals if they stop getting students! There was going to be a meeting with the president about Spellings's idea. Beforehand, we prepared for Greg a bunch of information. When he came back and we asked him how it went, he said, "Well, it was a pretty short discussion. When Margaret Spellings made her presentation, the president said, 'What problem are we trying to solve here?' She didn't have an answer. The president then just said, 'Well, let's move on'" [*laughs*].

General Thoughts on Economic Policymaking

Bowmaker: Can you give some examples of fallacies, misconceptions, or misinterpretations that affect policy debate in this country?

Rosen: Trade is the biggest one, and I think most economists would agree. Politicians from both parties have protectionist impulses and mercantilist tendencies. Whenever I hear them say, "I believe in trade, but it has to be fair," it makes my stomach tighten, because it just shows that they don't understand the benefits of trade.

Bowmaker: Which aspects of the institutional framework for making economic policy in this country work well, and which need to be reformed?

Rosen: This may be the bias of someone who worked in the executive branch of government, but it seems to me that a lot of the junk is coming out of Congress. I certainly viewed the Hill as the problem when I was in Washington. We were trying to figure out the right answer, while the Hill, in general, either didn't understand policy or just didn't care. A lot of policy was being driven by twenty-something staffers who certainly didn't know what they were doing. And so we spent as much time batting down bad ideas from the Republicans on the Hill as we did batting down those from the Democrats. I remember the Speaker of the House at the time was a guy called Denny Hastert. He was terrible! As far as I could tell, all he cared about was how much money was going to his district [*laughs*].

Personal Reflections

Bowmaker: What value has your public service had to you and to your university?

Rosen: In Washington, you deal with an enormous variety of questions. As an academic, your first instinct is to go to the literature. But often I couldn't find the answer in the literature [*laughs*]. And so I thought, "Oh, I'm going to have a great research agenda when I return to Princeton." But it turns out that those questions are not all that interesting to academics, which explains why no one had published anything about them. However, I did return from Washington feeling totally reinvigorated. Just being able to use my economist's skills in a different environment was incredibly refreshing, which meant that I was more enthusiastic about my teaching and research. I could enliven my teaching of microeconomics by drawing upon terrific examples from Washington. And as a footnote to my comment about my research agenda, I should add that I met people who subsequently became coauthors because they were really smart and had access to great data sets.

Bowmaker: How did your personality affect your style and approach as a policymaker?

Rosen: It had a big effect. I am not confrontational. That would mean that I did not come into meetings saying, "This is the way it has to be because your idea is dumb." Instead, I would be more likely to say, "Yes, I see your point, but did you ever think about it this way…" You don't change your personality just because you are sitting in a different office. It's the same style that I use when I am talking to my students. I try to understand their point of view and then convince them that mine has some merit.

Bowmaker: What were your strengths and weaknesses as a policymaker?

Rosen: My strengths were that I was good at delegating, which partly came from my experience as chairman of the Economics Department here, and I was effective at focusing on the key aspects of a given issue. I was also pretty honest. My weakness was that I might not have been sufficiently aggressive in presenting my views. If someone said something that was wrong, I may have been a little oblique when it came to correcting them. In other words, I could have been more forceful. I'll give you an example. A perennial problem in Washington is energy prices. Whenever the price of oil spikes, the West Wing goes nuts. There will be meetings in which a briefer from the Energy Department describes all sorts of ways to subsidize oil. You are sitting there knowing that those ideas are terrible. Sometimes, therefore, I wish that I'd been more assertive and told the meeting, "This just doesn't make any sense" [*laughs*].

Bowmaker: Which aspects of public service do you miss most?

Rosen: Being an academic is a lonely pursuit. And so I found it fun to be working as part of a team in Washington. Another thing that I found exciting was the challenge of seeing how close you could get to an answer to a problem in seventy-two hours, compared to the eighteen months I might spend on it as an academic. When someone said, "How's it going?" I couldn't give the stock academic response of, "Well, I'm just getting my head around this…" [*laughs*]. It was certainly a change of pace.

I was also starstruck when I met people whom I had only seen in the newspaper. For example, Karl Rove [senior adviser to the president] was a big surprise. From what I had read in the *New York Times*, I expected that he would appear in a puff of red smoke and there'd be a whiff of sulfur—an evil genius [*laughs*]. But in addition to being smart and personable, he was always very interested in what the right answer was to any policy question. I was enormously impressed. I think if you conducted interviews with those who worked in the West Wing during the Bush administration, I would be surprised if you could find anyone who spoke ill of him.

Edward Lazear (*left*), when chairman of the Council of Economic Advisers, with President George W. Bush (*center*) and Al Hubbard (*right*), director of the National Economic Council, in the Rose Garden of the White House on April 28, 2006. President Bush was speaking at a press conference on the economy.

27 Edward P. Lazear
Born 1948, New York City

Edward Lazear received an AB and an
AM in economics from the University
of California, Los Angeles (UCLA), in
1971 and obtained a PhD in economics from Harvard University in 1974.

Lazear taught at the University of
Chicago between 1974 and 1992 and
then moved to Stanford University,
where he has remained ever since. He
currently serves as the Morris Arnold
and Nona Jean Cox Senior Fellow at
the Hoover Institution and the Davies
Family Professor of Economics at Stanford's Graduate School of Business.

Lazear was commissioner of Presi-
dent George W. Bush's White House
Panel on Tax Reform in 2005 and then served as chairman of his Council of
Economic Advisers (CEA) between 2006 and 2009.

I interviewed Edward Lazear in his office at the Hoover Institution, in
Stanford, California. It was the middle of the morning on Wednesday, July
18, 2012.

Background Information

Bowmaker: Why did you become an economist?

Lazear: At the end of my freshman year at UCLA, I decided to study economics because I thought it would be a good prelaw major. But in my junior
year, I took a course from Robert Michael, who took me under his wing
and encouraged me to go into economics. I ended up working with him
and Ben Klein, another young professor at UCLA, and enjoyed the subject.
Then I went on to teach at the University of Chicago, where I met Sherwin

Rosen, my teacher and later my closest colleague; and Gary Becker, my dear friend and one of the greatest social scientists ever. They are the two most influential economists in my life. I probably learned more about economics from sitting in workshops with Sherwin and Gary at Chicago than from all the rest of my education.

Entering the Policy World

Bowmaker: What does an economist bring to the policy world that others do not?

Lazear: An economist has something to say about almost every policy issue. In the Bush administration, for example, national security and economic policy were kept very separate. As a result, I had little to do with it [national security]. But almost every other area of policy involved economics, and some from unexpected issues. I remember early in my tenure at the CEA, we were worried about pandemic flu. Should we close the borders? If we restrict trade, should it be people or goods or services? Those are economic questions because they involve trading off the costs and benefits of various policies.

An economist is also very good at thinking through fuzzy questions in a parsimonious, rigorous, and logical way. The beauty of our science, which some may view as a deficiency, is that we strip away the details and focus on what is important and, as a result, bring a clear head to a variety of different policy issues.

Bowmaker: In 2005, you became commissioner of the White House Panel on Tax Reform. What were your main responsibilities in this role?

Lazear: The president created a nine-person panel whose task was to design a reform of the entire tax code. I worked in very close contact with Jim Poterba, from whom I learned much, on designing a tax code that would not only be simple but also efficient in raising revenues in a way that discouraged the least amount of capital formation and had the smallest negative effects on labor supply and so on. It was a technical exercise in applied economics that you would even do in a university setting. We issued a report ["Simple, Fair, and Pro-Growth: Proposals to Fix America's Tax System"] in November of that year, and it has been textbook material for top economics classes, but the specific proposals have yet to be enacted.

Bowmaker: What were the main lessons that you learned from this initial experience?

Lazear: I learned that a person who is effective in government is someone who can propose policies that have some chance of actually being implemented. And they can be quite radical. If you read *Capitalism and Freedom* by Milton Friedman, who was one of the greatest policy economists of all time, you will find some ideas—like the all-volunteer army and school vouchers—that were not only consistent with good economics but could also have been enacted.[1]

As Chairman of the Council of Economic Advisers

Bowmaker: Why do you think President George W. Bush chose you to be his chairman of the Council of Economic Advisers?

Lazear: I believe John Cogan [colleague at the Hoover Institution] was instrumental in recommending me to the White House. But why was I chosen? There are certainly many other talented people in the economics profession, but I think part of it is that while my training is in labor economics and industrial organization, I benefited from spending so much of my career in wide-ranging seminars and workshops at Chicago, the NBER [National Bureau of Economic Research], and Stanford. As a result, I was fortunate to acquire the kind of breadth that is necessary for that kind of government job. When you are chair of the Council of Economic Advisers and the president asks a question, you can't reply, "I'm sorry, Mr. President, that's outside my area." You have to find an answer. That's not to say that you have to figure it out all by yourself, because there are people with more knowledge in a certain area who can help, but in the final analysis you are the guy who has to make the recommendation.

Bowmaker: Did he make it clear what he expected you to do for him?

Lazear: I came into the administration in 2006. By that stage, President Bush viewed his staff and advisers as having very well-defined roles. For example, he absolutely hated it if I ever said anything about politics. He once asked me, "Have you ever run for office?" [*Laughs.*] And, of course, he was right. You are

---

1. Milton Friedman, *Capitalism and Freedom* (Chicago: University of Chicago Press, 1962).

most valuable within government if you stay within your area of expertise, and the president was very effective in making sure we did just that. I think that is why we all treated each other with a great deal of respect.

Bowmaker: How did you go about establishing a comfortable working relationship with the president?

Lazear: As an academic, you don't ever think you're going to be sitting in the White House talking to the president of the United States. And so for the first few months, I didn't really know what I was doing. It took a while to figure out how I could be of value and see what kinds of information the president would need to know. I had to watch others, and it was a slow learning process. But gradually I began to understand what I could contribute to the story, and when I should back off and let other people take the lead. By the time I left the administration, I was one of the most senior people on the president's staff.

Bowmaker: When I spoke with Glenn Hubbard about his time as chair of the CEA, he described President Bush as being "very much a believer in the dynamic, Hayekian economy of business people groping toward a solution." Would you agree with that assessment of his worldview?

Lazear: The overwhelming impression I got of the president was that he was superb in two respects, which didn't come out in public. First of all, he was very levelheaded and extremely mature in his thinking. He was someone who could switch from one minute thinking about the war in Iraq to the next minute thinking about the collapse of Lehman Brothers, and have good perspective about each of those events.

Second—and this came as a big surprise—he was extremely analytic and very detail-oriented. When I presented some technical charts to him, he would say things like, "How does that relate to what you showed me on the previous chart?" or "How does that square with what you told me two months ago?" He had a tremendous memory. Of course, I wasn't surprised that he was smart. No one makes it to the office of president of the United States without being smart—there are just too many roadblocks along the way.

The president was also incredibly well-read. He would go to bed at 8:30 most evenings, read until 10:00, wake up at 5:00, read until 5:30, and be at work by 6.45. And then he would read for an hour on his exercise machine. These weren't picture books! He tended to read histories, often about other presidents. On the day he left office, he told me that during his presidency he had read seventy-nine books on Abraham Lincoln. People might not think of him as an intellectual or a deep thinker, but he certainly was.

If you read his book, *Decision Points*, you will learn about his logic and thinking through a variety of different issues, which is something that I saw on a daily basis.[2]

Bowmaker: Glenn Hubbard also described President Bush as being close to the very top among the politicians for whom he'd worked, in terms of his feel for economics. Is that true for you, too?

Lazear: Yes. He was like a smart MBA with a high-quality analytic mind who became the CEO [chief executive officer] of a top company. Because he had good judgment and was analytic, he would ask two types of questions. One would be technical questions. I remember showing him a chart on the payout associated with the Earned Income Tax Credit as a function of your income. One of my colleagues chimed in, "You can see, Mr. President, that people have an incentive to say that they have higher incomes because you receive payments as a function of the income that you earn." The president immediately said, "Wait a minute. That's true up to $35,000, but then you have an incentive to understate your income." He was right—the incentives switched once the slope of the function changed. It was impressive that he was so quick to infer those incentive effects. Whenever I was giving a presentation, he would interrupt me constantly with those sorts of comments.

Occasionally, he would ask for our judgment on a broader question, such as the auto bailout. On that issue as he often did, the president went around the room, and each of us articulated first how we thought we should proceed, and second put forward the evidence supporting that as the best policy.

Bowmaker: Were your economic philosophies in alignment?

Lazear: I tended to be at the more conservative end of our group. It's no secret that I am from the Chicago school that believes in the power of markets. And so there were some disagreements within the administration. For example, I was very close to the treasury secretary, Hank Paulson, but we didn't always agree on things as we were going through the process. On the other hand, we always had a tremendous respect for each other. And what is interesting is that while we might not agree at the beginning on an issue, we tended to converge to the same position.

---

2. George W. Bush, *Decision Points* (New York: Crown Publishers, 2010).

Bowmaker: During your term in office, the United States was, of course, hit by the financial crisis. When exactly did the CEA realize that the country was facing big trouble?

Lazear: It started in the summer of 2007, but surprises kept happening throughout the year. In this, we were not alone. The fact of the matter is that the entire economy was surprised.

Bowmaker: I would like to ask some questions relating to two major issues that you faced during the crisis: TARP [Troubled Asset Relief Program] and the auto bailout decision. First, in relation to TARP, the original vision for the program was to buy toxic assets from large banks, but you ended up capitalizing the financial sector. Why did the administration change its mind?

Lazear: There was some disagreement on that issue from the very start, and it was probably the most difficult period. As you say, we said at the outset that we would buy toxic assets and then ended up capitalizing the financial sector. What happened was that it became clear to the Treasury after initial attempts that buying up toxic assets would be neither feasible nor effective.

I will say, though, that the CEA definitely played an active role in deciding what to do leading up to those events—for example, in using the Exchange Stabilization Fund to guarantee the money markets when there was a run by institutional investors. We were the technical experts, and it was the role of the Treasury to implement. But the other agency that had the money was the Fed[eral Reserve], and during much of the crisis I think it was most important. It was the only agency with the resources to provide the bailouts, like them or not.

Bowmaker: What do you say to those who argue that there should have been conditions imposed on the money that was given to the banks?

Lazear: There were strict conditions of repayment on interest and so on. Whether they are viewed as fair by others is not for me to say.

Bowmaker: Can you describe the debate among the economic team about how the auto bailout ought to have been structured?

Lazear: Look, President Bush did not want to stick an incoming president with another major problem. Additionally, the costs to the economy, to the workers involved, and to the budget of the United States were too high. There was no Chapter 11 alternative available at the time because there was no private DIP [debtor-in-possession] financing available. We were in the middle of a financial crisis, so getting capital for troubled car companies was infeasible.

Bowmaker: Do you think a case could be made for arguing that the financial difficulties experienced by Fannie Mae and Freddie Mac in the summer of 2008 represented a great opportunity to close them down?

Lazear: I believe Fannie Mae and Freddie Mac have lasted too long in government hands. I have nothing to add beyond that.

Bowmaker: During the crisis, can you give some examples of when the president asked you about consensus among economists on certain issues?

Lazear: If we did a good job, he shouldn't have had to ask that question, because we would inform the president about the literature on an issue— including any controversies. Take the stimulus of 2008, for example. I remember telling the president that the evidence on the effect of a stimulus has not been very strong over the past thirty years. And I walked through the two views of a tax cut: Whether you are a Keynesian or a supply-sider, a tax cut is the right thing to do at this point. But the Keynesians think any transfer, particularly to low-income individuals, who have a higher marginal propensity to consume, would be better, whereas the supply-siders think in terms of cutting the marginal tax rate for those who have the most elastic response to it. And so it was very much a balanced approach to the issue.

Bowmaker: What was the most difficult intellectual economic argument that you had to make to the president during your entire time at the CEA?

Lazear: I'll give you an argument that was difficult analytically and technically but also fun. In the summer of 2008, the spot price of oil was around $145 per barrel, and there was talk in the press that this was all a result of speculation. The president and I were bike-riding buddies, and this was one rare occasion when we actually talked about economics on a ride. I told him that it could not be speculation, and he said, "Oh, really? I want you to provide a briefing for me on Monday." When the time came, I explained that speculators go into the spot market to buy oil when they think that its price will be higher in the future, because if that happens, they can then sell it at the higher price and make a profit on the spread. But I pointed out that in the summer of 2008, the oil market was backwardated, which means that the futures price is lower than the spot price. In that case, speculators would never go into the spot market to buy oil, even if they thought that the price will be higher in the future. Why? Because it's cheaper to just buy a futures contract in which the oil is delivered—say, thirty days from now—and then sold at the new high price. As a result, the speculations could not have been driving prices up in the spot market. It takes a while to think through that argument, but the president got it in an instant.

Bowmaker: Looking back, would you say that the president made his decisions quickly or slowly?

Lazear: We had a very formal and beautiful process that involved many levels of information gathering before coming to policy recommendations. It would begin with a meeting of the assistant secretaries, followed by a meeting of the deputy secretaries, and then it would be passed to us—the principal level. At each level, we would discuss issues over a period of a month or two, sometimes longer, and then a principals' meeting would take place. At the end of that meeting, we would come to either a consensus or a set of positions that reflected each person's view of the issue. If we had a consensus, we would have a meeting with the president a few days later and tell him that his advisers are unanimous in their thinking and give him a specific policy recommendation, including both its pros and cons. When there was disagreement, we would have a forty-five-minute to an hour meeting with the president, informing him that his advisers were divided. And then after going over the issue, he would say, "OK, let me think about it. I'll give you my decision later."

Bowmaker: How would you describe your relationship with Vice President [Dick] Cheney?

Lazear: The vice president was terrific. That partly reflects my own particular views of economics, because he was also very market-oriented, and so he and I were quite consistent in terms of how we thought about economic issues. I loved talking to him about economics. He had a very strong interest in the economy and was very knowledgeable because he had been a CEO, although he tended to be a little quieter than the president. Every week, we used to have something called an economic policy lunch, and the vice president would always attend. He preferred to listen rather than talk. I think that was because he was the most senior person there and didn't want to dominate the conversation. At some point, though, someone would get antsy and say, "Mr. Vice President, what do you think?" And then he would give an unbelievable five-minute lecture that summarized the logic of the previous fifty-five minutes.

Bowmaker: How influential do you think he was on economic policy?

Lazear: I think he was influential. I'm still very close friends with the president, and I know that he had tremendous respect for the vice president.

He felt that he was extremely supportive and almost ideal, because he had made it clear that he had no aspirations for higher office. He defined his role as someone who was going to tell the president—who was a very good listener—what he thought, and he was never offended if he didn't take his advice. He just offered it in the best and most honest way that he could.

Bowmaker: Did it make any difference that when you were working with the upper echelon of the White House staff, they may have only been interested in the politics of issues?

Lazear: I can't think of anyone in that group who I didn't like. We were in a foxhole together in 2008 with everything crumbling around us, and we worked very well as a team. We never did anything, and I mean *anything*, for political reasons. That just wasn't in President Bush's makeup. He was criticized for having a very strong view of the world, sticking to it, and not being very easily affected by public opinion. Yes, we may have disagreed occasionally, and some of us might have thought a particular policy was a bad one—but without exception it was never done because it was politically expedient.

Bowmaker: How would you describe your relationship with the Federal Reserve?

Lazear: I had a very good relationship with the Fed. I was pretty close to [Chairman of the Federal Reserve] Ben Bernanke, who had been my predecessor at the CEA. I didn't know him well as an academic because we worked in different areas, but I remember meeting him for the first time when I discussed one of his papers at an NBER conference about twenty-five years ago.

The CEA and the Board of Governors of the Fed had a monthly lunch meeting to talk about the economy. I don't know how things worked before or after my time, but we never discussed Fed policy. That was not permitted. In fact, it's not even allowed by law, because then it has to be a public hearing. We would only talk about the economy in relation to the latest data and theory. Most of us were PhD-trained economists—Ben Bernanke, Rick Mishkin, Randy Krozner, Don Kohn, and my group—and so we would chat about economics in the way that we would in a faculty lounge. There was a lot of give-and-take, and it was fun.

Of course, when there were serious issues because of the financial crisis, the Fed would want to learn about the White House's view, and we would talk further. But we were absolutely adamant in maintaining the independence of the Fed. We discussed this explicitly with the president, and he believed that it wasn't his role to influence the central bank.

Bowmaker: How would you describe your relationship with the Treasury?

Lazear: I worked very closely with the Treasury, which is the implementing arm of the administration. Sometimes I didn't agree with the way it was doing TARP, and I would tell Hank about it, but in the end it was the Treasury that was responsible for its implementation. That's not only the nature of government but of business, too. I saw my role as being chief economic adviser to the CEO, while Hank was the CFO [chief financial officer] with direct authority over the funds.

Bowmaker: How would you describe your relationship with the NEC [National Economic Council]?

Lazear: When I was at the CEA, Al Hubbard was the head of the NEC for most of the time. We had a terrific relationship, and we remain close friends. I would say Al was one of the most important policy people in the government behind the scenes. He had a very good analytic mind, held a Harvard JD-MBA, talked in a charming Tennessee accent, and had the ability to communicate well with Congress. We did the technical work, and then Al went up to Congress and used his political skills to make some of our policies happen. Al was eventually succeeded by his deputy, Keith Hennessey, who understands Congress as well as anybody, has an amazing grasp of the issues, and can synthesize better than anyone I know.

I know that there is not always a very complementary relationship between the CEA and the NEC, but I was very fortunate in having the opportunity to work with those two superb individuals.

Bowmaker: All things considered, can you point to a specific example of where you, as an economist, or the CEA, as an organization, were able to make a difference?

Lazear: You have to remember that the CEA is in an unusual position in the government. In some ways, the chair and the two members can be very powerful in that you have the president's ear, and in my case, in print because I built up a personal relationship with him. On the other hand, the CEA has no budget and does not administer anything at all. And so I thought of myself as an insider, not an outsider, whose only role was to advise the president. With that in mind, I think there were many times when we made a difference, certainly in terms of structuring the TARP.

Bowmaker: Because there was an ongoing major financial crisis, it was a fairly unusual presidential transition. Can you describe your interaction with the members of the [Barack] Obama economic team during this period, especially on issues relating to the financial crisis and macroeconomic conditions more generally?

Lazear: It was limited. The incoming Obama administration wanted a fresh start, and did not take up many offers to meet.

General Thoughts on Economic Policymaking

Bowmaker: Do you believe that if we were to raise the level of economic literacy in this country, economic policymaking would improve because the people would demand better policy?

Lazear: It's hard to take a negative position to that question. But I don't think good policy is prevented by the economic illiteracy of the public. Even when you have a room full of first-class economists, there will be disagreement, and so figuring out how to implement a particular policy is difficult.

Bowmaker: Do you think that the gap between economics research produced in universities and policymaking will increase or decrease over time?

Lazear: I think of academic economics as being the background for policy. The one thing that I learned as chair of the CEA is that you don't have time to think through economic analysis in that role. If you haven't already figured out a particular problem at some point during your career, you're not going to be able to do it on the spot. And so it's very important for an academic beginning a policy position to have a very large stock of human capital that can be applied immediately to policy issues. To the extent that you've been a serious scholar, you can then be an effective policymaker or adviser. When I went to the CEA, I can't think of anything that I learned in my thirty-five years of being an academic that was useless.

Bowmaker: Which fallacies, misconceptions, or misinterpretations affect policy debate in this country?

Lazear: One problem is that people confuse spending on health care and retirement with *government* spending on those things. As economists, we both know that every income elasticity is not 1, so as people get richer, all spending does not increase proportionately. If you look at the consumption bundle back in 1900, people spent a great deal more on food and housing as a proportion of their budget than they do today. And it's also true that as people get richer, they want to spend more of their income on health so that they can prolong and enrich the quality of their lives. But the question is how much of that spending should be guaranteed by the government, and how much of it should be done privately by individual choice. That's a decision that we have to think about more carefully.

Personal Reflections

Bowmaker: What value has your public service had to you and to your university?

Lazear: I never had any desire to be in the government. In fact, I turned down prior opportunities to do so. But I'm glad that I did it in the end. It is an enormous privilege to drive up and park your car at the West Wing of the White House and then go inside to your office. You almost have to pinch yourself. But it's tough because you work very hard. For three years, I worked fourteen hours every day, including weekends when I would have to read a 100–150-page reading folder that contained memos written by my staff. On Monday mornings, we would schedule meetings that were like miniseminars to discuss the issues in those memos. That was valuable to me because I learned a tremendous amount of economics from my staff. I had to think about every issue in areas that were not my own, such as international trade and international finance. This means that I am now able to comment on subjects in the media that I couldn't talk about before my three years at the CEA, which in turn is extremely valuable to Hoover—a public policy institute—and to my teaching at the Stanford business school.

Bowmaker: What were your strengths and weaknesses as a policymaker?

Lazear: My best skill for the CEA role in terms of the team aspect was that I'm broad in my economic research and knowledge, because I've had such great teachers and colleagues through the years. Also, I'm a pretty good expositor. That's important because economics is hard and not always intuitive. And so having an ability better than the average person to communicate in a clear way was valuable.

But I must tell you that when I went to the White House there was no step down in terms of the intellect of the people with whom I was dealing.

As an academic at Stanford and Chicago, I had spent my whole career with smart people, but people like Josh Bolten [chief of staff to the president], Joel Kaplan [deputy chief of staff for policy], and Keith Hennessey were intellects that matched any I've met in university.

My weakness was a lack of political background. In some sense, that was a strength because I always defined my role as being a technical one, which made me credible. In fact, whenever I went on TV explaining policies, I received many compliments from those in the other political party who told me that I played it straight. That was good. On the other hand, I was perhaps a little tone-deaf to the political aspects of certain issues and not very attuned to some of the realities that go on in Washington. I think of a predecessor, Glenn Hubbard, as being a more politically astute person than I am.

Bowmaker: As a policymaker, which decisions or outcomes were most gratifying?

Lazear: The entire autumn of 2008 was the most serious period of the financial crisis. If you look at the series of decisions that the economics team made at the time, I think we can pat ourselves on the back. I remember the meeting that we had on the afternoon of September 15, the day Lehman Brothers failed. Ben Bernanke opened the meeting by saying, "Mr. President, we're on the verge of total financial collapse." The president then went around the room asking each of us whether we felt that was the case. And it was true. One thing was toppling after another—Fannie Mae and Freddie Mac and Merrill Lynch had failed as well, Wachovia and AIG [American International Group] were going, and we were worried about Goldman Sachs and Morgan Stanley. But as terrible as the recession is, it is a far cry from the Great Depression. We don't have 25 percent unemployment, and we haven't lost 35 percent of GDP. I would attribute at least part of that to some pretty good decisions that we made during that period.

Bowmaker: On the other hand, there must be some things, in hindsight, that you'd like the opportunity to do differently. What are they?

Lazear: I certainly wouldn't claim that we did everything perfectly, and that in retrospect there weren't things that one could improve. For example, the three-week period involving TARP was chaotic, and the passage of the legislation that enabled it was not handled as well as it should have been. Part of that was political, because relations with Congress could have been better. And the structuring of the auto bailout might have been improved.

Knowing what we know now, we might have considered some kind of Chapter 11 bankruptcy.

I'll give you another example. People ask me, "Gee, when you bailed out AIG, why didn't you force Goldman Sachs and other banks to take a haircut?" You have to understand that this would have meant negotiating with those organizations over a period of a month. Everything was happening so quickly, and we just didn't have the time to do that. Yes, in retrospect, a haircut might have been appropriate and fair. But was it the first-order consideration? No. The first-order consideration was making sure that the financial sector did not fail, and that the economy didn't plunge into a truly Great Depression, which it did not do.

Henry Paulson (*left*), when secretary of the treasury, with Chairman of the Federal Reserve Ben Bernanke, listening to questions from senators during a Senate Banking, Housing, and Urban Affairs Committee hearing on Capitol Hill on February 14, 2008. The committee was holding a hearing on the economy and other financial matters.

28 Henry M. Paulson Jr.
Born 1946, Palm Beach, Florida

Henry Paulson Jr. graduated with a
bachelor's degree in English from
Dartmouth College in 1968 and
obtained an MBA from Harvard Business School in 1970.

After graduating from Harvard,
Paulson served as staff assistant to the
assistant secretary of defense at the
Pentagon until 1972, and he served as
assistant to John Ehrlichman (White
House domestic affairs adviser) from
1972 to 1973.

Paulson joined Goldman Sachs in
1974 and became a partner in 1982. He was cohead of the firm's investment
banking division from 1990 to 1994 and president and chief operating officer from 1994 to 1998, before becoming chairman and chief executive officer (CEO) in 1999.

Paulson was nominated by President George W. Bush in May 2006 to
succeed John Snow as secretary of the treasury. He was sworn into office as
the seventy-fourth secretary in July 2006 and served in this role until January 2009.

After leaving public office, Paulson spent a year at the Paul H. Nitze
School of Advanced International Studies at Johns Hopkins University as
a distinguished visiting fellow. In 2011, he founded the Paulson Institute,
an independent, nonpartisan think-and-do tank working to strengthen
US-China relations and achieve sustainable economic growth and environmental practices in both countries. Paulson is a senior fellow at the University of Chicago's Harris School of Public Policy.

I interviewed Henry Paulson at the offices of the Paulson Institute in
downtown Chicago. It was the middle of the morning on Monday, August
7, 2017.

Background Information

Bowmaker: How did you become first interested in economic policymaking?

Paulson: Early on, I had absolutely no interest in it. At Dartmouth College, I was an English major who loved Shakespeare and the Romantic poets. I took the obligatory introductory economics courses, but they didn't do anything for me, and because I placed a high premium on analytical rigor, I also took a lot of math classes.

After Harvard Business School, my first job was in the Pentagon, where I got my initial taste of policy. As a matter of fact, ironically, I worked on the loan guarantee that bailed out Lockheed. And then when I moved to the White House, my role was to work as a liaison to the Treasury. I was only there a short period of time, but I developed a keen interest in economic policy.

At Goldman Sachs, I gained practical exposure to markets—I lived in them. I was on the investment banking side and advised clients, including CEOs and heads of state in China and elsewhere, on economic policy–related issues. So I was used to operating not only as a principal in my capacity as CEO but also as an adviser to clients and was experienced in building relationships and finding common ground to get things done. One seminal experience for me took place in 1994, when I became chief operating officer of Goldman Sachs, a number of months after the firm had suffered severe trading losses that posed a real threat. Credit spreads on securities had blown out very quickly, and there was a liquidity crisis. That impressed on me the need for a big liquidity cushion and rigorous risk-management practices.

As Secretary of the Treasury

Bowmaker: Following more than thirty years spent working for Goldman Sachs, you were appointed secretary of the treasury in 2006 during the George W. Bush administration. How were you approached for the role?

Paulson: George Bush's chief of staff, Josh Bolten, approached me, and I turned the job down three times because my family wasn't enthusiastic, I enjoyed my role at Goldman Sachs, and I couldn't think of many people who had gone to Washington and left with a higher reputation than they came with. And as I thought about it some more, it occurred to me that maybe I was afraid I wouldn't succeed in D.C. As soon as that hit me, I said to myself, "Well, if it's a fear of failure that is driving me, I certainly can't let that be determinative. I owe a lot to our country." So when, remarkably, they came calling again, I ultimately accepted. I am very glad I did.

Bowmaker: Did you speak to previous secretaries of the treasury before you accepted the role?

Paulson: I obviously consulted with a number of people. For example, Jim Baker had recommended that I emphasize the importance of being the top economic adviser and spokesman on all domestic and international economic issues, and that it was important for me to be able to bring in my own team. President Bush agreed to those conditions and lived up to his commitment.

Bowmaker: Did President Bush make it clear what he wanted you to do for him, and did you make it clear to him about your intended approach to the role?

Paulson: During the sit-down I had with him beforehand, he talked about the importance he placed on entitlement reform and having me work on that issue, and how my practical knowledge might help in cutting off financing for terrorists or sanctioning rogue regimes like Iran and North Korea. I told him that I also wanted to play a major role in US-China policy because I thought, and still do to this day, that was the most important bilateral relationship. Handling that effectively would be very much in our interests, and in the interests of the rest of the world. He agreed with me.

Bowmaker: I would now like to turn to the issue of the financial crisis. When did you begin to suspect that there might be serious problems in the financial sector, and what were the events that generated these suspicions?

Paulson: Years before I left Goldman Sachs, I was quite concerned by market excesses. We had seen very low interest rates cause market participants to seek out higher yields all around the world. Risk was mispriced. At Goldman Sachs, we reacted by tightening up our risk-management processes and increasing our liquidity cushion. For instance, when I left Goldman Sachs, we had $50 billion in unencumbered Treasuries in a lockbox at the Bank of New York because we had learned that after having gone through the '94 crisis, in particular, liquid items can become illiquid very quickly. And assets that are supposed to provide diversity will often move together in very perverse ways when there is financial crisis.

In any event, when I came to Washington, the very first time I got together with the president and his economic team was at Camp David in August of 2006. He had asked me to speak about entitlement reform. As important as that was, I asked if I could speak about my concerns that we were overdue for a significant disruption in the financial markets based upon the leverage that I saw in the markets, as well as history. The president asked me what exactly would cause it. I told him I didn't know, but with twenty-twenty hindsight, it would be obvious [*laughs*]. I did talk about the derivatives market as well as hedge funds, but never once did I mention the mortgage market—I simply didn't see a once-in-a-seventy-five-year storm coming along. We were all aware of the subprime mortgage market, but ever since World War II there had not been a nationwide decline in housing prices. If you had a diversified pool of residential mortgages, the biggest risk you faced was that you got your money back too soon if interest rates dropped and people refinanced their mortgages.

The fact that I had a big concern caused me to immediately add some regulators to the president's working group on financial markets and hold regular meetings. That meant I was working with key regulators and Ben Bernanke [chairman of the Federal Reserve] and Tim Geithner [president of the Federal Reserve Bank of New York] for a year before the crisis hit. And I actually started working with Barney Frank, who was the chairman of the House Financial Services Committee, on Fannie [Mae] and Freddie [Mac] reform beginning in the fall of 2006, which proved to be very helpful.

I've got to say, though, even though I am a worrier and was at least as concerned as anyone else, right up until late in the fall of 2008, I, along with everybody else down there, underestimated the historic magnitude of what we were facing every step of the way. But even if I was omniscient, the excesses were already in the system—the horse was out of the barn, so to speak. And we didn't have an adequate regulatory system or the tools or the authorities we needed. As I just mentioned, I started working with Barney Frank in the fall of 2006, but it took Fannie and Freddie teetering on the edge in June of 2008 to get the reforms we needed from Congress to stabilize these institutions. And even in the darkest days of the crisis, the House voted down TARP [Troubled Asset Relief Program] the first time.

Bowmaker: Knowing what you know now about the aftermath of the Lehman Brothers bankruptcy, what would you have done differently over the weekend of September 13–14?

Paulson: Ben Bernanke, Tim Geithner, and I worked really hard to prevent the failure of Lehman. We believed at the time, and still do, that based on the authorities the Fed[eral Reserve] had, there was nothing they could have done that would have saved Lehman. And no one has yet suggested anything to us that we believe would have worked. Lehman was insolvent and had a very big capital hole. When Bear Stearns went down months earlier, we learned that a Fed loan to a disintegrating investment bank would not stop the panic and would not stop the run. And there were no emergency authorities to guarantee liabilities or put capital in a failing investment bank. Fortunately, though, we had J. P. Morgan as a buyer, and they even needed to guarantee the Bear Stearns trading book during the pendency of the shareholder vote to complete the deal.

After the Bear Stearns rescue, it was really clear to us that if Lehman were to go down and we didn't have a buyer, there would be a big problem. And so Ben Bernanke and I went to see [Chairman of the House Financial Services Committee] Barney Frank, laid out the problem for him, and said we need emergency resolution authorities to deal with a nonbank failure. He understood but told us, "You'll never be able to get them from Congress unless you come in and say that you think Lehman is going to go down, and it will be a disaster." Then, of course, Lehman would have gone down the next day.

My messaging also contributed to some of the controversy, misperceptions, and confusion around the Lehman failure. For instance, the weekend before we got the banks together—we call it Lehman Brothers Weekend—we announced that the government would not be putting any money into Lehman Brothers. That was a tactic, because I felt that was the only way we were going to get Wall Street banks to come together and collectively take these bad loans, which we knew the buyers weren't going to accept. All the while, we worked with the two potential reluctant buyers trying to persuade them to buy Lehman by continually emphasizing that they could leave behind the bad assets. Our tactic didn't work, but we came close. Then, in the aftermath of the Lehman failure, I didn't want to advertise that the United States government had no power to prevent the failure of an investment bank or to acknowledge the extent of our concerns, because that would have exacerbated the panic and Morgan Stanley would have failed immediately. So I talked about moral hazard, played down our concerns, and erred on the side of attempting to stabilize the markets.

The two other points I would make on Lehman.... First, we had three major financial institutions going down that weekend: Merrill Lynch, Lehman Brothers, and AIG [American International Group]. If Bank of

America had bought Lehman, then Merrill—which was much bigger than Lehman—would have failed, and that would have been worse. Secondly, the Lehman collapse jolted the political system. It created the first opportunity to go to Congress to get TARP authorities, which allowed us to recapitalize the financial system and avoid a catastrophe that I think would have rivaled the Great Depression. And so as bad as the Lehman failure was, as I look it now, the alternatives were worse.

The last point I would make is that while Lehman exacerbated the crisis by hurting the system and hurting many people, it was a symptom, not the cause. If you look at AIG, Merrill Lynch, IndyMac [the Independent National Mortgage Corporation], WaMu [Washington Mutual], Wachovia, and all of the European banks, they didn't go down because they were holding Lehman paper. The crisis which began in August of 2007 had been grinding on for over a year. And it was taking its toll. So a good number of banks were approaching failure or were on the brink of failure when Lehman failed.

Bowmaker: Your initial draft of the legislation that eventually became TARP was voted down by the Congress. Your draft was criticized as too terse and vague. Why did you believe that a Congress that was controlled by Democrats and that was generally suspicious of the George W. Bush administration would pass such a short draft, and on such short notice?

Paulson: Two issues are conflated there. First of all, I sent Congress a three-page TARP outline on Friday that was actually in response to Chris Dodd, chairman of the Senate Banking Committee, who said, "Hank, don't give us a fait accompli, work with Congress." So that was supposed to be the starting point, not a demand. What I should have done was to hold a press conference; I had a few other late-night press conferences during the crisis. We quickly got past this hiccup and in only eight days negotiated the TARP legislation with the congressional leadership. The House voted it down the first time, and that was a very stressful and difficult—but short-lived— period [*laughs*]. We had real trouble working with the House Republicans. There were some free-market ideologues and others who thought that they might likely lose their job in the election and didn't want to take a difficult vote. Fortunately, the House Democrats who were in control felt the responsibility to govern, and we had broad, bipartisan support in the Senate. So we got the TARP legislation in two weeks. And I believe that a big contributor to being able to get it in such a short period of time was the fact that my investment banking skills and client relation skills had helped me build relationships with the Democratic and Republican leaders of the House and the Senate during the year leading up to the crisis. We had some successful bipartisan achievements on a range of congressional legislation from trade to the stimulus to Fannie and Freddie before TARP was there.

Again, as I look at it, the excesses before the financial crisis brought out the worst in behaviors. But I think the crisis brought out the best when you look at the cooperation among regulators and between the executive branch and Congress on a bipartisan basis. I actually see the TARP legislation as a crowning achievement of all that. As a matter of fact, it is the last time Congress has enacted consequential legislation on a bipartisan basis.

Bowmaker: After the TARP legislation was finally enacted, the administration changed its focus—from buying troubled assets to instead directly infusing cash into banks. What was the reason for the change of focus?

Paulson: I would say to begin with that when the facts change, our ability to make real-time changes right there on the battlefield is a big reason why we had as much success as we did in stemming the crisis. Now, to get to the specifics, I had originally said we were not going to put capital in the banks. Instead, we were going to buy illiquid assets for two reasons. First, a big source of the problems for the banks were all these complex mortgage securities they owned, which were highly illiquid. So the theory was if the government provided some market for them, prices would rise, and this would allow us to recapitalize the banking system. And number two, the only precedent I had been aware of for a government putting capital in banks was when they were nationalized and given very punitive terms, which I had witnessed in Japan and read about in Sweden. So if this is the policy, the banks will only accept capital if they've got no other alternative. So they only take it just before they fail or after the fact.

But what happened in the three weeks from the time we started working to send things up to Congress until we got legislation was we had the two biggest bank failures in US history in WaMu and Wachovia, and six European countries had to step up and bail out their banks. So we realized we needed to do something which was quicker and more powerful than asset purchases.

Now, even though I said we weren't going to put capital in the banks, I should point out that we got the authorities with TARP to do so if necessary. And, fortunately, we came up with a better way to do so—one that had never before been done. Rather than try to distinguish between the healthy and the unhealthy banks, we offered to buy preferred stocks on very attractive terms, which allowed us to get out very quickly and recapitalize the banking system, putting capital into seven hundred banks. What we did was enormously unpopular because, understandably, the public wanted us to punish the banks. But it worked out very well for the taxpayer, because the money that went into TARP capital programs came back plus almost $50 billion. And, of course, it prevented a collapse of the financial system. Compare that to the model used by the Europeans, who only used the traditional nationalization approach: putting capital into relatively few banks just before they failed or after they failed. Many of their banks even today are undercapitalized, and look at how long it's taken them to try to claw their way back from the crisis, as opposed to the US.

When I explained to President Bush the need to reverse course and inject TARP capital into the banks, he said to me, "You've got to do what you've got to do to save the system, but how are you going to explain it to the world?" I told him, "I'm just going to say that we are going to put capital in the banks because we need to" [laughs].

Bowmaker: Fannie Mae and Freddie Mac have remained in government conservatorships for almost nine years. Is there anything that you could have done in early September 2008 to have avoided this lengthy period of indeterminacy?

Paulson: The simple answer is no, but I'm going to put that in context. The single most important thing we did to address the severe problems in the housing market was putting Fannie and Freddie into conservatorship. They were at the vortex of the crisis. Between them, they held $5.4 trillion in debt and mortgage-backed securities, which was nine times bigger than Lehman Brothers. They were in the market every week issuing at least $20 billion in debt and securities. We were in a race against time, because if they hadn't been stabilized before Lehman announced its earnings, it would have been a real disaster. And if one of them had failed, or even if one of their auctions had failed, it would have been a calamity. Just think about how many more foreclosures there would have been if they weren't backed by a US government guarantee, because they were the only source of mortgage funding.

Now, one other contextual point is that they had huge power in Congress. So when we nationalized them, we took not only their management teams by surprise, but we took Congress by surprise as well. The only way we could get the emergency reform legislation from Congress was with the stipulation that if we put capital in them, it had to be on terms that Fannie and Freddie approved. Fortunately, we also insisted on, and got, the power for the regulator to make subjective judgments on capital that other safety and soundness regulators have, and that was the authority used to put them into conservatorship. But the other issue was that we had emergency authority to guarantee or inject capital only through October of 2009. But Fannie and Freddie had long-term securities outstanding and needed to guarantee long-term mortgages. And so the only way we could stabilize them was to do some financial engineering to transform the powers we had into a long-term guarantee. That went against congressional intent, and I was even concerned for a while when we surprised Congress that I might be impeached. There was no will or ability in Congress to make any decision in terms of Fannie and Freddie's long-term form, what their business model would be, or what the level of government support would be. What I said when we nationalized them was conservatorship is a time-out, and we all know the current model of government support for private profit doesn't work. No one objected at the time.

I've heard some people argue, and I believe it's a flawed argument, that if we'd put them in receivership as opposed to conservatorship, somehow the government might have been forced to deal with Fannie and Freddie by now. I'd been planning on putting them into receivership, but my legal advisers convinced me that would be imprudent since we couldn't view their financial covenants—plus they had a lot of long-term hedges in place on their mortgage portfolio, and we thought we'd lose the value there. But whether they were in receivership or conservatorship, there's no way the government was going to remove the support before making a decision on what form these entities were ultimately going to take and, as I said, what the level of government support would be. Fannie and Freddie are just a prime example of the inability of government to deal with complex, politically difficult, and controversial issues when there's no forcing mechanism.

Bowmaker: Much of the Treasury's maneuvering to contain the financial crisis of 2008 took place in the shadow of a closely contested presidential election. Did the presence of the election and the campaigning make your job at the Treasury more difficult?

Paulson: [*Laughs*] of course, more difficult. The worst part of the financial crisis took place just a few months before a presidential election, which increased the volatility. George Bush was a terrific boss—a really strong leader during the crisis—who gave me great support. But he had a low level of public popularity at that time, and he was considered to be a lame duck. So we had a situation where if either presidential candidate had come out against TARP, I don't think we would have got the legislation, and it would have been a catastrophe. This was a very sensitive period.

Bowmaker: Did the outcome of the election make your job at the Treasury more difficult or easier?

Paulson: I'll say the following about the two candidates and the outcome. I was talking with Barack Obama and John McCain multiple times a week right up until Election Day. Obama was much easier to deal with. At one time he said to me, "Hank, I believe I'm going to be president. I don't want to inherit an economic wasteland, so if you believe the system is ready to go down and I can be helpful, give me a call." And the night we negotiated TARP with the congressional leadership, I actually called him, and he prevailed upon [Senate Minority Leader] Harry Reid to come down, which made a big difference.

McCain was in a much more difficult situation. He didn't like a lot of things we were doing. He was behind in the polls, and so the crisis was helping Obama and hurting McCain. It would have helped him, then, to come out against us, but he didn't. And the more and more I look back on it, I'm so grateful that he didn't. And actually he helped us get a number of the House Republicans to ultimately vote for TARP.

Now, in terms of the outcome of the election, I can tell you that the period from the election to when Obama was sworn in as president seemed barbarically long to me. And during that period, we had to put capital again into Citi; we had to step in and rescue Bank of America, as Merrill Lynch was announcing an almost $25 billion quarterly loss; and we had to rescue and restructure the auto industry. So this was a difficult period. But when I look back on it now, I am very grateful for the policy continuity across the administrations. President Obama selecting Tim Geithner as treasury secretary was huge, because Tim had been involved in all of our capital market stabilization programs. And then, despite the unpopularity of our programs and despite the pressure that President Obama had from members of his party—including a good number within his administration—to go in a different direction, Tim ultimately prevailed. They stuck with the programs that we had put in place, managed them flawlessly, and adapted a few of them expertly. For example, the stress tests were just a logical extension of our capital program, which worked very well.

I still believe that the hardest part of the response to the financial crisis were the controversial actions taken by the Bush administration to avoid a meltdown. Now, the Obama administration may view that differently. But the important thing for me is the continuity and the complementarity between us, and then the steps they took to revive the economy with a stimulus—plus, of course, the Fed's extraordinary monetary policy, which was key.

Bowmaker: How did you and your team at the Treasury work with others on the economic team, including at the Fed and in the White House?

Paulson: The first thing I would say relates to the very unusual, and maybe unique, way in which Ben Bernanke, Tim Geithner, and I worked together. We had different experiences and different skill sets, but we shared a strong mutual trust and appreciation of what each of us brought to the table, which allowed us to pool our talents and authorities to stem the crisis.

Ben is a brilliant economist. As you know, he is a scholar of the Great Depression, and he brought all his knowledge to bear on the problems that we faced. Tim is an expert policymaker and had been through a financial crisis working in the Rubin Treasury [during the time Robert Rubin was secretary of the treasury]. And I, as I said earlier, had a lot of practical experience in dealing with the markets and knew the players on Wall Street, which meant we were able to get real-time market information rather than looking at a Bloomberg screen.

I had a very smooth and very seamless working relationship with the CEA [Council of Economic Advisers], chaired by my friend Ed Lazear, and the NEC [National Economic Council], led by my friend Keith Hennessey. But the way the president wanted to work was that the core of the administration's response to the crisis would come from the Treasury. And so we developed the policies and programs and spearheaded the legislative efforts.

Bowmaker: Can you give us an insight into what it was like working for President Bush?

Paulson: Some of the public commentary has greatly underestimated this president. He'd gone to Harvard Business School; he'd been a businessman; he was really good on economic-related issues in terms of asking very smart questions; and during the crisis he was a calm, steady presence. He knew how to work with me. He said, "You're my wartime general." And when I continually brought him bad news, rather than giving me a hard time, he bucked me up by saying, "Just be glad you're here during this time. You spent your life preparing for it. Be grateful that you and I have a close relationship, and we've had an opportunity to work together. Imagine how bad it would be if this came early in an administration when a president and his treasury secretary were just beginning to learn to work together." I had negotiated the way the president and I would work together before I came to D.C., but I knew that if this didn't work, it would be my fault, not his. It was my job to make the relationship work. And I was really glad that I had a year to develop the kind of working relationship I had with President Bush before the crisis hit.

Bowmaker: What did you learn from President Bush?

Paulson: I learned a number of things. First of all, as I just mentioned, he was a strong leader with a very calm and reassuring presence. Secondly, he really knew how to delegate. Thirdly, he never personalized anything. He took all kinds of public abuse from people, but I never heard him in private or public say a bad word about anyone else. And lastly, he was politically savvy. For example, he gave me great advice in terms of dealing with Congress, and he knew how to get things done there.

Personal Reflections

Bowmaker: How did your personality affect your style and approach as a policymaker?

Paulson: Well, I'm practical and analytical. And I've always been decisive, so I've had to surround myself with people to slow me down so I didn't go too fast. This ability and willingness to make quick decisions when necessary was important. But I've also always been willing to change when I believe we've made a mistake. In crisis decision-making that's quite important, because you never have all the information you need to make a decision. And so you're always trading off doing something that's imperfect with doing nothing, which could be worse. But when the facts change, or your understanding of them changes, you need to be able to reverse yourself. Twice my willingness to change played a big role in our getting the policy right—first in nationalizing Fannie and Freddie and then in using TARP to put capital in the banks.

Bowmaker: As a policymaker, which decisions or outcomes were most gratifying?

Paulson: I am most gratified that we were able to work across party lines, among multiple branches of government and agencies, and spanning two administrations to get big things done that helped prevent the collapse of our financial system.

Bowmaker: On the other hand, there must be some things that, in hindsight, you'd like the opportunity to do differently. What are they?

Paulson: I would say the thing that I most regret is that I was never, ever able to convince the American people that what we did wasn't for Wall Street. We rescued the banks to save the financial system so that Americans could withdraw money from their mutual funds, get a home loan, get a loan for college, and allow small businesses to make investments and create jobs—all the things that you need a financial system to do to help our economy flourish and to help the American people.

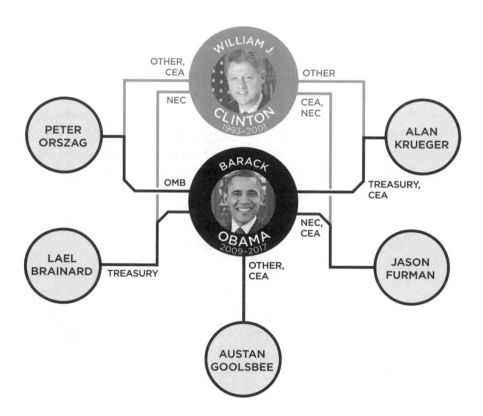

PETER ORSZAG

WILLIAM J. CLINTON 1993–2001

OTHER, CEA

NEC

OTHER

CEA, NEC

ALAN KRUEGER

OMB

BARACK OBAMA 2009–2017

TREASURY, CEA

LAEL BRAINARD

TREASURY

NEC, CEA

AUSTAN GOOLSBEE

OTHER, CEA

JASON FURMAN

VIII   Barack Obama Administration

Austan Goolsbee (*second right*), when a member of the Council of Economic Advisers, receiving cupcakes with Secretary of the Treasury Timothy Geithner (*third right*) during a surprise Oval Office celebration during the economic daily briefing in honor of their shared birthday on August 18, 2009. President Barack Obama (*left*) has his back to the camera.

29 Austan D. Goolsbee
Born 1969, Waco, Texas

Austan Goolsbee earned bachelor's and master's degrees in economics from Yale University in 1991, and obtained a PhD in economics from the Massachusetts Institute of Technology in 1995. He then joined the University of Chicago's Booth School of Business as an assistant professor of economics and has remained there ever since, currently serving as the Robert P. Gwinn Professor of Economics.

Goolsbee was an economic adviser to Barack Obama during his 2004 Senate campaign and senior economic adviser to Obama's 2008 presidential campaign. In the Obama administration he served concurrently as a member of the Council of Economic Advisers (CEA) and chief economist of the President's Economic Recovery Advisory Board, 2009–2010, before being chairman of the CEA in 2010–2011.

I interviewed Austan Goolsbee on two occasions. The first interview took place in his office at the Booth School of Business, University of Chicago, in the middle of the afternoon on Wednesday, December 19, 2012. The second interview took place in a visitor's office at the Booth School of Business, late in the morning on Saturday, January 7, 2017.

Background Information

Bowmaker: Why did you become an economist?

Goolsbee: As a kid, I wanted to be either an astrophysicist or a country music singer. And I spent a shockingly long time figuring out how I could combine them. Being an economist seemed to be the closest you could get [*laughs*].

Entering the Policy World

Bowmaker: What does an economist bring to the policy world that others do not?

Goolsbee: As an undergraduate at Yale, I took the last class that Nobel Laureate Jim Tobin ever taught and became his research assistant. He used to tell stories about when he was at the CEA under [President John F.] Kennedy— both that it was the highest honor and that the whole point of economics was to be able to deal with crises. I would say that economists have become more pervasive in government since Tobin's time, but our fundamental role remains broadly the same—namely, to bring an important and powerful economic framework to issues and to hold a high standard of evidence on data.

Bowmaker: Your entry into the policy world took place in 2004, when you were Barack Obama's economic adviser during his Senate campaign. How did that position arise?

Goolsbee: When you run for the Senate, it is like running for president in that you're asked about a bunch of national issues. But unlike running for president, nobody wants to help you because they don't know who you are [*laughs*]. And so his campaign advisers began calling around to find help on economic matters. They got in touch with Jeff Liebman, a friend of mine from the Kennedy School at Harvard, who said, "Look, I've never heard of this guy. You should at least call someone from the state of Illinois." Jeff gave them my name, and they called me. I said, "Oh yeah, I know this guy. It's the husband of Michelle Obama. I'd be happy to help." Michelle was a lot more famous than he was at the university at the time. I was asked to analyze the policies of Obama and his Republican opponent, Alan Keyes, who was a real bomb thrower from out of state that had been brought in when the Republican nominee resigned because of some scandal.

At a press conference, Keyes proposed that we should follow the lesson of the ancient Romans for slavery reparations and waive all the descendants of slaves from federal taxation for two generations. The campaign wanted an estimate of how much that would cost. I told them that it was a craziness, but I could give them a defensible guesstimate. I looked at the Current Population Survey and tried to match up income to how much people paid in taxes... and it came to something like five trillion dollars [*laughs*]. Later, Keyes proposed replacing the income tax with the sales tax. To prevent it from being regressive, he planned to exempt all spending on housing, food, and transportation, as well as any spending by senior citizens and the poor. The Obama campaign team wanted to know what the sales tax would have to be if those exemptions were granted. So I went and got the Current Expenditure Survey…and the rate came to something like 70 percent. During one of their debates, Obama said to Keyes, "I found an economist from the University of Chicago. His name is Professor Goolsbee. He says that the sales tax rate would need to be 70 percent."

After the debate, I went to the greenroom, which is where Obama and I met face-to-face for the first time. Everything else had been via memos from "Professor Goolsbee." He opened the door and said, "Who are you?" I said I was Professor Goolsbee. He was flabbergasted [*laughs*] and said, "WHAT?!? I thought I had a sixty-five-year-old guy with a tweed jacket and a pipe. You don't look anything like a professor. And what is with 'Goolsbee?'" I replied, "You've been telling everybody that you're the skinny guy with the funny name. You stole my bit. That's what I've been saying for the past fifteen years!" Never again has he called me Professor Goolsbee [*laughs*].

Bowmaker: You then served as his senior economic adviser during the 2008 presidential campaign.

Goolsbee: Yes. At the end of 2006, Obama said to me, "I've decided to run for president. The campaign [headquarters] is going to be in Chicago. Is this something that you could spend a lot of time working on?" At the time, I told him, "I don't know. My research is very important" [*laughs*]. But my wife said to me, "From the beginning, you thought he was very special. If he ran for president and lost, which he probably will, would you be kicking yourself that it was here in Chicago and you didn't do it?" When I replied that I would, she said, "Fine then. Take a year off from research and work on the campaign." Five years later, here we are.

Bowmaker: Did you view yourself as having strong policy positions by that stage, or simply as a hired professional advising Obama?

Goolsbee: I viewed my role as tapping into the collective brainpower of the economics profession so that I could bring sensible ideas to the campaign team that matched what they were trying to do. It seemed to me that the reason Obama entered the race was because the median family's annual income had fallen by $2,000 despite it being a boom [period]. If you looked at the data in the past, it appeared that the top had been going way up, the bottom had been going way down, and the middle class had basically moved about with the economy. This was the first time that pattern had diverged, and Obama viewed this hollowing out of the middle class as the biggest problem facing the country. I had to help come up with ideas to address the issue.

Bowmaker: How would you describe Obama's knowledge and understanding of economics before he became president?

Goolsbee: Obama is a very thoughtful guy who is notable in his ability to grasp economic concepts. I remember early on in the primary [season] when there was a debate about greenhouse gas emissions. There were those who favored a carbon tax, others who wanted a cap-and-trade system, and Republicans who opposed either policy. At one point, Bill Richardson [candidate for the Democratic presidential nomination] said, "Well, I'm for a cap-and-trade system and not a carbon tax because I don't want to hurt the middle class." Obama responded, "Wait, hold on. If you impose a cap-and-trade system that is of the same magnitude as the carbon tax, the impact is the same. It's just a question of who gets the permits." He was right about the incidence being the same, which is entirely economic theory. I think in a different life he could have been an economist.

Let me give you another example. In 2007, he brought in Larry Katz, Alan Krueger, and other labor economists to talk with him about how the middle class was doing. They went through their own evidence before Obama made the argument that in his view the reason why the savings rate went to zero in the 2000s despite it being a boom was because, as I mentioned earlier, the median annual family income had declined substantially. Of course, he didn't use the language of economists, but he was suggesting that the middle class had a consumption level that was based on what they thought was their permanent income. They hadn't been able to save because they had been hit by negative shocks that they hadn't anticipated. That's quite a sophisticated argument, and it wasn't something planted in his head by an economist. And by the way, that's also an example of how Obama likes nothing better than having several experts in the room with different views and Socratically quizzing them so that he can home in on the core issues. I attribute it to him being a law professor.

Bowmaker: Were your economic philosophies in alignment?

Goolsbee: Yes. My research is in two main areas—namely, tax and public policy regulation, and the so-called new economy. On the tax side, in particular, I was intimately familiar with the claims of some economists that a slightly more sophisticated version of the original Laffer curve exists, which means that cutting high income tax rates can either pay for itself or can generate much more reporting of income so that the revenue loss isn't so high and the deadweight loss is low. I didn't think this was supported by the evidence and was instead in agreement with Obama's general view that what we needed was tax relief for working people and investment in human capital.

Bowmaker: You were also part of the transition team when Obama became president. In hindsight, is there anything you might have known then that would have made making economic policy easier during the administration?

Goolsbee: One of the central debates about what would become the Economic Recovery Act stimulus bill fundamentally was a dispute of worldviews over the nature of both the recession and the recovery. It wasn't phrased that way, but that's what it was. There was one group of people saying, "Stimulus should be temporary and targeted because deep downturns are followed by strong rebounds, so we're likely to have a V-shaped recovery. And if we do, the last thing we want is to commit ourselves to, say, ten-year infrastructure programs because by the time that comes online, it's just going to be inflationary. We're already going to be recovering, so make the focus shifting activity into 2009 as much as you can." Then there was a second group arguing that this was a weird and different recession, and so the normal V-shaped recovery argument maybe doesn't apply. They believed, therefore, that the stimulus should be more long-lived. And then there was a third group—explicitly tied to the politics—who were saying, "Well, we need Republican votes, so let's make this as much about tax cuts as we can." We went back and forth about each argument during the transition, and ultimately, in the Washington way, the stimulus ended up being a third of each one. But if we had known at the time that it was going to look much more like a "normal" financial recession in that it wouldn't be a V-shaped recovery, then it would have heavily influenced the decision over what to put in the stimulus.

As Member of the Council of Economic Advisers

Bowmaker: Your formal entry into the policy world came in 2009 as a member of the CEA and concurrently as chief economist of Obama's Economic Recovery Advisory Board. As you began your roles, was there anything that surprised or frustrated you?

Goolsbee: The hardest adjustment was the fact that I went to Washington to race cars and found myself in the middle of a demolition derby in which car-racing skills were not so valuable. Everything is geared up for political battle. It is totally unlike the seminar room at the University of Chicago. Here the standard of evidence is astoundingly high, and the time frame in which we are able to answer questions is measured in years, not days or hours. It is an active debate in which everybody fundamentally loves each other. Washington is the opposite in every way—in terms of the standard of evidence, the time pressure, and the ability to have a conversation with those from the other side. For instance, Rahm Emanuel [Obama's chief of staff] was the king of pounding his fist on the table with a "Today we march!" attitude. "By five o'clock on Friday," he once said, "you will have a worked-out housing plan of how we will stave off foreclosure of millions of Americans." In the academic world, it's already difficult to do new research when you have one or two years to write the paper. In the policy world, doing it with three days' notice is impossible.

The whole period of the first nine months I was there in Washington is cloudy in my memory because it was so unbelievably stressful. Conditions were so bad that we didn't know whether there was going to be a depression or not. In the couple of months after Obama became president, he kept claiming that he would do whatever it took to prevent a depression. I was getting calls from colleagues who were economic historians telling me that the financial shock was bigger than the one in 1929, and so Obama should stop saying that there won't be a depression—it was destroying his credibility. He should work on a plan for what to do once the depression had started.

I had never been to Washington before, which meant I was constantly asking people whether this was a normal environment to be working in. For the first year and a half, I was told that it was 100 percent not usually like this. My formal entry into Washington, then, was not only frustrating and surprising, it was scary, too.

Bowmaker: In your view, was Larry Summers, as director of the NEC [National Economic Council], giving the president recommendations rather than options, which is typically the case in the honest broker role?

Goolsbee: Yes, he certainly was. But in fairness to Larry, I think his understanding with the president when he took the job was that he would not serve as the honest broker—he was hired because the president wanted his advice. And I certainly had amazing respect for his intellect. I saw many subjects where I thought the country was lucky to have somebody as smart as him. For example, let's go back to the transition. There was a proposal of the form that since credit was tight in the economy, why don't we have the government, which can still borrow at low rates, go into the mortgage business and basically give everyone an extremely low interest mortgage? I thought we ought to be nervous about that idea, given that we'd just gone through a horrible financial crisis brought on by a drop in real estate values and overleverage. And so even if you thought there was a 90 percent chance that people would pay back their loans, a 10 percent chance of the taxpayer having to eat a few trillion dollars of losses was a magnitude of exposure that was beyond the pale. It was just too risky. But I can still remember Larry saying to the proponents, "Look, I understand your argument that the government can borrow at, say, 1 percent, so why don't we issue a 2.5 percent mortgage to everyone in the country? But if you start thinking that way—that is, we're going to open up the government's balance sheet to sectors of the economy—why would you start with housing? Why not small business? Why not pick a bunch of things that are more job-creation intensive when we're in the middle of a recession?" I don't know if he thought of it on the spot or if it was just second nature to him, but his argument was completely correct. In other words, if you wanted to have a stimulus impact, which is essentially what we were arguing, why would you start with mortgages? You wouldn't. And so I think that kind of economic insight from Larry was often quite important. He wasn't always as great at being the broker-process type, though.

Bowmaker: At the time of the financial crisis, there was $750 billion of negative equity in housing. What do you say to those who argue that more could have been done to help homeowners? Could the negative equity have been written down, or would people have walked away from houses?

Goolsbee: We spent a lot of time thinking about that issue. My characterization of most of the critics is that you are living in a fantasy world if you think you could just write down principal that was pushing close to a trillion dollars. There was zero chance of having that amount of principal reduction to play with from the government, and if you put it onto the banks, they would all have collapsed. And beyond that, even if we somehow had the money, the issue then becomes one of who gets a payment. Let's say there were 15 percent of mortgages underwater, and the average mortgage was $200,000. That means you are handing a $40,000 check to several million homeowners, and they would disproportionately be ones that had not been prudent. Take someone who took out an 80 percent loan-to-value mortgage and had been diligently making their payments, while the person next door took out a 105 percent loan-to-value mortgage and stopped paying. Could you really send a $40,000 check to the neighbor? As I say, that would have been a problem even if we had the money, which we didn't.

Larry would instead pose the following question to us: If we had $20 billion or $50 billion, what would be the best use of that money to prevent foreclosure? To help answer that question, we went to the relevant economics literature, which suggested that people living in their homes valued them more than the market did. In other words, they don't want to leave, because they have kids in school and all their belongings in their houses and so on. If we could get the payments down to being affordable, then, people might continue to make them even if they were underwater. When there is $750 billion of negative equity, $20 billion of write-down is really a tiny drop in the bucket, whereas $20 billion of direct payment reduction in the short run is more than one drop in the bucket. And it's that type of thinking that led to the so-called HAMP [Home Affordable Modification Program].

I do think it would have been good if we could have had more principal reduction, and we put in various incentives for it—as they had tried in the Hope for Homeowners Act before Obama came into office. The puzzle was why the financial institutions weren't more amenable to it, given that foreclosure is not good for them either. Part of the answer is that we were dealing with securitized mortgages, so they didn't feel that they had the authority to make principal modifications to the loan. But a number of banks also felt that the American homeowner is almost pathologically honest and would keep paying the mortgage if they were underwater, so they wouldn't write it down. It was a tough problem.

Bowmaker: Can you take us through the auto bailout decision and your contributions to the debate?

Goolsbee: That was very fraught. There was disagreement within the economics team about its riskiness. If we save Chrysler, will that endanger GM [General Motors]? Will it be possible to rescue all of the auto companies when it's an economy of scale business, and so dividing a small pie among three companies might not work in a way that dividing it among two companies would? If we triaged and let Chrysler go, would that substitute demand to Ford and GM and thereby save them? But you had Ford, their direct competitor, arguing for a bailout of Chrysler and GM on the grounds that all of their suppliers also supply Chrysler and GM—so if those suppliers lose two-thirds of their business, they will go bankrupt and Ford won't get the parts they need. Polls were saying that 75 percent of the country opposed any rescue of the auto industry even when told that not rescuing them might cost one million jobs, and the automakers said they only had a couple of weeks before they would need to start liquidating. At one point, we had a meeting in Larry's office in which he asked something like, "If we rescue Chrysler, how many people here think that it will still be alive in five years?" The vote was exactly tied. So this was a big fat mess.

The team was arguing back and forth about it, and eventually there was a memo put together in which they were going to put both the pro side and con side to the president. But my understanding is that somehow the opposing arguments about the risks of doing Chrysler, too, were mostly removed. The president read through the memo at the next meeting and, I am told, said, "Is this a unanimous recommendation?"—sensing that something was too one-sided in the writing. When they replied, "No, I suppose not," the president said, "Why isn't Goolsbee here?" And so I was just working in my office when I receive a phone call telling me, "You're supposed to be at the Oval Office meeting." I didn't even know there was a meeting [*laughs*].

I run over, and when I go into the meeting, it looks like all the seats are full. There are only a limited number of places in the Oval Office— two couches, the president's chair, the vice president's chair, and a few extra chairs. They won't manifest more people than there are seats—that's just their policy. It turns out, though, that the vice president is not there that day, so the president says, "Just sit right there," which puts me right between the president and Larry sitting on the couch [*laughs*]. Larry had been the main advocate of saving both Chrysler and GM, whereas I was among the most vocal that doing both was risky. So when the president then said, "I understand that you have some qualms about this approach," and I walked through the main issues, Larry was looking at me with a real stink eye [*laughs*]. The president thought about it and said, "This is not something we can resolve in five minutes. Let's have a real meeting in the afternoon, go through the details, and then we will make a decision." At that meeting, everyone presented their arguments, and the president said, "I understand it might not work, but we've got to take a bet on American manufacturing. We can't afford to not do it." So it was done. My view was always that if the economists don't agree, and the price tag is more than

$10 billion, then the president at least needs to know what the options are and why there was a disagreement. In the end, of course, the president was proven right, and everything worked out better than anyone at the time could have imagined. He always had excellent judgment.

Bowmaker: How different was the kind of advising that you did as CEA member relative to before Obama became president?

Goolsbee: Once we got into government, it became much more formal, and you could see right away what a horrible job it is to be president of the United States. In December of 2008, I was present at his first briefing with those who had been picked for all of the major economic policy positions. There had been a huge snowstorm in Chicago, which meant that none of the cabs were running, and so seventy-nine-year-old Paul Volcker had to take the subway from the airport and traipse through the snow to get to the transition office [*laughs*]. Each person had a different part of the economy that we were going to tell Obama about. [Chair of the CEA] Christy Romer talked about GDP [gross domestic product]. "We are about to have an epically horrible decline of GDP," she told him, "maybe the worst in the history of the United States. We will need the biggest stimulus of all time, bigger than the New Deal as a share of the economy." Then [Treasury Secretary] Tim Geithner discussed the financial system, informing Obama that half of the major banks in the country may be insolvent, that we've already blown through the first half of the TARP [Troubled Asset Relief Program], that we don't know whether we're going to get the second half of TARP, and that the average cost to the taxpayer of the financial crisis might be 5–10 percent of GDP. I then talked about the housing market—the fact that house prices are down 15 percent, that they're expected to fall another 10 percent, which would mean that 30 percent of homeowners in the US will be underwater with $750 billion of negative equity. It just got worse and worse each time somebody spoke. When we had finished, I walked up to the president and said, "Mr. President, that has to be the worst background briefing that an incoming president has had since Franklin Roosevelt in 1932, and maybe since Abraham Lincoln in 1860." He looked at me in total seriousness and said, "Goolsbee, that's not even my worst briefing this week." At that moment, you just realize, "Oh, my God, you do not want this man's job." In our heart of hearts, all of us knew perfectly well how grateful we were that he was the guy who was on the hook to make the decisions and not us.

As Chairman of the Council of Economic Advisers

Bowmaker: Did President Obama make it clear what he expected you to do for him as chairman of the CEA?

Goolsbee: Not in a formal way. I had a long-standing friendship with the president, I had a decent idea of his worldview, and I knew the rest of the economic team and his political advisers pretty well. When I took over as chair of the CEA, I felt that my comparative advantage lay in promoting the issues ultimately found in the State of the Union address of 2011 relating to growth of the US economy, the competitiveness of American companies, investment in our workforce and infrastructure, and a subset of questions concerning the budget and taxation. It was clear that the case for outright, naked stimulus borrowed from the future had certainly changed, if not substantially lessened, from what it was in the first quarter of 2009. My predecessor, Christy Romer, came into the role standing at the edge of an abyss. The six-month period between the fourth quarter of 2008 and the first quarter of 2009 saw the worst GDP growth in the sixty-five years of official data. I inherited an environment of the first inklings of growth and signs of improvement in the job market.

In terms of the day-to-day contribution of the CEA, I already had a good grasp of this based on my experience as a member and from the advice that I received from former members and chairs of the CEA. I would say that there are three things they taught me in this respect. One is that although the CEA is quite important as an idea generator, it only ever wins on a policy issue the old-fashioned way   namely, by having a better argument, which also means that you have to have a fairly close relationship with the president. If he is not paying attention, that is an existential problem for the CEA. The second point is that the CEA tends to be most effective when it is not working on the most burning, front-rank issue of the day. Why? Because something as big as that is likely to involve so many constituencies that in some sense it won't be about the economics. On the other hand, for the next tier of issues, people tend to be a little more open to hearing the economic argument. For example, the question of the reform of Social Security is something which economists have an opinion about, but nobody is going to call us to hear our views. But take something like whether tax rates should be higher or lower on those with high incomes—there the CEA can serve as an evidence provider. And the third thing is that we can stop policy proposals that would be unhelpful, costly, and inefficient. The advice of Bill Nordhaus, another one of my teachers as an undergraduate at Yale and a former member of the CEA, was that the job of the CEA, like that of a successful gardener, is 90 percent pulling weeds and 10 percent planting seeds.

Bowmaker: Was there any frustration involved in working with White House staff who only wanted policies that would get the president reelected?

Goolsbee: I grew very fond of, and deeply impressed by, Obama's political team, particularly David Axelrod [senior adviser to the president]. I can't think of an example of when they would say, "We should do this policy because it would be really popular."

At that December 2008 meeting I described earlier, the first estimate of GDP growth for the fourth quarter of 2008 was negative 3.5 percent. On the basis of that figure, Christy Romer forecast that with the stimulus, unemployment would increase to 8 percent, and without the stimulus, it would increase to 8.9 percent. At the meeting, David Axelrod said, "I'm afraid that America has not had a 'holy shit' moment in which they see the conditions and say, 'Oh, my God, we have to do something.'" And then he says, "Take the document here that Christy has prepared informing us that we are going to need the biggest stimulus of all time. Are you telling me that we're going to pass this stimulus and the unemployment rate will still rise to 8 percent?" When she replied yes, Axelrod told us, "Well, this is going to be a fun messaging challenge." My point here on politics is that David Axelrod wasn't suggesting that we should avoid passing the stimulus because it would be difficult to sell—he never did that sort of thing. He was just warning us that it wasn't going to be fun.

Bowmaker: Did you work with the president's speechwriters and help vet his speeches?

Goolsbee: Yes. Most of his speechwriters were very good friends of mine from the campaign. In my opinion, they were some of the greatest public servants in America. Not only were they beautiful writers, but they cared and had an interest in policy, which sometimes speechwriters do not have.

There's a whole process around providing input to speeches. The president will sit with the speechwriters and explain his ideas to them. They'll come up with a draft, which will eventually be sent out to all the relevant agencies and offices who will then provide official comments. It's not casual. That said, there is an old Washington trick people sometimes make when they don't like something that's in a speech, and it used to drive me nuts. They would wait until the last minute before sending in their edits. That way, nobody gets to see them because they've been sent in so late [*laughs*]. Usually, though, Obama's speechwriters were a little inoculated to that trick, and so if they received suspicious-seeming edits by that stage, they would call around and ask what was going on, and then some bureaucratic brouhaha would follow. That happened when the Volcker Rule was under discussion.

I also remember one episode in particular when I became involved. I had been saying that the US workforce remained the most productive in the world, and the president liked that phrasing, and so it was put in the prototype of the State of the Union address. It was then sent around, and the CEA, being who they are, came back and told me, "They've adopted what you've been saying." When I replied I thought that would be good for us, they said, "No, no, we've checked the data, and technically Luxembourg has higher productivity than us." I just told them, "Please don't send in the edits and ask the president to say, 'Except for 250,000 workers in Luxembourg, we remain the most productive in the world'" [*laughs*].

Bowmaker: What did you learn about the role of the media in the policy world when you were chairman of the CEA?

Goolsbee: I guess I was a little more involved with the media than normal for a CEA chair. It was probably a holdover from the media work I did in the campaign, but I definitely tried to explain what we were doing as best I could. I think that sort of thing matters. Before I went into the government, it had always been my contention that the nation has been very generous to the economics profession, and so we owed it to America to explain what the subject is all about and what we do. The first thing that I learned is that if you can explain what you're doing, that makes a big difference as to whether you are able to get your policy through. The second thing is that if you can't explain something in a way that people understand, then maybe you don't fully understand either. And the third thing that I learned is that economic theories and facts are not tremendously popular even if they are well understood. For example, the economist's view is that all of life is about making trade-offs. People might acknowledge that's true, but it won't necessarily mean that they want to have to choose between things.

Bowmaker: All things considered, can you give an example of where you, as an economist, or the CEA, as an organization, were able to make a difference?

Goolsbee: I'm not a big fan of individuals taking credit for big policy moves of an administration. It doesn't really work that way. I do think, though, that we paid for ourselves fifty times over in the tens of billions of dollars of bad ideas that we helped block. For example, there was sentiment among some during the financial crisis that we should offer house price insurance. If you looked at the state of the housing market, you would see that afford-ability by any metric was as attractive as it's ever been, but people weren't buying houses. Their argument was that people must be afraid of house prices going down. If that's true, then the government should give every-body a guarantee that the price of their houses won't fall, and if it does, they will be reimbursed. That's another example of where the economics team had to politely just keep pointing out how much it would poten-tially cost, how it could induce behaviors that we don't necessarily want to encourage, and the like.

Bowmaker: You worked for Barack Obama for a long time. How did your relationship with him change over time? Can you describe how he changed over the period you worked for him?

Goolsbee: My relationship with him did change a fair amount, and in a way that's to be fully expected. If you had asked me in 2003 or 2004 about our relationship, I would have said that we were pals. But by the time he was elected president, everything became much more formal, as I mentioned earlier. We weren't pals anymore. Everyone ceased calling him Barack and began calling him Mr. President, and I didn't see anyone forget and slip back into calling him by his first name. There's just a certain distancing that takes place when you are talking to the guy who has to decide whether or not to take out Osama bin Laden.

As to how he's changed, I think he got more formal, too, partly because the demands on his time became more extreme. Before he arrived at the White House, he was the kind of thinker who enjoyed bringing in lots of different viewpoints around a table for a discussion that would involve him asking many questions. But once you get into the actual crush of events as president, you just don't have time to make decisions like that anymore. Everything becomes process oriented. Leisurely debates are a thing of the past. That said, my feeling was that his temperament remained pretty simi-lar to what it was even a long time ago.

Bowmaker: What did the president learn from you, and what did you learn from him?

Goolsbee: When I started out with Obama, the biggest misconception I had was that I thought, "Oh, campaigns must be about the policy people giving them the ideas, and then the message people figuring out how to explain the ideas." That's not how it works [*laughs*]. The themes of the campaign drive the message, and then it's more about which policies you have in the themes. In other words, policy people are not the center of the universe, and you need to recognize that fact. Once I did, I then viewed my role as the guy in NASCAR [National Association for Stock Car Auto Racing] who, when the driver pulls in for a pit stop, jumps over the wall, fills the tank with a gas can, changes the tire, and gets him back out on the track in thirteen seconds. The president is Dale Earnhardt Jr. Your job is to keep him driving. And so I don't know what the president learned from me—I was just doing my best to facilitate what he was trying to do.

But I learned many things from him, one of which was that he has a certain respect for a lot of different viewpoints and is able to distill from the cacophony something like a reasonable decision over and over again. It isn't just random. In my experience, he had amazing judgment on some quite tough calls, from whether we can afford to rescue both GM and Chrysler to whether we should offer X in exchange for Y in the budget negotiation, or to whether we should go after Osama bin Laden. I thought that was quite impressive.

Two, I learned he has a great temperament for a crisis. I don't think the public view of President Obama as a guy who doesn't get too hot or too cold and remains fairly steady is wrong. Now, there are moments when that makes people angry, and they say, "Why isn't he madder?" But there are other times, especially in crises, when it's more, "Thank God, that's the way he is"—not just for me personally, but for everybody.

The third thing is that the president has an ability to take a bunch of incoming anecdotes and merge them onto the data and cold analytics relating to the economy. When we were going through the housing program, for example, he was receiving letters from the public, and he'd come in and say, "Now wait, our policy is X and it's designed to prevent foreclosure, but I've just got this letter from someone who's saying it didn't help them. Can you go check this out?" The economists tended to reply, "Oh, this is only one anecdote. You can't base anything on that," or "Look, even with our policy, millions of people are still going to lose their homes. There's nothing we can do about it." That happened repeatedly in the case of housing when the banks agreed to do trial modifications. They would write down the monthly payment to an affordable level, but then you've got to check the borrower income, which takes months. And so the CEOs [chief executive officers] of the banks said to us, "We'll give them a trial modification, which means they'll get the lower payment, and then we'll start the process of checking their income. If it turns out that they don't have the income they said, they'll lose their modification, but they won't be worse off because they'll have already gotten six months of the lower payment. And if they do qualify, we'll just roll them into it." What happened during the trial modification, though, is that when the person started making a 40 percent smaller payment as the modification called for, a different part of the same bank would say, "This person only paid 60 percent of their monthly payment for six straight months. Commence foreclosure proceedings." That was the so-called dual tracking problem, which ended up being a huge issue that we had to deal with. The CEOs said, "Oh, we're so sorry. It was our mistake. The people can have their houses back." But they'd left their homes and taken all the copper wires out! That was an example of a complexity that the economists did not have in our data, but that the president was somehow attuned to by talking to people and getting their letters. I can't say that's something I learned to do myself, but at least I observed it, and it was very instructive. In the end, the economic worldview is not the be-all and end-all of everything we analyze.

General Thoughts on Economic Policymaking

Bowmaker: Do you believe that if we were to raise the level of economic literacy in this country, economic policymaking would improve because the people would demand better policy?

Goolsbee: Yes. My model of policymakers in Congress is that they're highly reflective of what their constituents think. The reason they couldn't make a deal on the grand bargain is our own fault as voters. Seventy-five percent of people in the polls said they agreed with the Republicans with respect to government spending being out of control, and 80 percent of people also said that they don't consider entitlements to be spending. When we hold those views at the same time, you can see why agreement couldn't be reached in Washington.

If there were more economic literacy, politicians would be less prone to making arguments that are not supported by the evidence. Again, take the issue of tax rates on high-income people. There is still a group who stand up and say, "We should cut high income taxes because that pays for itself and unleashes economic growth." There is a massive literature that goes against that argument, and it would be helpful if voters knew about it.

I also think greater economic literacy would make people more aware of thinking about trade-offs—not only in relation to government policy, but also in their own lives. There are large numbers of people in this country who have no savings and engage in economic activities that are fundamentally not sustainable. Economic literacy can help us make fewer of those mistakes.

Bowmaker: Do you think that the gap between economics research produced in universities and policymaking will increase or decrease over time?

Goolsbee: I think the dangerous gap that is growing is the difference between those who are interested in policy and those who are not. With the rise of the internet and every other form of entertainment, the world is becoming more and more niche oriented, and policy is now like the Golf Channel. Most people never see it, and the diehards can watch twenty-four hours a day. And once that is true, you have a much greater share of people who care about policy being those who are directly affected by it. That is a tough spot within which to be making policy. That said, there was a brief moment in 2009 when my mom in Abilene, Texas, said to me, "We need to deal with these 'too big to fail' banks. Why can't their capital requirements be higher?" [*Laughs.*] That was a great moment.

Personal Reflections

Bowmaker: What value has your public service had to you and to your university?

Goolsbee: It was an amazing experience that I wouldn't trade for anything, although it was highly stressful and frequently not all that fun. But I had consciously said that I wasn't going to Washington to find a new career— I would be coming back to Chicago. And I found that very helpful when I was thinking through issues, because I never felt that I better not say something in case my job was in jeopardy. I treated it a bit like a journey to the moon. Not many get to experience going to the moon, but it doesn't mean you want to live there.

In terms of the university, I know there are many graduates from Booth who felt it was value destroying [*laughs*]. Every time they saw me on TV defending the president or explaining his policies, they would call up the dean and say, "Why is the University of Chicago next to that guy's name?" I saw my colleague and friend Raghu Rajan at one point when I was in Washington. He said, "Are you coming back?" When I told him that I definitely was, he replied, "Well, some of the faculty are waiting for you with their knives sharpened…" But I have always believed that living in an environment where not everybody agrees with you is very healthy. Milton Friedman was a great debater, and when he once went to New York City, somebody said to him, "It must be hard to go to the heart of liberalism." He replied, "No, it's easy, because most people there have only been around those like themselves. They've never heard a smart conservative make an argument, so they're easily defeated." When I got to Washington, I found that to be true. The people there haven't been engaged in real idea wrestling with a great opponent for a long time, so they're easily pinned.

Bowmaker: How did your personality affect your style and approach as a policymaker?

Goolsbee: As you can probably tell, I don't take myself very seriously. My coping mechanism in a stressful situation is to make jokes. It turned out that both the president and his political team had a very good sense of humor, but oftentimes when I would make jokes in meetings, the rest of the economic team would have no idea what I was talking about [*laughs*]. Now, I don't know whether my personality was necessarily the most natural fit for the international part of the CEA role. I remember when I got back from a meeting at the OECD [Organisation for Economic Co-operation and Development] and Larry Summers said, "You were at the OECD? Austan Goolsbee is to the OECD as George Marshall is to Stephen Colbert" [*laughs*]. I had no problem with that [*laughs*].

Bowmaker: What were your strengths and weaknesses as a policymaker?

Goolsbee: I was probably best as a policy explainer—on a relative scale. And possibly more than the median CEA chair, I was interested in hearing from industry figures about the state of the economy. And so I would meet with, say, the CEO of FedEx or the CEO of Walmart to hear what they thought was happening in the economy in their data. I found that you could get more timely, and sometimes more accurate, information from talking to them.

My weakness as an adviser was similar to most academics who find themselves in Washington: we have no experience in building coalitions, and we are naive about how to bring people around on an idea. I remember when my chief economist found something that was wrong within the report of a policy proposal. It turned into an argument. He came to me and said, "In the academic world, if you read somebody's paper, found an error, and pointed it out to them before it was published, you would be thanked because it prevented an embarrassment. In Washington, if you say, 'Here's what's wrong and how we could fix it,' they think you are a jerk." As I say, I thought I was coming in to race cars, when what I really needed was more demolition-derby skills.

Bowmaker: As a policymaker, which outcomes or decisions were most gratifying?

Goolsbee: I believe historians are going to say the major accomplishment of the first two years of the Obama presidency was that there was no depression. Of course, they will say that the Fed[eral Reserve] also played quite an important role, as did some of the actions at the end of the Bush administration. But there were a lot of decisions that Obama made—such as those relating to bank stress tests, bank recapitalization, and the stimulus—that were instrumental in America avoiding going off a cliff. It could have been a catastrophe, and that is a significant achievement in my view. You have to remember that the financial shock at the end of 2008 was bigger than the one in 1929, and the financial sector is a larger share of the economy today than it was during the Great Depression.

Bowmaker: On the other hand, there must be some things, in hindsight, that you'd like the opportunity to do differently. What are they?

Goolsbee: On scores of small issues, I would reconsider things. On the big decisions, though, I am not sure that I would say that. I had been friends with the president for a long time, and I went to Washington to help him and to help him get us out of an epic crisis. He succeeded, and he did so with a fundamental dignity as a person that I think we will look back on longingly in the years to come. I would change one thing, though. Everyone told me that D.C.'s climate would be much milder than Chicago's, so I left my big coat back home. We were hit by a series of freak snowstorms including Snowmaggedon. So next time I would definitely dress better [*laughs*].

Peter Orszag (*left*), when director of the Office of Management and Budget, testifying before the House Appropriations Committee on the fiscal year 2011 budget with Timothy Geithner (*center*), secretary of the treasury, and Christina Romer (*right*), chair of the Council of Economic Advisers, on March 16, 2010.

30 Peter R. Orszag
Born 1968, Boston, Massachusetts

Peter Orszag graduated summa cum laude with an AB in economics from Princeton University in 1991. He then obtained an MSc and a PhD in economics in 1992 and 1997, respectively, from the London School of Economics, which he attended as a Marshall Scholar.

Orszag first served in government during the administration of President Bill Clinton. He was a staff economist at the Council of Economic Advisers (CEA) between 1993 and 1994 and then senior adviser and senior economist between 1995 and 1996. He was special assistant to the president for economic policy between 1997 and 1998.

Orszag then entered the private sector, working as an economics consultant, and he also taught economics at the University of California, Berkeley, between 1999 and 2000. He subsequently joined the Brookings Institution, where he worked between 2001 and 2007.

Orszag was appointed director of the Congressional Budget Office (CBO) in 2007 and then served as director of the Office of Management and Budget (OMB) in the administration of President Barack Obama between 2009 and 2010. He then was a distinguished visiting fellow at the Council on Foreign Relations before he joined Citigroup in 2011 as vice chairman of corporate and investment banking and chairman of the Financial Strategy and Solutions Group. In 2016, he joined investment banking firm Lazard Frères and Co. as vice chairman and managing director, and now serves as chief executive officer of Financial Advisory.

I interviewed Peter Orszag in his office at Lazard Frères and Co. in New York City. It was the middle of the afternoon on Monday, July 18, 2016.

Background Information

Bowmaker: Why did you become an economist?

Orszag: I studied economics as an undergraduate mostly because I was interested in public policy. Frankly, the economics classes seemed more insightful about policy questions than the public policy courses. I wasn't at all sure, though, that I wanted to go on and get a PhD in economics. In fact, I took the LSAT [Law School Admission Test] for law school, but I then won a scholarship to study in England. Since it didn't make sense to study law in that country, I am thus an economist [*laughs*].

Entering the Policy World

Bowmaker: What does an economist bring to the policy world that others do not?

Orszag: First, economists tend to have a certain comfort level with statistical analysis that people with other backgrounds are less likely to have. Second, and more importantly because it is at the heart of economics, there is a focus on how people respond to incentives, including any indirect and unanticipated consequences.

Bowmaker: Your entry into the policy world in Washington took place in 1994, when you were appointed as a staff economist at the Council of Economic Advisers during the Clinton administration. How did that position arise?

Orszag: One of my favorite undergraduate professors at Princeton was Alan Blinder, who joined the CEA at the very beginning of the Clinton administration. I was in Moscow working with [economist] Jeffrey Sachs when he called me up and said, "It must be cold there. Do you want to come to Washington?" I said yes because of Professor Blinder, and also since it was a new administration. I should add that I had spent the spring semester of my senior year in high school working for Tom Daschle, who was then a brand-new senator from South Dakota, and so I'd already had a little bit of Beltway Fever. I was excited to return to Washington.

Bowmaker: What did you learn from Joseph Stiglitz, with whom you worked closely when you were at the CEA?

Orszag: Joe was a very interesting chair of the CEA. First of all, he is incredibly creative and would approach issues differently than the typical government economist. He is certainly not the norm for someone who works in government. Second, he would pick out a few things that he really cared about. Normally, the things he focused on wouldn't have gotten much of the attention of the chair of the CEA. For example, I spent a large share of my time with Joe fighting the privatization of the US Enrichment Corporation, which at the time was a government corporation that enriched uranium for use in nuclear reactors. He was adamantly opposed to the privatization. Every time he met with Treasury officials, he would bring this up—so much so that they just got sick of his arguments about it. That was unusual, because most chairs of the CEA don't get involved in these heated battles. He would not give up.

I had a great experience with him. If you're willing to work hard, try your hand at lots of different things, and bring an academic perspective to an issue, he truly values you.

Bowmaker: When I spoke with Joseph Stiglitz, he told me that he tried to bring his sense of humor to the role. Can you give an example?

Orszag: My favorite Joe episode took place in 1994, when a few fishermen had been killing minke whales in violation of the International Whaling Convention. The US has something called the Pelly Amendment that requires us to retaliate through trade sanctions if a foreign government violates an international fisheries agreement. This happened right after the Norwegians had brokered the Arab-Israeli peace deal and just before they were about to host the Winter Olympics. When Joe and I went into a big interagency meeting about it, he decided that trade sanctions, which was the response being proposed, were not warranted in this particular case. And so he proposed boycotting the Olympics instead. I can still remember the State Department official turning to him irately and saying, "You do realize now you're equating the killing of a few minke whales with the invasion of Afghanistan"—which was what had triggered the previous boycotting of the Olympics. As only Joe could do, he paused for a second and put the sharp end of a pencil into his ear and rolled it around, which was a tendency of his. Then he said, "I guess you're right. But how about we calibrate our boycott and skip the events that we normally lose anyway? Like the ones with the skis and the guns?" There was just complete silence in the room for about a minute [*laughs*]. Nobody knew how to process what had been said. And so the meeting went on as if Joe didn't exist. Everybody completely ignored him. To this day, I still don't know whether it was a serious proposal on his part. He does have an impish way about him. I think part of Joe likes to say to himself, "Oh, that's an interesting idea. Why don't I throw it out there and see what happens?" [*Laughs.*]

Bowmaker: Can you tell us about how you interacted with Robert Rubin for the first time?

Orszag: Yes. When he was secretary of the treasury, I was a very young staffer but was present at a meeting he was leading. He said something like, and I am simplifying, "There are 1,000 of them and 10,000 of those, so that's something like 100 million." He had made a slight math mistake. And so I wrote a little note saying, "Secretary Rubin, there was a small error in your calculation. The number is actually 10 million. Peter Orszag." When he was rushing out the door, I handed it to him. Initially, I did not hear anything, and I thought to myself, "Well, he's busy, and that was probably a stupid point to make anyway." But about four or five days later, I was at my desk when the phone rang. The person on the other line said, "Can you please hold for Secretary Rubin?" To which the only answer is, "Of course." And so he picked up the phone from somewhere in Europe and said, "I brought a bunch of stuff with me on the plane. I was going through it, and your note was in there. I just wanted to call you back and say you were right." As a twenty-something staffer, I thought that was quite astonishing.

Bowmaker: What were the main lessons that you took away from your time at the Council of Economic Advisers?

Orszag: I learned that the CEA is a very important entity in helping the White House do its job better. It is remarkable. The structure is such that many of the senior staff members are academics who work there for a year or two and then rotate back, so it is hugely beneficial for academia to gain a perspective on how government actually works. Just as true is the fact that it is very important for an administration to have easy access to state-of-the-art academic economics. I think the current chair of the CEA, Jason Furman, is a tremendous example. He has done a phenomenal job of churning out high-quality, rigorous, and detailed white papers on everything across the board, from corporate structure and inequality (which I wrote with him)[1] to

---

1. Jason Furman and Peter R. Orszag, "A Firm-Level Perspective on the Role of Rents in the Rise in Inequality," paper presented at the "'A Just Society' Centennial Event in Honor of Joseph Stiglitz," Columbia University, New York, October 16, 2015.

the criminal justice system. It is a credit to the Obama administration that they're letting him run with it.

As Director of the Congressional Budget Office

Bowmaker: Why were you attracted to the position at the CBO?

Orszag: That's a dream job for someone with my background and interests. It is pretty much unprecedented, at least to my mind, to find somewhere like the CBO that not only has a massive amount of intellectual firepower but is also doing work that is directly relevant to important policy questions. It's been said that being director of the CBO is a challenging position, and there is no doubt that you have to deal with a great deal of pressure. But others have also described it as the best job in Washington, and I think that is the more accurate description.

Bowmaker: How did you balance being someone with strong policy views at the CBO, while at the same time being part of an institution that is supposed to be nonpartisan?

Orszag: What I tried to do at the CBO was to make it more open from the following perspective. Suppose you were a conservative Republican who wanted to accomplish X, or you were a liberal Democrat who wanted to accomplish Y, but you didn't know which levers to push to move toward your desired outcome. I felt like it was our job to help raise the curtain a little bit and help you migrate towards your goal, whatever it might be. I used the analogy, which many people at the CBO frankly didn't love, of the game of Battleship. In the past, people would say, "B14," and the CBO would reply, "Miss." So then they would say, "C22," which would be a hit. In both cases, though, the congressmen or senators didn't know why it was a hit or a miss, and they expressed their frustration. And so I tried to provide a bit more transparency and clarity. It was a case of saying, "Here are the policy interventions that would help you accomplish your objective," rather than saying, "Your objective is the right thing"—which is the typical meaning of someone having strong policy views.

As Director of the Office of Management and Budget

Bowmaker: When did you meet Barack Obama for the first time, and what were your impressions of him?

Orszag: Sometime in the 2004 to 2006 range when I was at the Brookings Institution, I was delighted to receive an invitation to meet Senator Obama. When you visit a senator, you always have to ask, "Where should I sit?" so that you don't sit in his or her seat. When I asked him, I remember he said, "Wherever you like." And then when we actually sat down, he said, "I've been looking over the Brookings website…" He had been reading our academic papers and wanted to talk about them, which I would say is highly unusual for a senator, and I remember at the time just thinking, "Wow, this guy…"

Bowmaker: How were you approached to become director of the OMB? It is well known that you didn't want to take the position because of your previous experience in Washington, which consisted of a lot of infighting. What made you change your mind?

Orszag: During the late summer of 2008, I was approached by some former colleagues. They were putting together transition teams, and their attitude was more of the ilk, "Would you be interested in…?" My response was, "I don't want to say no, but I have an important job now that I'm enjoying." Those conversations continued until immediately after the election, when the president's chief of staff, Rahm Emanuel, reached out and said, "You've got to do this." And so while I was happy with my work at that time, when a president asks you to go do something like this, you should generally go do it.

Bowmaker: Did President Obama make it clear what he wanted you to do for him?

Orszag: Yes. It was very clear that, in addition to the economic crisis, health care was going to be a big part of his first term. That is truly one of the most remarkable things that President Obama accomplished, and it was great to be asked to become involved.

Bowmaker: Was it established that you would have direct access to President Obama during your tenure? If not, how did you go about achieving this?

Orszag: My view has always been that if someone thinks you're useful, you'll have an audience with him or her. On the other hand, if you're not found to be useful, then all the guarantees and promises and reporting lines on paper in the world when someone is busy aren't going to get you very far. In other words, whatever is negotiated in advance is often a waste of time, because what matters is the content once you're in the seat. It is true that there were some attempts to curtail my access to the president, but inevitably a great deal of that type of positioning always takes place—which in retrospect just looks silly. Bob Rubin was famous for giving up personal face time with the president, and I think that just enhanced his stature internally. The general rule of thumb in the White House is that people will be fighting over access to the president, and that's something I could have handled better. Because of my previous experience in Washington, I knew it would be present, but I think I adopted a bit of a tit-for-tat approach, which in retrospect was unnecessary. In other words, you could argue that certain aspects of the process were far from optimal, but it's also the case that I could have responded better to the smaller things that really don't matter so much. That's on me.

Bowmaker: When I spoke with Austan Goolsbee, he told me that President Obama could have been an economist in a different life, such was his feel for the subject. Do you agree?

Orszag: The short answer is yes. Most good lawyers, like him, have an intuitive grasp of economics. Frankly, any intelligent adult who has been through various professional experiences often has that as well, because in today's world, you are exposed to economics all the time. I think the bigger challenge is taking that analytical framework and applying it to a job like the presidency of the United States that is unlike anything else. And it takes time to adjust, irrespective of your background. It is often forgotten that it took the Clinton administration a couple of years to get into any sort of rhythm.

Bowmaker: How did you and the president work together to get the Affordable Care Act from an idea to legislation?

Orszag: The first question was whether to do it at all. To the president's credit, he basically said, "Despite the fact that we're still clearly fighting the Great Recession, we're going to do it"—which, in retrospect, was the right thing. Those who say his focus should have just been on "jobs, jobs, jobs" overlook the fact that we had just enacted a massive stimulus bill, so the opportunity cost from a legislative perspective was pretty low. Congress wasn't going to do anything more on that front anyway. The second point is that there was a great deal of backbiting in the health debate about whether we should just do coverage expansion, or whether that should be combined with cost containment, or whether it should be deficit neutral. I always thought that the only political way of getting it done was to have the coverage expansion combined with the cost containment. And that was certainly the president's view.

Those on the left who believed we shouldn't have talked about costs at all weren't only ignoring the politics but were also being somewhat myopic. First of all, the bill would never have passed the Senate. Moreover, with regard to the progressive arm of the Democratic Party, if you did nothing to try to improve the 2020, 2030, and 2040 debt trajectory, then ultimately the programs that you care about—like food stamps and Social Security—would have been the ones ultimately under the most pressure.

Those on the right were obviously concerned that the deficit would blow up, and I remember being viewed skeptically by the deficit hawks for saying that health reform was entitlement reform. Yet the experience since then has been better than even I would have hoped, and this is a topic near and dear to my heart. The long-term fiscal outlook has improved fairly substantially, not entirely because of health care cost growth, but in no small part because of it. Now, it was possible to just cut provider rates—which is the traditional method of saving money in Medicare, but one that's also pretty ephemeral and not structural. It was only by changing the structure of the payment system that you would make sustained progress. And that couldn't get enough votes, in my view, without the coverage expansion. In other words, it wouldn't be possible to get something through Congress that was going to fundamentally change how health care was paid for without some coverage expansion being associated with it.

Bowmaker: Can you describe President Obama's frustration during the process?

Orszag: I think at some point he became frustrated about delivery system reform and cost containment because we kept telling him that we were doing everything we could, yet the CBO were continually saying, "We don't think this is going to do very much." The problem was that what we were proposing was very much out of the box, and the CBO is better at doing estimation when they can just say, "You just cut the reimbursement rate by X…"

Then, of course, the media commentary became, "This is all about coverage and it does nothing on cost," which was not really accurate if you take the time to look at the legislation. And so I do think President Obama became frustrated over both (a) the realization that the CBO was not going to say this was going to do what we thought it might do and (b) the press narrative. And by the way, so far it looks like we were basically right—that the legislation has done, if anything, more than expected to shift the delivery system in a good direction.

Bowmaker: During his presidential campaign, Barack Obama was adamantly opposed to individual mandates in health care, but he changed his mind when he became president. Why do you think this happened?

Orszag: Mario Cuomo once said we campaign in poetry and govern in prose. I think it's as simple as when the president worked through the details of an actual legislative proposal, the benefits of an individual mandate became clearer.

Bowmaker: Do you agree that there was significant policy disorder during the early part of the Obama administration?

Orszag: The reality is that we were dealing with a massive financial crisis and a new administration. When you put those two things together, it's not surprising that we found ourselves in a messy situation. If you look back at the history of other crisis-type moments, such as the Great Depression during the FDR [Franklin D. Roosevelt] administration, it always seems chaotic. It's only with the benefit of hindsight that you're able to say, "Well, of course this is the way things turned out."

In general, then, one piece of advice I give to people about working early on in an administration and/or dealing with a crisis is just to expect and tolerate that kind of uncertainty and disorder. It is inevitable. As I say, in retrospect, things will appear better and calmer, and I think that's the case now, too. Perhaps I have selective memory failure about my time in government, but when I look back on it, what are the big memories that stick out in my mind? We got the stimulus through, and we got health reform passed. All the things that can consume people in the moment, like "this" infighting or "that" infighting, seem pretty unimportant. And maybe that teaches us the perennial larger life lesson: we should realize the bigger picture and try to ignore the daily annoyances.

Bowmaker: Did your previous experience as head of the CBO help in your work as director of the OMB? Overall, how would you describe your relations with the CBO when you were at the OMB?

Orszag: I do think my previous work at the CBO helped while I was at the OMB, both in terms of understanding what the CBO does and in terms of Hill relationships. The relations between the CBO and the OMB occasionally became heated, especially during the health reform debate—mostly for reasons I discussed before—but in general were good.

Bowmaker: Overall, how would you describe your relations with the Council of Economic Advisers and the Treasury when you were at the OMB?

Orszag: The economics team had some differences of opinion, as any team would. I view that as a feature rather than a bug—if everyone thought exactly the same way and had the same views, what's the point of having a team?

Bowmaker: Why did you leave the OMB?

Orszag: There were multiple motivations. I had spent two years at the CBO and then a year and a half at the OMB, where I had done what I had wanted to do in terms of helping get health care reform enacted. The time had come to move on.

General Thoughts on Economic Policymaking

Bowmaker: Which fallacies, misconceptions, or misinterpretations affect policy debate in this country?

Orszag: It's not always the case that the masses are foolish, which tends to be the academic perspective. I'll give you two examples. In health care, academics argue that medical malpractice has no bearing on variation in costs, yet every practitioner says it's the most important factor. I think the academic literature is asking the wrong question, which tends to be of the form, "Do we see a correlation between costs in places in the US where liability, conditional on malpractice, is either higher or lower?" The answer is there is basically no correlation. But that misses an important point—which is that if I'm a doctor, I don't really care if my liability is $5 million, $10 million, $15 million, or $20 million. Even in the most restrictive cases, those numbers are still very high. I think the problem instead is the standard for being found liable in the first place, as opposed to the consequences, which is the main focus of the academic literature. The standard is typically "customary practice," but nobody knows exactly what it is, which leads to social contagion among doctors. That means if you're doing a lot of X, I will do a lot of X—in part because I mimic you, but also because that defines customary practice, especially in areas where the definition is *local* customary practice rather than *national* customary practice.

Another example of where academics tend to be dismissive of the popular view is free trade. For years, economists have been saying to everyone, "You don't know what you're talking about. Clearly, free trade is a good thing." I think it's well appreciated that, on average, it is indeed true. But what is meant by average here? Perhaps, in average *dollar* terms, it is true, but not when we consider the average *person*, which is more important politically. The lesson I take away is that the academic community should at least make sure that the empirical facts are so firmly on their side on this issue, otherwise the typical person will distrust the expert, and any accompanying mockery will be justified.

Relatedly, the policy world that's connected to academic economics tends to exaggerate the role of trade agreements on trade. Again, the academic view is that these agreements are good for trade. But let me give you an example that I find very illuminating. Up and down the Eastern Seaboard, ports are being deepened because of the larger ships that the expanded Panama Canal will now be able to facilitate. That could have as big, if not a larger, role in terms of trade with Asia, for example. In other words, we put all the emphasis on trade agreements and neglect the relevance of technology and transportation costs in driving trade outcomes.

Bowmaker: To what extent do you think that behavioral economics can inform policy debate?

Orszag: It's a very positive development that the White House and the UK government are sponsoring behavioral labs, because I think policy can only be better informed when the economic model being applied is not the one found in Econ 101. In my view, behavioral economics is attractive in many situations because it better predicts human behavior and outcomes than using a purely rational framework. My favorite example relates to enrollment in 401(k) plans. In most of those plans, workers don't participate unless they actively choose to. Under automatic enrollment, however, workers who fail to sign up for the plan become participants automatically. A number of economists, like Brigitte Madrian and Dennis Shea, have shown that automatic enrollment has been extremely effective in raising participation rates among workers, particularly among those who had previously the lowest participation rates.[2] How do you explain those results using the purely rational economic model? It is very difficult. One problem with automatic enrollment, though, is that it can mean that some workers simply passively keep the default contribution rate over time, when they might otherwise have chosen to contribute at a higher rate. But Richard Thaler and Shlomo Benartzi have devised something called the "Save More Tomorrow" program, in which workers agree (or not) up front that future pay increases will go towards additional contributions. They showed in one study that it led

---

2. Brigitte C. Madrian and Dennis F. Shea, "The Power of Suggestion: Inertia in 401(k) Participation and Savings Behavior," *Quarterly Journal of Economics* 116, no. 4 (2001): 1149–1187.

to a significant increase in contribution rates over time for those who participated relative to other 401(k) participants at the same firm.[3] If you want to change behavior, then you better understand why it is happening, and I think that's where the behavioral economics perspective is very attractive. But, frankly, its policy influence so far has been pretty limited. I think part of the reason is that it's not easy to find many more results from behavioral economics that are so compelling. Are there 20 clear-cut empirical findings like those of Madrian and Shea? Possibly. But are there 150 of them? I doubt it. And so when you combine that fact with the policy inertia that exists, then it shouldn't be a surprise that behavioral economics hasn't, up to this point, had a broad-scale impact.

Bowmaker: In your undergraduate thesis at Princeton, you wrote about the relationship between the Federal Reserve and Congress, and one of your conclusions was that "it is clear that Congress suffers from a lack of understanding of even the most rudimentary economics."[4] Twenty-five years later, do you still agree with this statement?

Orszag: That's a great question. I would say there are two countervailing trends. On the one hand, polarization is affecting Congress, which makes it difficult to have fact-based, intelligent debate. On the other hand, the rise of data journalism found in publications like the *New York Times* and *Vox* has meant that many members of Congress are responding to empirically driven, more popular discussions. But that's not an easy question for me to answer because these days I am spending more time with executives and board members than people from Congress.

Bowmaker: Which aspects of the institutional framework for making economic policy in this country work well, and which need to be reformed?

Orszag: One important issue for the economic agencies to address is how to recruit talent. The CBO, for example, is struggling to win horse races because the outside opportunities for economists have simply exploded in recent years. The government in general is suffering from that competition. But

---

3. Richard H. Thaler and Shlomo Benartzi, "Save More Tomorrow™: Using Behavioral Economics to Increase Employee Saving," *Journal of Political Economy* 112, no. S1 (2004): S164–S187.
4. Ryan Lizza, "Money Talks: Can Peter Orszag Keep the President's Political Goals Economically Viable?" *The New Yorker*, May 4, 2009, accessed March 9, 2019, https://www.newyorker.com/magazine/2009/05/04/money-talks-4.

when you consider the executive branch of government, the problem there is that many very talented people don't want to serve in positions because the confirmation process is a roulette phenomenon. Look at economists like Larry Summers, Janet Yellen, Alan Blinder, and Laura Tyson. They were in their midforties around fifteen to twenty years ago. They had some experience in government, clearly liked it, and wanted to serve in government again. And you can probably add another thirty to forty other economists like them. But I'm now in my late forties, and if you look at my cohort, I think that number is small—I could probably count those people on one hand. It's true that reflects a variety of forces, but I do believe it includes the fact that the confirmation process has become a major challenge.

Personal Reflections

Bowmaker: How did your personality affect your style and approach as a policymaker? For example, you have been described as being supremely self-confident when you were OMB director. Do you agree?

Orszag: I remember when that showed up in a press article somewhere. It's interesting because it's one thing when you can at least recognize the character when they write about you, but it's another when you have to say, "What are they talking about?" [*Laughs.*] And so "supremely self-confident" is not how I would describe myself, and I'm pretty sure that most people who know me well would agree with me, too. When I believe in something, I do try to convey my conviction, and maybe that comes off as "supremely self-confident." But frankly I mostly think that description was just bad journalism.

Bowmaker: What were your strengths and weaknesses as a policymaker?

Orszag: My connectivity to the think tank world, including my health care research, was a benefit, as was my experience at the CBO and my resulting relationships on Capitol Hill. We also had a president who liked empiricism, so my background was appropriate for that setting. In terms of weaknesses, I would include both the way I responded to the internal dynamics of the policymaking process and how I misjudged the nature of the economic recovery. I believed the macroeconometric models were right in that the recovery would be V-shaped rather than L-shaped. That was the big, substantive thing I got wrong. I did realize the mistake that I made by around mid-2010. In both cases, I like to think that having more life experience and a more varied professional career would have helped. I was still relatively young when I became OMB director.

Bowmaker: What value has public service had to you?

Orszag: Huge. There is nothing like it in the world. I remember reading a book called *The Wise Men*, which was about those who had served in government in the 1950s.[5] For example, Robert A. Lovett, who was [Harry] Truman's secretary of defense, found the day-to-day existence of earning a living after he returned to the private sector to be a difficult transition. Serving in a high-level government job is both an exhilarating and challenging professional experience. You have to deal with enormous time pressure, constant intrusion from the media, and very complex problems. As people say, "The issues wouldn't be reaching you if they were easy to solve."

---

5. Walter Isaacson and Evan Thomas, *The Wise Men: Six Friends and the World They Made* (New York: Simon and Schuster, 1986).

Lael Brainard (*right*), when undersecretary of the treasury for international affairs, meeting with President Barack Obama in the Oval Office on June 4, 2012. Also pictured are Timothy Geithner (*left*), secretary of the treasury; and Mike Froman (*center*), deputy national security adviser for international and economic affairs.

31   Lael Brainard
Born 1962, Hamburg, Germany

Lael Brainard graduated with a BA
with university honors from the College of Social Studies at Wesleyan
University in 1983 and obtained both
an MS and a PhD in economics from
Harvard University in 1989.

Brainard first worked in management consulting at McKinsey and
Company. She then joined the Sloan
School of Management at the Massachusetts Institute of Technology (MIT),
where she was an assistant professor
and then an associate professor of
applied economics between 1990 and
1996. Brainard was a White House Fellow between 1994 and 1995, and after
leaving MIT, she served as the deputy national economic adviser, chair of
the Deputy Secretaries Committee on International Economics, and deputy assistant to President Bill Clinton. From 2001 to 2008, Brainard was
vice president and founding director of the Global Economy and Development Program and held the Bernard L. Schwartz Chair at the Brookings
Institution.

She then served as counselor to Secretary of the Treasury Timothy
Geithner in 2009, and she was undersecretary of the treasury for international affairs from 2010 to 2013. During this period, she was the US representative to the G20 [Group of Twenty] Finance Deputies and G7 [Group of
Seven] Deputies and was a member of the Financial Stability Board.

Brainard took office as a member of the Board of Governors of the
Federal Reserve System in 2014, to fill an unexpired term ending in 2026.

I interviewed Lael Brainard in her office at the Board of Governors of
the Federal Reserve System in Washington, D.C. It was the middle of the
afternoon on Monday, August 29, 2016.

Background Information

Bowmaker: Why did you become an economist?

Brainard: Growing up as a child, I moved around quite a bit. I lived behind the Iron Curtain both in Poland and in East Germany prior to unification. I was struck by how much the opportunities afforded by society differed depending on a country's institutional and government structure, the extent of democracy and civil society, and the role of markets. Later, I learned the importance of economic integration in helping to not only bring about a better standard of living, but also to foster aspirations for a much more open and free society. And so I have believed for a long time that the US has a dominant role to play in terms of inspiring citizens in other countries to increasingly demand accountable government institutions.

Entering the Policy World

Bowmaker: What does an economist bring to the policy world that others do not?

Brainard: What I like about economics as a discipline is that it is very rigorous and applies systems thinking. It forces one as a policymaker and social scientist to not only be internally consistent and coherent with the recommendations one is making, but also to continuously validate those recommendations by reference to data.

Bowmaker: Your first taste of public service was when you were a White House Fellow in the 1990s in the Clinton administration. What did you learn during this time, particularly from Laura Tyson, for whom you worked?

Brainard: First of all, I arrived at the White House when the National Economic Council [NEC] was relatively new. It was trying to bring to the economic arena the kind of policy integration and interagency coherence that the National Security Council had been providing for nearly fifty years at that juncture. And so I thought the institutional goals were very compelling, because economic policymaking at the federal level had become very important. Laura Tyson had come from the CEA [Council of Economic Advisers] to take on the mantel of director of the NEC, and she could see how to use that policy coordination function to provide more rigorous recommendations to the president, to bring all of the Cabinet agencies together around a set of recommendations, and to ensure that those recommendations were grounded in appropriate data. I very much supported those efforts.

A week or two after I got there, we were in the early phases of the Mexican peso crisis, and that episode required the White House to work very closely with the Treasury and Mexican government—I was the coordinator—to come up with a response. One of the lessons we learned was the importance of having standing crisis fighting tools. We asked Congress for a crisis fighting fund that would help stabilize the Mexican financial markets and thereby prevent spillovers into the US markets, while Mexico in turn would be required to undertake very important institutional and policy reforms. But the political dialogue that was necessary for members of Congress to get comfortable with such an idea itself spilled over into the market arena, as these things tend to do. It became clear in that episode, then, that it was crucial for there to be some standing crisis fighting mechanisms because at the height of a crisis, it is not a reasonable thing to ask Congress to authorize new facilities. But by the same token, the debate and dialogue can be market destabilizing. And so that set of lessons ultimately led us to use standing authorities, and then to work closely with the international partners. That has always been a very important part of my thinking in all the financial crisis fighting that I have done since—from my work in Asia or the euro area, or to seeing it applied to our own circumstances.

Bowmaker: Did you get a sense of how President Clinton felt about the US's response to the peso crisis?

Brainard: I do remember that my first close interaction with President Clinton and his team of advisers was during the response to the peso crisis. His own response was just the kind one would expect from a chief executive, which was to recognize that it was deeply in our interests to help Mexico find a path to stabilize their markets and to democratize their institutions. He also started talking about how this set of actions—providing temporary bridge loans to Mexico—polled unfavorably with 90 percent of the US population, but he was going to follow through because it was the right thing to do. In the end, his instincts proved outstanding. In our system, there are some decisions that do weigh heavily on the shoulders of the president, and that was certainly a canonical example of where it was all negative from a short-term political point of view—but looking at the medium term, it was clear that we had to stabilize the economy of our nearest neighbor to the south because of the potential negative spillovers to us if we hadn't done so.

Bowmaker: Were you able to get a sense of President Clinton's operating style during your initial interactions with him?

Brainard: Yes. I'll give you an example from just after the midterm elections of 1994, when the president found himself confronted with a very radically changed political environment in which he would no longer have support from the majority in Congress. We were preparing him for his trip to the APEC [Asian-Pacific Economic Cooperation] meetings that year, and I was present at the briefing. I remember that he was listening, but he needed only a tiny fraction of his brain because he is a very, very quick study. And then he launched into an analysis of the election and what it would mean for his policy agenda—in particular, how it would impact the things that he could and couldn't get done. It was all off the top of his head and very impressive.

Bowmaker: Your first major government appointment was as the deputy national economic adviser and chair of the Deputy Secretaries Committee on International Economics during the Clinton administration. How did this come about?

Brainard: Gene Sperling took over at the NEC at the beginning of the second term, and his expertise was on the domestic policy side, so I think it was just a natural thing for him to want someone as a deputy who was very comfortable with overseeing the international arena. That would help make his tenure at the NEC integrated, and together we could continue to establish the agency as a policy coordinator and manager of policy execution. The section of the NEC that I worked with went hand in glove with the National Security Council [NSC], so I think on the part of Sandy Berger, the NSC adviser, there was a sense that my assuming the deputy role would provide the kind of ongoing continuity that had been developed between those two agencies.

Bowmaker: During your role, how useful was your academic and consulting research?

Brainard: I have always tried to bring my research to bear on policy activities and decision making, in general. When I was in the private sector at McKinsey, I worked in an interesting variety of industries, many of which had been challenged by international competition and were in the process of either adapting or finding themselves unable to continue to thrive. And as an academic at the business school at MIT, I would seek opportunities to walk around factory floors or to meet with people who were engaged in industry-specific research, to continue to ground my thinking in how firms operate internally. For example, if you are a senior executive at a large private-sector firm, you are likely to respond to incentives differently than government civil servants or government decision-makers might assume. For me, then, it is very helpful to have a much more granular sense of the effect of government on the private sector and similarly to understand how the dynamism of the private sector can be reflected in government policy.

Bowmaker: You then spent eight years at the Brookings Institution, where you founded and headed the Global Economy and Development Program. Which aspects of your work at a think tank proved to be most useful to take into the rest of your career?

Brainard: Brookings was a good moment to step back and reflect on how some of the largest and most dynamic emerging economies were affecting some of the assumptions that we had been making in the economic arena. And so during that period, I spent a lot of time—in particular looking at China, India, and Brazil—trying to think about how to better incorporate some of these markets, as well as emerging markets, into local governance, and how to better reflect their growing economic importance into some of the international institutions that were so paramount in my financial crisis work.

I also thought very hard about how the emergence of those countries would affect the challenges faced by different types of workers in the US economy, whether they be in the manufacturing or services sectors, or whether they be high school or college educated. In particular, I developed a very good sense of China's effect on the US economy by looking at just the size of the workforce and the distortions that I saw in currency markets and capital investment patterns. That certainly informed my work when I arrived at the Treasury.

As Undersecretary of the Treasury for International Affairs

Bowmaker: How did you come to be appointed undersecretary of the treasury for international affairs?

Brainard: I was originally slated to go over to the State Department, but in the wake of the election I received a call from the White House asking whether I would be willing to instead contemplate joining the Treasury to help Secretary Geithner, since the financial crisis was raging at that point, and his hands were overfull. Of course, I was happy to accept such a great opportunity.

Bowmaker: As principal policy adviser to Treasury Secretary Tim Geithner, did he make it clear what he wanted you to do for him?

Brainard: I had spent a very rich and lengthy period at the White House interacting with the Treasury, including when Tim Geithner was undersecretary, so since I already knew what the role entailed, we didn't need to have a very complicated set of discussions about it. But I do think the view of Tim and his chief of staff, Mark Patterson, was that the financial demands on the domestic front had to be his dominant focus—which meant he needed someone on the international side who could hit the ground running from day one and take a huge amount of the burden off the team in the front office that was already stretched very thin.

Bowmaker: As someone who had previously held the role, did Tim Geithner offer any advice about the position?

Brainard: That's a good question. Along the way, there were moments when he gave me advice on particular policy initiatives or challenges that laid ahead of us. And, of course, he weighed in on policy directions that he wanted the country to take. In general, I would say his approach was for the United States to lead by the quality of their ideas rather than by resting on their laurels. That accorded very well with my own inclinations, and I think he also brought a quite activist approach to the role, which similarly was something that was well aligned with my own instincts. We didn't see problems as resolving themselves—rather, we would push our team, as well as ourselves, to continue to work hard to get international partners to either accept our proposals or to work with us to modify them in ways that could actually be implemented to strengthen the global economy. We recognized that the US economy was flat on its back and needed as much of a supportive international environment as could be possibly created.

Bowmaker: Would you agree that asserting economic leadership was a challenge in the wake of a financial crisis caused by what may be termed "American preferences in economic and financial policy?"

Brainard: One of the earliest things I did when I came into the role was to participate in trying to both finalize our G20 agenda, and then to reach agreement on those items that we thought were most important. They included fiscal support and financial reform of certain types. As you suggested, many countries wanted to lay the blame for the very precarious state of global financial markets and terrible state of global aggregate demand, growth, and trade at the feet of the United States. So I thought it would be most effective to assume a posture of humility and to acknowledge the deep flaws in the US regulatory system, in US financial markets, and in US economic policy that certainly created the crisis in our country, and then to take responsibility as a team for putting solutions on the table. My hope was that by being humble about our own past mistakes, and by not shying away from taking responsibility and being accountable, our negotiating counterparts would be more willing to hear our proposals based on their merits.

Bowmaker: Was the task made more difficult given that the US's economic advantage over the rest of the world has declined in recent years?

Brainard: A number of our counterparts—senior officials, finance ministers, and perhaps even leaders—did want to critique both the American approach and American economic system. But at the end of the day, nobody else was willing to step up and play a leadership role. I think the reality is that the US recovery was the most important objective for most of those same countries. They wanted to see a resurgence of US demand and a resurgence of US financial resilience, because that was crucial for their own economic strategies. And secondly, while it was easy to critique the US, there was no country with a serious plan that wanted to put itself forward as the proposer of solutions, and so in that sense it still fell to us. Now, we did work very closely in the first instance with the UK, because they were chairing the London summit. During that period, they had their own incredible story to tell on financial regulation, so they certainly weren't any stronger than we were. But similarly they did take it upon themselves to put proposals on the table. On the other hand, there were other countries, like China, who were activists within their own borders and not at all willing to take the lead in proposing solutions for the world. And, of course, it wasn't too much longer after the London summit that the continental Europeans began to grapple with some of their own problems.

Bowmaker: How difficult was it to make the case to Congress that the US needed to be so deeply involved in other countries' finances?

Brainard: It varied. Over the course of the first few years of the recovery, we asked the development banks to work with us, and at the behest of the G20, to put a lot of trade finance on the table, because it had essentially collapsed at that point. And the amount of money that they were able to come up with was materially important for many emerging markets and poor countries in particular, who were finding it difficult to sustain their safety nets at a time when both trade and growth had fallen. Since the development banks stepped up into that breach, it was only natural that we would then go and propose to recapitalize those institutions because they were really stretched. But there was a general assumption at that point—we are talking 2010 and 2011—that there was no way Congress would be willing to fund new capital for these institutions. In fact, I think historically we had never gone and asked Congress for recapitalization of every single one of the development banks. And not only was it an unprecedented ask, but we were dealing with a Republican majority of the House and a Democratic majority of the Senate. And so, contrary to all predictions, you can imagine how delighted I was to be able to work equally with committee leadership in both the House and Senate to make sure those institutions were reauthorized and funded.

While it was relatively easy to make a compelling case to Congress that in order for the US to thrive, the rest of the world had to thrive, too, it was a bit more difficult as we entered the euro area crisis. That was not the typical kind of financial stabilization case in the sense that the euro area as a whole is quite a wealthy part of the world. And it was less obvious to members of Congress that we should help intervene, given that we had our own needs, and that certainly led to a complicated set of discussions. On the one hand, they did acknowledge that the euro area mattered hugely to American vitality and financial stability, but on the other hand, the rationale was less clear for why the IMF [International Monetary Fund] should be backstopping in Greece, as opposed to having the Europeans be responsible for the members of their own monetary area. I was sympathetic to that argument.

Bowmaker: You have been described as a tough negotiator. Do you agree?

Brainard: In general, people do think I'm polite [*laughs*]. But I accept that when I go into a negotiation, I usually know what I want to get out of it, because that has been based on agreement ahead of time through the interagency process of the White House. And I usually arm myself with a lot of deeply researched knowledge about the priorities of our negotiating partners. What matters to them politically? Where are they in their own political cycle? What matters to them economically? How much authority do the individual players have? If they do have the authority to make commitments, is there some kind of parliamentary procedure needed to ratify them? Given the best possible information on these questions, I will then try to get the best possible outcome.

Bowmaker: How do you handle difficult people during negotiations?

Brainard: First of all, you have to understand whether you are dealing with a personality issue, or if it's the case that your negotiating counterpart is at risk of losing their job if things don't come out the right way. In other words, are they much more constrained than you realize? But I also tend to employ self-deprecating humor and diversion sometimes in negotiations. The G20 meetings are probably the best example. If there is a big time zone change in the host country, they'll tend to wear everybody down with a full day of meetings that are really just a recitation of talking points. And then they'll have dinner followed by negotiations at 10 o'clock in the evening. For someone like myself who has flown into Asia, for example, you're already at a huge disadvantage because of the time zone, and so in those circumstances, you have to remain very detail-focused and recognize that in the room you have many different countries with many different interests and levels of knowledge. You have to make clear that there's not a single word or sentence that you're just going to let go—that you're going to hang on to the very last second. With that in mind, then, I think making jokes along the way can help you get what you want. For example, in the early years, I was sometimes the only woman in the room, which meant I was already seen as a slightly unusual kind of creature. And since people don't know what to make of you anyway, I think when you make even the corniest of jokes, they tend to laugh, it diffuses tension in the room, and they then try to arrive at a compromise.

Bowmaker: How about dealing with cross-cultural differences?

Brainard: I certainly try to be as attentive as I can to the reality that English is not the first language for most of my negotiating counterparts. So I'm very aware that I'm at a huge advantage, because those negotiations are in English in almost all cases. This means that I aim to be as open and as flexible as possible in offering up alternative English words. Remember, I grew up as a child in an environment that always involved multicultural settings, such as schools, so I try to be as sensitive as I can. But I also recognize that there is a real risk that the underlying substance of what I am attempting to say may be lost in translation, so I am very much attuned to avoiding that kind of unforced error.

Bowmaker: In your experience, to what extent can concepts from game theory be used to explain behavior in international negotiations?

Brainard: First of all, you are often going to confront the same negotiating partners, which means there is usually some element of repeated game negotiations. And my general sense is that there is a little bit of a temptation for somebody who is young, and maybe a political appointee in government for the first time, to see the potential for a big win. But if it's such an overwhelmingly lopsided win, then it may actually end up playing out badly politically for your negotiating partner, because you can no longer negotiate with them on subsequent issues. In other words, it is not really a win for them. So in reality, I always tried to give everybody something they needed to make it politically feasible and always tried to give as much honor and dignity in the process as possible. In a game-theoretic framework, that rules out zero-sum wins.

Bowmaker: How useful were macroeconomic models in your work in international economic policymaking at the Treasury?

Brainard: When you're living in a world of imperfect information, I think it is very difficult to make good policy judgments without having an underlying model in your head. For example, when we first realized the extent of the Greek debt crisis, we quickly put together an analysis of how this might spill over more generally into the euro area and then came to the table at the G7 meetings with not only a much greater sense of urgency than even some of our European counterparts, but also with a pretty good feel for where the solutions might lie to arrest the contagion. That was based on an understanding of financial stability concerns, how macroeconomic considerations like debt dynamics and growth dynamics interact, how you might have spillovers within a currency area, and how a currency area might constrain the potential responses. In other words, it was an underlying set of economic models that helped inform the analysis and recommendations, even though we were not successful in the end [*laughs*].

Bowmaker: You have worked under two different presidents—Bill Clinton and Barack Obama. How would you compare and contrast their operating styles?

Brainard: I've had an unbelievable opportunity to work with two of the smartest presidents, and perhaps world leaders, in modern times. They both brought the ability to grasp very complicated material in depth very quickly and to make assessments about how they wanted to come out on a set of very complicated decisions very quickly.

In their interactions with foreign leaders, President Clinton used many more of his own personal ideas in deciding where to take a conversation and to pursue a certain goal, whereas President Obama has very clear objectives— agreed to ahead of time—that he wants to accomplish in a meeting. That means with President Clinton, for example, he might just decide to go at an issue from a completely different angle, leaving his advisers sharply inhaling and thinking, "Is he taking this agenda to the finish line that we want?" But they almost always breathe a sigh of relief at the end, because his approach tends to be even better. It's just that you can't know that *ex ante* [laughs].

General Thoughts on Economic Policymaking

Bowmaker: Which fallacies, misconceptions, or misinterpretations affect policy debate in this country?

Brainard: I think sometimes what is seen as a fallacy is actually referring to how the same set of policy developments might be experienced very differently by different groups of people. For example, take the trade arena. There is nothing in the economic theory of trade that says it is good for everybody. Yes, it can deliver benefits on aggregate, but it is also redistributive in that some groups stand to win, while others stand to lose. And unless there is a mechanism to spread the benefits, then it is not incorrect for certain groups to argue that trade is not in their best interests. In the US context, certain groups of workers have faced absolute losses because they lose further through curtailment of health or retirement benefits. In my view, we haven't traditionally coupled trade policies with meaningful approaches to help those who may be adversely impacted.

Personal Reflections

Bowmaker: What are your strengths and weaknesses as a policymaker?

Brainard: I try to be fair-minded and challenge my own preconceptions, which is something that I ask others to do as well. For example, I'll meet with people here at the Fed[eral Reserve] and say, "This is how I see the economy, but tell me what I am missing." And similarly I try to be emotionally detached, which is something that I have to work hard at—how to separate my own personal investiture versus the policy outcome itself. And that will mean that if a superior policy proposal comes to light in a process, I will try to be open-minded enough to perceive its advantages. Since I tend to have very strong inclinations to avoid any form of bias, I will make sure that I'm allowing myself to listen to alternatives in a reasonable manner. But I can also be impatient, which comes partly from being very outcomes-oriented, so I have to check myself a little bit there, too, because I realize that there are benefits to focusing on the process itself.

Bowmaker: As a policymaker, which decisions or outcomes were most gratifying?

Brainard: I've been very, very focused on currency manipulation and distortions, and by the time 2013 rolled around, I had proposed and succeeded in getting some very strong language in both the G7 and G20 about exchange rates. I feel good about it because we started with nothing on imbalances in currencies.

Our analysis, recommendations, and intense engagement were also all in the absolutely right direction in relation to the euro area crisis, but we couldn't get the fiscal piece agreed in a meaningful way because of the time it took for the ECB [European Central Bank] to be able to get the political support it needed. As I say, though, we came at it with the correct spirit.

In addition, we had some great successes in proposing new funds in climate change and food security that were agreed and implemented while I was at the Treasury, and of course recapitalizing and reforming all the development banks was also a big plus. And we helped create a big regional infrastructure initiative called Power Africa, which was another good outcome.

Bowmaker: On the other hand, there must be some things that, in hindsight, you'd like the opportunity to do differently. What are they?

Brainard: When the China WTO [World Trade Organization] negotiations were ongoing, we did not foresee that China's exchange rates would become so badly distorted, and so we failed to put in a strong currency chapter. At the time, though, China was coming off the Asian financial crisis and had maintained a relatively strong value of its currency throughout that episode. Instead, we put a lot of energy, subsequently wasted by the [George W.] Bush administration, into getting a China-specific safeguard of Section 421 of the Trade Act of 1974, which allows the US to take action against Chinese import surges. So I think that imbalance was one that introduced an enormous distortion into the global economy for a good eight years leading into the financial crisis, because China quickly developed a hugely undervalued currency and a current account surplus that essentially went from zero to 10 percent. There were clear material effects on US manufacturing workers, given the sheer size of China and the extent of the undervaluation. Even though it didn't have a currency chapter, Section 421 could have been potentially used for exchange rates, and that is one of my regrets.

Alan Krueger (*far right*), when chairman of the Council of Economic Advisers, meeting with President Barack Obama (*far left*) in the Oval Office on August 10, 2012. Also pictured are Mike Froman (*second left*), deputy national security adviser for international and economic affairs; David Plouffe (*third left*), senior adviser to the president; Jacob Lew (*third right*), chief of staff; and Gene Sperling (*second right*), director of the National Economic Council.

32   Alan B. Krueger

Born 1960, Livingston, New Jersey
Died 2019, Princeton, New Jersey

Alan Krueger graduated from Cornell
University in 1983 with a BS in industrial and labor relations and obtained
an AM and a PhD in economics from
Harvard University in 1985 and 1987,
respectively.

Krueger was an assistant professor of economics and public affairs at
Princeton University between 1987
and 1992. He then served as Bend-
heim Professor of Economics and
Public Affairs at Princeton until February 1, 2019, and he was the James
Madison Professor of Political Economy there until his passing on March 16, 2019.

In government, Krueger served as chief economist of the Department of
Labor between 1994 and 1995, during the administration of President Bill
Clinton. He returned to government during the administration of President
Barack Obama and served in the Department of the Treasury as assistant
secretary for economic policy and chief economist between 2009 and 2010.
He also served as chairman of the Council of Economic Advisers (CEA)
between 2011 and 2013.

I interviewed Alan Krueger in his office at Princeton University, in Princeton, New Jersey. It was the middle of the afternoon on Monday, August
8, 2016.

Background Information

Bowmaker: Why did you become an economist?

Krueger: When I started college I had the intention of being a lawyer. And I
was particularly interested in labor law. I attended the Industrial and Labor

Relations School at Cornell, and I fell in love with economics when I was there, in part because I realized that it was a tool for achieving important social goals. That's such an obvious point, but I had no idea about it at the time. For example, I remember studying the economic impact of the Civil Rights Act, and I just told this to Lyndon Johnson's daughter a week ago. It was mind-opening that economics could provide insights on such a critical issue. I also took a course by Bob Hutchens on social insurance, which really excited me. Bob inspired me to study economics and to become interested in social insurance programs. And then I worked on my senior thesis with John Burton, on worker's compensation insurance.

By my junior year I thought there was a good chance I wanted to go to graduate school in economics, but I still ended up applying to both law school and economics PhD programs. I was just lucky that I got into Harvard, and I was very fortunate that Larry Summers returned to the university at the same time that I started. He was a great adviser. Richard Freeman was also there, and Larry Katz arrived at the end of my four years in graduate school. He became a great friend and mentor. So I have to say that things all just fell in place.

Entering the Policy World

Bowmaker: What does an economist bring to the policy world that others do not?

Krueger: I think economists bring a lot to the policy world. For one, a knowledge of the policy. For another, a commitment to the view that the policy should be evaluated using appropriate tools. I'll never forget when I was on the Clinton health care task force in 1993. I went to a meeting as the head of a group that was supposed to do economic analysis of the health care plan. I remember talking to a woman who worked for [Treasury Secretary] Lloyd Bentsen and was a senior person at the Treasury Department. She said, "I like to get the policy right first and then worry about the economic impact." I thought that was completely backwards, and she said it without a hint of irony. I believe you need to start from basic principles and think about what it is we want to achieve, what are the best means for achieving it, what are the unintended consequences, and what are the magnitudes of certain effects. It is extremely valuable to understand how to weigh those trade-offs. But I don't think economics has a monopoly on wisdom—there is a lot that we don't understand about the economy. In that respect, it is important that economists not be doctrinaire when they work in the policy process as well.

Bowmaker: Your first major entry into the policy world in Washington took place in 1994, when you were appointed as chief economist of the Department of Labor. How did this appointment arise?

Krueger: It came about because Larry Katz was the first chief economist. [Secretary of Labor] Bob Reich created the position because he wanted to give economists an opportunity to learn about how the government worked. And I think he also wanted the credibility from some top-notch economists on the staff, particularly in dealing with the National Economic Council [NEC]. He also told me that he wanted to have an economics group to keep him honest—to fact-check him and to make sure he wasn't making errors.

Larry did the job for about a year and a half and did it extraordinarily well. When he was ready to return to Harvard, I suspect that Bob Reich told him to draw up a list of candidates to replace him. I came down for an interview with Bob Reich, whom I had never met previously. He asked me a bit about my research and about my views of the economy. What I remember most, however, was when the meeting ended, he said he wasn't sure which direction he wanted to go in. I thought the interview had gone went quite well [*laughs*]. I didn't think it was pro forma, but I was a little surprised that I hadn't won him over. Anyway, a couple of days later he offered me the job.

Bowmaker: By this stage in your career, did you view yourself as having strong policy positions or simply as a hired professional serving the president?

Krueger: I viewed myself as someone who was part of a policy team with certain goals for the economy. But in terms of the means for how you get there, I think I'm open-minded. And I think it's also important—and difficult for an academic to get his head around—that if you work for a Cabinet member, then your job is to support that person. Now, you could disagree with him and explain why, but you have to make sure you share the same goals as your principal. Then your job is to determine how you meet your principal's goals as best as possible. That's the way I always viewed my role.

I'll give you an example. When I was nominated for assistant secretary of the treasury, I had my hearing with the Senate Finance Committee. Senator [Max] Baucus was chairman of the committee, and he said, "Professor Krueger, can you just tell us two or three of your highest policy priorities?"

I replied, "Senator, I have one priority: I just want to see the economy improve. We're losing far too many jobs, and too many people are suffering. Frankly, I'm willing to consider anything that'll help. I think it's too important a time to come in with strong suppositions about what's going to work." He said that was a very good answer [*laughs*].

Bowmaker: As you began your position, was there anything that frustrated or surprised you?

Krueger: When I worked in the Labor Department in '94, '95, I never thought I'd come back to the government. I didn't particularly enjoy it, and I didn't think I learned all that much that was useful for my academic career. I thought before I went to Washington that I would learn about some policies I didn't know about, that it would teach me new regression discontinuities and provide some new opportunities for conducting research. There was some of that, but much less than I expected. And I also thought that we would be expanding some of the Great Society programs on the margin, but we ended up defending the New Deal. The reason for that is because Newt Gingrich and Dick Armey took over the House of Representatives. And it was the first time the Republicans had controlled the House for forty years. They wanted to roll back a tremendous amount of the social safety net and worker protections. And so we spent a great deal of time protecting and defending programs that I think are very much in the interest of the US economy and American workers.

I would say the one thing that did surprise me the most was how powerful the Treasury is in economic policymaking. It is next door to the White House.

I was also surprised by how confrontational it all was and how difficult it was to try to find some common ground with Congress. Everything that we did was viewed by both sides as an existential fight. I thought that was very unfortunate, because it was not the environment that I was accustomed to. While I now have a thicker skin, my view is that economics should aspire to be a science. We can have our differences, but there are boundaries in terms of debating, disputing, and resolving them. In dealing with the political environment in Congress, the boundaries were totally different, which was both frustrating and unpleasant.

Bowmaker: After leaving the role in August 1995, you swore that you would never return to Washington because of the pressure and sense of overwhelming responsibility. How did Tim Geithner manage to convince you to take on the position of assistant secretary of the treasury for economic policy almost fifteen years later?

Krueger: Yes, I told my wife that if I ever say I want to go back, remind me of the bad experiences I had. But when I joined the Treasury Department in 2009, it was a very different environment. Tim Geithner called me up in December 2008 and told me he had just been nominated for treasury secretary. I said, "Congratulations." And he replied, "I don't know if that's the right word. But it's going to be my job, and I'd like you to be assistant secretary for economic policy." I didn't know Tim particularly well, and I asked him what the job entailed. I said, "Is it like being the chief economist?" He told me that he could give me that title, too, which helped to define the job. But the sales pitch he made was, "Come to the Treasury Department, and we'll do big, consequential things. This is a time when the economy really needs your help." That was a sales pitch I couldn't turn down—the economy was contracting at an 8 percent annual rate, and we were losing 800,000 jobs a month.

I went through vetting, which is a long and tedious process. And I had learned from my experience in the Clinton administration that the beginning of an administration is a better time to participate because more is achieved then, and also more of the practices and precedents get set then. On a personal level, I think people make more binding relationships as well. There is a greater sense of going through the trenches together in the beginning. When I started at the Labor Department, Larry Katz had already laid a lot of the groundwork, and so this time I said I would really like to begin on day one. But the vetting took a bit of a while. I remember calling up the chief of staff in the first week of February 2009, which was only about two weeks after inauguration. I said, "Look, if this is going to be a six-month process, and you're going to wait until after I'm confirmed before I can start, you can find someone else. I know a lot of important issues are being decided now, and the economy needs a lot of help." Because of my urging, they were able to clear me a lot sooner, so I started February 10. And it was like drinking from a fire hose!

Until you are in the midst of a crisis, one has no idea what it's like—how many issues the Treasury Department and treasury secretary have to juggle. It felt on many days like the entire US economy was dependent on the Treasury for support.

Without having been in the government before, I think it would have been extremely difficult, because as an academic you work in a very different environment. For example, the way a memo is supposed to look is just not something academics are accustomed to. Government meetings are very different from those in academia—knowing who the different individuals are, and knowing the different departments involved on a particular issue. And so I think having served as the chief economist in the Labor Department helped to prepare me for the whirlwind of policymaking that I joined at the beginning of the Obama administration.

Bowmaker: Which innovations did you introduce at the Treasury when you held the position of assistant secretary of the treasury for economic policy? I am interested, in particular, to learn about the monthly sessions that you provided to the noneconomists working for Geithner.

Krueger: That innovation, which I carried over to the White House, related to when Tim Geithner asked me to give him a weekly briefing on where we were in the economic recovery. Tim asked for the briefing to cover: What's changed in the last week? What's stronger than we think? What's weaker? How does our forecast change? I said that I would be happy to do it, but that I don't think the economy changes so quickly that it makes sense to do it on a weekly basis. And even if it does change that quickly, we don't get the data in real time to know whether it changed on a weekly basis, so we should do it on a monthly basis. He reluctantly agreed and said he would come to the first couple of briefings, which would make all of the other senior staff attend. Tim actually never missed a briefing, so he must have found it useful.

At the first briefing I needed to do some basic things, like explain what GDP [gross domestic product] is, its different components, and their weights. And I did a basic shift share analysis by having a particular component of GDP grow at a certain rate and then multiplying that by a share to get the contribution to GDP growth to a first order. I think it was very healthy for the department, because everybody was talking about the economy at that time and people were experts in their areas, but they weren't trained as economists or hadn't studied economics for a long time.

And it was good for my staff, too. Briefings like that often focus on the risks to your forecast. What can go wrong? I think that's an important exercise. But what I tried to do was to list the upside potential also. Why only look at the downside? I had my staff go through an exercise where we would actually poll them and say, "What do you think is the upside potential?" That practice continued after I left, and when I got to the White House, I thought I would do the same thing for the president.

There were a couple of other innovations that seemed extremely valuable to me at the time. One is that I suggested we do *pre-mortem planning*. I learned this from my friend and colleague Danny Kahneman. It's based on the idea that people tend to be overly optimistic—they don't think about what can go wrong. Instead, we should put people in a frame of mind where you say, "OK, this failed. We now have a crisis on our hands. Let's do a pre-mortem. What are all the reasons this policy could have failed?" Then you try to address them beforehand. I did it with the Treasury debt auctions. Suppose you have a failed auction—what do you do? The fear I had was there were some auctions that were thinly subscribed at certain times. And if you have a failed auction, it could lead to a financial panic. And so how do you calm the markets? Who writes what the secretary says? Where does the secretary say it? When does the secretary say it? Go through those steps so that you're prepared. The example I like to use is 9/11 and Rudy Giuliani. He was, in my judgment, a completely failed mayor who had one good day—on 9/11. In retrospect, it was a good day only because his words were soothing, and he prepared for that. But his planning was awful. He put the city's control center in the World Trade Tower: it got destroyed when the buildings came down. He should have known that that was a target. But what he had done was prepare for the event of a disaster, and he had scripted out language like, "We don't know what the ultimate death toll will be, but it will be a burden too great for any of us to bear." Those turned out to be very soothing words at the time. And so I approached a lot of the programs that we were working on with that same type of mind-set. How do we think about what might go wrong? I went around to some of the assistant secretaries or people running the programs and said, "What would we do if this fails?" and "What are the steps that we would take?" I think that's very useful for thinking about how to avoid problems and how to deal with them should they occur.

Then I did some other useful things which should have already been done. For example, the Treasury Department has close contact with several of the financial regulators. The treasury secretary meets regularly with the chair of the Securities and Exchange Commission [SEC] and with the head of the Commodity Futures Trading Commission. We had the Flash Crash in early 2010, when the stock market fell 800–900 points in a day and then regained a lot of what it lost. We didn't know what was causing it at the time. One obvious concern was that it was some type of a cyberattack. Secretary Geithner said to me that I should figure out what's going on. But

I didn't know who to call at SEC—I didn't know who their chief economist was. And so after that experience I had a regular monthly meeting with the chief economists of all the regulators, who didn't know each other.

Bowmaker: In those two years working for Tim Geithner, what did you learn about his approach as secretary of the treasury, as well as his mode of thinking?

Krueger: I have enormous respect for Tim. I think he handled the crisis extraordinarily well and with tremendous grace. He never let the criticism bother him. He knew his goal was to put a floor under the financial system so that it could support a recovery, and he's written that the great irony of financial crises is that the solution requires rescuing those who were involved in bringing about the crisis in the first place. But if you don't do that, the innocent suffer much more. I think his heart and his sympathies were with the innocent bystanders who are the collateral damage from the financial crisis. He wanted to reduce that damage as much as possible and put the economy on an upward trajectory.

Tim was a dedicated public servant. He was criticized for having come from Wall Street and for being too soft on Wall Street, but he never worked on Wall Street. I think he was too slow to respond to those criticisms. Yet he was able to float above it in a way in which very few people can. The only other person I know who was also able to rise above the criticism and remain at peace with himself is President Obama. They have very similar personalities. Tim was able to take a perspective of, "You know, the people who are criticizing me are just doing what is in their role; they don't fully understand the issues. They're doing it often for political reasons. I'm here to do a job, and I will do it." His equanimity in that environment was remarkable to me and was a very valuable lesson.

He was multitasking all the time and was a very quick study. I thought he must have been a great student, because he was able to absorb and internalize what he needed to know very quickly. Of all the hearings I went to, I think there was only one when I felt obligated to pass him a note. I had put a statistic on inequality in his written testimony, and a congressman said, "That's really remarkable. Would you mind repeating that?" He was having a little trouble finding it, so I handed it to him. It was seamless.

Bowmaker: When you were at the Treasury, Larry Summers was director of the National Economic Council. How much interaction did you have with him?

Krueger: Larry called me up before I started at the Treasury and said, "I'd really like you to take this job. And even though you might deserve something higher ranking, I'll look out for you." And he did. He would often call me—when he probably should have called the CEA—if he missed the unemployment insurance number or the GDP number the night before it was released. He certainly trusted me on things where he thought I was knowledgeable. There were some issues where I had expertise which he didn't know about, and it was not always easy to persuade him that I actually knew something, but I always felt like he had my back. I enjoyed working with Larry.

One time he asked me and my staff to help him write a big speech he gave at the Peterson Institute [for International Economics]. It was tremendous fun. Larry ran an operation which was a little bit like a fraternity house. I would go to his office every night at 6:30, but he would not be able to get down to focus until 7:30. His staff would order some food using his credit card, and he would say, "How did the sushi get here?" And they'd explain that they used his credit card to buy everybody dinner [*laughs*]. Larry would drink a Diet Coke, by the way. And we would go into his office with some research which he would browse through. It had to do with why Okun's law was off—companies were overreacting because of fear. Larry would look through it and compliment us by saying, "This is a substantial amount of work. I am impressed. Here are five other things to do…" I would tell him, "Oh, I thought about doing that…" And so we would do that work for the next day. Then he would take out his tape recorder and dictate his remarks. At a certain point, he would get to an area where he would say something which I didn't think was quite right. I would have an expression on my face that looked a little bit pained, and he would say, "What's the matter?" I would tell him why it wasn't quite right, and he would look really unhappy and think about it. Then he would figure out a clever way to say what he wanted to say, and a smile would appear on his face [*laughs*]. This would go on until about midnight, when he would finally hand the tape to his young staff to type up. The next day he would start over with the research that we did. He would look at his remarks, say, "More active verbs and shorter sentences when you transcribe it for tomorrow," and dictate it through again. Around 11:30 at night, quarter to 12:00, one of his staff members, Manasi Deshpande, who is in a wheelchair, would say, "I'm sorry, Larry, I need to leave. The last handicap bus leaves at midnight." Larry would tell her in an empathetic way, "I can give you a ride home." People don't see that side of him.

Bowmaker: Did you get a sense of how Larry Summers interacted with the other members of the economic team when he was director of the NEC?

Krueger: There were times when Larry and Tim disagreed. And I'm sure Tim found it frustrating to have to go over the same arguments with Larry. There was one meeting where Tim said, "Larry, you're so good at arguing either side. What are the arguments you would make on the other side of this issue?" I said to Tim as we were driving back, "I thought that was really clever." He replied, "I've been wanting to do that for fifteen years" [*laughs*]. But they got along quite well. I would describe them as almost like brothers joined at the hip. When they argued, they would soon patch up. It's the way I get along with my brother. We used to fight, and then ten minutes later we were the best of friends [*laughs*].

As Chairman of the Council of Economic Advisers

Bowmaker: Can you describe how you came to be appointed chairman of the CEA in 2011?

Krueger: I like to tell people I took a sabbatical from the government for ten months, after my term of service came to an end in November 2010. I felt like I gave a solid two years, and I also thought that public policymaking was going to slow down because of the upcoming midterm elections. When I came back to Princeton, it was relatively easy to reengage in research and particularly in teaching, because I taught a course on the Great Recession. I didn't expect to return to Washington because I thought that the president would have other choices for chairman of the CEA. But as fate had it, I got a call from Mark Patterson, the chief of staff of the Treasury—the same person who I had said to, "Look, if you can't get me in the building in the next week or so, why don't you choose somebody else?" He's a real gem at the Treasury Department and someone who doesn't get the credit he deserves for the role he played in rescuing the country from the financial crisis. Anyway, Mark told me that the president was going to reopen the search for chairman of the council and asked if I would be interested in being a candidate. My wife wasn't thrilled about the idea, so I had to tell him I'd think about it. Then when I got back, I said, "You're certainly welcome to consider me, but I don't really know enough about the type of arrangement that the president wants." However, it turned out I was the only candidate at that point.

I came down to Washington for meetings with Pete Rouse, the deputy chief of staff, and with Jack Lew, who I didn't know particularly well then. And I also met with Austan Goolsbee. Bill Daley, chief of staff at the time, was not available, so he asked me to come down a second time, and I'll never forget what happened. It was early July of 2011 and I was at the NBER [National Bureau of Economic Research] Summer Institute in Cambridge, and I was going to fly from there to Washington. I realized that I brought a really old pair of shoes with me—the heels had worn through, and they were dangerous to walk on. It turns out that there's a shoe cobbler right across the street from the hotel where the NBER meeting was being held, in Kendall Square. And so I left one session and was taking my shoes to have them fixed when I bumped into Rebecca Mas, the wife of one of my colleagues, Alex Mas. Rebecca and I were chatting, and I saw out of the corner of my eye that a toddler had gotten away from his mother and was several feet ahead of her. He was running and had a big grin on his face. Then I saw a big SUV barreling up the street, and it made a right into the parking garage next to the Kendall Park Mall. The kid was going to get run over by the car, so I instantly ran and grabbed him. And fortunately I was big enough that I was over the grill, so that the driver saw me and jammed on the brakes. It was a remarkable feeling. There was a homeless guy around the corner who saw what had happened and said to me, "You're a hero. Could you save me?" I didn't really know how to respond, but I felt really good when I met with Bill Daley. I thought to myself, "Even if I don't take this job, these are the kind of everyday contributions that make a difference in people's lives. And if I take this job and it's a frustration, and nothing good passes through Congress, I still made a difference in the world."

When I came down to see Daley, we met over lunch, and ten minutes into it, President Obama walked in. I suspected it was planned. He said, "Oh, Alan, so nice to see you. I didn't realize you'd be here. You look great. You have that glow that people have when they leave the administration. What have you been doing? How long are you going to be here? I'd really like to meet with you if you can." Of course, for the president you have as much time as you need [laughs]. My afternoon was free, so I said, "I'd be happy to meet with you anytime." "That's terrific," he replied. "I'll ask my secretary to try to set something up." So I went over to the Oval Office. He said, "Look, I would offer you the job today, except I'm not allowed to until the FBI [Federal Bureau of Investigation] finishes the vetting. I think you're the right person for the job, so let's not waste time. Tell me everything we should ask for in the jobs bill next month. Don't think about the politics of it. The politics is my job. You focus on the policy. What are the best economic proposals to make to create more jobs? What'll give us the most bang for the buck? What's the best thing to do for the economy?" We had a wonderful discussion. And it was a discussion I thought about on the way down to Washington, because I had hoped, of course, that I'd meet with the president or other senior advisers. I had a list of things to raise with him, and he was terrific about it. He followed up on all of them—in particular some of the proposals for unemployment insurance reform.

Bowmaker: At your meeting with Bill Daley, did you ask for anything in advance that might help the CEA if you took the job?

Krueger: I thought I would ask for just a couple of things that were very important for the CEA. One was moving all of the offices back to the EEOB [Eisenhower Executive Office Building]. After 9/11, the staff of the CEA were moved to G Street, behind the World Bank. I said to Bill Daley, "I think it's important for the CEA to be all in the same building and for us to work together." He replied, "Oh, I didn't know you weren't in the same building. I'll make sure that that happens." And we got great office space. The chairman's office in particular is on the corner of Pennsylvania Avenue and West Exec, which overlooks the White House and Blair House. And the members have excellent offices with a great view of the White House, and the staff are not far away either. We have nice conference rooms as well. Sometime during the [George W.] Bush administration they named a conference room after David Bradford, who served on the CEA for the first President Bush and sadly died in a fire. I thought it was good for continuity to keep the name. I thought it'd be nice to have all the former chairmen and members come back and celebrate that we had moved back to the EEOB. All of them—people like Alan Greenspan, Charlie Schultze, and Martin Baily—said, "This space is nice, but we used to have a view of the Washington Monument." They were so nostalgic for their space. I would trade a view of the White House for a view of the Washington Monument any day [laughs].

The thing that was difficult to ask for related to getting access to a 7:00 am meeting at the White House, which involved all the key political staff. Tim Geithner would go to those meetings, too, and Larry Summers did as well. But CEA was not invited. I thought it was important for us institutionally to try to get into those meetings. Austan told me, "You should ask to get into them. But he'll tell you that it's not policy, it's politics." So I said to Bill Daley, "I understand there's this 7:00 am meeting. I think it would be very good for the Council of Economic Advisers if I could go, because that would help me understand the agenda. And we could help support the president's agenda that way, too." Bill replied, "I've got nothing against you coming, but it's more of a communications and political meeting, not policy. You won't find it useful." I told him, "I'm not a morning person, and if it's not useful I'll stop coming. I'd much rather be able to sleep in for half an hour in the morning." I had him over a barrel [*laughs*]. In the end, I never missed a meeting, and Bill kept to his word—he permitted me to keep going.

Even the stuff discussed at those meetings that wasn't relevant was often very interesting to me. For example, I learned about the killing of Colonel [Muammar] Gaddafi in Libya at those meetings. But I think there were decisions made where it was quite important that I was present, like those relating to regulations where I knew about their benefit-cost analyses. I had more influence because I was able to go to those meetings, and I understood better the way the White House worked.

Bowmaker: Apart from Austan Goolsbee, did you ask for advice from former chairs of the CEA either before taking on the role or after accepting it?

Krueger: I spoke early on to Alan Blinder. He's been a close colleague, good friend, and also tennis opponent for almost thirty years. In fact, I talked to Alan probably before I talked to anybody else. He and I arranged to play tennis shortly after Mark Patterson, the chief of staff of the Treasury, asked me if I was interested in the job. Amazingly, Alan knew that they had reached out to me. My guess is they asked Alan for advice about who they should call, and I know Bill Daley is a fan of Alan's and trusts his judgment. I felt a little bit uneasy because I wanted to keep things as confidential as I could, but given that Alan already knew, I didn't see any harm in having further discussion with him. And he offered me very good advice. He said one thing—which I hadn't full anticipated—is that you'll grow as a person if you do it. I thought more about what I would contribute, and I didn't think about the lessons that I would learn, which was extremely valuable.

Alan Greenspan called me up when my nomination was announced. I had become friends with Alan when I worked at the Treasury Department, and I still have lunch with him at least once every two months. Greenspan told me that the most important job he ever had was being chairman of the CEA for Jerry Ford. He loved the range of issues and told me about how he advised him. He also said that you need to learn the best way the president absorbs information. Is it by discussions? Is it talking to him during a football game? Is it sending him memos? Can he read graphs? Everyone absorbs information differently, which I knew already because I had worked for Bob Reich and for Tim Geithner. But I think that is extremely important for an adviser in any capacity.

I also spoke to Glenn Hubbard, who was supportive. I spoke to Marty Feldstein often. Marty, more than any other of the past chairmen, made an effort to come down to Washington and to meet with me.

I often say that I have more in common with the past chairmen and members of the CEA than I do probably with random economists in the profession. We care about the same issues and know about the same issues. The range of disagreement is not nearly as great as many people might expect. The main commonality at the time, of course, was the fact that the economy was still in a lot of trouble. Economists had different views about how to get out of that trouble, but I think that there was more pessimism than in retrospect was warranted. There was a tremendous amount of fear that there would not be sufficient momentum at the end of 2011, beginning of 2012—especially once the sequester kicked in—to allow the economy to continue recovering. In other words, there were worries that we would fall into a second dip. I remember at one point asking Marty Feldstein about the upside. He, by the way, was very encouraging. I think by nature he is an upbeat and optimistic person. But when he looked at the economy he just saw a lot of negative signs. And so I asked him, "Well, why do you think I should still take this job?" He was glowing in recalling his time working for President [Ronald] Reagan. He told me that it was an experience that continued to give benefits throughout the rest of his life. It changed his outlook and the network of people with whom he interacted.

Bowmaker: How did you think your approach would be different to that of your predecessor, Austan Goolsbee?

Krueger: I had a couple of views about following Austan. One is I'm not as comfortable doing media as he is. I'll tell you a funny story related to it. When I first met the president, he said to me, "I think you'll be great for this job because I've worked with you and know you. I think you'd be perfect at this moment when we're so focused on trying to increase job creation. But there are some things that come with the job that relate to defending the administration. For example, did you watch the Republican debate last night? Did you see when they asked, 'Would you be willing to take $10.00 of spending cuts for every $1.00 of additional tax revenue?' None of them raised their hands and said they would take that deal. That's insane. We need to bat that down, and so some of the job is responding to the other side when we have disagreements. Austan Goolsbee was the best person in the administration, including me, on television. You'll need media training." His presumption that I wasn't going to be as good on television as Goolsbee was funny [*laughs*]. At least he was being honest with me.

Bowmaker: How did you set about establishing a comfortable working relationship with President Obama?

Krueger: I knew him beforehand, which helped. The other thing—and it probably helps every CEA chairman—is the fact that I didn't have a constituency. In other words, CEA is the only Cabinet member which doesn't feel obliged to represent some special interest. I think presidents know that. When President Obama announced my nomination he said, and the words were beautiful, "I rely on the Council of Economic Advisers to give me unvarnished, objective advice about what's going to do the most good for the most people in this country." So I had that benefit of the doubt, which I think CEA has earned over the years, and which I felt like I maintained with President Obama. But it is still a challenge to figure out what's the best way to advise the president if you're the CEA chairman. I thought I would start with the same process that I had at the Treasury of having a monthly briefing on where we are in the recovery. That consisted of a cover memo and about 20–25 pages of PowerPoint slides.

I'll never forget the following story, because I was going to brief the president in person in a meeting on a Monday, and on the Friday before, I sent it to [Director of the NEC] Gene Sperling, who thought it looked good. I said, "That's great—I'm going to put it in the president's briefing book over the weekend." But Gene told me, "I don't think you should do that. I find meetings often go better if people don't see the material in advance. If they see it in advance, they might ask unrelated questions." I thought, "That's crazy. If he sees it in advance, he'll ask more thoughtful questions." Plus you still don't know whether the president had time to read his briefings, and so I put it in his briefings book. He walked into the meeting, gave me the thumbs up, and before he sat down said instantly, "Alan, those slides were fantastic. I want you to do that every month." That gave me an enormous amount of information because (a) I knew that he read them, (b) I knew that he liked them, and (c) because he had read and concentrated on them, I didn't need to go slide by slide—I could just give an overview and have a discussion. I found when I had briefed the president during the campaign in 2007 that he is brilliant at synthesizing. He doesn't need to review slides after he's seen them, and he doesn't want to be lectured to—he wants to have a dialogue. And I didn't feel the necessity to take up all of the time. I thought I could just summarize very quickly some of the key points, and then we could have a discussion. That briefing went extremely well.

The other thing that I did over time is I had a core set of slides that take some effort to absorb when you see them for the first time. What are things indexed to? Are they indexed to the previous trough or peak? What are you comparing? Which recoveries are you comparing? And when you compare the current recovery to other recoveries, where is it doing well, and where is it underachieving? Why is it underachieving in those areas? Then I had, in addition to the core material, some bonus slides that would relate to topics that I thought would be of interest at the time to the president. For example, if he was going to give a big speech on manufacturing, I would have three or four pages on that sector. What was very interesting to me is I thought the core was really useful, but I wasn't sure about the bonus material. After the election, the president asked me to his small dining room and said, "Alan, I think you're doing a great job and want you to continue. I understand you're going to need to go back to Princeton at some point, so I'm not asking for a commitment for the full term." That was very nice, because for many Cabinet members that's what he asked for. I said, "Thank you, Mr. President. I'm really touched. Are there ways that I could do my job better?" He replied, "I like the monthly briefings, but the core material doesn't seem to change much. The bonus slides are great." I thought there was information in the core material [laughs]. So I changed the balance, and I started to add more bonus material.

The president also told me early on that the most stressful fifteen minutes he had every month was when I came over to brief him on the unemployment situation. I thought, "Oh, my goodness, the president's got Iraq, Syria, and Libya on his plate. The economy's clearly getting better at this stage. Why is this the most stressful fifteen minutes?" But I tried to do everything I could to lower the stress level for him. When it was good news, I tried to brief the president earlier in the day. At one point—and I thought this was totally unfair—he told me that I have a horrible poker face. He once teased me that he could always read the news on my face [laughs].

I thought, "Yes, if I arrive early you can read the news that it's good news, and if I arrive at the time I'm supposed to then it's not necessarily so good."

Bowmaker: How would you describe President's Obama feel for economics? When I spoke with Austan Goolsbee, he told me that President Obama could have been an economist in a different life, and Peter Orszag agreed.

Krueger: I think for the time we were facing, he was an outstanding economist—he made excellent judgments. I think his formal training in economics might have been limited. He was a lawyer and thought about issues like a policy wonk. His father was an economist, and I suspected he had a special spot in his heart for economists for that reason.

I think his intuition for economics is excellent. I'll tell you about an early briefing I was giving to the president. I think it's very important to say, "Look, here's what I think about the economics of this issue. Here's how confident I am. But you should be aware there are other views." This particular issue on international tax policy was really complicated, and the evidence was quite weak. I started by saying, "Mr. President, I was asked to brief you on the economics of this issue. Let me begin by telling you that the evidence is not dispositive." He interrupted me and said, "When is the evidence ever dispositive in economics?" I liked the word "dispositive" because it's a good legal term. I said, "Well, Mr. President, we're much less dispositive on this issue than we are on many others." And so I then went through the logic and economic theory of my position. Someone else at the meeting said, "Mr. President, I know Alan said X, but maybe a slim majority of the economics profession would make a different argument and take the other side." The president cut him off. He said, "Alan's a smart guy and my chief economist" and then repeated what I had said. This person replied, "Oh, I agree with Alan. I just wanted to make the point..." But the president had sent an extremely useful message, which is, "I appointed Alan to be the chairman of the CEA. I trust his judgment." He didn't want to see debates like that in front of him. He preferred it if I reflected the views of the profession and administration on those issues. And I think I did it in a balanced way where I made the other views quite clear—even on issues like the minimum wage, where my work, at least initially, was not the consensus in the profession.

He also would read pretty widely. This bothered some other members of the administration. He's the first president to have an iPad—my good friend Reggie Love gave it to him as a birthday gift. So the president will go on the web and find an IMF [International Monetary Fund] study and ask you if you've read it. On one occasion, I was told, "The president's fishing around for stuff. We need to make sure that we're all aware of what information he has so that we can constrain him." I didn't think that was an appropriate job for me to do. I actually thought it was great that the president availed himself to more information. It is embarrassing, though, when the president hands you an IMF study and you're not aware of it, which happened to me one time. But he also asked me about studies, fortunately, that I was aware of, had read, and could say something intelligent about. And he liked it when I would give him studies to read. What he told me at one point was that he felt like he wasn't getting enough input. One thing Larry Summers brought to the table was a broad knowledge, the ability to inform the president on any subject, and to engage him intellectually. That may have been missing after Larry left. The president once told me, "If you ever see an article you think I should know about, send it to me. Write me a one- or two-page cover memo summarizing it. If I think it's interesting, I can skim the article. Give it to me on Friday evening because I've got more time to read on the weekends." I took that to heart. About every other week I would give him something to read.

Bowmaker: Were your economic philosophies in alignment?

Krueger: By and large. I would say I learned from the president. He believes the rise in inequality has affected consumption. And it's quite a plausible view—one that more and more people are coming around to. And I did some work where I calculated how much the shift in income to the top 1 percent has affected aggregate consumption. It's enormous. And so that's an area where I would say he's influenced my economic view.

Bowmaker: You are a data-driven economist. Do you think this was an advantage as CEA chairman, as opposed to being someone whose academic work was largely grounded in theory?

Krueger: I think being an empiricist helped me to do my job enormously. But I also think that being eclectic helps. I came away much less doctrinaire about the right way to do economics, because sometimes the president would ask me a question and my obligation was to give him the best answer. And sometimes the best answer was from a computational model where the parameters were all made up, but there was nothing else. And I thought it's better to give him the best answer that we have, rather than have some other department just go with special interest. I would try to explain where it was that I thought the evidence and the modeling was more convincing. I did go through an exercise where I looked at all the policies I worked on, which was over sixty. I said to myself, "Did we have any evidence? Any data at all?" Overwhelmingly, we did. It could be about the size of the problem. That would be at a minimum. Then I said, "How much of the time was the evidence observational and germane to the policy we were considering?" That was about half the time. Then I said, 'How much of the evidence was based on a randomized controlled trial [RCT]—the gold standard?" It was 10 percent, so only six of the roughly sixty issues. And finally I said to myself, "Well, in how many cases could I conceive of doing an RCT experiment, where we could actually yield experimental evidence?" That was about half of the time. So I think we can expand on that margin, which will help inform policymaking. But in the middle of a financial crisis you don't want to say, "Why don't we do a random experiment on TARP [Troubled Asset Relief Program] and give some funds to a random subset of the systemically important banks?" I could see how you might say, "Let's exploit this regression discontinuity." But even that's hard, because FDIC [Federal Deposit Insurance Corporation] often wouldn't share information on who just missed the threshold. That was sensitive information.

One thing which also helped was having been editor of the *Journal of Economic Perspectives*, because economists tend to be very narrow and specialized, especially in the US. As the editor of that journal, I had to represent the whole profession—which meant economic theory, experimental research, laboratory experiments, field experiments, and so on. That was extremely valuable, because the chairman of the CEA is responsible for representing the agency on a wide range of issues. Sometimes you can bring someone along with you at a meeting. I remember when I brought Jim Stock [a member of the CEA]. You couldn't imagine a better person to bring along for time-series econometrics or macroeconometric questions. It was Jim's first meeting with the president, and it was held in the Roosevelt Room. Some issues were going to come up which Jim had briefed me on, and I thought it would be nice for him to attend. I prepared Jim by saying, "You're going to sit off the table. You're probably not going to get to say anything." During the meeting, the president asked me a question, and I said, "Mr. President, I'll give you my answer. But I'm going to turn to Jim Stock, who's the world's greatest expert on this, and he can pitch in." I tried to give Jim a heads-up that I was going to call on him, even though I previously told him he probably wouldn't get to say anything [*laughs*]. I gave my answer, and then Jim elaborated a little bit. Then the president asked a follow-up question, and Jim said to the president, "Good question." That's what you would say to a student who asked a good question. The president said, "I know, that's why I asked it." Jim said to me afterwards, "I can't believe I said 'good question' to the president" [*laughs*].

Bowmaker: Related, some of your papers and research findings have been considered quite controversial. Did the experience of having to strongly defend your work help when working in a policy environment where disagreement is part of the landscape?

Krueger: I don't know if it helped. Having been involved in academic controversies has made me somewhat more gun-shy. I find it uncomfortable when people challenge me, and I especially find it unpleasant when people challenge my integrity—because I may get some things wrong, but it's never with ill intent or because I'm pushing a particular view. What I've done in my career to avoid that is I often move on after researching an area, because I think what happens to many economists is they publish a paper that becomes their identity, and then they spend the rest of their career defending it. I'd rather other people defend or criticize it, because I don't want to be someone who is typecast as always in a particular corner. One of the things I tried to do was treat the CEA chairmanship like it was a dignified position, meaning that I didn't need to respond to every criticism from a junior researcher at the Brookings Institution or the American Enterprise Institute. When I worked for Tim Geithner and he got criticized, the communications staff would say, "You need to respond by writing an op-ed." He'd reply, "It's beneath the dignity of the office to respond to it." Now, I didn't go quite that far, but I thought that it was a bit unbecoming for the chairman of the CEA to engage in fights over data, especially with junior researchers. I think that's a mistake some past chairmen have made.

Bowmaker: I was interested to learn that Vice President Joe Biden, when asking you to predict the unemployment rate on Election Day in 2012, said, "The problem with you smart guys—and I include the president in this—is you're too worried about making a mistake. Tell me what's in your gut." What are your thoughts on his view?

Krueger: First of all, I love Joe Biden. He always says, "I'm not an economist. You guys are the economists who have the hard job of putting the economy back together. That's harder than foreign policy." I would tell him, "You're a behavioral economist. You understand human nature far better than the rest of us." He was really a delight for me to get to know. Early on, I flew with him to Iowa, where he gave a speech in the basketball stadium at Iowa State. On the way back, he said to me—and this was at the end of 2011—"What do you think the unemployment rate's going to be on Election Day?" At that time it was around 9.2 or 9.3 percent. I didn't want to give an answer because I didn't see the point, and so I said, "We're going to go through a process as part of the budget, and we'll come up with revised economic forecasts for the budget in a few months." He said to me, and he pointed his finger at my chest, "The problem with you smart guys— and I include the president in this—is that you're too scared about making a mistake. Christy Romer [when Chair of the CEA] said the unemployment rate wouldn't get above 8 percent. She was wrong. So what? I don't care if she was wrong. In your gut, what do you think the unemployment rate's going to be?" And so I couldn't dodge the question. In my gut I thought it was going to be below 8 percent. I thought the pace of job growth would continue, because the economy was going through a natural healing process. And I thought the long-term unemployed would drop out of the labor force, which is a tendency the longer a recovery goes on. I preferred a situation in which they would exit unemployment by finding jobs, and I worked to that end. But I felt that the typical dynamic of labor force withdrawal would take place. So I said, "I think it's going to get below 8 percent." And he replied, "Huh. Huh," and then walked away. Now, I would have thought, "Well, he asks lots of people these questions. I doubt he really remembers what they said." And I can also say as an economist I don't pay too much attention to people's forecasts. Tim Geithner always used to ask me about the blue chip consensus. My view was, who cares about the blue chip? And he would also ask, "What does this guy at Morgan Stanley think?" He seemed intent on knowing what the chatter was.

Anyway, the vice president never followed up with me on that particular issue until October 2012, when the unemployment rate did fall from 8.1 percent to 7.8 percent. I'll never forget we were looking at the report the day before. It was a very good report. And I did the thing that I normally do, which was to reach the president early. He was on Air Force One, and it's not so easy to call the president on that plane. You have to use a secure phone, which is like an old walkie-talkie where two people can't talk at once. The president said, "Alan, you probably saw my debate with [Mitt] Romney last night. I could use some good news. I hope you have a lollipop for me." And I said, "Well, sir, I do. The unemployment rate dropped." I paused a moment for some emphasis, "It dropped from 8.1 per cent"—and again I paused for a moment to make sure he heard the next number—"to 7.8 percent." The president took everything on his desk, and he threw it up in the air [*laughs*]. The photographer gave me a photo of it. He said to me afterwards, "When you were on the phone with the president, we didn't know if it was good or bad news." The president said to me, "Alan, that's great news." And I went into a few more details. I said, "Mr. President, you once told me if it's good news to give you every detail. I'll send you the whole report—all fifty pages." He replied, "Well, that's really great. You're the employee of the month." I thought that I was only the messenger. This was an accumulation of a lot of hard work from many people. The next morning, while I was walking out to the beach on the front lawn of the White House (as they call it, because there are some umbrellas to shade the cameras from the sun), the vice president called me. He said, "I just heard the news. This is marvelous. You were the only one who was brave enough to make a forecast. And you were right. I love you for that."

Bowmaker: Did you have many opportunities outside the formal policy environment to speak with the president about economics?

Krueger: I've only seen the president relax on a few occasions. One was when he went to Camp David, where he was an incredibly gracious host and he loved showing us around. I actually got to play tennis with him—he was my doubles partner. Another was at the inaugural party at the White House after he was reelected. And on Air Force One he could roam around. One time I was in the staff compartment just beyond his office. Once we took off and then got to cruising altitude, I went back and did a briefing for the press on the infrastructure proposals the president was going to make. This was a close connection with the president, because when I first met him in 2007 we talked about infrastructure investment, and he said come back with an infrastructure plan. We were going to the port of Miami, where the tunnel underneath it was built in part with funds from the [American] Recovery [and Reinvestment] Act. I gave the briefing and made a good joke when I said, "Here's a view of where we are in the recovery from 30,000 feet." I came back and was walking into my cabin when I saw a shoe coming from a leg that's sitting in my chair. The president had moved from his cabin to my chair [*laughs*]. And so I took the seat next to him, and we had a very nice discussion. Then we landed. The president went down the front steps, and the staff went down the back steps. They told me that I was going to go in a certain van, and as I was walking over to the van, one of his advance people tapped me on the shoulder and said that I could drive in the limo with the president. I had no idea the president selects who he wants to accompany him.

There was one time when I went into the Oval Office with the jobs report and told him the unemployment rate is elevated, but if you break it down by short-term and long-term unemployment, the short-term unemployment rate's back down to normal. What is keeping the unemployment rate high is long-term unemployment—they're either going to leave the labor force or we're going to help them find jobs. The president said to me, "I imagine that the long-term unemployed are typically middle-aged men who were displaced from blue-collar manufacturing jobs." I went back to my office and started to look into it. What the president said actually describes 6 percent of the long-term unemployed. Twenty-nine per cent at that time were from the service sector. The recession was so deep that long-term unemployment was rampant, and it was almost random who became long-term unemployed once people lost their jobs. I decided that I would put together a memo for the president on long-term unemployment, and that we should have a task force to try to address it. My staff and I put together a 25–30-page document—probably four or five pages of memo, and then the rest were graphs and slides. It was fascinating and extremely useful background for the task force that was then set up. The chief of staff, Dennis McDonough, had read it and said, "Alan, that memo was so excellent, why don't you summarize it at one of those 7:00 meetings?" I did, but I didn't get feedback from the president on it. So when I was next in the car with him, I thought I'd ask him. I said, "Mr. President, did you have a chance to read the memo I sent on long-term unemployment?" He looked at me and said, "We discussed it." I said, "No, sir, I don't think we did." He was very puzzled and then said, "Oh, I discussed it with Dennis." It dawned on me that that was why Dennis wanted me to present it to the senior staff, because the president probably said he thought it was very informative. And the president did a great job summarizing it when I was in the car with him. It was also a good occasion to talk to him about economics rather than television shows, which we sometimes did when we were in the car together [*laughs*].

Bowmaker: Did President Obama always make it clear what he wanted his economics team to do for him?

Krueger: My experience was that the president set very clear directions and wanted us to come back with consensus recommendations on key issues, and highlight where we couldn't agree when we couldn't reach a consensus. That certainly happened with the auto bailout, where Austan Goolsbee and I were on the side that recommended bailing out GM [General Motors] but not Chrysler, while others said bail out both of them. The president listened to both sides, and in retrospect I think he made the right decision. Austan and I were both wrong, and we have written a paper about it.[1]

After the Recovery Act, the president told us to go back to the drawing board because we needed more ideas to strengthen the recovery. That set off a project where I was very proud to be involved. I championed a couple of programs that were part of the proposal, and Larry Summers had the job of kicking the tires. For example, we did an enormous amount of work on a new jobs tax credit to encourage companies to expand on the margin, something like what Jimmy Carter did in the seventies. An enormous amount of research analytical effort went into structuring that program, and Christy Romer has said that it was the best work that she was involved in during the administration. Larry was concerned that there wasn't enough demand and the elasticity of substitution was small. He was focused on income effects, not substitution effects, but after a while he came around to thinking, "Well, I don't love this, but there's a lot of support for it by other people who I respect. And it will give small businesses more money, and they're credit constrained, so it will have something of an income effect." And so he let it go forward. Before he reached that point, there were meetings with the president describing the different policies and telling him that we weren't all aligned yet. The president would say, "Go back to work." I heard that in one meeting, which I didn't get to go to, he was frustrated and disappointed that we hadn't given him options at that point. So I never felt like he wasn't on top of things and giving clear guidance.

Bowmaker: How would you describe your relationship with the NEC during your time as chairman of the CEA?

---

1. Austan D. Goolsbee and Alan B. Krueger, "A Retrospective Look at Rescuing and Restructuring General Motors and Chrysler," *Journal of Economic Perspectives* 29, no. 2 (2015): 3–24.

Krueger: Gene Sperling and I worked well together. He does certain things extraordinarily well, like relating to the press. He once paid me a compliment when he said, "You went out to the front lawn of the White House at least a hundred times and never screwed up." I never felt like I hit anything out of the park, but not screwing up I take as a high praise [*laughs*]. Gene, on the other hand, has an ability to put out a phrase or a quote that really resonates.

He also works very hard. I found sometimes he was disorganized, which was frustrating. And there were some times when I felt like we disagreed, and it would have been easier if he got to my issue sooner. But I think we have similar values. Sometimes we have different views about how to get there. One of the things I also learned is I tend to let the best be the enemy of the good too much. And politics is never going to be perfect. I think that's something that Gene understood better than I did at the time.

Bowmaker: How about your relationship with the Treasury?

Krueger: I thought it would have been better than it actually turned out to be. The Treasury is a little bit of an island to itself in that it has the attitude that it is the lead department when it comes to making economic policy. So it was a little bit easier interacting with the Treasury when I was at the Treasury than when I was at the CEA [*laughs*]. But I tried to do some things which I think were useful for building relationships with the Treasury. Let me give you an example. When I was at the Treasury, my office would receive the GDP and unemployment insurance claims from the CEA the day before those statistics were announced. My office would prepare a memo for the secretary from the bare-bones spreadsheet CEA would provide us, and I would brief him. When I became CEA chairman, I invited my successor at the Treasury, Jane Eberly, over to my office to look at the whole report at 5:30 in a secure environment so she could prepare as much as she wanted.

By the way, I saw the risks of getting the data the day before. The worst thing that could happen to the credibility of the administration is if it leaks out and political people are talking about it. That made me nervous. I told my staff to wait until you see it on television the next morning before sending an email to all the White House staff. I didn't want them to look at the clock and say, "It's 8:30, I can send this." It doesn't matter if you send it sixty seconds late. What are you going to do to make the economy better if you get this sixty seconds earlier? But it does matter if you send it sixty seconds early if the clock is off. Think about it. You can really screw things up, and there have been some mishaps in other administrations. I think caution was correct in that area, so I tried to restrict the number of people who could possibly have early access to the data, such as those in the front office. I didn't want people reading our body language when we had the news. And I wouldn't even call up my wife because I didn't want her to say, "He was in a good mood, which must mean good news."

Bowmaker: Related to the previous few questions, how great was the temptation to compromise or even sacrifice your viewpoint in order to preserve good personal relations?

Krueger: I didn't find that an issue. As I said earlier, the president told me to give him the best economic advice, and that he would handle the politics. He always kept to his word. And Eddie Lazear, by the way—who I consulted after I got the job—told me to stay in my own lane. He said he once ventured into gay marriage and realized afterwards that it's not his job to advise the president on that issue. I thought that was right.

Bowmaker: All things considered, can you give an example of where you, as an economist, or the CEA, as an organization, were able to make a difference?

Krueger: In some ways I think I made a bigger difference at the Treasury. We had a lot of authority at the time because the Democrats controlled the House and Senate, so there are parts of the Affordable Care Act and the Dodd-Frank Act that I could point to that I worked on. There was also the small-business lending fund that was part of the small-business bill, which is a really interesting illustration of how nobody makes a difference in that you're part of a giant team—but the team makes a difference. When the president told us to go back to the drawing board and come up with some new ideas for job growth for the State of the Union address, Tim Geithner convened a small group of us and said, "Blue sky, what would you do to raise job growth and increase credit to small businesses?" Of course, the political people were all thinking about how we could use TARP, but I said, "Look, here's how I would do it as an economist. We've been good at giving capital to banks. Let's give capital to banks at a certain interest rate, say 5 percent. If they increase their lending to small businesses, we lower the interest rate to 1 percent. If they reduce their lending to small businesses, we raise the interest to 7 percent. That gives them an incentive, and it's on the margin because it's based on what they did before." Tim liked it, but Gene Sperling opposed it pretty strongly initially because he felt that we were putting our fate in Congress's hands. He bumped into Austan Goolsbee and said, "Tim asked us for some ideas to increase small business lending. What would you do?" Austan replied, "I would give the banks more capital, and if they increase their lending I'd give them more money." Gene called me up and said, "I talked to Austan, and he had your idea. There's no diversity of opinion in your field." I thought that was hysterical. It just showed that economists have a framework for thinking, so I kept pushing the idea and wrote up a memo on how to do it.

Tim played it a bit coy because he always valued—much more so than me—the implementation risk and burden and the ability of the government to pull it off. But it turned out I had a very important ally. Towards the end of the deliberation process, I was in my kitchen in Princeton on the weekend when we had a critical conference call, including Herb Allison, who was the head of the TARP office that would have to implement this policy. Gene had made his pitch for his policy, and I had made mine. Herb said he liked my proposal but said the only thing he didn't like about it was the penalty if banks didn't increase their lending. He said he didn't like "a disincentive in an incentive program," which was funny to me [*laughs*]. I was willing to compromise and take out the penalty, so Tim called it the Krueger-Allison proposal. We had a meeting on the following Monday, and Gene wanted to re-litigate it. And then he called another meeting the next day [*laughs*]. There were no new arguments and no new evidence in either follow-up meeting. So I said, "Gene, when you see a movie and you like it, you go back a second and third time." We were just rehashing the exact same arguments, but he was just hoping to change his mind. Tim thought that was really funny, because he said his sister had read the same book, *Black Beauty*, three times [*laughs*]. And so Tim stayed firm, Larry was OK with it, Peter Orszag liked it, and the president was very happy with it.

To Gene's credit, he worked on the political side to try to sell it, and it passed almost exactly along the lines that I described. But the implementation was not as good as I had hoped because FDIC dragged their feet in setting protocols, which taught me that you really need to think about the implementation side of things. So while I can honestly say that it was my idea, it was not sufficient—it took an army to get it passed and implemented, which makes what you do in the government totally different from what you do in academia.

Bowmaker: Can you give an example of when the CEA was able to kill a bad idea?

Krueger: Many CEA chairs say that their greatest contribution was killing bad ideas. Greenspan tells me that every time I meet him. But I think it's different when you're there in the middle of a crisis. If you start with the presumption, "Well, the economy's going OK," then the desire to do something is probably going to be an adverse thing. On the other hand, if you're there in the middle of a financial panic, sitting on the sidelines is a mistake. So I had less of that experience.

But there were some bad ideas in the education area. For example, there was a desire to try to punish universities if they were raising tuition very quickly. To me that made no sense. For one thing, many universities give a lot of financial aid. They're raising the sticker price, but low-income students are finding the university more affordable. Secondly, universities do more than educate students. And the way the proposal was laid out would have reduced National Science Foundation and NIH [National Institutes of Health] grants to universities that were raising tuition too quickly. One thing had nothing to do with the other, so that was something I was able to stop.

But by and large, I found that we were looking to do things. For example, in the budget negotiations, we were looking for ways to reduce growth in entitlement programs and looking for ways to raise revenue. There are some ways of raising revenue that are better than others. The idea of a repatriation holiday is one that is not liked by the economic staff throughout the administration. Businesses might love it because it's just gravy for them, but we killed it. And I'll tell you a related funny story. There was a lot of support, as I mentioned earlier, for a new job tax credit. The day after the president said he wanted a tax credit for companies who expanded their payroll by hiring unemployed workers, Senator Chuck Schumer said, "Thank you very much. That's a great idea. Orrin Hatch and I are going to introduce the HIRE [Hiring Incentives to Restore Employment] Act, inspired by the president. If you hire somebody who's been unemployed for more than sixty days, you don't have to pay payroll tax for that worker the rest of the year." That was valued at, say, $15 billion, whereas our proposal was more like $50 billion. And the HIRE Act is not operating on the margin—if you have a lot of turnover, you're going to hire people anyway. It's easy to explain and simple to administer compared to what we wanted. While we thought our program was much more bang for the buck, their program wasn't terrible, and it was a step in the right direction. But I was still a little despondent because that's where all the oxygen went. And amazingly, six weeks later Congress passed it. It was maybe a third of what we wanted in terms of job creation, but it was actually something. Greenspan said to me, "Why are you down about that? You got a third of what you wanted, which is victory. They'll think it's helpful." And I did think it was good because it turned the discussion towards hiring, and I did my best to make people aware of it. When the repatriation holiday idea came up at another time, Gene said, "Why don't we use the money to require the companies to invest more in hiring workers or in investing in infrastructure?" I'll never forget Larry's response. He said, "Gene's idea sits perfectly at the intersection of schlock and policy. He took an idea that we don't like, and he married it with ideas that we do like to make it potentially politically feasible" [*laughs*]. In a way, I also thought it was a brilliant thing that Gene had done. Maybe I was too negative about letting the best be the enemy of the good.

General Thoughts on Economic Policymaking

Bowmaker: As an economist who has used its principles in his work, to what extent do you think that behavioral economics can inform policy debate?

Krueger: Behavioral economics provides a more realistic and more useful model of behavior, and when it comes to public policy, understanding how people respond to incentives is critical. The field was represented in our discussions during the Obama administration—for example, when we talked about how we were going to try to generate more consumer spending and protect investors. I would say the Consumer Financial Protection Bureau is spawned by thinking about behavioral economics. And it also played a role in the Affordable Care Act. Before having a mandate, we had long discussions about whether the default could be that you were enrolled, and that it would be hard to change from the default.

In the midst of a crisis, I think behavioral economics is really important. And certainly when you meet with business people, they represent behavioral economics. We had the former CEO [chief executive officer] of Bank of America come in, and he said that the two greatest motivators are greed and fear. That sounds like a Bruce Springsteen song, but decisions are tied up with emotions, which can be found in Adam Smith's work.

When Robert Lucas gave his presidential address to the AEA [American Economic Association], he said we focused too much on the business cycle and on unemployment and not enough on growth. But if you use behavioral economics and say people's identity and sense of self-worth is connected to their job status and their future prospects, because of hysteresis, you want to much more forcefully address unemployment. That is something that motivated me when I was in government.

Behavioral economics mattered in other ways, too. For example, I learned from Danny Kahneman's work on life satisfaction that people are miserable when they're commuting to work. That influenced my thinking on infrastructure investment, because if people can commute to work faster, mass transit is better for their utility.

Personal Reflections

Bowmaker: What value has your public service had to you?

Krueger: The personal rewards are tremendous. And I think there have to be personal rewards because you're going to get criticized by the press at times—that goes with the territory. You have to hold the view that what you're doing is beneficial for your country, which is something that I learned from Tim Geithner. He could care less what was written in the press. His feeling was that he was out there to do the right thing. If people screamed for him to resign or said he was a tool of Wall Street, he would just chuckle and shrug it off.

Now, there are financial costs. The Treasury Department paid a salary of $152,000 a year, with no summer money, and I had to get a second place to live in Washington [*laughs*].

Bowmaker: How did your personality affect your style and approach as a policymaker?

Krueger: That's a very good question. What I often say is that being an academic and being a policymaker involve very different skills, and some of them are personality related. Lingering is one of those skills. What do I mean by lingering? Hanging around after the meeting to push your agenda, or hanging around in the West Wing to buttonhole somebody. We had someone at the Treasury who used to linger in the West Wing so much that the chief of staff called up and said, "One of your guys is lingering here all day long. Can you bring him back to the Treasury?" It's not something that comes naturally to me. I want to go back to my office and do work. But a lot of the work takes place outside of the meetings. There's a famous saying that when there's a meeting in the government the academics say, "What's on the agenda?" while the real politicians say, "Who else is going to be there?"—because the agenda often changes.

The president once said to me that he doesn't want any drama in his briefings. I'm not a dramatic type of person, so I think that my personality meshed well with his. But one of the things that I observed is that it's easier to get face time with your principal if you're concerned about some imminent threat. And creating drama around these threats can be in someone's interest in terms of making themselves more important. That can happen on the economic side. For example, at one point California thought it had a budget crisis. I believed it was fictitious—they needed to solve their problems, and it would be a big mistake for the federal government to bail them out. But others created tremendous drama around it. They thought it would sink the US economy, and so we needed imminent involvement. I think I had the right view, especially in hindsight, and Larry did a brilliant job of analyzing it and walking it down. But that's an example of how you could create drama around a particular issue. I was never interested in doing that. I think I was always able to keep things in proportion.

Bowmaker: What were your strengths and weaknesses as a policymaker?

Krueger: I was a little reluctant sometimes to speak up, especially early on when I was at the Treasury. And then I went through the experience of seeing some friends who complained about AIG [American International Group] bonuses, and I thought, "You know, I own some of this policy. People are going to remember me for what's happening here." That emboldened me to be more forthright and to argue my positions more frequently and more strongly. But I'm not necessarily the most articulate, and certainly there were times when I felt a bit tongue-tied with the president. And one of the things which shocked me about him was that he was perfectly happy to call on me even though I wasn't on the agenda. He did that at a Cabinet meeting once, and also at a meeting with CEOs. That was a little unusual, because I don't recall him doing that very often with others—particularly at a Cabinet meeting, which tends to be scripted. And so after the first time when he did it and I was tongue-tied, I always thought, "What would I say if he called on me?"

I also tried to make the memos and the emails interesting. If Tim Geithner sent me to a meeting in his place with the president, I would always immediately write him about what happened. And I would try to write it a little bit like a novel, so he would want to read it. And he actually did. He told his special assistant once that he appreciated reading my emails.

And the president was a very good reader. I once told Valerie Jarrett [senior adviser to President Obama] that I had read some of Walter Heller's [chairman of the CEA, 1961–1964] memos to President [John F.] Kennedy. What surprised me is that some of them were quite funny. She said that the president could use some humor. So I started to hand draw a smiley face if an economic report had good news. And I tried to write memos in a style that wasn't just drab—something he would want to read.

I think the president is probably happiest when he's in his study at 10:00 at night and reading important memos with ESPN on in the background. He can be alone with his thoughts. And he's also a good writer. I have always thought that writing is thinking. The people who don't write clearly probably really don't understand the ideas themselves. And in economics it's too easy for people to get by if they write poorly—they can obscure it with math.

Bowmaker: There must be some things, in hindsight, that you'd like the opportunity to do differently. What are they?

Krueger: In hindsight, my biggest economic regret is that we weren't able to get a budget deal at the end of 2012. I think that I should have made the argument that pushing for the right compromise on tax revenue was a mistake. Just to recap, [Speaker] John Boehner started out by saying he is in favor of additional revenue and a reduction of tax expenditures; he never mentioned raising tax rates. He began at $800 billion, and the president was at $1.6 trillion. Boehner went up to a trillion, and the president came down to 1.4. A reasonable compromise, then, was somewhere between a trillion and 1.4. The president reached out to him and said, "Look, there's got to be some way we can make a deal here. We're not that far apart. You can even use a different baseline when you talk to your folks if you want, so you can say it was a trillion." But Boehner walked away because his interpretation was that the president wanted too much tax revenue. I think what I should have done was to make a case that Boehner would not go higher than a trillion.

And another thing is that at one point the Republicans wanted to raise the Medicare age to sixty-seven. The president's view was that's unfair to low-income elderly who haven't had the benefit of life expectancy increasing, which is right. On the other hand, the Affordable Care Act helps them quite a bit. And I think I probably should have argued that a deal could have been reached where the Republicans actually accepted the Affordable Care Act and made it work, especially for sixty-six-year-olds and sixty-five-year-olds. That was a plausible trade for raising the Medicare age and the rest of the budget deal.

But my job wasn't to negotiate—it was to look at different options and to think about their pros and cons. I felt very effective internally in terms of the components that the president put on the table during the negotiations, but I regret that a deal did not happen. I once asked the president if he was frustrated by the budget situation, and his answer was very interesting. He said, "That doesn't bother me anymore. There's time to get that worked out. What bothers me are the things we're doing that are potentially irreversible—like climate change, which is a real threat." I thought that was the absolutely right perspective to take.

Jason Furman (*far right*), when chairman of the Council of Economic Advisers (CEA), meeting with President Barack Obama (*center*) in the Oval Office on March 5, 2015, following a CEA meeting. Also pictured are Abigail Wozniak (*far left*), CEA senior economist; Jessica Schumer (*second left*), CEA chief of staff and general counsel; Jeffrey Zients (*third left*), director of the National Economic Council; Maurice Obstfeld (*third right*), CEA member; and Betsey Stevenson (*second right*), CEA member.

33   Jason Furman
Born 1970, New York City

Jason Furman graduated with a BA in social studies from Harvard University in 1992. He then obtained an MSc in economics from the London School of Economics in 1993 and an MA in government and a PhD in economics from Harvard University in 1995 and 2003, respectively.

In 1996, Furman first worked in government as a staff economist at the Council of Economic Advisers (CEA) during the administration of President Bill Clinton. He then served as senior adviser to the chief economist and senior vice president of the World Bank, before returning to government as special assistant to the president for economic policy in 1999.

He was a senior fellow at the Center on Budget and Policy Priorities from 2004 to 2006 and a senior fellow in economic studies and director of the Hamilton Project at the Brookings Institution from 2006 to 2008. Furman was economic policy director for Barack Obama's presidential campaign in 2008 and a member of the presidential transition team. From 2009 to 2013, he was principal deputy director of the National Economic Council (NEC), and he served as chairman of the CEA from 2013 to 2017.

Furman is now Professor of the Practice of Economic Policy at Harvard Kennedy School, and he is also a nonresident senior fellow at the Peterson Institute for International Economics.

I interviewed Jason Furman in his office at the CEA in Washington, D.C. It was the middle of the afternoon on Friday, December 2, 2016.

Background Information

Bowmaker: Why did you become an economist?

Furman: I became an economist for three reasons. One, I loved math, physics, and politics, and economics was a great way to combine them. Two, when I was thirteen years old, I was very interested in foreign affairs and asked my father's friend, who was a political science professor, if he could recommend something for me to read regularly. I thought he would say *Foreign Affairs*, but instead it was the *Economist*, which I have read every week ever since. And last, when I was growing up, my father was doing a PhD in economics, which he never finished.

Entering the Policy World

Bowmaker: What does an economist bring to the policy world that others do not?

Furman: With economists, everything comes in threes. One thing is an independent mind-set. Many people in the policy process are very oriented around the team they're on, or their own perspective, and so tend to find more evidence that supports their point of view and dismiss any evidence that contradicts it. Economists, on the other hand, revel in finding counterintuitive ideas and take seriously any evidence that's critical of their own views. And I think that ultimately leads to better thinking.

Two, economists have a set of tools that they use in their critical inquiry. Almost every policy question has some theoretical component to it, where understanding incentives, budget constraints, or prices can help you answer it. But there will also be an empirical component to it, and so knowing the appropriate data sources to use and how to understand causality is helpful.

And last, economists bring subject-area expertise. For example, you could be an expert in tax policy or health policy or international exchange rates. I would say, though, this is the least important of the three, because I've found that most of the policy questions I've gotten in government are ones that haven't been studied in the past or haven't been answered in the academic literature.

Bowmaker: Your formal entry into the policy world took place in 1996 during the Clinton administration, when you were approached by Joseph

Stiglitz to work as a staff economist at the Council of Economic Advisers. When I spoke with Joseph Stiglitz, he told me that he made life "interesting and vibrant" for you. How so?

Furman: I had no plans to go into government and work on applied economic policy. But when Joe heard my name from someone else, he called me up for an "interview." What that consisted of was him talking to me for half an hour straight about all the things he was excited about at the time. At the end, even though I had barely gotten a word in, he offered me the job and I accepted. Much of what we did together concerned the things that we had spoken about over the phone. For example, the unemployment rate was getting lower and lower, and it was thought that would trigger inflation. And so we did work to help establish that in fact, the natural rate of unemployment had fallen, and how that opened up space for not having premature contractionary policy. But what Joe really introduced me to was a taste for a wide variety of issues and how economics had something to offer on all of them, as opposed to just sticking to a narrow specialty.

By the way, I should also mention the second reason why I came to Washington. I was in love with a woman, and she was moving here. I thought I should chase her because she wasn't nearly as interested in me. Everything worked out—I'm chair of the CEA, and I'm also married to that woman.

Bowmaker: Which things, in particular, did you learn from Joseph Stiglitz that you were able to draw upon when you eventually became chair of the CEA?

Furman: Something that Joe did very well as chair was that he didn't just engage in the internal policy process—he used speeches and reports as tools to help change the dialogue in economics. In other words, he put new ideas forward and changed the way people thought. That's something I have tried to do as chair. In particular, I learned a certain amount from him about the power that a speech can have if it's analytically rigorous and brings new data and a new perspective to bear on policy discussion.

Bowmaker: During this time, you were also working at the National Economic Council, which was early in its development. Can you tell us what you learned about the role played by the NEC, and how it interacted with the Council of Economic Advisers?

Furman: I'm a big believer in a division of labor. Someone once asked one of my predecessors, Charlie Schultze, what the world would be like if

President [Jimmy] Carter had always taken his advice. Charlie responded, "If that were the case, I would've given him different advice." At the CEA, then, we can give the best economic advice, but I wouldn't want the president to always follow it because sometimes it couldn't pass Congress—in which case you haven't helped anyone. Other times, it could blow up and leave Congress to pass a law undoing your executive action—in which case you haven't helped anyone again. And so the president has to consider many factors, which is where the NEC comes in. It brings the CEA's economic advice, but also a perspective about communications and legislative strategy, and sets a table upon which all of those views can be aggregated. I think that's a very important function. The world works better when the NEC isn't claiming to be the sole expert about economic policy, but it also works better when the CEA isn't claiming to be giving advice about communications and legislative strategy. The NEC makes that division of labor possible, actually empowering CEA to play the economic role.

Moreover, NEC also enforces the process, so it is not Treasury deciding Treasury issues unilaterally and [the Department of] Commerce deciding Commerce issues unilaterally. Instead, all of the decisions are made in a teamlike process with everyone sitting around the same table led by NEC. This means that Treasury, Commerce, [the Department of] Labor and other agencies all give up a bit of their prerogative in exchange for a greater say in everyone else's issues. And it means that CEA has a seat at the table on every issue—without even giving anything up because we had not a specific area to begin with.

Bowmaker: After you completed your PhD at Harvard in 2003, you were involved in the presidential campaigns of Wesley Clark and John Kerry and then joined the Center on Budget and Policy Priorities. Gene Sperling has suggested you were the behind-the-scenes hero of the defeat of President [George W.] Bush's privatization plan of Social Security during this period. Can you tell us about the work that you did and, in your view, the specific role played by you?

Furman: When every administration puts forward ideas, it likes to de-emphasize the trade-offs that are associated with them. And so when the Bush administration suggested setting up individual accounts for Social Security, it never supplied the full set of details and information—such as the impact it would have on short-run debt, on the long-run solvency of Social Security, or on those individuals from different parts of the income scale. What I did, then, was to take the different bits and pieces of the plan as they came out and put together an analysis so that people could see how it would affect both them and the economy. And I think they understood that it wasn't a free lunch and, in many ways, would be quite harmful and costly. In terms of being the behind-the-scenes hero, though, I would just say that my job at the time was to analyze plans, and the Bush administration created a very large vacuum in that area that I helped to fill.

Bowmaker: What have you learned from Greg Mankiw, a former chair of the CEA and your former PhD adviser, over the years?

Furman: One lesson I didn't learn very well is that he kept trying to get me to come back to graduate school to finish my PhD as I found new and exciting things to do in Washington, and I put it off for years. But when Al Gore lost the 2000 election, it did at least have the side benefit of making me go back to Harvard—where the most important thing I learned from Greg was the importance of critical thinking rather than just finding evidence that confirms your own biases. In both our personal friendship and in his writing, he continues to challenge me today. I disagree with him on a decent amount, but occasionally he'll persuade me that he's right, and even when he doesn't, he makes me smarter in terms of how I think.

Bowmaker: By 2008, you had been appointed economic policy director for Barack Obama's presidential campaign. Your appointment drew criticism from labor unions and antiglobalization activists, who argued that you defended Walmart's business model in a 2005 paper on the grounds that the firm's low prices are helpful to poor people. How did you respond to the criticism?

Furman: The most important response was to tell everyone that the decisions on the campaign were being made by Barack Obama, not by me. And then I emphasized that I'm very open-minded and pretty eclectic in my views, some of which I share in common with those on the right, middle, and left sides of the political spectrum. For example, when it comes to Social Security or tax policy or minimum wage, I am largely in agreement with the same people who were criticizing me over Walmart. And I've worked closely with labor unions in the last eight years of this administration. Yes, we disagree on some areas like trade, but I think that's healthy. And ultimately I hope I've had a good relationship with them, because I've always had time to listen to their views.

Bowmaker: What did you learn about how Barack Obama thought about economics during your role in the campaign?

Furman: The most important thing I learned was how much he thought about economic policy, but not from the perspective of politics. In October of 2008, he would have conference calls with his advisers, who would want to talk to him about political strategy—like whether to do a negative ad about John McCain or whether to visit a certain state. All he wanted to talk about was the financial crisis, particularly the question of whether we should buy up toxic assets or do equity injections, which is something that we spent a great deal of time thinking about during that month. It was a very important question for the future of the economy, but utterly irrelevant for his odds of becoming the next president of the United States. On a campaign trail, you're supposed to be maximizing your chances of becoming president, not figuring out what is needed to save the economy.

The second thing I learned is that he and I share a very deep respect for markets and think that they are the most powerful force for the creation of wealth. But left to their own devices, markets can have a self-destructive side and certainly don't guarantee that wealth is divided in a way that we would think is fair. And so understanding how to make sure that you're retaining and centering your economy around a market, but fixing the parts that are wrong so that can everyone can share in the benefits, is his economic philosophy. And it's certainly mine, too—which is why it's been a complete pleasure to work for him for eight years.

Bowmaker: You were also part of the transition team when Obama became president. In hindsight, is there anything you might have known then that would have made making economic policy easier during the administration?

Furman: First of all, nobody had lived through a financial crisis like that one. Tim Geithner and David Lipton [both former undersecretaries of the treasury for international affairs] had experienced something similar in other countries, but it was a new and unparalleled circumstance in the United States. I think we did a very good job in getting the economics right, and our recovery compared to other countries is a vindication of our strategy. What I wished I had known was a little bit more about the politics. What surprised me is that I thought Congress would be much more eager to come back and do more economic stimulus after passing the initial [American] Recovery [and Reinvestment] Act—that they'd say, "We still have tough economic times, so we need to take some more medicine." Instead, the reaction was, "Things are a bit worse than anyone expected, which means the stimulus didn't work. So let's not do any more." I would like to have understood just how difficult it would be to get more through and, even more troubling, to have been aware of the fact that the magnitude of the negative shock would actually be correlated with the difficulty in getting something done. The worse the economy was in 2009, the more the stimulus was blamed, and the less desire there was for another one—when in fact more was needed.

As Deputy Director of the National Economic Council

Bowmaker: From your perspective as deputy director of the NEC, how did the different players on the economic team interact in the debate over the size of the stimulus?

Furman: There was a lot of economics brought to bear over the debate, like figuring out the multiplier for different forms of stimulus, which we did during the transition. And then once we got into government and we argued over subsequent rounds of stimulus, there was even one Cabinet-level meeting that Larry Summers chaired in his office in which two different papers were presented that had original algebraic models and empirical calibrations underlying them. One held the perspective that when monetary policy is at the zero lower bound, fiscal stimulus could help pay for itself, while the other argued that fiscal stimulus can reduce confidence and hurt the economy. It was as rigorous a debate as I've ever seen in my more than ten years in government and the World Bank.

In the end, most of us thought that the stimulus should be as big as possible, which was about $1 trillion. Our political advisers said that we had no chance of getting that amount—the best we could hope for was around $900 billion. And then because of a holdup by three Republicans, that was ultimately pared back by another $100 billion. I was very much of the view that we needed to do as much as possible. The constraints were political, not economic, and in the worst-case scenario in which we did too much, then the Fed[eral Reserve] could always offset it. And so to me there was very little danger of doing too much, but a great deal of risk in doing too little. And I would have also used the Recovery Act as an opportunity to not just make a one-time change in policy, but to have improved automatic stabilizers and built in a response in advance that was contingent on the economy, and not reliant on further action from Congress. For example, there could have been tax cuts every year until the unemployment rate was below 6 percent. Or every time the unemployment rate was elevated, unemployment insurance benefits could have been extended or state fiscal relief increased. Things might have turned out to be even better than they did.

Bowmaker: Do you think a case could be made that the president ought to have been exposed to more debates from economists outside of the economic team who had different viewpoints?

Furman: I think we've always tried to do a good job of presenting the president with a range of perspectives, and not just from those who work for him. We've done so in a number of different ways. One, during the transition, we called about thirty economists to get their views on whether we should do a stimulus and, if so, what should be its size and composition. We wrote up all their views in three or four lines, put it together in a memo, and sent it to the president-elect.

Two, we routinely do a written daily economic briefing for the president which often includes an academic paper. For example, we might summarize a recent NBER [National Bureau of Economic Research] paper on some issue of relevance, and we don't just show him ones on which we agree—we send in a whole range.

Third, we bring in different groups of economists to see him—like Greg Mankiw and Joe Stiglitz, who have served different presidents, but others too, like Ken Rogoff, who has never worked in government.

And last, even if I wanted to have a monopoly on information for the president, which might have been nice for me, he happens to have an iPad and is constantly reading, learning, and asking questions. And so it just isn't an option to pretend that your view is the only one, because he is going to be exposed to other perspectives, and that is only good for the world. For example, Angus Deaton's research on mortality was something that he came across directly, and he had many questions about why it was happening, how it related to the economy, and what could be done about it. Likewise, he was very struck by some research on the decline in the male labor force participation rate and pushed us to understand exactly what it meant.

Bowmaker: What did you learn from Larry Summers, the director of the NEC, during your time as deputy director?

Furman: The most important thing for an economist to bring to government is skepticism, self-doubt, and critical thinking. Larry Summers is superlative in all those areas. People might think of him as somebody who is very confident and drives his views through, but he subjects any idea he has—or any idea that anyone else has—to a huge amount of critical scrutiny. He really knows how to kick the tires. When you're on the receiving end, it can be very difficult, but when you watch him apply it to himself, it weeds out a lot of bad, lazy, and sloppy thinking and creates a filter through which the better ideas do get through and prosper.

As Chairman of the Council of Economic Advisers

Bowmaker: You were appointed as chairman of the CEA in 2013. Did President Obama make it clear what he expected you to do for him?

Furman: He didn't give me a detailed job description. He assumed I had been around the White House long enough to understand being chair of the CEA is a reasonably well-defined role.

Bowmaker: The president had indicated during his 2014 State of the Union address that the odds of Americans rising up the economic ladder were declining. However, a new study by Raj Chetty and coauthors had indicated that while mobility was indeed low, it had been flat for around fifty years.[1] Gene Sperling suggested that you had a "classic Jason Furman moment," in that you were "savvy enough to know, if misinterpreted, it would be used against the president."[2] Can you tell us about the work you did behind the scenes to convey the White House's position to reporters the day before the study came out, and the memo that you cowrote to the president about the issue?

Furman: There is less research on mobility than you might think, and even less research on how mobility has changed over time. And so Raj Chetty and his coauthors did some very important research that produced some

---

1. Raj Chetty, Nathaniel Hendren, Patrick Kline, and Emmanuel Saez, "Where Is the Land of Opportunity? The Geography of Intergenerational Mobility in the United States," National Economic Bureau of Research Working Paper 19843, http://www .nber.org/papers/w19843. Published in *Quarterly Journal of Economics* 129, no. 4 (2014): 1553–1623.
2. Zachary A. Goldfarb, "Economist Jason Furman Is the Wonkiest Wonk in the White House," *Washington Post*, February 12, 2014, accessed March 4, 2019, https:// www.washingtonpost.com/lifestyle/style/economist-jason-furman-is-the-wonkiest -wonk-in-the-white-house/2014/02/12/7e14b7bc-8e8f-11e3-b227-12a45d109e03_story .html?noredirect=on&utm_term=.ea728377d9e9.

very striking results. I had a chance to read it in advance and wanted to make sure the president understood it, since he's a very fact-based person and believes in science. Some of his earlier statements on this issue were a little broad, although not unreasonable based on the information available at the time. This new research showed that just because people's likelihood of moving up or down in a rank ordering had not changed over time does not mean that mobility had not gotten worse. Because when inequality gets worse, and you're stuck in the same place in the income distribution, that's more consequential than if inequality has gotten better and you're stuck in the same place. And so it was the intersection of unchanged mobility plus increased inequality that was the real problem, not either one by themselves. I had to make sure that reporters understood that point, while at the CEA we did a three-or-so-page memo and had an opportunity to talk with the president about it at the edge of another meeting, just to make sure he understood it as well—which he did. We don't want to ever base our arguments for policies on information that is wrong.

Bowmaker: How does President Obama like to process and absorb information?

Furman: He does better with reading in advance. In a conversation, he wants to interact more and talk about how everything fits together. And so you're much better off if you can get the information basis that you need through writing in advance. Then you can jump straight to the conversation. What he tends to not have a lot of patience for is a forty-page PowerPoint presentation with five facts on each page and someone sitting there and going through it for him slowly. He is someone who absorbs information quickly.

Bowmaker: Robert Rubin and Larry Summers have both suggested that you are one of the few outstanding economists who is also able to navigate politics in Washington. Do you think this comes purely from experience, or is it an innate ability?

Furman: I think it was a revealed preference. As I said earlier, when I was in graduate school, I had no intention whatsoever of working in Washington. But from the first moment I arrived here, I discovered that I liked combining politics and economics—trying to figure out how to explain things clearly to people and working on a wide range of issues rather than the very narrow topics that you can sometimes do in the academy. I realized pretty quickly, then, that that was my comparative advantage, and it was the reason why I stayed for four years instead of one, which was my original intention. And I only went back because I didn't have an option to stay any longer, thanks to George W. Bush.

Bowmaker: It is noticeable that during your chairmanship, the CEA has done more white papers and speeches than in the past. What are the costs and benefits of this arrangement?

Furman: The benefits are substantial in a few different respects. One is we have a great platform to shape how the public and the economics profession understand a variety of issues. For example, the work we have done on labor force participation, competition, patents, or the pricing of coal have all affected the policy dialogue and moved it in the direction where economists are interested in solving problems for which we don't know the answer. Some have told me that our work gave them the idea to do more research on a particular area. I think that's great. Two, sometimes I'll do a speech that won't be related to a policy proposal, but in the course of it, we'll discover that it should have a proposal. For example, for the fiftieth anniversary of Joe Stiglitz's teaching, Peter Orszag and I wrote a paper about competition and inequality [see chapter 30]. Originally, I wrote it because I wanted to honor Joe and have something to say at his conference, but five different executive actions ended up emerging from it—in areas ranging from technology to airports to the beer industry. It turns out that competition has many aspects beyond antitrust associated with it.

Going the other way, we also did internal research for a policy process on conflict of interest for retirement brokers. We discovered that when they receive a payment based on what security they advise you to buy, they tend to provide bad advice, which is costly. The administration decided to go ahead with the policy, in part because of our research. They asked us to turn the memo that we did into a report so that everyone could see their argument for following the policy, and I think it has held up pretty well and made a convincing case. But the downside, of course, in doing more white papers and speeches is that there is a trade-off in terms of time.

Bowmaker: When you want to run ideas by other economists, do you ever reach out to former chairs of the CEA?

Furman: I think it is a critical function of the CEA to bring in knowledge from the outside, and the great thing is that people will return the calls of almost anyone here, including research assistants. I speak with Joe Stiglitz all the time—he was very helpful to me in dealing with the recent economic crisis in Puerto Rico—and I talk regularly with Greg Mankiw, Christy Romer, Alan Blinder, and many others. But I also bounce ideas off specialists. For example, when we were worried about the cost of imprisoning people, I reached out to Jens Ludwig, an outstanding economist who is head of the NBER's program on crime. He said, "Look, you first need to look at the cost of crime because it is distributed very unequally, with the poor being the most affected. As a result, you ought to be concerned with not just how to reduce the cost of overincarceration, which is a big problem, but also how to reduce crime itself." And he helped to convince us that it was a good idea to emphasize the importance of policing in dealing with crime, and that we could use some of the money saved from imprisoning fewer people to have more police. That's something we brought to the attention of the administration.

Bowmaker: I would like to ask a couple of questions about time management. First, how do you balance time managing your staff, conducting economic analysis or making speeches, and speaking with the president or other principals about economics?

Furman: I probably don't do a good job of it because every day is different. But one aspect of time management that has worked well for me—against the advice of others—is to write the first drafts of memos and speeches. I was told that, as a principal, I should let my staff do it. I'm a fast writer, though, and I find that it's easier for me to get something 85 percent of the way there and then hand it off to somebody else than it is to start with something from somebody else that's not what I envisioned, and I have to rewrite it.

Bowmaker: How about the balance between your professional and personal lives?

Furman: My wife and I would both give different answers to this question. When I was at the NEC, I just couldn't do it. One, we had a financial crisis on our hands, and two, I didn't decide when I worked—there would be a conference call at a given time, and we had to prepare for it. At the CEA, it's more often the case that a lot needs to get done, but I have a little bit more say in when it gets done. Now, I usually get home around 6:45 p.m., spend until 9:00 p.m. with my children, and then work as late as is necessary. That's just so much better than when I was getting home at 9:00 p.m. or 10:00 p.m., and my children were already asleep.

Bowmaker: All things considered, can you give an example of where you, as an economist, or the CEA, as an organization, have been able to make a difference?

Furman: One of my rules is that we should be making a small contribution to big things and a big contribution to small things. One example is conflict of interest in retirement brokers, which I mentioned earlier. Many people helped craft a solution to the problem, but I don't think it would have happened without our work here.

There were also some obscure issues that we spent a lot of time on, too, such as management of the electromagnetic spectrum. More of it had to be freed up with a set of auctions that involved two sides buying it from broadcasters and then selling it to internet providers. I was part of the team that made sure there was more competition included in the process.

At the same time, I'm also very proud of my contributions to some very big topics when I was at the NEC, such as the Recovery Act and the Affordable Care Act. I'm under no illusion that they wouldn't have happened without me, but hopefully I helped defend and improve them through my work.

Bowmaker: You have worked for Barack Obama for a long time. Can you describe how he has changed over the period you have worked for him?

Furman: It's easier to see change when you go away from somebody for a while and then return. But when you see somebody every week, any change you see appears to be so gradual. I would say, though, that he continues to place policy first and remains optimistic about his ability to persuade others of his ideas and to be able to work together to get things done. That's very much his temperament, and you saw it in the types of fiscal deals he was pursuing in 2011–2012, and in the way he has dealt with President-Elect [Donald] Trump. But I've also seen him become someone who is enjoying his freedom a little bit more since he is less politically constrained in what he says and does. That being said, he didn't do the Affordable Care Act in 2009 because he thought it was a great thing politically—he knew it would be costly in that respect, and wanted to go ahead anyway.

Bowmaker: How has your relationship with him changed over time?

Furman: My relationship with him has gotten better. I hope he has developed a higher level of trust in me and that I've gained a higher level of understanding of what he is and isn't interested in, and how to process and provide him with the information that he needs. I have also discovered that he likes science fiction and, in particular, appreciates the work of one Chinese science-fiction author that I have a lot of fondness for, as well. And so five years ago, I would never have thought to strike up a conversation with him about a Chinese science-fiction novel, but now I do so regularly.

Bowmaker: What have you learned from the president, and what has he learned from you?

Furman: I won't be presumptuous enough to say what, if anything, he's learned from me, except many specific pieces of information. But I've learned from his attitude. The day after Trump won the election, everyone in the White House was devastated. The president came in with his head held up high. He talked about how we had done a great job, how there were checks and balances in the system, and how America was a strong place. Just watching him helped me learn to be that way and to become a better leader of my team.

General Thoughts on Economic Policymaking

Bowmaker: Which fallacies, misperceptions, or misconceptions affect policy debate in this country?

Furman: One is that the world is zero-sum, and so trade is about winners and losers. The basic lesson of economics teaches us that somebody always values a good or service more than another person, meaning that an exchange can be mutually beneficial. The second biggest fallacy, which oddly is the exact opposite of the first, is that people have an enduring belief that they can always get something for free. For example, that you can require a business to offer a benefit to an employee without having to worry that it may make it less likely to hire that person or reduce the wages that it would pay him or her.

Bowmaker: Which aspects of the institutional framework for making economic policy in this country work well, and which need to be reformed?

Furman: We have a team-oriented approach to policy in the United States. The Treasury Department, for example, can weigh in on the Labor Department's issues, and vice versa. That's then refereed and adjudicated in the White House and has led to a broader range of ideas and a better discussion and debate of policy than I see in other countries. But I think Congress can be quite weak at times in terms of its analytical abilities. Although it does have the CBO [Congressional Budget Office] and the Joint Committee on Taxation to draw on, it has fewer economists and less of an orientation around policy, which can sometimes lead Congress to rely more on outsiders—with politics receiving a large weight in decisions. Of course, it's totally appropriate that politics plays a role, but it often does so more than it should. If anything, then, to have greater technical expertise serving where the laws are ultimately passed could lead to better economic policy in this country.

Bowmaker: To what extent can economics research produced in universities be used to help inform policy debate?

Furman: Many economists put more time into describing and understanding how the world functions than recommending policies to change it. But some academic research can be very useful. Take the very specific issue of for-profit colleges that charge a great deal of money to students. Often those students end up not doing very well when they graduate, but you might argue that the colleges also take in a different set of students who are more difficult to teach. And so perhaps they help them in ways that other schools can't. There is academic research that has looked at for-profits and helped inform how we've regulated the industry to capture the best of it and mitigate the consequences of the worst of it.

Bowmaker: How do you think the role of the CEA has changed over time, and how will it continue to evolve?

Furman: The creation of the NEC has helped to free up the CEA to do more of what it should, which is to focus on the substance and the economics and not to think too much about the politics and how it all fits together. Before we had the NEC, most CEA chairs were a little less academic in their background, although I'm more the exception than the norm because I have more in common with a Herb Stein or a Charlie Schultze than a Harvey Rosen or a Greg Mankiw. Looking ahead, I certainly hope that President Trump makes use of the CEA, because I have enormous respect for the role that it has played in both Democratic and Republican administrations. The chair of the CEA does not always get his or her way but I think for the most part is pushing in the right direction and helping make things better, or at least less bad. We've been on a seventy-year streak of doing so, and long may it continue.

Personal Reflections

Bowmaker: How does your personality affect your style and approach as a policymaker?

Furman: Because I did this job as a junior person, I can picture what it means to be one of them. And so I try to empower my staff and encourage

them to speak up and disagree when it is necessary. I have sufficient confidence in my relationship with the president, and with those in the West
Wing, that I'm not worried that if somebody else shines, then that's going
to make me look less good. In fact, it's precisely the opposite. When everyone at the CEA does well, it makes us as an organization look better, and it
makes me personally look better. I try, then, not to micromanage—I aim to
be encouraging of initiative, to be transparent, and to run the organization
in a way that is as flat as possible. That's something from which I benefited
when I was here in 1996, and I continue to do so because what I've just
described helps bring the best out of people.

Bowmaker: What are your strengths and weaknesses as a policymaker?

Furman: In terms of strengths, I have a wide range of interests, know a little
bit about many things, and know who to call on a lot of different topics. In
terms of weaknesses, I'm sure I have many of them—with the biggest one
probably being that an answer to your question isn't immediately coming
to mind for me. But when I think about it, I may not delegate as well as I
should, and while I am balanced in that I try to see all sides of every issue, it
does sometimes create the Harry Truman problem of having a two-handed
policy adviser who says, "On the one hand … but on the other hand," when
what you want is someone with one hand.

Bowmaker: As a policymaker, which outcomes have been most gratifying?

Furman: Number one is the Recovery Act and everything else that went
into saving the economy from falling into a second Great Depression. A
close second is the Affordable Care Act, which is the most important piece
of legislation in half a century in this country. Many people contributed to
it, and I was one of them. Also very important to me are the tax cuts for
low-income households—expansions to the Earned Income Tax Credit and
the Child Tax Credit—that I played a major role in designing and legislating
while at the NEC. In 2009, I watched the president sign them into law on a
temporary basis, and then, unusually for a CEA chair, I was called upon in
2015 to negotiate making them a permanent part of our tax structure. I was
constantly on the phone with both parties in Congress to figure out a trade
that would give something that Republicans wanted, which was more certainty about taxes for businesses, and something that Democrats wanted,
which was more certainty about taxes for low-income households. I had
to mix and match those things and trade them off each other. There was

an economic and analytic component to it, but there was also a great deal of holding hands, getting people to trust each other, and figuring out how to move forward together, which we ultimately did. When the president signed our compromise into law, that was enormously gratifying because it reduced poverty and encouraged work.

Bowmaker: On the other hand, there must be some things that, in hindsight, you'd like the opportunity to do differently. What are they?

Furman: For the country as a whole, the biggest disappointment is that we weren't able to pass comprehensive immigration reform and do it in a way that would provide a path to citizenship for the people here, while also bringing in more talented people that can contribute to our economy. In terms of issues that I've worked on personally, I spent more time on business tax reform than probably any other single topic in the last eight years in the administration. I helped craft the president's framework to lower the rates, broaden the base, and reform the international tax system, but we have never been able to get it through Congress. I hope it can happen in the future and in the way that we proposed it: revenue neutral rather than at the expense of the deficit.

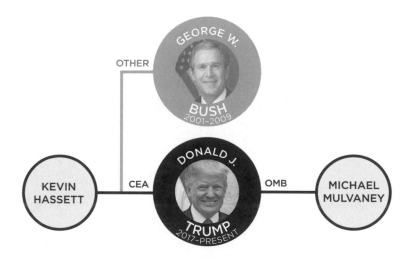

OTHER

GEORGE W. BUSH
2001–2009

DONALD J. TRUMP
2017–PRESENT

KEVIN HASSETT

CEA

OMB

MICHAEL MULVANEY

IX Donald Trump Administration

Kevin Hassett, chairman of the Council of Economic Advisers, holding the *Economic Report of the President* (released the previous day) at the Brady Press Briefing Room at the White House on February 22, 2018.

34   Kevin A. Hassett
Born 1962, Greenfield, Massachusetts

Kevin Hassett graduated with a bachelor's degree in economics from Swarthmore College in 1984 and obtained a PhD in economics from the University of Pennsylvania in 1990.

Hassett was an assistant professor of economics at Columbia University's Graduate School of Business between 1989 and 1993 and an associate professor there between 1993 and 1994. He worked as an economist in the Division of Research and Statistics at the Board of Governors of the Federal Reserve System between 1992 and 1997 and then joined the American Enterprise Institute (AEI), first as a resident scholar and then, between 2014 and 2017, as the State Farm James Q. Wilson Chair in American Politics and Culture.

He was chief economist and senior economic adviser in the John McCain presidential campaigns of 2000 and 2008, respectively; economic adviser in the George W. Bush presidential campaign of 2004; and economic adviser in the Mitt Romney presidential campaign of 2012.

In early 2017, Hassett was nominated by President Donald Trump to become chairman of the Council of Economic Advisers (CEA). He was confirmed by the Senate on September 12, 2017, and sworn in the next day. On May 31, 2019, Hassett informed President Trump that he would be resigning from his position.

I interviewed Kevin Hassett in his office at the CEA in Washington, D.C. It was the middle of the afternoon on Friday, November 10, 2017.

Background Information

Bowmaker: Why did you become an economist?

Hassett: I began studying economics as a freshman at Swarthmore College in 1980. I didn't start out as an economics major, but I was very interested in the subject, in part because the little town I grew up in—Greenfield, Massachusetts—experienced very hard times that were actually similar to those that many other mill towns around the country went through back then and indeed have experienced more recently. For example, during my childhood, the Greenfield Tap and Die Corporation and the paper mill in Turner Falls both shut down, and many kids' parents lost their jobs. It was an extremely negative time from an economic standpoint. But when I arrived at Swarthmore, an astonishingly gifted faculty made me realize that economics could help me understand not only what was going on in the place where I grew up but could maybe lead me to develop policies to go back and turn it around.

Entering the Policy World

Bowmaker: What does an economist bring to the policy world that others do not?

Hassett: Economists bring devotion to data and an authoritative voice about data to the policy world. If a particular policy is being considered, and someone has tried it before, there might be evidence that can inform the debate. And so it is the economist's job to be an honest arbiter of that evidence.

Bowmaker: What did you learn about the intersection between policy and politics during your work as an economic adviser on several presidential campaigns?

Hassett: What I learned the most is that presidential campaign policy development is very, very difficult because not only are the stakes very high—if you put out a number that's incorrect, it can cause a huge embarrassment for the candidate—but also you have very little staff. And so one of the reasons why the Open Source Policy Center [at AEI] was developed was because I thought that maybe policy debate isn't as rich as it could be, if people had the tools to get the correct numbers for their ideas. Today, everyone across the political spectrum can get a score for their tax idea, can get distribution tables, and can even get a dynamic score if they choose to. In other words, I wanted a tool that would help campaigns have more confidence as they developed their own policies and explored their own ideas. But many, many people—not just Democrats and Republicans, but also ordinary citizens and college students—have been taught how to use the software so that they too can be their own private CBO [Congressional Budget Office] or a joint tax committee. I encourage you to go fiddle around with it [*laughs*].[1]

As Chairman of the Council of Economic Advisers

Bowmaker: How were you approached for the role as Chairman of the Council of Economic Advisers, and why do you think you were chosen?

Hassett: My introduction to Trump's people came originally through the Open Source Policy Center. They found our tool, and I started to help them use it to explore the president's tax ideas. I was approached by someone on the transition team about the CEA role and interviewed first by [Secretary of the Treasury] Steve Mnuchin and [Director of the National Economic Council] Gary Cohn, and then ultimately by the president himself. But you'd have to ask them why they chose me. Amongst the set of bad choices, maybe I was the least worst [*laughs*].

Bowmaker: How would you describe the interview process?

Hassett: It was a case of them asking me what I thought the role of the CEA is in the White House, what my management style would be, and so on. They didn't say anything like, "Geez, I've always been saying XYZ. Are you going to support me or fight me on it?" That wasn't part of the conversation at all.

Bowmaker: Was that the first time you had met Donald Trump? If so, what were your first impressions of him?

Hassett: Yes, that was the first time I had met President Trump. I thought he was a very easy guy to be around, very gracious and easy with compliments. He was also inquisitive—conversations with him can go on for a long time because one question leads to another question. I was very favorably impressed. In fact, meeting with President Trump was something that helped me be more excited about the job.

---

1. See Open Source Policy Center (website), accessed February 3, 2019, https://www .ospc.org/.

Bowmaker: Did you consult with former chairs of the CEA both before and after you accepted the role? If so, what did they tell you?

Hassett: Yes, I talked to many former CEA chairs. Jason Furman is a good friend of mine, and he gave me a lot of advice—including in a binder of FAQs [frequently asked questions]—about what the job entails, so that at the confirmation hearing I would be able to respond to questions about my role and duties with full information. I'm sure it would have been much trickier without his advice, because I might have appeared to not have a clue about what the job was all about.

Austan Goolsbee told me that once I began the job I should be wary of something called "potted plant duty." This is when a politician is giving a speech, and you're standing right next to him or her. That can put you in an uncomfortable position as an economist, especially if the politician is taking questions. And so Austan said that one of the most important skills that the CEA chair needs to have is knowing when to be out of town [*laughs*]. I've only been out of town once—and it was a scheduled event—so I'm not really doing anything about it, but I think the idea of watching closely what kind of things you get involved in publicly is important.

The different CEA chairs seem to have different attitudes towards that aspect of the job. Alan Greenspan virtually never appeared in public when he was CEA chair, and I've spoken with him about it. His confirmation hearing was the day after [President Richard] Nixon resigned, so he came in at a very turbulent time when a steady hand was required here in the EOB [Executive Office Building]. That was one approach. But other people like Austan—who is so charismatic and intelligent—were probably on TV every day if we went back and looked.

Bowmaker: Under the Trump administration, the chairman of the CEA no longer has Cabinet-rank status. Do you worry the position has been downgraded because the views of economists can be inconvenient for those involved in policymaking?

Hassett: I don't worry about that at all. I think that the CEA at the moment is wound right into the White House in a way that's probably pretty similar to what it typically is. If I were designing the CEA from scratch as you go back to the '46 act, then I wouldn't want it in the Cabinet, because our job is to not be political but to provide objective analysis, and there are many aspects of the institutional design of the CEA that guarantee that is the case. For example, we recruit PhD economists who take a year or two of leave from their universities, which means that the CEA staff turns over enormously all the time. And so you get a good read of what the economics profession thinks about an issue at a point in time, rather than something that has been built up as the staff position over time.

Bowmaker: But do you think President Trump himself is interested in hearing the views of economists?

Hassett: I think to his surprise President Trump really enjoys interacting with the CEA and consuming our products. For example, if he thinks there's an important message in our output that we should share with the American people, he'll say, "Kevin's giving the presser [press conference] today instead of [White House Press Secretary] Sarah [Huckabee Sanders]."

Before I came in and really got to know President Trump, there was some talk about him being hostile to economics and economists. And so one of the things I've learned is that's just absolutely not true.

Bowmaker: How do you handle being in a position where current administrative policy on immigration and trade, in particular, is in conflict with what you have advocated in the past? For example, it seems that the problem with immigration as President Trump sees it is that there are too many American-born workers who are competing for the same jobs as immigrants, while on the issue of trade, it seems that raising tariffs is his preferred approach. Do you think your own views in these areas will cause the CEA to have less influence than would otherwise be the case?

Hassett: I reject the premise of your first question. On the issue of trade, I certainly support the president's objectives. I think they'd be good for global welfare. In my view, he genuinely wants to move towards a world where we have fully reciprocal deals that are symmetric. And so the goal is not to raise tariffs.

In terms of immigration, I'd have to review the literature before I talk about it. I know there is a recent paper by George Borjas on the topic that has received some negative criticism, but again I haven't educated myself on this question enough to be able to form an opinion.[2]

In any case, certainly there are times when my views are different than the president's—I can't talk about them because of executive privileges—but

---

2. George J. Borjas, "The Wage Impact of the *Marielitos*: A Reappraisal," *Industrial and Labor Relations Review* 70, no. 5 (2017): 1077–1110.

he doesn't punish me. On the contrary, he encourages debate, and he likes to hear multiple opinions.

Let me give you a simple example to illustrate my point. As you can see, I have cheddar Goldfish [crackers] on my desk here. The president would never say, "Look, we've got to have cheddar Goldfish for a snack. Explain why that is the right answer." There has never been a meeting when that happens. Instead, it's always, "Hey, I'm thinking we should have cheddar Goldfish for a snack. Does anyone think we should have something else?" Then you might say, "Well, how about an apple, because it'll be healthier for you?" He'll reply, "Oh, you're right, maybe we should have an apple." The president is very open to other ideas and enjoys debating matters, and he does so extremely graciously and collegially.

Bowmaker: Do your meetings with President Trump tend to be more structured, like Barack Obama's, or more wide-ranging, like Bill Clinton's?

Hassett: Meetings with President Trump always begin in a very structured way and usually focus on a specific objective. If we resolve the issue in less time than is required—and if his schedule allows—then sometimes we'll talk about how the economy is doing. But it's not a social gathering if you're meeting in the Oval Office [*laughs*].

Bowmaker: Have you been given access to important meetings with the president?

Hassett: I'm certainly with the president every time that I need to be. In any well-organized White House—and this is a well-organized White House—there are deputies' meetings and principals' meetings. In terms of the nuts and bolts of policy creation, it's very often the principals' meetings where the key decisions are made and presented to the president. In my time here, there hasn't been a policy decision principals' meeting where the CEA wasn't represented. And so again I think the CEA right now is doing exactly what the CEA always does.

Bowmaker: How would you describe President Trump's understanding of economics relative to other politicians for whom you have worked?

Hassett: President Trump is a very successful businessman who knows a lot about how businesses work. If you talk about tax law with him, for example, then he'll immediately know well how a particular law changed in a particular way, and he'll tell you what his company would do. We're in the middle of a tax debate at the moment, and many decisions have had to be made—sometimes very urgently. The thing that jumps out the most to me is that having been at a big operation—and probably having paid his fair share of taxes—President Trump really understands how the corporate tax world works. He knows exactly what depreciation is, what happens if it's accelerated, or if there's expensing. And he knows how his firm would act. And so I'd say in terms of economic intuition and getting right to the key substance, he's more of an insider to the economic process than Senator McCain or President [George W.] Bush or Mitt Romney. But I think Romney and Trump are much similar. If I had to break up the people I've worked closely with into two groups, I'd put Romney and Trump in one group and McCain and Bush in the other group. They're all great guys in their own way, but in terms of relative strengths, it's the people who have been running businesses who very quickly understand what happens if you go to expensing, for example, and how that will have an impact.

Bowmaker: So would you describe President Trump as being detailed oriented as opposed to being a big-picture person?

Hassett: I wouldn't pick one or the other. On the one hand, when you go into the Oval Office with him, he embraces the details. He likes to talk about them and is effective at thinking about them, because if you're running a business, the details matter a lot. On the other hand, he's definitely a big-picture guy. It's his communication that there are three big pillars—maybe four, if you count repatriation—to the tax bill. They are nonnegotiable. In other words, he wouldn't sign a bill if it didn't meet those objectives.

Bowmaker: A couple of years ago, you and Joseph Sullivan wrote a paper reviewing the literature about the impact of uncertainty on the economy.[3] Do you accept that President Trump, relative to previous presidents, creates more uncertainty with his actions?

Hassett: It's possible that President Trump creates more uncertainty with his actions because he's extremely ambitious in the policy space. But in addition to uncertainty—which is about the second moment of the distribution [the variance]—he's also doing things that move the first moment [the mean] significantly. For example, when he was elected, I think the expected tax rate for 2019 went down because people believed he might be able to get a tax bill through. And I think one of the reasons why there's

---

3. Kevin A. Hassett and Joseph W. Sullivan, "Policy Uncertainty and the Economy," American Enterprise Institute, August 2016, accessed March 4, 2019, http://www.aei .org/wp-content/uploads/2016/08/Policy-Uncertainty.pdf.

been so much optimism in response to the president's promises is that people are focused more on the opportunity from the first moment than the second moment.

Bowmaker: Ultimately, do you think it is reasonable to hold presidents accountable for what happens to the economy?

Hassett: What economists should do is study individual policies and evaluate honestly what they accomplish. And then, of course, if you're writing a history of a president, it would be fair to hold them to account for policies that they chose. But the state of the economy is something that is determined by a lot more than just policy. For example, President Obama arrived at the White House right at the start of the Great Recession. I think some of the policies he pursued could have been better, but it would be wrong to look at the growth rate on average for the first couple years of his administration and say that was a metric of his success as a policymaker.

Bowmaker: The first three months of your role as chairman of the CEA have been spent on the tax bill and also writing the *Economic Report of the President*. I have some questions relating to your work there. First, do you think that the tax bill will make multinationals bring more profits back to the US now that they are no longer paying a big tax penalty to do so?

Hassett: Yes. The economic literature is very clear that profit location is extremely responsive to changes in tax rates, and so we would expect that there would be a massive amount of relocation to profits and repatriation of past profits in response to the tax bill.

Bowmaker: Did you think that greater profits being repatriated to the US under the new tax regime will lead to more employment and investment within the US, or will it go to share buybacks and dividend payments and other payments to those who own parts of the company?

Hassett: The simple answer is all of the above. But when we're talking about repatriation, there is a stock and a flow issue. The stock issue is that there is a massive amount of previous profit that has accumulated overseas, and those trillions can all come back right now because of the way the tax bill was written. But there is also that much smaller incentive for future profits to be located abroad, which is the flow issue. And so with this stock being so large, one of the things we'd expect to see when it comes home is that it will lead to more employment, more investment, more dividends, more share repurchases, more bonuses, and more wages.

Bowmaker: In your role as chairman of the CEA, you slammed the Tax Policy Center's critical analysis of the Trump administration's tax reform plan since it contained "many fictions" and "scientifically indefensible" conclusions.[4] Some observers, notably Larry Summers, have taken exception to your impugning the integrity of the think tank. Looking back, is there anything you might have said or done differently?

Hassett: No. You can go back and cut and paste whatever you want out of my talk. There has certainly been a lot of noise from opponents of the tax bill, not just from Larry Summers. But I haven't heard anything substantive that would make me rethink or reconsider anything I said. When Glenn Hubbard was CEA chair, left-leaning economists all said that the CEA had become a partisan place. There was a *Slate* article written about him.[5] When Greg Mankiw was CEA chair, Paul Krugman accused him of being a partisan hack because of his forecasts. And Eddie Lazear got the same treatment.

I think that it's a real honor to serve your country and be here. But one of the sacrifices you make is that there are people out there who will decide you're a worthy target for some political reason, and it's just part of the job to be gracious when that happens. And so I take the example of Glenn, Greg, and Eddie seriously when I think about how I should respond to critics. But the other thing about that criticism is that very often in public debate, people try to win arguments either with what Jeremy Bentham says is the lowest form of argument—appeal to authority—or to silence arguments with bullying.

I believe that it's the job of the CEA chair to respond to good arguments and to demonstrate that they won't be cowed by bullying. And I think I've done that effectively. But as I say, this is not the first time it's happened. At least in my memory, it happens every time there's a Republican as the CEA chair.

Bowmaker: Your own model suggests that the Trump administration's tax plan will not lead to as much deficits or debts as implied by the range of

---

4. Prepared remarks by Council of Economic Advisers Chairman Kevin Hassett before the Tax Policy Center-Tax Foundation, October 5, 2017, accessed March 4, 2019, https://www.whitehouse.gov/sites/whitehouse.gov/files/documents/TPC%20-%20 Hassett%20Speech%20-%20FINAL%20FINAL.pdf.

5. Chris Suellentrop, "Glenn Hubbard: First-Rate Economist. Tax-Cut Champion. Presidential Yes Man," *Slate*, January 22, 2003, accessed March 4, 2019, https://www.google .com/amp/s/slate.com/news-and-politics/2003/01/council-of-economic-advisers -chairman-glenn-hubbard.amp.

views that characterize the mainstream. If you are wrong, what would you recommend as an appropriate policy response?

Hassett: If we're wrong—and it becomes an urgent policy matter—then a fiscal consolidation of some form would be required. And if that is the case, the place I'd start is the fiscal consolidation literature, so that we could learn from the ones that worked. In fact, I wrote a paper with Andrew Biggs and Matt Jensen on that very subject.[6]

Bowmaker: President Trump has promised to spend $1.5 trillion on infrastructure, but nothing seems to have materialized in this area in the first year of his administration. Why?

Hassett: It's true that we haven't had a bill yet, but we have studied it extensively—there is a whole chapter written about it in the forthcoming *Economic Report of the President*. One of the big problems we found is that private capital is not drawn into the infrastructure space very much because of ridiculously long delays—eight to ten years, in some cases—to get a permit for a project. The president has instructed his Cabinet to come up with a plan to get that down to two years. And so while I agree that legislation is difficult in this space, it is definitely something we're ambitious about. Even without legislation, I think we've made a lot of progress in trying to create a climate so that municipalities will have an easier time getting permits when they have projects that they want to do. But if you also reduce government uncertainty in this space, then you can potentially attract a lot of private capital, too. That's one objective where we've enjoyed significant success in the first year.

Bowmaker: When I spoke with Greg Mankiw, he told me that he was skeptical about the value of the *Economic Report of the President* because of the incredible amount of work it takes to put it together every year, and that it takes resources away from other aspects of the White House policy process. Do you agree?

Hassett: When a president is elected, his first *Economic Report* is an opportunity to describe to future historians what his worldview is, how he thinks about the economy, and what policies he intends to pursue. And so I think

---

6. Andrew G. Biggs, Kevin A. Hassett, and Matthew Jensen, "A Guide for Deficit Reduction in the United States Based on Historical Consolidations That Worked," American Enterprise Institute Economic Policy Working Paper No. 2010-04, December 27, 2010, accessed March 4, 2019, http://www.aei.org/wp-content/uploads/2011/10/20101227 -Econ-WP-2010-04.pdf.

it's an important responsibility for the CEA chair to put an enormous amount of effort into it, because it's going to help people think about how well the administration accomplishes its objectives over time. Go back and read the first one for John F. Kennedy, then read the first one for Ronald Reagan, and then read the first one for Barack Obama. There's a heck of a lot of really interesting information in those reports about the way in which those presidents intended to govern. Again, it's very useful for economic historians and for anyone who wants to understand those presidents. If I'm around that long, maybe the fourth one won't feel as impactful as the first one, but I'm certainly going to be very proud of our first *Economic Report*. We've devoted a massive amount of time to it, and it was right to do so.

Bowmaker: How has the first three months in your role been different than you expected?

Hassett: The biggest surprise for me is just how many different things we have to work on every day—there is an economic angle to almost everything. One of our junior people here said that it is like all gas pedal and no brake. As you know, the tax debate is a big part of what is going on right now, but a small part of each of my days because there are so many other urgent policy matters that I have to attend to. I would estimate that I have to help inform fifteen different debates each day, which is seventy-five different debates each week. And sometimes it is about a specific policy issue that you know nothing about, like how renewable standards work. But people who have been here in the past can be extremely generous with their time to help you figure out that kind of issue. For example, Jim Stock is one of the most brilliant economists who has ever been at the CEA. I just love his work. Jim is doing some very interesting research on renewable fuel standards that grew out of the work he did here, when the CEA had to weigh in on the subject.

I certainly wasn't planning to be chair of the CEA throughout my career, and I'm surprised and humbled that I'm here now. But I think that having worked at AEI for twenty years and advised presidential campaigns and having had to think about how both the policy process and political process work has helped me be effective in knowing where to look for expertise. The problem in government is that when you're gathering information, you have to make sure it is coming from trusted sources. There is always a risk that people will lie to you. And so as I say, the social network of economists I built up before I came to the CEA has been extremely valuable in guaranteeing that I will receive an honest read about how to think about a specific issue.

Personal Reflections

Bowmaker: How does your personality affect your style and approach as a policymaker?

Hassett: Something that is very important in policy advising is humility: you are not so confident that your model is so perfect that you disregard criticism and disregard data. As you mentioned earlier, you should be thinking, "What if it doesn't work?" In other words, as well as preparing for being right, you should also be preparing for being wrong—because you don't have a monopoly on the model of how the world works.

Mick Mulvaney (*far left*), director of the Office of Management and Budget, receiving a pen from President Donald Trump (*center*) after the latter's signing of an executive order titled "Comprehensive Plan for Reorganizing the Executive Branch" in the Oval Office on March 13, 2017. Also pictured are Linda McMahon (*second left*), administrator of the Small Business Administration; Ryan Zinke (*third left*), secretary of the interior; Nikki Haley (*fourth left*), ambassador to the United Nations; Ben Carson (*back center*), secretary of housing and urban development; Mike Pence (*third right*), vice president; Rick Perry (*second right*), secretary of energy; and Elaine Chao (*far right*), secretary of transportation.

35   John Michael Mulvaney
Born 1967, Alexandria, Virginia

John Michael "Mick" Mulvaney graduated with a degree in international economics, commerce, and finance from
the Georgetown University School of
Foreign Service in 1989 and obtained a
JD from the University of North Carolina at Chapel Hill in 1992.

Mulvaney practiced commercial
transaction law at James, McElroy and
Diehl from 1992 to 1997 and then
started his own firm, Mulvaney and
Fisher, where he continued to practice commercial transaction law until
2000. He then joined his family's real
estate development business, and in
2009—three years after completing the Owner/President Management Program at Harvard Business School—he became a minority shareholder in and
owner and operator of Salsarita's Fresh Cantina, a privately held regional
restaurant chain.

His political career began in 2006, when he won an open seat in South
Carolina's House of Representatives, and two years later he was elected to
the South Carolina Senate. In 2010, he won a seat in the US House of Representatives by defeating fourteen-term Democratic incumbent John Spratt,
and in doing so, he became the first Republican since 1883 to represent
South Carolina's Fifth Congressional District.

Mulvaney was nominated as director of the Office of Management and
Budget (OMB) by incoming President Donald Trump in December 2016 and
was confirmed by the Senate on February 16, 2017. President Trump also
appointed Mulvaney to serve as acting director of the Consumer Financial
Protection Bureau under the Federal Vacancies Reform Act, which allows the
president to appoint an interim replacement without Senate confirmation.

He served in this role from November 2017 to December 2018, and then became acting White House chief of staff.

I interviewed Mick Mulvaney in his office at the Eisenhower Executive Office Building in Washington, D.C. It was early in the morning on December 15, 2017.

Background Information

Bowmaker: What attracted you to study economics as an undergraduate?

Mulvaney: I honestly don't have a specific memory of what attracted me to study economics as an undergraduate. I do know that I'd never even heard of economics until I got to college—I didn't take the subject in high school—and all I understood were basic English words like supply and demand. At Georgetown, microeconomics was my introduction to the subject. I absolutely hated it. I was pretty good at math, but I still couldn't grasp micro, and I almost failed the class. In fact, the only reason I passed the final exam was because I answered the extra credit question correctly. This will mean nothing to you but everything to the gentleman on your left [an OMB staff member sitting in on the interview], since the question asked for the name of the next coach of the Notre Dame Fighting Irish football team. They had just fired Gerry Faust, so the job was open. Because I was a Minnesota Gophers fan, I knew that Lou Holtz had a clause in his contract at Minnesota that allowed him to break it if he received an offer from Notre Dame. The extra five points moved me from a D to a C [*laughs*]. I took macro the next year, and I absolutely loved it—it made sense to me. I really liked the fact that it was a multivariable type of world where all sorts of inputs were involved. It was fascinating. And at the time that I was studying macro, I was taking a lot of Spanish language and culture classes. Spain and Portugal were joining the EU [European Union] during this period, and I managed to weave the two things together—which was cool.

As Director of the Office of Management and Budget

Bowmaker: When did you first meet Donald Trump, and what were your impressions of him?

Mulvaney: I had bumped into Donald Trump on the campaign trail a couple times, but mostly just to shake his hand. He wouldn't have known me from

Adam's house cat. The very first time I met him properly was in Trump Tower about a year ago this week, for the OMB job interview. My first impression of him was the same impression I have now, which is he is a high-energy, spirited, results-driven individual. He is the exact same person today that he was a year ago, and my guess is that that's true twenty years ago as well. What you see on TV is the real Donald Trump. So many politicians are different when you meet them in person. Donald Trump is Donald Trump all the time—the same mannerisms, the same energy, the same everything.

Bowmaker: How were you approached to become director of the OMB, and why do you think you were approached?

Mulvaney: I can't remember how I was approached. Someone may have called my chief of staff and said the president wants to interview you for the OMB director job. That's probably what happened. Why was I approached? I think they thought about trying to give the job to Jeb Hensarling—he is close friends with Mike Pence. But he didn't want the role because he was going to be House Financial Services Committee chairman. My guess is that Pence asked Jeb who he might recommend instead, and Jeb gave him my name. At the same time, the transition team most likely reached out to [Speaker] Paul Ryan, and Paul probably gave them my name as well.

Bowmaker: In your first official meeting with President Trump, did he make it clear what he wanted you to do for him?

Mulvaney: No. The meeting was entirely personal. We talked more about golf than we did about the Office of Management and Budget. Donald Trump had no idea about the Office of Management and Budget. That's not a slam on Donald Trump. No incoming president already knows what the Office of Management and Budget does. Hillary Clinton didn't know what the Office of Management and Budget does, and she'd been First Lady for eight years and then a senator. No one knows what this office does, so it doesn't surprise me that he didn't either. As I say, the interview was entirely personal. Did he think he could work with me? Clearly, he thought that he could.

The decision he was trying to make was the following. He had Wall Street people lined up for this job, and he had me. And I think what he was trying to figure out was, "OK, I've got some of my transition team saying I should put a business person in OMB, and some of my transition team saying I should put someone with a government background in OMB. Let me talk to Mulvaney and see what happens." And I believe I was able to satisfy him that I knew enough about the government side to fill that space, but that I could also fill the other role, too, because the president knew about my private-sector background in real estate. In other words, when he came to the decision, he was probably thinking, "I don't want a Wall Street guy for the job—I want a Washington guy for the job. But if we're going to take a Washington guy, I want a Washington guy who also has private-sector experience. Mulvaney fits that suit."

Bowmaker: Did you consult with former directors of the OMB either before or after you accepted the role?

Mulvaney: Yes, I did. In fact, I met with my Democratic predecessor, Shaun Donovan. He's a really nice fellow. He actually reached out to me and asked if I wanted to come down here to talk with him. I had known both Mitch Daniels and Rob Portman [directors of the OMB during the George W. Bush administration] a little bit, so I had the chance to speak with them, too. Obviously, you don't want to spend too much time doing that kind of thing before you get the gig, because you don't want to presume confirmation— which is always a fine line that any Cabinet nominee walks. But they were all very gracious. You have to remember that this is not the most partisan of jobs. I don't even consider us bureaucrats as much as I do technocrats. The red building you can see across the street is pretty much the OMB, and the folks inside make the gears move on government, but they're not Republicans or Democrats in the sense that they don't bring their political views to work. So the point is that you can't be hyperpartisan in the way you manage the job. And I think that's something we have seen from those who have done the job well. For example, Mitch Daniels is a tremendous Republican, but he had the ability to shift gears. And I would argue that Shaun Donovan and Rob Portman were the same way, too.

Bowmaker: Has your governmental experience given you an advantage in your relationship with President Trump relative to his other advisers?

Mulvaney: I certainly think so, and the president appreciates it. It especially came out during health care, because the only people in the Cabinet at that time who had any elected office experience were me, Mike Pence, Jeff Sessions, Tom Price, Mike Pompeo, and Dan Coats. Having some folks— although not all of them were involved in health care—who understood the nuances of the House was helpful. But I'm just as candid with the president that I don't pretend to understand the Senate, because I don't. The Senate and the House are two very, very different places.

Bowmaker: How do you handle being in a position where current adminis-trative policy is in conflict with what you have advocated in the past?

Mulvaney: That's easy. The budget that I write is not the budget I would write if I were president. But I'm not the president, which means that I write the president's budget. My job, as I see it, is to give the president various options on various spending levels and various ideas on various programs. I will advo-cate for what I would support most if I were the president. But I also give him the merits of the other arguments as well. I try obviously to influence the out-come, like everybody does here—that's part of what we do as advisers to the president. But ultimately the president makes the call. And if you can't then get behind the team effort, you shouldn't be on the team. I have absolutely no difficulty at all espousing very energetically a position that is not entirely my own, because I've had my say, and that's all you can really look for.

Before he left office, I used to tell John Boehner that one of the reasons I didn't think he was very effective in his role as Speaker was that he didn't let the conservative wing of the party have its say. I can't tell you how many times I told John, "Give us a vote on an amendment, and even if it fails, we'll still vote for your bill. But if you don't give us a vote on an amend-ment, we're not going to vote for your bill because we haven't participated in the process, we haven't had our say." Being here allows me to do just that, and that's something that the president wants to do.

One of my favorite conversations was after I had the job interview with the president, and I went to talk to Steve Bannon [White House chief strate-gist for the first seven months of the Trump administration], who I didn't know very well. I asked him, "Steve, what are you all looking for in an OMB director?" He said, "What do you mean?" I replied, "Well, if you're looking for a yes-man, I'm not your guy. I'm going to have my opinions, and I'm going to push them." He then told me, "That's what the president wants." In other words, he doesn't want groupthink. And in hindsight, if you think about it, everything becomes very clear. The president put together a group of people who might not agree on very much at all, but they're all very smart, and he has confidence in them. He wants to see what ideas bubble up. My favorite example of this is me, the right-wing nut job from rural South Caro-lina; and [Director of the National Economic Council] Gary Cohn, the glo-balist Democrat from Goldman Sachs. I have probably worked more closely and productively with Gary than anybody I ever worked with on the Hill. And I think the president looks for those types of abilities. He wants me to be the right-winger that I was in the House and wants to be able to know that when we settle on something that isn't all the way over to the right, that I can still espouse that position for the team. I feel as if I've been able to satisfy him in that respect.

Bowmaker: How does President Trump like to receive and absorb information?

Mulvaney: The president is still at heart a businessman. So his grasp of this whole process is as a businessman, not as a lawmaker. He doesn't look at things in the same way that Paul Ryan or [Senator] Elizabeth Warren would. When you're a legislator, substance is something, but process is almost everything. The House has its rules, and so does the Senate. The president, on the other hand, is an executive, which means he wants a summary that relates to results. For example, he would be much more interested in knowing the impact of a particular proposal relating to the tax bill than being told, "OK, here's how we can secure fifty-one votes in the Senate to get it." He wants to know whether it is a good plan. Because he figures if it is a good plan, then the lawmaking process should fall into place behind it. We've certainly seen that on the tax bill. We didn't have as much luck as we wanted to on health care, but I don't think we've given up on it.

Bowmaker: Is the president a reader or a listener?

Mulvaney: Both. And I haven't found a sweet spot on that yet. People suggest all he does is watch television all day. I have four articles on my desk that he has signed and cut out of the newspapers and sent to me to read. He devours information. And the one thing that no one has written about yet is that people who have interacted with him accuse him of having a short attention span or not being detail oriented. I learned the hard way that that is not the case. During the first budget in March of this year, I mentioned to him something about a program that I wanted to change. He asked me, "How much does that save us?" I told him, "That's $110 million." He said, "OK," and we moved on to the next topic. Six weeks later I came back to him with a revised version, and that same program for some reason came up on the piece of paper. Again, he asked me, "How much does that save us?" I told him, "That's $113 million." He paused, looked at me, and said, "Six weeks ago you told me it was $110 million. Why did it change?" Now, that's a $3 million change in a $4 trillion budget. So the people who think that he is not detail oriented do so at their peril. He can take in the details very, very quickly, and he does. It's just that he spends his time and energy on the big picture.

Bowmaker: How would you describe President Trump's understanding of economics?

Mulvaney: His understanding of economics is very much what you would expect from a businessman: practical. So he knows what interest rates do to an economy. He knows what tax rates do to an economy. He knows what encourages somebody to invest. He knows what encourages someone to move overseas, and he also knows what encourages somebody to come back.

Bowmaker: When you disagree with the president, what strategy do you find most effective in changing his mind?

Mulvaney: You do the same as you would with any executive: simply try to lay out the facts and arguments. Social Security Disability Insurance [SSDI] was a classic example. He told me that he didn't want to deal with it because it is Social Security. I said, "Mr. President, even though it's called Social Security Disability Insurance, it's not Social Security. The Social Security that most people consider is old-age retirement. The Disability Insurance component of Social Security is only called SSDI because it is administered through the Social Security Administration and the tax system. It has no more to do with old-age retirement than food stamps does. It's just another kind of welfare." And so after several meetings and discussions about it, he gave me permission to make proposals to change SSDI.

The president was also very public on how he changed his mind on the Afghanistan policy. He came in and listened to the generals, who made a series of cases over the course of several weeks. The president changes his mind for the reason most intelligent people do: he gets more facts, better facts, and different facts. And when the circumstances change, sometimes his opinions do as well.

Bowmaker: Does the president encourage debate during meetings? Are those meetings more structured, like Barack Obama's, or more wide-ranging, like Bill Clinton's?

Mulvaney: The president has already guaranteed debate by virtue of who is in the room. I'll be in there with Steven Miller [President Trump's senior adviser for policy]. Steve and I might not see eye to eye on a particular topic, and yet we are both invited to the meeting. Now, if he knows that Steve Miller and I see eye to eye on an issue, there's no reason to have both of us in the meeting. So he'll go find somebody else on that other topic who has a different opinion.

The meetings themselves are not remarkable for their style, at least not in my mind. Perhaps I've gotten used to it by now. I can only compare it to the business meetings that I had in the real world and on the Hill. Does the president jump around a little bit more? Yes. But that's just maybe because the folks I worked for in the past were a little more structured.

Bowmaker: Does he reach decisions quickly or slowly?

Mulvaney: I think he wants to reach decisions quickly. But there are things he knows are so important that you cannot make a snap decision. The Afghanistan policy, for example, was not arrived at quickly. In fact, we had a dedicated Cabinet meeting at Camp David for a weekend to go over it. And he was very meticulous. He went around the table for two and a half hours to give everybody their chance to weigh in. Even I was able to put forward my budgetary and political perspectives. So while I think he likes to make quick decisions and will do so when he can, he knows that the gravity of certain things dictates that you take a longer look at them.

Bowmaker: I would now like to ask you some specific questions about two economic policy issues—namely, your first budget proposal and tax reform. First, how do you justify to both the public and to those within the White House your budget proposal that has led to accusations of heartlessness, since it includes cuts to highly sensitive programs?

Mulvaney: What's more heartless, asking somebody to try and get off welfare or saddling your children with a generation's worth of debt? You tell me. And I would ask the same question of the Obama administration or the Bush 43 administration. You don't get $20 trillion in debt by one party sticking it to you. It is a bipartisan effort to run up this debt. You see it right now on the Hill with this end-of-the-year spending. They are falling over themselves to run up the deficit on the Hill. Again, my only question is what's more heartless, asking Texas to do without a dollar of hurricane relief or asking your grandkids to pay it back? If it's that important, let's pay for it ourselves. That's always been my attitude. One more time: if it's really important to do something—whether it is hurricane relief or food stamps or national defense—we should pay for it and not ask somebody else.

Bowmaker: Why do we need tax reform?

Mulvaney: We need tax reform right now because we have a tax structure that prevents the American economy from firing on all cylinders. To use an analogy, there is a restrictor plate on the engine. In NASCAR [National

Association for Stock Car Auto Racing] and Formula One motor racing, they put a device on the engine to prevent it from functioning at its highest efficiency levels for safety reasons. Regulation does the same thing to our economy, and so does our tax code. I can make the argument that the primary reason American companies have set up overseas has less to do with our trade policies than it does with our tax policies. There is a huge tax advantage to moving overseas, which acts as a limitation on how our economy can function. And so if we can fix our tax code, it will encourage firms to invest here.

When you move away from the corporate side and onto the individual side, the idea of the tax code is starting to be undermined by a belief that it is unfair, that it doesn't treat everybody the same. And the truth of the matter is that it doesn't. The tax code long ago ceased being primarily a tool to raise money for the government and has morphed into a tool for behavioral engineering. It's a case of, "We want you to buy more solar cars, so here is how we will change your tax code" and "We want you to buy this type of house, so here is how we will change your tax code." And it has become as bizarre as the following example. If you and I make the exact same amount of money, but your kids go to college and my kids join the military, you pay less tax than I do. A growing number of people see those types of anomalies as being unfair, and that's why I think individual reforms are so important. Hopefully, it will start to rebuild confidence that similarly situated people will be treated the same, that you don't need someone to prepare your taxes for you, that you're not better off if you hire a lobbyist. As a government, I think there's a fundamental value to the institution of the tax code being not only credible but also broadly respected

Bowmaker: How do you respond to critics who argue that the tax bill is simply a giveaway to the wealthy?

Mulvaney: When I go on CNBC and CNN, they accuse the tax bill of being a giveaway to the rich, and when I go on Fox, they accuse it of being a tax increase on the rich. Keep in mind that the "giveaway to the rich" narrative was going to be out there regardless of what we did. We could have raised the top marginal rate to 40 percent, and the Democrats still would have said it is a giveaway to the rich. All I can tell you is that I think what we're doing is good policy. Lowering the top rate is good policy. Limiting the state and local tax deduction is good policy. Go back to the example I just gave you about the fairness in the tax code. Ceteris paribus, we are the exact same person, but you live in New York and I live in South Carolina. I pay more federal tax than you do. I don't think that's fair. In fact, I spoke to a group of state lawmakers, and they said, "You're eroding our tax base." I told them, "No, you're eroding ours." Unless we change the law, if New York raises its taxes next year, the amount of your adjusted gross income that's available for the government to tax goes down because your deduction for state and local gets bigger. I don't think that's fair, so it's good policy to get rid of it. What is the impact of doing so on an individual? I have no idea. What do we know? There will be a tax reduction in every single tax bracket. May there be individuals who have a different outcome because of their very unique circumstances? Sure. That's always the case when you end up painting with a broad brush, as any national federal tax policy will do.

The politics of envy in this country doesn't sell. In other words, I don't care that you are doing better than I am. What I care about is whether or not I'm doing well, and whether or not I'm being treated fairly. In our example, you're a rich person and I'm a middle-class person. You tell me that the tax plan is going to give you a huge tax cut. I don't care, as long as I feel like I'm being treated fairly. If you get a $10,000 tax break because you paid $100,000 in taxes last year, I don't feel bad if I get a $1,000 tax break because I paid $2,000 in taxes last year. Some people might look at that and say, "Oh, I'm only getting $1,000 and you're getting $10,000." But I shouldn't care. What matters is that I'm getting $1,000, and I used to pay $2,000. It's a fair system. And I think that's why the Democrats have always struggled on selling this as a giveaway to the rich—people don't buy it as long as they feel like they're being treated fairly. I believe our tax bill is able to do just that.

Bowmaker: Can you describe how you have interacted with Gary Cohn and [Secretary of the Treasury] Steve Mnuchin on tax reform? How would you assess your relative contributions?

Mulvaney: At the very beginning of the process, I would describe it as 45 percent Gary, 45 percent Steven, and 10 percent me. I was involved in helping look at some of the larger macroeconomic parameters—what we thought was achievable in terms of added GDP [gross domestic product] through tax reform, and how we could give an incentive to firms to invest in the United States. I've been out of it for several weeks now as the rest of the economics team have taken over the discussions on the Hill, but I continue to help with the messaging of the tax plan.

Bowmaker: Speaking of the rest of the economics team, the chairman of the Council of Economic Advisers no longer has Cabinet-rank status under the

Trump administration. Do you think this might have reduced the influence of the CEA?

Mulvaney: No. Everybody knows [Chairman of the CEA] Kevin Hassett is a genius, and everybody wants to work with him. That's just the way it is. He goes to senior staff meetings in the morning, and he has an equal say in them, just like I do as a Cabinet member.

Bowmaker: What does an economist bring to the policy world that others do not?

Mulvaney: You're asking the exact wrong person. I was never a practicing economist, but it's hardwired into my system to the point where I could sit and talk to Kevin Hassett about capital investment all day long. I'm a geek like that. So it's better to go ask somebody who doesn't have any economics background what Hassett brings to the table. What I will tell you is that he is the smartest person in the Old Executive Building. Having him on the team has been extraordinarily helpful. He does have an ability that many economists lack, which is to translate economic theory and practice into the real world. In other words, he's done a really good job of allowing us to translate the message from the lens of macroeconomic theory and econometric analysis to what you can say in a television interview. And the nice thing about Kevin is that he won't put any work out if he can't back it up. He's not in the political spin business, he's in the economics business—and he knows that everything will be raked over coals. His research has to be academically defensible. And I think that his detailed study that argued that reducing the top corporate tax rate from 35 percent to 20 percent would mean that the average American household would receive a $4,000 a year benefit is one of his best pieces of work.

Bowmaker: Gary Cohn is portrayed by the media as being the president's chief economic adviser. Is that an accurate description?

Mulvaney: I think Gary certainly fits that mold. He will tell you that the president of course also turns to Kevin Hassett, both directly and through Gary, and to the treasury secretary, and to me. But it is absolutely accurate to say that Gary Cohn is the chief economic adviser to the president, and he's doing a damn good job at it. I see him a couple times a week, and we do hang out socially a little bit as well. Like I said earlier, I've probably worked more productively with Gary than anybody else during my whole career in Washington.

Bowmaker: Do you think it matters that he is not a professional economist?

Mulvaney: No, because Gary understands the markets. If we're looking to add more technical economists, we can find them—although no one will be as good as Kevin Hassett. But getting somebody like Gary, with his understanding of the financial markets and the capital markets, is much harder to come by.

Bowmaker: Why is it so important to understand markets in that role?

Mulvaney: Keep in mind that everything we do here moves markets. I teach an hour-long class on political economy. When I walk in, I tell the graduate students, "Look, I'm not here to talk to you about economics, because I don't know anything about it. What I know about is politics." And then I draw the aggregate demand formula [aggregate demand = C [consumption] + I [investment] + G [government spending] + X [exports] – M [imports]]. That's a political formula, because everything we do here affects one of those variables. You want to boost C? Let's give a tax rebate. You want to boost I? Let's do something to our corporate tax code. You want to boost G? That's obvious! You want to boost NX [net exports, which is X – M]? Let's do something else with fiscal policy. So we are macroeconomics in this office. And that's why I think having that combination of Gary, with the private-sector market-related experience, and Kevin, with the technical genius, has been extraordinarily productive for us.

Bowmaker: It seems like Gary Cohn is not acting as the honest broker in his role as director of the National Economic Council. Is that a fair assessment?

Mulvaney: What do you mean?

Bowmaker: Since the Clinton administration, the director of the National Economic Council has traditionally coordinated the different views of the government agencies on an issue and then presented them to the president.

Mulvaney: I'm not sure that's how I would describe what we do here. All we want is for Gary Cohn to be the chief economic adviser to the president. There have been many occasions when someone has brought me something from a budgetary standpoint, and I have said, "Look, I have to get Gary on this right now, because this will move markets." And the president also relied on him very heavily during the discussions about the Federal Reserve chair replacement, to the point where Gary was considered for that job—and rightly so. I thought he would have been a good choice.

Bowmaker: How much interaction have you had with Janet Yellen at the Federal Reserve?

Mulvaney: I saw her yesterday. I now sit on FSOC [Financial Stability Oversight Council] as a result of my temporary appointment to CFPB [Consumer Financial Protection Bureau]. But I had regular interactions with the Fed[eral Reserve]—both with Dr. Yellen and Dr. Bernanke—when I was on the Monetary Policy and Trade Subcommittee of the Financial Services Committee on the Hill. I have to say that I would have been a lot more hawkish on monetary policy than either of them have been. I am more of a Dr. John Taylor type of guy. I worry long term about the structural impact of having had a zero interest rate policy for eight years. Many people don't realize that it has absolutely brutalized the Social Security Trust Fund. We have a $2 trillion trust fund, and we have only been able to invest in one thing, which is government securities. I have raised this issue with Dr. Yellen because I wanted her to increase interest rates earlier.

Bowmaker: As you just mentioned, you have been appointed Consumer Financial Protection Bureau acting director. How did that position arise?

Mulvaney: I think the president tasked Gary Cohn with trying to find a replacement when they thought that Richard Cordray might leave to go run for governor of Ohio. I don't know if you know this or not, but one of the reasons everybody agreed that I was a good choice was that, number one, I had tremendous exposure to the CFPB during my work on the Hill. As I just mentioned, I was on the Monetary Policy and Trade Subcommittee, and that had jurisdiction over the CFPB. No one did more hearings on the CFPB than I did. So it's not like I woke up the day after the president appointed me and said, "What's the CFPB?" I have been following the CFPB very closely. Number two, and this probably goes underappreciated, is that I think they wanted somebody who could handle the environment and circumstances, since it is a fairly high-profile position. I have been an elected member of Congress who has been put through the ringer a couple times during a fairly provocative confirmation process.

Bowmaker: How do you balance your two roles?

Mulvaney: I always laugh when people say, "Oh, you can't do two jobs at one time." There are 500 people who work here at OMB, and there are 1,600 people who work across the street at CFPB. I'm pretty good at math, so that is 2,100 people. There are 82,000 people who work at [the Department of] Health and Human Services, and we have one HHS secretary. My point, then, is that it can be done. The way you do it is by having the right team in place. Delegation is the key to the high-level functioning of the executive branch of government. It starts with the president: he delegates down to the Cabinet secretaries, and they put their teams together. The biggest challenge I face over the CFPB is that of the 1,600-person staff, I am the only political appointee. So I'm trying to fix that and bring more people in, because here at the OMB I have a team of 35–40 people who are political appointees. Once we get a team over there, there's no reason why one person can't run it all.

Bowmaker: What have you learned from President Trump, and what has he learned from you?

Mulvaney: What have I learned from Donald Trump? That if you hit a lot of fairways, you can play golf into your seventies. He's better than I am, and it really pisses me off. But seriously, I will say the following. The man's energy levels are stunning. He's seventy-one years old. My parents are seventy-five. If my dad did what this gentleman does for a week it would kill him, and my dad's in decent health. President Trump doesn't sleep. He works all of the time, he's always up, and not just awake—he always has high energy. It's just bizarre to watch. And I think it just goes to show you the lesson learned is if you really like what you do, age is not a limitation.

What has he learned from me? I'd like to think he's learned a little about the subtleties of lawmaking in Washington, D.C. I'm not Paul Ryan. And I'm not Donald Trump. I haven't spent all my life in government, like Paul has. I haven't spent all my life in the business world like Donald Trump has. I've done both. And so maybe I've been able to help him bridge between those two worlds.

Personal Reflections

Bowmaker: How does your personality affect your style and approach as a policymaker?

Mulvaney: I don't have any personality. They tell me here that I should start every speech with a joke, but it has gotten to the point where I say to them that I can't do it, because budget people with economics degrees don't have a sense of humor. What I will say to you is that I like my jobs—they're fun— and I think I'm productive at them. I would hope the president thinks hiring me was a pretty good decision. But you'd have to ask other people how my personality affects what I do.

OMB staff member: Let's go for a beer, Simon [*laughter*].

Conclusion

Before beginning this book, I had little experience engaging with policy-makers. Over the years I spent conducting these interviews, however, I came to appreciate what it means to interrupt a successful and distinguished career as an academic, investment banker, lawyer, business consultant, or corporate executive to lend one's economic expertise to the president of the United States. To be sure, working at the White House inevitably brings its fair share of difficult moments, yet the very willingness of this group of people to discuss candidly what must be, at times, disappointing outcomes speaks volumes about the passion and commitment with which they approached their roles. Indeed, observing their boundless enthusiasm in person only intensified my admiration for them.

In approaching this work, I did not intend to provide a critical analysis of each policymaker's tenure or even of each president's economic legacy. While I certainly recognize the importance of that endeavor, it is a task beyond the ambitions of this book. Rather, my goal was to show through these firsthand accounts the scope and complexity of the issues—both professional and personal—faced by an economic policymaker working at the highest level. I trust I have achieved this objective and preserved for posterity the colorful personalities, the highs and the lows, and the sometimes volatile relationships that have characterized much of the past half-century of economic policymaking in the White House.

This period of time has seen the breakdown of Bretton Woods, rampant inflation, tax reform, the collapse of communism, the longest peacetime economic expansion in US history, 9/11, the financial crisis of 2008 and the Great Recession that followed, and the recent seismic shift in the political landscape. Each presidential administration faces specific crises, is shaped by the president's personality and agenda, and requires support from a Congress whose views frequently shift with the political winds. Against this backdrop, the experiences captured herein demonstrate that even the most well-prepared professionals can struggle to find their footing in a role that has no suitable training.

Despite the unique circumstances faced by each person interviewed in this book, nine common themes emerged from our conversations about working for nine different presidents. These themes cut across all administrations and are likely applicable to future economic policymaking work. Whether you are a student, teacher, curious citizen, or prospective policymaker, I hope these themes provide you with a connection to the men and women whose often overlooked work shaped your life.

It Is Hard to Say No to the President

> And so with all the good intentions of explaining to him why I couldn't, wouldn't, and shouldn't take this job, I heard myself saying, "Yes, sir, I'll do my best"—which was my first lesson in how hard it is to say no to the president in the Oval Office.
>
> —W. Michael Blumenthal

Many policymakers shared the view that when the president called, a sense of duty arose within them—one that both dispelled any initial personal reservations and transcended political viewpoints. It was understood that the opportunity to serve the president was also a call to serve the country; to put their skills to the test, sometimes at a moment of crisis; and to work on issues that would touch the lives of millions of Americans.

While some policymakers received advanced notice that their call from the president was approaching, others heard it out of the blue. Both situations seemed to leave little time to prepare as much as anyone would have liked. Many leaned on the flexibility of their spouses, moved across the country, divested their businesses, filed endless paperwork, and accepted the impending invasion of privacy for the chance to serve at the highest level in the executive branch.

The Learning Curve Is Steep

> I think one of the keys to being effective as you enter the policy world is to know what you don't know. So I had an immensely steep learning curve in all of the six and a half years that I was there, and that was something I liked about being in government.
> —Robert E. Rubin

No matter how knowledgeable or experienced the policymakers were before they arrived in Washington, the specific set of economic challenges they faced were almost always unprecedented, complicated, and fraught with the potential for wrong turns or unintended consequences. While many saw this as an attraction—the economic puzzles and demanding circumstances made their roles thrilling and professionally rewarding—not surprisingly, the learning curve proved steep. In particular, the policymakers needed to learn quickly about how to operate in the large, multifaceted executive branch; to work with others to respond to political, rather than economic, concerns; and to navigate the president's personality, management style, and agenda.

Sooner or later, each policymaker confronted issues outside of his or her strengths and comfort level. To adapt, many reached out for advice to predecessors from both sides of the political aisle. A common bond seems to form among those who serve in the executive branch that made those conversations friendly and supportive. It appears that most of the policymakers who work with the president in policy roles develop an institutional sense of responsibility and want to be available to advise whoever comes next. It is these professional courtesies and kindnesses that facilitate the transition for each policymaker.

The President Makes the Final Decision

> At the end of the day, you lay out your recommendation to the president and he makes the final decision—which, by the way, is something that you have to get your mind around: you only *recommend*, even if you are a Cabinet member.
> —Stephen Friedman

For most of the policymakers, the White House was unlike any other work environment they had experienced. The academics were accustomed to the luxury of time, developing their ideas in a setting characterized by high standards of evidence and among generally collegial peers. The corporate executives were used to following their own chains of investigation, delegating freely and acting according to their own expertise. In the White House, however, it was the president's personality, management style, and political agenda that dominated the context of every dilemma and decision. In addition, no matter how complex were the challenges they faced, the expectations for viable solutions moved at lightning speed, with the media being ever present, probing, and ready to pounce on missteps.

The policymakers focused on providing advice and putting forward recommendations, with the president making the final call since he must synthesize the viewpoints fielded from many competing and often opposing voices. Each policymaker had to accept the fact that on many issues, their argument would not necessarily prevail, and the president would not always choose a solution that adhered to the soundest economic principles.

Politics Trumps Economics

> When you are sorting through options, it is sometimes frustrating as an economist to see things dismissed because they are not politically acceptable, and similarly things being done for political reasons that don't embody the absolute best economics.
> —Janet L. Yellen

Many of the policymakers reported that the presidents they served strived to identify the best policies first and address politics second. However, few major initiatives on any president's agenda can move forward without, for example, congressional approval. Therefore, political realities inevitably shaped White House decisions. In most cases, the policymakers conceded the political maneuvering to the president and the legislative staff, which often resulted in a solution that was not first best from an economic perspective.

In this respect, the poor economic literacy of the electorate appeared to be a significant impediment to the pursuit of sound economic policy. The policymakers provided numerous examples of how there is often a gross misunderstanding of the fundamentals of economics, from the difference between the national debt and the federal deficit to the impact of taxes and the gains from international trade. If elected officials are indeed as much followers as they are leaders—that is, if they are highly reflective of the public's thinking on an issue—then one can see quite clearly how politics trumps economics in Washington.

A Good Relationship with the President Is Key

Sound economics is an essential input to policy, but the ability to input it depends greatly on the personal relationships between an elected leader and his advisers.
—Michael J. Boskin

Establishing a close and comfortable working relationship with the president was crucial to determining a policymaker's impact at the White House. First and foremost, this required an assessment not only of the president's interest in economics, but also of his understanding of the subject. Second, the policymaker needed to learn the best way the president absorbed information. As one might expect, presidents varied substantially across these dimensions.

The timing of a policymaker's arrival at the White House also shaped the experience that followed and often affected his or her ability to be effective. Early in a presidency—indeed, during the campaign itself—personal relationships and circles of influence begin to form, which makes it the most opportune time to advance the president's agenda. Once the precedents and practices of the presidency have been established, however, it becomes more difficult to make an impact.

Receiving a Respectful Hearing Is Paramount

From his experience in the Carter administration, Stu Eizenstat told me that a person could have advocated for an issue for twenty years and seen the president go against them but be loyal if they had felt that they had had a fair chance to represent their views.
—Gene B. Sperling

Given the complex and challenging nature of the White House environment—and the accompanying external constraints—most, albeit not all, of the policymakers recognized that their ability to effect change single-handedly would likely be limited in most circumstances. For a number of the policymakers, this was one concern that had loomed large in their minds before accepting the appointment in Washington.

However, effective teamwork during moments of crisis drove many of the most rewarding aspects of serving the president that were recalled by the policymakers. For several academics, this was also a rather surprising feature of their experience, given the somewhat solitary nature of their profession. One lesson from this collaborative environment was that even if a policymaker had been on the losing side of a debate, as long as he or she had had the opportunity to put forward an argument and it was listened to respectfully, then that person would be more likely to support the final decision.

There Is a Natural Tension with the Media

> [The media are] always looking for a story line, and government officials are always open to questions and serve as a fair target. You need to learn to accept that as a fact of life in the public sector.
> —John W. Snow

The media are a participant in the economic policymaking process, and their role has expanded significantly over the past half-century—including in their ability to draw and sustain attention to specific issues, their capacity to change the discourse around a policy debate by how it is framed, their ability to highlight the role played by the key players in the policymaking process, and of course their capacity to act as the primary conduit between the public (which learns about how government policies will affect it) and the government (which receives feedback about public opinion on its policies).

While most of the policymakers recognized that the media are unquestionably part of the Washington landscape, it is also true that they emphasized the pitfalls encountered when balancing media interest with the desire for discretion. Some discovered whom they could trust by tracking which meetings resulted in media leaks and which did not. In other instances, the policymakers simply learned the hard way—from the president's response to the markets' reaction—to be careful about what is said in public statements.

Economic Policy Is the Toughest to Make

> Economics is not just a dark science where you put a lot of data into a computer, and it comes out with the right policy. So much depends on how people perceive their situation and how they react to circumstances.
> —Stuart E. Eizenstat

Formal training in economics—or a practical exposure to the field—brings a unique framework, a set of tools, and a way of thinking that is very useful for addressing complicated policy issues. There is a focus on how people respond to incentives, including any unintended consequences; an understanding of markets and individual choice; an ability to identify cause and effect; a healthy respect for data; a cost-benefit analysis of government; and an awareness of trade-offs. Indeed, it can be argued that economics can contribute to thinking about almost every policy problem.

However, the policymakers also acknowledged that economics can rarely provide a straightforward and unambiguous answer to most policy issues. This implied that making policy recommendations to the president involved dealing with the uncertainty associated with the impact of different policy options. Part of the problem, of course, relates to the unpredictability of human behavior—which the standard rational economic model cannot always explain, but which may be better understood through the lens of behavioral economics. Therefore, when the inherent deficiencies of economic science are combined with political and legislative constraints, one can make the case that economic policy is the most challenging of all to make.

Serving the President Is an Exhilarating Experience

> I remember George Bush 41 telling me that when his father left the Senate and went back to his role as a partner at Brown Brothers, he realized that once you've been in government it transcends anything you do in business. At the time I thought, "Well, I'm not sure about that," but the truth of the matter is he was right.
> —Nicholas F. Brady

To be sure, having the rare opportunity to serve the president and help advance the economic policy of the United States represented a career-defining moment for the policymakers and brought tremendous rewards.

Being intimately involved in a wide variety of economic issues that affected the well-being of the nation both broadened and deepened their perspectives on those same issues; being able to see firsthand the intricacies of government machinery in Washington allowed the policymakers to understand the gulf between policymaking in theory and its real-world implementation; and being in a team-based setting exposed them to a fascinating array of extremely smart and intellectually inquisitive people.

This is not to say that the experiences of the policymakers were always characterized as being positive and fun. They were sometimes deeply frustrating, often somewhat hostile, and invariably highly stressful. Indeed, for those who worked through the highest stakes of an economic crisis, it is difficult to imagine a more physically and mentally demanding professional environment. Yet it is rather revealing that despite these downsides, almost none of the policymakers regretted taking on their respective roles. Moreover, it appears that many of them will encourage their younger colleagues to enthusiastically embrace the opportunity when the president calls.

Photo Credits

George P. Shultz

p. 10, US Federal Government / Oliver Atkins

p. 11, Courtesy of Hoover Institution

Paul A. Volcker

p. 22, Trinity Mirror / Mirrorpix / Alamy Stock Photo

p. 23, Courtesy of Volcker Alliance

Alan Greenspan

p. 42, Gerald R. Ford Presidential Library / Ricardo Thomas

p. 43, Chris Bott / Alamy Stock Photo

Charles L. Schultze

p. 60, Ken Hawkins

p. 61, Courtesy of Brookings Institution

W. Michael Blumenthal

p. 74, Keystone Press / Alamy Stock Photo

p. 75, Agencja Fotograficzna Caro / Alamy Stock Photo

Stuart E. Eizenstat

p. 96, Courtesy of private collection of Stuart Eizenstat

p. 97, Courtesy of Covington & Burling LLP

Arthur B. Laffer

p. 114, Bettmann / Getty Images

p. 115, Courtesy of Laffer Associates

Murray L. Weidenbaum

p. 138, Ronald Reagan Presidential Library / Michael Evans

p. 139, Courtesy of Weidenbaum Center on the Economy, Government, and Public Policy

Martin S. Feldstein

p. 156, Ronald Reagan Presidential Library / Pete Souza

p. 157, Courtesy of Harvard University

Nicholas F. Brady

p. 172, George H.W. Bush Presidential Library and Museum

p. 173, Bill Denver

David C. Mulford

p. 184, George H. W. Bush Presidential Library and Museum

p. 185, Courtesy of Hoover Institution

Michael J. Boskin

p. 202, Bettmann / Getty Images

p. 203, Courtesy of Stanford University

Gene B. Sperling

p. 222, William J. Clinton Presidential Library / Ralph Alswang

p. 223, Bloomberg / Contributor

Robert E. Rubin

p. 254, William J. Clinton Presidential Library

p. 255, Courtesy of Council on Foreign Relations

Lawrence H. Summers

p. 266, William J. Clinton Presidential Library / Ralph Alswang

p. 267, Courtesy of Harvard University

Joseph E. Stiglitz

p. 280, William J. Clinton Presidential Library / Bob McNeely

p. 281, Courtesy of Columbia University

Alice M. Rivlin

p. 296, William J. Clinton Presidential Library / Bob McNeely

p. 297, Courtesy of Brookings Institution

Janet L. Yellen

p. 322, William J. Clinton Presidential Library / Sharon Farmer

p. 323, Federal Reserve / Alamy Stock Photo

Jacob J. Lew

p. 336, William J. Clinton Presidential Library / Sharon Farmer

p. 337, Courtesy of Columbia University

Paul H. O'Neill

p. 358, David Hume Kennerly / Getty Images

p. 359, Bloomberg / Getty Images

R. Glenn Hubbard

p. 376, Newscom / Alamy Stock Photo

p. 377, Courtesy of Columbia University

John B. Taylor

p. 388, Dave Chan / Getty Images

p. 389, Courtesy of Hoover Institution

John W. Snow

p. 402, Newscom / Alamy Stock Photo

p. 403, Courtesy of JWS Associates LLC

Stephen Friedman

p. 420, Stephen Jaffe / Getty Images

p. 421, Courtesy of Stone Point Capital LLC

N. Gregory Mankiw

p. 432, Courtesy of private collection of Gregory Mankiw

p. 433, Courtesy of Harvard University

Harvey S. Rosen

p. 448, Bloomberg / Contributor

p. 449, Courtesy of Princeton University

Edward P. Lazear

p. 464, Mandel Ngan / Getty Images

p. 465, Courtesy of Hoover Institution

Henry M. Paulson Jr.

p. 480, Mark Wilson / Getty Images

p. 481, Courtesy of the Paulson Institute

Austan D. Goolsbee

p. 496, Newscom / Alamy Stock Photo

p. 497, John Zich

Peter R. Orszag

p. 516, Kristoffer Tripplaar / Alamy Stock Photo

p. 517, Courtesy of Lazard Frères and Co.

Lael Brainard

p. 532, White House Photo / Alamy Stock Photo

p. 533, Board of Governors of the Federal Reserve System

Alan B. Krueger

p. 546, White House Photo / Alamy Stock Photo

p. 547, Courtesy of Princeton University

Jason Furman

p. 580, Veterans Administration / Alamy Stock Photo

p. 581, Courtesy of Harvard University

Kevin A. Hassett

p. 600, Newscom / Alamy Stock Photo

p. 601, Executive Office of the President of the United States

John Michael Mulvaney

p. 614, Newscom / Alamy Stock Photo

p. 615, Executive Office of the President of the United States

Index

Note: Figures are indicated by "f" following page numbers. Footnotes are indicated by "n" following page numbers.